A DICTIONARY
of
VOCAL TERMINOLOGY

By the same author

BEL CANTO: PRINCIPLES AND PRACTICES
THE FREE VOICE: A GUIDE TO NATURAL SINGING
VOICE: PSYCHE AND SOMA
ESSAYS ON THE NATURE OF SINGING

A DICTIONARY
of
VOCAL TERMINOLOGY

AN ANALYSIS

---

by

CORNELIUS L. REID

R E C I T A L   P U B L I C A T I O N S
P.O. Box 1697   Huntsville, TX 77342-1697

Ed. No. 560

International Standard Book Number: 0-915282-07-0
Library of Congress Card Number: 81-86074

Recital Publications Reprint Edition
1995

Reprinted from the original 1983 edition of
Joseph Patelson Music House, New York.

RECITAL   PUBLICATIONS
P.O. Box 1697   Huntsville, TX 77342-1697

Ed. No. 560

To

WANDA

_____

For Her Patience, Love and Understanding

The author wishes to express his gratitude and appreciation to The Ford Foundation, whose generous grant has provided both the time and the encouragement necessary to an adequate treatment of a vocal terminology, old and new, which should be familiar to those who sing and to those who develop or are otherwise concerned with the human voice.

ACKNOWLEDGMENTS

I would like to express my gratitude to Bruce Kramer and to my pupils Peggy Dufour and Archibald (Tony) McDowell III: their generous assistance, clear thinking, knowledge, editorial skills and enthusiastic cooperation have appreciably enhanced the value of this work. If errors of logic or oversights have been committed, they are mine.

I would also like to take this opportunity to thank those publishers who have graciously permitted the use of their copyrighted materials, as well as those laborers in the field who have seriously addressed themselves to the difficult problems related to vocal pedagogy and supplied reasonable solutions.

I am especially grateful to my friend and colleague Richard Dyer-Bennet for sharing his stimulating ideas, and to Dr. Elsworth Baker for guiding me to an understanding of natural functioning.

C.L.R.

Anatomical illustrations are reproduced by the kind permission of the following publishers, authors and artists:

Figure 1. S. W. Jacob, C. A. Francone, and W. S. Lussow, *Structure and Function in Man,* Fourth Edition (Philadelphia: W. E. Saunders, 1978), p. 181.

Figure 2. James E. Crouch, *Functional Human Anatomy,* Third Edition (Philadelphia: Lea and Febiger, 1978), p. 385.

Figure 6. Reprinted from *CIBA Clinical Symposia: The Larynx,* Volume 16, Number 3 (1964) Plate I, p. 70, Frank H. Netter, M.D., Illustrator.

Figure 7. Reprinted from *CIBA Clinical Symposia: The Larynx,* Volume 16, Number 3 (1964) Plate II, p. 71, Frank H. Netter, M.D., Illustrator.

Figure 8. Reprinted from *CIBA Clinical Symposia: The Larynx,* Volume 16, Number 3 (1964) Plate III, p. 74, Frank H. Netter, M.D., Illustrator.

Figure 9. Reprinted from *CIBA Clinical Symposia: The Larynx,* Volume 16, Number 3 (1964) Plate IV, p. 75, Frank H. Netter, M.D., Illustrator. CIBA Pharmaceutical Company, Division of CIBA-GEIGY Corporation.

Figure 17. Crouch, p. 476.

Figure 19. Wallace O. Fenn and Hermann Rahn, Editors, *Handbook of Physiology,* Section 3: Respiration, Volume 1 (Baltimore: American Physiological Society), p. 312. "Physiology of the Upper Airway," by Dr. Donald F. Proctor.

Figure 20. Crouch, p. 205.

ILLUSTRATIONS

An Index of Terms will be found beginning on page xi.

The Index of Names will be found beginning on page 447.

The Bibliography will be found beginning on page 449.

Index of Terms

INDEX OF TERMS

INDEX OF TERMS

INDEX OF TERMS

INDEX OF TERMS

INTRODUCTION

This dictionary has been prepared in response to a pressing need to define and analyze those terms and expressions in common usage by the vocal profession from the early seventeenth century to the present, as well as those introduced into the lexicon by members of the various scientific disciplines concerned with the subject. In so doing, every effort has been made to be as objective as possible. However, since we are all in a sense victims of time and place, cultural attitudes and aesthetic preferences, background and training, personal experience and psychological predisposition, my only claim is that the opinions, observations and representations made concerning the contributions of others are as fair and objective as possible under the circumstances.

Two late nineteenth century authorities engaged in separate yet related disciplines established the basic premises upon which the following analyses have been structured. The first premise was introduced by Dr. Gordon Holmes, a New York throat specialist, when he observed that "Voice is nothing but the movement of air and the activity of muscles." The second is contained in a comment made by Manuel Garcia to the effect that "All control over the tone is lost once the vocal cords become vibratile." More recently, these views were corroborated by Frederick Husler and Yvonne Rodd-Marling, who stated that "The sounding of a resonance chamber is always a secondary manifestation, the result of muscular movements in the vocal mechanism."

The opinions quoted above reflect a profound insight into the vocal process, on the one hand recognizing that the generation of sound waves takes place within the larynx and that the quality of the ultimate tonal product equates with the quality of the muscular coordination operative within the throat parts, and on the other hand relegating metaphysical concepts and symptoms associated with "placement" and "nasal resonance" to an observed phenomenon rather than a functional principle. All of the analyses made, therefore, are based upon Dr. Holmes' formulation: the various tone qualities brought under discussion are related to those muscle systems which prompted their emergence.

The development of procedures based upon the above premise is complicated by the fact that few of the muscle systems involved in phonation are subject to volitional or direct control, and to change their habitual patterns of response is extremely difficult. However, these systems do react in a predictable manner to specifically arranged patterns of pitch, intensity and vowel to yield tone qualities commonly recognized as "registers." Consequently, by observing the consistent parallels between stimulus and response, and through dependence upon the awakening of what is recognized as a "singer's instinct" and the relinquishing of outerimposed disciplines, it is possible to make contact with the innate functional logic by which the vocal mechanism is governed. Under these conditions, as G. B. Lamperti so astutely remarked, "There is no 'attack,' no 'mouth position,' no 'tongue control,' no 'fixed chest,' no relaxing this or that muscle, no stiffening of any part of the body, in fact, nothing that would not spring from instinctual utterance."

It was Sir Morell Mackenzie who observed a century ago that "the whole secret of fine singing" is to be found in the functional relationship between the two vocal registers. These homogeneous tone qualities, traditionally recognized as chest register and falsetto or head voice, result from a particular ratio of tension shared between the two muscle systems which tauten the vocal folds, a coordinate relationship profoundly influencing both the suspensory muscles which stabilize the larynx and those responsible for adjusting the pharyngeal cavities in order to define and resonate the vowel. These muscle systems, which are reflexive and cannot be acted upon, comprise the sum and substance of those functional elements taking place at the onset of phonation.

Upon reflection, what at first looms as an insuperable difficulty stands forth as the very strength of the pedagogic process. Since involuntary muscle systems cannot be acted upon, the avenues of approach necessary to an effective solution of vocal problems are limited. There is a special advantage to be gained through the functioning of a reflexive system, however: its ability (when properly stimulated) to respond naturally, rapidly, with absolute precision, and with a minimal amount of fatigue. If this advantage is to be exploited, the principles and practices employed during training must be directed toward the stimulation of those involuntary muscle systems within the vocal tract whose function is directly responsible for the quality of the ultimate tonal product but which cannot be consciously regulated or controlled. The mechanical principles which govern registration overcome this difficulty, since at all levels of expertise they stimulate the laryngeal muscular systems into consistent and *predictable* types of tonal response.

There are other persuasive reasons why vocal training must be structured so as to stimulate reflexive movement: 1) the ideal position of the larynx is unknown, and like quality, which usually represents a present technical status rather than an intrinsically natural quality, it can only be conceptualized and experienced *after* vocal problems have been eliminated; 2) the mass per unit length, tension, mode and rate of vocal fold vibration are not susceptible to improvement by means of respiratory and/or articulatory controls, and 3) the desirable position of the involuntary muscular systems engaged in phonation is incapable of being replicated either through verbalization or by example. Again, it is because of the natural, reflexive movement characteristic of registration that it becomes possible to establish these delicate adjustments.

With such considerations foremost in mind, it is obvious that the procedural options available for the development of vocal skills are circumscribed. A simple solution would be at hand were arbitrary adjustments of peripheral areas, *i.e.,* special breathing techniques, a precise positioning of the tongue, jaw and mouth, and/or emphasis on resonance capable of effecting a desired technical reconstruction. This is not possible, however, because the imposition of volitional controls violates a cardinal rule governing the behavior of all complex muscular activities:

if but one member of a muscular complex is reflexive, *all members of the system must be treated as though they, too, were reflexive.* This principle precludes any hope of attaining a viable solution to vocal problems through recourse to mechanistic methods. The statement of Lamperti quoted above embraces this overall concept, implying that spontaneous, natural movement cannot be achieved through the imposition of outer-imposed disciplines. All of the analyses and value judgments expressed by the present writer have been predicated upon this understanding.

The parallel relationships known to exist between registration and tone quality, whether perceived as chest register or chest resonance, head voice or head resonance, reveal the functional origins of all sounds capable of being produced by the human voice. These tone qualities, like colors and odors, can only be described in generalities or by comparing them to other more familiar phenomena. Nevertheless, just as the trained eye can arrive at a just estimate of the proportions among the primary colors required to make varying shades of green, purple, orange, *etc.,* so, too, can tone qualities be estimated, analyzed and understood by relating them to their functional origins. Indeed, the analogy between sound and color is precise— vocal tone is the product of frequencies that are created by movements of the vocal folds, which are tautened by their associated musculatures, and the frequencies perceived as color result from a blending of pigment. Perceptual changes from sight to hearing occur only because of the extremely wide difference in the vibrational frequencies of the two media. What is clearly evident, therefore, is that the harmonic spectra of varying tonal qualities, which find their origin in registration, are quite as discernible to the trained ear as is color to the trained eye. By observing these relationships, the mechanical principles governing the functional capabilities of the mechanism will stand revealed, and the possibility for gaining effective control over an essentially reflexive organic system will become increasingly apparent.

Despite the difficulties to be surmounted, it is nevertheless the author's hope that this dictionary will accomplish these objectives: 1) foster a more perceptive insight into natural functioning and the principles which govern that process; 2) make those terms introduced by scientists more familiar and understandable to students, singers, and teachers of voice; 3) acquaint scientists with the significance and etymology of vocal terms from the perspective of the voice teacher, and 4) provide a basis upon which a standard terminology can evolve which will strike a balance between aesthetics and natural functioning. If this Dictionary of Vocal Terminology succeeds in this, it will have fulfilled its purpose.

C.L.R.

A DICTIONARY
of
VOCAL TERMINOLOGY

A

A♭ Tenor: a tenor voice limited in range and quality.

Several factors may contribute to this deficiency: 1) the chest register forced beyond its natural terminating point (E—F above middle C); 2) an undeveloped head register, and 3) the constrictor tensions always present in an imbalanced registration.

To attribute the problems of the A♭ tenor to a lack of "support," incorrect "placement," or improper "breath control" is to direct attention away from the real cause of his difficulties and preclude any possibility of solving them.

See Bel Canto
Falsetto
Modern Methods
Register
Resonance
Vowel

Abdomen: possibly from the Latin word *abdere,* "to hide;" that portion of the body which lies between the thorax and the pelvis.

The abdomen contains a cavity (the abdominal cavity) separated by the diaphragm from the thoracic (chest) cavity, and is lined with a serous membrane, the peritoneum. The abdominal cavity contains the viscera and is enclosed by a wall (abdominal wall or parietes) formed by the abdominal muscles, vertebral column and the pelvic bones. In the expiratory phase of respiration, the muscles of the abdominal wall contract and pull inward, moving the abdominal contents upward. This motion permits the diaphragm to relax and return to its dome-shaped form, with the result that the lungs become compressed, expelling the breath.

See Breathing
Emotion
Energy

Abdominal Control: a technique for stabilizing tone and conserving breath through conscious manipulation of those muscles associated with expiration, *i.e.,* the diaphragm, the abdominal muscles, and the muscles of the lower back and flanks.

Experience has demonstrated that attempts at abdominal control usually fail to conserve either breath or tonal energy and ignore several functional laws: namely, that correct tone production results from the existence of a state of balanced tension within the entire respiratory tract, from the palatal muscles to the pelvic floor; that the concentration of energy and attention to any particular respiratory element (including the abdominal muscles) upsets this balance; that when either expiratory or inspiratory tension predominates, the glottal space reflexively widens, thereby making it more difficult for the vocal folds to approximate or adduct, and further, that the muscular and membranous tissues which fill the space between the tracheal rings narrow the aperture on exhalation and widen it as they relax during inhalation.

ABDOMINAL PRESSURE

From this it is apparent that attempts at abdominal control introduce a number of negative factors which, unless abdominal pressure is effectively counterbalanced by the inspiratory process, result in muscular interference. If the respiratory (vocal) system is to be brought into equilibrium, the expiratory muscle system must balance with its natural inspiratory antagonist, thus permitting the costal muscles and the lowered diaphragm to assist in holding the breathing mechanism in suspension. Under these circumstances, the vocal folds are free to approximate and respond to the positive action of the laryngeal muscles which draw them into tension.

Acting upon the abdominal muscles to the exclusion of other important members of the respiratory system is inhibitory, and it disrupts the natural equilibrium without which the mechanism cannot be maintained in balanced tension.

See Breathing

Abdominal Pressure: pressure engendered in the abdomen and thorax by the conscious manipulation of the abdominal muscles associated with expiration.

Proponents of abdominal control maintain that abdominal and thoracic pressure should be gradually increased with each rise in pitch and intensity to conserve energy and provide tonal "support." A further belief is that abdominal tension helps to lower the diaphragm, expand the rib cage, widen the flanks, and approximate the vocal folds. Collectively, these activities are thought to regulate air compression, thereby assuring tonal steadiness and controlling the rate of breath flow.

Whether or not this is true is open to question. Abdominal pressure energizes the expiratory system, and by so doing, causes the inspiratory muscles to relax. In the absence of a counterbalancing factor, the glottis (the space between the vocal folds) opens reflexively. Since, under these conditions, the vocal folds must be forced to approximate, the inevitable consequence is an increase in constrictor tension. Should, however, abdominal pressure be resisted by the intercostals, a desirable balance of tension will have been achieved. Attempts to exert abdominal pressure without proper muscular antagonism, however, disturb the natural equilibrium of the system, with the result that greater abdominal pressure must be exerted to compensate for the energy loss.

A more interesting and reasonable theory concerning abdominal pressure moves in a different direction, proposing that it is laryngeal function which controls breath expenditure; that is, breath expenditure is determined by the coordinative efficiency of the laryngeal musculature, which draws the vocal folds into tension and stabilizes the larynx. If this is true, then abdominal pressure, or indeed any other pressure system, is incapable of stimulating these systems into improved patterns of response, and consequently fails to offer a viable solution to what constitutes the crux of the vocal problem.

Research by the French scientist Raoul Husson reinforces the latter viewpoint. After considerable experimentation he advanced his neurochronaxic theory, which proposes that the vocal folds, independent of breath pressure, vibrate as a neurological response to the singer's will. The combustible element which energizes and vitalizes them (and, for that matter, all muscles and body substances) is oxygen. Thus, if the vocal mechanism is functioning harmoniously, the energy derived from respiration will be used to maintain an equilibrium within the entire phonatory tract. Contrarily, if the mechanism is not precisely balanced, a corresponding amount of breath will be wasted. Any breath wasted in singing, therefore, can be attributed to faulty muscular coordination—not to respiratory deficiencies which could be improved by special breathing techniques. Faulty laryngeal muscular coordination is the cause, respiratory dysfunction the effect.

The movement of involuntary muscles lies at the core of the functional process. If the mechanism is to be brought into equilibrium, these muscle groups must be stimulated to perform in a manner consonant with nature's laws. Volitionally controllable muscles (such as those associated with abdominal control) should rarely be acted upon, since to do so carries with it no assurance that the vocal mechanism will remain free from interference. In the absence of an equilibrium, however, breath pressure must be used, since the energy wasted must be supplemented in order to sustain phonation.

See Breathing
   False Vocal Cords
   Neurochronaxic
      Theory

Abdominal Tuck: an abrupt contraction of the abdominal muscles at the onset of phonation.

Also called the "intercostal lift," the abdominal tuck is advocated by proponents of abdominal breathing and tonal support. It is accomplished by expanding the rib cage during inhalation and then driving the abdominal muscles and diaphragm upward and inward. Advocacy of this practice is based on three misconceptions: 1) that breath can be controlled during phonation; 2) that tone, which is nothing more than vibrations moving within a column of air, can be "supported," and 3) that the diaphragm (which, physiologically, relaxes in ascent and tenses in descent) can support tone by being pushed upward. The functional equilibrium essential to the proper production of tone is destroyed by this practice, and, pragmatically, it is a procedure which does not work.

See Breath Control

Abduct: from the Latin prefix *ab*, meaning "away," and the verb *ducere*, "to draw;" to move away from a median line, plane or midpoint. In singing, used with reference to the separation of the vocal folds.

See Vocal Folds

Abduction: a widening of the glottal space; a separating of the vocal folds to permit air to pass through the trachea into or out of the lungs.

Above the Breath: from the Italian *sopra il fiato*, a late nineteenth century pedagogic directive meaning that tone should be energized in the air spaces above the larynx (notably, in the antra, sinuses, and so-called "head cavities"), probably in an attempt to "get the tone out of the throat."

The directive to sing "above the breath" dates from an era when vocal instruction was geared to the replication of sensations of vibration which the teacher considered worthy of emulation. Directives to sing "above the breath" are nebulous and do not appear to be functionally useful.

Absolute Pitch: unfailing accuracy in pitch recognition. Many singers possess absolute pitch, but it is a gift which offers neither a functional advantage nor an indication of musical potential. When learning to sight sing, it is an advantage; when transposing, it is not.

Absolute pitch would seem to predominate with females, although no studies have been made to verify this assertion.

Acoustic Illusion: an aural deception concerning the nature, origin, or function of sound.

Paradoxically, almost everything connected with the vibratory sensations experienced during phonation seems to camouflage functional origins. Scientific investigation has established, for example, that "nasal" and "head" resonance are concepts without basis in fact, and that, along with impressions such as "forward" and "back," they are symptoms of specific types of laryngeal muscular coordination. Tones sound "forward" or "heady," for example, when they are the products of a well-balanced registration and proper laryngeal suspension, whereas they sound "back" or "nasal" when constrictor tensions have narrowed the laryngeal orifice. To cite another example, pitch is functionally neither "high" nor "low"— only a greater or lesser number of vibrations per second. Similarly, the apparent relaxation associated with efficient muscular coordination (whether it be in athletics, dancing or vocalization) is an illusion created by the absence of muscular interference.

See **Register**
  Sensations of
  Vibration

Manuel Garcia warned against the danger of treating illusion as reality when he cautioned not to be deceived by "mere appearances." Effective vocal pedagogy deals with things as they are—not as they seem to be.

Acoustics: the science of audible sound.

The acoustical studies most pertinent to vocal pedagogy are those which analyze the nature of various elements of voiced sound (*e.g.,* simple and complex sound waves, fundamentals and their partials, the properties of resonance, and vowel forms).

See **Aerodynamic**
  Theory
  Bernoulli Effect
  Reed Theory
  Resonance
  Standing Wave
  Vibrating String
  Theory

Although a basic knowledge of acoustics may serve to dispel theoretical misconceptions (such as tonal "placement" or "projection"), acoustic principles are analytical rather than creative: that is, they analyze the final product rather than propose techniques for improving the coordination of the total respiratory system, which is the source of voiced sound. A creative pedagogic approach, on the other hand, influences the manner in which the respiratory muscles adjust to articulate various pitch, intensity, and vowel patterns and to create a favorable resonance adjustment. Acoustic analysis can be an important pedagogic tool, however, since its results can contribute to the formulation of concrete functional principles based upon reality rather than illusion.

See **Neurochronaxic**
  Theory

Activator: in acoustics, an energy source responsible for setting a vibrator in motion. The breath is said to be the vocal activator, although a considerable body of scientific evidence contradicts this theory.

Adam's Apple: slang expression for the larynx, or "voice box." The term is probably derived from the fact that the larynx is significantly more prominent in men than in women.

See **Larynx**

Adduct: Latin, *adducere*, "to draw toward;" to move toward a median line, plane or midpoint. In singing, it indicates the approximation of the vocal folds as they become vibratile.

See **Register**
  Vowel

Adduction: a drawing together of the vocal folds to accommodate the frequency of higher pitch levels. In adduction, the posterior portions of the vocal folds approximate and press together, thereby shortening the anterior segment, which is left free to vibrate. The adduction of the vocal folds is achieved by the contraction of the thyroarytenoids in response to rising pitch and increased muscular tension. In phonation, as the pitch rises and greater portions of the vocal folds adduct and make contact, the glottal space becomes smaller and the vibrating surface of the cords thinner. An exact parallel to this process is the working of the common zipper, which, when made to close, gradually reduces the aperture above the adducted parts.

A precise adduction of the vocal cords is an indication that the vocal mechanism is working effectively as a unit, and it demonstrates that each tone of the musical scale has its own ideal ratio of registration. An unforced adduction of the vocal cords is largely dependent on two factors: 1) a well-developed, properly balanced registration, and 2) a proper laryngeal suspension.

See **Abduction**
    Larynx
    Vocal Folds

Adjustment: a rearrangement of physical parts made in response to changing conditions.

The vocal mechanism is comprised of three essential units: 1) the organs of respiration; 2) the vocal generator (larynx) and its surrounding pharyngeal resonators, and 3) the articulators. Each of these must be adjusted, "tuned," or positioned, if they are to function effectively in the production of sound. Since almost all of the muscular systems important to the qualitative properties of phonation are involuntary, neurological considerations (concepts, innervation) play a dominant role in the production of vocal tone. One of the essential difficulties in vocal training, therefore, is to understand and properly utilize the predictable correlations known to exist between stimulus and the reflexive movements of interior laryngeal processes, and to change (readjust) the response pattern of a poorly coordinated involuntary muscular system.

See **Breathing**
    Coordination
    Laryngeal
      Suspension
    Larynx
    Register
    Resonance
    Vocal Folds
    Vowel

Aerodynamic Theory: a theory proposed by Daniel Bernoulli, a Swiss scientist, dealing with the velocity, resistance, and pressure of air in motion.

Many scientists and vocal theorists believe that the aerodynamic laws discovered by Bernoulli are a factor in vocal fold approximation, but the number of reputable dissenters who have raised serious doubts as to its applicability indicates that this premise is purely speculative.

See **Bernoulli Effect**
    False Vocal Cords
    Puff Theory
    Sigh Tones
    Standing Wave
    Yawn-Sigh

Aesthetics: the abstract science or branch of philosophy that deals with the qualitative properties of beauty.

Any discussion of aesthetics inevitably includes art and technique. It is necessary, therefore, to be clear as to the meaning of all three if the role of aesthetics in the creative process is to be understood. Aesthetics is concerned with evaluating things of beauty, art is the use of skill and imagination in the production of those things, and technique is the ability to perform or produce them.

One of the glories of Western vocal culture has been its success in uniting art and aesthetics with functional health, a success based upon mechanical principles which utilize the natural action of the organic systems involved in phonation in a natural way. Art, aesthetics, technique, quality, and feeling have long been recognized to depend upon function, which, when efficient, gives ready expression to artistic intent. Certainly it is clear that when the vocal muscles are poorly coordinated, artistic demands cannot realistically be met because of limited quality and freedom.

The establishment of aesthetics as a primary basis for training the singing voice has been a serious impediment to vocal progress. This is because many aesthetically pleasing sounds can be produced under unsatisfactory technical conditions. For example, tones can be attractive and lovely (even if superficially) despite visible signs of vocal abuse such as a trembling of the tongue and jaw, a manifestation fairly common among many notable artists. Neither tremulous qualities nor the underlying muscular tensions which produce them can be subject to correction unless aesthetics is subordinated to those concerns related to function. In developing technical skills during training, therefore, aesthetics must give way to functional needs if performing success is not to be too strongly dependent upon personal charisma, musical sensitivity, and/or an extraordinary vocal potential.

To bring aesthetics, art, and function (technique) into proper perspective, it is essential that a distinction be made between the *art of singing* and the *process of learning to sing*. Artistic singing is a communicative experience falling directly within the province of aesthetics, and is to be judged on that basis; the process of developing vocal skills involves the isolation, development, and reintegration of those muscular systems whose activity determines the extent to which skill and imagination can be given expression.

In the final analysis, aesthetic sensitivity can only be fully expressed through technical mastery. Because training methods based upon aesthetics do not address themselves to function, they are incapable of effecting a real technical improvement.

See Bel Canto
Imagery
Modern Methods
(To) Progress
Vocal Study

Affective Expression: spontaneous sounds, usually made in response to an emotional stimulus. Laughing, crying, yawning, sobbing and screaming are all forms of affective expression, as are exclamations and similar responses.

Although it cannot be proven that he possessed even the simplest form of structured music, primeval man nevertheless possessed a facility for affective expression, and consequently an ability to sing. Infants use affective sounds such as cooing, gurgling, and wails of anger and frustration to communicate feelings and desires, sounds which must be considered a primitive form of singing. Singing itself, even in its most sophisticated form, must be considered an extension of affective expression, as opposed to speech, which is an acquired skill and a product of intellectual development.

It is this intrinsic capacity for affective expression that establishes the vocal mechanism as a singing instrument and leads to the conclusion that it is a double- rather than a single-valve instrument. During the production of those sounds associated with affective expression, the false vocal cords (the upper valve) close. This closure of the upper valve is imperative for singing, and occurs when the laryngeal and respiratory musculature is properly balanced. The false vocal cords are particularly well suited to act in this capacity since their downturned lower borders are perfectly designed to check the breath flow. Thus, they narrow to seal off all but a small portion of the opening into the pharyngeal cavity lying immediately above. The true vocal folds are not well constructed for this purpose—their upturned margins are designed (when closed) to prevent air, food particles, and other foreign matter from entering the lungs, rather than to resist air pressure.

Singing as a sophisticated form of affective expression, therefore, establishes a consonance between a physical positioning of the false vocal cords and the vibratory characteristics of the true vocal folds, and, additionally, between breath flow and emotional expression. The key to achieving this precarious psychophysical equilibrium is to utilize functional principles which will encourage natural, free, spontaneous movement. Practices which simulate yawning and coughing, and the use of expressions such as *ha, ha, ha*, because of their association with affective expression, are, when used with discrimination, helpful in gaining a sense of healthy, expansive movement within the throat parts.

Poor coordination among the numerous laryngeal muscles responsible for phonation destroys the natural link between affective expression, kinesthetic perception, and the cognitive powers of the mind. In the final analysis, it remains within the province of the functional principles that govern registration and pharyngeal resonance to lessen inhibitory tensions and facilitate spontaneous affective expression.

See **Kinesthesia**

Afferent: a term indicating the direction in which information is conveyed from a sensory receptor to the central nervous system. For example, when touching a hot object, the message "hot" is relayed from the finger to the brain along an afferent pathway. The brain then sends a motor impulse back to the finger via an efferent pathway. The processing of the information moving along the afferent and efferent pathways involves sensory receptors and nerves which make up the somatic and autonomic nervous systems.

It is important to note that all of the cranial nerves which give motor supply to the tongue, pharynx, and suspensory and laryngeal musculature (the glossopharyngeal, vagus, and trigeminal) also possess sensory branches which relay sense impressions of pain, pleasure, temperature, comfort and discomfort from these diverse areas to the brain. It is the impulses moving along different pathways that make the singer kinesthetically aware of his vocal mechanism and its functional state and condition. This awareness is crucial to the learning process since a "feel" for the right physical coordination during the production of vocal tone becomes a concrete reality and represents a special kind of "knowing."

See **Anxiety**
Autonomic Nervous System
Kinesthesia
Limbic System
Sensation
Somatic Nervous System

Affricate: a consonant whose production involves the tongue, lips and velum. The term is derived from the Latin *affricatus,* meaning "a rubbing on or against." Technically, an affricate is a stoppage of sound followed by a fricative (*e.g., pf*).

See **Consonants**

Agility: facility in singing swift musical passages accurately, smoothly, and evenly.

All voices which are correctly used will be agile, but all voices which are agile are not necessarily being correctly used. For example, some light voices which are products of a "mixed" registration can run with agility, despite the presence of considerable throat constriction. In such instances, however, the runs are rarely "clean" (*i.e.,* with each pitch precisely formed). Furthermore, such voices are seldom able to swell and diminish effectively—particularly in the lower range, where tones tend to fade out.

See **Registration, "Mixed"**

Agonist: in anatomy, a prime mover; a muscle opposed in action by another muscle, called the antagonist.

AIR STREAM

See Coordination
Laryngeal
Suspension
Register
Resonance

The human body is so arranged that the muscles attached to the skeletal framework are paired in the manner of a complex system of pulleys. Thus, for every action (muscular agonist) a countermovement can be made because another muscle or muscle group is performing as its natural antagonist. A correct technique of singing finds these largely involuntary processes in equilibrium not only with themselves, but with each other.

Air Stream: an aerodynamic term used with reference to the movement of air through the glottal space.

The expression "air stream" would appear to be inappropriate when applied to the singing voice. In a correct technique of singing, breath does not "stream" or "flow," but is emitted in a series of tiny puffs. These create pressure variations whose rhythmic disturbances of the surrounding air space are analogous to the visual impression received when a stone is thrown on the water: one is certain the water is moving in an outward direction, whereas in reality it is moving up and down. In both instances, however, a stream of air or tidal movement would disrupt the rhythmic pulsations and their resulting waves of sound or water.

The concept of air flow often appears in research papers in connection with the Bernoulli Effect. There are serious gaps in this theory, however: 1) no continuous streaming process occurs during phonation; 2) suction does not play a significant role under ordinary sound pressure, and 3) there are no low and high pressure regions of any significance within the mechanism to cause air to stream.

One of the tests applied in the nineteenth century to measure technical efficiency and breath expenditure during phonation was to hold a mirror close to the lips; if it remained unclouded, the vocal function was considered to be correct. A mirror could not possibly remain unclouded if breath were moving through the throat cavities in a stream.

In singing, when the technique is correct, that breath which does escape through the glottal space is minimal, and it trickles rather than flows.

See Aerodynamic
Theory
Bernoulli Effect
Breathing
False Vocal Cords

Alto: the lowest voice among women and boys, and the highest among men.

Derived from the Latin *altus*, meaning "high," the term "alto" originated in Renaissance music from the relative position of this voice to the tenor, which was assigned the melody. In early operatic terminology, alto meant the lower of the two falsetto voice types that were popular until the early part of the nineteenth century; the higher was referred to as the "soprano." In modern terminology, alto (or, more properly, "contralto") refers to the relatively rare, lowest female voice whose singable range should extend from D below middle C to the second B♭ above middle C. The term is also occasionally used to refer to the male alto, or countertenor, who sings in church choirs of men and boys.

See Castrato

Alveolar: a term derived from the Latin *alveolus*, meaning "small cavity," referring specifically to the sockets of the teeth.

See Consonants

Alveoli: tiny air sacs within the spongy tissue of the lungs through which oxygen is passed into the blood stream.

Amplitude: the distance between the crest and trough of any tonal oscillation.
When the technique is correct, the amplitude of the tonal pulse is directly pro-

10

portionate to both pitch and intensity. Amplitude is greatest, for example, when a high pitch is sung loudly. If the intensity is lowered, the amplitude is decreased; likewise, if pitch is lowered and intensity remains constant, the amplitude is also decreased.

Furthermore, the amount of energy required to sustain phonation is also proportionate to the amplitude of the tonal pulse: the greater the amplitude, the more energy is expended in singing, and *vice versa*. An accurate visual analogy of the relationship of amplitude to energy is presented by a child on a swing, where the amplitude of oscillation is dependent on the amount of energy expended in maintaining the movement.

See **Vibrato**

Anchored in the Chest: a figure of speech used to describe a sensation experienced when the cricopharyngeal muscle, which pulls the cricoid cartilage down and back, is brought into tension.

The feeling of the voice being "anchored in the chest" is experienced by a singer when the cricopharyngeal muscle works in conjunction not only with other members of the suspensory system (the thyrohyoids, sternohyoids, palatolaryngeals, stylopharyngeals, the omohyoids, and the sternothyroids), but also with the arytenoids, whose contraction approximates the vocal folds. When these systems coordinate effectively with the posterior cricoarytenoids and the cricothyroids, the mechanism produces tones which are open-throated, "ringing," and free.

From the standpoint of vocal mechanics, an anchored tone is a by-product of registration, since this symptom will not appear unless the chest register is properly developed and holds synergetically against the pull of the head voice. Pedagogic attempts to promote tonal "anchoring" by means of imagery, advice to depress or volitionally lower the larynx, or the employment of any device designed to act upon the mechanism not only fail to address themselves to the problem, but offer solutions which adversely affect all areas of vocal technique.

See **Cricopharyngeal Muscle**
Laryngeal Suspension
Register
Resonance

The impression of tones being "anchored in the chest" is common to all good vocalization and implies that a reasonably high level of technical skill has been attained.

Antagonistic Muscle(s): a muscle or muscle group whose contraction directly counters that of another muscle or group, known as an agonist, which opposes it. Ideally, all antagonistic muscle pairs should be maintained in a state of equilibrium, or balanced tension. In this state, all tones will be produced economically, since each primary muscular contraction (agonist) will be balanced by its natural antagonist.

See **Equilibrium**

Antrum: a body cavity; a sinus, especially the maxillary antrum.

Anxiety: uneasiness or disquietude of mind.

Anxiety seriously disrupts communication between the voluntary and involuntary muscular systems and the vegetative and nervous systems, fragments the personality, and limits personal expression. Most singers are afflicted by anxiety to a greater or lesser degree. For many, it is merely a matter of temporary, controllable performance "nerves." For others, however, it is a chronic, apparently insurmountable problem resulting from various deep-rooted neuroses.

APPARATUS

Chronic anxiety is a serious pedagogic concern since its physical manifestation often immobilizes the very muscles most crucial to the vocal function. In addition, the muscular armoring associated with anxiety frequently places the body in a state of permanent rigidity, making it difficult, if not impossible, to establish contact with movements which are free and natural. Curiously, however, some singers who suffer from chronic anxiety are able to cope with their inner tensions and make their neuroses work *for* rather than *against* their functional capacities. According to the theories advanced by Wilhelm Reich, and endorsed by Elsworth F. Baker, M.D.,[1] different types of "armoring" (primary and secondary layers) are reflected in specific types of physical and psychic reaction. Those who succeed in breaking through a secondary layer are those who are able to react in a more outgoing manner.

A second category, anxious singers who repress their feelings, presents a special problem. Not only do they resist, but the suppression of their anxiety is accomplished by bringing the swallowing muscles into tension, which inadvertently constricts the throat. Even when forcing themselves as an act of will to be more aggressive, those falling within this category find it difficult to relinquish the safe hold they maintain on their throats and feelings, and the use of greater energy is often counterproductive: the more vigorously they work to open up, the harder the constrictor muscles tend to resist. This is not to say, however, that the resistances peculiar to either of the types described cannot be broken down. With time and patience a more open-throated resonance can be achieved, in which case the singer will gain on two levels: he will have freed his voice and freed himself of many psychological inhibitions.

A possible explanation for the contradiction in behavior between the two broad types described is this: those who suppress their anxiety by minimizing the ebb and flow of natural respiration cause the damned-up energy to move into the internal organs where it is bottled up, whereas those less armored are able to release energy into the muscle system. From this it should be evident that the manner in which energy is utilized represents the qualitative factor in rhythmic sensitivity, in one's capacity to identify emotionally to a given stimulus, and in one's general capacity for motility. *Psychologically, singing is an aggressive act.* For one to "open up," energy must move into the muscles rather than turn inward.

If emotion is understood to be a process of bodily expansion, of moving out, it will then be clear that anxiety not only arrests organic motility, but inhibits healthy emotional expression as well. That this has an adverse effect upon the vocal process goes without saying, for whatever the degree of chronic muscular contraction brought on by anxiety, to that degree will the vocal process and respiration be impeded. Here, obviously, is an aspect of interference having nothing to do with singing *per se*. For this reason, among those who are equally talented, some will forge ahead and progress while others will pull back, literally being forced to remain within the boundaries set by their psychic tensions. In sum, the fears underlying psychic tensions arouse a profound distrust of involuntary movement and thus act as a serious impediment to vocal progress.

Apparatus: in anatomy, an arrangement of a number of physical parts acting together in the performance of some special function.

The term "apparatus," as used in vocal nomenclature, refers not only to the vocal

[1] Elsworth F. Baker, M.D., *Man in the Trap* (New York: Macmillan Company, 1967), pp. 4, 29.

See **Breathing and Emotion**
Emotion
Energy
Limbic System

folds and the muscles that directly act upon them, but also to the cartilaginous structures of the larynx.

See **Larynx**

Appoggiare la Voce: Italian, "to lean on the voice."

Taken at face value, this early pedagogic directive appears to be nonsense, since vocal tone, like that produced by all other instruments, is merely a series of complex sound waves that cannot be "leaned" upon.

The structure of the vocal mechanism, however, suggests a possible explanation for the coinage of such a phrase. The larynx, a respiratory organ which is also a part of the digestive tract, can be moved up and down to permit swallowing and ingestion. When used as a vocal organ, this mobility permits it to function efficiently as a primary resonator. Four paired suspensory muscles participate in stabilizing these movements, and when held in balanced tension, they coordinate to provide the resistance necessary to energy economy. When the suspensory muscles are maintained in equilibrium, the singer is able to "lean on the voice" and sing without fatigue.

See **Laryngeal
  Suspension**

Approximate: to draw together. In phonation, the term is used to refer to the closing of the glottal space as the vocal folds come together.

Arched Palate: a backward and upward movement of the soft palate made possible by a contraction of the tensor and levator muscles.

A volitional arching of the palate is commonly practiced in an effort to enlarge the upper pharyngeal cavities, which adjust to form and resonate the vowel. The device is ill advised on several counts: 1) the control of isolated functional areas results in a lowering of overall effectiveness, increasing rather than decreasing the possibility of throat constriction; 2) certain vowels (*oo*) cannot be produced with an arched palate, and in energizing higher partials for tonal brilliance, the palate must be lowered somewhat, and 3) some voiced consonants (*m*) require that the nasal passages remain open, while for others (*wh*) they must remain closed, in which case a consistently arched palate inhibits an essential flexibility of movement.

While an arching of the palate will occur reflexively during "covering," it also takes place when the face is forced into an artificial smile, especially when accompanied by a lifting of the facial muscles. This latter practice is not only unattractive, but, by raising the larynx, it stiffens the throat parts and causes the voice to sound "shrill." The disadvantage of singing with a volitionally arched palate is that it represents an attempt to institute direct control over processes which are essentially reflexive. Such a practice is both unnecessary and unnatural.

See **Covering,
  (To) Cover
Formants
Hum
Laryngeal
  Suspension
Modern Methods
Register
Resonance
Vowel**

Articulation: the physical process involved in uttering consonants.

Articulation and the articulatory processes are important to phonation because it is by these means that words are clearly delineated. The muscular processes involved, however, must be considered separate and distinct from vowel formation, although both must function as a coordinate unit. The reason for this is clear: each vowel has a particular tonal form and resonance characteristic that requires a relatively fixed cavity adjustment, whereas the muscles of the tongue, lips, jaw and face must be highly mobile for the articulation of consonants. In most instances, articulatory demands must be subordinated for a considerable time during training to the needs of the tonal form, for unless tone production can be made independent of articulation, a clear enunciation of text is virtually impossible. In good singing, neither tone nor articulation is sacrificed for the other.

To achieve this cooperative independence of tone and articulation, the mouth must be "detuned" as a resonator. All vowels must be resonated pharyngeally so that the tongue, lips, jaw and facial muscles may remain relaxed and ready to move freely. When tone becomes independent of articulation and *vice versa,* the voice will emerge freely and easily, the tone quality will be pure, articulation, clean, the face, expressive, and the text easily understandable.

Articulatory Processes: those portions of the body (namely, the tongue, the hard and soft palates, teeth, lips, jaw and facial muscles) which are used in forming consonants.

Artificial Channeling: the misdirection of conscious effort, which produces muscular movements that impede spontaneous, natural movements.

Singing methods which attempt to consciously control function (such as those founded on "breath control," voice "placement," or nasal "resonance") inadvertently encourage artificial channeling.

Arytenoid Cartilage: a ladle-shaped, tough, whitish tissue of gristly texture, which connects the larynx and the arytenoid muscle. The word "arytenoid" is derived from the Greek word for ladle.

Arytenoid Muscles: one of the two muscle groups responsible for the phenomenon of registration. The group itself is comprised of the transverse arytenoids, the oblique arytenoids, and the cricoarytenoids. When tensed, these are responsible for yielding tone qualities commonly recognized as "chest voice."

Aryvocalis: muscle fibers embedded within the thyroarytenoid.

Aspirate: a semi-consonant formed by the gradual closing of the vocal folds, which allows air to escape unchecked (*e.g., he*).

Attack: to initiate vocal tone; the physical events that take place as tone is generated within the laryngeal pharynx.

Two important factors are involved in the physical process which yields vocal tone: 1) the tensing of the vocal folds, which enables them to meet the requirements of various pitch-intensity patterns, and 2) the positioning of the larynx and pharyngeal cavities, which results in tonal amplification or resonance. At the inception of vocal tone, the muscle groups responsible for these two processes move from relaxation to balanced tension. The precision of the attack is determined by the efficiency of these movements.

The ascription "attack" is singularly inappropriate to describe the onset of phonation, since it implies an aggressive beginning which can only be successfully executed by those whose technique is extremely well advanced. A superior concept is the old Italian expression *con slancio,* which means "to launch;" the underlying impression is one of gentleness rather than forcefulness, of allowing the physical mechanisms involved to come into motion rather than acting upon them.

See Consonants

See **Intrinsic Musculature of the Larynx**
Register
See **Vocal Folds**
Vocalis Muscles

The ideal tonal attack is to "let" the mouth open, think the vowel and tonal form, and then "hear" vibrations appear within the thought form, without acting upon them. The vocal folds can easily be approximated neurologically by "thinking" them to close, and it is this phenomenon which prepares the mechanism for phonation and makes a clean attack one without pre-tension or guttural noises.

See Con Slancio
    Onset

Auditory Feedback: sound sensations perceived by a singer after he has produced them.

Auditory feedback creates a dichotomy between the singer's initial tonal concept and his perception of the sounds he has produced for these reasons: 1) the realization of the singer's original tonal concept is limited by the degree of faulty muscular coordination present in his technique; 2) the sound heard is the product of vibratory impulses transmitted through the external atmosphere, which differ in phase from those radiated through the skeletal framework by bone conduction, and 3) the perception of the sound marks a shift in concentration from "sending" to "receiving," *i.e.*, conceptualizing to listening.

The conflicts introduced by auditory feedback can only be resolved by changing the singer's attitude toward quality. If both the concept and its translation into sound are evaluated on the basis of functional mechanics (*i.e.*, registration and resonance) rather than on aesthetics, discrepancies between the two can easily be reconciled. By treating concepts in this way, qualitative evaluation can take on a new dimension: one which unites mechanical function with its concrete realization in sound.

See Ear
    Functional
      Listening
    Hearing
    Masking
    Self-Listening
    White Noise

Auditory feedback is a problem with which each singer must learn to cope. Its successful resolution depends upon an ability to learn to "hear" functionally.

Auditory Nerve: a nerve attached to the central spiral of the snail-like cochlea (the inner ear) and inserted into a perforated bone called the modiolus. The auditory nerve enters the back of the cochlea, its external section uniting with nerves belonging to the semicircular canals and dividing into two parts, which form the eighth cranial nerve.

See Basilar Membrane
    Ear
    Organ of Corti
    Eustachian Tube

Autonomic Nervous System: the nervous system which innervates the visceral organs, glands, cardiovascular and involuntary muscles, and telegraphs somatic impulses to the central nervous system.

The autonomic nervous system is divided into two parts: the sympathetic and the parasympathetic. Both are concerned with visceral or involuntary functions that cannot be consciously regulated or controlled.

The parasympathetic system is related to vegetative reactions such as digestion and the redirecting of blood from the skeletal muscles to the viscera. The sympathetic nervous system increases the flow of blood to the skeletal muscles, speeds the heart rate and respiration, and functions as a personal and nonintellectual response to environmental pressures. Emotional reactions brought on by anxiety, performance nerves, and other emotional stimuli are both processed and "remembered" by this system. It is quite possible that methods devoted to breath control were originally instituted to bring this system into equilibrium.

See Afferent
    Breath Control
    Cerebellum
    Cerebrum
    Emotion
    Kinesthesia
    Limbic System
    Somatic Nervous
      System

The autonomic nervous system is active in the production of energy, reacting to environmental pressures and determining whether bio-energy will be rigid or free.

B

Back: See Too Far Back.

Back Vowels: See Vowel, Front and Back.

Baritone: the male voice type whose range (the second G below middle C to A♭ above middle C) lies between that of the tenor and bass. Although the modern baritone's range is practically identical with that of the pre-Romantic tenor, the baritone timbre is noticeably richer and heavier.

As opera developed during the course of the nineteenth century, various musical and dramatic demands created a need for special vocal categories. Thus, baritones came to be classified as "lyric baritones," "French baritones," "Verdi baritones," "dramatic baritones," or "Heldenbaritones."

Although some baritones function successfully in many different musical styles, subcategorization appears to have some artistic justification, since vocal music frequently requires specific tonal weights, textures, and coloration for optimum performance.

Baritone-Tenor: a male voice whose technical deficiencies disguise its true timbre and make classification difficult.

The tonal compass of lyric baritones and dramatic tenors is almost identical, and until technical problems have been worked out satisfactorily and the true voice quality established, the ambiguity of classification cannot be resolved. An additional vocal classification offers nothing in the way of a solution to this and related problems.

Basilar Membrane: a membrane encased within and lying at the base of the cochlea, dividing it into three parts, or canals: the scala media, the scala tympani, and the scala vestibuli. The tentacle-like end of the basilar membrane, together with the lamina spiralis, forms a partition between the scala tympani and the other two canals; when sound waves pass from one canal to the other, the membrane vibrates sympathetically.

Movements of the basilar membrane cause the hair cells protruding from the organ of Corti to be stimulated at their base, "broadcasting" an electrical current through the tissues nearest them. Since these fibers are incapable of carrying the full range of frequencies the brain is capable of registering, it is believed that they send symbolic representations and "information" by means of coded messages. These are communicated by a technique much the same in principle as that used when data is simplified and processed into a computer. Once coded, the messages being delivered along the auditory nerve are then relayed to the brain.

See **Ear**
Masking
Organ of Corti

Bass: the lowest male voice type.

Within this general classification, four subcategories are commonly recognized: 1) the *basso cantante* or "singing bass," whose range should extend from the second F below middle C to G above middle C; 2) the *basso*, whose range should extend from the second D below middle C to F# above middle C; 3) the *basso buffo* or "comic bass," who specializes in character acting and whose range is identical to that of the *basso,* and 4) the *basso profundo* or "deep bass," a vocal rarity whose range extends from the second C below middle C to the E above middle C.

Since lower voices must employ more chest register than the higher voice types, bass voices are frequently considered intrinsically inflexible and unwieldy. This is not true, however, since the well-used bass voice (particularly the *basso cantante*) is not only sonorous, but extremely facile in the execution of rapid passages.

Bass-Baritone: a male voice type whose ideal range extends from low F to high F#. The voice quality of the bass-baritone is somewhat lighter than that of the *basso cantante* and heavier than that of the dramatic baritone.

The term "bass-baritone" has acquired a somewhat derogatory connotation over the years through its association with poorly developed male voices of limited range. While the term is sometimes misapplied, the bass-baritone is nevertheless a legitimate vocal category with an operatic repertory peculiarly suited to its textural properties and range, *e.g.*, Mozartian and Wagnerian roles.

Beginner: an inexperienced or unskilled singer; a novice.

See **Exercises**
Modern Methods
Practice
Vocal Study

Pedagogically, beginners form a rather strange category, since experience and skill in singing do not necessarily go hand in hand. One may have studied for many years, and technically still be a beginner; conversely, one may never have studied at all, and because of superior natural gifts, be technically advanced. Protracted study and performance may add up to experience, but unless the experience is constructive, its negative aspects will leave the singer worse off than a beginner, since he will have to "unlearn" most of what he has so carefully studied before real progress can be made.

Bel Canto: Italian, "beautiful singing;" a style of singing characterized by brilliant vocal display and purity of tone.

The term Bel Canto is commonly used to refer not only to a style of singing, but also to an era of operatic history, to a musical style, and to a pedagogical technique for training the singing voice. The era itself began in the early part of the eighteenth century and flourished until the middle of the nineteenth.

Whether the musical style or the pedagogic technique which made its execution possible came first is difficult to say, but it is certain that the functional principles used by voice teachers of the time produced singers possessing special qualities.

The interaction between musical style and the quality of its executants was indicated by Estaban Arteaga, who, in an article appearing in *Le Rivoluzioni del Teatro Musicale Italiano* (Venice, 1785), observed "But nothing contributes so much to clarify Italian music at the time as the excellence and abundance of the singers."

As opera grew in popularity, composers took advantage of the exceptional technical prowess exhibited by the prominent artists of the period, and the elaborate ornamentation and bravura display contained in these works afford considerable insight into their vocal abilities. What appears evident, in measurable terms, is that these singers possessed powerful voices which were extensive in range, flexible, capable of sustaining long phrases with ease, and able to swell and diminish at will. In addition to these technical accomplishments, the Bel Cantists were also musicians of the highest order, and one of the required skills was an ability to spontaneously improvise and embellish a melody during a performance.

Careful examination of the available evidence related to early teaching practices explains why the vocal art blossomed so dramatically in the eighteenth and nineteenth centuries. Through necessity, the founders of the art of Bel Canto became, in essence, natural scientists. They observed the manner in which the vocal organs were prone to respond and formed conclusions on the basis of those observations. By simply observing, they were able to grasp the fact that the response was not always uniform, and that the lack of uniformity was caused by differences in the dynamics of the musical figure or phrase being sung. From this, it was but another logical step to conclude that the functional reaction of the vocal organs is predictable, *i.e.*, that a definite correlation exists between a particular type of musical stimulus and vocal response. Implicit in this understanding was the fact that "voice" was recognized to be a product of a mechanism, or mechanisms, without any mechanical function of its own, and that voice "building" was primarily a matter of coordinating more effectively those purely involuntary physical activities taking place within the vocal organs proper.

The structure upon which early training had been based was one in which functional laws were formulated, understood and utilized on a practical basis. Procedures to improve physical coordination were clearly predicated upon a belief that the vocal mechanism is self-regulatory, and will, when properly stimulated, respond naturally in a natural, *i.e.*, functionally healthy, way. Proof of this is to be found in a statement by Mancini:

> Art consists of knowing where nature directs us, and to what we have been destined; understanding at once the gifts of nature and cultivating them easily, man can perfect himself; how sure is harvest for the attentive farmer, who has observed and understood the different seeds, which are fecund in diverse types of earth.[2]

[2]Giam Battista Mancini, *Practical Reflections on Figured Singing*, translated by E. Forman (Champaign, Ill.: Pro Musica Press, 1967), p. 115.

Given this understanding, it is evident that a direct parallel was recognized to exist between plant growth in response to specific combinations of soil, moisture and sunlight, and vocal growth in relation to equally compatible arrangements of pitch, intensity and vowel, *i.e.*, a vocal exercise as elemental as a single tone or a musical phrase.

Procedures for cultivating the voice (in what would be more properly called coordinating the laryngeal muscular system responsible for the production of vocal tone) centered on the development and integration of the two vocal registers, which were termed the *voce di petto,* or "chest voice," and the falsetto. Years of experience with the falsettists and *castrati* had indicated that various patterns of pitch, intensity, and vowel evoked responses which were both predictable and radically different. Thus, vocal exercises for the stimulation and recoordination of the involuntary muscles yielding those "voices" were constructed on the principle that vocal tone did not have to be "produced," but happened reflexively, and that the mechanism itself constituted a self-contained ecological system. In this system, the selected exercise established an environment which, when congenial to the growth needs of the mechanism, enabled it to flourish like a well-tended garden and develop in its own way and time in accordance with nature's laws.

From the standpoint of utility, the most impressive aspect of early training was that the techniques employed were not mechanistic. There was a total absence of "do this" instruction, and a natural phenomenon was dealt with in a natural way. What appears evident is that vocal development was accomplished by stimulating involuntary muscular activities within the laryngeal pharynx by means of carefully selected vocal exercises. The physical constitution of these exercises, when properly proportioned, were observed to elicit response patterns which indicated an improved functional condition and a greater inner freedom.

The natural laws upon which Bel Canto training procedures were founded have been admirably summed up in this century by Edmund J. Myer:

> Nature was the great teacher and not man. Man, when he bases his teaching upon his own ideas of voice, is too artificial; hence, artificiality. Witness the many ridiculous things singers are (now) taught to do. With such the effort is to make the voice, to compel it, instead of *allow* it. Nature teaches differently. The voice is in Nature, and by a study of Nature and Nature's laws the voice is allowed to develop; is allowed or induced to reveal itself instead of being made, compelled or forced.[3]

[3]Edmund J. Myer, *Position and Action in Singing* (Boston: G. Schirmer, 1911), p. 9.

With these remarks, Myer touches upon the essence of early pedagogic thought, practice and belief. It was this understanding of the vocal mechanism and "voice" that led to the formulation of functional principles during the seventeenth and eighteenth centuries which, because they are valid, are as valid now as they were then.

The influence of Italian teaching extended to England and the Continent. In Germany, Agricola translated Tosi's *Observations*, and training methods based upon registration were instituted by Marpurg, Mattheson, Hiller, Lasser, von Engelbrunner, and other prominent teachers of that country. Mattheson, stressing his agreement with Mancini, found all voice types (including the soprano) to be capable of producing a falsetto. Rameau, Mengozzi, Fétis, Blanchet, and the German, Martini (born Schwarzendorf), established Italian training methods in France, where their influence can be recognized by the terms *voix de poitrine* and *voix de tête*. Tosi, Tenducci, Corri, Lanza, and, much later, Garcia, brought the Italian vocal tradition to England.

The essence of the art of Bel Canto, both the musical style and the pedagogic technique for training the singing voice, is to be found within its naturalness and simplicity, and it is there that one must look in order to understand it.

Bel Canto, Functional Basis of: formulations and techniques developed as a consequence of the observation of the parallel relationships that exist between natural, reflexive organic movements and their corresponding expression in tone quality, and the physical composition of the musical phrase by which these movements were stimulated.

These relationships are analyzed below in the order of their importance.

REGISTRATION

The first of the numerous parallels to engage pedagogic interest was registration. This phenomenon was recognized as early as the fourteenth century, when an Italian named Marchetto reported that one of the vocal tricks of his time was to pass from the chest register to the falsetto after the manner of a yodel. The two registers were known at the time as the *vox integra* and the *vox ficta*. That these "voices" became a matter of serious pedagogic concern is evident from the writings of many prominent teachers who emerged during the eighteenth century. The first of these was Pier. Francesco Tosi (1647—1727), who described them as follows:

> *Voce di petto* is a full voice, which comes from the Breast by Strength, and is most sonorous and expressive. *Voce di Testa* comes more from the Throat than from the Breast, and is capable of more volubility. *Falsetto* is a Feigned Voice, which is entirely from the Throat, has more volubility than any, but of no substance.[4]

Some years later, Giam Battista Mancini (1716—1800), a pupil of the illustrious Bernacchi, expressed himself similarly:

> The voice ordinarily divides itself into two registers, one called the "chest," the other the "head," or falsetto. Every student, whether a soprano, alto, tenor or bass can easily know the difference between these two registers. The great art of the singer consists in acquiring the ability to render, imperceptible to the ear, the passing from one register to the other.[5]

Manfredini (1737—1799) was another who recognized the importance of registration to voice production, as is evident from one of his chapter headings, which reads "On combining the chest voice with the head voice, vulgarly called falsetto." Continuing with respect to joining them, he added the following:

> . . . this is to be accomplished not by forcing the high chest tones but rather by reinforcing the lower tones of the falsetto, or else doing the opposite, if the chest tones happen to be weaker and deficient and the falsetto tones plentiful and strong.[6]

Qualitatively, all who expressed an opinion concerning the falsetto recorded it as being "breathy," "veiled," weak in its lower extension, and literally a false tone. Because of its close proximity to the chest voice, it was also recognized that, when properly integrated with that mechanism, the falsetto would modify and become a true tone quality of exceptional beauty.

The gap between the chest register and the falsetto, or head voice, came to be known as the "break" or "bridge" (*il ponticello*). To eliminate this gap and so unify

[4]Pier. Francesco Tosi, *Observations on the Florid Song,* translated by Galliard (London: Reeves Bookseller, Ltd., 1926), p. 22.

[5]Giam Battista Mancini, *Practical Reflections on the Figurative Art of Singing* (Milan, 1776), translated by Pietro Buzzi (Boston: The Gorham Press, 1912), p. 58.

[6]Vincenzo Manfredini, "Dell' unire la voce di petto colla voce di testa, la quale volgarmente chiamasi falsett," *Regole Armoniche,* second edition (Venice, 1797), p. 61. Cited and translated by Philip A. Duey, *Bel Canto in its Golden Age* (New York: Kings Crown Press, 1951), p. 116.

the functional activities of the two basic mechanisms, advanced singers were introduced to the art of the *messa di voce,* or the swelling and diminishing of a single tone. Specific details for accomplishing this juncture were recorded by Isaac Nathan (1791—1864):

> The rule experience pronounces infallible is this: when the singer after having cultivated the lower tones (which form the basis and give the character to his voice) arrives at the *break* or meeting of the registers *di petto* and *di testa,* let him proceed to the feigned voice, alone; let him increase its power by swelling, and let him gradually unite it with the chest voice rather by its own enlarged volume than by any exertion of the latter—thus affected, the junction will be imperceptible, and once gained will never be lost. It is only by voices so formed, that the higher effects of the heart can be produced, or that the qualities so often lauded be realized.[7]

[7]Isaac Nathan, *Musurgia Vocalis* (London: Fentum, 1836), p. 146.

An important element of the above procedure, one designed to encourage the appearance of the "feigned" voice was to 1) change from an *oo* vowel to *ah,* and 2) reduce the level of intensity at the point of register transition, since it was found through experience to be impossible to sing a pure falsetto on this vowel under these conditions. The result was that the tone quality modified reflexively, taking on a "singy" quality, to emerge as the head voice. By utilizing this simple exercise, the falsetto was transformed into a truly legitimate tone quality—one which, with proper development, could become powerful, flexible, and extensive in range.

The adoption of the *messa di voce* and other exercises utilized in early training was a direct result of the observation of the parallel relationships that exist between musical stimuli (varying combinations of pitch, intensity, and vowel) and the mechanics of registration. Through the skillful manipulation of these basic musical elements, early training became a dynamic process in which the vocal muscles could be coordinated more effectively, and a faulty technique could be thoroughly restructured.

The two-register theory and the techniques to be employed in unifying the registers were, with few exceptions, generally agreed upon until the middle of the nineteenth century, or shortly before Garcia invented the laryngoscope (1854). This change in viewpoint appears to have coincided with the ending of the era of the *castrati.*

With the ascendency of the *prima donna,* the relationship between the falsetto and the head voice became more difficult to discern. To sing is to coordinate, and with women's voices this means that the falsetto, acting conjunctively with the chest register, finds its textural properties modified to become the head voice, the effect being expressed in a dramatic extension of the upper tonal range. Because the lower portion of the head voice is often weak and breathy (betraying the influence of the falsetto, whose essential characteristic is breathiness), it was essential that this tonal area be reinforced. The result was a quality transformation that introduced a third tonal texture, one commonly misnamed "middle."

The confusion surrounding the mechanical derivation of the lower tones of the female head voice led Mathilde Marchesi (1821—1913), teacher of Melba, Calvé, Eames, and other prominent singers, to make this declaration:

The three registers of the female voice are the Chest, Middle and Head. I use the term Middle and not Falsetto (the word used by some professors of singing) firstly, because the word Medium (middle) precisely and logically explains the position that this register occupies in the compass of the voice, and, secondly, to avoid all confusion that might be caused by the term *Falsetto*, which belongs exclusively to men's voices. Falsetto, which signifies *Falso* (false), that is, *in place of the true,* is a term that has been used in Italy from the earliest period in the history of the art of singing, to indicate certain *piano* effects in the high tones of the tenor voice.[8]

[8]Mathilde Marchesi, *Bel Canto: A Theoretical and Practical Vocal Method,* edited by Philip L. Miller (New York: Dover Publications, Inc., 1970), p. xiv.

On the basis of earlier theoretical opinion, which viewed registration as being common in all essentials to all voice types, male and female, the information supplied by Marchesi is patently false. What it does indicate, however, is that the question of registers occupied the thinking of serious teachers of voice from the earliest times until the end of the nineteenth century, and that registration was the foundation upon which Bel Canto training procedures succeeded in "building" the vocal techniques that will forever remain a source of astonishment and wonder.

PURITY OF INTONATION

In addition to their stated concerns for registration and register development, early teaching practices placed considerable emphasis upon purity of intonation, a postulate which referred to an unblemished tone quality or "nothing but the vowel." Tosi made this clear in the following statement:

> Let the master attend with great care to the voice of the scholar, which, whether it be *di petto* or *di testa,* should always come forth neat and clear, without passing through the nose, or being choked in the throat. . . . Let the scholar be obliged to pronounce the vowels distinctly . . . if the fault is not the master's, it is the singers', who are scarce got out of their first lesson.[9]

[9]Pier. Francesco Tosi, *Observations on the Florid Song,* translated by Galliard (London: Reeves Bookseller, Ltd., 1926), pp.18, 25.

While the expression "purity of intonation" represented an admired attribute of Bel Canto instruction, details as to how this was to be accomplished are scanty. In the absence of instruction other than to "pronounce the vowels distinctly," it must be assumed that the different vowels were known to be capable of both influencing and being influenced by registration. Justification for this assumption is provided by Isaac Nathan in his discussion of the "feigned voice:"

> Should my observation on the "feigned" voice appear obscure and the tyro find any difficulty effecting its practice, or in distinguishing it from the falsetto, which is not improbable from the seeming affinity the two sounds bear to each other, he may at once satisfy every doubt upon that point by exercising his falsetto on different vowels, in which attempt he will discover it to be physically impossible to articulate the Italian broad *a*, but the "feigned" voice will against all resistance instinctively become the vehicle of its intonation—at this crisis the two qualities of tone must be instantly detected.

> The tyro having thus far satisfied his ear in distinguishing the "feigned" voice from the falsetto, should endeavour to blend those two qualities of tone by commencing with his falsetto upon any given sound, and whilst in the act of prolonging that sound, change the vowel without taking breath, as

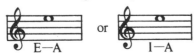

this will decidedly effect the desired union, which having been accomplished, the next object must be that of uniting the "feigned" voice with the *voce di petto.*

Let every note be begun in the "feigned" voice as softly as possible, by swelling gently, and immediately returning to the first *piano;* as the voice increases in power and quality let the swell be increased, yet with caution; the slightest irregularity or roughness being a sign that the singer has exceeded the development of which his organ is capable.[10]

[10]Isaac Nathan, *Musurgia Vocalis*(London:Fentum, 1836), p. 145.

In view of the fact that "purity of intonation" was referred to in a casual rather than specific way by early authorities, one is forced to conclude that this goal was achieved by other means, *i.e.,* by improving the functional capabilities of the vocal organs through the use of various vowels in conjunction with the development and integration of the two register mechanisms. Many teachers have subsequently cited the advantages to be gained by utilizing the Italian *ah,* some even advancing the exaggerated claim that a precise pronunciation of the verbal text will improve function. The question arises, however, as to whether or not the benefits provided by the use of the Italian *ah* (or any vowel) are intrinsic to the vowel itself, or, as Nathan suggests, merely vowel sounds best adapted to a bridging and/or development of the registers.

On the basis of the information supplied by the instruction manuals of the time, it is evident that "purity of intonation" as it equates with the vowel and tonal purity must be considered both a means and an end. With so much emphasis placed on the development and integration of the vocal registers, it is certain that the *use* of a given vowel was considered the means, and the *achievement* of vowel purity an end result.

The above postulate is readily supportable when evaluated on a functional basis. A vowel (tone quality) can only be as pure as the coordinative (mechanical) process will allow. Thus, it is evident that registration (which directly affects the coordinative process) was considered a means for gaining access to the functioning parts of the mechanism itself, and when properly developed, "allowed" the vocal organs to respond to the concepts of tonal purity so greatly admired. The achievement of this goal, together with the "inexhaustible respiration" so commonly noted, obviously did not depend upon mechanical processes contained within the vowel or tone quality alone, but upon the physical coordination of the laryngeal musculature.

BREATHING

The subject of breathing, from a mechanical standpoint, did not occupy a position of great prominence in early training. Theoretical opinion varied widely, ranging from Vincenzo Cirillo's (1623—1667) remark *"Mio dio!* If God has not taught you how to breathe, it is time you were buried" to Pacchiarotti's "He who knows how to breathe knows how to sing." Specific breathing techniques (abdominal, intercostal and/or clavicular) did not engage pedagogic interest; this shift in emphasis was a late nineteenth century development that probably coincided with an increasing demand for great volume of tone to match the heavy orchestration of later operatic works.

Explanations advanced during the Bel Canto era as to the most efficient technique to be employed in managing the breath generally favored a slightly elevated chest position (as reflected in the posture of a good dancer), but greater concern was shown for avoiding audible breathing, breathing in the middle of a word, and using the breath wastefully. The avoidance of wasteful expenditure could perhaps be said to represent a form of breath "economy" (although the expression was never used), yet it is more likely that the directive was issued to counteract the natural tendency of most beginners to "push" their voices and dissipate energy by over-singing. The prevailing attitude toward breathing was, as Manfredini (1737—1799) so aptly phrased it, to "take the breath in the requisite manner and at the proper time."[11]

Mancini, the most eloquent spokesman of the period, was fully aware that good breathing habits depend upon efficient laryngeal activity (the development and integration of the vocal registers), and while breath compression was known to be important as an energy source, breath was not considered to be the instrument itself. This insight is implicit in the following statement:

> The air from the lungs acts upon the larynx in singing, just as it acts upon the head of a flute that is leaned to the lips for playing. The lungs are not the actual organs of the voice; they merely furnish the material, the air. . . . I conclude by saying that it is not enough for one to have merely an elevated chest and a capacity for big noise to become a successful singer.[12]

Isaac Nathan, a direct descendant of the Porpora School, summed up the attitude of early nineteenth century pedagogy with reference to breathing:

> The lungs, like an organ, must depend upon a current of air for the production of sound. The singer should first take an inspiration, as if to sigh, taking care to take so much breath under command, that one note might be continued at pleasure; gradually increasing or diminishing the sound without labour. The chest being thus inflated, it should be an object to sound the note as softly as possible, before any of the breath expires, gradually increasing the sound to the fullest extent of the voice, and diminishing it in the same ratio, until it is scarcely perceptible to the ear.[13]

The statements quoted above, representing the substance of early theoretical postures with respect to breathing, contain no information to justify the belief that the *mechanics* of breathing occupied a place of importance in early training, and, indeed, suggest that something is missing. Cirillo's comment says too little, while Pacchiarotti's, if taken literally, claims too much. Certainly such a broad assertion as Pacchiarotti's stands in direct opposition to fact, since it is evident that many sing well who breathe incorrectly, just as there are many who sing badly but breathe properly. On neither a theoretical nor a pragmatic basis can a direct parallel be discovered between the two events. Mancini's assertion that it is "not enough to have merely an elevated chest position" surely admits the possibility that other, more important principles are responsible for a free tonal emission. Nathan, in stressing the necessity for utilizing the breathing technique he advocated, used it

[11]Vincenzo Manfredini, "Dell' unire la voce di petto colla voce di testa, la quale volgarmente chiamasi falsett," *Regole Armoniche*, second edition (Venice, 1797), p. 78. Cited and translated by Philip A. Duey, *Bel Canto in its Golden Age* (New York: Kings Crown Press, 1951), p. 116.

[12]Giam Battista Mancini, *Practical Reflections on the Figurative Art of Singing* (Milan, 1776), translated by Pietro Buzzi (Boston: The Gorham Press, 1912), p. 53.

[13]Isaac Nathan, *Musurgia Vocalis* (London: Fentum, 1836), p. 121.

in conjunction with the act of swelling and diminishing, and by implication directly linked the art of breathing with the mechanics of registration.

It was left to later authorities to clarify the importance of breathing to the phonative process. One of the most persuasive was William Shakespeare (1849—1931), a notable singer and pupil of the younger Lamperti. His explanation concerning the "voice of the breath" follows:

> [Its] meaning can only be that the voice should be trained to respond fully to a breath pressure which we are able to control and economize so that none escapes in waste. . . . The old singers judged whether the vocal cords were acting naturally, or whether they were squeezed out of the right position, by two signs. First, when rightly produced the note should be sung with comparatively little breath, and this, combined with a proper control, gave rise to the system of practicing before a lighted taper, or a mirror, or against the finger, in order to discover if the note sounded full to a breath pressure which would last twenty to thirty seconds without causing the candle to flicker, or tarnishing the mirror, or unduly warming the finger. Supposing the note to have been wrongly produced, the singer was compelled to use greater breath pressure than he could control.[14]

[14]William Shakespeare, *The Art of Singing* (Bryn Mawr, Pa.: Oliver Ditson Co., 1898), pp. 24, 25.

Commenting further, he stated that "under this system, it was found that the right note produced the most sound with the least expenditure of breath." And later, he stated "The second sign was the unconscious action of the larynx."

The substance of these remarks indicates that it was not a controlled technique of breathing which either regulated the rate of breath expenditure or assured a correct technique of tone production, but that breath expenditure was understood to be controlled by function. The procedures to be adopted to improve function centered on techniques for stabilizing the larynx and developing and integrating the vocal registers. Shakespeare's opinion agreed substantially with the view expressed by Garcia, who, while supporting Pacchiarotti's dictum, nevertheless did not consider the *mechanics* of breathing important enough to dwell on them either extensively or in detail. In his last work, *Hints on Singing*, seven full pages were devoted to the subject of registration, and to breathing, only seven lines.

With the rather sketchy information recorded as to the mechanics of breathing, it might be advantageous to search elsewhere for an explanation of its importance to phonation. If, therefore, a distinction is raised between the *process of learning to sing, i.e.,* the acquisition of skills one did not formerly possess, and the *art of singing*, or the tasteful utilization of skills already acquired, the statement of Pacchiarotti quoted above may be justly considered rational and included as an important functional element in vocal study. One must sing with feeling, and the emotional commitment, once made, must be free and yet restrained, spontaneous and at the same time controlled. Since the respiratory function is disturbed under emotional stress, the vocal organs (the mechanical process resulting in "voice") must be maintained in equilibrium. Consequently, feelings must be regulated and brought under discipline.

In his expression of feeling, therefore, the artist must learn to strike a balance between natural functioning and control over natural impulses. He must learn how to make others laugh and cry without laughing and crying himself; he must learn to be involved, yet aloof; to feel profoundly, yet stop short of being overwhelmed by his feelings. It is the "cool head, but warm heart" often cited by so many great singers. By "feeling with his breathing," the artist is able to regulate, control and maintain this precarious balance. Breathing techniques developed with this end in view, however, are concerned not with the mechanics of function, but with the mechanics of feeling.

The importance of respiratory equilibrium to the emotional projection of the music and text in artistic singing has been described by Shakespeare in the following terms:

> With the great singer a never ceasing pressure of breath is maintained, alike when he is singing his softest notes and when he is making his most dramatic effects; but through his natural production the effect reaches the audience as intensity of emotion, and so touches the soul, without the hearer being reminded of the force of the breath and effort employed. Should this become apparent the artistic effect is destroyed.[15]

[15]William Shakespeare, *The Art of Singing* (Bryn Mawr, Pa.: Oliver Ditson Co., 1898), p. 42.

The artist in performance, therefore, should have already acquired the technical skills necessary to establish himself as a professional, and these skills must, through practice, become ingrained in the subconscious. In company with the instrumentalist, the singer must take his technique for granted as he immerses himself in the communicative experience. To do otherwise is to produce tone, perhaps even beautiful tone, without ever addressing oneself to the *art* of singing.

If Cirillo's "*Mio Dio!* If God has not taught you how to breathe, it is time you were buried" is evaluated within the context of a learning process, it makes good sense. Restructuring the vocal mechanism is primarily a matter of developing and integrating the registration, and this cannot be accomplished effectively while maintaining a direct concern for stabilizing the breathing mechanism. A respiratory (synonymous with vocal) equilibrium is possible only when *all* participating elements of the breathing apparatus are well coordinated, with the parts in perfect agreement with the whole. The primary goal of training, therefore, is to utilize those functional principles which assist in bringing the entire vocal mechanism into balanced tension. This objective is implicit in the comments of Mancini, Nathan, and Shakespeare, all of whom indicated that other factors (notably registration as it affects the physical dimension of the vocal folds) form the functional core of a mechanism which, when well coordinated, makes good breathing habits possible.

At higher levels of technical expertise, Pacchiarotti's statement can also be said to be true. With the vocal mechanism already in equilibrium, the primary concern of the artist is to identify with his material on a physical, intellectual and emotional level without upsetting the precarious balance among all of the forces involved. Neither the process of learning how to sing nor artistic singing, however, can be achieved by protruding the abdomen, "elevating the chest to make a big noise," or revealing to the audience the "force of the breath and effort employed." Nor, since an equilibrium is self-supporting, should an overt effort be made to control separate elements of the respiratory process. If Pacchiarotti's "knowing" is equated with "knowing how one feels" and knowing how to regulate the intensity of one's emotional commitment, then his statement is not only true, but essential to artistic expression.

POSTURE

A good physical presence and correct posture were considered in Bel Canto training methods to be essential both to the learning process and to effective public performance. Tosi stressed this point in the following statement:

> He [the teacher] should always make the scholar sing standing, that the Voice may have all its organization free. Let him take care, whilst he sings, that he get a graceful posture, and make an agreeable Appearance. Let him particularly correct all tricks of the head, of the body and particularly of the mouth; which ought to be composed in a manner (if the sense of the words permit it) rather inclined to a smile, than too much gravity.[16]

Manfredini concurred with that opinion:

> When singing, one should always hold one's head firm and straight; neither should one make any unbefitting motions with one's shoulders, arms, or any other part of one's body; on the contrary, one should hold oneself in a noble posture, and sing while standing in order that the voice might come out more easily, particularly when studying and when one must [make an effort] and is anxious to [be successful in] being heard.[17]

All of the advice noted above is easily acted upon and requires no vocal expertise. It does, however, mark both a point of beginning and a desired end result of good vocalization. All "tricks of the head" and other mannerisms are posturings that should be avoided regardless of time and place. As is true with other doctrines formulated during this era, the proposals should be followed by all who sing, or attempt to sing, regardless of changes in vocal style or *genre*. Artifice is not art, and posturings have no place in either private or public performance. Since a correct posture is one of the few things a singer is able to accomplish volitionally, negligence in this area of vocal presentation is inexcusable.

THE MOUTH

The shape and opening of the mouth received considerable attention from early theorists. Mancini once again emerges as the most fertile source of information, describing its functional importance with this statement:

> It is necessary that the student learn this good principle, and know how to open the mouth well; and know how to open it according to the rules, and not at his fancy. I value this knowledge of how to open the mouth well in a beginner, and the knowledge of how to place it well, so much because it is the source for the clarity of the voice and the neatness of the expression; thus on the contrary the defective position of the mouth spoils the voice absolutely, renders the cantilena disgusting, the singer ridiculous and repulsive because of the change which it makes in the face.[18]

Continuing, Mancini made this comment:

> There are many who sing with their teeth closed and firmly so. To sing thus between the teeth is the greatest defect; it is a defect that completely betrays the voice, because one cannot hear its extension, and it does not retain the neatness nor the clear articulation of the words.[19]

[16]Pier. Francesco Tosi, *Observations on the Florid Song,* translated by Galliard (London: Reeves Bookseller, Ltd., 1926), p. 56.

[17]Vincenzo Manfredini, "Dell' unire la voce di petto colla voce di testa, la quale volgarmente chiamasi falsett," *Regole Armoniche,* second edition (Venice, 1797), p. 66. Cited and translated by Philip A. Duey, *Bel Canto in its Golden Age* (New York: Kings Crown Press, 1951), p. 116.

[18]Giam Battista Mancini, *Practical Reflections on the Figurative Art of Singing* (Milan, 1776), translated by Pietro Buzzi (Boston: The Gorham Press, 1912), pp. 29, 30.

[19]*Ibid.,* p. 30.

Mancini further advised the following:

> Every singer should position his mouth as he positions it when he smiles naturally, that is, in such a way that the upper teeth be perpendicularly and moderately separated from those below.[20]

According to Mancini, a smiling position was not to be rigidly maintained:

> One should not believe however, that for this reason the mouth should be deprived of its customary motion, and one should admit its necessity, not only to interpret the words, but also to expand and clarify the voice to that degree taught by the same art.[21]

Mancini was even more explicit in his instructions:

> He [the singer] should be careful not to make contortions with his mouth, and thus make himself look convulsed . . . thinking that will help them. Instead it makes them appear ridiculous, and they acquire unmendable habits. . . . Now if the faulty position of the mouth, as I said, mars the beauty and expression of the voice, how much more will it spoil the amiable features of the singer? Features which are exposed at that moment to a public which is there ready to praise or censure him?[22]

Excessive opening of the mouth was considered a vocal fault until the end of the nineteenth century, when "covering" became fashionable. The maximum opening formerly permitted was usually measured optimally by placing two fingers between the teeth; the singer was never allowed to exceed that amount of opening. This practice offers two distinct advantages: it facilitates the economic articulation of consonants, and by minimizing movement, simplifies the combining of tone with articulation.

EXERCISES AND PRACTICE

The vocal exercises providing the materials which, through supervised practice, were used to either condition or recondition the vocal organs, were the necessary accouterments of the vocal objectives of the period. These exercises ranged from the elemental to the difficult. In early stages of training, single tones were utilized to inculcate a sense of vowel purity and establish the registers in their rightful place, leading "insensibly," as Tosi insisted, "from the easy to the difficult." After considerable progress had been made, the student was introduced to the study of *solfeggio,* then songs to combine tone with text. It is of the utmost importance to note in this connection that tonal purity with respect to the production of vowels preempted concerns for articulation, a fact strongly emphasized much later by Shakespeare:

> It may be adopted as a principle that he who can sustain naturally the vowel sounds can in similar freedom articulate the consonants. In other words, "Take care of the vowels and the consonants will take care of themselves."[23]

More sophisticated vocalises incorporated studies in agility, the staccato, the legato, the shake (trill), the portamento, appogiature, gruppetti, the turn, diatonic and chromatic scales, and finally the improvisation of cadenzas.

[20]Giam Battista Mancini, *Practical Reflections on the Figurative Art of Singing* (Milan, 1776), translated by Pietro Buzzi (Boston: The Gorham Press, 1912), p. 30.

[21]*Ibid.*

[22]*Ibid.,* p. 95.

[23]William Shakespeare, *The Art of Singing* (Bryn Mawr, Pa.: Oliver Ditson Co., 1898), pp. 24, 25.

HYGIENE

Considerable emphasis was placed during the Bel Canto era on the care of the singing voice through personal hygiene. Strict rules were laid down: hygienic practices included the most appropriate wines to be consumed, some of which were to be diluted with water (for young singers and those with higher voices), others undiluted (for lower voice types and those who have reached maturity), as well as those wines most appropriate for the different seasons of the year. Spicy food, nuts, milk and the imbibing of cold drinks when overheated were to be avoided, and overeating was frowned upon. Lighter foods were preferred to those heavier, greasier, and less easily digestible, and singing was forbidden until at least two hours after mealtime. Comfortable clothing that permitted freedom of movement was another recommendation.

Although singers were advised to seek medical assistance when throat discomfort persisted, many home remedies were used for the cure of minor irritations, colds, and hoarseness. All were derived from natural sources—among them the eating of raw garlic, myrrh placed under the tongue, tea made from fennel (an herb belonging to the carrot family), benzoin dissolved in water, and the chewing of sweet gum or gum of the storax tree.

The attention given to personal hygiene is indicative of the seriousness with which vocalists of this period addressed themselves to their art, and it is apparent that in matters pertaining to health an obligation was felt not only to themselves, but to the audiences who expected so much of them.

CONCLUSION

The training procedures outlined above centered on problems related to natural functioning and succeeded in creating a remarkable era in vocal history. Many singers were produced whose technical accomplishments can only be described as astonishing. Some idea of their proficiency has been left for posterity by Mancini, who recalled the feats of Cavaliere Baldassare Ferri:

> He had in the highest degree all the characteristics of perfection in every style; he was gay, proud, serious, tender at will; his pathos captivated the heart. In one breath he sang a scale up and down two full octaves, trilling continuously, and marking all the chromatic steps with so much accuracy, even without accompaniment, that if the orchestra during the improvisation sounded the note which he was singing, whether flat or sharp, one would instantly hear an agreement of pitch so perfect as to surprise everyone.[24]

[24]Giam Battista Mancini, *Practical Reflections on the Figurative Art of Singing* (Milan, 1776), translated by Pietro Buzzi (Boston: The Gorham Press, 1912), p. 6.

[25]*Ibid.*, p.7.

Career longevity was an additional benefit often derived as a result of Bel Canto training, and it is reported of Cavaliere Matteucci that he still possessed, when past eighty years of age, a voice "so florid and clear, and used in every way with such flexibility and agility, that every listener, not seeing him, believed him a youth in the flower of his years."[25]

The accomplishment of Matteucci (while perhaps exceptional) is not atypical of the singers of the period, many of whom retained an undiminished vigor and freshness of voice at an age when singers of the present time have long since retired. Of great significance from the standpoint of pedagogy is that the vocalists of this period learned their craft and developed technical skills which far exceeded their original capabilities. That these skills were acquired is evident for several reasons:

1) the voice of a boy soprano or boy alto before puberty is, no matter how exceptional, extremely limited when compared to the vocal virtuosity of a *castrato;* 2) it is not likely that the seven to nine years of intensive vocal study to which these young singers were subjected were given over to the consolidation of skills already possessed, and 3) descriptions of the course and results of vocal study can be found in the statements of contemporary writers. Among the latter, one made by Mancini concerning the training given Antonio Bernacchi, a pupil of Pistocchi, is most illuminating. Although not gifted with a good voice, Bernacchi studied assiduously, and according to Mancini

> . . . did not hesitate to undertake any trial, no matter how disastrous, how painful, and to apply himself for a prescribed time, according to the precepts of the master, to whom he did not fail to go each day for wise counsel. During the time of this study, he not only did not sing in church nor theater, but let no one hear him sing except his most intimate friends.[26]

With respect to the results this study produced, Mancini continued thus:

> My pen would presume too much if it believed itself able here to relate all the praises which this great man earned. It is enough for me to say that he was universally admired, and that he became one of the first figures in the Profession of Singing, as has been indubitably attested by all who heard him. . . . The scholar should read from this fact the profitable reflection that an assiduous study under a great master can render a bad voice good.[27]

The functional basis upon which Bel Canto training procedures were founded is as relevant now as in former times for two compelling reasons: 1) the principles are both physiologically sound and utilitarian, and 2) when correctly applied they can develop, as Mancini asserted, a "bad" voice into a "good" voice, and assure career longevity. Intensive interest is currently being shown by scientists in one of the basic tenets of early training: the vocal registers, what they are, how many, and how they function. As these investigations continue, it will be demonstrated that Bel Canto training procedures, which differ both in theory and in practice from modern methods, are demonstrably superior. Because of this superiority, these procedures should be restored to their rightful place in modern training. To do so would make it possible for those who aspire to perfect their vocal skills to claim their rightful heritage.

The end result of the study discipline demanded by the early teachers of Bel Canto was to free the mechanism, reveal its innate beauty, and provide a medium of artistic expression limited only by individual potential and the skill of the teacher. This training discipline, now only adhered to by instrumentalists, was both rigorous and effective. Its reward was the satisfaction gained from having achieved an artistic stature of the highest order.

Bellows: a device for producing a stream of air under pressure.

In singing, the term is used by proponents of abdominal breathing, who contend that the abdominal muscles (especially the diaphragm) must be forcibly pushed upward and inward during exhalation in order to activate the vocal folds. The bellows concept, however, like all aspects of abdominal control, contains inherent

[26]Giam Battista Mancini, *Practical Reflections on the Figurative Art of Singing* (Milan, 1776), translated by Pietro Buzzi (Boston: The Gorham Press, 1912), pp. 7, 8.

[27]*Ibid.*

See Breathing
    Emotion
    Falsetto
    Falsetto or
      Head Voice
    Kinesthesia
    Laryngeal
      Suspension
    Middle Register
    Modern Methods
    Register
    Resonance
    Standing Wave
    Vowel

contradictions: 1) the diaphragm contracts (and flattens) during inhalation and relaxes (and rises) during exhalation; 2) the diaphragm is a reflexive muscle, and cannot be consciously controlled, and 3) concern for any isolated muscular activity introduces compensatory tensions and tonal stiffness by undermining the respiratory equilibrium characteristic of correct vocalization.

Belting: the practice adopted by "pop" singers (particularly women) of driving the chest register too high in the tonal range.

Belting is not a legitimate use of the mechanism and is extremely detrimental to vocal health. "Belters" frequently develop nodules on the vocal folds that require either long periods of rest or surgery for their removal.

Bernoulli Effect: a physical principle first advanced by Daniel Bernoulli, an eighteenth century Swiss scientist, that deals with the velocity, resistance, and pressure of air in motion.

The Bernoulli Effect refers to a sucking action that occurs as air moves from a low to a high pressure region. In singing, this sucking action, according to some theorists, is caused by increased pressure in the trachea, which, when the vocal folds are reasonably approximated, causes a complete narrowing of the glottis. Thus, if the breath flow is sufficient, the air, moving more rapidly through the narrowed passage, sucks the vocal folds together. Theoretically, the folds adduct because of an air stream exiting from the lungs, rather than, as conventionally believed, being brought together by muscular contraction.

On the basis of neurological evidence, it does not appear that aerodynamic laws are applicable to the vocal function. To quote Dr. Barry Wyke with respect to the prephonatory tuning of the vocal folds:

> Electromyographic studies of the motor unit activity in the intrinsic laryngeal muscles that is associated with phonation (both in speech and song) have shown that just as phonatory expiration is initiated, the inspiratory activity in the posterior crico-arytenoid muscles is suddenly (but only temporarily) reduced by some 70 percent, while at the same time, there is a brief high-voltage burst of motor unit activity in the vocal fold adductors—resulting (as mentioned earlier) in rapid adduction of the vocal folds shortly before the expiratory air stream reaches them, and thus prior to each vocal utterance.
>
> This is the process of prephonatory tuning of the vocal folds, during which—as a result of reciprocally coordinated adjustments of the discharge frequency in the individual components of the corticobulbar tracts that project to the motoneurone pools of the abductor and adductor vocal fold muscles—the tension, length and mass of the vocal folds are repeatedly preset to the degree required for each forthcoming phonemic utterance. Depending upon the phonatory circumstances, the interval between this prephonatory adjustment of the activity of the vocal fold musculature and the beginning of each utterance may vary from as little as 50 msec to as much as 520 msec—but the intervals are generally shorter in trained speakers and singers than in untrained individuals.[28]

[28]Barry Wyke, M.D., "Neurological Aspects of Phonatory Control Systems in the Larynx: A Review of Current Concepts," in *Part II: Respiratory and Phonatory Control Mechanisms. Transcripts of the 8th Symposium: Care of the Professional Voice,* Juilliard School, New York City, June 1979, edited by Van Lawrence, M.D. (New York: The Voice Foundation, 1979), p. 43.

If the substance of these findings is true, then suction is not a factor in phonation nor is the Bernoulli Effect operative. Other objections which tend to deny the validity of the Bernoulli Effect during phonation are the following:

1. The alternate compressions and rarefactions taking place during phonation occur *below* the glottis, as well as above, and the strong air flow essential to the Bernoulli Effect would disrupt these oscillating patterns;

2. There is insufficient air flow under the normal pressures used in singing to create a suction effect (when the technique is efficient only about 36 cc of air is used per second);

3. The vibrating vocal folds produce periodic impulses during which time the breath escapes in tiny "puffs," the folds remaining closed longer than they are open. Consequently, the concept of "breath flow" and "stream of breath" is inappropriate; without a steady air flow, the Bernoulli Effect is inoperative;

4. A clean tonal attack does not include breath flow, or "wild air," but is the result of an immediate approximation of the vocal folds in response to a mental concept;

5. When the mechanism is in equilibrium, it is not breath pressure or air flow that generates vocal tone, but breath compression. In the latter instance, the compression stores enough oxygen to energize the muscles and body substances, making them, provided they are well coordinated, responsive to electrical impulses directed through the nervous system by will power;

6. There is an implicit rejection of the obvious presence of a supraglottal pressure system (ventricles of Morgagni) to counter the subglottal pressure built up within the trachea, and

7. The concept of air flow (necessary to the Bernoulli Effect) violates the acoustic function of the standing wave, which, when operative, strengthens the pressure oscillations within the laryngeal pharynx and intensifies the resonance characteristics of the tone produced in inverse ratio to the amount of effort expended.

From the standpoint of function, efforts to apply the Bernoulli law of aerodynamics to the vocal process, either theoretically or practically, overlook the importance of the right structural design to its successful operation. Just as some aircraft fly very well, others badly, and some not at all, voices also vary in their functional efficiency. For any physical law to become operative during phonation, the vocal apparatus must be positioned properly, *i.e.,* coordinate effectively. This efficiency is dependent upon the precision with which those muscular adjustments take place that hold the vocal folds in balanced tension, stabilize the larynx, and ensure a harmonious interplay among other muscle groups lying in peripheral areas.

For the practical teacher of voice, the problems encountered during training are not those which require familiarity with Bernoulli's law. His responsibility is to understand the functional principles which will help coordinate the vocal muscles more efficiently. Once these systems learn to participate correctly in the phonative act, all valid scientific theories concerning phonation will have been made operative. The Bernoulli law of aerodynamics is an interesting posualte, but, even if correct, it can neither indicate nor demonstrate how the vocal mechanism is to be stimulated so that, like a well-designed aircraft, it can best utilize a natural law.

See Aerodynamic
    Theory
  Breathing
  Coordination
  Energy
  Neurochronaxic
    Theory
  Standing Wave
  Vocal Training
  Wild Air

See Functional
Listening

Big Voices: a term used to describe voices that are well resonated and opulent, as opposed to those that are loud and somewhat noisy.

One of the characteristics of a "big voice" is that its size is more impressive to the listener than to its possessor. Conversely, a loud voice is heard by the listener as being rather small, while to the singer it appears to be very powerful. Big voices carry, loud voices do not. An interesting attribute of a big voice is that its qualitative properties obscure quantitative considerations. Acoustically, a big voice is the product of regular vibratory impulses; a loud voice produces vibrations which are irregular and diffused.

(To) Bite Into the Tone: a pedagogic device designed to make the voice "ring."

The concept of "biting into the tone" is based upon an intuitive sense of the actual physical processes taking place during phonation. Fiberoptic scopes, for example, have shown that when singing *ah* in the lower octave of both male and female voice types, the epiglottis, or lid above the glottis, partially closes. Commencing at B, however, the lid opens in response to a forward tilting of the thyroid cartilage as the contracted cricothyroid muscles stretch the vocal folds. When accompanied by a slight lowering of the velum (soft palate), the oropharyngeal cavity narrows and becomes more compact in size. Qualitatively, this compactness produces a ringing tone quality possessing considerable thrust and carrying power.

In contrast to the dynamics of "covering" (which features a lowering of the larynx and a corresponding elevation of the soft palate), the device of biting into the tone is designed to achieve an adjustment similar to that of the *voix claire*, but too often without having established those prerequisites (*i.e.*, a well-balanced registration and a resonance adjustment free of constricting tensions) necessary to its successful execution.

When properly executed, the feeling of biting into the tone is one of incisive movement from a wider to a more closed pharyngeal opening; this contrasts with the sensation experienced when, for example, biting into an apple. Correct execution, therefore, is important. Otherwise, biting into the tone, while imparting brilliance to the tonal product, will inadvertently introduce an undesirable "twangy," nasal quality.

An exercise most favorable to the successful cultivation of tonal "bite" is one using an octave jump. In many instances, it is helpful to sing *ah* on the tonic and change to an *ee* vowel on the upper octave, since this vowel forces the mouth to close slightly and obliges the oropharynx to narrow. Other practices utilize the so-called "open" vowels (associated in the twentieth century with vocal tract elongation) and "closed" vowels (a more compact pharyngeal adjustment), an association through which concepts related to vowel "size" (large and small) have come into being. Provided the throat is relatively free of constricting tensions, and the change of adjustment is made with incisiveness and precision, the effect of the exercise is one of "biting into the tone."

Errors to be avoided in utilizing concepts related to "biting into the tone" are associating this procedure with "nasal resonance," or attaching undue importance either to breathing techniques or to the position of the mouth. Moreover, since the usefulness of this practice depends upon the singer first having gained a sense of natural movement within the throat parts, and consequently a considerable degree of technical skill, it is a device reserved for those more advanced.

The directive to "bite into the tone" is of limited value. Pedagogically, it embraces no functional principle, is incapable of increasing the tonicity of flaccid muscles, and provides no means for improving the physical coordination within the laryngeal musculature, nor does it serve to eliminate muscular interference. Under certain technical conditions, however, it does help gain reasonably effective contact with the laryngo- and oropharynges as resonators. When mistakenly associated with "nasal resonance," however, it is a concept which inevitably promotes throat constriction.

See Covering,
    (To) Cover
Natural Movement
Stretchers of the
    Vocal Folds
Vowel Size

Bleat: a fast, tremulous tonal pulse caused by pharyngeal constrictor tensions.

See Tremolo

Blending the Registers: the unification of a two-register mechanism into a functional unit.

A "blended" registration is the antithesis of a "mixed" registration: the former implies a proper development and coordination, whereas the latter implies one which is incorrect. An indispensable exercise for blending the registers is the *messa di voce,* or the swelling and diminishing of a single tone. Whatever the procedure used to combine the registers, however, permanent blending, or mutation, should be postponed until each mechanism has been developed independently to its fullest potential.

See Register

Bocca Ridente: Italian, "smiling mouth."

Bocca ridente was a pedagogic device introduced by the early teachers of Bel Canto. One of its essential purposes was to avoid grimaces and to present a pleasing appearance. An additional consideration was the natural tendency of this mouth position to aid in the production of brighter tone qualities.

Not all theorists agreed upon the usefulness of this practice, but the prevailing belief was, according to Mancini, that "every singer should position his mouth as he positions it when he smiles naturally." However, Mancini modified this statement considerably when he cautioned that "the mouth should not be deprived of its customary action, and one should admit its necessity, not only to interpret the words, but also to expand and clarify the voice."[29] If the face is to reflect the sentiments of the text, both artistic expression and vocal freedom require that the mouth remain mobile. Under these conditions, neither the facial expression nor the articulation will interfere with the tone, nor the tone with the facial expression or articulation. A constant smiling position of the mouth mitigates the achievement of this objective.

Technically, a smiling mouth position raises the larynx slightly and strengthens the higher partials to add brilliance to the tone. It also encourages "spreading" when singing in the upper tonal range, and as all devices, must be used occasionally and judiciously.

[29]Giam Battista Mancini, *Practical Reflections on the Figurative Art of Singing* (Milan, 1776), translated by Pietro Buzzi (Boston: The Gorham Press, 1912), pp. 30, 31.

See Facial Muscles

Bone Conduction: the radiation and transmission of vibratory impulses generated within the larynx to peripheral areas of the skeletal framework.

Vibratory impulses transmitted by means of bone conduction are responsible for many misconceptions regarding tone production, and particularly resonance (*e.g.,* belief that tones are amplified in the nasal passages, the chest and head, and the facial mask, as well as concepts related to higher or lower "placement"). Since these anatomical parts are incapable of performing as resonators, some other type of activity must be responsible for those symptoms, which, while illusory from the standpoint of resonance and placement, are nevertheless very real. The logical point of origin for all such symptoms is the laryngeal pharynx.

Acoustically, because of the frequency and phase distortion that occurs as impulses generated within the larynx pass through a dense rather than a more elastic medium, the singer "hears" his own tone quality differently than would be the case were he able to listen objectively, *i.e.,* to perceive the air-conducted sound waves without being confused by the natural dichotomy between these sensations and those which are experienced because of bone conduction. This dichotomy, which usually stands in direct conflict with the preconceptualized memory-pictures that set the physical process in motion, is one the singer must resolve satisfactorily if he is to develop valid tonal concepts.

Bone conduction is an important by-product of tone production. Because it is the source of those sensations of vibration so commonly felt by singers, especially those perceived as nasal "resonance," an understanding of their derivation should lead to a revision of current theories concerning phonation, and thereby place contemporary instruction on a more solid footing.

See Hearing
    Modern Methods
    Register
    Resonance
    Self-Listening
    Sensations of
        Vibration

Bottled Up: a phrase used to describe tones which are the product of pharyngeal constriction, and which therefore appear to be "caught," "swallowed," or "bottled up" in the throat; "throaty."

Bravura: Italian, "bravery."

In singing, "bravura" is used to describe the brilliant execution of coloratura passages to be sung in a heroic manner. Provided their techniques are correct, all voice types are capable of singing bravura passages with strength, precision and beauty of tone.

Break: an interruption of the tonal flow that results from any of several functional conditions, such as the following:

1. A developmental discrepancy between the two registers at the point of their juncture;
2. A predominance of chest register in the tonal area above its natural limits;
3. An attempt to sing too loudly in the lower range of either the falsetto or head voice;
4. The collapse of an open-throated resonance adjustment, and
5. The sudden release of constrictor tension which occurs when the throat-opening muscles become operative.

Although tonal breaks are sometimes disconcerting to the student, they are not necessarily bad, since a break may be nature's way of protecting the mechanism or the audible sign of changing technical conditions. The register "break" in the female voice is important in tone "coloring" for dramatic effect, especially in *verismo* opera.

See Register

Breakthrough: a vocal phenomenon which occurs at the precise moment constricting tensions are replaced by a more effective and open-throated resonance adjustment.

Since one of the express purposes of a vocal exercise is to break down muscular interference, breakthroughs are normal when these have been well selected and properly executed. A breakthrough is easily recognizable because of a dramatic change which occurs in the tonal character as a "tight," constricted production is suddenly released and muscular activities shift to an opposing system. For those afflicted by throat constriction, a breakthrough, while slightly traumatic psychologically, is an encouraging sign of vocal health.

Breastbone: the bone running down the front of the thorax (chest); the sternum.

The breastbone performs no functional task, but, being attached to the rib cage, moves in response to whatever breathing habits the singer chooses to adopt.

Breath: air received into and expired from the lungs during the act of respiration. Phonologically, breath is a voiceless expiration of air, and should never be confused with the mechanics of breathing.

See Energy
Vital Capacity

Breath Capacity: The consensus among investigators is that some 500 cubic centimeters of tidal air passes in and out of the lungs during normal respiration. In maximum inhalation and exhalation, another 1500 cubic centimeters of supplemental air is normally added. The extreme limit of vital capacity, or maximum breath that can be exhaled after forced inhalation, has been shown to vary in adults from 2200 cubic centimeters to as much as 5000 cubic centimeters. According to authorities, a properly produced tone sung at a medium level of intensity will expel breath at the rate of 36 cubic centimeters per second, whereas the expulsion rate with poorly used voices will rise as high as 280.

What seems to emerge from the above is this: vital capacity is irrelevant to phonation. Even singers with the lowest capacity should have more than enough breath to manage the longest musical phrases, provided they sing correctly.

See Breathing
Vital Capacity

Breath Compression: the condensing of molecules within a restricted area to create a self-energizing source of pressure.

In singing, breath compression occurs when the lungs have been inflated and then the breath release is checked by the action of the two valves which block (or partially block) its point of exit. The first valve, the glottis (the space between the vocal folds), reflexively closes when a balance of tension has been established between inspiratory and expiratory muscular tension. The second valve, the false vocal cords, narrows when precise contact has been established with diaphragmatic contraction, a downward movement which occurs whenever pressure is raised within the throax (chest). The expansion of the ribs and flanks which takes place in conjunction with increased thoracic pressure is natural. Therefore, any volitional effort made to assist an outward movement of the rib cage is burdensome and unnecessary. It is due to the narrowing of the false vocal cords that the air both above and below the vocal folds is maintained above atmospheric pressure; this condition is essential to free vocalization.

BREATH CONSCIOUSNESS

Contemporary accounts of early training methods had little to say concerning breath compression, but the theory was certainly familiar to many. This is evident from a rare commentary on the subject by Giovanni Battista Lamperti (1840—1910), subsequently quoted by William Earl Brown:

> There is no "attack," no "mouth position," no "tongue control," no "voice placement," no "fixed chest," no relaxing this or that muscle, no stiffening any part of the body, in fact, nothing that would not spring from instinctual utterance.[30]

[30]William Earl Brown, *Vocal Wisdom: Maxims of Lamperti,* edited by Lillian Strongin (New York: Arno Press Inc., 1931), p. 64.

An essential feature of the coordination which leads to the state of equilibrium described by Lamperti is a balancing of motor power with a controlling force: pressure versus resistance. With specific reference to the vocal function, this means that if the vocal folds are to be freely vibratile, primary resistance to the compression buildup must be provided by the narrowing action of the false vocal cords, a role for which they are ideally suited because of their down-turned angulation.

A radical functional difference exists between the procedures related to breath pressure and breath compression. With the former, reliance is placed upon applied muscular energy to propel and regulate the movement of air from the lungs and to steady the tones being emitted; these procedures involve manipulation of the abdominal, intercostal, and/or clavicular muscles. The compression theory, on the contrary, permits the rate of breath release to be controlled by a narrowing of the upper valve through which breath must pass, *i.e.,* the false vocal cords. Thus, when the technique is correct, the glottal space is narrowed by an unimpeded contraction of those laryngeal muscles (the cricothyroids and the arytenoids) which regulate the length, tension, and mass of the vibrating membranes. The result is that the glottal space closes willingly, rather than being forced to close by wrong muscular effort.

Although not widely accepted, the compression theory holds a definite advantage over the breath pressure theory, since the former allows regulation of the breath flow to take place by natural means rather than through consciously controlled and overt muscular action. With the false vocal cords narrowing the aperture at the point of tonal exit, the ever-changing balances between pressure and resistance are easily managed and fall within the province of a natural and instinctive singing sense.

Physically, the essential difference between these divergent concepts is that under the breath pressure theory, the true vocal folds are required to act as the resisting agent (a role for which they are poorly designed), whereas in the compression theory, this role is assumed by the false vocal cords. The benefit to be gained by utilizing breath compression to generate energy and sustain vocal tone is that the mechanism becomes virtually self-sustaining, self-regulating, largely innervated by the will, and easily maintained in equilibrium. As a result, the voice "sings itself" in an apparently relaxed and effortless manner through instinctual and musical dependencies, rather than being "managed" and manipulated.

Breath Consciousness: an acute awareness of breathing as a vocal problem, malaise common to many who practice methods whose purpose is to control the expenditure of breath.

All methods of breath control foster a self-conscious attitude, which engender bodily stiffness and exacerbates rather than alleviates breathing problems. Breathing problems, left alone, normally correct themselves once the laryngeal musculature becomes well coordinated and the vocal mechanism responds more naturally and efficiently.

See **Breathing and Emotion**

Breath Control: an attempt to limit breath expenditure through some system of consciously controlled breathing.

There are three such systems: 1) thoracic (also called costal or rib breathing); 2) clavicular (chest or shoulder breathing), and 3) diaphragmatic (or abdominal) breathing. Each of these systems is founded upon the belief that it is efficient use of the breath that improves function.

Important studies carried out by the Bell Telephone Laboratories, as reported by Douglas Stanley, offer convincing proof that no system of controlled breathing either improves the quality of the tone production or fosters breath economy.[31] Wesley A. Wiksell demonstrated more recently that such a dependency is without substance, finding that "attempts to control specifically those types of breathing result in lowered effectiveness."[32] These and other studies seem to agree that the institution of direct control over the breathing apparatus is not an effective procedure for developing vocal skills.

Both experimentally and experientially, it is evident that no controlled technique of breathing reduces the amount of breath expenditure or improves function. The contrary seems to be true, and it is function, *i.e.*, an efficient muscular coordination within the laryngeal pharynx (a coordination which approximates the vocal folds and narrows the glottal slit), that limits breath consumption and heightens the effectiveness of other muscular systems involved. This conclusion is reinforced by logic, since the respiratory system is so complex that efforts to bring a limited group of muscles under conscious control would inevitably disrupt the natural coordination of the total system. What is certain is this: when the laryngeal muscles coordinate effectively, little or no excess breath will escape—in effect, the properly functioning mechanism itself controls and regulates the breath.

Breath Expulsion: the amount of breath loss sustained during phonation.

The rate of breath expulsion is determined by the size of the glottal opening and the general vibratory pattern traced by the moving vocal folds. Each of these factors is in turn governed by 1) the efficiency of the muscular movements occuring within the laryngeal pharynx, *i.e.*, registration, and 2) the resonance adjustment assumed by the laryngeal and oral pharynges. Since registration is an adjustment made in response to pitch and intensity (an adjustment which regulates the length, thickness and elasticity of the vocal folds), and resonance characteristics are determined by tuning the pharyngeal cavities to energize the frequency bands responsible for vowel quality, the size of the glottal slit and the amount of air that escapes is regulated by the efficiency with which these functional activities coordinate.

To a certain extent, the quantity of breath moving through the glottal slit can be attributed to the pressure exerted by the action of the breathing muscles. For the skillful singer, however, breathing has more to do with an orderly exchange of carbon dioxide for oxygen than with breath pressure. The small amount of breath that does escape through the glottis when conditions are right has to do with the undulating movement of the vocal folds, not breath pressure. During these move-

[31]Douglas Stanley, *The Science of Voice* (New York: Carl Fischer, Inc., 1929), pp. 52, 61.

[32]Wesley A. Wiksell, "An Experimental Study of Controlled and Uncontrolled Types of Breathing," *Studies in Experimental Phonetics*, Giles Wilkeson Gray (ed.), *University Studies*, No. 27 (Baton Rouge: Louisiana State Univ. Press, 1936), pp. 99–164.

ments the vocal folds separate briefly, at which time a tiny puff of air escapes. These puffs coincide with a healthy tonal movement known as a vibrato.

In an inferior technique, the regularity of these puffs, as well as their identification with intensity (greater amplitude with high intensity, reduced amplitude with reduced volume), is replaced by erratic sequences. The result is an increase in breath expulsion, the presence of "wild air" (breath that has not been converted into tone), and breathing problems that have nothing to do with any particular method of breathing. When the mechanism is maintained in a state of equilibrium these syndromes disappear, and the question becomes one of normal breath loss, which is a minimal factor in tone production.

While under ideal technical conditions breath loss is negligible, this criterion cannot be used as a gauge by which technical efficiency is to be judged. Many who sing with a severely constricted throat are capable of sustaining very long phrases, whereas others who sing more freely cannot do so. The sole criterion should be whether the tone production is open-throated or working through a constriction. During training, for example, when interfering tensions are being broken down, excessive effort is often required to accomplish this end, and breath loss may be momentarily excessive.

To sing long phrases when the throat is constricted is both technically and aesthetically undesirable. When one is *learning* to sing, breath expulsion may often be extremely high; when one has learned *how* to sing, it is always low.

See **Puff Theory**
Wild Air

Breath Management: the institution of volitional muscular controls over the respiratory function whose design and purpose is to steady the tone and regulate breath expenditure.

Breath Pressure Theory: a theory that recognizes breath pressure to be the actuating and regulating force that, when directed against the resisting vocal folds, stimulates and controls their movement; a postulate virtually synonymous with breath control.

One reason for the ready acceptance of the breath pressure theory as a viable pedagogic tool in recent years is that, with the exception of the diaphragm, the respiratory muscles are largely subject to volitional control, whereas the musculature responsible for vocal fold tension and laryngeal stabilization is not. Without a means for stimulating an involuntary muscular system, especially when there is an obvious need to institute some kind of control to facilitate the learning process, the breath pressure theory appeared to offer a practical, if mechanistic, basis upon which vocal skills could be developed.

There are serious weaknesses in the arguments generally advanced in support of the breath pressure theory. The vocal folds, while being asked to resist (through tension) the breath pressure directed against them (in which case the degree of tension would have to be directly proportionate to the degree of pressure being exerted), are also being required to maintain their elasticity in order to accommodate quickly and easily to fluctuating melodic patterns. Another serious weakness is that the angulation of the vocal folds (which are shaped like a Gothic arch) is not designed to effectively resist a pressure buildup from below without stiffening. This obvious conflict of interest between resistance and motility is unlikely to be resolved as long as the breath pressure theory is accepted without challenge.

While it may be argued that the breath pressure theory must be operative when the mechanism is limited in freedom because of imprecise muscular coordination, such a viewpoint is unsupportable when the mechanism is in balanced tension. Thus, a dependency upon breath pressure is either unnecessary, or a compensation for the energy dissipation which results because of technical limitations. It would seem, therefore, that the breath pressure theory has been devised to accommodate the needs of the average singer, who, because of a poorly functioning instrument, finds his energy resources depleted too rapidly. These resources must be supplemented, the conventional solution being to press breath into the system, check it in some way by a special technique of breathing, and thereby control its expiratory flow. The consequence is a superimposition of additional tensions, which serve to lock in those vocal faults already present, thus furthering the continuance of effortful, rather than natural, free vocalization. As a result, an effect—excessive expenditure of breath—has been substituted for the cause, *i.e.*, poor laryngeal muscular coordination. It is the energy loss which results from muscular interference that creates excessive demands upon the breathing apparatus—demands which it cannot adequately meet.

If the breath pressure theory does not seem to offer a reasonable solution to the crucial vocal problem of breath loss, some other principle must exist to offer a viable alternative. Traditionally, the vocal organs have been considered to be a single-valve instrument in which the vocal folds act as the valve. Many important theorists, however (including Lunn and Myer), have suggested that the mechanism is comprised of two valves rather than one. According to this theory, the false vocal cords, located above the vocal folds, serve as the upper valve, and narrow to create supraglottal pressure by impounding air within the ventricular sacs. In this way an equilibrium is maintained between sub- and supraglottal pressure, each system mutually counteracting the other. This leaves the vocal folds free to create the pressure variations necessary to pitch without having to act as resisting agents.

While a number of practical teachers of voice, theorists and scientists disagree with the formulation outlined above, the concept nevertheless enlists an impressive array of supporters. Foremost among the latter are J. Piguet, G. Decroix and J. Libersa, French scientists who concluded from their experiments that the frequency of the vibrations of the vocal folds is independent of the strength of subglottal pressure.[33] The most compelling aspect of their findings, on a pragmatic level, is that under these conditions it becomes possible for the vocal mechanism to function in an apparent state of relaxation, and, as is evident experientially with great singers, to produce the voice without visible signs of effort. Without supraglottal pressure to counterbalance subglottal pressure, this ease in singing would not be possible.

On the basis of the known anatomical structure of the vocal mechanism, there appears to be no other alternative for neutralizing subglottal pressure than the inflation of the ventricular sacs, which is caused by a narrowing of the false vocal cords. If breath compression is substituted for the conventional view of breath pressure, a source of self-generating energy will be found readily available. When properly utilized with other forces which are maintained in equilibrium, compression will obviate the necessity for having to act overtly upon the respiratory system, *i.e.*, using abdominal pressure or other techniques for directing breath against the vocal folds. Breath compression, built up by inflating the lungs during the act of

[33]J. Piguet, G. Decroix and J. Libersa, *Comptes Rendus* Vol. 242 (Paris: Academy of Sciences, 1956), p. 1223.

inspiration, is self-energizing. It does not disturb the precarious balance between inspiratory and expiratory tension (a balance essential to a natural closing of the glottal space); it preserves the independent movement of the two muscle systems which draw the vocal folds into tension (the arytenoids and the cricothyroids); it permits the false vocal cords to narrow to 1) create a supraglottal pressure system, and 2) regulate and control the rate of airflow, and, in general, makes possible the continuance of a state of equilibrium throughout the vocal mechanism.

A practical alternative to the breath pressure theory, therefore, is to consider the volume of air inspired as 1) a source of oxygen, which acts as the combustible element to vitalize the muscles and organs of the body, 2) air particles within the pharyngeal tract waiting to be set in motion by the vibration of the vocal folds, and 3) a source of compression and subglottal pressure that, through supraglottal pressure built up because of a narrowing of the space between the false vocal cords and an impounding of air within the ventricular sacs, permits the vocal folds to become freely vibratile. Those who have achieved this pressure equilibrium often refer to phonation as "drinking in the tone," or as the Italians express it, *inhalare la voce*, to inhale the voice.

In the final analysis, it is the singer's skill in establishing and maintaining an equilibrium throughout the entire respiratory tract which eliminates the need for breath pressure and breath management, as it is function which regulates the rate of breath expenditure and makes overt controls unnecessary. Those who sing correctly renew their breath at the beginning and end of a phrase because they lack oxygen, not breath.

Breath Support: the exercise of direct control over the respiratory muscular system for the purpose of ensuring tonal steadiness and regulating breath expenditure; largely synonymous with breath control. The dominant muscle groups involved in the practice of tonal support are the intercostals, the diaphragm, and the abdominals.

There are several inherent fallacies in all techniques designed to "support" the tone. Among them are the following:

1. Vocal tone is nothing more than pressure variations created by an oscillating movement of the vocal folds whose frequency determines pitch. It is a physical impossibility to "support" these vibratory patterns;
2. The amount of breath expenditure is regulated by 1) a narrowing of the false vocal cords (which occurs when the intercostals, the diaphragm and the abdominals are maintained in balanced tension, *i.e.*, an equilibrium that is self-supportive), and 2) the size of the glottal opening, which, in turn, is determined by the manner in which the vocal folds are stretched and brought into tension by the contraction of the cricothyroids, the arytenoids and the vocalis muscles, *i.e.*, registration;
3. The diaphragm is without proprioceptive nerve endings, and therefore without sensation. Thus, it is impossible to exercise any control over diaphragmatic movement except through the reflexive act of breathing;
4. The abdominals cannot be acted upon without involving other members of the respiratory system, particularly the diaphragm and the intercostals, and a movement favorable to one is not necessarily beneficial to the others. Furthermore, none of these activities necessarily improves the intricate movements taking

place within the laryngo- and oropharynges, *i.e.,* those which adjust the vocal folds to a desired length and tension, and position the resonating system;

5. An excessive push of the abdominals (as in weightlifting) forces the false vocal cords to close, whereas during phonation they should merely be narrowed;

6. When any one member of a muscular system is purely involuntary (as is the case with the diaphragm and most of the laryngeal muscles involved in phonation), the entire system must be treated as though all of its movements were involuntary. This is especially true when the functional purpose requires quick reflexive movements, and

7. If the goal of good pedagogy is to help the student sing in a manner consonant with nature's laws, it is necessary to depend upon refined concepts, an awakened instinct for singing, and delicate muscular coordination as a total experience, rather than devote attention to isolated peripheral parts, if the complex sound-producing mechanism is to be brought into equilibrium.

The utilitarian value of breath support as a pedagogic practice is highly suspect. It is not based upon a valid functional principle, it leads to a self-conscious awareness of the body, confuses ends with means, and overlooks the fact that in an ideal technique all of the muscular systems involved are in equilibrium, which means that they are self-supporting. When the tones produced by the singer are unsteady or ill-formed, attention must be directed toward those aspects of technique which lie at the root of the problem, *i.e.,* activity within the laryngeal pharynx and its surrounding musculature. The real question, therefore, is not one of supporting the tone with the breathing muscles, but improving the coordinate relationship of a highly complex system of laryngeal muscles, which lies beyond volitional control. No known system of "breath support" addresses itself to this problem.

See **Bel Canto**
Laryngeal
  Suspension
Modern Methods
Register

Breathiness: a tone quality largely consisting of "wild air" (air that has not been converted into vibratory impulses), which passes unchecked through the vocal folds.

A breathy tone quality is attributable to the following:

1. The exclusive use of the head voice, which has not been properly coordinated with the chest voice in its lower extension (a weakness characteristic of women's voices);

2. A "mixed" registration, which finds the two muscle systems, the cricothyroids and the arytenoids (heard as the head voice and the chest voice, respectively) both undeveloped and imbalanced, each mechanism conflicting rather than coordinating with the other;

3. A faulty laryngeal suspension and a consequent failure of the laryngo- and oropharyngeal cavities to select and energize those frequencies which define and resonate the vowel, and

4. An overall misapplication of energy distribution throughout the entire phonatory tract.

See **Laryngeal**
  Suspension
Modern Methods
Registration,
  "Mixed"
Resonance
Vowel

The unvocalized breath escaping during phonation is reflective of technical problems that do not easily yield to correction. The muscle systems involved, most particularly the thyroarytenoids (being involuntary), can neither be acted upon directly nor improved by breathing techniques, but must be stimulated by the application of those principles governing the mechanics of registration.

BREATHING

Breathing: the act of inhalation and exhalation that exchanges oxygen for carbon dioxide, the oxygen intake providing the combustible element that vitalizes the muscles and body substances; in singing, commonly considered a source of pressure to initiate and sustain phonation.

To fully comprehend the significance of breathing to vocalization, a clear distinction must be made between breathing and breath. Breathing is the act of respiration; it is accompanied by contractions and expansions within the respiratory system, a complex of muscles and cartilages synonymous with the vocal tract. Breath, on the other hand, supplies oxygen to the system; through combustion (the formation of compounds of body substances with oxygen), oxygen creates energy. The function of breathing is to supply and regulate the production of energy within the total system.

Some method of breath control is central to almost all systems of vocal training. There are a number of reasons for this. First, all spontaneous and natural movement, synonymous with vocal, physical and psychological health, is an outgrowth of spontaneous and natural breathing. Second, since the singer with vocal problems invariably wants for breath at the end of phrases and is usually a victim of tonal unsteadiness, the conclusion often made is that faulty breathing lies at the root of the trouble. Also, of all the functions responsible for producing tone (exclusive of the articulators), breathing alone is subject to volitional control. Breathing merits special consideration for two additional reasons: 1) because higher levels of energy expenditure absorbed into the vocal mechanism during phonation demand greater breath intake, and 2) because of the reflexive interplay between respiration and the movement of the vocal folds.

While a more ample supply of oxygen is needed during phonation than in normal respiration, qualitative use of the breath (conditioned by the coordinative relationship between concepts and physical response) is far more important than the quantity inspired. Quantity is not of overriding importance; what *is* important is a proper attitude toward the manner of inspiration as tone is initiated.

All known systems of breath management concern themselves with the quantity of air inspired rather than its qualitative use, and thereby overlook a basic truism: *efficient breath intake depends upon a full release of expiratory tension.* The physical act of phonation, therefore, does not begin with inspiration (a perfectly natural reflex, provided there is no residue of expiratory tensions to stand in the way), but with a conscious release of expiratory tension. It is the singer's failure to fully release expiratory tension at the onset of phonation that gives rise to so many vocal and breathing problems.

Emotional factors further complicate the respiratory process. A basic human characteristic is to erect defenses against anxiety by restricting respiration (hence the sigh of relief when danger, real or imagined, has passed). Consequently, natural inspiration, which is perfectly automatic when expiratory tension has been properly released, is impaired.

There are two reasons why this release is crucial: 1) because inspiratory movement becomes inhibited and breath has to be "taken" rather than inspired reflexively, and 2) because a sufficient discharge of carbon dioxide is impossible, with the result that the organic systems suffer because of an oxygen deficiency. Muscularly, this failure leads to early fatigue, while at the same time organic vitality

44

is diminished because the alveolar gas from the respiratory dead space has not been transferred efficiently. Consequently, the respiratory reflexes are slowed, and the diffusion of oxygen into the blood stream is improperly converted, *i.e.*, poor oxygenation of the blood results in a lowering of general energy output.

In order to understand fully the essential role which breathing plays in the vocal process, it is necessary to examine the reflexive interplay between respiration and the movement of the vocal folds. Normally, when the folds are under either inspiratory or expiratory tension they open reflexively, and close briefly when tension is being transferred from one cyclic phase to the other. Inasmuch as the phonative act requires an approximation of the folds so that their edges run parallel without touching, it may be seen that this process is subverted whenever inspiratory or expiratory muscles work independently. The specific nature of the problem, therefore, is that natural breathing forces the vocal folds apart, when in order to vibrate properly, they should be together. Thus, some means must be found for neutralizing both inspiratory and expiratory tension so that the act of breathing is not permitted to disturb the free movement of the vocal folds, or for that matter, to constrict the throat. This is the essential nature of the breathing problem.

One technique for curbing the reflexive opening of the vocal folds while breathing is to commence singing just before the completion of the inspiratory cycle, a practice known as "singing on a gesture of inhalation." This will serve to eliminate breath pressure as an activating source of energy, and hold inspiratory muscular tension against the reflexive expiratory movement which accompanies phonation. In effect, a balance will be established between what would normally be an "in" and "out" movement of the breathing muscles. With the glottal space now closed, the abdominal wall will hold position (without being held), with the result that a genuine feeling of body poise will be established. Above all, the glottal space will remain closed without being forced to close by the registration.

Another device for closing the glottal space is to inspire comfortably, without raising the chest or tensing the shoulders, and pause for a fraction of a second before phonating. This practice is particularly useful for those involved with repertoire, in which vocal technique is combined with musicianship and interpretation to evoke mood and atmosphere. Utilizing the breath in this manner, however, applies mainly to those who are technically well advanced.

It is of the utmost importance to note that the pause before singing stops the breath, thereby arresting respiration without closing the throat; this should be distinguished from holding the breath, which would induce wrong tension. Stopping the breath momentarily before singing, when done correctly, should maintain the entire body in a poised attitude that admits the possibility for natural movement. Technically, stopping the breath creates a balanced pressure between the thoracic muscles of inspiration and the abdominal muscles of expiration. Holding the breath inhibits natural movement, as it causes a stiffening of the expiratory muscles. Inability to fully release expiratory tension is one of the direct causes of throat constriction.

With the glottal space closed by either of the techniques suggested above, the muscles drawing the vocal folds into tension are able to respond without interference. With this freedom, provided the registers are effectively coordinated, the singer is able to concentrate on interpretative matters. Because the vocal folds approximate without interference, singing becomes quite effortless. If at the same time the larynx is well positioned, all basic technical problems will have been solved and breathing itself will becomes economical, self-regulatory, and virtually independent of conscious control.

Short of the time when really advanced training begins, instruction in breathing should involve those aspects of technique which encourage naturalness of posture. There should be no raising of the chest or tensing of the shoulders, no pulling in or pushing out of the abdominal wall, no direct effort to expand the rib cage, and no indulgence in the often burdensome chore of breathing too deeply. The amount of breath to be used, the manner in which it is inspired, and the way it is utilized as a vital force will in the end be determined by the efficiency of the motor response within the laryngeal pharynx, *i.e.*, by the precision with which the laryngeal muscles engaged in phonation position themselves. When this condition exists, the healthy movement potential of the respiratory system will assert itself, minimizing breath flow and relieving the vocal folds and their associated musculatures of undue pressure.

Since technique is merely the manner in which something is done, a correct technique of breathing, *i.e.*, one of functional rightness, obviously represents an important phase of the vocal process. But to attempt to control function through control of the breath, as is commonly practiced, appears to be patently unwise. Certainly breath is wasted and presents an obvious problem when the mechanism functions poorly, and there is no question that excessive energy is required to inject and sustain tonal vitality when the muscular coordination is at odds with itself. But shortness of breath and dissipation of energy are effects of a functional condition, not causes, and to confuse one with the other is to obscure the issue.

It is the clear consensus of numerous scientific studies that breathing techniques fail to improve either overall function or breath expenditure, and that breath economy is due to an efficient coordinative process within the laryngeal musculature. Empirically, it is also evident that breathing techniques are superseded in importance by function, since it is evident that there are those who breathe incorrectly and sing extremely well, just as there are those who breathe correctly and sing quite badly. Good breathing habits help, but do not ensure, a good vocal technique. Throat constriction, nasality, a restricted tonal range, lack of resonance, inflexibility, and an inability to sustain even moderately long phrases without running out of breath fall within the province of function rather than breath management.

TYPES OF BREATHING

From the beginning of the twentieth century to the present, it has been thought that proper breath management will ensure a correct tone production. The techniques developed out of this belief center upon overt physical manipulations designed to enlarge the rib cage and abdominal area, and/or push the abdominals inward and upward against an expanded and elevated chest position. The purpose of these procedures is to steady and "support" the tone and to control the rate of breath expulsion. Because they act upon that which will act upon itself (natural inflation of the lungs will reflexively engage abdominal tension, lower the diaphragm, and expand the rib cage), breathing "techniques" are essentially unnecessary and unnatural. One does not have to expand to breathe; expansion occurs as a consequence of having breathed fully. The breathing techniques currently in vogue are listed below.

ABDOMINAL or DIAPHRAGMATIC BREATHING: the concept that was formally introduced by Dr. Louis Mandl in 1855, and has since been widely accepted as a valid precept by the vocal profession. In its present form, the concept of abdominal breathing includes two separate and mutually opposed concepts: 1) an effort to force the descent of the diaphragm through expansion of the lower abdominals, and 2) an inward and upward abdominal pressure designed to push the free ribs apart and expand the chest cavity. Both systems operate on the almost universally accepted breath pressure theory.

Those who practice abdominal breathing (as described in the first category) usually employ exercises designed to develop abdominal pressure and strengthen an outward and downward (inspiratory) movement. Many devices are employed to strengthen this movement, among them the wearing of broad belts or corsets to push against, and singing while lying prone, with weights (usually books) placed on the abdomen. The inherent dynamics of these practices reflect an attitude toward tone production which considers physical strength, rather than precise coordination, to be the essence of correct function.

The second approach to abdominal breathing possesses certain commendable features. Unlike the unphysiological and unsightly protrusion of the belly that is often the result of the first technique, the inward and upward movement of the abdominal muscles anticipates resistance from the inspiratory system, with the object of reducing tracheal pressure, closing the glottis, controlling the rate of breath flow by narrowing the space between the false vocal cords, and steadying the tone. This process involves an extremely complex coordination between the lower and outer abdominal muscles, the large back muscles, the inner chest muscle, the intercostals, the diaphragm, and the suspensory muscles responsible for adjusting the laryngeal position.

In this arrangement, the contraction of the muscular fibers of the diaphragm effects the movement of the ribs, the nature of this movement depending upon the degree of abdominal muscular activity, as well as the degree of activity in the intercostal system. If abdominal muscular activity is greater than the inspiratory tension generated, then the movement will be one of expiration. Conversely, if inspiratory tension predominates, the abdominals will undergo an alteration in their pattern of expansion. During the act of phonation, therefore, abdominal pressure must be countered by inspiratory tension; otherwise, the precarious equilibrium between two opposing forces will be destroyed. These muscle systems are shown in Figure 1, below.

There are two important reasons for maintaining this equilibrium: 1) the glottis will remain closed without being forced to close by the registration, and 2) when expiratory tension is absent, there is a limit to the amount of pressure that can be applied by the abdominals. This dependence upon effective inspiratory tension is due to the fact that the lower ribs form the point of attachment to the abdominal muscles. Thus, the downward pull of the abdominals is able to oppose the upward pull of the ribs, the effect of which is to firm the walls of the thorax. This reflexively narrows the opening between the false vocal cords, closes the glottis, and serves to minimize breath flow. Ideally, however, these events should occur naturally and with a sense of total equilibrium. Voluntary control of individual abdominal muscles is impossible, and when it is attempted, it raises the danger of creating muscular interference.

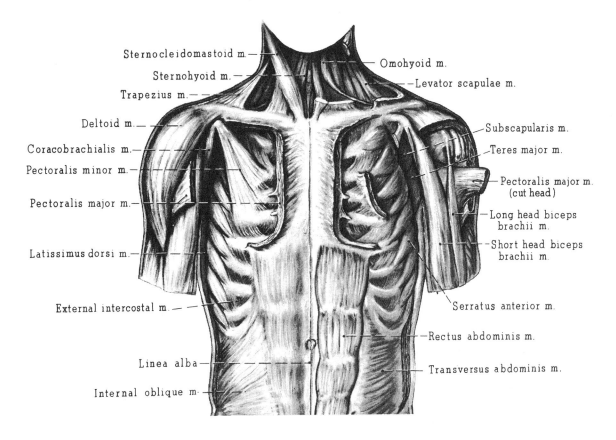

Sternocleidomastoid m.
Sternohyoid m.
Trapezius m.
Deltoid m.
Coracobrachialis m.
Pectoralis minor m.
Pectoralis major m.
Latissimus dorsi m.
External intercostal m.
Linea alba
Internal oblique m.
Omohyoid m.
Levator scapulae m.
Subscapularis m.
Teres major m.
Pectoralis major m. (cut head)
Long head biceps brachii m.
Short head biceps brachii m.
Serratus anterior m.
Rectus abdominis m.
Transversus abdominis m.

Figure 1. Muscles of the abdomen and thorax, from S. W. Jacob, C. A. Francone, and W. S. Lussow, Structure and Function in Man, *Fourth Edition (Philadelphia: W. E. Saunders, 1978). By permission.*

In those instances where control over the breathing mechanism is sought through diaphragmatic manipulation alone, nothing positive can be said. Conscious control over diaphragmatic movement is impossible, since 1) this muscle is without proprioceptive nerve endings and impervious to both volitional control and sensation, and 2) it flattens reflexively during inhalation and rises when breath is being discharged, during which time it is relaxed. Consequently, it is a physical impossibility to push up with the diaphragm for any purpose whatsoever.

ANXIOUS BREATHING: a restriction of respiratory motility brought on by fear, usually imagined.

The entire body, and especially the respiratory system, responds to pleasure by expanding and responds to fear and anxiety by contracting. When expansive movement is encouraged during training, the anxious student will often respond to the feelings aroused by inhibiting the respiratory function. The specific nature of this physical inhibition is an inability to fully release expiratory tension ("holding" caused through fear of "letting go"), with the result that both inhalation and exhalation become shallow.

It is the "holding" through inhibition that lies at the root of many singers' vocal troubles. A mechanism which depends upon expansive movement to function properly will, under stress or because of chronic anxiety, become partially or even totally immobilized due to the constricting tensions introduced from this source. The "shallow breathers" so familiar to all teachers of voice are in fact anxiety-ridden and literally incapable of taking a deep breath.

Anxious breathing creates undesirable tension throughout the entire respiratory tract, and is most conspicuous in the region of the throat. This tension constantly interferes with the free action of the vocal muscles and yields a constricted tone quality. In such instances, anxious breathing not only fails to properly innervate the vocal mechanism, but also, because it deprives the body of necessary oxygen, actually debilitates it.

AUXILIARY BREATHING: another name for rib, or intercostal breathing; usually an exaggerated expansion of the rib cage, a practice which tends to stiffen the body because of the excessive amount of breath inspired.

BACK BREATHING: a preparatory attempt to increase the amount of air taken into the lungs by expanding the latissimi dorsi (back muscles), which connect with the oblique abdominal muscles that stretch sideways and backwards.

The directives to "fill the small of the back with air" or "breathe into the back" are devices specifically designed to increase breath pressure and provide additional "tonal support." Since back breathing techniques relieve an unnatural arching of the small of the back, release back tension, and permit the respiratory musculature to participate more effectively in the vocal process because of improved posture, a transitory benefit is often derived by utilizing them. As is true with all attempts to exercise direct control over isolated functional areas, however, back breathing runs the long-term risk of tensing and partially immobilizing other parts of the vocal mechanism, and inhibiting the coordination between the larynx and other respiratory muscles.

BELLY BREATHING: slang for abdominal or diaphragmatic breathing; a practice usually associated with an unsightly protrusion of the stomach.

CLAVICULAR BREATHING: pertaining to the collarbone; the process of inhaling by elevating the chest and pulling up the ribs by means of muscles which normally move the shoulders; also known as scapular (shoulder blade), high chest, and shoulder breathing.

Foremost among the many deficiencies of clavicular breathing is that it attempts to expand the upper rib cage, which has a minimal range of movement, consequently limiting the amount of air that can be inspired. Another fault is that it attempts to push up with the diaphragm (which relaxes in its upward movement) with the intent of forcing the abdominal wall inward and upward to expand the rib cage. A great deal of compensatory muscular effort is therefore required in order to sustain phonation.

High chest breathing further creates unnecessary muscular interference because of the concomitant tension brought to bear on the neck muscles, without which the chest cannot be raised. Additional disadvantages are the following: 1) loss of contact with the expiratory musculature, which must balance with the muscles of inspiration if the glottal slit is to narrow properly; 2) an inability to provide the desired control over intrathoracic pressure, and 3) a tendency to interfere with the proper working of the larynx. Clavicular breathing not only locks the upper torso into a fixed, semirigid posture, but also immobilizes the rest of the respiratory mechanism as well.

COSTAL BREATHING: pertaining to the ribs; also known as thoracic, or rib breathing.

Costal breathing is virtually identical with normal respiration, except that, because of the greater amount of breath inspired, it involves an increase in the transverse dimensions of the thoracic cavity. In taking a costal breath, the singer is usually required to concentrate on holding the ribs in an expanded position. The weakness of costal breathing is that it excludes the antagonistic action of the abdominals (the most powerful muscles of expiration) and thus fails to establish an effective balance between inspiratory and expiratory tension.

FORCED BREATHING: the use of excessive breath pressure to generate and sustain vocal tone; a practice based upon the belief that a great quantity of breath is necessary to ensure tonal vitality and "control" the mechanism.

INTERCOSTAL BREATHING: an exaggerated form of costal breathing, which, because of the increased amount of air inspired to fulfill the requirements of sustained singing, causes a fuller expansion of the rib cage.

Because intercostal tension coincides with a lowering of the diaphragm (and relaxation of the diaphragm coincides with relaxation of the external intercostals), the function of the intercostals is purely inspiratory and primarily reflexive. Neither the diaphragm nor the intercostals can perform effectively during phonation unless they are maintained in balanced tension with their natural antagonists, the abdominals. Achievement of this equilibrium tends to be natural, provided other elements of the vocal mechanism coordinate efficiently, notably the ratio of tension shared between the muscle systems which regulate the physical dimensions of the vocal folds, *i.e.*, registration, and the suspensory muscles which stabilize the larynx.

One of the prevalent misconceptions with respect to this and other types of respiratory control is the assumption that, since breathing can be either voluntary or involuntary, direct control over these muscle systems will have a salutary effect on laryngeal functioning. This assumption is demonstrably false. A correct technique of breathing is easily mastered, and difficult to maintain only when the respiratory system is disturbed because of poor muscular coordination within the vocal tract itself. It is efficient laryngeal functioning, not respiratory control, that equates with breath economy and a correct tone production.

NOSE BREATHING: a preparatory technique in which breath is inhaled through the nose with the mouth closed.

Although occuring naturally during quiet respiration, nose breathing is not practical in singing for several reasons:

1. Excessive inspiratory effort is required;
2. It does not, as some believe, "open the pharyngeal resonators;"
3. It takes too long;
4. It is noisy;
5. It tends to tense and raise the chest, and
6. It prohibits the respiratory parts set in motion during inspiration from recovering in time to make swift, easy adjustments for phonation.

Perhaps nose breathing was introduced by singers to prevent accumulated stage dust or cold temperatures in rehearsal halls from drying out the mouth and throat during inhalation.

PRONE BREATHING: as its title suggests, the practice of breathing while lying on one's back.

Breathing while lying prone is apparently an attempt to help the singer sustain the inspiratory tension characteristic of respiratory equilibrium, and is sometimes accompanied by placing books or other heavy objects on the chest or stomach. It is pedagogically impractical for several reasons:

1. The ribs cannot expand as freely when prone as when standing;
2. Vital capacity is greater when standing, and
3. Singing is a coordinated activity, and exercises conducted in a fashion not customary or normal to the singing experience are ineffective.

SHALLOW BREATHING: a respiratory cycle during which only a minimal amount of tidal breath is inhaled and exhaled.

Proper oxygenation of organic systems is impossible when breathing is shallow, and shallow breathers do not adapt readily to the phonative process. There are two reasons why this is so: 1) the muscle systems involved are held too rigidly, and 2) the amount of air inspired does not meet the energy needs of the mechanism. Isolated from psychological factors, the physical problem centers on the general inadequacy of the events that transpire when carbon dioxide is exchanged for oxygen.

Even in normal respiration, approximately 150 cc of the air inspired never reaches the alveoli, which means that in shallow breathing the possibility of achieving an adequate oxygen-carbon dioxide exchange is proportionately reduced. The result is that the air trapped in the dead space (an area in the trachea and bronchi in which air, free of oxygen, remains despite the natural ebb and flow of the respiratory cycle) accumulates too much carbon dioxide. Unless this gas is adequately discharged, an excessive amount of carbon dioxide is drawn back into the lungs with each inspiration. Thus, the lungs, even though a fresh supply of air has been taken, contain too high a proportion of carbon dioxide, and consequently almost immediately stand in need of oxygen replenishment. The shallower the breath taken, the greater the proportion of inspired air that is unable to participate in alveolar ventilation.

The significance of this fact to vocalization is this: since only that air which reaches the alveoli sacs oxygenates the vital organs of the body, an excess of carbon dioxide within the dead space deprives these systems of the combustible element required for their vitalization. Because his oxygen supply is deficient, the shallow breather is obliged to re-oxygenate prematurely, *i.e.*, before the natural respiratory movement has been completed, with the result that tension is built upon unrelieved tension. This becomes a vicious cycle, leaving the singer with the feeling of being constantly depleted of oxygen because of his inability to release the requisite amount of carbon dioxide. Breathing problems, therefore, and especially those pertaining to shallow breathing, may be seen to center on the *expiratory* process—a failure to expel sufficient quantities of carbon dioxide from the lungs, rather than, as commonly believed, with the inspiratory process.

The physical difficulties encountered by the shallow breather are many, and possess definite psychological implications. Some singers find it physically impossible to inspire fully, and since phonation, like all physical activities, is energized by the oxidation of inspired breath, they lack the requisite energy for sustained singing. In almost every instance, these singers are victims of emotional repression and the physical rigidity that results from unreleased anxiety. At the root of all shallow breathing lies anxiety, an emotional state which, because of its defense mechanisms (physical ridigity, or armoring), makes vocal problems most difficult to cure.

The physical associations between shallow breathing and anxiety are apparent. Without oxygen there can be neither combustion nor production of energy. Heat and kinetic energy depend upon oxygen, and a free exchange of oxygen for carbon dioxide is essential to healthy organic life. Energy output, therefore, can be diminished by reducing the amount of oxygen introduced into the system. Thus, through shallow respiration, intensity of feeling will be lowered, and anxiety will be decreased.[34]

[34]Elsworth F. Baker, *Man in the Trap* (New York: Macmillan, 1967), p. 22.

See **Anxiety**
 Dead Space
 Energy
 Natural Movement
 Register
 Rhythm

Since emotional intensity is held at tolerable levels by reducing the respiratory process, the breathing mechanism may be seen to be the somatic counterpart of emotional repression and psychological factors synonymous with energy. To be effective, training procedures must confront this problem, as a correct technique of singing depends upon kinetic energy that has been built up from potential energy and released, not suppressed. The principles governing registration are extremely useful in this connection, since they vitalize the muscles, release feeling, and promote spontaneous movement.

SILENT BREATHING: respiration without phonation.

Silent breathing exercises are of little pedagogic value, since the vocal problem is learning to coordinate the movement of respiratory muscles (in particular, the vocal musculature) *during* phonation.

SUSTAINED BREATHING: slow, deliberate respiration.

Sustained breathing is sometimes used to improve respiratory reflexes and alleviate bodily stiffness. The conceptual error consistently committed in utilizing this drill is to concentrate on the inspiratory process rather than the expiratory function, which is the source of the problem. Inspiration, the most natural of all reflexes, only constitutes a difficulty because of a common inability to release expiratory tension, a tendency which is a by-product of anxiety.

See **Anxiety**
 Emotion
 Energy
 Rhythm

Breathing and Emotion: Feeling and breathing are integral parts of the communicative experience, and spontaneity, natural functioning and natural breathing are largely dependent upon uninhibited respiration. However, phonation often interferes with the normal ebb and flow of natural breathing, because in singing, tonal duration requires the maintenance of a narrowed glottal position for protracted periods of time. This narrowed position must remain constant regardless of the level of emotional involvement. Consequently, unchecked emotions cause the vocal bands to lose their tonicity, thus depriving them of their capacity to approximate properly. In two critical areas, therefore, spontaneous emotion can often work against the singer's vocal interest: it may disturb both reposeful breathing and the coordinative process which closes the glottal space.

All emotive processes stimulate the diaphragm and associated respiratory muscles, and act upon the larynx. Overstimulation of the diaphragm, the respiratory organs, and the throat parts causes a breakdown in physical control, a luxury the singer cannot afford. Prevalent misconceptions with regard to diaphragmatic control and breath management, therefore, may stem from the need to control emotion. Thus, what is thought to be breath control is really an effort to establish emotional control.

It is entirely possible that all or most breathing techniques were originally based upon a concern for the need to bring "feeling" under control. To be an artist, one must learn how to make others laugh and cry without succumbing to real laughter or tears; one must be involved yet aloof, to feel profoundly yet not be overwhelmed by one's own emotions. Dealing with intensity of feeling is learning to sing with "a cool head, but a warm heart." By "feeling with his breathing," the artist is able to regulate, control and maintain this precarious balance in a very effective way. Breathing techniques developed with this end in view, however, are not concerned with breath flow, but with the maintenance of an emotional equilibrium.

To free and regulate feeling through respiratory control is not an insurmountable difficulty. The encouragement brought on by success minimizes "performance nerves," and with growing confidence the singer becomes able to deal effectively with the problems centering upon respiratory equilibrium. With those unable to overcome their psychological inhibitions, free respiratory movement remains a continuing problem, and it is perhaps for this reason so much attention has been placed upon breathing techniques in recent years. Those who are afraid of their feelings and cannot express them easily do have a breathing problem, but it is one which is psychological rather than functional, *i.e.*, the repression of their feelings inhibits the respiratory function, and consequently both respiration and vocalization are disrupted.

Biologically, inhibited respiration performs the function of reducing the production of energy in the organism. The reason for this is clear. If a smaller amount of energy is created, the motor impulses generated will be less intense, and as a result easier to deal with. Thus, the reduction of energy output also results in the reduction of anxiety. Since inhibition of respiration is the psychological mechanism for suppressing anxiety and repressing feeling, the singer experiences difficulty in energizing his voice properly, as well as in relating to the emotional content of the music. As a consequence, he finds himself unable to move spontaneously, and fails to adapt easily to the vocal process.

While it does seem hazardous to generalize in such matters, it is nevertheless apparent that singers fall into two broad psychological categories—three, if the compulsive singer who seems bent on destroying his vocal resources is included. First, there are those who control their anger through repression, by means of muscular armoring, and second, those who are able to break through one or more layers of restrictive tension and find release for their hostility and aggression through positive action. Of the two types, the latter is far easier to train. Those who direct their anger outwardly do release their feelings; they are less inhibited, and consequently able to function more effectively. The majority of successful singers appear to belong in the second category, and reveal a singing style which, while limited and rather one dimensional on an emotional level, nevertheless possesses an aggressive quality that projects a certain vitality across the footlights.

Breathing Exercises: various pedagogic procedures which purport to improve the vocal function by regulating the mechanics of inspiration and/or expiration.

Most of these exercises, and the pedagogic theories from which they are derived, are based on the assumption that the vibration of the vocal cords is initiated, controlled and regulated by a special technique of breathing. Breathing exercises, whether silent or coupled with phonation, are directed toward three major objectives: 1) an increase in the vital capacity of the lungs; 2) provision of "tonal support," and 3) control of the rate of expiratory flow.

While breathing exercises may improve posture and physical appearance, increase vital capacity, and promote general health, they are nevertheless questionable aids in the development of vocal skills. Their greatest limitation is that neither phonated nor nonphonated breathing exercises exert any positive influence on functional mechanics, *i.e.*, improve the coordination between the respiratory process, the laryngeal musculature responsible for stretching the vocal folds, and the suspensory muscles that enable the larynx to operate as a primary resonator of vocal tone. Indeed, silent exercises would seem to subvert correct function. Both inspiratory and expiratory tension reflexively widen the glottal space and separate the vocal folds; in singing, however, the glottal space must be narrowed and the vocal folds drawn into approximation to produce pitch. Even when coupled with sustained phonation, breathing exercises direct energy and attention to localized areas, a practice which upsets the respiratory equilibrium essential to correct vocalization. Singing is a coordinated activity, and exercises practiced in a fashion not customary or normal to the singing experience are bound to fail.

Psychological attitudes play an important role in respiration, and it is evident that the positive physical and emotional effects which breathing exercises can sometimes produce are limited in their application. Although some singers manage to benefit because they are able to release anxiety and emit a "sigh of relief" through deep respiration, or by practicing "sigh tones," others become "breath conscious" and increasingly inhibited. Shallow breathers who cannot sigh heavily or inspire fully present special problems, but in all cases the difficulty is with expiration rather than inspiration, for unless the expiratory muscle system has fully completed its cycle, proper inspiration is impossible. With inabilities of this kind, undue emphasis on breathing exercises worsens an already difficult situation, increasing rather than diminishing psychological resistance. When this happens, the singer becomes "tied up" with his breathing, and perpetuates a cycle that must be broken if progress is to be made.

It is a curious but revealing coincidence that specialized breathing exercises originated not only from the time of the heavy orchestrations of late nineteenth century vocal writing, but also from the era when the so-called "Bel Canto" tradition was lost. As the demand for full, opulent voices increased, less attention was apparently directed to the functional mechanics of vocal development, and more to the subjective impressions of singers (many of whom had "natural" voices) who possessed the requisite power to be heard in large houses over modern orchestras. Thus, the pedagogic concerns of training the singing voice were gradually diverted from the core of the functional process (*i.e.*, registration) to secondary concerns such as resonance and volume.

Bridge: the transition from chest voice to head voice (approximately E, F, F# above middle C).

The term is a translation of *il ponticello,* "the bridge," the Italian reference to the register transition. Bridging the two mechanisms gracefully and imperceptibly requires a great deal of technical finesse—particularly for tenors and mezzo-sopranos, who, because the register transition falls in the middle of their singing ranges, must either effect a successful juncture or sing with a divided registration.

See **Register Break**

Brilliance: a tonal quality caused by the concentration of energy in the upper partials (harmonics) of the tonal spectrum, particularly in the frequency range of 2800—3400 cps.

Vocal quality depends upon the strength with which the various harmonics are energized in relation to the fundamental, and scientists are uniformly agreed that tonal brilliance is an essential property of laryngeal resonance. Whether this is true of all brilliant sounds, constricted or open-throated, has not yet been clearly determined.

See **Twenty-Eight Hundred**

Broca's Area: the left-front portion of the brain (named for the French scientist Paul Broca), which governs articulate speech.

Bronchi: the two main branches of the trachea, or windpipe, through which air passes into the lungs.

See **Breathing**

Buccal: pertaining to the cheeks or mouth.

Buffo: Italian, "comic."

In opera, the term *buffo* is associated with certain male roles requiring comic, or character, acting. Thus, some roles are designated as *tenore buffo* or *basso buffo* (there is no female counterpart). A comic work in which such roles appear is called an *opera buffa.*

Building on the Soft: a pedagogic practice originally designed to join the two register mechanisms, the chest voice and the head voice, into a functional entity.

In its original context, as used in the nineteenth century, "building on the soft" was a preliminary exercise to set the groundwork for a well-executed *messa di voce.* By balancing the registers properly within an open-throated resonance adjustment, both soft and full-voiced singing shared the same resonance characteristics, and were therefore logical extensions of each other: increases in intensity, at an advanced level, became merely increases in tonal strength.

With the passing of time, however, the two mechanisms became associated with their accompanying sensations of vibration and resonance, and the relationship between registration and pitch-intensity patterns became blurred, and was ultimately forgotten. As a result, the exercise lost its validity as a building process and its usefulness was defeated. Voices so trained inevitably become smaller and smaller, more constricted, and eventually of little artistic value.

A correct technique of singing softly engages both registers at all times and actually tends to combine them, since either register, when operating as a relatively separate entity, requires high levels of intensity to maintain its own functional identity. Unless soft tones can be swelled to full voice, the registers have not been sufficiently developed and integrated to justify the continuance of this pedagogic practice. As a general rule, correct soft singing represents the art of producing the voice, and its consistent use is inadvisable until the final stages of technical development. To develop a student's vocal potential, emphasis should be placed on building, not restraining.

See **Bel Canto**
   Modern Methods
   Register

Buoyant Voice: an acoustic impression conveyed when the periodicity of the vibratory impulses is regular, and the amplitude of the oscillations increases and decreases in correspondence with variations in intensity.

See **Vibrato**

A buoyant voice, regardless of its size and weight, retains those properties of lyricism common to all voices which are correctly produced.

Buzz: a tone quality infused with those properties of sound heard, for example, when sustaining the consonant *z*, or when standing too near a double bass viol.

The buzz in a tone is attributable to any one or a combination of all three possible sources: 1) a good, but approximate, tuning of the laryngeal pharynx; 2) a slightly nasal quality imposed on the former condition, and 3) pressure variations, which result from puffs of air that escape during every undulating movement of the vocal folds.

A "buzzy" tone quality can represent technical attributes ranging from the desirable to the undesirable, depending upon the strength of the nasality present. A precisely adjusted mechanism, however, does not produce a "buzzy" tone quality, but one that is pure and well focused, *i.e.*, in the sense that a picture is in focus when the mechanical parts within the camera are precisely adjusted to the object being filmed. The nasal "twang" and characteristics recognized by many to represent nasal "resonance" are examples of undesirable types of "buzz." A buzzy quality is not an ascription applicable to the tones produced by great singers, which are clear, ringing, and well defined.

C

Carrying Power: a tonal characteristic which enables some sounds to be heard in an auditorium more clearly than other, apparently louder, sounds.

Several factors account for this phenomenon: 1) an absence of irregular vibrations (*i.e.*, noise); 2) a specific physical coordination effecting an acoustical coupling of the laryngo- and oropharynges, which perform as a double resonating system, making it possible to reinforce two separate frequency bands simultaneously, and 3) the presence of tonal "ring," a quality identified by scientists as resonance centered within the laryngeal pharynx, this resonance being a concentration of vibratory energy in the region of 2800—3400 cps.

One of the essential muscular activities responsible for carrying power is a strongly tensed cricopharyngeal muscle, whose function it is to draw the larynx slightly down and back.

See Coupling
  Laryngeal
    Suspension
  Suspensory
    Mechanism

Cartilage: a gristly tissue usually connected to bones. The larynx is totally comprised of cartilaginous material.

See Larynx

Castrato: an emasculated male singer, either a soprano or an alto.

Although the practice of castration had been common to many early civilizations, including the Roman Empire, it only emerged as an accepted social phenomenon in fourth century Italy, when Pope Sylvester, following the edict of St. Paul to "let your women keep silence in church" (I Corinthians 14:34), established the Schola Cantorum, to which boys with exceptionally promising voices were sent to be trained as choristers. The practice of castrating boys for this purpose ended shortly after the accession of Pope Leo XIII (1878—1903).

The rather sexless voices of the *castrati* perfectly fitted the performance of early church music. However, it was soon discovered that their powerful voices were equally well suited to both the declamatory and florid styles of early opera. The *castrati* or *evirati* ("emasculated ones"), as they were sometimes called, soon became the operatic "superstars" of their day, complete with exorbitant fees, exaggerated lifestyles, rivalry with other singers, devoted fans, *etc.* All the major operatic composers of the seventeenth and eighteenth centuries, including Monteverdi, Handel, Gluck, and Mozart, wrote music for *castrati;* although Mozart referred to them in private as "screaming eunuchs," he nevertheless wrote at least two operatic roles and a solo motet, *Exsultate jubilate,* specifically for *castrati.* Many, notably Caffarelli (1710—1783) and Farinelli (1705—1782), whose tenure and prominence at the Spanish courts of both Phillip V and his successor, Ferdinand VI, are notorious, became celebrated international personalities. The last *castrato* to sing in opera appeared in London in 1844.

Physiologically, the *castrati* could be said to possess the vocal organs of children in the bodies of grown men. Luchsinger and Arnold,[35] for example, reported that, in a 1909 dissection of the body of a 28 year old *castrato* performed by Tandler and Gross of Italy, the thyroid cartilage was quite small and the thyroid notch, or "Adam's apple," did not protrude as it does in the normal adult male larynx. They further reported that the length of the vocal folds amounted to only 14 millimeters— almost exactly the dimensions of the folds of an average coloratura soprano. This abnormality enabled the *castrati* to exceed the power potential of the female voice, and is thought to be responsible for the "inexhaustible respiration" for which these singers were famous.

Qualitatively, the *castrato* voice was in all probability an acquired taste phenomenon, although eighteenth century writers universally acclaimed the great power and beauty of those voices. It is doubtful, however, whether their tonal qualities would appeal to modern ears. The closest modern approximation is in all likelihood the sound produced by present-day countertenors. After the Church banned the barbarous practice of castration, one of the last of these unfortunates was recorded at an advanced age in the early years of the twentieth century. It is not an attractive sound.

Caught in the Throat: See Too Far Back.

Cavity Tone Theory: a theory advanced by the British scientist Wilfred Willis in 1830 which states that tonal timbres are determined by the natural frequency of their resonators. His experiments with vibrating reeds of different pitches demonstrated that the concentration of energy within the harmonic spectrum remains constant regardless of the pitch of the fundamental.

More recent studies have shown that vowel quality is largely determined in a similar fashion and that it, like timbre, is dependent on the manner in which energy is distributed over the harmonic spectrum. Each vowel activates four to six prominent areas of frequency (called "formant regions" or "frequency bands"), at least two of which must be strongly reinforced if the vowel quality is to be well defined. If these two areas are not strongly energized, the lack of energy concentration will be reflected in a distortion of the vowel quality and a devitalization of resonance.

Pedagogically, the cavity tone theory demonstrates that the definition and resonation of a wide spectrum of vowel qualities depends upon the availability of a series of adjustable cavities that can be "tuned" either separately or together. Since the laryngo- and oropharynges fulfill these requirements, it is here that the primary source of both vowel definition and tonal resonance is to be found.

Willis' cavity tone theory would appear to offer a reasonable explanation of vowel formation, and by inference points to the need for coordinating the pharyngeal muscular systems responsible for positioning these cavities into improved patterns of response if this tuning is to be efficient.

Ceratopharyngeus: a part of the middle constrictor muscle of the tongue that attaches to the greater horn of the hyoid bone.

[35]Richard Luchsinger and Godfrey E. Arnold, *Voice-Speech-Language* (Belmont, California: Wadsworth Publishing Co., Inc., 1965), p. 191.

See Masculine Voice

See Coupling
    Formants
    Register
    Resonance
    Twenty-Eight
      Hundred
    Vowel

Cerebellum: the "small brain."

The cerebellum is divided from and positioned below and to the rear of the cerebrum, with a surface structure composed of gray matter containing cells and fibers which connect with other areas of the brain. These bundles of fibers receive impulses from the motor centers of the cerebrum, the semicircular canals of the middle ear, and directly from the skeletal muscles, and transmit outgoing impulses to the cerebrum, down the spinal cord, and to the muscles. The result is that nerve impulses are transmitted through their respective motor centers, innervating the body walls and helping to maintain posture, equilibrium and the tone of the voluntary musculature.

The function of the cerebellum centers on properties associated with the instincts, receiving and transmitting tactile, kinesthetic, auditory and visual stimuli that are subconsciously perceived. It is these perceptions which the singer must learn to identify with and trust; in essence, they account for what is recognized to be a "singing sense." Vocal study is directly concerned with awakening this instinct for sound making, and until the mechanism has been well coordinated muscularly, instinctual, spontaneous responses must be given precedence over the cerebral aspects of learning.

See Instinct
Natural Movement

Cerebrum: the largest part of the brain; that part of the brain which fills the entire upper portion of the skull.

The cerebrum is made up of gray and white matter; the latter, located beneath the gray matter, consists of three types of fibers, which link all the areas of the brain, and the brain with the spinal cord. All mental activities, intelligence, reason, will, memory, and other areas of consciousness are governed by this portion of the brain. The "intellectual" singer depends almost exclusively on cerebral controls to develop his vocal skills, rather than the instinctual responses governed by the cerebellum, and it is this that makes such singers so difficult to teach. Vocalization involves such a complexity of forces—physical, instinctual, emotional and mental— that to rely on cerebral processes exclusively destroys the equilibrium of energies necessary to singing. Singing involves the totality of the individual and sums up the totality of the human experience. This demands that the physical, intellectual, instinctual, and emotional properties of each individual are brought into balance and fully exploited. Excessive dependency on any one factor, to the partial exclusion of others, destroys this balance and aborts the learning process. It is a notorious fact that the "intelligent" singer rarely sings either well or "naturally," *i.e.,* spontaneously.

See Cerebellum
Limbic System

Cervical Vertebrae: those segments of the spinal column which are located above the shoulders.

Some theorists believe that the cervical vertebrae are the transmitters of tonal vibrations from the laryngeal area to the chest, since the cricoid cartilage of the larynx is connected to the spine in this region. This theory offers a possible explanation for the illusion of "chest vibrations" experienced by many singers in the lower tonal range. A more likely explanation, however, is that these symptoms occur because of tracheal resonance and vibratory impulses radiating through the skeletal framework because of bone conduction.

Changing Note: a pitch on which a new tonal color is introduced in singing—most often at a point at which a change takes place when shifting from one register balance to another.

Although many believe that "changing notes" are located at specific intervals in the harmonic series, this correlation is unlikely. Too many individual exceptions violate the rule, and since changing notes ("lifts" or "breaks") do not occur when the vocal registers are perfectly balanced, it appears that the supposition is baseless. More reasonable is the concept that changing notes are physiological rather than acoustic phenomena that reflect slight imbalances at the segmentation points relative to registration.

Some teachers try to categorize voices by the location of changing notes in the tonal scale, since it would appear that heavier voice types might have slightly thicker vocal folds, and consequently lower changing notes than their lighter counterparts. This practice, however, is exceedingly dangerous, as breaks and noticeable changing notes often indicate the presence of technical limitations, and cannot be considered fixed installations.

To establish vocal categories on the basis of changing notes, or even tonal range, is an *a priori* judgment. It leads to an acceptance of a status quo, the avoidance of making necessary changes, and procedures which avoid the employment of those functional principles which alone are capable of developing the voice properly.

See **Register**
Register Segment
Segmental
Vibration

Changing Voice: a voice whose function is being modified by the physiological effects of puberty.

Chanting: in Western civilization, the singing of psalms and canticles in the liturgies of the Roman Catholic and Anglican churches. The Roman variety, commonly referred to as "Gregorian Chant" in deference to its founder, Pope Gregory I (590—604), is monophonic and in free rhythm, whereas Anglican chant is customarily harmonized throughout and metered at cadences.

Chanting, one of the oldest vocal practices, possesses many opportunities for the development of vocal skills: 1) it combines singing and speaking into a unified process; 2) it develops skill in the shaping of a melodic line, and 3) it increases rhythmic sensitivity. The study of chant, or plainsong, should be incorporated into every music curriculum, since it contains the basic elements of phrasing upon which all Western music is founded.

Chest: the thorax; that part of the body enclosed by the ribs and breastbone.

Chest Resonance: See Resonance, Chest.

Chest Voice: a pedagogic term, both inaccurate and misleading, commonly used to refer to the lower and heavier of the two register mechanisms. The term, like "chest resonance," is a misnomer, since any vibrations experienced in the thoracic region are the result of bone conduction or other transmiting agents; they are neither produced nor resonated within the chest cavity. These tones originate and are resonated within the laryngeal pharynx.

"Chest voice," inaccurate as it may be, is commonly used to refer to those tone qualities which respond to high levels of intensity in the lower pitch ranges. Functionally, these qualities result from the parallel positioning of the vocal folds by the cricothyroid and arytenoid muscles in a "thick" adjustment (*i.e.*, the vibratile mass is increased by a preponderance of arytenoid tension). The term "chest voice," however, usually implies some form of coordinate relationship between the combined falsetto, or "head voice," and the "chest register"—the latter, a term reserved for the lower mechanism in its isolated form.

See **Register**
Resonance

Chesty Voice: a descriptive term commonly applied to a voice that is dominated by the chest register, or to the voice of a singer who belts popular songs.

In a "chesty" voice, the resonance characteristics associated with the chest register extend too high into the middle and upper pitch ranges, with the inevitable result that the larynx rises, the tongue tenses, the ratio of registration is not allowed to change, the head voice is shut off, and high notes become difficult or impossible to produce. Singers who pride themselves on having "big" voices commonly fall into this error.

See **Belting**

Chewing Bread: a remedy for vocal disabilities advanced by E. Froeschels (1952); originally, without the bread, a "breath" chewing exercise.

Bread or breath chewing was instituted as a relaxation method by Dr. Froeschels to overcome disorders of voice and speech. While masticatory movements are inherited, inborn abilities (sucking, biting, swallowing and other phases of eating), they are inadequate when applied to communication. Singing and speech are acquired skills, and are served and learned by secondary cortical patterns which differ from the inborn primary centers associated with respiration and other life-sustaining, reflexive functions. For one who is "tied up" physically and psychologically, relaxation is a precondition for effective positive action, but positive action further requires muscular contractions, and these are either well or poorly coordinated. It is the problem of muscular coordination which lies at the root of the vocal difficulty. When solved, the articulators will become facile and free in their movement, unless under stress of a nervous or psychic disorder.

See **Cerebellum**
Lip Trill

Choked Tones: those tones whose quality indicates the presence of throat constriction.

The principal cause of throat constriction is faulty coordination among the muscles which adjust the vocal folds and the pharyngeal resonators. Psychological problems can also encourage throat constriction. Pedagogic practices such as "covering," "nasal resonance," "breath control," and tonal "placement" exacerbate this condition when it exists and tend to create it when it does not. The cure for "choked" (constricted) singing is the institution of procedures that encourage natural movement within the interior processes of the vocal function. Registration is a key factor in effecting this transformation.

See **Closed Tones**
Constriction

Clavicle: the collarbone.

Clavicular Breathing: See Breathing, Clavicular.

Cleft Palate: a congenital malformation of the roof of the mouth.

CLOSED TONES

Closed Tones: a somewhat ambiguous term used to indicate 1) a constricted tone quality, 2) covered tones, and 3) closed vowels.

See **Resonance**
Vowel

With the exception of throat constriction, the qualities listed above have become associated with a narrow mouth opening. But since all vowels should be resonated pharyngeally, regardless of whether they are "open" or "closed," the correspondence between mouth position and tone quality should not be considered a fixed equation. Poorly resonated sounds are often referred to as "closed," because they are produced with some amount of throat constriction. The continued inclusion of the expression "closed" in the vocal lexicon is another example of the difficulties encountered when attempting to develop a precise vocal nomenclature.

Closely Coupled: See Coupling.

Closers of the Vocal Folds: the internal thyroarytenoid (vocalis muscles) and interarytenoid muscles, which participate in approximating the vocal cords, and thereby narrow the glottal slit. These muscles work in conjunction with the cricothyroids and arytenoids, antagonists which hold the vocal cords in balanced tension for phonation.

See **Registration**

Clustered Formants: See Formants.

Clutch: to suddenly constrict the laryngeal muscles and pharynx, and thereby "collapse" the existing resonance adjustment; a situation commonly brought on because of nervous tension.

See **Anxiety**

Coaching: instruction which is primarily concerned with the interpretive aspects of vocal music: correct pitches and time values, reasonable tempi, the proper pronunciation and inflection of languages, musical style, musical form, phrasing, and the tonal coloration required to project the words and music with feeling and intelligence.

A good coach should be able to make interpretive suggestions which will utilize a singer's strengths, camouflage his weaknesses, and in general foster artistic and technical growth. The coach should not, however, take on the responsibilities of a voice teacher, a role for which he is usually unqualified either by experience or by training.

Coarse Tones: vocalized sounds possessing a rough, uncultivated quality.

Tonal coarseness is characteristic of an uncoordinated chest register, whether the voice be male or female, but even when the registers are fairly well integrated, the voice will sound coarse if the resonance adjustment is poor.

See **Cavity Tone Theory**
Harmonic Theory
Relative Pitch
    Theory

Acoustically, coarse tones are the product of higher, odd-numbered harmonic partials (the ninth, eleventh and thirteenth), which add certain dissonant elements to coarsen the tone quality.

See **Ear**

Cochlea: the spiral cavity which forms the inner ear.

Cold Voice: 1) a voice that has not been "warmed up" or prepared for vigorous vocalization, or 2) a voice that lacks feeling and warmth.

Colla Voce: Italian, "with the voice."

Colla voce is frequently found in piano or orchestral accompaniments, and instructs the accompanist or conductor to "follow" the singer in passages or phrases where the technical or communicative requirements of the music demand freer treatment.

Collapse of the Vocal Mechanism: a breakdown which occurs when one or more parts of the vocal mechanism are either functionally inoperative or weakly developed. An inward tilting of the thyroid cartilage, rather than a forward movement, is one of the more obvious symptoms of a collapsed mechanism.

Collapsed Falsetto: See Falsetto, Collapsed.

Collapsed Resonators: a constriction within the laryngo- and oropharynges caused by the inability of the suspensory muscles to stabilize the larynx, and/or an imbalanced registration.

Laryngeal stability is essential to resonance, since the intrinsic and extrinsic muscle systems which either insert or originate there depend upon that stability to function properly. When the thyroid cartilage tilts inward, for example, neither the oropharynx nor the articulatory processes can move freely, nor can the vocal folds approximate easily when the position of the larynx is either too high or too low. Throat constriction is unavoidable when the laryngeal and associated musculatures are poorly coordinated.

Collapse of the resonating system and its concomitant throat constriction causes a reduction in tonal vitality, a deficiency which inevitably inclines the singer to force his voice.

See Constriction
(To) Force
Laryngeal
   Suspension
Resonance

Collapsed Tones: vocalized sounds which lack resonance, and therefore lack musicality.

Collapsed tone qualities are the result of 1) the failure of the vocalis muscles and the arytenoids to adjust properly, or 2) a faulty laryngeal position. Either deficiency distorts the natural adjustments necessary for efficient phonation.

Collapsed tone qualities are frequently the product of vocal practices which encourage throat constriction, such as consistent "marking," nasal resonance, and breath control.

Collar of the Larynx: the muscular ring, formed by the aryepiglottal folds, which comprises the upper portion of the larynx. This ring-like structure forms a link between the arytenoid muscles of the larynx and the epiglottis.

(To) Color the Voice: to make adjustments in the tonal texture of vocalized sound that reflect emotional responses to the music or text. Functionally, tonal coloration is achieved by subtle variations in the balance of registration, and by adjustments made for resonance. Descriptive terms like "soft," "sweet," "brittle," "rich," "edgy," "hard," "bright," "dark," "ringing," *etc.*, are all verbal representations of tonal coloring.

The ability of the vocal organs to respond to the singer's concept of "color" is due to the fact that the vocal folds can produce a given pitch and adjust for the vowel in various ways. For example, a longer vibrating surface harmonically enriches the fundamental tone and introduces a dark, rich tonal texture, whereas a shorter vibrating surface reduces the energy concentrated in the fundamental, intensifies the strength of the higher partials, and produces a brighter tonal texture.

The resonance adjustment also affects tonal coloration, since a long throat column is always associated with dark tone qualities, whereas a shorter, more precisely tuned coupling of resonance cavities coincides with brighter qualities.

Coloratura: a translation from the German word *Koloratur,* signifying vocal ornamentation.

The word coloratura is not, as commonly supposed, derived from the Italian language, where the proper expression for "coloring" would be *colorazione.* The Italian term to indicate rapid scales and embellishments is *fioritura,* meaning "flowery."

In its accepted sense, coloratura can mean 1) turns, rapid scales, trills and similar embellishments, 2) the singing of these ornaments, and 3) a high soprano who specializes in this style of singing.

When functioning correctly, all voice types are capable of singing coloratura passages swiftly and accurately. However, voices of higher range are generally more adept at florid singing than are their heavier counterparts, since the head voice they are obliged to depend upon is by far the more agile of the two mechanisms. Thus the "coloratura soprano," or *soprano leggiera,* the highest of all female voices, is generally the most flexible because of the two and a half octaves of head voice that make up the body of her tonal range.

Coloratura Soprano: the highest of all female voice types, with a compass extending from G below middle C to G in altissimo; a voice noted for extreme agility in executing rapid scale passages.

While the coloratura soprano is capable of sustaining an exceedingly high tessitura, she is consequently confronted with special problems. Because her high range is weak in overtone structure and the product of strongly reinforced fundamentals, she must take care that her voice does not "spread" and become shrill. A special limitation is found in altissimo, where vowels become neutral and cannot be delineated clearly. It is for this reason that the upper tonal range of the coloratura soprano requires a subordination of the text to the tone production, and her altissimo singing is never concerned with a verbal text unless the music is badly written for the voice.

Colpo di Petto: Italian, "stroke of or against the chest."

When the vocal mechanism is well coordinated, all energy expended in singing is directed into the maintenance of an equilibrium, and the singer feels that there is a point of resistance against which he can "press" or "lean." This feeling of resistance is primarily the result of a precise coordination between the respiratory system, the false vocal cords, and the suspensory muscles of the larynx.

The feeling of being able to "stroke against the chest" is reserved for those singers who experience a balance of muscular tension into which energy can be directed without being dissipated, and who are able to produce their tones forcefully without pushing. The physical action of a *colpo di petto* is similar to that of the staccato, except that the tones are more chest register-dominated and located in the mid and lower tonal ranges, and the resonance engages a deeper laryngeal position—hence, the term *colpo di petto*.

Combination Tone: a vocalized sound which is the product of a combined action of the two register mechanisms; acoustically, a combination of difference and summation tones.

Pedagogically, the term "combination tone" is not useful, since strictly speaking it is physically impossible to sing a legitimate tone that is not combined, *i.e.*, one without some degree of register coordination. To carry any meaning, therefore, it must be prefaced with a descriptive adjective.

The acoustic definition of a combination tone does not apply to the production of vocal tone.

See **Register**

Compass: vocal range; a term used in reference to both a singer and a musical composition.

Complemental Breath: inspired breath taken in excess of tidal air, or that amount taken during normal respiration.

The act of phonation requires the use of complemental air since the demands upon the breath rise above normal usage. Complemental air (about 1600 cc or above) is sometimes of abnormal concern to the singer, who often feels obliged to inflate the lungs in excess of his needs. Complemental breath is, however, necessary to phonation because of the need to build up compression, provide a more ample supply of oxygen to the system, and sustain long musical phrases.

See **Supplemental Breath**
Vital Capacity

Complex Tone: a sound with overtones; a sound composed of the sum of a series of pure sound waves.

A pure tone (*i.e.*, one without overtones, a sine wave) is exemplified by the vibrations set in motion by a tuning fork. All vocal tones, however, are complex sounds, and the composite of the sine waves, or sinusoids, erects a harmonic structure which determines the qualitative properties of the tone produced. Complex sounds can be analyzed acoustically by an oscilloscope and plotted in graph form to produce a read-out, which can be useful in assessing vocal problems and progress.

See **Sine Wave**

Components of Sound Waves: the partials or harmonics which comprise a complex sound. Partials are integral multiples of frequencies contained within the fundamental or basic tone.

Compression Wave: part of a sound, or that phase of a sine wave whose motion compresses the adjacent air particles as it moves away from a vibrating source.

Con Slancio: Italian, "impetus or impulse," referring to the onset of phonation; conceivably derived from *lanciare,* "to launch."

Concept: See Mental Concept.

Concone Exercises: See Exercises.

Conditioned Reflex: a response pattern which, through habit, becomes automatic.

A healthy vocal technique is not a conditioned reflex, but a condition in which the vocal mechanism is *ready* to respond naturally and spontaneously to a given stimulus. The singer who has acquired an efficient technique has acquired vocal freedom: that is, he is no longer subjected to learned responses, but has learned to respond. Thus, if the word "sing" sets up a conditioned reflex in which the coordinative process becomes fixed and invariable, then regardless of its merits, the technique of the singer is limited by his conditioning. To remove these limitations, a training program must be instituted which will serve, in effect, to recondition a conditioned reflex. Until this has been done, spontaneity is impossible, and vocal expression is at best contrived, calculated, and cerebral.

See **Energy**
Natural Movement
Register

Congesting: an accumulation of energy which finds both the intrinsic and extrinsic muscles of the larynx maintained in an almost constant state of unrelieved tension, a condition which requires an excessive amount of breath pressure to be directed against the vocal folds.

Congesting is usually associated with thoracic (high chest) breathing, its visual manifestations being tongue stiffness and, because the capillary vessels cause the veins in the neck to bulge, redness of face.

See **(To) Force**
Mechanistic
Methods
Resonance

Congesting results from 1) an effort to "make" resonance, 2) improper breathing habits, and 3) an imbalanced registration. It is to these areas of interest that pedagogic attention must be directed if the tone production is to be free.

Conscious Control: arbitrary, mechanistic control of the voluntary muscles used in phonation.

Conscious control, fostered by proponents of tonal "placement" and special techniques for breathing, is usually manifested physically by prepared (often exaggerated) tongue and mouth positions, facial expressions, and body posture. Since virtually all of the important muscles engaged in phonation lie beyond the singer's power of volitional control, efforts to institute effective controls through conscious effort abort the vocal process and create problems more serious than those they were designed to solve.

Consonants: those phonemes or units of sound used in forming words that are not sonants, or sustained sounds.

The word "consonant" is derived from the Latin verb *consonare*, "to sound together." Generally, consonants introduce, connect, or conclude the vowel phonemes, which are sustained. This is not always the case, however, since many consonants (*e.g., m, n, l, f, v, s, z, h* and *r*) can be sustained independently.

Consonants are articulated by the lips, teeth, and tongue, and by the soft and hard palates. They have been grouped by authorities into two distinct categories, one based on their acoustic properties, and another on the manner of their production or articulation.

Acoustically, consonants are referred to as either "voiced" or "unvoiced." A voiced consonant is accompanied by laryngeal vibration (*e.g., m, b*); an unvoiced consonant is not (*e.g., k, t*). Further distinctions are provided by the terms "plosive," "fricative," "nasal," and "glide," which refer, somewhat arbitrarily, to the manner in which sound is emitted. For example, a voiced plosive (so named because sound is released in an abrupt, explosive manner) is the phoneme *b;* its unvoiced counterpart is the phoneme *p.* A voiced fricative (whose sound is produced by friction) is the consonant *v,* its unvoiced counterpart, *f. M* and *n* are typical nasal consonants, and both are voiced. *R* and *j* are voiced glides, since their sounds are accompanied by a gliding movement of either the tongue or the lips. Various combinations of consonants are considered distinct phonemes, each with its own acoustic description. For example, there is both a voiced and an unvoiced *th,* as in the English words "these" and "thought." The unvoiced fricative *sh* (as in the English word "should") finds its voiced counterpart in the soft *g* of "garage," *etc.*

Nomenclature based on the manner of consonant articulation uses terms like "labial" (formed by the lips), "lingual" (formed by the tongue), "dental" (using the teeth), "alveolar" (using the gum ridge), "palatal" (using the hard palate), "velar" (using the soft palate), and "glottal" (an abrupt approximation of the vocal folds). Although some consonant phonemes, such as *b, p, m* and *w,* fall comfortably into one of the above classifications (in this case, "labial"), many phonemes require a combination of articulatory terms. Thus, we have "labial-dental" (*f, v*), "lingua-alveolar" (*t, d, l, s, z*), "lingua-dental" (*th*), "lingua-palatal" (*r, j*), and "lingua-velar" (*k, g, n*) consonants. The adenoidal *n* sound, which can be produced with the mouth open, is considered a glottal consonant.

Fortunately, vocal training is rarely concerned with the technicalities outlined above. More important to the singer is the realization that the formation of vowels and the articulation of consonants involve two distinct muscular processes whose actions must be coordinated for clear, effective communication. The reason for this is clear: each vowel possesses a particular tonal form and resonance characteristic which requires a relatively fixed cavity adjustment, whereas the muscles of the tongue, lips, jaw, and face must always be highly mobile for the articulation of consonants. Vowels, therefore, must be formed pharyngeally so as not to interfere with the articulatory processes, and the articulation of consonants must occur without interrupting the resonance characteristics necessary to each vowel.

Recent studies carried out in France by Nicole Scotto di Carlo (1979) refute the contention that strongly energized articulation is essential to a successful projection of the verbal text. According to di Carlo, and on the basis of the evidence provided by most singers, the opposite seems to be true. An over-articulated text, especially in English, does not come clearly across the footlights. Therefore, something is obviously wrong with the theoretical propositions that have been put into practice. The substance of di Carlo's findings are quoted as follows:

> We have shown in this research that articulation has particularly disrupting effects on the beauty of the vibrato, the continuity of the legato, the aesthetics of attacks, sustained phrases and releases, which are generally considered to play a considerable part in the quality of singing.

> The training methods based upon articulation or *consonantal emphasis* are therefore to be systematically avoided, as they are bound to endanger the precarious balance

CONSOVOWELS

[36]Nicole Scotto di Carlo,"Perturbing Effects of Overarticulation in Singing," *Journal of Research in Singing* Vol. II, No. 2 (July 1979), 23.

that the singer has to reach if he wants to preserve both the intelligibility of the text and the aesthetic value of the music.[36]

The concepts essential to an understanding of the relationship between tone and text may be summed up briefly as follows:

1. When vowels are impure and ill defined, it is necessary to compensate for this deficiency by overstressing the consonants;
2. When consonants are strongly articulated and the vowels remain impure, the text may be discerned, but the voice will have lost its essential properties of communication, *i.e.*, the tonal colorations which infuse the text with subtleties of feeling that rise above word meanings;
3. When vowels are purely produced and well resonated, and the consonants are weakly articulated, the text will still be difficult to hear. The feeling will be communicated, but the specific linguistic guidelines will be absent, and
4. When the vowels are produced purely and the consonants are stressed in proportion to their tonal strength, the text will emerge with clarity and definition, while at the same time the voice quality will convey those subtleties of meaning that cannot be verbalized.

The functional climate in which clear enunciation is realized exists when the entire vocal tract, from the pelvic region to the palatal muscles, is maintained in balanced tension. This equilibrium results from a properly developed and well-integrated registration, genuine laryngeal resonance, and superior linguistic skills. Under these technical conditions, all energy expended during phonation will be distributed equitably throughout the total system, with the result that both the tone and the text will fuse into an entity that truly reflects the singer's innermost thoughts and feelings. To overenergize consonants at the expense of the tonal form, or to subordinate clean articulation to the interests of tonal resonance, is to break down this precarious equilibrium and undermine the communicative experience.

Consovowels: consonants (also called "semi-vowels") comprised of voiced sounds which can be sustained (*e.g., m, n, l, r, v* and *z*).

Constriction: in singing, a narrowing of the pharynx that is caused by muscular interference.

Throat constriction is generally the result of the inability of those muscle groups which adjust the vocal folds to meet the changing demands of pitch, intensity, and vowel (registration), and of those which position the larynx as the primary resonator of vocal tone (resonance), to function efficiently. As constriction becomes habitual, however, energy is misdirected away from spontaneous, natural movements into compensatory movements, which impede natural functioning. Throat constriction invariably leads to a loss of vocal freedom, power, range, resonance and flexibility.

Although throat constriction may assume many guises, two of the most common are the following: 1) a condition in which the hyoid bone and tongue are depressed, the laryngeal orifice is partially covered by the epiglottis, and the thyroid cartilage is collapsed inward, and 2) one in which the genioglossus and hyoglossus muscles are relaxed, the tongue and hyoid bone are elevated, and the base of the tongue drawn backwards. Under these circumstances, it is impossible either for the vocal folds to be positioned properly, or for the laryngo-, oro-, and nasopharynges to function effectively as resonators.

Once the singer has acquired a constricted technique, the cure is very difficult, since it involves a complete reversal of habitual muscular movements. Attempts at reversing the action of the involuntary muscles used in singing are not only physically difficult, but also, in many instances, psychologically threatening to the singer.

Contrabasso: the lowest male voice type (also called *basso profundo*), whose range extends from two octaves below middle C to the F above middle C.

Contraltina: See Countertenor.

Contralto: the lowest female voice type, whose range extends from D below middle C to high B♭. Known for its unusual tonal weight and warmth, the true contralto is a rarity.

Contratenor: See Countertenor.

Control: the ability to direct or restrain the functioning of the vocal mechanism. Basically, there are four types of vocal control:

1. That which is governed by hearing;
2. That which is regulated by an awareness of sensations of vibration;
3. That which is made possible by the arbitrary positioning of volitionally operable parts of the vocal mechanism, such as the tongue, mouth, and uvula, especially those having to do with the breathing apparatus, and
4. That which is based upon instinct, an understanding of natural movement, and the functional logic by which the vocal mechanism is governed.

Of the four approaches listed above only the first and last, used conjunctively, are essential to the development of legitimate vocal control. These are discussed below under their appropriate headings.

HEARING

The kind of hearing necessary for the attainment of this objective is a special talent which must be carefully cultivated. Instead of "producing" qualities which reflect an aesthetic preference, the singer must learn to recognize the innumerable combinations of tone quality yielded as a result of the exercise patterns projected by the teacher. An essential feature of these exercises is to induce, essentially through the mechanics of registration, new and unfamiliar qualities. These qualities represent important changes in the response pattern of a complex of laryngeal muscles whose movement lies beneath the threshold of consciousness, and which are consequently inaccessible to direct control.

It is in this way that the singer learns to equate the numerous tone qualities he is capable of producing with their corresponding functional origins. Through careful cultivation, it is possible thereby to grow into an understanding of the qualitative properties associated with the two register mechanisms, the relationship between a wide assortment of tonal colors and their functional origins, and the specific nature of the adjustments formed by the throat parts—whether open-throated or constricted, too "heady" or too "chesty," "thick," "dry," "ringing," "brittle," *etc.* Simultaneously, the singer will have gained a profound insight into his own natural tone quality.

Other advantages are to be gained from attentive listening. Differences will be discerned in the tonal pulse, and the singer will soon learn the types of tonal oscillations, together with their variants, perceived as a vibrato, tremolo or wobble. Attentive listening will further enable him to detect the slightest imperfection in vowel quality, and most important of all, to "hear" that the voice is capable of moving from pitch to pitch without the aid of overt, prepared, or consciously controlled movement.

Since a valid subjective attitude toward quality is exceedingly rare as a natural gift, "trained listening" must be inculcated under the guidance of a skillful teacher. When properly developed, these perceptions will refine concepts and encourage natural movement, two essentials to vocal progress. For the talented, this will lead to an understanding of the functional logic by which the vocal mechanism is governed.

INSTINCT

The fourth category is as important as the first, for it is the release of the "singer instinct" through improved function and encouragement of spontaneity that allows free natural tone production to be developed.

Controls growing out of spontaneity and understanding of natural movement are diametrically opposed to all others in principle. This is because the singer, not having prescience, cannot know how to control and use his instrument properly until *after* he has learned to sing freely and naturally. In essence, for a long period of time, the only controls one is capable of putting into effect are the very controls to be relinquished.

SENSATIONS OF VIBRATION

Attempts to control function through the duplication of sensations of vibration thought to be desirable can be marginally successful at best. First, if the sensation one is attempting to duplicate is one's own, the procedure arrests progress, since it is only through change that improvement can be made. If sensations of vibration (which are ultimately the products of compensatory tensions) are not allowed to change, the coordinative process which produced those sensations will not be able to improve, and technical progress will again be at a standstill. The perfectly sung tone is a coordinative act which is free and exhilarating as a total experience, and notable for a lack of localized sensation. Second, if the sensations one is attempting to duplicate are someone else's, progress is even less likely. In this instance, the singer is not only limited by the technical efficiency of the example, but also by the fact that a physical symptom (*e.g.*, a sensation of vibration) is always the reflection of a physical condition. Thus, in order for the sensations of vibration experienced by one individual to be felt by another, the two would have to be emotionally, psychologically, physiologically, kinesthetically, and functionally identical. The probability of this happening is remote.

ARBITRARY ADJUSTMENTS

Mechanistic controls are at best minimally helpful. The vocal problem centers around the fact that all important muscle groups involved during phonation are involuntary. These cannot be directly energized, and to attempt to do so inevitably invites muscular interference and compensatory tensions. Arbitrary tongue and mouth positions will sometimes predispose interior muscles to react differently, but this procedure fails to exert a profound influence on the coordinative process. Special techniques for breathing exacerbate technical problems by encouraging stiff, self-conscious physical attitudes that inhibit natural movement.

The inherent danger in all methods of direct control is that they tend to discourage natural movement. In fact, the feeling of being able to control one's voice by overtly acting upon the mechanism is not necessarily desirable. While such controls may be reassuring, they are usually related to habits which should be discarded. Risk is an inherent factor in vocal freedom, and if progress is to be made, one must venture upon uncharted seas in search of new experiences. Imposed controls are self-limiting; those associated with freedom are not. It is therefore essential to abandon all controls during training, for only then can progress be made.

See Breathing
Energy
Functional Hearing
Functional
Listening
Register
Resonance
Self-Regulation

To learn to sing freely, one must learn to "let go:" to respond, instead of attempting to master a series of learned responses. The best kind of control is that which finds the mechanism functioning as a self-regulatory instrument, and operating in accordance with procedures founded upon a belief that organic activities are inherently rational. The ultimate vocal control, therefore, is that arrived at *after* contact has been made with the logical movement potential of the mechanism. Outer-imposed disciplines do not lead to that kind of control.

Conus Elasticus (Cricovocal or Cricothyroid Membrane): the tough, cone-shaped lining of the larynx, consisting of a strongly developed layer of elastic tissue (covered both on its inner and outer sides by a thin layer of mucosa) which extends from the superior border of the cricoid cartilage to the upper limit of the true vocal folds. Since one portion of the conus elasticus is attached to the arytenoid cartilages and its process and the remainder to the vocal folds, it is considered to be instrumental in adjusting their length.

See Larynx

Coordinated Falsetto: See Falsetto, Coordinated.

Coordinated Registration: a physical adjustment in which the qualities of both the head voice and the chest voice are combined.

See Register

Coordination: the combined action of two or more muscle systems engaged in the execution of certain complex movements.

Phonation is the end product of complex muscular movements taking place within the throat parts. No muscle (with the possible exception of the sphincter) is capable of acting alone; a muscle is steadied or opposed by the contraction of one or more muscles or muscle groups that oppose or work in conjunction with it, and as a result, coordination of the largely involuntary muscle systems responsible for "voice" is extremely difficult, and requires a special technique of teaching and learning.

COORDINATIVE PROCESS

The procedures to be adopted in the development of vocal skills must embrace functional principles which are philosophically opposed to those applicable when dealing with volitionally controllable activities. The concept of registration promulgated during the Bel Canto era was based upon this premise, and an essential feature of the instruction was a notable absence of "do this" instruction. By avoiding explicit directives, the teachers of that era recognized that the involuntary muscle systems to be coordinated could neither be directly acted upon nor controlled, either by the will or by the intellect. Implicit in early commentaries on the subject was an understanding that it is the *idea* of movement that causes movement, and that all overt controls and manipulative devices are inhibitory.

Science has verified the soundness of this approach, since it has been discovered that the core of the functional activities associated with phonation is recorded, stored and evaluated in the cerebellum rather than the cerebral cortex. According to Willard R. Zemlin, the cerebellum is a motor regulatory system which functions in much the same manner as certain electrical circuits known as feedback loops: the information with respect to organic movements travels by afferent and efferent pathways to record the character, extent, and rapidity of involuntary movements. It is from such information that this "second brain" evaluates and regulates those involuntary movements taking place below the level of consciousness.

Instruction designed to improve a present technical status by changing or modifying the coordinate interplay among the relevant muscular systems may therefore be seen to depend upon procedures which stimulate *reflexive* movement. The specific elements of this stimulus, contained in a musical idea to which the student need only respond, has led to the formulation of those principles long known to govern registration.

Coordination of the various vocal muscles, especially those within the throat parts, is indispensable to the development of vocal skills. Inevitably, the quality of the ultimate tonal product will be a direct reflection of the quality of that coordination.

Coordinative Process: those movements which occur in response to a musical stimulus embracing four basic elements: pitch, intensity, vowel and duration.

Core: the essence of a well-formed tone.

Functionally, the tonal "core" is caused by a harmonious muscular coordination among those muscle groups which position the vocal folds to meet changing demands of pitch, intensity and vowel (registration) and among those which establish the larynx as the primary resonator of vocal tone (resonance). A well-developed, well-integrated registration and an effective resonance adjustment form the core of an efficient vocal technique.

Corti: See Organ of Corti.

Costal: pertaining to the ribs. The term is derived from the Latin word *costa* or "rib."

Costal Breathing: See Breathing, Costal.

Countertenor: a falsetto-dominated male voice type (also called "contraltina" or "contratenor") whose range extends from F below middle C to the second F above middle C.

Functionally, countertenors sing in a "mixed" falsetto, which, because some coordinate relationship has been established with the chest voice, may possibly justify inclusion of this category among other voice types recognized as legitimate. A considerable body of musical literature has been written, especially in England, to accommodate the special characteristics of the countertenor. The rather monochromic and effeminate quality intrinsic to this type of tone production contains little emotional thrust, and does not wear well on extended listening.

All countertenors sing in a "mixed" registration with its concomitant throat constriction.

See **Falsettists**
Falsetto
Mezzo Falso
Male Alto
Registration,
"**Mixed**"

Coup de Glotte: an expression introduced by Manuel Garcia, a prominent nineteenth century vocal teacher and the inventor of the laryngoscope, to describe and explain the mechanics of a proper attack.

Garcia's description of the *coup de glotte,* together with that advanced by his most illustrious pupil-teacher, Mathilde Marchesi, is somewhat puzzling. It is, to use Garcia's own words, "the neat articulation of the glottis that gives a precise and clean attack to the sound." Garcia further describes this action in the following statement:

> . . . the stroke of the glottis is somewhat similar to the cough, although differing essentially in that it needs only the delicate action of the lips and not the impulse of the air. The lightness of movement is considerably facilitated if it be tried with the mouth shut. Once understood, it may be used with the mouth open on any vowel. The object of this is that at the start sounds should be free from the defect of slurring up to a note or the noise of breathing.[37].

[37]Manuel Garcia, *Hints on Singing,* translated by Beata Garcia (New York: Edward Schuberth Co., Inc., 1894), pp. 13, 14.

As a disciple of Garcia, and as the teacher of Calvé, Melba, Eames, Alda, and other prominent singers, Mathilde Marchesi possessed qualifications that cannot logically be challenged. Nevertheless, in her theoretical statements concerning the *coup de glotte,* her position appears to have reinforced certain of the negative connotations which surround the practice of this device. According to her account, the *coup de glotte* requires "a sudden and energetic approximation of the lips of the glottis, an instant before expiration commences." Continuing in her comment on the subject, she modifies the concept called by many the "shock" of the glottis by suggesting that it is a "natural movement of the vocal organs, and that the pupil has only to bring under his will this spontaneous action *which has been developing since the first cry at the moment of birth.*"[38] She then re-emphasizes the fact that the *coup de glotte* is a "natural and spontaneous organic action."

Despite the contradiction implicit in Marchesi's definition ("a sudden and energetic approximation" vs. "a natural and spontaneous organic action"), one must assume that the proper execution of the *coup de glotte,* carried out in order to insure a clean attack and eliminate breathy tone qualities, was, in safe hands, a constructive pedagogic procedure. Both Garcia and Marchesi were highly cultivated and refined musicians, and it is inconceivable to conclude that either of them

[38]Mathilde Marchesi, *Bel Canto: A Theoretical and Practical Vocal Method,* edited by Philip L. Miller (New York: Dover Publications, Inc., 1970), p. xii.

approved of a rude, energetic approximation of the vocal cords in the form of a tonal explosion.

As is true with so many loosely verbalized statements, the principle underlying the *coup de glotte* has been misinterpreted, and having been translated into studio practice by less skilled teachers, it has become a caricature of the original. As the ideal answer to a recurring pedagogic problem, however, the *coup de glotte* must be accepted with some reservation, for it would seem that there are safer options available to remedy breathy tone qualities and a slovenly attack.

For those inclined to master the subtleties of a well-executed *coup de glotte,* it might be suggested that the most advantageous point of beginning is to practice the staccato. For the following reasons, the staccato provides a conceptual and kinesthetic understanding of the manner in which the vocal mechanism can be effectively stimulated:

1. It is impossible to sing staccato without using the larynx as a resonator;
2. The staccato makes the singer aware of the manner in which the vocal folds and the laryngo- and oropharynges can move quickly and precisely from a relaxed state to an open-throated resonance adjustment, and
3. In producing a staccato, the vocal folds yield vibrations which are not encumbered with breathiness or extraneous noise elements.

See **Attack**
   Dans la Masque
   Laryngeal
      Suspension
   Register
   Resonance
   Vowel

By pursuing this and similar alternatives, it is possible that a proper execution of the *coup de glotte* will suggest itself, and that, under skillful tutelage, it will come to regain its place as both an effective teaching tool and an artistic effect.

Coupling: the joining of two or more elastic systems (either two oscillators, a vibrator and a resonator[s], or adjoining cavities having an interconnecting channel or divider) in which the frequency of their vibratory motion is either complemented or modified by an exchange in their energies.

A system is said to be "loosely coupled" when the difference between two or more sources of actual or potential vibration is slight. The factors involved in loose coupling are 1) the natural frequencies of two oscillators, 2) that of a vibrator and a resonator(s), and/or 3) two or more sources of potential resonance. A system is "tightly" or "closely" coupled when the difference between their natural frequencies is wide. In such a coupling, if either the cavities or the vibrator are so "tuned" or adjusted that the vibratory energy of one system dominates that of the other, it forces the weaker source of potential vibration to conform to the movement characteristics of the stronger. Should a second or third resonator be added, the periodic force exerted by each will further modify the vibratory impulses given off by the total system.

The British physicist Sir James Jeans drew attention to the pendular movement of two clocks to explain the coupling of oscillating bodies, taking into account such variables as weight, distance and frequency. A minimal exchange of energy takes place, for example, when the clocks are placed some distance apart, *i.e.,* loosely coupled. In such a state, each remains unaffected by the movement of the other, regardless of any discrepancies in their motion. When brought into closer proximity, however, *i.e.,* closely coupled, the difference in their frequencies provokes an interaction which, provided the clocks are of comparable size and weight, results in a perfect compromise between the times they would have kept had they been moving independently. Moreover, should one timepiece be larger and of sturdier construction, the greater energy imparted by its motion will force the weaker to alter its frequency until it conforms to that of the larger. Thus, the elements of a coupled oscillating system can be indifferent to one another (as in loose coupling), either dominate or be dominated by one another when the rate of oscillating movement differs (as in close coupling), or, because their frequencies are identical, move in rhythmic harmony with one another.

The coupling of a vibrator and a resonator occurs when, for example, a tuning fork is held over a cylinder sharing the same natural frequency. If the natural frequencies of the fork and the column of air are identical, the strength of the vibrations, perceived as resonance, will be optimal. If they differ slightly, the frequency will vary in accordance with the manner in which their energies have been exchanged. In this type of "loose coupling," the pitches of each are generally pulled slightly out of tune. If the length of the vibrating column of air dominates the vibratory pattern of the vibrator, the system is "closely" or "tightly coupled," and the energy needed to maintain the vibrations must be increased.

With respect to cavity coupling, if the individual systems share the same frequency, their resonances will again be "loosely coupled," a "close" coupling being characterized by a wide difference in their resonance frequencies.

Coupling, whether "loose" or "tight," is common to both musical instruments and the human voice. With instruments, coupling takes two forms: 1) the forcing of a vibrator to tune to the frequency of an adjacent column of air (*e.g.*, reed instruments), and 2) that in which a solid body (*e.g.*, a violin or piano) is forced to vibrate at the natural frequency of external or internal strings.

With the voice, however, where adjustment of the pharyngeal cavities and the vocal folds offers a wider variety of options, coupling can take many forms, either or neither element taking control over the vibratory motion. When, for example, qualities described as "too open" are produced, it is the vibrator which has dominated the resonator, whereas in "covered" singing it is the resonator which dominates the vibrator, forcing the vocal folds into a conformation dictated not by the pitch, intensity and vowel pattern being sung, but by the acoustical properties of the cavities lying above them. Thus, under certain technical conditions, either system can be made to prevail over the other.

In a correct technique of tone production (which produces a "seamless," legato tone connection throughout the vocal range), neither the vibrator nor the cavity dominates the other. In such instances, the vocal folds adjust to a length and thickness ideal for the tonal pattern being sung, while at the same time the pharyngeal cavities select and energize those frequencies which define the vowel in the most efficient manner possible. In effect, it is like setting two clocks side by side that are of the same size and weight, and that keep the same time: there is a minimum of friction between the two sources of oscillation, and the loose coupling results in optimal efficiency.

Coupling of the vocal resonators during phonation involves the pharyngeal and oral cavities, the former being by far the more important of the two. Functionally, the interconnecting channel which separates the laryngo- and the oropharynges is far more subtle than the line of demarcation which separates the pharynx from the oral (mouth) cavity. With the former, the division is effected by the position of the epiglottis; with the latter, by the narrow channel formed as a result of the position assumed by the base of the tongue. Since the various cavities can be "tuned" either separately or together, and since these in turn can be "tuned" to the vibratory pattern of the vocal folds, the vocal mechanism is able to resonate a diversity of vowel qualities over a wide pitch range.

An important fact concerning acoustic coupling and resonance is that a cavity possesses no energy of its own, but responds to that supplied by a fundamental tone generated at the vibratory source. Thus, it may be concluded that 1) the vocal generator and primary source of vibratory energy is located within the laryngeal area, and 2) vowels are defined by adjustments made within the oropharynx.

There are many cavities accessible to the sound waves moving through the vocal tract into the outer atmosphere, and they can be coupled in a variety of ways. Those to be considered are the following:

1. The antra and sinus cavities of the head;
2. The nasopharynx (the area directly behind the nose);
3. The mouth;
4. The oropharynx (the area directly behind the mouth);
5. The laryngeal pharynx, and
6. The trachea (the tube below the laryngeal pharynx through which air is conducted to and from the lungs).

Since the antra, sinuses, nasopharynx and trachea are nonadjustable, for the most part highly damped with mucus, and remote from the tonal source, they cannot be considered important elements in cavity coupling. The mouth is equally ineffective when used in this capacity. Its fleshy walls increase the amount of damping, it is too mobile to influence the formant structure in any positive way, and its air space is constantly being disturbed because of the movement of the tongue during the articulation of consonants. Therefore, it is the two remaining cavities, the laryngo- and oropharynges, that are responsible for the production and resonation of vowel phonemes, because they can be tuned either to different frequencies or to the same frequency, i.e., they can be tightly or loosely coupled.

Ideally, the laryngeal pharynx is consistently tuned to energize vibrations of approximately 2800—3400 cycles per second (a concentration which accounts for the so-called "ring" in a tone), while the oropharynx adjusts to select those frequencies which define the vowel. Thus, a coupling of the resonators in response to the pitch, intensity and vowel pattern being sung involves these three factors:

1. A laryngeal adjustment that, regardless of the tracing of the melodic pattern energizes those frequencies which cause the tone to "ring;"
2. A tuning (adjustment) of the oropharynx so that it selects and energizes those frequencies associated with a given vowel quality, and
3. A shaping of the mouth that facilitates (but does not ensure) the proper formation of these cavities.

It is important to realize within the latter context that the oropharynx, while it patterns its position after the adjustment assumed by the mouth, should retain its ability to tune to a uniform vowel quality even though the mouth cavity is mobile. This is most practical, since it is obvious that a constant vowel quality and a constant mouth position in performance are aesthetically and functionally undesirable. Indeed, a proper tuning of the resonators will mean that both the cavity adjustments and the mouth movements necessary to the articulatory processes are completely independent, even when they coincide.

While an understanding of acoustic coupling should provide a more profound insight into the nature of the vocal problem, it is not a solution. From the standpoint of a viable vocal pedagogy, the crucial factor is not acoustic analysis but knowing how to stimulate the involuntary muscular systems involved in these diverse positioning processes so that the size, shape and type of pharyngeal cavity formation, the vibratory pattern of the vocal folds, and the physical dimensions or cross-sections of the connecting passages are precisely adjusted and free of interfering tensions.

Technical training leading to an efficient coupling of the pharyngeal resonators depends upon those mechanical principles known to govern registration, for if the muscular contractions which draw the vocal folds into tension do not coordinate effectively, other elements of the system cannot avoid constricting. If, however, the registers are well developed and properly balanced, and if the resonance adjustment is precise, the mechanism will be properly coupled. As a result, the singing voice will be free, resonant, and beautiful.

Covering, (To) Cover: to make a change of resonance adjustment by "darkening" those vowels phonated in the area of the primary register "break" (E—F♯ above middle C), and also at the so-called "upper break" in women's voices, lying an octave above, in order to avoid tone qualities which are commonly perceived to be "too open." Covering is generally used in conjunction with "closed" vowels, *e.g.,* *oh, oo.* It is also used when singing *sotto voce,* or when a "darkening" of the tone quality is appropriate as an interpretive effect.

Covering forms the substance of most training methods that are currently in vogue. Technically, it is a device for coupling an acoustic system in such a manner that the cavity dominates the vibrator. This practice alters the physical conformation of the vocal folds, and consequently realigns the registration. Covering, therefore, is a device used to overcome inequities in the balance of tension shared between the two muscle systems (the cricothyroids and the arytenoids) which tauten the vocal folds.

Covering plays an important role in the development of vocal skills, since it confronts problems related to either the strengthening or the vigorous use of the chest register (a process which unavoidably *energizes* that mechanism, causing a widening of the gap between it and the head voice), and the need to bridge the *passaggio* with reasonable facility. Since a proper bridging is the final and most difficult stage of technical development, coordination of the two mechanisms must be approximate rather than precise for a considerable period of time. For this reason, covering, which effectively addresses itself to the problem of register tran- sition *before the basic mechanisms are capable of fine tuning,* possesses a functional importance which should not be ignored. It is a pedagogic misconception, however, to consider covering a permanent good; it is rather a device that compensates for a discrepancy in the registration without correcting it.

The impermanent value of covering as a pedagogic device is apparent when this training technique is compared to the art of the *messa di voce,* or the swelling and diminishing of a single tone without distorting the vowel. In executing the *messa di voce,* the ratio of registration will change precisely with fluctuations of intensity, while the resonance adjustment, *i.e.,* the vowel quality, will remain constant. Covering reverses this procedure: the balance of registration is an approximation at best, and the resonance adjustment is significantly altered, as it results in, or is caused by, a distortion of the vowel quality. As long as the practice of covering is thought to be a permanent good, vowel purity, a seamless voice, and the artistic swelling and diminishing of a single tone will remain a lost art.

HISTORY AND BACKGROUND

The history of "covering" began with the career of Gilbert-Louis Duprez (1806—1896), who reputedly became the first tenor to sing a high C in chest voice. Duprez first used this new technique when he was twenty-four, and he called it *voix sombre, couverte,* or *en dedans.* The literal meaning of the latter term is "inside," but in a vocal context it probably signifies "self-contained" or "directed inward," as opposed to outgoing or open.

Whether or not Duprez actually sang in chest voice up to the high C is open to question. The vocal organs function in accordance with natural law, and it is quite impossible to carry a chest register adjustment (where the thickness of the vocal folds is too great for the fundamental frequency) beyond an A♭, a major third below, even by straining. The problem, however, may be one of nomenclature; if it had been said that Duprez was the first to sing a high C full voice in the manner of Mario del Monaco, the statement could be accepted at face value, since he, too, sang high C with a chest register-dominated technique.

The covered technique introduced by Duprez departed radically from the Italian Bel Canto emulated by French vocalists. At this juncture in the development of opera, the *castrati* reigned supreme in both accomplishment and popularity, and the capabilities of the tenor voice had never been vigorously exploited. Lyricism, flexibility, and the ability to sustain long phrases were the essential requisites. The qualitative properties of the tone production reflected an excessive dominance of the head voice, a condition which permitted the voice to soar effortlessly, but without "thrust" or ring. By abandoning these aesthetic objectives and the functional principles essential to their realization, Duprez introduced a style of singing based upon dramatic declamation. He became the first dramatic tenor.

While the covered style of singing was inimical to the taste and linguistic characteristics of the Italians (who have always preferred a more "open" type of tone production), the impact of Duprez' new technique did succeed in expanding the horizons within which the tenor voice had been so long confined. In Italy, however, teachers remained faithful to the traditional principles upon which their art had been founded, and developed training techniques whereby full-voiced singing in the more "open" style would produce ringing high tones without loss of flexibility, and without distorting the vowel, *i.e.,* without abandoning the principles upon which a successful execution of the *messa di voce* depends. An example of this lyric dramatic singing style can be heard on recordings made by Fernando de Lucia (1860—1925), who, according to authorities, epitomized the successful combining of both the florid and *verismo* style popular during the latter half of the nineteenth century.

In France, disenchantment with the Duprez dramatic declamation, which was antipathetic to the innate Gallic sense of refinement and elegance, ultimately led to the adoption of the *voix mixte*, a pedagogic procedure that reduced the weight and tension of the chest voice by infusing it with a strong admixture of the head voice. While the use of this device was once widespread, its popularity has been superseded by singing *dans la masque*, a technique introduced much later by Jean de Reszke.

During the twentieth century, events have again come full circle, and the majority of the world's singers are now being taught to cover as a basic tenet of instruction at all levels of technical expertise. This popularity is not difficult to understand. The more heavily orchestrated music being composed, the larger opera houses, and a demand for greater tonal opulence led singers to push the chest register in order to cope successfully with this repertoire. "Covering" appeared to be the answer, because by energizing the chest voice and "darkening" the tone quality, a much greater amplitude of volume could be quickly developed.

Economics has also played an important role in the general acceptance of this technique. Years of patient study are required to develop the technical skill necessary to sing full voice without opening the seams in the "break" area. Furthermore, as dramatic roles have enjoyed increasing popularity, those who sing them have been tempted by the additional inducement of receiving higher fees. Since the mechanics of covering can be quickly learned by those already in possession of a well-developed instrument (and for those less skilled, it offers what appears to be an easy solution to a difficult technical problem), the practical reasons for adopting this method would appear to be compelling. Nevertheless, the rapid decline in vocal skills during the past half century, and the alarming failure of brilliant young vocalists to develop their potential, would appear to be directly attributable to an excessive and literal application of the technique of covering that was originally introduced by Duprez.

THE TECHNIQUE

The first scientific account of "covering" was published in 1840 by two French physicians, Diday and Pètrequin, who found that covered singing involves a lowering of the larynx and a simultaneous arching of the velum, an adjustment that enlarges the throat cavity. More recent investigators concur with this finding, but provide more detailed information. The consensus now is that in covering, the epiglottis is more elevated, the hyoid bone is more erect, and the glottis is positioned at a higher level in relation to the cervical spine. In addition, the vocal folds and the ventricles become more elongated, and the throat cavity is broadened by a widening of the space between the base of the tongue and the epiglottis. Acoustically, covering weakens the second harmonic (in an "open" tone production it is strong), but compensates for this deficiency by concentrating a greater amount of energy in the fundamental.

Among the inherent limitations of the adjustment associated with covering is the fact that it represents an imprecise tuning of the mechanism. Because of this absence of sharp tuning, covering is capable of, and indeed demands, a great deal of physical force if high levels of intensity are to be sustained. Richard Luchsinger (1949), a German physician who devoted careful study to every aspect of the vocal function, proved conclusively that breath volume per second and general energy expenditure is far greater in "covered" singing than it is in "open" tone production. It is not surprising, therefore, that with the acceptance of "covering" as an ultimate good, methods devoted to breath control and "support" came to assume overriding importance.

One of the essential features of covering is that in approaching the "break" area (E—F# above middle C) the vowel is changed from *ah* to *uh* or *oh*. This involves a rather arbitrary adjusting of the tongue, a rounding of the lips, a narrowing of the mouth position, and a corresponding depression of the larynx. The acoustic effect of this manipulation is to lower the frequency of the pharyngeal cavities so that they select and reinforce the lowest formant. Since a cavity with a smaller aperture at its point of exit resonates a lower pitch, lip rounding accompanied by a narrowing of the mouth position also tends to modify the vowel. Coincidentally, as demonstrated by the studies of J. Tarneaud of France (1932) and R. Schilling of Germany (1925), as the vowel shifts to *uh* or *oh,* a change takes place in the physical dimension of the vocal folds that devitalizes the chest register, modifies its "too open" quality, and brings in more head voice.

The practice of covering, therefore, is widely at variance with early tradition, where specific exercises were designed to neutralize the tonal dependency on any mouth position and thus free the articulatory processes. An early exercise designed to accomplish this objective was one in which the pupil was required to sing and clearly delineate all five vowels while holding a pencil between the teeth. This exercise led to a complete independence of tone and text, and eliminated the necessity of preparing any special mouth position in order to "control" the tone. In comparison, covering may be seen to be manipulative and restrictive, whereas the earlier dependency on pharyngeally resonated vowels was freeing.

Concepts related to covering have become more complex with the developing interest in phonetics. Today, covered tones and uncovered tones are used interchangeably with "covered vowels" and "uncovered vowels." To further confuse matters, phoneticians consider "front" and "back" vowels with reference to the position of the tongue ("high-back," "mid-back," "low-back," "grooved," "flat," *etc.*) whereas voice teachers generally believe that "covered vowels" are "forward" and "open vowels" are "back," and that these are synonymous with "closed" and "open" tones. When these concepts are thrown together with prevailing beliefs that upper tones are "placed" or resonated "higher," and lower tones placed "lower," the confusion in which the subject is now enveloped may be readily grasped.

In opposition to these concepts, science has verified that 1) the pharyngeal cavities adjust and interadjust to select and energize those frequencies necessary to the articulation of a given vowel, 2) these cavities are located at the back of the mouth and in the throat, and 3) the physical conformation of the vibratory surface of the vocal folds and the size of the glottal space influence vowel quality. Moreover, the root of the tongue (which differs structurally and functionally from its forward, more visible portion) is innervated by the glossopharyngeal and vagus nerve. Thus, its movement during phonation is governed and determined by other movements within the oro- and laryngopharynges (to which it belongs), and not by a volitional positioning of its forward part. Consequently, it is evident that both the terms and the techniques employed by phoneticians and the vocal profession at large are without functional orientation for the singer.

The practice of covering is largely the concern of the male singer. While all voice types, male and female, are governed by the same functional principles, the range of the female voice lies an octave higher. This places the *passaggio* in the low portion of the female voice, where the tension is slack, whereas in male voices the "break" occurs in the upper part of the voice range where the tension is fairly high. It is therefore less crucial that women resort to covering (with the possible exception of contraltos and dramatic sopranos), and the process of covering rarely constitutes a problem unless the chest register is "pushed" too high and too loudly.

It is for the above reason that the problems encountered in weightier voice types are more complex and time consuming than those encountered in lighter voices. This is not to suggest that voices singing in a higher tessitura should not develop and integrate the chest voice with the head voice, but simply that within this context, covering in the "break" area usually presents no difficulty. Instead, the problem in balancing the registers in lighter voices occurs an octave above the "break:" when the chest register has not been solidified in its lower tonal range, vowels must be "rounded" to assure a proper entry into the head voice without the encumbrance of a chest register "drag."

The difference between older practices and covering can be summarized as follows: in a "seamless" voice, the registers rebalance very precisely for each tonal pattern sung within a constant resonance adjustment and without altering the vowel, but covering changes both the vowel and the registration. In the latter instance, the readjustment of the vowel resonators is directly proportionate to the degree of vowel distortion present—a condition which, in turn, forces a change in the register balance. These modifications are often appropriate to earlier stages of technical development, but not to more sophisticated levels of vocalization.

PEDAGOGIC SIGNIFICANCE

The pedagogic significance of covering is that it points up the limitations inherent in training methods based upon 1) efforts to "cover up" technical faults by imposing qualities thought to be aesthetically more desirable, and 2) manipulation of peripheral areas (tongue, uvula, mouth and lips, and special techniques of "breath control"). These practices skirt the real issue and are not viable substitutes for a more demanding, but ultimately superior procedure based upon functional principles which effect changes at the core of the coordinative process, *i.e.*, the involuntary muscular systems within the laryngeal pharynx. Regardless of the methods adopted or the theoretical stance assumed, however, one fact stands clear: the difficult transition points experienced by singers, which have led to such pedagogic panaceas as "hooking," lifting "up and over," getting the tone "forward," "high and low placement," and "covering," all direct themselves to difficulties that are related to registration.

The mechanistic training methods based on the precepts noted above have not proved successful. Few singers appearing before the public could justly be said to have more than marginally fulfilled their potential, and the throat constriction that is the logical outgrowth of such practices is encouraged rather than cured by these techniques of tone production.

In the final analysis, vocal training and artistic singing should be founded upon principles which agree with the laws of physics, physiology and acoustics. Short cuts are not the answer. What is patently clear is that all music, whether dramatic or lyric, and whether composed by Monteverdi, Mozart, Wagner, Verdi, Strauss, or Berg, can best be sung when the mechanical parts responsible for producing vocal tone work in accordance with nature's laws. The practice of covering does not conform to those laws.

The history of great singers and singing is replete with names of those who used their voices lyrically and in the true Bel Canto tradition even when the voices were heroic in size. Frequently, these voices are described as being "unusual" and "exceptional," but this fact remains: while they are rare, these singers nonetheless are exceptional not because of any anatomical superiority, but because they use their voices exceptionally well, and avoid such unnecessary and inhibitory devices as "covering." Duprez had a short career. He was able to sing at one dynamic level (high), and he had little flexibility. His was at best a limited technique. In large part, those limitations were and are the equivalent expression of "covering."

Crack: See Break.

Creak Voice: See Loft Voice; Pulse Register.

Cricoarytenoid Muscles: part of the complex muscular system which causes the arytenoids to rotate upon the cricoid. Also called the "posticus," the cricoarytenoids are believed by some scientists to assist only in silent breathing.

Cricoid Cartilage: that cartilage which forms the base of the larynx; familiarly known as the "ring" cartilage because of its similarity to a signet ring. The posterior cricoarytenoid muscles originate in the cricoid cartilage, and that cartilage also serves as a point of attachment for the longitudinal fibers of the esophagus.

Cricopharyngeal Muscle: a suspensory muscle which arises from opposite sides of the cricoid cartilage and encircles the gullet, and whose function is to draw the larynx slightly down and back.

By stabilizing the larynx, the cricopharyngeal muscle establishes an essential independence between laryngeal function as it is concerned with stretching the vocal folds, the processes involved in articulation (particularly movements engaged in by the base of the tongue), and the adjustments made by the oropharynx to define and resonate the vowel. Failure of the cricopharyngeal muscle to contract during phonation results in an unnatural elevation of the larynx and is one of the principal causes of vocal malfunction, particularly as it is reflected in throat constriction and tongue and jaw tension.

Although the cricopharyngeal muscle assists in peristaltic movement (swallowing) and is a factor in the laryngeal "tuning" necessary to sustained vocalization, its role in speech is passive. It is, however, a factor in affective expression, and lends support to the contention of many that affective expression is to be considered a primitive form of singing.

Cricothyroid Muscle: a muscle which joins the cricoid and thyroid cartilages, and, by pulling the cricoid cartilage forward and downward, stretches the vocal folds.

See Register

Crooning: a style of singing adopted by singers of popular music during the 1930's and 1940's.

"Crooners," whose soft, sentimental style of singing may have resulted from technological innovations in tonal amplification during this period, must always rely on a microphone for audibility. Functionally, crooners suffer from the limitations of a "mixed" registration and from the vocal strain which results from a collapsed larynx.

See Registration, "Mixed"

Cuneiform Cartilages: Latin, *cuneus,* meaning "wedge;" a pair of small, wedge-shaped cartilages imbedded within the fleshy tissue of the aryepiglottic folds.

The cuneiform cartilages, or cartilages of Wrisberg, are one of nine which comprise the skeletal framework of the larynx. Together with the epiglottis, the aryepiglottic folds and the arytenoids, they form a ring, known as the "collar of the larynx," which, by performing a sphincter movement, helps protect the lungs from the intrusion of liquids and foreign matter.

The cuneiform cartilages are probably a vestigial remnant of a phylogenetically earlier period, since their primary function (together with the epiglottis and aryepiglottic folds) is to assist olfaction (smelling) in lower animals, whose survival depends upon a heightened sensitivity to odors even though the mouth remains open.

See Collar of the
    Larynx
    Larynx

Cupo: Italian, meaning a dark, hollow tone quality; sometimes used in combination with other effects, such as *sotto voce;* possibly derived from *cupola,* a dome-shaped ceiling resembling an inverted cup, whose acoustic properties enrich orchestral and vocal sound. In the latter sense of its meaning, *cupo* is a "round" sound, neither covered nor spread, capable of being produced only when the technique is highly advanced, and hence, rarely heard.

Cupped tones are frequently confused with "covered" tones. The two, however, share nothing in common. A cupped tone is the product of 1) the contraction of the tensor-veli-palati muscles, and 2) resistance to the breath exerted from beneath the vocal folds by the partial closing of the false vocal cords (located above the true vocal cords), which, in turn, causes the ventricular sacs (found between the false and true vocal cords) to inflate. These movements establish a pressure system above the vocal folds which gives the aural illusion that the tone is "contained" and reflected downward as tone is reflected from a domed ceiling. Cupped tones are therefore an acoustic phenomenon. Covered tones, on the other hand, are products of throat constriction which result from changing the vowel for the upper notes of the tonal range in the absence of a precisely balanced registration.

See Covering,
    (To) Cover
    Glottis
    Register
    Resistance

Curve: a unit of tonal movement traced on graph paper by an oscillograph. The curve is formed by the oscillograph's projecting tonal movement (vibrations yielded by a sounding musical instrument) against time. The ascending portion of the curve indicates the period of compression and the descending portion indicates the period of rarefaction.

CYCLE

Cycle: in acoustics, a complete vibration; the sum of a compression period and its subsequent period of rarefaction.

Cycles Per Second (cps): the number of times a complete sound wave (comprised of an alternating compression and rarefaction phase) occurs within the designated time span.

D

Damping: energy depletion which occurs 1) during free vibration (for example, the "dying down" of a pendulum or a tuning fork), and 2) because of the surface quality of the resonator or reflecting agent (soft surfaces increase the amount of damping, hard surfaces lessen it). Inertia, heat, and the pull of gravity are also important factors in determining the rate of damping.

A vibrator is said to be lightly damped when energy is lost slowly and gradually. It is heavily damped when the vibratory impulses recede quickly. A room is heavily damped when filled with thick drapery materials and overstuffed furniture, all of which absorb sound. An empty room is reverberant and lightly damped because of the hard reflecting surfaces and the absence of soft, plushy materials. Acoustically, softer surfaces are not responsive to high partials, and they reduce both reverberation and tonal brilliance.

In singing, light damping depends upon sharply tuned resonators which hold energy dissipation to a minimum and produce brighter tone qualities. To achieve this, the laryngeal and oropharyngeal cavities must be adjusted so that they present firm reflecting surfaces that select and energize but a few of the frequencies present within the complex tone emitted by the vibrator. Excessive flaccidity of the oropharynx, coupled with an imprecise tuning of the larynx (*i.e.,* collapsed and/or positioned too high or too low), de-energizes the high partials and causes the tone to appear "unfocused."

Damping is an important factor in the resonation of vocal tone, however, since certain areas of a coupled resonating system must present a softer surface if reactive coupling (which causes the voice to break and leap into a higher octave) is to be avoided. This is a task for which the oropharynx is particularly well suited.

Damping, or dampening, is a term commonly used within another frame of reference—as, for example, when the vocal folds come together and cease vibrating as they adduct when the pitch rises. In such instances, the amplitude of vibration is decreased through pressure having been exerted on the vibrator. The touching of felts on the strings of a piano when the damper pedal is pressed down is similar in principle to this type of damping.

See **Adduction**
Coupling
Dark Tone
Resonance

Dans la Masque: French, "in the mask;" a pedagogic directive to "place" vocal tone in the facial mask (*i.e.,* the frontal sinuses, the antra, and the nasopharynx) for tonal amplification or resonance.

The appearance of concepts related to singing *dans la masque* marks the second major point of departure from early Italian training procedures (the first was the gradual abandonment of those principles and practices associated with registration, which occurred after Manuel Garcia's invention of the laryngoscope in 1854 led to a proliferation of register-related terms). This second shift was the combined result of increasing pressure upon teachers of singing to produce "big" voices to match the sonorous orchestral textures of late nineteenth century operatic music, and increasing concern for the apparent strain placed upon the vocal mechanism when singing this music. It was also the product of a growing antipathy for Garcia's *coup de glotte,* which, in the hands of those less competent, had rapidly degenerated into a vocal aberration. More generally, concepts related to singing *dans la masque* reflect the gradual transition in pedagogic interest and emphasis from "singing into the voice" (*appoggiare la voce*) to "singing on resonance."

The principal advocates of singing *dans la masque* were H. Holbrook Curtis, a noted throat specialist, and his friend, the great tenor Jean de Reszke. Their express purpose, according to Curtis, was to avoid the excesses of the misused *coup de glotte* and to "take the attack from the vocal cords." Their suggested means for accomplishing this was to precede a vowel phoneme with "a labial consonant M, P or B [so] that the shock of the glottis is reduced to a minimum."[39]

[39]H. Holbrook Curtis, *Voice Building and Tone Placing* (New York: D. Appleton & Co., 1900), pp. 142, 158.

There are a number of facts that raise serious doubts as to the advisability of singing *dans la masque*—either as an antidote for vocal abuse or as a constructive pedagogic practice. One reservation is that such efforts channel energy away from the tonal source (the vibrating vocal folds and laryngeal musculature) into peripheral areas where muscular interference and compensatory tension are much more likely to be encountered than avoided. Furthermore, the concept defies acoustic laws, since 1) vocal tone, the movement of air particles set in motion by the vibrating vocal folds, cannot be "placed," and 2) the small, highly damped nasal cavities and passages are unsuited for effective resonation. Frederick Husler and Yvonne Rodd-Marling stressed these points in the following statement:

> Opinions vary as to whether anything, apart from the pharynx and the nasal and oral cavities, can be considered to act as a resonator (*e.g.,* windpipe or thorax). There is no need, however, for the voice trainer to concern himself unduly with such questions. He can safely leave the singer his useful fictions (*e.g.,* the sinuses as sound amplifiers) but he himself must realize that the sounding of a resonating chamber is always a *secondary* manifestation, the result of muscle movements in the vocal mechanism. Whether, for instance, the nasal cavity acts as resonator or not, depends on the behaviour of the palato-laryngeal muscles which keep it open, and—this appears to be still more important—which stretch the vocal folds in a particular way. (When singing with closed mouth the voice has to pass through the nasal cavity, yet "non-nasal" sounds can be produced, as well as so-called "nasal" ones, according to what takes place in the mechanism of the throat.) It goes without saying that the *first* causes for the various *acoustic* phenomena that occur in singing lie in the vocal organ itself, and it is these that the voice trainer must learn to hear.[40]

[40]Frederick Husler and Yvonne Rodd-Marling, *Singing: The Physical Nature of the Vocal Organ* (New York: October House, 1964), p. 72.

The fundamental difference between the concerns of Dr. Curtis and those of Husler and Rodd-Marling is that the first-named advocates a mechanistic approach that attempts to "make" resonance (which may be real or imaginary), whereas Husler and Rodd-Marling focus attention on those activities taking place at the tonal source, *i.e.,* the laryngeal pharynx, within which sound impulses are both generated and resonated.

On a purely pragmatic level, procedures designed to encourage singing *dans la masque* and to promote so-called "nasal resonance," although widely accepted, have not been successful. Students who have been trained by these methods have not fulfilled their vocal potentials, and "natural" singers and well-established professionals who have been encouraged to rely upon them often suffer a decline in their vocal power during what should have been their physical and vocal prime.

Although the practices of singing *dans la masque* and with nasal resonance have been discredited by scientific research, these methods are still highly regarded and widely practiced (even in Italy, where they conform neither to the language nor to the great vocal tradition of that country), whereas the *coup de glotte,* a widely misunderstood and misused device, remains to this day a universally discredited procedure for training the singing voice. This is but another example of a tendency displayed too frequently in modern pedagogy: the concern for symptom rather than process, for tone rather than tonal source, and for effect rather than cause.

The practice of singing *dans la masque* and the theories related to that practice should be categorically abandoned, since they invariably violate fundamental scientific laws. They have failed to meet the needs of practical pedagogy, and they represent radical departures from earlier, more successful training procedures, which, through instinct or by design, were based upon sound physiological, functional, and acoustic principles. These principles, whose practical application led to a great Golden Age of Song, are immutable, and sufficient to the demands of all good vocal music, whether it is by Monteverdi, Bellini, Donizetti, or Mozart, by Verdi, Wagner, or Strauss, or by any contemporary composer who writes well for the voice.

Dark Tone: a vocalized sound whose warm, rich tonal characteristics result from a de-energization of the inharmonic partials and overtones in its harmonic spectrum, a process that is usually accomplished by depressing the epiglottis.

At its best, all tonal coloration is the product of a reflexive tuning of the vocal resonators in response to musical, textual, and emotional stimuli. Thus, the skillful vocalist should be able to produce "dark" tones in response to moods of introspection, sadness, extreme warmth, *etc.*, without upsetting the coordinative process and without vowel distortion.

Dark tones should not be confused with "mouthy" or "thick" vowel qualities, or with "covering," each of which involves a faulty concept of resonance and is the product of an improperly developed and balanced registration.

The genuine tonal warmth associated with dark tone qualities is most attractive, but to be fully effective, it must be combined with a certain amount of tonal brilliance.

Dead Space: that part of the respiratory tract (the trachea and bronchi) in which inspired air accumulates during inspiration without reaching the alveoli of the lungs, and consequently without participating in the oxygen/carbon dioxide exchange.

Air within the respiratory dead space accounts for almost 150 cubic centimeters of the 500-or-so cubic centimeters inspired during normal, quiet breathing. Because this dead space exists, the efficiency with which the bodily organs are oxygenated is adversely affected by shallow breathing habits.

Decibel: an acoustical unit used to measure the relative loudness of sound; one-tenth of a bel.

A decibel is that unit of sound approximately equal to the smallest degree of intensity that can be perceived by the human ear. Thus, a sound of one decibel is at the lower end of the threshold of audibility, a sound of ten decibels is ten times that loud, and a sound of twenty decibels, a hundred times greater.

The human ear is capable of tolerating up to about 130 decibels before the pain threshold is reached. Thirty to forty decibels, or d.b., is the approximate level of normal speech intensity.

Deep Tone: a vocalized sound whose rich tonal characteristics result from a full coupling of the pharyngeal cavities, an adjustment which intensifies resonance within the laryngeal and tracheal area.

See Coupling

Genuine tonal depth is impossible without a well-balanced registration and an absence of muscular interference. The volitional imposition of tonal depth is to be avoided since it results in a lowering of the larynx, a practice which engenders throat constriction and tongue and jaw stiffness.

Depressed Larynx: See Lowered Larynx.

Depressor Muscle: either of two sets of paired suspensory muscles, the sternothyroids and cricopharyngeals, whose contractions work in natural opposition to those of the suspensory muscles that elevate the larynx (*i.e.*, the stylopharyngeal, thyrohyoid, and palatal muscles).

See Laryngeal Suspension

When contracted, the sternothyroid muscles pull the larynx downward and forward, and the cricopharyngeal muscles pull it downward and back. Since a precise balance of tension or equilibrium among the suspensory muscles is a prerequisite of so-called "open-throated" singing, effective coordination of the depressors and elevators of the larynx (*i.e.*, a precise resonance adjustment) is one of the fundamental goals of vocal training. The pedagogic challenge is to encourage such movement with a minimal amount of articulatory manipulation, and without recourse to practices designed to gain volitional or direct control over these and related involuntary activities taking place within the vocal mechanism.

Developed Falsetto: See Falsetto, Developed.

Dialect: a regional variety of language usually transmitted orally, and differing distinctively in rhythm, phraseology, idiom, and pronunciation from the standard spoken language.

Diaphragm: the large dome-shaped partition formed by muscles and connective tissue that separates the thorax (chest) from the abdomen (stomach).

During inspiration, the diaphragm contracts (*e.g.*, flattens) to enable the lungs to fill with air; it relaxes to its natural dome-like shape during expiration. Thus, the diaphragm descends when tensed and moves upward when relaxed.

Neurologically, the diaphragm is innervated by a single phrenic nerve (which connects to either side) that originates from the third to the fifth cervical nerves. Thus, as part of the autonomic nervous system, the diaphragm cannot be willfully energized or overtly acted upon. Furthermore, since this reflexive muscle is totally lacking in proprioceptive nerve endings, it is impossible to experience any sensation of its movement whatsoever. On the basis of these facts, pedagogic directives such as "support with" and "push upward with the diaphragm" are impossible to execute, since if one could "push" with the diaphragm, he could only push *downward.*

Pedagogic procedures initiated with the express intent of pushing the diaphragm "up" or "in" mistake diaphragmatic action for abdominal muscular tension. What creates the illusion of diaphragmatic activity is that the abdominal wall is pulled inward during expiration, and consequently moves the abdominal contents upward. As a result of the upward abdominal pressure, the visceral contents compress the lungs and deflate them. Since either inspiratory or expiratory tension widens the glottal space to permit the passage of air, both abdominal pressure and the relaxation and elevation of the diaphragm during phonation is undesirable.

See Breathing

Diction: the pronunciation and enunciation of words during speech or singing.

Ideally, in both speech and singing, the vowel form carries the emotion and meaning of language, and consonants delineate it. Under these circumstances, so-called "singers' diction" is identical to that of everyday speech. However, normal speech patterns are so frequently careless, slovenly and nasal (*e.g., buh-loh* rather than *bee-loh*) that they lack color and definition, and become relatively unintelligible, when sustained in singing.

It is almost paradoxical that American singers usually have better diction when singing in foreign languages than they do when singing in their own, and singers of other nationalities are often more clearly understood when singing in English than Americans. This phenomenon results, in part, from the serious effort made by American singers to master vowel phonemes somewhat different from those to which they have been accustomed. The concentrated attention given to the proper articulation of the vowel phonemes in these cases, while it improves and clarifies both their tone production and diction when singing in a foreign language, is rarely carried over into their mother tongue.

It is possible that the lack of intelligibility so frequently experienced when listening to an English text sung by Americans stems from an assumption that their pronunciation is correct. Indeed, this belief is often encouraged by advice to "pronounce in singing as you would in speech." Since Americans rarely take pride in the cultivation of good speech habits, such directives say, in effect, "bring your careless speech habits into the song form." The result is usually impure vowels, overarticulation of consonants, and generally poor diction.

The English language itself is not the problem. On the contrary, since some foreign and American artists sing intelligible English, it is certain that 1) the English language can be sung clearly and distinctly, and 2) when it is not clearly delineated, something must be wrong with either the singer's tone production or the way he is pronouncing the vowels and articulating the consonants.

It has often been suggested that diction can be improved by overarticulating the consonants, but as Nicole Scotto di Carlo of France pointed out in a recent study, the reverse is true. To promote good diction, therefore, it is important to 1) display greater concern for vowel purity and the avoidance of schwa vowels, and 2) revise the tone production. Singer's diction is careful diction, and when the technique is efficient and vowels are produced purely, neither English nor any other language should pose a problem in communication.

Diction Singing: a technique of singing and a method of teaching singing predicated upon the erroneous belief that good diction (*i.e.,* precise pronunciation and enunciation) fosters correct vocalization.

Good diction unquestionably enhances technical proficiency, but it is relatively ineffective in the face of technical deficiencies. Limited range, poor resonance, shortness of breath, throat constriction and tremulous movements of the tongue and jaw, for example, are problems related to poor physical coordination within the laryngeal pharynx that can neither be corrected nor alleviated by improved diction. Like so many other pedagogic "imperatives," the equation "good diction fosters correct vocalization" needs to be reversed: correct vocalization fosters good diction, or at least admits the possibility of good diction.

Good diction is the product of a free vocal technique, and the mechanical principles upon which this freedom is founded have to do with registration and laryngeal suspension, not pronunciation.

Diet for Singers: See Vocal Hygiene.

Diffused Tone: a vocalized sound whose "breathy," "unfocused," ill-defined tonal characteristics result from an absence of energy concentration in the first and second formants of its harmonic spectrum.

The first and second formants of the harmonic spectrum are those areas upon which vowel definition depends. Consequently, "diffused" tones invariably lack not only general tonal vitality but precise vowel definition as well. All diffused tone qualities are the result of faulty concepts and poor physical coordination.

Digastric Muscle: either of two paired muscles, each of which consists of two bellies originating from the point of the jaw and the base of the skull near the ear, that are united by a central tendon whose contractions raise the hyoid bone to which the muscles are attached; the "biventor" muscle.

Contractions of the digastric, or biventor, muscles pull the hyoid bone up and forward or back, depending upon which belly contracts more strongly (*i.e.,* that attached to the jaw, or that attached to the skull).

Diphonia: See Diplophonia.

Diphthong: a speech sound consisting of two successive vowel phonemes, the first of which is generally stressed (*e.g.,* those sounds represented by the English alphabet letters "o," pronounced *oh-oo,* and "i," pronounced *ah-ee*).

Diphthongs in English are often represented by one alphabetic symbol, as in the examples cited above, although they can be indicated by two or more letters (*e.g.,* the *oh-oo* of the word "roam," the *ah-oo* of the word "bough," *etc.*).

In a diphthong, the stressed vowel phoneme is called the "sustained" vowel, and the unstressed vowel, the "vanishing" vowel. In sung English, the former should be sustained for the duration of the note, and the latter articulated crisply and unobtrusively at the end of that duration, or just prior to the articulation of the next phoneme.

The diphthong should not be confused with the glide, in which the second of two successive vowel phonemes is sustained (*e.g.,* the Italian word *più*), or with the liaison, in which both vowel phonemes are stressed equally (*e.g.,* the English word "coordinate").

See Glide
    Liaison
    Vowel

Diplophonia: the simultaneous phonation of two distinct pitches; diphonia.

In diplophonia, each of the two vocal folds vibrates at a different frequency. It should not be confused with dysphonia, in which the false vocal cords are made to vibrate as a substitute for normal vocal vibration (*i.e.,* that of the true vocal folds).

See Disphonia

Double Consonant: two successive consonant phonemes.

In singing, the vowel phoneme preceding a double consonant, regardless of the language being sung, should always be sustained for its full notated duration, and the double consonant should be articulated at the end of that duration (*e.g.,* the English word "bold," sung *boh-ld*) or just prior to the articulation of the next phoneme (*e.g., boh-lduh-r* as in "bolder" or *bah-bee-noh* as in the Italian word *babbino*). To do otherwise is to interrupt the legato tonal flow so essential to good singing.

See Consonants

Double Plosive: two successive plosive consonant phonemes (*e.g., k, p, t,* or *d*) separated by a stop or plosion (*i.e.,* a momentary interruption of vocal vibration).

A double plosive is found in the English word "wept," which is sung *weh-p-t.*

See Consonants

Double Resonator: a system consisting of two or more adjustable cavities that can be used singly, or coupled so that each selects and energizes separate bands of frequencies.

Wheatstone and Helmholtz were the first scientists to prove the need for double resonators in the production of vowel sounds and the enhancement of resonance. Others, notably Douglas Stanley, Wilmer T. Bartholomew, Gunnar Fant and Joel Pressman, have further shown that it is the oropharynx (a flexible cavity) and the laryngeal pharynx which serve this purpose in the human resonating system. Mastery of this tuning process, which lies beyond the singer's power of effective volition, constitutes one of the primary objectives of vocal training.

See Coupling
    Forced Vibration
    Formant
    Helmholtz
      Resonator
    Indirect Control
    Register

Dramatic Voice: any voice that is full-sized and motivated by a dramatic temperament.

"Dramatic" voices are common to all vocal categories. Thus, one hears reference to the "dramatic coloratura," "dramatic soprano," *soprano drammatico, soprano giusto,* and Wagnerian soprano;" to the "dramatic mezzo;" to the "dramatic tenor," *Heldentenor,* "heroic tenor," *tenore robusto,* and tenore scrio; to the "dramatic baritone" and "Verdi baritone," and to the "Wagernian bass."

Genuine dramatic voices are a rarity. Too often, those who have reasonably opulent voices are pushed into the dramatic repertory and pay the price by losing the lustre and tonal beauty natural to their voices. Even those with dramatic potential should resist the temptation to undertake these roles too soon, since the mechanism must be fully mature (which, in most instances, is not until about the age of forty) and used with understanding before it can sustain such singing without recourse to undue strain and effort.

Drill: a physical or mental exercise designed to achieve a particular objective.

In singing, there are drills for any number of purposes: for velocity, legato, staccato, *etc.* However, exercises and drills possess no intrinsic value: they are only as effective as the manner in which they are executed.

A truly effective exercise and drill is one that helps improve the coordination among the muscles that adjust the vocal folds and among those that position the laryngo- and oropharynges for tonal amplification, or resonance. Rote or "mindless" practice of drills and exercises, therefore, is absolutely useless.

See Exercise
   Register
   Resonance

Drink In the Tone: a pedagogic directive given to encourage the duplication of a sensation which often accompanies a well-formed tone.

Paradoxically, the directive "drink in the tone" is not totally without foundation in fact. When the technique is efficient, for example, the pharyngeal resonators produce what is known as a standing wave, an acoustic phenomenon common to brass instruments and the human voice that returns almost eighty percent of the sound energy generated to the sound source. The significant element in the awakening of this sensation is that the mechanism is maintained in equilibrium, with the chest register holding synergetically against the pull of the head voice (*i.e.*, the resistance of the arytenoids against the pull of the cricothyroids), the larynx stabilized by its suspensory muscles, and the pharyngeal cavities precisely "tuned" to the vibrator.

Many teachers, past and present, have incorporated the concept of "drinking in the tone" into their teaching practices. The sensation is not uncommon among fine singers and can be traced to the Bel Canto tradition, where it was known as *inhalare la voce.* William Shakespeare, for example, relates that his teacher, Francesco Lamperti, observed that "the breath of a good note should feel as though it comes toward one," *i.e.*, as though it is being inhaled.

See Bernoulli Effect
   False Vocal Cords
   (To) Project
   Resistance
   Standing Wave
   Yawn-Sigh

As is true of so many sensations of vibration experienced by those who sing well, this directive cannot be acted upon or conjured up at will unless it has already registered as a prior experience. "Drinking in the tone" is symptomatic of a healthy technical status, and that equation cannot be reversed.

Driven Tone: a vocalized sound whose aggressive tonal characteristics result from excessive and misdirected effort.

A driven tone is almost invariably the result of an absence of equilibrium among the vocal muscles, and it makes the voice quality hard, unresilient, and devoid of tonal nuance.

See (To) Force

Dry Throat: the perception of an absence of moisture in the mucous membranes that line the entire vocal tract (especially those of the mouth and the laryngo- and oropharynges).

Dry-throatedness in singing can result from nervousness, certain varieties and stages of the common cold, the use of antihistamines, dust and poor ventilation, or improper use of the vocal mechanism. It can also accompany the production of a pure falsetto and reflect a state of inner tension and anxiety.

See Anxiety
   Emotion
   Falsetto
   Phlegm

Duration: continuance in time; a length of time during which a vocal tone is sustained.

The sustained quality of vocal tone and the vibrato are two of the important factors that make singing functionally different from speech.

See **Sing As You Speak**
Vibrato

Dynamic Adjustment: a term used to describe a technical status free of wrong tension that ensures a smooth transition from one tonal range and intensity level to another.

A dynamic adjustment cannot be acquired unless the inherent contradiction between two basic functional activities is reconciled: 1) stabilization of the larynx without "locking" the registration, and 2) developing and integrating an ever changing registration without disturbing the laryngeal adjustment. This means, among other things, that the blade of the tongue remains mobile while its base firms to form the forward wall of the oropharynx, thus enabling the latter to perform effectively as a resonator.

See **Bel Canto**
Laryngeal
  Suspension
Modern Methods
Register
Resonance
Static Adjustment

Dynamics: variation and contrast in volume or intensity.

See **Intensity**
Volume

Dyne: a unit of force that measures speed in relation to mass, length, and time (*i.e.,* that measures acceleration through space).

Within a vocal context, dynes are used to determine the pressure of air moving through the glottal space.

See **Aerodynamic**
  Theory
Bernoulli Effect

Dysphonia: the inability to phonate or utter voiced sounds.

Dysphonia can be either temporary or chronic, congenital, or the result of damage to the vocal organs. It is usually caused by one of the following:

1. A chronic hoarseness resulting from structural abnormalities of the vocal organs;
2. A state of emotional hysteria;
3. Glandular deficiences, or
4. Vocal nodules or polyps resulting from improper use of the vocal mechanism.

In some chronic cases of dysphonia, the false vocal cords are induced to vibrate in lieu of the true vocal folds. This condition is known as "ventricular dysphonia."

See **Diplophonia**
Emotion
Nodule

E

Ear: the mechanism of hearing; the ability to distinguish slight differences in sound, especially between nuances of pitch and tonal quality.

As the mechanism of hearing, the ear receives stimuli from air which has been forced into motion by a vibrator. It then transmits vibratory impulses to the brain, where they are evaluated and stored. Physically, the human ear consists of the following elements:

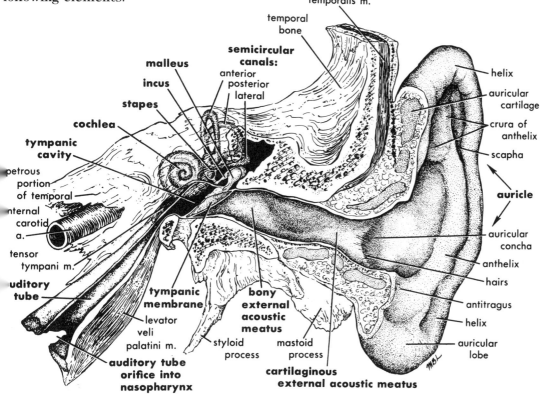

Figure 2. A general view of the left ear, showing the auditory tube and the external, middle, and inner ear. From James E. Crouch, Functional Human Anatomy, *Third Edition (Philadelphia: Lea and Febiger, 1978). By permission.*

1. The external ear (*pinna* and external auditory canal);
2. The middle ear (*tympanum*), a cavity connected to the external ear by the tympanic membrane ("ear drum"), to the pharynx by the Eustachian tube, and to the inner ear by a series of three small bones called the "hammer," "anvil," and "stirrup," and
3. The inner ear (*labyrinth*), which contains the cochlea and semicircular canals.

The function of the outer, middle, and inner ear is to gather sound waves. These sound waves are converted into mechanical energy by motion of the tympanic membrane, then into hydraulic pressure waves, and finally into electrical impulses by the basilar membrane.

One is said to have "an ear for music" if he possesses acute auditory discrimination. The singer, however, must go even further, and combine hearing perception with a kinesthetic awareness of the physical movements involved in phonation, and at the same time reconcile these with aesthetic preferences based upon emotional and psychological attitudes. Thus, hearing acts as a governor which evaluates and regulates the diverse forces at work during the phonative process. Hearing is a special gift which must be carefully nurtured and refined if the vocal mechanism is to realize its fullest potential.

See Auditory Nerve
     Hearing
     Eustachian Tube
     Functional
        Listening
     Limbic System
     Organ of Corti

Ease of Production: an ability to sing a wide range of pitches within prescribed limits, at any intensity, on any vowel, and without fatigue.

Ease of tone production is the result, not the cause, of a correct vocal technique, and while it is often said that "to sing easily is to sing well," the reverse is more accurate: "to sing well is to sing easily." However, not even this statement can always be taken at face value, since, when technical freedom has been newly acquired as a consequence of the voice-building process, the unaccustomed absence of compensatory tensions will place the entire burden of effort on muscles which, never having been used, are flaccid. Thus, when an open-throated tone production is new, vocalization will usually be momentarily more effortful.

The attempt to solve vocal problems by singing easily is a procedure which merely indicates a willingness to avoid difficulties, to stay within limitations, and to make permanent a status which is comfortable because of habit, even if it is incorrect. An effortless approach to tone production will rarely solve technical difficulties or relieve interfering tensions.

Echo Tones: qualities (most commonly associated with high sopranos) which are flutelike, apparently disembodied, and used for special interpretive effects. Functionally, an "echo" tone is a soft *mezza voce,* produced with too little chest register connection, and consequently not fully open-throated, since it cannot be swelled smoothly to full voice.

Edema: a swelling due to the infusion of water into muscle tissue. The condition is usually pathological, but can be brought on because of vocal abuse.

Edgy Tones: vocalized sounds which are aesthetically too brittle or shrill. "Edgy" sounds, unlike those which possess genuine resonance and tonal "ring," are products of throat constriction, which is brought on by an imbalanced registration.

Efferent: See Afferent.

Emotion: a term derived from the Latin *emovere,* meaning to "move out," or engage in expansive movement.

An ability to identify satisfactorily with the phonative process on an emotional level is a component as important to the learning process as overall talent and a gift for physical coordination. It plays an important role in determining the type of tone quality (and instruction) to which the singer finds himself instinctively drawn, and it is also reflected in physical attitudes. The ability to "move out" freely and spontaneously is predicated upon an absence of physical blockages brought on by emotional tension. Regardless of the rightness of the functional principles being applied, movement potential will inevitably be inhibited by psychological tensions. To expand one's technical horizons and communicate with emotional sensitivity involves a psychological risk that must be taken if technical improvement and artistic maturation are to become a reality.

See Anxiety
    Breathing and
    Emotion

Emotional Identification: a psychological predisposition which intuitively draws one to certain types of musical expression. Aesthetically, this predisposition is manifested by a preference for a particular kind of tonal quality, voice type, musical style, *etc.,* and often by an aversion toward qualities which fail to agree with that preference.

Emotional Listening: a distortion of aural perception and objectivity which reflects a personal attitude toward another artist or performer; taste conditioned by those prejudices that are always acquired during a learning process; aesthetic ideals.

Frequently, a listener identifies so strongly with a particular performer that communication supersedes all other considerations to the extent that even the basic elements of music (pitch, vowel quality, tonal beauty) are no longer objectively perceived. This is also true of vocal training, where various manifestations of constriction (*e.g.,* "nasal resonance," "ping," and "twang") are often accepted as legitimate aesthetic goals.

Although singing and listening are emotional experiences, the emotional identification most desirable depends upon two elements: 1) technical freedom, which provides a wide latitude of expression, and 2) aesthetic and communicative values. The first allows the singer to make a personal artistic statement with taste and intelligence; the second, to reach the heart and mind of the listener. In the best sense, emotional listening rises above mundane prejudices and lifts both artist and performer to a higher realm of sensitivity, feeling, and understanding.

Empathy: the ability to perceive how another person thinks and feels through kinesthetic identification.

Empathy is a sympathetic reaction by which a free feeling in the throat is experienced when listening to a fine singer, or conversely one by which localized tension is experienced when listening to a singer whose voice is constricted. Empathy is not to be confused with psychological projection. In essence, it is "listening" with the body.

See Kinesthesia

Empirical: based on observation or practical experience rather than on scientific principles.

Generally the starting point of any scientific discipline, empirical observation was of necessity the sole basis of early training methods. By observing without prejudice the numerous parallels that exist between stimulus and response (culminating in formulations which led to a Golden Age of Song), early teachers developed an approach to vocal training that was based on nature and free of mechanistic controls.

On the basis of historical evidence and the failure of modern methods, it is clear that empiricism still offers the most satisfactory solution to the problems confronted in the development of vocal skills.

See Bel Canto
Holistic Pedagogy
Modern Methods
Natural Movement
Register
Vowel

Empiricists: those who form conclusions based upon experiment, observation and experience; a name ascribed to the early founders of the art of Bel Canto, their training methods, and the principles they formulated on the basis of observed phenomena.

Empty Falsetto: See Falsetto.

(To) Emulate: to attempt to equal or surpass in accomplishment.

For the student of singing, emulation of the great artists is both natural and desirable, since they are the gauge by which all creative strivings should be measured. Emulation, however, should never be confused with imitation, which is essentially destructive and noncreative.

See Imitation

Energy: work performed by a body to overcome inertia, as distinguished from force (something that moves an object or body) or power (measure of the rate at which work is done). Units of work and energy are both measured in ergs, and power is expressed in watts.

There are many sources and types of energy (atomic, solar, chemical, electrical turbine, water power, *etc.*), but those most applicable to phonation are elastic potential (the energy imparted when work is done to distort the natural state of body possessing elastic properties), kinetic energy (the work done to change the body from a state of rest to a state of motion), breath compression, and the neurological impulses which innervate the vocal mechanism.

Oxygen is essential to the generation of energy through these sources, since without oxygen there can be neither combustion nor the production of energy, neither movement nor organic life. The response capability of physical energy when stimulated neurologically, therefore, is regulated by the state and condition of biological functions, *i.e.*, general health and psychological predisposition, mood eating habits, muscular tonicity and physical coordination. An important fact relative to energy is that it is never lost, but merely takes other forms.

In singing, the energy liberated through oxidation represents a means by which the vocal mechanism is able to move from relaxation to a state of balanced tension in response to neurological stimuli. The amount of energy expended depends upon the quality of the concepts which set the physical processes in motion, and the amount of friction (muscular interference) within the systems involved. Whether the vocal mechanism is well or poorly coordinated, however, when this process has been completed, the work that has already been done in preparation for phonation undergoes a transformation and becomes potential, or stored energy.

A visual example of the processes involved in moving from a position of rest to one of balanced tension is supplied by the archer, who, in preparing an arrow for flight, has applied force to draw the bowstring. After the tautened bowstring has been stretched, the archer, the bow and the bowstring are in a state of equilibrium, at which moment the work done becomes transformed into potential energy. With the release of the arrow, the potential energy within the drawn bow changes into kinetic energy (Greek, meaning "to move"), to be further transformed during flight because of friction, heat and the pull of gravity.

Since every change that takes place in the universe represents a transformation of energy from one form to another, it is evident that the vocal mechanism is governed by those same physical laws. Thus, the principle of energy transformation is the same in archery and phonation, the only difference being the medium. When, for example, the muscles engaged in phonation are brought into tension, the vocal folds represent potential (or stored) energy. As the folds become vibratile, potential energy is transformed into kinetic energy, setting in motion those compressions and rarefactions of the surrounding air particles perceived as sound or vocal tone. Like the arrow in flight, the amount of kinetic energy concentrated in the sound waves produced is seemingly dissipated because of heat and friction.

Another law of physics applicable to the vocal function is that of inertia, which holds that an object or body is disposed to continue in its existing state, whether at rest or in motion, until some force acts upon it. Thus, once the vocal folds become vibratile they tend to continue their movement. The duration factor is determined by the quality of the concepts by which the mechanism is innervated, the extent to which the total system is capable of being oxygenated, physical coordination, an innate vigor, and the inevitable losses to heat which occur as these processes are transformed into sound waves. When combined with kinetic energy, and provided a source of effective resistance is available, these laws minimize the use of force and overt muscular activity, and cause a well-produced tone to be virtually self-sustaining.

In applying these physical laws to the vocal function, it is probable that energy is utilized in the following manner:

1. "Instruction" by means of concepts which prompt the mechanism to move;
2. Innervation of the vocal folds and a "setting" of the pharyngeal resonators through neurological impulses, which cause vibrations to appear in response to the will rather than in response to force or breath pressure;
3. Work done as the muscle systems which tauten the vocal folds and adjust the

pharyngeal cavities for resonance move from relaxation to balanced tension;

4. The storing of potential energy as the vocal tract maintains the tonal form in consequence of prephonatory tuning;

5. The transformation of potential energy into kinetic energy as the vocal folds become vibratile;

6. A further transformation of kinetic energy into those disturbances of the surrounding air particles perceived as sound, and

7. Continued movement resulting from kinetic energy, which causes the vocal folds, like a plucked string, to maintain their vibratory pattern in a state of free vibration for a certain period of time, until the transformation of kinetic energy into sound waves is complete.

An additional source of energy which vitalizes the vocal mechanism is that derived from breath compression. Like the air in an inflated balloon, compressed breath provides a source of power because molecules have been crowded together and "work" to rectify the discrepancy between the density of the air contained in the lungs and that of the outer atmosphere. If energy expenditure is to be economical, it must be harnessed (as with the steam boiler, the combustion engine, the sailboat, *etc.*) so that a greater proportion of the available pressure is contained. Since the vocal folds are poorly angulated to offer effective resistance to the compression build-up below the glottis, some other source capable of resisting subglottal pressure must be available as an alternative if subglottal pressure is to be effectively countered.

Nature provides such a mechanism by a narrowing of the false vocal cords and a resultant inflation of the ventricular sacs, thereby creating a balanced pressure system. The immediate effect of this arrangement is to do the following:

1. Maintain compression effortlessly without recourse to respiratory controls;

2. Minimize breath loss and ensure tonal steadiness because of a natural regulation of breath flow;

3. Use the oxygen inspired almost exclusively to oxidize the muscle and organic systems involved;

4. Reduce the amount of overt muscular activity to that which is essential, *i.e.* maintain an equilibrium throughout the vocal tract, and

5. Make the vocal folds solely responsive to neurological stimulation without having to resist subglottal pressure, thereby enabling them to freely create the host of pressure variations (which find potential energy transformed into kinetic energy with the requisite speed, and without impairing their elasticity.

If sub- and supraglottal pressure are to effectively counter one another, other components of the vocal mechanism must function properly. To accomplish this the two muscle systems (the cricothyroids and the arytenoids) which adjust the vocal folds to a mass, length and elasticity dictated by varying combinations of pitch, intensity and vowel, must first be brought into balanced tension. Since these muscle systems respond reflexively to specifically arranged patterns containing these tonal elements, they can (when properly stimulated, and because they can be made to respond either separately or as a coordinate unit) be trained to function harmoniously, not only in and of themselves, but also with respect to other elements engaged in the production of vocal tone.

The positioning of the larynx and the pharyngeal cavities for resonation of the vowel is another prominent factor in energy economy. The interaction among the muscle systems responsible for these adjustments (the infra- and suprahyoids, the palatals, the tongue muscles, *etc.*) is far more complex and difficult to realign than the activity of the vocal folds, whose physical contour can be effectively altered by applying those principles known to govern registration. Unless the muscle systems responsible for adjusting the resonating system are free of constricting tensions, the efficiency of other muscle groups (such as the coordinated activity of the abdominals and internal intercostal muscles) is seriously disrupted. In the absence of genuine resonance, the singer's only alternative is to force his voice, a procedure that is always uneconomical and self-defeating.

Efficient tone production requires that the transformation of energy from one form to another be accomplished with a minimum of artificial channeling. The formula for a transformation of optimum efficiency is as follows: potential energy equals kinetic energy minus that energy which has changed form because of heat or friction in meeting some opposing force. The energy used in singing, therefore, must be replenished primarily because of these factors:

1. An absence of equilibrium among the muscle systems involved, *i.e.,* muscular interference;
2. A build-up of carbon dioxide, which requires that a fresh supply of oxygen be inspired to ensure the continuance of oxidation;
3. A weakening of sound waves through heat and friction because of the resistance of adjacent air particles;
4. Biological functions, which act as regulators of energy output, and
5. Psychological attitudes, which either inhibit or foster expansive movement.

If, as Dr. Gordon Holmes (1880) so astutely observed, "voice" is nothing more than "the activity of muscles and the movement of air," then it is apparent that "voice," as sound, has no mechanical function of its own, but is the product of other functions. Thus, the energy expended during phonation must be channeled so as to stimulate into improved patterns of response those muscle systems which tauten the vocal folds and position the larynx and the pharyngeal cavities for resonance. When this has been successful, the minus factors (energy which has changed form because of heat or friction in meeting some opposing force), which require that energy be replenished at a faster rate than is either convenient or efficient, will have been removed.

In view of the fact that the important muscle systems engaged in phonation are not subject to direct control, the pedagogic problem is to discover and utilize principles which will encourage reflexive, spontaneous and natural movement, improve the "activity of muscles," bring diverse systems into a high state of tonicity, and thereby transform potential energy into kinetic energy in the most efficient manner possible.

Training methods used prior to the twentieth century successfully addressed themselves to this problem. In large part, this success was assured because the principles and practices employed stimulated the appropriate muscle systems within the vocal tract so as not to violate their logical movement potential. As a result of having observed the existence of consistent parallels between stimulus and response, voice teachers of that era established rational control systems based upon nature whereby the involuntary muscle systems functioning at the tonal source could be reconditioned without having to be acted upon directly.

Modern methods, unlike those of an earlier era, generally proceed in a direction contrary to that necessary to achieve the objectives outlined above, and they abandon principles known to stimulate natural movement for directives which act upon the mechanism. Among the outer-imposed disciplines used to subject the mechanism are special techniques of respiratory "control" to minimize breath loss, a direct effort to increase vital capacity in order to "support" the voice, correct pitch problems, and cure tonal unsteadiness, advice to "sing on resonance," and/or "place" the voice into the facial mask, as well as directives which include imagery and imitation.

The emphasis on vital capacity, breath "control," "support," "placement," and similar directives is ineffective because these methods 1) are incapable of improving either the ratio of tension shared between the muscle systems which adjust the vocal folds, or their tonicity, 2) interfere with prephonatory tuning (a setting of the vocal folds which occurs before air has moved below the glottis, and that is a reflexive adjustment governed by neurological control systems), and 3) do not address themselves to problems related to laryngeal suspension and stabilization. The "activity of muscles" is hindered rather than helped by such arbitrary controls, especially when those muscles are mainly involuntary. As a result of these and other substitute measures, training procedures based upon the above directives merely compensate for vocal faults (an absence of equilibrium) without curing them. Under these circumstances, energy economy becomes an unattainable goal.

What is at issue here is a confusion between cause and effect. While a mechanism functioning in equilibrium makes it appear that respiration is the controlling factor in phonation, and indeed that it controls function, in reality it is function which determines both the rate of breath expenditure and the economical use of energy. Two factors must be present to ensure this economy: 1) a well-balanced registration, and 2) a properly positioned larynx. Unless energy is concentrated into the functional activities taking place at this level, the vocal mechanism cannot function properly, nor can concepts be effectively transformed into reality.

The successful channeling of energy during phonation is measurable, and finds expression in a wide tonal range, flexibility, genuine resonance, beautiful tone quality, and an absence of fatigue—attributes possessed by all those whose technique of tone production is correct.

Energy Distribution: the arrangement, points of concentration, and general distribution of overtones with relation to the fundamental.

Every sung tone has its distinctive quality, and this quality is determined by the number, frequency, and relative intensity of its component parts, *i.e.*, the energy distribution of the overtones within the fundamental. Within each tone, energy assembles into groups, so that certain areas of overtone content are stronger than others. Each concentration of frequencies is called a "vowel band," and these vowel bands are heard as a particular vowel quality. Harmonic partials or overtones that are present but lie outside the vowel band itself impart additional characteristics of sound such as "brilliance," "shrillness," "thickness," *etc.*, according to the way they are dispersed over the harmonic spectrum.

See Artificial
    Channeling
    Bel Canto
    False Vocal Cords
    Holistic Pedagogy
    Laryngeal
        Suspension
    Modern Methods
    Natural Movement
    Register
    Resonance
    Standing Wave
    Vowel

Energy distribution is dependent upon several factors, including these:

1. The vowel and its frequency bands, or formants;
2. Tonal "coloring" and emotional response;
3. The manner in which the length, thickness, and contour of the vocal cords are adjusted in response to pitch and intensity (*i.e.,* the registration), and
4. The adjustment of the pharyngeal cavities responsible for tonal amplification— especially the laryngeal pharynx, the oropharynx, and the postnasal pharynx (*i.e.,* resonation).

Enlarged Pharynx: an overly opened throat.

Pedagogic directives such as "open the throat" or "vomit the tone" often encourage students to overopen the throat, and thereby to confuse an enlarged pharyngeal adjustment with open-throatedness. An open-throated resonance adjustment does not mean that the pharynx is expanded: on the contrary, a feeling of genuine open-throatedness is one of compactness, or the concentration of energy.

Those who consciously try to enlarge the pharyngeal aperture usually do so by an excessive distention of both the oropharynx and the mouth. This practice prohibits genuine laryngeal resonance and makes articulation extremely awkward. Although the pharynx may indeed expand somewhat when the resonance adjustment is precise, the size of the aperture is not important.

Efforts to enlarge the pharynx usually destroy the fine tuning that is essential to genuine laryngeal resonance, and increase muscular interference. A better description of a tone quality recognized to be "open-throated" is one "free of constrictor tensions."

See Covering,
(To) Cover
Resonance

Enunciation: the act of pronouncing articulate sounds; often mistaken as being synonymous with articulation and pronunciation. Enunciation is said to be clear when vowels are well formed and the articulation crisp.

Epigastrium: the upper part of the abdominal wall, frequently confused with the diaphragm.

Epiglottis: a thin, yellowish cartilage at the base of the tongue which folds over the glottis during peristaltic movement.

The natural function of the epiglottis is to direct food into the esophagus and prevent its entrance into the lungs. Choking, from food getting caught in the throat or other causes, is an example of the problems encountered when the epiglottis fails to function properly.

Because of its intimate association with swallowing, the folding of the epiglottis, when accompanied by a rising of the larynx and an inward collapse of the thyroid cartilage, is one of the most common manifestations of throat constriction. Since swallowing is a natural, habitual act, singers invariably identify more readily with this constricting process than with the pharyngeal expansion characteristic of an open-throated resonance adjustment.

Equilibrium: an equal distribution of tension between two or more opposing forces.

The muscular complex engaged in phonation is in equilibrium when all of the muscle groups involved brace or otherwise stabilize one another. For example, the muscles which stretch the vocal folds are in equilibrium when the ratio of tension shared between them is proportionate to the pitch, intensity, and vowel pattern being sung.

When the technique is correct, all muscles throughout the vocal tract will be in a state of self-maintained equilibrium. Apart from the vocal folds, the most important among these muscles are those controlling the inspiratory and expiratory process, including three layers of abdominal muscles (extending from the pelvis to the inner ribs), and the diaphragm, which descends with each intake of breath and, with the intercostals, moves the rib cage outward. A correct technique of singing finds these processes in equilibrium not only with themselves, but with each other.

See Coordination
Registration,
Ratio of
Tonicity

Regardless of the amount of physical energy brought to bear upon the mechanism when it is maintained in equilibrium, it will be absorbed economically as long as the muscular tonicity is sufficiently high.

Esophagus: a passageway through which food and liquids pass into the stomach; also known as the gullet.

The esophagus is made up of longitudinal fibers (some of which attach to the cricoid cartilage) that connect the hard palate to the diaphragm. The mouth of the esophagus is attached to the upper tips of the arytenoid cartilages, and since it can pull down on the arytenoids, it can close the glottal space. As it pertains to singing, however, this movement is undesirable, since it engenders a rise in the laryngeal position, thereby placing a strain on the lateral cricoarytenoids and consequently constricting the throat.

Eustachian Tube: the auditory canal; a small canal that leads from the middle ear to the nasopharynx.

The function of the Eustachian tube is to equalize pressure on the inner surface of the tympanic membrane (eardrum) with that of the outer atmosphere, and to drain any excess mucus. Although the pharyngeal opening of the tube remains closed under normal conditions (except when swallowing, yawning, or sneezing), the tube itself remains open.

The Eustachian tube is strongly affected during phonation by the behavior of a broad complex of pharyngeal muscles: the salpingopharyngeals with which they interconnect, the palatopharyngeal muscles, and the superior constrictor. When these muscle groups and other laryngeal muscles with which they coordinate create neck tension, the Eustachian tube will close. The result of this interference is that the pressure on opposite sides of the eardrum will be unequal, and the singer, regardless of the acuity of his hearing perception under normal circumstances, will hear his voice improperly, and may sing out of tune without realizing it.

See Neck Tension

Even Scale: a linear vocal pattern in which each tone is perfectly graduated in proportion to its neighbors.

Although the term "even scale" is misleading, the basis upon which this concept is founded is correct in principle. No two pitches, whether produced by the voice or by any other instrument, are ever identical. Therefore, the so-called "even" scale, commonly considered a series of identical tonal qualities, is actually an "evenly graded" scale, *i.e.*, a succession of vocalized sounds that share identical resonance characteristics and for which the ratio of registration for each pitch differs from, but matches, that of its neighbors.

Efforts directed toward the achievement of an even scale through absolute uniformity of quality and tonal texture "lock" the registration and seal in vocal faults. Such practices limit the functional capacity of the mechanism and make the voice colorless and qualitatively uninteresting.

Exaggeration: an overstatement.

In early stages of development, exaggeration is a useful device for establishing new conceptual response patterns. Once an idea has been grasped, however, the execution must be refined and performed more tastefully.

Exceptional Voices: those singing instruments in which precise coordination among the muscular complexes involved in phonation, an instinct for singing, musicality, and the ability to communicate effectively, have fused into a rather precarious equilibrium.

The "exceptional" element of an exceptional voice is not necessarily due to anatomical peculiarities, *i.e.*, the mechanism itself, but to the fact that all contributing elements function at a high level of efficiency.

Exercises: musical patterns designed to improve the coordinate relationship among those muscle groups responsible for producing tone.

The purpose of a vocal exercise is to encourage natural movement, to remove muscular blockages, to strengthen that which is correct, to develop and properly integrate the vocal registers, and to effectively position the larynx so that it provides the open-throated resonance so essential to good singing. To get at the functional core of the vocal apparatus, one must know what scale patterns to select, when and how to use them, and why they can be expected to work. Each exercise must be selected on the basis of individual needs, and while certain patterns may be generally applicable, each must nevertheless be used at the right time under the right circumstances. *No vocal exercise possesses intrinsic merit.* Its sole importance is its suitability as a problem solver and the manner in which it is executed. Rote exercises are virtually useless.

Listed below are some elemental exercises designed to achieve specific functional objectives:

1. Simple musical patterns (*e.g.*, sustained tones, triads, and arpeggios), to be used with specific combinations of intensity and vowel, whose express purpose is to either separate or combine the two basic register mechanisms, to establish a proper laryngeal suspension, and, when used in conjunction with *solfeggi*, to combine tone production with articulation. Until such time as considerable technical progress has been made, these exercises should always be sung legato to ensure consistency of resonance, to maintain a direct relationship between the upper, middle and lower tonal ranges, and to include loud and soft singing, as well as all shades of vowel coloration;

2. Trills at all stages of training. For the beginner, these will serve to loosen throat tension, but they cannot be expected to sound like two distinct pitches. A true trill can only be executed when the technique has achieved a high state of excellence;

3. Arpeggios sung staccato in order to gain a sense of free laryngeal activity. This should lead to an understanding of natural, involuntary movement within the laryngeal area, and, through kinesthetic awareness, open up the possibility for effective control without recourse to direct control;

4. An octave jump which includes an appoggiatura. By slackening the energy used in singing the upper octave, the pitch should be allowed to fall to the seventh without losing tonal vibratility. This should be followed by a rapid return to the octave. Mechanically, this is achieved by a reduction in laryngeal firmness (so that the tone almost flattens to the seventh) with a reinstitution of the true pitch by means of laryngeally centered energy. This device should achieve two objectives: 1) to "let" the tone, in effect, "spin" as though self-vibratile, and 2) to develop a sense of free laryngeal resonance. Unlike the staccato, which is executed by a rapid narrowing and opening of the glottal slit, this exercise is designed to identify with a natural movement of the suspensory muscles which position the larynx, and represents a rapid oscillation between a state of balanced tension (for the upper octave) and partial relaxation (as the slackened energy permits the pitch to lower). This exercise is most helpful in gaining a sense of laryngeal equilibrium, and

5. Velocity exercises, which have a twofold purpose: 1) to encourage spontaneous, natural movement, and 2) to by-pass the singer's tonal concepts, which on a subjective basis are always somewhat incorrect, thus allowing new qualities to introduce themselves.

See Laryngeal
    Suspension
    Register
    Resonance
    Trill

Exercises prepared by Concone, Bordogni, Nava and others have largely outlived their usefulness, as there is now extant a wealth of vocal literature which serves the same technical purpose and possesses the additional advantage of being presentable for performance.

Expiration: the discharging of inspired breath from the lungs.

Physically, breath is expired by the contraction of a complex series of abdominal muscles: notably, the rectus abdominus, transverse abdominus, external oblique, internal oblique, transverse thoracic, and latissimi dorsi. Their natural opponents, the inspiratory muscles, contract for inspiration. When these two muscle systems are in balanced tension, the glottal slit closes and the vocal folds become freely vibratile.

See Breathing
    Energy
    Register

Expression: the representation of thoughts and feelings through some medium.

Expressive singing is a complex amalgamation of verbal expression (expression through words), musical expression (expression through sound), and self-expression. Although feeling may be refined through disciplined thought and language, it is sound itself—its quality, texture and inflectional nuance—which raises the communicative experience in singing to its highest level. Personal feelings can be an embarrassment unless they reveal an inner vision which establishes a common bond between the performer, the audience and the material being presented. To succeed in this is the ultimate responsibility of the artist.

External Intercostal Muscles: one of three muscle groups separating the ribs whose contraction elevates the rib cage.

External Oblique Muscles: thin, flat expiratory muscles which extend from the lower eight ribs to the crest of the pelvis, whose function is to compress the abdominal contents in forced expiration.

External Thyroarytenoid Muscle: one of the muscle bands comprising the vocal folds.

The thyroarytenoid originates below the thyroid notch (some fibers attaching to the middle cricothyroid ligaments), and inserts into the base of the arytenoid cartilages. By drawing the arytenoid cartilages forward toward the thyroid cartilage, the thyroarytenoid muscles shorten the vocal folds. Acting against its antagonist (the cricothyroid muscle), the contracted thyroarytenoid firms and tenses the vocal folds. Acting alone, this contraction shortens the vocal folds.

See **Intrinsic Musculature of the Larynx**
Thyroarytenoid Muscle
Vocal Folds
Vocalis Muscles

Extrinsic Laryngeal Muscles: muscles which extend from the exterior of the larynx to other parts of the body.

Many of the extrinsic laryngeal muscles attach to such structures as the hyoid bone, the mandible, the sternum, the clavicle, and the shoulder blades, while others, like the inferior and middle pharyngeal constrictors, form the pharyngeal wall.

The extrinsic laryngeal muscles are responsible for controlling the vertical movements of the larynx and shaping the pharyngeal resonating system, and, because the sternothyroids hold synergetically against the contraction of the cricothyroids, they play an important role in determining the ratio of registration.

See **Laryngeal Suspension**
Register
Vocal Folds

F

Facial Muscles: external muscles of the head and neck which can be divided into two groups: muscles of facial expression and muscles of mastication.

The facial muscles form an integral part of the vocal mechanism because of a direct neurological connection with the larynx, the larynx and the diaphragm, and the larynx and the inner ear. To a certain extent, the entire pharyngeal tract is conditioned and influenced by mouth positions and facial expressions. A smiling mouth position brightens the tone; spreading the lips tends to spread the tone, and the forming of a round mouth position aids in the production of a rounder tone quality. While these facial expressions may be used on occasion as technical devices, it is important to realize that the singer who phonates properly has established a condition whereby the tonal form is almost completely independent of posturings and prepared mouth positions, thus leaving the face to reflect the meaning and emotional content of the text and the music.

Tones which depend upon any particular facial expression for their efficiency are being produced incorrectly.

See **Bocca Ridente**

False Elevators of the Larynx: the muscles which attach the tongue to the hyoid bone, *viz.*, the mylohyoid, the digastric, the stylohyoid, and the geniohyoid.

The false elevators of the larynx are active during perastaltic movement, *i.e.*, swallowing, and consequently they are inhibitory to an open-throated tone production when tensed. Singing with a high larynx is symptomatic of this tension, and indicates that some degree of throat constriction is present.

See **Constriction**
 Open Throat

False Vocal Cords: the two fleshy folds similar in appearance to the true vocal folds, forming what Garcia (1855) described as the superior glottis. These folds, or ventricular bands, lie above the true vocal folds, and are separated from them by narrow, horizontal cavities known as the ventricles of Morgagni. Because the false vocal cords move with the arytenoid cartilages, they are thought to assist in bringing about a closure of the glottis.

Some authorities believe that the false vocal cords and ventricular sacs are vestigial remnants of the air sacs found in mammals and other animals, but their primary function now appears to be limited to the prevention of the passage of air from the trachea (as when lifting weights), and to the production by their mucosa of a lubricating agent to protect the vocal folds.

One of the earliest theories concerning the function of the false vocal cords was advanced by Runge (1753), who termed the ventricular bands "ligamenta superiora," and thought them to be responsible for the production of low tones, whereas the true vocal folds, or "ligamenta inferiora," he thought responsible for the production of high tones. For many years it was thought that the false vocal cords were the source of falsetto tone qualities, but with Garcia's invention of the laryngoscope (1854) both of these theories were proven to be without substance. On the basis of laryngoscopic observation, Czermak (1859) concluded that the false vocal cords only functioned as a vibrator pathologically, *i.e.*, under conditions of true vocal fold dysphonia.

At the turn of the century, Charles Lunn and Edmund J. Myer drew attention to another functional possibility when they advanced the double valve theory. This theory contends that both the true and the false vocal cords regulate air flow, the narrowed aperture of the false cords offering, according to Lunn, "a point of resistance," which, in addition to controlling the rate of air flow, creates the supraglottal system necessary to an effective countering of subglottal pressure. While their views have not been widely accepted, this concept is not without merit. In theoretical terms, at least, the proposition receives solid support from other physical and acoustical phenomena.

One piece of physical evidence that supports Lunn's thesis is the difference between the angulation of the true and the false vocal cords. The false cords, unlike the true vocal folds, are perfectly designed by nature to control air flow because of their downward angulation. Because of this peculiarity, they function in much the same manner as the locks which control water levels in a canal. In both instances, increased pressure is met by increased resistance; the greater the pressure, the stronger the tendency of the opening to narrow. Thus, the resistance offered is not accomplished by force, but occurs because a basic engineering principle has become operative. Observation of the false vocal cords during loud and soft singing lends support to this premise, since they narrow as intensity is increased and separate somewhat when it is lowered.

When technical conditions cause the false vocal cords to narrow, they not only limit the amount of breath flow, but also compress air into the ventricular sacs, or pouches, which form a cavity between the true and the false vocal cords. This creates a source of pressure above the vocal folds capable of resisting and equalizing subglottal pressure. On the basis of this theory, it is through the presence of a balanced pressure system on opposite sides of the vocal folds that the latter are relieved of what would otherwise be abnormal tension. When other functional activities coordinate with a reflexive narrowing of the false vocal cords, the vocal folds become self-vibratile and are free to create the pressure variations responsible for pitch.

An early experiment conducted by Johannes Müller (1843) on excised larynges tends to support the above hypothesis. While testing the position, tension and vibratory nature of the vocal folds in response to varying degrees of air pressure he was led to the following conclusions: 1) that when the ventricular folds were inflated (an operation which depends upon a narrow passageway), the tones produced sounded louder and fuller; 2) that concurrent with a depression of the epiglottis, the quality became darker and the tone slightly lower in pitch, and 3) tha a drawing together of the false vocal cords appeared to be caused by an overpressure in the lungs.

Another piece of evidence to indicate a pressing need for a supraglottal system to counter subglottal pressure has been introduced through a series of experiments conducted by Carl Müller (1876) and duplicated in this century by Richard Luchsinger, a German physician. In this experiment a small slit was cut into a stretched goatskin, which was placed over a cardboard tube. When air under high pressure was directed against the vibrator (the slit in the goatskin) from the lower end of the tube, the desired high tone (d⁴ or 2349 cps) could be produced only when the space above the membrane was confined, which was done by placing a plate 5 to 10 mm. above the vibrating surface.

It was visually apparent to both investigators that the membranous margins performed only vertical vibrations without a horizontal component, *i.e.*, they produced what in the human voice would be described as a "flute" or "whistle" tone. Of singular interest in this experiment is the fact that no sound could be heard until a source of pressure was created above the goatskin to counteract the pressure build-up from below. In principle, certainly, this experiment indicates some need for a source of counterpressure both above and below the vibrator to fulfill the normal requirements known to exist when any system is in equilibrium.

Perhaps the strongest argument in support of the functional utility of the false vocal cords has been recently advanced by Janwillem van den Berg. On the basis of X-ray pictures taken of the larynx during phonation, he discovered that the false vocal cords not only narrowed, but also functioned as a low-pass filter to remove some of the higher harmonics. This, he found, provided more tonal richness and warmth. Beckmann (1956) concurred with van den Berg, finding that when the ventricles were plugged with soft cotton (using excised larynges) the higher harmonics were reduced in strength.

The role assigned the false vocal cords by van den Berg is acoustically important, but a result of much greater significance to come out of these X-ray studies is the discovery that the false vocal cords narrow when the tone is rich and full, and separate when the tone production is poor. Together with Husson (1935) and Luchsinger (1949), van den Berg also observed that the ventricles changed slightly with changing vowels, a reaction that is surely an indication of their importance to phonation.

Whether or not the false cords perform as a low-pass filter does not alter the fact that they do narrow. Four facts would appear to emerge from the above experiments:

1. The false vocal cords do narrow during correct tone production;

2. By narrowing, they limit, regulate and steady the breath flow;

3. Because they partially block the exit to the oral cavity, they build up a pressure system above the true vocal folds, and

4. When narrowed to cause the ventricular pouches to inflate, they help make the tones produced sound louder and fuller.

FALSE VOCAL CORDS

One of the by-products of the regulatory function of the false vocal cords is the circulation of air in a clockwise and counterclockwise direction along the sides of the ventricular sacs, a movement which gave rise to the vortex theory. It is also possible that the counterbalance between sub- and supraglottal pressure is responsible for the presence of a standing wave (a pattern of vibratory motion which finds sound waves being reflected back toward the tonal source) within the vocal tract. It is not inconceivable that this type of tonal reinforcement, when combined with a proper coupling and adjustment of the pharyngeal cavities, provides the vocal mechanism with its extraordinary powers of resonance.

While conventional opinion maintains that the true vocal folds owe their motion to the resistance they provide to the breath pressure directed against them, this theory remains questionable. One reason for doubt is that the vocal folds are not well constructed for this purpose, since their under portions slant upward. This conformation is ideal for permitting puffs of air to escape to create the pressure variations responsible for pitch, but not for resisting or controlling the breath flow without stiffening or losing the essential elasticity of the vocal folds.

The neglect of the false vocal cords as a pedagogic concern is perhaps attributable to the fact that they are not subject to direct control. They reflexively narrow, however, when the intercostal muscles hold in opposition to abdominal muscular tension, as in the case of weightlifting, coughing, defecating, and holding one's breath. Under such conditions, the diaphragm tends to maintain its lowered position while thoracic pressure is increased.

The role played by the false vocal cords during phonation partially explains the success of some abdominal breathing techniques. However, those who adopt this practice are not regulating breath flow because of abdominal muscular control, but are limiting it by a reflexive and subconscious narrowing of the false vocal cords. To expect other elements of the mechanism to benefit from this type of breath control is unrealistic, since these controls do not necessarily have either a positive or a negative effect on other aspects of laryngeal functioning.

In order to bring the total musculature of the vocal mechanism into equilibrium, problems related to registration and laryngeal suspension must be given priority. When the proper ratio of tension is shared between the two muscle groups which regulate the size of the glottal slit (registration), and the larynx and the pharyngeal resonators are correctly adjusted, the respiratory system and other peripheral functions will balance themselves naturally. As a result, the rate of breath flow will be negligible and the pressure systems above and below the vocal folds will be equalized. With the mechanism maintained in equilibrium in this manner, the singer will become conscious of his breath being *under control,* as opposed to being *controlled.* One of the ingredients essential to this technical status is a supraglottal pressure system which has been established and maintained by a narrowing of the false vocal cords.

Although insufficient studies have been made on the function of the false vocal cords, it would seem that their importance is greater than heretofore realized. Since the more conventional view (which contends that the true vocal folds perform both as a vibrator and as a resisting agent) has not proven successful, currently accepted "precepts" should also be challenged and questioned in the light of this alternative theoretical possibility.

See Breathing
     Damping
     Energy
     Laryngeal
       Suspension
     Modern Methods
     Puff Theory
     Register
     Standing Wave
     Vortex Theory

Falsettists: male vocalists, usually those who sing the alto part in church choirs that exclude women; not to be confused with the *castrati*, or *evirati*, who enjoyed popularity during the seventeenth and eighteenth centuries.

Falsetto: Italian, *falso*, meaning "false;" also known by some early theorists as the *voce di gola*, or "throat voice," which, according to Isaac Nathan (1791—1864), describes a quality "where the throat appears to be the chief organ connected with the production of sound . . . called a throat voice, termed in Italian, falsetto;" any false tone quality; one which possesses important functional properties, yet is without artistic merit.

To ascertain the precise nature of those qualities which distinguish a falsetto and establish its legitimate boundaries is not easy. Historically, falsetto tone qualities had succeeded in gaining the attention of theorists as early as the fourteenth century, when they were referred to by Marchetto as the *vox ficta*. In later centuries, owing to the rapid development of vocal skills and the popularity of the *castrati*, it was apparent that this mechanism was capable, when trained correctly, of taking on new dimensions. By joining it "imperceptibly" to the chest register in a coordinate relationship, its quality could be modified, its range, flexibility and power increased, and its "falseness" transformed into a thoroughly legitimate tone quality.

The potential legitimacy of the falsetto through modification is clearly indicated by the changes in terminology recorded from the early seventeen hundreds to the present. Tosi, Manfredini, Mancini and Corri wrote of the "falsetto or head voice," an indication that a definite correlation existed. Manfredini summed up the viewpoint generally shared during this era with a chapter heading "On combining the chest voice with the head voice, vulgarly called falsetto." With respect to joining them, he wrote "This is to be accomplished not by forcing the high chest tones but rather by reinforcing the lower tones of the falsetto, or else doing the opposite, if the chest tones happen to be weaker and deficient, and the falsetto tones plentiful and strong."[41] Early German sources (Hiller, Lasser, von Engelbrunner) reflected the influence of Italian models, referring to the two register mechanisms as "chest or natural and falsetto or artificial." Mancini specifically stated that "The great art of the singer consists in acquiring an ability to render imperceptible to the ear, the passing from one register to the other."[42]

The fact that the two register mechanisms can either be separated or combined in a variety of ways has led to difficulties with respect to nomenclature. Early authorities, even the majority who acknowledged the existence of but two register mechanisms, spoke of the "falsetto or head voice," either undisturbed by the ambiguity or assuming that everyone knew why they were similar yet different. Apparently the head voice was tacitly recognized to be a falsetto-derived tone, or one reflecting some type of coordinate relationship with the chest register. Garcia helped clarify this issue, asserting that the falsetto and the head voice were two distinct entities. After pointing out that the falsetto sounded "dull" and "hoarse," he further stated that "the falsetto (a term often misapplied and confounded with the head voice) is naturally the more veiled of the two, and requires a greater expenditure of breath."[43]

This confusion of identities was later encouraged when, on the basis of laryngoscopic evidence (where it was found that the vocal folds presented a longer and

See Castrato
Falsetto
Male Alto

[41]Vincenzo Manfredini, "Dell'unire la voce di petto colla voce di testa, la quale volgarmente chiamasi falsett," *Regole Armoniche,* second edition (Venice, 1797), p. 61. Cited and translated by Philip A. Duey, *Bel Canto in its Golden Age* (New York: Kings Crown Press, 1951), p. 116.

[42]Giam Battista Mancini, *Practical Reflections on the Figurative Art of Singing* (Milan, 1776), translated by Pietro Buzzi (Boston: The Gorham Press, 1912), p. 58.

[43]Manuel Garcia, *Hints on Singing,* translated by Beata Garcia (New York: Edward Schuberth Co., Inc., 1894), p. 8.

thinner vibrating surface for the mid-tonal range), the terms "middle" or "mixed" register were reintroduced, supporting what until then had been a minority opinion, and leading to the erroneous conclusion that there were three vocal registers rather than two.

William Shakespeare, a pupil of Giovanni Battista Lamperti, was one among many who confounded the difference between the falsetto and head voice, as is clear when he referred to the "middle" register as being a "mixed voice," one "occasionally termed by the Italian masters falsetto. . . . Of course this has no reference to the English term falsetto."[44] The latter remark is, of course, a direct reference to the male alto voice common to English church choirs. A contemporary exponent of Bel Canto, Ida Franca, also spoke of the falsetto as being synonymous with the "mixed" register.[45]

From the above remarks it is apparent that the falsetto lies in a pitch range immediately above the chest voice, with its lower four tones overlapping the latter mechanism. It is also evident that it can be used in many ways, functioning either as an isolated entity, or combining to a greater or lesser extent with the chest register to produce what would be more properly called "a falsetto-derived tone." In any event, it is certain that the falsetto cannot in its pure form be classified as "falsetto or head voice," "middle register," or "mixed register" at one and the same time. Until a mechanical principle has been formulated to establish the origins of this quality, none of the terms used above will have any real significance.

To arrive at a physical and qualitative understanding of an isolated falsetto, it is essential to examine the function of the two muscular systems responsible for drawing the vocal folds into tension. There are two such systems, the arytenoids and the cricothyroids, each of which is capable of working as a coordinate functional unit or independently. When the falsetto is isolated, the cricothyroids tense while the arytenoids are relaxed, an imbalance which causes the glottal space to open widely.

Because of the absence of arytenoid (chest voice) connection and the inability of the vocal folds to produce the pressure variations known as a pitch vibrato, the tone quality produced under these technical conditions sounds "false." Since the cricothyroids share a common facet with the pharyngeal constrictors, the natural tendency of the falsetto (unless a high rate of breath expulsion is maintained) is to constrict. Thus, when the falsetto combines, as it can, in an almost infinite variety of ways with the chest register to become the head voice, its qualitative properties will also reflect those influences brought to bear by the type of adjustment assumed by the pharyngeal resonators, *i.e.*, open-throated or constricted. A valid insight into the type of head voice being produced is therefore impossible without understanding those characteristics natural to each of its constituent parts.

When reference is made to a pure, isolated falsetto, or one in which the cricothyroids are tensed without engaging a counterpull or synergetic "hold" on the part of the arytenoids, its tonal range is confined to B below middle C to its upper octave. Within this compass the tones will possess the following identifiable features:

1. A range limited to, at most, an octave for all voice types, male and female;
2. An extremely "breathy" and "hooty" tone quality;

[44]William Shakespeare, *The Art of Singing* (Bryn Mawr, Pa.: Oliver Ditson Co., 1898), p. 34.

[45]Ida Franca, *Manual of Bel Canto* (New York: Coward-McCann, Inc., 1959), p. 15.

3. A high rate of breath expulsion, which restricts tonal duration to two or three seconds at best;
4. Little or no aesthetic value;
5. Total absence of tonal pulse, and
6. An inability to diminish without reflexively engaging some chest register tension, thereby modifying its quality.

In sum, the falsetto is literally a false tone. When tones become clear and the range extensive, when tones can be swelled and diminished, when there is a natural vibrancy, or when the mechanism becomes flexible, then the falsetto can no longer be said to be pure.

Judged by the above criteria, a singer who might be described as capable of singing and sustaining beautiful falsetto tones could not be using a pure falsetto, but a *falsetto-derived tone,* a somewhat coordinated falsetto—one in which, to a degree, the chest register acts as a participating agent. Tonal clarity, the ability to sustain tone, the presence of a musical quality, and other normally desirable features cannot exist without some measure of coordinate action with the arytenoid muscle system (the chest register). A pure falsetto is without chest register connection, does not sustain, and is far from beautiful.

The falsetto, while present, is more difficult to isolate in the female voice than it is in the male voice. To sing is to coordinate, and the range and intensity requirements of repertoire cannot be met unless the registers are combined. This is not to suggest, however, that the falsetto does not exist in women's voices, but simply that, since it habitually combines, it is not easily separated.

If a "mixed" registration and its concomitant throat constriction are to be corrected, isolating the falsetto, even with women's voices, is an essential first step. Regardless of the singer's sex, however, once the falsetto has been isolated the pitch range, the tone quality, the symptoms and the gradations of intensity natural to it will be identical for all voice types.

Since with both sexes the falsetto is usually undeveloped and poorly integrated, it must be disengaged if technical progress is to be made. As a consequence of this separation the entire coordinative process, even though largely involuntary, can be restructured. Because the falsetto is "hooty" and enlarges the pharyngeal opening through excessive breath expenditure, several advantages will have been gained by pursuing its development: 1) a weakened and improperly functioning mechanism can be revitalized; 2) its accompanying "mixed" registration and inevitable throat constriction will be afforded relief, and 3) the chest register, less impeded in its action by muscular interference, will benefit vicariously. Consequently, regardless of whether the voice is male or female, the falsetto, when properly developed, acts as a freeing agent.

A raw chest register and the "hooty," pure falsetto are the basic mechanisms which Garcia and others described as a series of homogeneous sounds, or tone qualities, yielded by a particular type of physical arrangement within the laryngeal musculature. When they function as isolated entities, since only half of the muscular systems responsible for positioning the vocal folds are engaged, each must be considered, in a sense, false.

Physically, all falsetto tones incapable of being expanded to full voice represent a breakdown of equilibrium among the muscle systems (the vocalis, the crico-thyroids, and the arytenoids) responsible for approximating the vocal folds. This breakdown, however, is often desirable, since the separation and development of the falsetto as an independent unit is an essential pedagogic device. With the mechanisms isolated, they are manipulable, and each can be properly exercised and strengthened before being ultimately brought into balanced tension. Were it not possible to isolate the chest register and the falsetto, the possibility of curing a "mixed" (improperly joined) registration and other serious vocal faults such as throat constriction would be remote.

The specific techniques for isolating and developing a pure falsetto are as follows:

1. Selection of an exercise employing but a single tone;
2. Utilization of pitches extending from B below middle C to the octave above, a range consistent with all voice types, male and female;
3. Selection of appropriately high levels of intensity;
4. Establishment of a tone quality which is hooty, breathy, without vibrato and incapable of being sustained, and
5. Use of the *oo* vowel exclusively.

The intensity scale pattern of a pure falsetto is extreme, commencing softly and breathily in its lower tonal range (those tones shared in common with the chest register) and mounting rapidly in intensity as the scale is ascended. High levels of intensity imposed upon the lower falsetto tones will cause an improper juncture with the chest register, a condition which results in a "mixed" registration. (See Figure 3.)

Figure 3. Pitch and intensity range of a pure falsetto common to all voice types, male or female.

While all of these factors are important to the isolation of the falsetto, of special importance is the selection of the *oo* vowel. When properly used, this vowel elicits a predictable response on the part of the vocal muscles, ensuring that the vocal folds assume the position of an inverted V. As a result of this widening of the glottal space, the tone quality becomes breathy and "hooty," and takes on those characteristics associated with a pure falsetto. Thus, proper vowel selection is as indispensable to the production of a pure falsetto as pitch and intensity.

The acoustic reason for this phenomenon was not fully understood until recent experiments with cavities and vibrating members supplied evidence that cavity selection (for example, forming an *oo* vowel) not only energizes the lower formants, but also, as is the case with reed instruments, forces the vibrator (the vocal folds) to adjust its physical dimensions to conform to the acoustic properties of the resonator, *i.e.*, the pharyngeal cavities, a reaction which tends to minimize the influence of the chest voice. This influence is clearly discernible when observing the difficulty so many singers experience in solidifying the *oo* vowel and making its resonance characteristics match those of the more "open" vowels.

By phonating the *oo* vowel in conjunction with the proper pitch-intensity pattern, a student therefore achieves several objectives, learning how to do the following:

1. Produce an isolated falsetto;
2. Recognize its textural properties and natural boundaries;
3. Develop and strengthen it without having it "mix" improperly with the chest register;
4. Sharpen his listening perception, and
5. Correctly evaluate the origins of the almost infinite number of falsetto-derived tones that can be produced, *i.e.*, those that are to be avoided and those that are to be encouraged and cultivated.

Another important advantage is that by encouraging a "hooty" quality and a high rate of breath expulsion, the student will, by literally having blown the throat parts open, reverse the natural tendency of the thyroid cartilage to collapse inward (as it does in a wrongly produced falsetto), and, through instinctual awakening, kinesthetically learn how to assume an open-throated resonance adjustment which will ultimately maintain and stabilize itself. These factors combine to form a special kind of "knowing."

The qualitative properties of a pure falsetto are modified, as previously stated, by the cavity formation that establishes its resonance characteristics. Two apparently different types of pure falsetto reflect this influence: 1) a falsetto which is toneless, the throat being pushed open by excessive breath flow, and 2) one equally pure and breathy which, however, finds the pharyngeal cavity performing as a resonating agent. What remains the same in both instances is the shape and function of the vocal folds; what changes is the adjustment assumed by the pharyngeal cavities.

Different authorities attach different names to these functional conditions: a collapsed falsetto as opposed to a supported falsetto, oral falsetto as distinct from a pharyngeal falsetto, a pure falsetto as separate from a coordinated falsetto, and special classifications such as developed, integrated, mixed, *etc.*

None of the terms listed is completely satisfactory, the possible combinations of falsetto-derived tones being virtually limitless. Those most common to the profession are described below.

COLLAPSED FALSETTO: a term introduced by Husler and Rodd-Marling to denote an "unsupported" falsetto, a type of muscular imbalance which causes the hinged thyroid cartilage to tilt inward and narrow the pharyngeal opening; one of the many types of falsetto which cannot be developed into a full-voiced, legitimate tone quality.

As described by the above-named authors ("an extremely thin, breathy tone quality which cannot be modified"), the collapsed falsetto indicates the presence of a "mixed" registration, usually brought on because of a premature effort to combine the falsetto with the chest voice.[46] When the falsetto is produced easily and with a low rate of breath expulsion, and appears to be collapsed and incapable of being ultimately expanded to a full, legitimate tone quality, it is a type of falsetto which is throaty and pedagogically useless.

[46]Frederick Husler and Yvonne Rodd-Marling, *Singing: The Physical Nature of the Vocal Organ* (New York: October House, 1964), p. 59.

COORDINATED FALSETTO: a falsetto-derived tone quality indicating the presence of some degree of chest register tension. The heavy sense of overlay in a coordinated falsetto is due to the strong contraction of the cricothyroid muscles and the relatively weak participation of the arytenoids. There are obviously numerous balances of tension which, when combined with the variables operative within the laryngeal adjustment, produce many types of coordinated falsetto. Some of these qualities can be used for legitimate *pianissimo* effects; others, less well coordinated, are sometimes used for comic effect. The technical function of a well-coordinated falsetto is to bridge the gap between the chest and falsetto register mechanisms and to pave the way for the proper execution of a *messa di voce*. The emergence of the head voice represents an intermediary stage in the combined activity of these two mechanisms.

DEVELOPED FALSETTO: a falsetto which has been strengthened without a coordinate relationship having been established with the chest register.

In developing the pure falsetto, single tones must be used exclusively within a range confined to B below middle C to its octave. The only suitable vowel for this purpose is *oo*. Although the intensity will be low where the falsetto overlaps the chest register and extremely high in its upper portion, all falsetto tones must be sung as energetically as the preservation of their innate tonal characteristics permits. To avoid having this mechanism "mix" improperly with the chest register, it must remain breathy, straight (without noticeable oscillating movements) and toneless.

A mistake to be avoided in developing the falsetto is to act upon the assumption that these tones can become legitimate without a radical change of texture. As long as the falsetto is pure (isolated) it will remain a literally false tone quality. Attempts to strengthen it by injecting a ring into the tone quality will cause it to combine improperly with the chest register, an engagement which will narrow the glottal opening.

In the best sense of its meaning, a developed falsetto is merely a condition which finds the cricothyroids, operating alone, exercised to a point where they have reached their optimum strength potential.

During training, of course, the stage of development outlined above should be employed judiciously. The vocal mechanism must always be considered a totality, the sole reason for isolating any of its constituent parts being to effect those improvements necessary to performance economy. Unless one understands the register mechanisms in their isolated forms, however, developing the voice at more sophisticated levels of tone production depends upon procedures largely based on chance. Knowledge of the principles which effectively stimulate the registers, whether to isolate or combine them, eliminates this element and precludes the likelihood of unnecessary failure. Falsetto development is basic to a positive restructuring and/or refinement of technical and artistic ambitions.

INTEGRATED FALSETTO: a falsetto which, either by training or by nature, operates with some degree of coordinate relationship with the chest register.

The processes involved in promoting falsetto integration reverse those adopted when developing a pure falsetto. The intensity must be lowered, the musical figure lengthened, and the vowel *ah* substituted for the hooty *oo*. The effect of such a procedure will be to reflexively stimulate chest register participation and gradually transform the falsetto into a semi-legitimate tone quality—one which with further development will become fully integrated into the technique.

If care is taken to ensure that the pharyngeal resonators are free of constricting tensions during the development and integration of the falsetto, a logical progression will take place. From a pure falsetto, first oral and then pharyngeal, the quality will further modify to become what is recognized as a falsetto-derived tone, and will ultimately emerge as the head voice. Coincidental with this development, the quality will become increasingly clear and "singy," the range will extend outward in opposite directions, the voice will become extremely mobile, all vowels will assume uniform resonance characteristics, the voice will sustain easily, and the articulation of consonants will become more natural and effortless.

MIXED FALSETTO: a combined registration which finds an excessively dominant falsetto improperly joined to the chest voice, with the result that the activity of each seriously interferes with that of the other. A mixed falsetto is always accompanied by throat constriction.

ORAL FALSETTO: a pure falsetto without laryngeal resonance. An oral falsetto lacks vibrato and possesses no musical qualities. It is breathy and difficult to sustain, even briefly. The so-called "oral falsetto" is not resonated in the mouth cavity, but in the oral pharynx, with the laryngeal pharynx neutralized and detuned. The quality characteristics of the oral falsetto are similar in kind to those heard when blowing over the top of a bottle.

PHARYNGEAL FALSETTO: a pure falsetto which is resonated within both the laryngo- and oropharynges. The pharyngeal falsetto possesses more body and tone than the oral falsetto and represents the second stage in the development of a legitimate head voice quality.

PURE FALSETTO: the tonal equivalent of a physical arrangement which finds one of the stretchers of the vocal folds, the cricothyroids, tensing, while their opposers, the arytenoids, are relaxed. The pure falsetto differs from other forms of the falsetto in that no coordinate action takes place with the chest register (arytenoids), whereas other forms have some. With regard to resonance characteristics, the pure falsetto without laryngeal resonance is termed "oral" falsetto; when the laryngopharynx is active, the pure falsetto is referred to as the "pharyngeal" falsetto.

SUPPORTED FALSETTO: a semi-legitimate tone quality, indicating the presence of some degree of laryngeal resonance and chest register participation, which causes the tone quality to be clear and "singy."

A distinctive feature of the supported falsetto is its ability to sustain and use less breath than the chest voice. Since the vocal folds become approximated because of arytenoid (chest register) tension, it is apparent that this type of falsetto has developed out of the pure falsetto. Under proper guidance, a supported falsetto is capable of being further transformed into a completely legitimate, full-voiced tone quality.

The semi-legitimate quality of a supported falsetto represents an important transitional stage that leads to an ultimate integration of the two basic register mechanisms.

SUMMARY

The falsetto is important to the voice-building process because when properly employed, it is capable of inducing changes in the behavior patterns of those laryngeal muscles which lie beyond volitional control, but which are nonetheless responsible for positioning the vocal folds. Its use, particularly with male voices, is almost always essential, but in those rare instances where the mechanism is extremely well formed, it is unnecessary. As a mechanism, the falsetto can be used in a variety of ways. The difficulty is one of proper selection. It can be isolated, strengthened and trained to work cooperatively with the chest voice, or through misuse it can become the direct cause of a gradual or even precipitous technical disintegration.

While an understanding of functional mechanics is essential to the success of the voice-building process, it must be remembered that the ultimate goal of training is to unite and integrate, rather than divide, the two basic register mechanisms. The invention of the *messa di voce* (the swelling and diminishing of a single tone) by the early Italians led to the fulfillment of this objective. By understanding how the basic register mechanisms work in their more primitive form, therefore, the inner mechanics of this artistic device can be perceived, and with patience and skill, ultimately mastered. The falsetto-derived tones (head voice or coordinated falsetto), without which the execution of this artistic effect would be impossible, are in turn dependent (whether through training or by nature) upon a well-developed falsetto register.

See Bel Canto
Cavity Tone Theory
Chest Register
Covering,
   (To) Cover
Formants
Helmholtz
Reed Theory
Register
Resonance
Standing Wave
Vowel

Falsetto or Head Voice: a rare ambiguity in early vocal nomenclature which finds two terms used interchangeably to designate what was recognized to be but one register mechanism.

In view of the fact that pedagogic procedures from the beginning of the vocal art to the final years of the nineteenth century were designed to combine the falsetto with the chest register, it is evident that the head voice is a falsetto-derived tone quality resulting from a coordinate relationship between two mechanisms which, in their isolated form, are aesthetically deficient. The expression "falsetto or head voice," therefore, was probably used synonymously in recognition of the optional possibilities available: the falsetto concept was employed with reference to elemental developmental procedures, the head voice to more sophisticated levels of tone production. It is also possible that the expression "falsetto or head voice" was used as a reminder to the student that the head voice could not be developed, evaluated, or effectively controlled and regulated without knowledge of its functional origins.

It must be concluded, therefore, that the virtual synonymy of "falsetto or head voice" was neither an ambiguity nor a careless use of language, but (as in contemporary nomenclature, where a distinction is often made between chest "register" and chest "resonance") an effort to show that pitches in one and the same tonal area can be produced in either an isolated or a combined registration.

See Middle Register

Fatigue: a symptom indicating a physical state of being which, depending upon the specific nature of its origin, may be either a warning signal or evidence that a constructive vocal change is taking place.

The negative aspects contributing to vocal fatigue are the following: 1) poor physical coordination, resulting in misuse of the vocal organs; 2) strain, or exceeding the physical limitations inherent in a present technical status; 3) unwise selection of repertoire; 4) protracted periods of singing with insufficient rest, and 5) anxiety brought on by a fear of the expansive movement which frequently accompanies rapid progress.

A positive aspect of vocal fatigue is that experienced during a dramatic transition from a poor technique to one which finds the vocal mechanism functioning more efficiently. With the muscular systems involved responding in an unaccustomed manner, and consequently with lowered muscle tone, such fatigue is momentarily inevitable and quite natural. If, however, the new coordinative process conforms to the logical movement potential of the muscle systems engaged, the symptom of fatigue experienced will be of short duration.

Relief of vocal fatigue caused by malfunction depends upon the isolation, independent development and reintegration of the two basic register mechanisms, the chest voice and the falsetto.

See Bel Canto
Falsetto
Modern Methods
Registration,
"Mixed"

Fear: an emotion, ofttimes real, sometimes imagined, causing muscular contractions which interfere with the vocal process. Among the fears most frequently encountered are those of expansive movement, the revelation of inner feelings without inhibition, and sometimes, success. Muscular interference caused by anxiety constitutes the single greatest impediment to the learning process.

See Anxiety
Emotion

Feigned Voice: Italian, *voce di finte;* an archaic term used to describe a falsetto-derived tonal quality representing a juncture between the two register mechanisms, the chest voice and the falsetto.

The precise meaning of the feigned voice is obscure, but during the seventeenth and eighteenth centuries it was doubtless considered to be virtually synonymous with the falsetto. Domenico Corri (1746—1825), a pupil of Porpora, was one of many who used these terms interchangeably, describing the tonal area directly above the chest register as "feigned or falsetto." Isaac Nathan (1791—1864), the only writer to define the feigned voice, used this term within a different context; he observed that in addition to the chest register, the falsetto and the head voice

> There is a fourth kind of voice, which is but little appreciated, consequently rarely cultivated—and since I cannot trace any sponsors, either among the Italian, or English, who have given a name to this peculiar style, I shall call it the *feigned.* I am aware that the falsetto is considered a feigned voice; and certainly that voice must be feigned which is produced by artificial constraint, and that does not consequently seem to come forth naturally from the chest; but the quality of sound that

FEIGNED VOICE

[47]Isaac Nathan, *Musurgia Vocalis*(London:Fentum, 1836), p. 117.

I allude to is not that which is produced in the throat, and already distinguished under the name *falsetto;* nor is it the *voce di testa.* It is a sweet and soft melodious sound wafted from afar, like unto the magic spell of an echo.[47]

That this vocal effect was considered by Nathan to be important to the joining of the two register mechanisms is evident from the following account:

> There is a break, more or less, in the voices of both sexes, but more particularly in that of the male, between the *Voce di petto* and *falsetto:* that precise part of the vocal organ where the *Voce di petto* forms this juncture with the *falsetto* is by the Italians called *Il Ponticello,* "the little bridge:" and singers who can with safety carry this *Voce di petto* over this little bridge may truly sing its praises. It should here be an object with the Singer to contrive to blend the two qualities of tone, at their juncture, in such a manner that the transition from one to the other may not be perceptible to the ear. This cannot be accomplished without the aid of the feigned voice, which may be justly considered the only medium or vehicle by which the *falsetto* can be carried into the *Voce di petto.*

> Should my observations on the feigned voice appear obscure, and the Tyro find any difficulty in effecting its practice, or in distinguishing it from the *falsetto,* which is not improbable from the seeming affinity the two sounds bear to each other; he may at once satisfy every doubt upon that point by exercising his *falsetto* on the different Vowels, in which attempt he will discover it to be physically impossible to articulate the Italian broad *a,* but the *feigned* Voice will against all resistance instinctively become the vehicle of its intonation—at this crisis the two qualities of tone must instantly be detected. Hence it is evident that the *falsetto* is entirely governed by the contracted aperture of the mouth, the formation of which having no influence whatever in the production of the *feigned* voice: the intonation of the former is chiefly produced in the small cell or cavity above the arch of the mouth, called the *internal nose;* and the latter is formed at the back part of the head and throat, just above the glottis, where the uvula is situated. *The Veil of the palate* becomes elevated, which obstructs the sound from traversing the nasal passages, and is consequently compelled to pass direct and pure through the mouth.

See Bel Canto
      Covering,
        (To) Cover
      Falsetto
      Falsetto or
        Head Voice
      Middle Register
      Modern Methods
      Register

[48]Isaac Nathan, *Musurgia Vocalis* (London: Fentum, 1836), pp. 144–145.

> The Tyro having thus far satisfied his ear in distinguishing the *feigned* voice from the *falsetto,* should endeavour to blend those two qualities of tone by commencing with his *falsetto* upon any given sound, and whilst in the act of prolonging that sound, change the vowel without taking breath. This will decidedly effect the desired union; which having been accomplished, the next object must be that of uniting the *feigned* voice with the *Voce di petto.*

> Let every note be begun in the feigned voice as softly as possible, by swelling gently, and immediately returning to the first piano: as the voice increases in power and quality let the swell be increased, yet with caution; the slightest irregularity or roughness being a sign that the singer has exceeded the development of which his organ is-as yet capable. Any unsteadiness or tremor of voice is to be remedied by taking the note *softer;* a contrary course only serving to increase and confirm the defect.[48]

The employment of those techniques associated with the development of the feigned voice undoubtedly helped account for the incredible facility of those trained in the Bel Canto tradition.

File la Voce: Italian *filare*, "to spin;" to decrescendo to *pianissimo;* to "spin out" the voice.

Fixed Pitch Theory: a pedagogic theory based upon the premise that a resonance cavity or cavities, when incited to vibrate, yield not only their own natural frequency but also those of the harmonic overtones or partials in tune with them; the so-called "formant theory."

The fixed pitch theory largely explains vowel production, since on the basis of this theory, the acoustic properties of a cavity can be awakened regardless of the fundamental.

See **Relative Pitch Theory**
Resonance
Vowel

Flageolet Register: a term used to describe the flute-like tonal quality characteristic of the uppermost extension of lighter female voice types; the so-called "flute-voice" or altissimo.

Strictly speaking, the "flageolet register" is not a register at all, but merely an undeveloped tonal quality produced by a segmenting of the vocal folds which takes place above high C. Because the membranous margins of the vocal folds perform vertical vibrations without a horizontal component, this segmenting action reduces the number of upper partials in the harmonic spectra of the tonal product to yield the "floating," "disembodied" tonal characteristics commonly associated with this type of tone production.

See **Falsetto**
Register
Segment

Flanks: a complex of respiratory musculature which consists of the lower intercostal muscles, the origins of the diaphragm at the lower thoracic wall, the muscles of the lower back, and those of the upper abdominal wall.

See **Respiratory Scaffolding**

Flat Singing: phonation that is consistently under pitch.

"Flat" singing generally results from an imbalanced registration and other technical faults, rarely because of a hearing deficiency. The cure resides with a change in vocal method.

See **Hearing**
Pitch
Register

Flexibility: agility in moving from one pitch to another.

Throughout the history of singing, vocal flexibility has been one of the ultimate objectives of vocal study. Of itself, however, a flexible voice is not necessarily indicative of vocal health. Any voice that is head register-dominated will in all likelihood be flexible, but optimum flexibility without loss of pitch definition can only be achieved after the muscle systems involved in the production of vocal tone are precisely coordinated and free of constricting tensions. If the voice is not to "flutter" through scale passages it must possess a vibrato, and a true vibrato depends upon a free vocal technique. Since a vibrato is the consequence of a free vocal technique and not its cause, flexibility is not one of the primary objectives of vocal training.

See **Register**
Resonance
Tremolo
Vibrato

Floating Tone: a vocalized sound which creates the impression of disembodiment and/or self-vibratility.

Since vocal tone is merely the product of moving air particles, and since air particles do not "float," the impression that the tone "floats" is an acoustic illusion.

Pedagogic attempts to encourage the production of "floating" or "spinning" tones through aesthetic concepts or imagery, without the inclusion of valid mechanical principles, are bound to fail of their purpose.

See **Register**
Resonance

123

Flute-Voice: See Flageolet Register.

See **Tremolo**
  Vibrato

Flutter: a tremulous tonal movement that results from nervousness, throat constriction and/or a "mixed" registration.

Focused Tone: a vocalized sound whose clear, vibrant, well-defined tonal characteristics, vowel purity and apparent ease of production result from a precisely tuned resonance adjustment.

Since vocal tone is conveyed by sound waves that emanate from the tonal source polydirectionally, it is impossible for a singer to consciously "place," direct, or "focus" vocal tone, and attempts to do so are usually made at the expense of functional mechanics.

Functionally, a "focused" tone is analogous to a photograph that is considered to be in focus: both are products—not causes—of a precise mechanical adjustment.

See **Breath Control**
  Placement
  Resonance
    Adjustment
  Standing Wave

Just as in order to produce a clear, well-defined picture, the photographer must learn to adjust the interior mechanism of his camera to accommodate such changing factors as light, distance, and his mental impression of the object being photographed, so the singer must learn to allow the interior processes of his vocal organs to adjust to changing conditions of pitch, intensity, vowel, and musical concept. Only in this manner can a singer learn to have a "well-focused" voice.

(To) Force: the use of excessive energy to compensate for an absence of muscular equilibrium within the vocal tract; to "push."

Although tonal forcing often results from tensions brought on by anxiety, poor technique, misconceptions and imprecise physical coordination, it is both detectable and correctable because of its effect upon the vocal folds and their associated musculatures. Technically, forcing occurs when the focal folds adjust to the wrong length and thickness for the pitch-intensity pattern being sung, a condition which deprives them of their natural elasticity. This, in turn, disturbs the resonance adjustment, making it impossible for the pharyngeal cavities (the laryngo- and oropharynges) and the suspensory muscles which stabilize the larynx to function properly. Consequently, since the mechanism is not in a state of balanced tension, lost energy must be replaced by an excessive use of force.

See **Coordination**
  Ease of Production
  Energy
  Equilibrium
  Kinesthesia
  Kinetic Energy
  Register
  Resonance
  Vocal Study

It has been frequently suggested that forcing can be eliminated by reducing the amount of energy applied, a misconception based upon the relaxation fallacy. While easing off may sometimes prove a useful preliminary step, the real cure for forcing lies elsewhere. Since energy dissipation and forcing are caused by muscular interference within the laryngeal pharynx, this problem cannot be solved by withholding energy, but by redirecting it.

When, through training, the coordinative process yielding vocal tone has been brought into equilibrium, it is impossible to force—regardless of the intensity being sung or the amount of energy being expended.

Forced Vibration: vibratory impulses which move in the period of an applied force rather than the natural frequency of the vibrator or medium.

In musical instruments, there are two types of forced vibration: 1) that in which a vibrator is forced to tune to the frequency of a vibrating column of air (*e.g.*, reed instruments), and 2) that in which a solid body (*e.g.,* a violin or piano) is forced to vibrate at the natural frequency of external or internal strings. With forced vibration the element of duration, as in maintained vibration, depends upon the application of an external or supplemental source of energy for its continuance.

Forced vibration becomes a factor in tone production when "covering" (usually in the area of the register "break," where tones often sound "too open") is a technical necessity. It is by means of this device that the vocal folds are literally forced into an adjustment they would not assume naturally because of an absence of precise coordination between the arytenoid and cricothyroid muscle systems which draw them into tension. Thus, in covering, the air column shaped by the pharyngeal cavities forces the vibrator to tune to the natural frequency of the resonating system.

Forced vibration of the second category is responsible for those sensations of vibration often experienced during phonation in the chest and head, as well as for those symptoms perceived as nasal "resonance." These symptoms are commonly mistaken to be a product of cavity resonance, but in reality they are merely vibrations transmitted through the skeletal framework by means of bone conduction, the strength of the symptoms being dependent upon the amount of energy generated within the laryngeal pharynx.

See Bel Canto
Covering,
(To) Cover
Formants
Modern Methods
Register
Resonance
Standing Wave
Vowel
Vowel Modification

Formants: a resonance cavity or a series of cavities which, when incited to vibrate, energize the harmonic partials or overtones to which they are tuned; the band of frequencies energized by such cavities; also known as "resonances."

There are two types of formants: 1) clustered, so named because the first two frequency bands are close together, a "tuning" which infuses the tone quality with mellowness and depth, and 2) separated, where the first and second formants are widely spaced, a distribution of energy which imparts brilliance and "ring" to the tone quality. The so-called "closed" vowels are associated with clustered formants; "open" vowels are associated with those that are separated. In adult males, the first formant ranges between 250—700 cps and the second between 700—2500 cps; 2800 cps and above is the range for the upper frequencies. Formant frequencies are somewhat higher for women than men, and still higher for children.

According to Johan Sundberg, changes in the physical dimensions of the vocal tract alter the formant frequency (a longer tract equates with a lower frequency, a shorter column with higher), its upward or downward movement depending upon where the cross section of the standing wave undergoes a change.[49] It is for this reason that various vowel sounds can be "colored," or modified, and made "darker" or "brighter." Thus, formants are strengthened or weakened because of the type of adjustments occurring within the vocal tract, *i.e.,* a lowering or raising of the larynx and soft palate, a broadening or narrowing of the pharyngeal isthmus, a forward tilting or retraction of the thyroid cartilage, and, marginally, the position assumed by the articulators.

It is due to the ability of the vocal resonators (the laryngo-, oro-, and nasopharynges) to selectively reinforce certain groups of partials (formants) that specific tonal characteristics recognized as vowel, timbre, resonance, *etc.,* owe their being.

It has been agreed among scientists that higher formants are resonated within the laryngeal area, and those which are lower within the oropharynx. When the

[49]Johan Sundberg, "Acoustics of the Singing Voice," *Scientific American* (March, 1977), 82–85.

resonators are properly "tuned" as they adjust in response to both tonal concepts and the vowel, the appropriate formant regions will be strongly energized, and the tone may be said to be well produced.

Considerable stress is currently being placed by investigators on what is known as the "singer's formant" (strongly energized frequencies ranging from 2500—3400 cps, regardless of the pitch, vowel, or dynamic level being sung), but these investigators seem to have little regard for the physical processes mentioned above to which the formants owe their being. Pharyngeal cavity adjustments made in response to the vowel, for example, can vary remarkably, ranging anywhere from open-throated to constricted, well-coupled to badly coupled. Sundberg was quick to point this out, noting that any constriction or expansion within the vocal tract affects the standing wave, and consequently lowers or raises the frequencies, an event which has a correlative effect upon both the pitch and the amount of energy used. It is the singer's physical skill in shaping the pharyngeal cavities in response to a tonal concept that is responsible for successfully energizing the desired formants. Thus, the amount of formant energy developed during phonation represents the product rather than the cause of the physical adjustments taking place.

The strength with which the formant frequencies are energized is not limited to cavity formation, but also depends upon two additional factors: 1) the physical dimension of the vocal folds in relation to the pitch, intensity and vowel pattern being phonated, and 2) the quality of the neurological stimulation.

In the first instance, vocal fold activity is determined by the quality of the registration, *i.e.,* shared tension between the cricothyroid and arytenoid muscle systems that results in their being either imbalanced in a variety of ways or well coordinated. Since an imbalanced registration upsets the equilibrium essential to a proper laryngeal suspension, to adjust the pharyngeal cavities precisely when the vocal folds are poorly innervated is clearly impossible. Registration profoundly influences pharyngeal cavity formation, and consequently is a key factor in determining the strength with which formant frequencies are energized.

Just as it is commonly recognized that the tensing of the vocal folds yields qualities known as "registers," and that these spring into being in response to specifically arranged patterns of pitch and intensity, it is also evident that their physical conformation is correspondingly influenced by pharyngeal cavity adjustments made in response to the vowel. This interrelationship has been demonstrated by the French scientist J. Tarneaud, who observed that the dimensions of the folds, if the pitch-intensity pattern remains constant, will vary with changing vowel patterns (cavity adjustment). He further noted that they are longer and thinner in "covered" singing, and thicker and somewhat shorter in an "open" tone production.[50]

The conclusions of Tarneaud point out other parallels many teachers of singing recognize to exist, and it is evident that the physical dimensions of the vocal folds not only correlate with "covered" and "open" singing techniques, but also with 1) open vowels, chest register-dominated tones, and a more open mouth position, and 2) closed vowels, head register-dominated tone qualities, and a relatively closed mouth position. While a precisely tuned pharyngeal cavity coupling can resonate all vowels (except for the highest pitch range of the female voice) without relying upon specifically prepared jaw, tongue and mouth positions when the registers are

[50] J. Tarneaud, "Du rôle fondamental du larynx dans la différenciation du timbre des voyelles," *Comptes Rendus* (1941), 212, 286.

well developed and properly integrated, this is impossible when they are not. Should the chest register be pushed beyond its legitimate boundary (E to F# above middle C), to cite one possibility out of many, the tone quality tends to become "too open," "shouty," or, as is particularly true with the upper tonal range of women's voices, "spread." This results in underenergized and shifting formants.

Formants may thus be seen to reflect the influence of a particular balance of registration. Whereas cavity adjustments have to do with vowel quality and the resonance properties of the tone, *i.e.*, determining whether the production will be open-throated or constricted, registration has to do with other tonal properties, including texture ("heady," "soft," "chesty," "robust"), intensity, and flexibility of movement. Of the two, it would appear that the precision with which the vocal folds position themselves is more important, since any imbalance would disturb the natural equilibrium of the suspensory muscles which stabilize the larynx, and such an imbalance would adversely affect the pharyngeal resonators. The enlarged physical dimensions of the vocal folds which prevail when the chest voice is overly dominant in its upper extension causes the larynx to rise and the throat to constrict, a condition which alters the cavity adjustment responsible for selecting and energizing the proper formants.

It is a faulty adjustment of the vocal folds in relation to the pitch-intensity pattern being sung (registration) which has led to the popular remedy known as "covering." In covering, the vowel is deliberately changed from *ah* to *oh*; this device is commonly resorted to when approaching the "break" area. The result of this practice is to readjust the resonators (the laryngo- and oropharyngeal cavities) so that they dominate the vibrator, forcing the vocal folds to change their length and thickness. This is a technical compromise (useful at certain stages of development) to avoid the "too open" tone qualities caused by an overly aggressive chest voice. Covering energizes the low formants, and by setting up a condition where the vocal folds must become longer and thinner, helps increase the participation of the head voice (provided this mechanism is developed and ready for use), a procedure which correspondingly minimizes the activity of the chest voice. The modification of vowel and tone quality that results is expressed acoustically by the manner in which energy is distributed over the harmonic spectrum.

Under ideal technical conditions, modifications of this description are unnecessary, since in a well-balanced registration all tones, regardless of the vowel, pitch, or intensity level being sung, will be nicely "rounded" without recourse to artificial manipulation. Electroacoustic investigations carried out by Gemelli, Sacerdote, and Bellussi (1954) lend support to this view.[51] Their studies indicate that both open and covered singing are aspects of tone color, and that neither technique is desirable when permanent. They further proved, as might be expected, that when both extremes of "production" are avoided, the higher harmonics are more evenly distributed throughout the vocal range.

The quality of the neurological stimulation stemming from concepts related to quality and resonance further influences the formant structure. Inasmuch as the vocal mechanism is innervated by will power, the clarity or opaqueness of the concepts formed is of paramount importance to a proper stimulation of the vocal mechanism. The difference between what the singer wills to happen and what actually transpires, however, usually reveals a conflict between an aesthetic ob-

[51]A. Gemelli, G. Sacerdote and G. Bellussi, "Analisi Electroacoustica della Voce Cantata," *Bollettino della Società Italiana di Fonetica sperimentale, Fonetica biologica, Foniatria, Audiologia* 4 (1954), 3, 4. Translated by Godfrey E. Arnold, M.D. and Evelyn Robe Rinkbeiner, Ph.D. and cited by Luchsinger and Arnold, *Voice-Speech-Language* (Belmont, California: Wadsworth Publishing Co., Inc., 1965), p. 105.

jective and one's technical capability for realizing that objective. Since each tends to be conditioned by the other, the effect upon the formant structure of the tone produced is far-reaching. A proper reconciliation of concepts in order to promote technical improvement and energize the formant structure efficiently is an intangible process. Since the tones produced by the singer are a reflection of function, functional concerns, *i.e.*, registration and adjustment for resonance, supersede all others.

Two possible avenues of approach can be taken in order to energize a given formant structure. The one, advocated by Sundberg and shared by a majority of voice teachers, is based upon the supposition that effective control over formants can be obtained by positioning the jaw and the blade and tip of the tongue, by setting mouth positions, and by lip-rounding. This viewpoint implies that muscular activities within the laryngeal area can be governed and determined by a programmed behavior of peripheral parts. Lip trills and tongue exercises, however, do not relax, loosen, or open the throat, nor do they have any positive effect on the physical coordination of those involuntary muscles lying within the throat parts that are essential to phonation. Furthermore, if, when articulating the "Tra, la, la la" 's from Thomas Morley's *My Bonnie Lass*, for example, the formants and the standing wave were to be dependent upon the position of the blade and the tip of the tongue, as Sundberg suggests, both the articulation and the tone production would be interfered with to such a degree as to nullify their effectiveness.

The second alternative moves in a contrary direction and deals with the problem at its source—innervation of the muscle systems involved in adjusting the vocal folds and the pharyngeal resonators. When these have been properly stimulated, the jaw, tongue and lip positions will accommodate themselves to the needs of the tonal form.

There is, of course, some correspondence between the articulators and the tone produced. It cannot be assumed, however, that because the posterior portion of the tongue rises when producing an *ee* vowel and flattens for an *ah* that these adjustments, once made, necessarily ensure a correct coordination within the throat parts, *i.e.*, that the registers will be well balanced and the pharyngeal cavities finely tuned and free of constricting tensions. If arbitrarily selected jaw, tongue and lip positions (which can be assumed volitionally) would energize the formants properly and eliminate vocal faults, pedagogic problems would be vastly simplified. Since these volitional acts can be mastered very quickly by anyone possessed of average talent and intelligence, it is obvious that a correct positioning of the articulators is not a crucial factor in promoting technical proficiency. The development of vocal skills goes far beyond such simple remedies; from a pragmatic point of view, arbitrary positionings of the articulators should be discarded in favor of more important functional interests.

From the standpoint of practical pedagogy, until such time as the concepts, the physical coordination as it affects cavity coupling and adjustments for resonance together with a well-developed and properly balanced registration, are in effect vitalization of the desired formant structure will remain an analytical gauge of technical efficiency, or a description of what happens during phonation, rather than an important adjunct to the creative process.

By locating the source of resonance and establishing an acoustic basis to accoun for vowel quality, the formant theory has made it possible to rescue vocal pedagogy from the mythology which has dominated it for so long a time. The formant theory has conclusively proved that 1) vowels are both resonated and defined because of the shape of the pharyngeal cavities and because of the physical dimensions of the vocal folds, and 2) neither the primary nor the secondary resonator of vocal tone is located in the nasal passages or in the facial mask, as is commonly believed.

If the principles upon which a revised pedagogy is founded are to serve a constructive purpose, they must include techniques for stimulating an involuntary laryngeal muscular system into improved patterns of response as it moves from relaxation to a state of balanced tension. As a result of such procedures, the articulatory processes, freed of imposed disciplines, will assume positions dictated by laryngeal functioning. When encouraged to react spontaneously to properly selected stimuli, *i.e.,* vocal exercises, all of the muscle systems involved in the phonative process will adjust reflexively in a manner consonant with their natural movement potential.

Forward Placement: See Placement.

Forward Tone: a term used to describe a vocalized sound that creates the impression and/or sensation of being resonated in the area of the facial mask, or at the lips or teeth.

The concept of a "foward" tone evolved during the latter part of the nineteenth century, when pedagogic interest began to center on those symptoms which appeared to be associated with resonance, as opposed to traditional formulations based upon registration. The result of this shift in emphasis was to make the symptoms of vibration (aroused by a particular register balance, formerly recognized as "head" voice) a direct object of study. Since in a "head" voice-dominated technique the tone *appears* to be forward, it was assumed that by encouraging this symptom through proper "placement," the throat would be freed of constricting tensions and the mechanism would function more efficiently.

There are serious flaws in this reasoning: 1) it is impossible to evoke a symptom without first having established the conditions which arouse that symptom; 2) the muscle systems responsible for the qualities recognized as "head" voice or "forward" tones meet with the lower constrictors, and consequently tend to increase rather than decrease those constricting tensions which make the tone appear to be "too far back," and 3) these sensations are not the product of resonance in the sinuses, antra, or nasal passages, but of bone conduction, by means of which viratory impulses are radiated from the tonal source, the laryngeal pharynx.

As Manuel Garcia once observed, "the real mouth of the singer ought to be considered the pharynx,"[52] and it is within this area—more specifically within the laryngo- and oropharynges—that all resonation of vocal tone occurs.

Fossa: a depression or small cavity; either of the two nasal fossae or cavities.

Fourier's Theorem: a theory advanced by the French scientist Jean Baptiste Joseph Fourier in 1822 that established a formula for analyzing the qualitative aspects of vocal tone in terms of harmonics.

See Bel Canto
Bernoulli Effect
Coupling
Energy
Fixed Pitch Theory
Helmholtz
Lip Trill
Modern Methods
Register
Relative Pitch Theory
Resonance
Standing Wave
Vowel Formant
Vowel Manipulation
Vowel Modification

See Bel Canto
Dans la Masque
Kinesthesia
Modern Methods
Nasality
Placement
Resonance
Sensations of Vibration
Sinus Tone Production

[52]Manuel Garcia, *Hints on Singing*, translated by Beata Garcia (New York: Edward Schuberth & Co., 1894), p. 12.

FRAGMENTATION

According to Fourier, each complex sound wave, whether it is produced by a voice or by another instrument, is comprised of a series of pure (sine) waves, and each fundamental frequency includes harmonic partials or overtones that are integral multiples of the fundamental. Therefore, according to Fourier, each musical tone has a distinctive acoustic representation.

Fourier's theorem, along with the findings of Helmholtz, laid the foundation for the science of sound. The usefulness of Fourier's theorem to vocal pedagogy, as well as other more recent studies in the fields of acoustics, physiology and anatomy, would appear to be limited. This is because the movement of air molecules heard as "voice" is physically due to the activity of muscles. Thus, the analysis of vocal tone, while it may comment on the quality of that activity, cannot change it.

An understanding of Fourier's theorem, like other bodies of scientific knowledge, may promote better theorizing, but it is relatively unimportant to the creative experience faced in practical pedagogy.

Fragmentation: a division of the whole into parts; a state of disunity.

There are several types of vocal fragmentation: 1) that which takes place as the vocal folds are drawn into tension by the contraction of those muscle systems with which they are affiliated to produce tone qualities commonly recognized as "registers;" 2) "breaks" which occur because of vocal abuse, and which usually appear on pitches other than those normally associated with proper vocal fold segmentation, and 3) those abrupt stoppages which interrupt tonal continuity because of constricting tensions brought on by anxiety. Types two and three are both physically and psychologically complex, and unless treated with skill and patience, they do not easily lend themselves to correction. Contrarily, vocal fragmentation attributable to register imbalances is a normal technical condition indicative of vocal health.

Despite the contention of many that a fragmented voice is one that is being improperly used, this judgment is difficult to justify. Many of the world's greatest vocalists, especially those capable of undertaking dramatic roles, do not have a seamless tone production, and while their technique may not be flawless their merits certainly outweigh their faults. It is no coincidence, however, that the high levels of intensity required to cut through a heavy orchestration tend to separate the voice into two parts and to leave a weakened area, or "hole," between them. The means of correction of this problem before the twentieth century (when the principles governing registration were both understood and practiced) was to control the "break" area and smooth the *passaggio* by lowering the intensity of the upper tones of the chest voice, and, through the practice of the *messa di voce*, to strengthen the lower tones of the weakened mechanism (the falsetto, or head voice) until the scale became equalized. Without this and similar options, voices so fragmented will, it is true, fall into disrepair.

A slight fragmentation of the voice, or division of the registers, is desirable for all but the most advanced levels of technical training, since once these "mechanisms" have been completely integrated, further development is impossible.

Free Throat: a condition which exists when the vocal mechanism, whether by nature or through training, is unencumbered by constricting tensions.

To sing with a "free throat," the muscle systems engaged in phonation must be

See Bel Canto
   Falsetto or
     Head Voice
   Messa di Voce
   Modern Methods
   (A) Seamless Voice

so stimulated that they move naturally and spontaneously. A successful training program, therefore, is one which addresses itself to this phase of the vocal problem, since all peripheral tensions involving the tongue and jaw which result in tonal unsteadiness and breath loss will be eliminated once the interior muscular processes function in conformity with their natural movement potential.

In contemporary methodology, the acquisition of a free-throated tone production is founded upon procedures which seek to remove vocal faults by "placing" the voice properly, by "supporting" the voice with the breath, and/or by relaxation. None of these manipulative devices, however, relieves wrong tension at the tonal source (the laryngeal pharynx), or helps develop and bring into balanced tension the muscular systems which generate vocal tone and determine its qualitative properties. Unless principles are applied which effectively restore lost motility to an exceedingly complex involuntary muscular system, the possibility of freeing the throat parts of restricting tensions is remote.

See Bel Canto
    Breath
      Management
    Laryngeal
      Suspension
    Modern Methods
    Natural Movement
    Open Throat
    Register
    Resonance
    Vowel

Free Vibration: an oscillating movement that continues after all applied energy has been removed; the orderly movement of air particles that continues in the natural period or frequency of the vibrator, or energy source, until the initial vibratory impulse has been dissipated.

A visual analog of the movement of air particles that occurs during free vibration is the movement of a free-swinging pendulum.

See Forced Vibration
    Maintained
      Vibration
    Resonance
    Standing Wave

French Nasal: any of a series of vowel phonemes represented in written French by a vowel and a concluding nasal consonant (*e.g.,* *m* or *n*) which is silent (*i.e.,* unvoiced).

With rare exceptions, the techniques employed in the sounding of French nasals attempt to direct and concentrate tonal energy into the facial mask, *i.e.,* the sinuses, antra, and the nasal passages. Since, however, this procedure constricts the adjacent pharyngeal muscles, the tone quality becomes "pinched," "white" and somewhat "pointed." The resultant nasality accounts for the generally inferior voice quality of those who have adopted this method and carried it to its logical conclusion. Fortunately, there is an alternative, nasality being easily avoided by instituting procedures which utilize the larynx (the source of tonal "ring") as a resonator, while at the same time "tuning" the oropharynx to energize those frequencies known to define and resonate the vowel. French nasals produced in this manner result in superior tone qualities, a healthier tone production and a more correct French pronunciation.

See Nasality
    Resonance
    Vowel
    Twenty-Eight
      Hundred

Frequency: the number of complete cycles that a vibrator (a string, membrane, the vocal folds, or some other sound source) traces within a time unit of one second.

The basic unit of measurement used to determine frequency is called a period, or a single vibration consisting of one complete compression and rarefaction cycle. These cycles, or pressure pulses, which periodically disturb the air particles surrounding the sound source, are perceived as pitch. Higher pitches equate with higher frequencies.

Acoustically, each frequency or pitch generated by a sound source is called a fundamental. According to the law of vibrating strings or membranes, the oscillations produced by a vibrator also produce harmonics or overtones that are integral multiples of the fundamental frequency. Thus, a string or membrane not only vibrates along its full length, but divides into segments of halves, thirds, fourths, fifths, *etc.* The manner in which the fundamental and its overtones are arranged determines the qualitative properties of the ultimate tonal product.

The range of frequencies perceivable by those with above average hearing is generally considered to extend from 16 to 20,000 cycles per second. Few of the frequencies lying above 9,000 cycles per second are influential in determining vocal tone quality.

Frequency Band: an area of frequencies or overtones energized to the exclusion of other areas of potential vibration, and perceived by the listener as a particular vowel quality or timbre.

In singing, the vocal mechanism is intuitively adjusted so that certain frequency bands are selected and energized at the expense of others. The skill with which these adjustments are made, either consciously or subconsciously, determines both the purity of the vowel and its resonance characteristics.

Science has proved that a well-produced voice will have energy concentrated in only two or three frequency bands, whereas one less well produced will spread the same amount of tonal energy over a much wider spectrum, resulting in tonal products that are diffused or "unfocused."

Fricative: See Affricates.

Frontal Sinus: either of the two sinus cavities located in the forehead.

Fry Voice: See Vocal Fry.

Full-Throated Tone: a well-resonated vocalized sound that results from a well balanced registration, a precisely adjusted laryngeal position, and an absence of constrictor tensions.

Full Voice: *forte* singing which utilizes the resources of the vocal mechanism to the fullest extent, regardless of its technical condition.

Although full-voiced singing is synonymous in certain respects to "loud" singing it is qualitatively different, the latter being acoustically diffused and the product of poor laryngeal muscular coordination. Loud singing is synonymous with "forcing."

Full voice is also used on occasion to distinguish a legitimate tone production from that described as "half voice."

Function: the natural action characteristic of a mechanical or organic system.

Within a vocal context, function is suitably described as natural or unnatural, healthy or unhealthy, well-coordinated or awkward, blocked or free. Inasmuch as the vocal folds and the laryngeal muscles must be positioned during phonation to meet specific tonal requirements, how these muscles adjust (function) is of paramount importance if the voice is to be well produced and free of muscular interference.

Function and technique are synonymous, the qualitative properties of the one equating with the efficiency of the other.

See Aesthetics

Functional Hearing: aural perception in which the listener is pleased by vocalized sounds that are well produced and displeased by those which suffer from varying degrees of dysfunction.

Functional hearing is the medium by which most listeners evaluate vocal performance, and is a perception based upon aural impressions and empathetic reactions. The level at which each individual identifies with these impressions is determined by natural aptitude, psychological predisposition and training.

Except for a general feeling of pleasure or displeasure with respect to tone quality, aural impressions perceived by most listeners are not subjected to analysis until some type of tonal unsteadiness commands the attention. Without knowing "why" this unsteadiness is offensive, the listener perceives that something is amiss. Although this level of perception is somewhat elemental, it is nevertheless an important aspect of functional hearing.

Scientific data has revealed the essential differences between aesthetically acceptable oscillating movements and those that are objectionable, establishing that in an ideal technique the periodicity is relatively fixed for all pitches (occurring about 6.0 to 6.8 cps), whereas the amplitude will consistently vary and correlate with changes of pitch and intensity. Fluctuations natural to the vibrato (as this type of movement is called) are not perceived as such by the listener, but heard as a "centered" pitch of clear, vibrant, beautiful tone quality.

Oscillograph tracings of tonal movements have supplied information which explains the nature of these movements. When, it has been shown, a correctly produced high tone is sung *forte* and the tone appears to be steady and without perceptible movement, it is in fact oscillating almost a half step in pitch. The same amplitude and level of intensity sung on a pitch an octave lower, however, is obtrusive and becomes aesthetically objectionable. Similarly, the oscillating movement that was agreeable when the high tone was sung *forte* becomes disagreeable when the intensity is reduced to *mezzo forte,* and extremely unpleasant when it is further reduced to *piano.*

A negative reaction to tonal movement develops, therefore, when these oscillations depart from an established norm and move erratically. When the periodicity is either irregular or too rapid, and the oscillations fail to increase and decrease in proportion to increases and decreases in intensity, the quality is immediately perceived as being tremulous, wobbly, or the result of what is often inaccurately described as an "excessive" vibrato. Since these faults are associated with a severely unbalanced registration and throat constriction, it is not unusual, when listening to a singer afflicted by these problems, to experience personal discomfort, feeling one's own throat become "tight" empathetically.

On a more sophisticated level, those who have learned to recognize the textural properties contributed to the ultimate tonal product by each of the vocal registers will be quick to estimate its physical condition (as does the skilled mechanic, who, by listening to a motor, is able to detect the source of the problem); because they have the tools at their disposal which will stimulate an involuntary laryngeal muscular system into improved patterns of response, they can remedy the fault.

FUNCTIONAL LISTENING

Of singular interest in all of these examples is the intimate relationship that exists between perception, function and aesthetics. All those sensitive to vocal sound, although listening on different levels, nevertheless identify empathetically with the singer and "hear" muscular imbalances as part of a broad listening experience. For the teacher of singing, functional hearing, combined with a knowledge of functional principles, is indispensable to a successful resolution of vocal problems and must be brought to the highest degree of refinement.

Functional Listening: aural perception in which the listener evaluates tonal qualities for their intrinsic health and as a reflection of a coordinative muscular process rather than for their aesthetic value.

Not all healthy sounds yielded by the vocal organs are agreeable, nor are all agreeable sounds healthy. In many instances, in fact, aesthetic judgment limits progress, since some vocal qualities having little or no aesthetic value can be extremely useful when reconditioning poorly conditioned reflexes. Two such cases in point are the rather crude chest register sounds often produced by females in early stages of development, and the male falsetto. Neither sound possesses aesthetic properties, but both are extremely important to the restructuring process.

The abilities to hear functionally and to empathize with a singer are indispensable attributes for the teacher of singing.

Functional Logic: the "sense" possessed by muscles and organs regarding their own natural movement potentials.

There is a natural and economical way for muscles to respond and adjust during phonation, just as there are many ways that are unnatural and inefficient. The muscles "know" this and protest through visible and audible symptoms when wrongly stimulated. Some of these visible symptoms include facial grimaces, tongue and jaw tremolos, a shaking of the body, shortness of breath, and premature fatigue. Audible symptoms include erratic tonal movements (tremolos, wobbles, and other forms of tonal unsteadiness), "pinched" and constricted tonal qualities, out-of-tune singing, shrillness, distorted vowels, *etc.* All these symptoms of abuse spontaneously disappear when the vocal muscles have been encouraged to respond in accordance with their natural movement potential.

The cure for these symptoms is not to be found in such currently popular remedies as relaxation exercises, advice to sing easily, nasal resonance, or special techniques of breathing and breath "control," but by redirecting energy into the muscular systems that yield vocal tone in such a way that they respond more efficiently (*i.e.,* in a manner that is more in keeping with their natural movement potential).

A correct technique of singing operates within the framework of natural law and assists the muscular processes involved to respond in keeping with an innate functional logic. When so encouraged, the faulty tensions which inhibit freedom of movement will release themselves, permitting the vocal muscles to respond more correctly.

All natural functioning is logical, and if one is to sing naturally, contact must be made with the functional logic by which the movement potential of the vocal organs is governed.

Fundamental: the lowest frequency of a complex sound wave; the frequency which usually determines that property perceived by the listener as pitch.

Complex tones are comprised of a fundamental tone and numerous harmonic partials or overtones, whose frequencies of vibration are integral multiples of the fundamental. These various frequencies are produced by a string, reed, membrane, *etc.*, capable of vibrating both as a whole and in parts at the same time. For example, when a string is tuned and forced to vibrate at 262 cycles per second (yielding the pitch heard as middle C), it will also divide itself in half, in thirds, in fourths, *etc.*, and produce overtones with frequencies of approximately 524 cps, 786 cps and 1,048 cps, *etc.*

During phonation, the fundamental frequency is determined by the length, tension and mass of the vibrating vocal folds, and by pressure variations created by puffs of air which escape through the glottal space.

See Fixed Pitch Theory
  Formants
  Puff Theory
  Relative Pitch
    Theory
  Resonance
  Standing Wave
  Vowel

Furrowed Tongue: a grooved, "V-shaped" tongue, whose distorted shape is caused by throat constriction.

See Groove of the *oo*

Fuzzy Tone: a vocalized sound whose tonal characteristics are poorly defined.

"Fuzzy" tones result from an imprecise adjustment (tuning) of the pharyngeal resonators, *i.e.*, the laryngo- and the oropharynges, due to a dissipation rather than a concentration of energy within those frequency bands necessary to tonal (vowel) purity.

The presence of fuzzy tone qualities is an indication that the vocal folds are not fully approximated, and in some cases it can indicate the presence of an incipient nodule condition. Fuzzy tones are always a product of poor laryngeal muscular coordination, and consequently reveal an improper vocal technique.

See Cavity Tone Theory
  Focus
  Formants
  Nodule
  Registration,
    "Mixed"
  Vowel
  Vowel Modification

G

Gag Reflex: a natural throat-opening response associated with regurgitation; sometimes used as a pedagogic device.

The gag reflex can be induced by touching the base of the tongue with one's finger to stimulate the initial stages of retching. Since the gag reflex releases throat tension, causing expansive movement, it can be both psychologically and vocally useful.

Garcia: Manuel Garcia (1805—1906), famous teacher of singing and inventor of the laryngoscope.

See **Bel Canto**
Modern Methods
Voix Mixte

Generator: the mechanical processes which, when set in motion, produce those vibratory impulses perceived as "voice."

The larynx, pharyngeal cavities and their associated musculatures serve as the generators of vocal tone; fuel and the resultant combustion is supplied by oxygen intake. The quality of the vibratory impulses produced by the vocal generator is determined by the clarity or opaqueness of concepts, physical coordination, and the vigor of the neurological impulses involved.

See **Breathing**
Energy
Emotion

Genioglossus: muscle fibers which extend from the chin to the hyoid bone and to the side of the pharynx.

The genioglossus muscle fibers are influential in positioning and moving the tongue. Together with the glossoepiglottic folds, which attach the tongue to the epiglottis, these muscles stiffen and move awkwardly whenever constrictor tension is present in the laryngeal area.

Geniohyoglossus: a muscle unit composed of the genio- and hyoglossus muscles, the latter performing as a tongue depressor.

Geniohyoid: a part of the muscular system, attached to the jaw, which pulls the hyoid bone forward.

Gesture: a reflection of thought and feeling expressed as bodily movement. Gestures should be minimized during training in order to heighten awareness of interior, involuntary muscular movements.

Gesture of Inhalation: the sensation of initiating phonation before the inspiratory cycle has been fully completed.

Singing on a gesture of inhalation is designed to 1) circumvent the natural tendency of the trachea (windpipe) to contract on exhalation, and 2) avert the reflexive widening of the glottis, which occurs when either inspiratory or expiratory muscular tension is predominant.

In the first instance, since the muscular and membranous tissue which constricts the windpipe relaxes on inhalation, imagining that phonation begins before the inspiratory cycle has been completed conceivably becomes a psychological aid in reducing throat tension. The purpose of the second is to avoid interference with the approximation of the vocal folds and to assist in the establishment of one of the preconditions essential to their self-vibratility. Singing on a "gesture of inhalation" may therefore be considered a technique for both mentally and physically preparing the vocal folds for phonation.

In addition to the desirable qualities mentioned above, singing on a gesture of inhalation promotes a poised posture, which is both pleasing to the eye and helpful in maintaining a state of equilibrium throughout the entire vocal tract, assuring that all energy directed into the vocal mechanism will be absorbed economically.

The practice of singing on a gesture of inhalation should be reserved for advanced stages of training if attitudes which develop because of "body consciousness" are to be avoided.

See Breathing
  Natural Breathing
  Register
  Self-Regulation
  Singer's Stance

Get It Out of the Throat: a directive based upon the fallacious notion that throat constriction (which creates the impression that the voice is "caught in the throat") can be corrected by "placing" or "directing" the tone away from one part of the mechanism to another deemed more suitable.

The advice to "get it (the voice) out of the throat" runs counter to the laws of acoustics and also overlooks the fact that 1) the vocal mechanism or sound source is situated in the throat, 2) the laryngo- and oropharynges are primary determinants of vowel quality and resonance, and 3) since the throat parts themselves can be either constricted or free-moving, the pedagogic problem is to put into effect those functional principles which, when operative, will replace constrictor tensions with muscular activities that open the throat.

When procedures are instituted which will succeed in stimulating the laryngeal muscular systems to replace wrong tension with movements that are natural and free, a directive such as "get it out of the throat" will be recognized as having no pedagogic value.

See Bel Canto
  Modern Methods
  Natural Movement
  Register
  Sensations of
    Vibration
  Standing Wave

Glide: sounds resulting from the movement, or a gliding, of either the tongue or the lips, or both, during the articulation of consonants. *L, r, w* and *i* are considered glides.

Glottal Action: strictly speaking, not an action at all, since the size and configuration of the glottal space is determined by the length, thickness and general contour of the vocal folds. Acoustically, a disturbance of air particles within the laryngeal area that is set in motion by the vibrating vocal folds.

Glottal Fricative: a syllable or word beginning with *h*. A glottal fricative is sometimes called a glottal aspirate.

Glottal Plosive: See Consonants.

Glottal Pulse: See Vibrato.

Glottal Register: a term sometimes used synonymously with vocal fry. — See Vocal Fry

Glottal Stop: an interruption of vocalized sound by a quick, precise approximation of the vocal folds.

    The glottal stop is used in speech, especially in languages of Teutonic origin, for the following reasons: 1) to separate syllables that end and begin with vowel phonemes (*e.g.*, "the ear"); 2) to prevent ambiguities of meaning (*e.g.*, "some ice" as opposed to "some mice"), and 3) to interrupt tonal flow after a so-called "stopped" consonant (*e.g.*, "football"). — See Consonants / Coup de Glotte

Glottal Stroke: a tonal attack in which the vocal folds are deliberately struck together in order to avoid breathiness.

    The glottal stroke is a dangerous practice which induces throat constriction and is a vocal aberration growing out of a misinterpretation of Garcia's *coup de glotte*. — See Coup de Glotte

Glottal Vibrations: sound waves set in motion by the movement of the vocal folds.

Glottis: a reed-like structure; the air space between the vocal folds.

Grainy Tone: a tonal quality subjectively evaluated as being rough-edged, coarse-textured and impure.

Greater Horn of the Hyoid: the conical-shaped end points of the hyoid bone, connected by means of the thyrohyoid membrane to the thyroid cartilage. The greater horn of the hyoid forms the points of attachment for the hyoglossus and thyrohyoid muscles and the middle constrictor of the pharynx.

Groove of the *oo*: an expression occasionally used to describe the adjustment or "placement" for the production of high tones which finds the blade of the tongue set in a V-shape.

    The purpose of "grooving the *oo*" is to utilize the mouth as a resonator and inculcate a sense of the tone being "brought more forward." Such a setting, however, ignores the fact that vowels are formed, defined and resonated within the pharyngeal cavities, and fails to consider that both "open" and "closed" vowel phonemes require a consistent "tuning" of the larynx to those frequencies in the range of 3,000 cps. Moreover, it makes the desired independence between the tonal form and the free movement of the articulators all but impossible. — See Cavity Tone Theory / Formants / Register / Resonance / Vowel

    Grooving the *oo* does not improve laryngeal functioning, and indeed promotes throat, tongue and jaw stiffness.

Groove of the Tongue: an adjustment of the tongue which makes it furrowed.

The concept of the grooved or furrowed tongue was first introduced by Lilli Lehmann (1848—1929), who proposed that the tip of this member should be positioned against the lower teeth, with the rear portion held high and away from the throat, and then formed into a furrow. She confined this practice to the mid-tonal pitch range, believing it to be unnecessary and even inhibitory elsewhere.

To consider the articulators (the tongue, lips, mouth, jaw, *etc.*) a controlling influence in phonation is a serious misjudgment. The concept is mechanistic and unnatural, and it moves away from concerns related to laryngeal stabilization and pharyngeal cavity formation as they affect resonation of the vowel. In addition, it fails to utilize those functional principles (registration) known to bring the vocal folds into an equitable ratio of tension for the pitch-intensity pattern being sung.

Grooving the tongue, therefore, is a practice which addresses itself to none of the problems of physical coordination mentioned above, and as a device it is more likely to cause tongue stiffness and to increase throat constriction than it is to promote technical improvement. Even the contradictory advice to "relax the tongue" avoids the central issue, since by implication the tongue is already tense and cannot relax until throat tensions have first been released. Exercises involving a protrusion and retraction of the tongue are equally valueless for the same reason, for if there is wrong tension within the pharyngeal cavities, the tongue will stiffen in spite of all efforts to relax it or set its position.

Unless training procedures incorporate principles designed to improve the involuntary muscular processes taking place within the pharynges, no position of the tongue, grooved or flat, will succeed in making a positive contribution to tone production. On the contrary, if the vocal mechanism functions properly at the tonal source, all peripheral concerns affecting the articulators will regulate themselves without conscious effort. Under these conditions the tongue will be flexible and free with or without "grooving."

See Bel Canto
  Laryngeal
    Suspension
  Modern Methods
  Register
  Tongue
  Vocal Study
  Vowel

Guttural Register: a group of tones lying below the pitch range of the chest register proper; that is to say, an octave and a sixth below middle C.

While without aesthetic value, this so-called "growl" register (not really a register at all since there is no separate musculature to account for its presence) can be marginally useful with those who suffer from a chronically raised and constricted larynx, since it cannot be produced unless the body is completely relaxed.

The growl register is similar to what modern scientists refer to as "vocal fry."

See Register
  Vocal Fry

Guttural Tone: a harsh, rough tone quality produced by a stiff laryngeal adjustment and a "mixed" registration.

There is a fundamental difference between having a guttural voice and the production of guttural sounds. Those who possess the former *always* speak or sing gutturally; the latter are capable, as in the case of German pronunciation, of making guttural sounds in a functionally correct manner that is both euphonic and beautiful

H

Habit: a conditioned behavior pattern without appropriate reference to an outer stimulus, ranging from the thoughtless to the compulsive.

The majority of those who study and perform sing incorrectly. Consequently, the learning process is largely one of eliminating bad habits. Central to this process is the replacement of learned responses in favor of learning to respond. In a free vocal technique one does not respond by habit, but in a manner appropriate to the character of the stimulus.

See **Natural Singing**

Half Voice: phonation at low levels of intensity, frequently for artisitic purposes, but often in order to reduce the fatigue factor and "save" the voice.

When singing half voice, or *mezza voce* (Italian, "middle of the voice"), both registers must always be engaged; otherwise the tonal product will lack substance and vitality, and the mechanism will tend to constrict.

See **(To) Mark**
    Register
    (To) Save the Voice

See **Coup de Glotte**
    Onset

Hard Attack: an overly vigorous initiation of vocal tone.

Hard Palate: the bony, anterior part of the roof of the mouth.

See **Standing Wave**

Harmonic: See Harmonic Partial.

Harmonic Partial: a simple component of a complex tone; a tone sounded in conjunction with the sounding of a fundamental tone whose frequency of vibration is an integral multiple of that of the fundamental; a harmonic, overtone, or partial.

See **Frequency**
    Fundamental
    Harmonic
       Spectrum

Harmonic Series: an infinite series of partials or overtones whose frequencies are integral multiples of the first partial or fundamental frequency.

Harmonic Spectrum: the relative intensities of harmonic partials or overtones in relation to the intensity of the fundamental tone; a graph that illustrates this relationship.

Harmonic Theory: a theory of vocal resonance which states that the resonators merely augment harmonics which have already been produced by the vocal vibrator (*i.e.*, the vocal folds).

The harmonic theory was advanced in 1885 by the German physicist Hermann L. F. Helmholtz in his book *On the Sensations of Tone.* Helmholtz' theories were highly influenced by the work of an earlier British physicist, Sir Charles Wheatstone. For this reason, the harmonic theory is sometimes referred to as the "Helmholtz" or "Wheatstone-Helmholtz" theory.

Many pedagogues view the harmonic theory as the direct antithesis of the so-called "puff theory" advanced by the British physicist E. W. Scripture in 1906. Scripture maintained that during phonation the vocal vibrator emits puffs of inspired air that determine pitch and then move on to excite the vocal resonators, which in turn superimpose their own frequencies, both harmonic and inharmonic, onto vocal tone.

Neither of these theories completely explains the complex nature of vocal resonance, although taken conjunctively they provide a reasonable, if oversimplified, explanation of this phenomenon. What these theories do suggest is that the effective resonation of well-defined vowels presupposes the availability of a series of cavities capable of being tuned either separately or together. Since the trachea, the larynx, the pharyngeal cavities and the mouth serve this purpose, it is here that the source of vocal resonance and vowel definition is to be found. It is due to the adjustability of these cavities that the singer is able to produce resonant tones over a wide pitch range.

See Coupling
Energy
Helmholtz
Puff Theory
Resonance

Harsh Voice: one of rough-textured quality, the result of poor coordination among the vocal muscles.

See Bel Canto
Chest Register
Falsetto or
Head Voice
Middle Register

Head Register: a term traditionally, if incorrectly, used synonymously with head voice to denote falsetto-dominated tone qualities.

Strictly speaking, the head register is not a register at all, since there are but two basic register mechanisms, the chest register and the falsetto. The head voice is a falsetto-derived (coordinated) tone quality.

Head Resonance: see Resonance, Head.

Head Voice: tone qualities produced through the coordinate activity of both register mechanisms, the chest register and the falsetto, but with the falsetto strongly dominant; so named because the sensations of vibration evoked as a result of this physical arrangement appear to be concentrated in the head cavities.

The term "head voice" is so commonly thought to be the end result of tonal energy having been concentrated in the facial "mask," a condition of "resonance" achieved by means of tonal "placement," that the functional basis upon which the concept was originally founded has been lost. It is important, therefore, if development of the head voice is to be carried forward and reassociated with a mechanical principle, to trace the origins of this concept.

When voice culture was in its formative stage (circa the fourteenth century), two mechanical functions were recognized. One was the *vox integra* (later to become the *voce di petto,* the natural or chest voice), the other the *vox ficta* (or falsetto). This division of the voice into two parts continued almost to the beginning of the seventeenth century; it was a technical condition which left the voice restricted in range and somewhat limited in expression. Caccini (circa 1546—1618), for example, preferred the *voce di petto* to the falsetto, and it is evident from the music written for the voice during his era that, since range extension was not yet a consideration, the "natural" voice answered the expressive needs of his time.

It was not until the seventeenth century that the functional potential of the vocal organs came to be exploited, at which time it was discovered that by combining these two "mechanisms" the vocal range could be extended, the voice would become more supple and expressive, and the quality characteristics throughout would become clear, vibrant, full-bodied and flexible.

The necessity for blending the *vox integra* and the *vox ficta* was commented upon by Pier Francesco Tosi (1647—1727) as follows:

> A diligent Master, knowing that a soprano, without the falsetto, is constrained to sing within a narrow compass of a few notes, ought not only to endeavor to help him to it, but also to leave no means untried, so to unite the feigned and the natural voice that they may not be distinguished; for if they do not perfectly unite, the voice will be of divers registers.[53]

Giam Battista Mancini (1716—1800) was less ambiguous in his assessment of the registers. While ignoring the concept of the "feigned voice," he noted the existence of two registers, apparently using the falsetto and head voice synonymously. This is implicit from the following: "The voice in its natural state is ordinarily divided into two registers, one of which is the chest, the other the head or falsetto,"[54] Mancini further believed this division to be found in every voice type, soprano, alto, tenor and bass.

Domenico Corri (1746—1825), a pupil of Porpora, also recognized these mechanisms, as well as the need for coordinating them, when he made this statement:

> After he [the pupil] has ascertained the compass of the Natural voice, his great study should be to contrive to unite the Natural voice with the first note of the falsetto, to unite them with nicety, that the union may be imperceptible.[55]

Regardless of how the chest register and the falsetto are joined to suit the taste of different times and cultures, the fact remains that new tonal qualities emerge as a result of this process. Because the upper tones of the chest register were known to be "strong and robust," whereas the corresponding pitches sung in falsetto are breathy and weak, it is obvious that the difficulty, then as now, consists in effecting a smooth juncture. Once joined, however, the resultant quality becomes that commonly recognized as the "head" voice.

Of singular importance to contemporary pedagogy and an understanding of the head voice is the fact that the mechanisms to be joined share a number of pitches in common and respond to three of the basic elements comprising musical tone, *i.e.,* pitch, intensity and vowel. The emergence of the head voice, therefore, is assured mechanically, and indeed can only be arrived at, by arranging these ingredients in appropriate combinations to provide an environment which might be described as a microcosmic ecosystem.

[53]Pier. Francesco Tosi, *Observations on the Florid Song,* translated by Galliard (London: Reeves Bookseller, Ltd., 1926), p. 23.

[54]Giam Battista Mancini, *Practical Reflections on Figured Singing,* translated by E. Forman (Champaign, Ill: Pro Musica Press, 1967), p. 20.

[55]Domenico Corri, *The Singers Preceptor* (London: Chappell & Co., 1810), in *The Porpora Tradition,* edited by E. Forman (Champaign, Illinois: Pro Musica Press, 1968), p. 66.

Despite minor confusions prevalent with respect to terminology (falsetto, feigned voice, head voice), the two-register theory was almost uniformly agreed upon by theorists until the beginning of the nineteenth century. There are three reasons why these concepts came to be modified: 1) the ascendancy of the *prima donna;* 2) the need for opulent voices to cope with the more heavily orchestrated music being composed, and 3) an increase in size of the opera houses in which these works were performed.

Two great teachers of voice dominated the vocal scene during that century, Manuel Garcia (1805—1906), who invented the laryngoscope, and Francesco Lamperti (1813—1892). Each believed the two-register theory was applicable to men, but that women's voices were made up of three. Garcia called these Chest, Falsetto, and Head, while Lamperti referred to them as Chest, Mixed, and Head. The reason Garcia advanced to explain the lesser number of registers in the male voice was that after puberty, men's voices dropped an octave in pitch, consequently making the head voice inaccessible. In Figure 4A these are displayed as they appear in Garcia's *The Art of Singing*, and in Figure 4B as they would appear in musical notation.

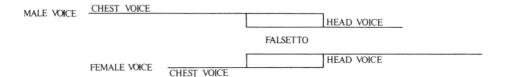

Figure 4A. Demonstrating the relative positions of the chest, falsetto and head voice in the tonal range, reported by most early writers as being applicable to all voice types, male and female. (After Garcia, The Art of Singing.*)*

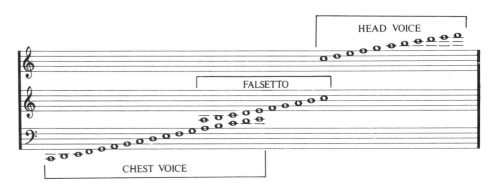

Figure 4B. Showing the approximate pitch ranges of the chest register, falsetto and head voice as these are positioned in musical notation. (Reid.)

If Corri was correct in stating that the natural (chest) voice must be joined "nicely" with the first note of the falsetto so that the union is "imperceptible," then the significance of Lamperti's use of the term "mixed" should be obvious. If one is not to be, as Tosi warned, "constrained to sing within a narrow compass of a few notes," then it is clear that if the head voice is to appear, the two registers, the chest and the falsetto, must be combined. It is by means of this process of "mixing" the falsetto with the chest register that the head voice becomes a functional reality.

The muscle groups most active in the production of head tones are the crico-thyroids and the sternothyroids (both of which act as stretchers of the vocal folds), and the arytenoids, which hold against their contraction. The ary- and thyrovocalis muscle fibers running through the vocal folds are also influential, since their contraction, together with that of the thyroarytenoids, assists in closing the glottal space.

When singing in the head voice, the arytenoids (whose contraction is responsible for those sounds recognized as a chest register quality) are not as fully engaged in the holding process as is ideal. It is for this reason that singers who use the head voice exclusively possess rather light, lyric voices. To the degree that the arytenoids participate, weight and solidity will be added to the tone qualities produced.

Hearing: the process, function, or power of perceiving sound; aural perception of the motion of sound waves which enter the auditory canal and set the tympanic membrane in vibration.

In the mechanical process of hearing, the vibrations received by the external ear are transmitted by means of the auditory ossicles stretched across the middle ear to the organ of Corti, which is located in the inner ear. As they traverse their path, the tonal oscillations create a rhythmic disturbance of the fluids of the inner ear, and consequently stimulate the nerve endings of the organ of Corti. These impulses are then conveyed to the center of hearing in the temporal cortex, where they are perceived as sound and evaluated qualitatively. It is through hearing that the brain perceives external musical stimuli, which it then conceptualizes and transforms into neurological impulses that innervate the vocal organs.

Hearing in singing is a complex phenomenon. Not only must the singer learn to hear melodically, harmonically, functionally, and qualitatively, but he must also learn to reconcile contradictions between auditory sensations perceived through external and internal means. Thus, the singer must learn to discriminate between vibratory sensations he receives from air-conducted sound waves and those that are radiated away from the tonal source by bone conduction. All these factors must, in turn, be related conceptually and kinesthetically to their functional origins in registration and resonance. Reconciliation of these diverse elements is especially difficult when, during training, the mechanism is being restructured, at which time most of the constituent elements are in a state of flux. This adds an additional psychological dimension to the problem, as resistance to change because of anxiety often introduces an impediment which will forestall any hope of real technical progress.

Hearing perception and learning what to listen to and for require a willingness to respond to changing patterns which, while temporary, are unavoidable if technical difficulties are to be overcome. Adapting to these changes obviously constitutes a special kind of ear training, a process complicated by the fact that the singer's instrument is his own body. Unless he learns how to "tune" it, and to understand its qualitative potential and physical limitations through hearing acuities which bring rightness of function and qualitative perceptions into agreement, his vocal problems will remain unsolved.

See Bel Canto
   Falsetto
   Falsetto or
      Head Voice
   Illusion
   Messa di Voce
   Register
   Stretchers of the
      Vocal Folds

See Anxiety
   Auditory Feedback
   Bone Conduction
   Emotion
   Kinesthesia
   Mental Concept
   Register
   Resonance
   Self-Listening
   Vowel

The role of hearing in vocalization is extremely complex. Within limits, it is an acquired skill which through "education" can be brought to an exceedingly high level of sensitivity.

Heavy Mechanism: the chest register.

Since the chest register is active in the lower tonal range of all voice types, responds to high levels of intensity, and is "heavier" or "weightier" than the head voice, the term "heavy mechanism" is not wholly inappropriate. The term itself probably derived from laryngoscopic observation of the vibrating folds; one of the first references to grow out of these investigations described the chest register as "lower thick."

Whether "heavy mechanism" or "chest register," however, the important thing is not so much one's choice of terms, but knowing how to apply the functional principles which predispose the vocal folds to reflexively adjust to the desired configurations. Utilization of these principles not only assures the development of a heavy mechanism when this is desirable, but also assures that it will be developed properly.

See Bel Canto
   Modern Methods
   Register

Heldentenor: See Heroic Tenor.

Helmholtz: Hermann L.F. Helmholtz (1821—1894), a German philosopher and scientist.

The father of physiological acoustics, Helmholtz demonstrated that quality depends upon the order, number and relative intensity of the overtones or harmonics present in every musical tone, drawing parallels between these and the physical conformation of the cavities that act as resonators. Out of these experiments Helmholtz advanced the fixed pitch theory, showing that the frequencies awakened to produce a particular vowel quality are independent of the pitch of the note upon which the vowel is sung. This concept is of crucial importance to an understanding of vocal resonance, since the cavities of the throat and mouth (particularly the laryngo- and oropharynes) are capable of functioning as a coupled system which can be tuned either separately or together.

See Fixed Pitch Theory
   Relative Pitch
    Theory
   Resonance

Although in his later writings Helmholtz anticipated modifications in his theory because of possible differences in vibratory reactions to surface quality, hard or soft, the fixed pitch theory he formulated does not take these factors into account.

Helmholtz Resonator: a hollow sphere made of spun brass with an opening at one end that is used for acoustic experimentation.

In his experiments with resonance, the nineteenth century German physicist Hermann L. F. Helmholtz used many such resonators of varying size, length of neck, and width of aperture to provide new insights into the nature of sound. He proved, for example, that if cavity size remains constant, cavities with longer, narrower necks resonate lower frequencies, and those with shorter necks and wider apertures resonate higher frequencies.

See Fixed Pitch Theory
   Formants
   Puff Theory
   Relative Pitch
    Theory
   Resonance
   Vowel

Functionally, the vocal resonators (*i.e.,* the laryngo- and oropharynges) operate on a similar principle, and must therefore be adjusted or "tuned" if the voice is to resonate tones over a wide range of pitches.

Heroic Tenor: a male voice type of exceptional power and "ring" whose natural tessitura is slightly lower than that of the so-called "dramatic tenor."

The true "heroic tenor" is ideally suited for the heavier Wagnerian roles. It is not a common voice type.

Hertz: a synonym for one cycle per second, or cps.

Acousticians substituted the term "hertz" (usually abbreviated "Hz") for cycle per second in recognition of the contribution made to the science of sound by the German physicist Heinrich R. Hertz (1857—1894).

See Cycle

High Baritone: a male voice type whose legitimate tonal range extends from low G to A above middle C.

The voice of the "high," or "lyric" baritone is of slightly lighter weight and texture than those belonging to other categories, and is extremely well suited for many nineteenth century French and Italian operatic roles.

High Chest Breathing: See Breathing, Clavicular.

High Formant Vowel: a vowel phoneme whose second formant is widely separated from the first, as opposed to a low formant vowel, which finds the two closer together.

See Formants

High Frequency Consonant: a consonant phoneme whose articulation activates frequencies in the upper part of the harmonic spectrum.

High frequency consonants can be either "voiced" or "unvoiced" and are produced by forcing breath through a restricted aperture. Common examples of high frequency speech sounds are the phonemes f, v, and s. The sibilant s produces particularly high frequencies because its tonal energy is tightly concentrated and must often be consciously de-energized during performance.

See Affricate
Consonants

High Larynx: a condition in which the larynx is elevated to a considerably higher position than that which is functionally desirable.

When the larynx is raised abnormally, the thyrohyoid muscle which connects it to the tongue contracts with little or no counterpull from its natural antagonists, the sternothyroid and cricopharyngeal muscles. Under these circumstances, the lower respiratory musculature arising from the pelvic floor finds a higher than ideal point of contact with the vibrating vocal folds, and the entire respiratory system is thrown out of equilibrium.

See Coupling
Lowered Larynx

Singing with a high laryngeal position encourages throatiness, limits the tonal range, and is one of the principle causes of vocal strain.

Resonance

High Register: the head voice.

The use of the term "high register" is not inappropriate, although "upper" would be even more precise, since this mechanism is located above the chest register in the tonal range of all voice types.

See Falsetto or
Head Voice
Head Voice

Hoarseness: vocal dysfunction that is characterized by tonal roughness and/or harshness.

Hoarseness usually results from a severe cold, a "mixed" registration, or an absence of genuine laryngeal resonance. It sometimes results, however, from temporary abuse of the mechanism (*e.g.*, oversinging), or occasionally from more serious pathological conditions (*e.g.*, nodules on the surface of the vocal folds, or polyps).

When hoarseness occurs, the singer should refrain from singing for a few days. If the condition is or becomes chronic, however, he should seek medical advice. If medical examinations reveal no apparent cause for the hoarseness, the condition is most likely attributable to poor vocal technique. In this instance, the only cure for hoarseness is a change of vocal method.

See Nodule
    Polyp

(To) Hold: to sustain; to cause to be or remain in a particular situation, position, or relation; to maintain a particular vocal adjustment.

Although in a very real sense the skillful singer "holds" or "maintains" a desirable physical (resonance) adjustment, the term "hold" often carries with it a negative connotation, *i.e.*, that of maintaining an unnatural or undesirable physical adjustment in a state of unrelieved tension. In this sense, a "held" tone is symptomatic of "gripping," "throatiness," and muscular interference. Such stiffening of the throat parts often results from conscious or subconscious desires to gain direct control over the vocal mechanism and/or to maintain a certain preconceived tonal quality whether or not it is in keeping with the natural qualitative potential of the mechanism.

See Control
    Equilibrium

(To) Hold Against a Pull: See Register; Synergy.

(To) Hold the Breath: to prevent the escape of inspired air from the respiratory tract by closing the glottis.

The role of the respiratory musculature in phonation differs in all essentials from those reflexive movements that occur during normal respiration. In normal breathing, both inspiration and expiration are accompanied by a reflexive opening of the vocal folds, whereas in sustained vocalization the membranes must remain approximated. The purpose of "holding the breath," therefore, is to circumvent this tendency by suspending the respiratory process momentarily prior to phonation. This procedure establishes a balance of tension between the inspiratory and expiratory process and "catches" the vocal folds while in their closing phase. As a result of this equilibrium, the vocal folds do not have to be forced into approximation and the vocal mechanism is ready to respond at optimum efficiency. Thus, "holding the breath" is a technique which could be said to assist in the regulation of a natural process in a natural way.

The state of readiness achieved by a momentary holding of the breath prior to phonation is one of the legitimate properties of what is familiarly known as "the singer's stance," and is similar to that posture assumed by a good dancer, who, while poised and ready to move, is neither relaxed nor stiff.

See Breathing
    Equilibrium
    Singer's Stance

Hole in the Voice: a weak area or gap in the tonal range.

The gaps, breaks, or "holes" in the voice which sometimes disrupt the tonal flow are of two kinds. The first and most serious usually occupies a position in the mid-tonal range and is attributable to the presence of nodules or polyps on the vocal folds, in which case the advice of a qualified physician is imperative. The second type is more common with women than men and lies immediately above the point of register transition (E—F above middle C for all voice types); it is caused by an overly energized chest register having been driven too high in the tonal range, a practice which correspondingly de-energizes the head voice and separates the register mechanisms. Both types of "hole" share certain symptomatic similarities (breathiness) and cover a span of 3—4 semitones.

To eliminate the gap or hole in the voice, it is necessary to reverse those procedures which have created the imbalance. This is accomplished by strengthening the lower portion of the head voice until it meets the upper tones of the chest voice with equal strength and intensity, a practice which involves a reduction in chest register participation. Another solution is to sing quietly and smoothly throughout the tonal range using arpeggios of an octave and a third or fifth, passing to and fro across the register "break" without increasing or decreasing the volume. During the Bel Canto era, this process was known as "building on the soft," a preparatory step essential to a successful execution of the *messa di voce.*

If the "hole in the voice" is not addressed as a problem, the register mechanisms will remain too widely separated, a condition which will foster a continual undermining of the entire functional process.

See **Bel Canto**
     Messa di Voce
     Register

Holistic Pedagogy: training theories and practices which address the learning process from the standpoint of total response; in singing, a pedagogic approach designed to improve an existing voice quality by means of abstract concepts, hearing, imagination, breathing techniques, imitation, resonance and tonal "placement."

Holistic pedagogy is based upon Gestalt philosophy (*Gestalt,* German, meaning "the form of something, a shape or entity"), a doctrine founded on a belief that the whole is not only greater than the sum of its parts, but is often perceived as a separate and unique entity. As a philosophy, holism attempts to mentally unify an assortment of seemingly unrelated events or functions. In its negative aspects, this tends to equate the significance of that which is being perceived with one's ability to perceive, and as a result that which is truly significant is frequently overlooked.

The premise that conceptual awareness and development begin with a perception of the whole and ultimately lead to a recognition of the contributing elements has strongly influenced contemporary vocal pedagogy. To quote Dr. Barry Wyke, the noted neurologist:

> Phonation should, therefore, be regarded realistically as one (albeit complex) component in the holistic behavior that is audible communication, giving expression to the speech (and singing) processes that have been required in the brain of each individual. Thus I would submit that when singing teachers or teachers of dramatic actors are teaching their pupils to do what they do they are not teaching them to control their respiratory muscles, they are not teaching them to control the adductor muscles of their vocal folds, they are not teaching them to adjust the position of the tongue in the mouth or the palate or the pharynx—instead, they are teaching (or rather, they should be teaching) their pupil's brain to integrate all of this kaleido-

[56]Barry Wyke, M.D., "Neurological Aspects of Phonatory Control Systems in the Larynx: A Review of Current Concepts," in *Part II: Respiratory and Phonatory Control Mechanisms. Transcripts of the 8th Symposium: Care of the Professional Voice,* Juilliard School, New York City, June 1979, edited by Van Lawrence, M.D. (New York: The Voice Foundation, 1979), p. 43.

[57]*Ibid,* p. 47.

scopic array of neuromuscular control systems into an efficiently functioning form of precisely coordinated behavior, out of which will emerge (hopefully) an intellectually meaningful and satisfying product.[56]

Wyke's assessment of the vocal process is significant both for what it proposes and for the absence of a just solution to the vocal problem. The magnitude of the difficulties confronted during the course of normal vocal rehabilitation creates dimensions which do not easily lend themselves to correction through holistic pedagogy alone. The reason, as made clear by Dr. Wyke in a subsequent comment, is that "the speaker and singer automatically pretunes his vocal fold musculature into a state that he has learned from past experience to be appropriate for the particular sound that he wishes to utter—but with degrees of accuracy that vary with his acquired vocal skills."[57] Since vocal training is concerned with improving the degree of accuracy that represents the singer's vocal skills, the likelihood of improvement by means of holistic pedagogy alone is remote.

It is true that the singer must be taught to develop concepts which will bring a "kaleidoscopic array of neuromuscular control systems into an efficiently functioning form of coordinated behavior," but since both concepts and the physical coordination among the involved muscular systems are at odds with themselves and each other, it is imperative that the student be presented with options other than those which are merely habitual and familiar. This implies a need for conceptual and physical changes, which, if new sensations are to be correlated and perceived, can be a part neither of the singer's preconcept nor of his kinesthetic experiences, and which are therefore momentarily incomprehensible. If the technique is to be restructured, at least certain parts of the mechanism must be susceptible to manipulative controls of a reflexive nature, and they must be capable of being isolated and made to function without muscular antagonism. Otherwise, the singer will pretune "his vocal fold musculature into a state that he has learned from past experience to be appropriate for the particular sounds that he wishes to utter—but with degrees of accuracy that vary with his acquired vocal skills." It is not until the final stages of vocal training (or when singing) that the integration of responses should be a consistent pedagogic objective.

There are two avenues of approach to be adopted in effecting profound changes in habitual behavior patterns, each capable of by-passing the singer's preconcept and of providing a wealth of new information to be recorded and evaluated without reference to habit or prior conditioning. The first has to do with the restoration of lost motility.

Restoration of lost motility is made possible through an understanding of those techniques associated with the stimulation of natural movement. The basic premise upon which these procedures are founded is elemental: spontaneous movement is free, natural movement, and natural movement can be stimulated through a total rhythmic commitment to the exercise patterns undertaken. Once a freer response to a rhythmic impetus occurs, the involuntary muscular activities responsible for "voice" will of themselves clearly indicate how they prefer to adjust, and an inner impetus will prompt them to move this way and not that way. At this juncture, the student's latent talent will surface and his intuitive "feel" for singing will incline him to do that which is functionally correct.

150

Contact with natural organic reactions in the manner described is a function of kinesthesia, or a perception of the position, movement and tension of muscles, tendons and joints. These perceptions are transmitted by means of sensory receptors, and since these reach the cerebellum and not the cerebral cortex (and consequently produce no consciousness of localized sensation), there is a considerable body of functional activity occuring during phonation that is (like rhythm) felt and sensed as a total event rather than as separately apprehensible components. To intellectualize the learning process by imposing a system of direct controls, therefore, is to ignore that vast array of kinesthetic activity responsible for making the voice "feel" right and neglect the encouragement of what is known as the "singer's instinct." Furthermore, since feeling and instinct based upon kinesthetic perceptions cannot be verbalized, replicated through imagery or imitation, or acted upon until after the sensations have been experienced, the focal point of pedagogic concern is to create an ambiance within which new experiences can be apprehended as a result of spontaneous movement. Thus, training the vocal mechanism is not a process of adopting learned responses (by adjusting the tongue or the uvula, by special breathing techniques, nasal "resonance," or "placement"), but one in which the student is encouraged to grow into new experiences by learning to respond.

The spontaneous reaction of the body to a rhythmic pulse, or intensity-patterning, falls precisely into the context of holistic, or Gestalt, philosophy. In this way, since a rhythmic commitment to the élan of a musical exercise often yields tone qualities not entertained in the student's preconcepts (although anticipated by the teacher), the mind of the student is able to discard old concepts and adopt those more in conformity with a physiologically healthy functional potential. In this sense, the teacher is indeed able to train the student's mind to "integrate neurological control systems into an intellectually meaningful and satisfying product." If the right exercise patterns are not projected, however, neither the ultimate tonal product nor the communicative experience will represent the best that the performer has to offer.

In the final analysis, methods devised to stimulate natural movement through rhythmic identification supersede all other theoretical considerations, and were it not possible to stimulate natural movement, all hope of reconditioning an involuntary muscular system, rechanneling misdirected energy, or discovering new tone qualities and new sensations, would have to be abandoned. Without the availability of procedures designed to restore lost motility, the student would never be able to discard familiar sensations and quality concepts that form a part of his non-freedom, or grow into an experience never previously experienced.

The second option available for promoting fundamental changes in the behavior pattern of neuromuscular control systems, and for developing them independently so that they can ultimately be coordinated more efficiently, is the factor of registration. When properly stimulated, these reflexive mechanisms will accomplish the following objectives:

1. Separate the vocal folds (as when singing in pure falsetto, in which case arytenoid muscular tension is minimal);
2. Draw them together (as when singing in an isolated chest register, where the vocal folds are approximated but without the normal cooperation of the cricothyroids), and

3. Combine these two register mechanisms into a functional unit, which finds arytenoid and cricothyroid tension equitably distributed.

Since each of the above objectives is obtainable by projecting specific pitch, intensity and vowel patterns that prompt their emergence, a means is provided for gaining direct access to, and bringing under control, a seemingly inaccessible complex of involuntary muscles. By admitting the possibility for such manipulations, certain muscular systems can be exercised singly or together, and, because of differences in the textural properties yielded, made to directly influence concepts. Were it not possible to extract certain functional elements from the whole (a departure from the holistic approach), restructuring the technique and learning to sing in the fullest sense of its meaning would be impossible.

Vocal training should both begin and end with holistic pedagogy, at the beginning, to gain a sense of singing as a total communicative experience; at the end, to integrate all of the diverse elements into an effective form of communication which constitutes the art of singing (as opposed to the process of learning how to sing). Since, during the learning process, the whole is imperfectly perceived because of conceptual misjudgments and functional limitations, unless attention is given to restructuring the parts (while continuing to work within the framework which treats vocalization as a single coordinative act), the interaction between free and interfering tensions will reduce the parameters of the singer's technical ability and leave his potential unfulfilled. Holistic pedagogy is an important factor, but not the only one, to be considered during the voice-building process.

Hooking: a technique for effecting a change in registration when moving from the upper tones of the chest register to those immediately above the register "break," *i.e.,* the head voice.

The negative factor in hooking is that it involves a change in resonance adjustment, as well as registration, and generally introduces a constriction of the throat and a distortion of the vowel quality. While this may be more desirable than singing tones which are "too open," *i.e.,* dominated by an energized chest register, hooking nevertheless tends to be aesthetically offensive, and it limits further technical development.

Hooty Tones: tone qualities which are somewhat breathy and hollow.

A hooty tone is characterized acoustically by a strongly energized fundamental with weak upper partials, a condition brought about because of a "mixed" registration. In this particular type of register imbalance, excessive breath pressure must be used, with the result that there is an accumulation of wrong tension within the laryngeal area and an absence of genuine tonal "ring."

While a "hooty" tone quality is appropriate for use in developing a pure falsetto, it has no place in a legitimate tone production unless used for special interpretive effect.

Hum: a vocalized sound made with the lips closed.

Humming possibly serves to relax the throat parts and tongue, as well as induce greater head register response, but these benefits are limited to a relatively narrow pitch range. Because it is impossible to hum without the nasal passages being open, humming is frequently used as a pedagogic device to release those constricting tensions which cause the levator palati muscles to close the entrance into the nasal passages. The value of humming is limited, however, since it tends to raise the larynx as the pitch rises, and to constrict the throat.

When called upon to hum in performance, the singer must be careful to incorporate certain aspects of legitimate tone production, *i.e.*, a stable laryngeal resonance adjustment (avoidance of a raised larynx) and a continuing infusion of energy into the laryngeal area, to ensure the presence of genuine tonal vitality. This necessarily requires the cooperation of both register mechanisms, which presents a difficulty since very little arytenoid (chest register) activity is involved in humming, and open-throated singing is impossible without a properly coordinated chest voice. The fact that the chest register requires a certain amount of mouth opening to function presents a further difficulty, and the closed-mouth hum in the upper tonal range obviously cannot bring about an open-throated resonance adjustment.

Continued practice of humming as a pedagogic device would seem inadvisable and ultimately counterproductive.

See **Open Hum**
   Register
   Resonance
   Twenty-Eight
   Hundred

Hum-on-the-Tongue: an exercise based upon the French nasal sounds *in, an, on, etc.*, and produced by placing the tongue loosely between the teeth; a concept introduced by William Vennard, who later modified it to an "open hum" sung on an *ae* vowel.

The pedagogic value of the hum-on-the-tongue is questionable. To position the tongue loosely between the teeth will, of course, draw its base forward to enlarge the oropharynx. Peripheral movements, however, do not have a positive effect on the interior vocal processes taking place within the throat parts, as both laryngeal and oropharyngeal adjustments are in large part determined by the efficiency of the registration.

The hum-on-the-tongue is often thought to be helpful in "getting the tone forward and into the nasal passages" to relieve throat constriction and improve resonance. The device, however, fails of its intended purpose. There is little or no resonance within the nasal passages, and throat constriction is encouraged rather than relieved by this technique. All vowels, including French nasals, should be resonated pharyngeally, and it is the presence of laryngeal resonance particularly that makes a sharp distinction between nasality and what appears to be genuine nasal resonance. The hum-on-the-tongue is not a factor in achieving either vocal freedom or genuine resonance.

See **Energy**
   French Nasal
   Nasality
   Register
   Resonance
   Tongue
   Vowel

Husky Tones: qualities reflecting a partial malfunction of the mechanism or a pathological condition.

When malfunction or failure of the vocal folds to approximate is the cause of huskiness, the solution lies within the mechanics of registration and techniques for relieving the underlying constrictor tensions that are always associated with this condition.

Pathological huskiness due to inflammation caused by infection, nodules, or an allergic reaction requires the attention of a physician.

See **Nodule**
   Register
   Resonance

See Larynx

Hyoid: Latin derivative of the Greek *hyoeides:* Y, *upsalon*, plus *eidos*, meaning "form;" therefore, having the shape of the Greek letter omega (Ω) in its lower case.

Hyoid Bone: a crescent-shaped bone, located at the root of the tongue, from which the thyroid cartilage, or Adam's apple, is suspended.

Hyoglossus Muscle: a muscle which connects the larynx to the tongue, and, when throat constriction is present, extends laryngeal muscular tension from the tongue to the jaw muscles.

Hyperfunction: overuse of the vocal muscles through incorrect and/or prolonged periods of singing.

Hypofunction: lessened and reluctant activity resulting from continued overuse of the vocal muscles.

I

Illusion: perception of things as they appear to be rather than as they truly are.

Illusion, whether it be the illusion of reality or the reality of illusion, exerts both a misleading and a disruptive influence on the formation of value judgments made with respect to vocal technique. For example, there is little tonal resonance in the frontal sinuses (vibrations perceived as emanating from that area are caused by bone conduction), the head voice is no "higher" (except for tonal range) than the chest voice, and pitch height is an acoustic illusion created by an increase in the number of vibrations per second, a "position" due to greater or lesser degrees of horizontal vocal fold tension. The feeling that the tone is "out of the throat" when the mechanism is free of muscular interference is without basis in fact (sound is generated within the laryngeal pharynx and resonated in the throat cavities), and the impression that the tone production appears to be without tension and a product of "relaxation" is symptomatic of a physical condition rather than reality (movement is impossible without muscular contraction, *i.e.*, tension). Those who believe that tone can be "focused" or "placed" are also victims of illusion, since tone can only be focused (as the lens of a camera is adjusted to bring an object into focus) by reflexive adjustments which occur within the throat parts.

Attempts to develop technical skills by acting upon symptoms which are the product of illusion are bound to fail of their purpose. In the first place, all effective tonal control has been lost once the vocal folds become vibratile; in the second, the muscles which draw the vocal folds into tension, together with the suspensory muscular system which stabilizes the larynx, are not subject to volitional control, and any effort made to act upon them directly raises the danger of bringing into tension those muscles associated with swallowing, a consequence that would be an open invitation to throat constriction.

See Imagery
Kinesthesia
Mental Concept
Modern Methods
Placement
Register
Standing Wave
Vowel

Imagery: psychological, mental, or visual concepts used in the pedagogic process, usually as a substitute for explicit instruction.

To a certain extent, vocal instruction is impossible without imagery, since even the most elemental scale pattern must be conceptualized before it can be executed. However, the successful realization of a preconcept depends upon an ability to respond, which in turn is a matter of physical coordination. Since the student has presented himself in order to overcome obvious physical disabilities, the use of imagery cannot be considered pertinent to the central issue. Imagery, therefore, is not an important factor in the voice-building process.

IMAGERY

The projection of imagery falls under two general headings: 1) mimicry, and 2) sensual awareness. In the first category, directives such as "imitate a steamboat whistle" or "produce a hooty tone quality" are often useful in the conceptualization of a pure falsetto, provided, of course, the proper pitch, intensity and vowel pattern has been selected. The suggestion to "sound like a man" is similarly helpful when working with women who have difficulty in identifying with the chest voice. To "let go" and respond rhythmically and spontaneously to the exercise pattern projected without concern for an aesthetic result is another important aspect of the constructive use of imagery. Marginally, a concept which contains the advice to "think high but feel the tone well anchored in the chest" is useful at more advanced levels of training, especially when a stable laryngeal adjustment is being combined with a strongly energized head voice.

Imagery as commonly practiced, however, is often destructive. Directives such as "sing on the breath," "place the tone in the facial mask," "feel your throat to be a long, flexible tube," "focus the tone against the hard palate," and "feel as though there is a large grapefruit in your throat" are without merit. They neither are founded upon a valid mechanical principle, address themselves to problems related to muscular interference, nor contain elements capable of assisting in the development and coordination of the vocal registers. Unless the student's vocal mechanism is so coordinated by nature as to yield the desired sensations, dependency upon this type of imagery is bound to fail of its purpose.

The fundamental weakness of any type of imagery as a pedagogic tool is that it fails to come to grips with reality by elevating symptoms to a position of greater importance than those conditions which are responsible for producing them. This false dependency is glaringly exposed when dealing with problems related to quality. Except in those rare instances where the voice is already well formed as a gift of nature, the natural quality of the singer's voice is unknown. It cannot be "imagined," therefore, until the vocal mechanism has been trained to function correctly. The crucial functional activities taking place during phonation operate below the conscious level. Consequently, they must be stimulated into improved patterns of response by means other than concepts based upon imagery.

The replication of vibratory sensations that have not yet been experienced is futile and does not serve any functional need. More constructively, the attention of the pupil should be directed to those modifications of quality (as well as their accompanying symptoms) that occur as the vocal organs, through the mechanics of registration, are stimulated into improved patterns of response. These changes are associated with growth and are impermanent—the student need only observe them. It is through the teacher's skill in projecting exercises that stimulate spontaneous, natural movement that these changes are facilitated and technical improvement made.

The one area in which imagery can be most effectively employed is interpretation. One can, for example, "see" a pastoral scene or feel the melancholy of a hopeless love and successfully identify on emotional terms with a particular mood. Thus, imagery may be justly considered a legitimate part of the creative process. While helpful, it is not, however, an important adjunct to the voice-building process.

Whether imagery plays a positive or negative role in voice training depends upon the soundness of the functional principles employed and the skill of the teacher in applying them. One of the errors to be guarded against when imagery is used is misinterpretation by the student, whose sense of vocal reality is limited conceptually and functionally.

Imagination: in singing, the ability to form images of that which has not yet been perceived by the senses or present in reality; the ability to synthesize abstract ideas and translate them into physical reality.

Imagination is indispensable to creativity, but does not provide a secure basis upon which to build a viable vocal pedagogy. Development of vocal skills is virtually impossible unless the instruction is founded on those principles governing natural function, *i.e.*, registration.

See Illusion
(To) Progress

Imitation: an attempt to duplicate those attributes observed in others.

Imitation comes naturally to the aspiring artist, but is inherently dangerous. For example, to attempt to imitate the tonal beauty and artistry of another is destructive when such faults as throatiness, nasality, breathiness, impure vowels, and a limited range are problems which have not yet been solved. Another misjudgment is to imitate the tonal resource of a mature vocalist when one's own voice is, albeit well formed, still immature. One must learn to emulate artists without imitating them, yet do so within the framework of one's present abilities. Each artist possesses his own uniqueness; to succeed, those who strive to become artists must discover their own. The basis upon which artistic singing is founded is a correct vocal technique, that is, well-defined mental concepts and a precise physical coordination, which depends upon procedures designed to stimulate an involuntary muscular system. Such corrective measures center on the mechanics of registration, not imitation.

Imitation of an admired artist is a logical error for a young student to make on his own, but for a student to be encouraged during training to imitate his teacher's technique of tone "production" is inexcusable. A successful pedagogy is based upon solid functional principles that should be adapted to the student's special needs, which vary from pupil to pupil. To imitate a teacher of unfulfilled promise who has either failed as a professional singer, or who has had a career cut short prematurely because of unsolved vocal problems, cannot serve those needs.

To prevent this pattern from repeating itself, teachers must question their procedures and embark on a search for functional principles that produce positive results. Functional mechanics, it will be discovered, are not related to imitation or acoustic illusion, but to the reality of the muscular movements occuring in the laryngeal area during phonation. Rarely will imitation, on any level, lead to functional freedom; generally, it precludes the possibility of artistic development.

See Breathing
Kinesthesia
Modern Methods
Register
Resonance
Standing Wave
Vowel

Imposto: Italian, "placed."

Like the original meaning of *messa di voce*, "imposto" indicates a pre-existent condition rather than a process which requires overt action. The term should not be considered synonymous with tonal "placement" as it is recognized today, since this concept was not extant during the seventeenth and eighteenth centuries.

See Cavity Tone
Theory
Messa di Voce
Nasality
Placement
Resonance

Indirect Control: the ability to regulate involuntary or subconscious functions by means of volitionally controllable factors to which they react.

Access to the physical parts involved in phonation that are not subject to direct control is made possible because of the nature of reflexive movement. For example, while it is impossible to consciously adjust the vocal folds to any specific length and tension, or to "order" them to create the pressure oscillations necessary to the sounding of any given pitch, one can nevertheless sing the desired pitch, knowing that the vocal folds will adjust reflexively in a reasonably appropriate manner. The qualitative aspects of the adjustment made can be subsequently improved by the utilization of carefully selected pitch-intensity patterns (registration), which will induce them to respond in a way more in keeping with their natural movement potential and an innate functional logic.

Vowel concepts cause similar reactions within the throat parts, and cavity tuning for tonal resonation is always made in response to a specific type of vowel quality. Thus, by selecting appropriate combinations of pitch, intensity and vowel, it is possible to influence the manner in which the vocal folds, as well as the cavities of the throat and mouth, position themselves.

See **Kinesthesia**
Laryngeal
   Suspension
Mechanistic
   Training
Natural Movement
Register
Resonance
Vowel

What in effect is direct control over seemingly inaccessible parts of the vocal mechanism is made possible because of three factors: 1) skill in manipulating the vocal registers; 2) a perceptive insight into the influence of the vowel on cavity formation, *i.e.*, resonance, and 3) knowing how to stimulate the organic systems involved to promote spontaneous natural movement. Used judiciously, the principles inherent in these processes will assist in eliminating muscular interference and establishing a free vocal technique.

The successful development of vocal skills and the avoidance of mechanistic methods are impossible without the utilization of indirect controls.

Individuality: those inherent qualities peculiar to an individual that distinguish one individual from another.

Voices are the reflections of personality. Since no two people are identical, no two voices will ever be exactly alike. The ultimate goal of vocal study is to develop an individual's uniqueness to the fullest; the achievement of this goal is essential to becoming an artist.

Inferior Fold: the lower part of the thyroarytenoid, or true vocal cord.

Inferior Pharyngeal Constrictor: the lowest of three paired muscles, connected at either end to the thyroid and cricoid cartilages, whose contraction constricts the pharynx.

Inflection: modification of vocal pitch or timbre to express the grammatical relationship or emotional content of words.

There are three types of pitch inflection in speech: downward, upward, and double. Downward inflections are the most common pattern in English and generally express simple statements. Upward inflections imply questioning attitudes. Double inflections are usually associated with expressions of doubt, irony, and so-called "double meaning."

The difference between inflectional patterns is one of the factors that distinguishes speech from singing. Whereas in speech there is an almost continuous upward or downward inflectional glide, in singing, the same meaning must be expressed within the framework of fixed melodic patterns.

Infrahyoid Muscle: that part of the laryngeal muscular system which lowers the larynx, or when maintained in balanced tension with the suprahyoids, stabilizes its position.

See Suspensory
Mechanism

Infralaryngeal Muscle: a muscle whose contraction pulls the larynx downward.

See Laryngeal
Suspension

Inhalare la Voce: See Drink In the Tone.

Inharmonic Partial: an overtone whose frequency is not an integral multiple of the fundamental frequency.

Inhibition: an inability to express feelings spontaneously.

Anxiety lies at the root of all inhibition, which results from an intuitive fear that contact is about to be made with deeper layers of feeling. Inhibition is generally marked by physical contraction, which, by checking both feelings and their concomitant expression in movement, enables the singer to maintain a strong defense against anxiety. The expansive movements associated with vocal progress, therefore, pose a threat to the security of that defense system.

Emotional inhibition is a common cause of serious vocal problems. If these self-imposed limitations are to be overcome, the singer must face the fears aroused because of expansive movement and risk the consequences. While to do so requires courage, for those who dare the rewards are highly satisfying technically, artistically and personally. Those who prefer to remain bound by their inhibition, however, can never learn to sing freely.

See Anxiety
Emotion
Energy

Innervation: the stimulation of a muscle or organ by nerve impulses directed from the brain through the central nervous system.

In singing, the vocal mechanism is said to be well innervated when at the moment of attack the response is spontaneous and natural. Self-conscious attitudes developed out of practices designed to act upon the mechanism directly (special breathing techniques, placing the voice "forward" or in the facial mask, *etc.*) lack spontaneity and lead to a poor innervation of the mechanism.

See Attack

Insertion: the attachment of a muscle to any part of the bodily framework other than its point of origin.

Inspanning: a series of complex muscular activities in which the tensing and approximation of the vocal folds is affected by contractions involving the suspensory muscular system.

Inspanning involves all four muscle groups comprising the laryngeal suspensory system, and the process is further complicated because of the participation of the omohyoids, which connect the hyoid bone to the shoulders, and the sternohyoids, which connect it to the sternum, or breastbone. When tensed, these muscles lower the tongue, and consequently (since the tongue and larynx are connected by the thyrohyoid muscle) lower the laryngeal position. In an efficient technique, this movement tends to counteract the constricting influence of the swallowing muscles during phonation. When the technique is inefficient, however, the swallowing muscles pull the larynx back and up while the omohyoids and sternohyoids struggle to pull it down and back. This confusion is one source of the muscular interference that results in "throaty" singing.

See (To) Force
  Laryngeal
    Suspension

Inspiration: 1) the act of taking air into the lungs, and 2) the animation, influencing, or guiding of a student by those aspects of personal commitment that move the intellect or emotions.

In the latter sense, inspiration is indispensable to vocal study. If, on the other hand, it is used as a substitute for a real understanding of vocal mechanics, the inspirational approach will soon outlive its usefulness.

See Breathing

Instinct: an innate capacity to respond in a manner that appears rational but is in fact spontaneous and below the threshold of conscious control.

Those who adapt easily to the processes involved in learning how to sing possess an instinctive sense of physical coordination. The latter, since it conforms with nature's laws rather than with man's, is generally more to be trusted than theoretical knowledge or posturing. Instinct, an integral part of vocal success, is often separate from other essentials such as musicality or intellectual and emotional probity.

See Kinesthesia

Intensity: the amplitude of pressure variations that results from vibratory impulses passing through an elastic medium (*e.g.*, air or water); magnitude of loudness or volume; extreme depth of feeling.

The emotional aspects of intensity exert a profound influence on both tonal coloration and loudness. Intensity, therefore, whether emotional or acoustic, is an important element in constructing patterns intended to develop and coordinate the muscles involved in phonation, especially those responsible for the phenomenon of registration.

See Loudness
  Register
  Volume

Intensity Vibrato: tonal oscillations whose amplitudes increase and decrease in direct proportion to changes in intensity.

In the well-used voice, the intensity vibrato corresponds to the violinist's finger vibrato: its oscillations increase and decrease in direct proportion to loudness and emotional content. A true intensity vibrato is reflective of a healthy vocal technique and is characterized by a vibrant, vital tonal quality without noticeable fluctuations in pitch. A noticeable pitch oscillation indicates the presence of vocal faults.

See Tremolo
  Vibrato
  Wobble

Interarytenoids: the transverse and oblique arytenoids, whose contraction approximates the edges of the vocal folds.

Intercostal Breathing: See Breathing, Intercostal.

Intercostal Lift: a combination of costal (rib) and clavicular breathing that according to its proponents, assists in "supporting" vocal tone.

Since vocal tone is nothing more than vibrations moving through space, it cannot be "supported" any more than it can be "placed" or controlled in any fashion once the vocal folds become vibratile. Moreover, attempts to tense any one area of muscular activity at the expense of another (as with the intercostal lift) merely undermine and disturb the equilibrium essential to a correct tone production. Shortness of breath and tonal unsteadiness cannot be cured or even alleviated by methods based upon the intercostal lift, nor can the natural movements so essential to free vocalization be achieved by practices which serve to promote muscular interference.

See Breathing

Intercostal Muscles: three sets of muscles that are lodged between the ribs and that control their movement.

Of the three sets, two, the interni and intimi, contract to assist in expiration; the third, the externi, contracts during inspiration. In singing, these should be maintained in balanced tension.

Interference: the inhibition of free, natural movement by compensatory muscular tensions.

Interference is caused by three negative factors: 1) conceptual confusion (which can result from a lack of experience, a faulty self-concept developed out of a natural tendency to imitate admired artists, improper training, unrealistic goals, *etc.;* 2) poor physical coordination, and 3) psychological barriers. Regardless of the cause of interference, however, removal of these impediments to progress is the direct responsibility of a qualified teacher. Rarely can interference be removed through self-help.

Internal Intercostals: the interni, or intercostal muscles that pull the ribs downward during expiration.

Internal Thyroarytenoids: the so-called "vocalis muscles" that form the muscular rims of the vocal folds.

The internal thyroarytenoids perform a unique function in that they are capable of contracting independently, and it is due to this that the middle portion of the glottal space is able to close completely.

See Thyroarytenoid
  Muscle
Vocalis Muscles

International Phonetic Alphabet: a set of symbols devised and modified between 1886 and 1938 by the International Phonetic Alphabet Association to record, facilitate, and standardize the pronunciation of the world's languages.

Although the International Phonetic Alphabet contains well over fifty symbols and diacritical marks for recording and guiding the pronunciation of languages, the symbols most commonly used for Western languages (and consequently for most sung texts) are the following:

Vowels

(*ee* phonemes)	(i) as in the English word	*beet*
	(ɪ) as in the English word	*bit*
(*ay* phoneme)	(e) as in the English word	*pay* with silent *y*
(*eh* phonemes)	(ɛ) as in the English word	*pet*

INTERNATIONAL PHONETIC ALPHABET

Vowels

	(æ) as in the English word	*back*
	(a) as in the English word	*bask*
(*ah* phonemes)	(ɑ) as in the English word	*calm*
	(ɒ) as in the English word	*hot*
	(ɔ) as in the English word	*bawl*
(*uh* phonemes)	(ə) as in the English word	*the*
	(ʌ) as in the English word	*cut*
	(ɜ) as in the English word	*word* with silent *r*
	(ɝ) as in the English word	*word*
	(ɚ) as in the English word	*per*
(*oh* phoneme)	(o) as in the English word	*tone*
(*oo* phonemes)	(u) as in the English word	*boot*
	(ʊ) as in the English word	*foot*
(foreign phonemes)	(y) as in the French word	*salut*
	or in the German word	*Hütte*
	(ʏ) as in the French word	*sûr*
	or in the German word	*Hüte*
	(ø) as in the French word	*peu*
	or in the German word	*Hölle*
	(œ) as in the French word	*feuille*
	or in the German word	*Höhle*
(nasal phonemes)	(ɛ̃) as in the French word	*faim*
	(ɛ̃:) as in the French word	*feindre*
	(ã) as in the French word	*en*
	(ã:) as in the French word	*tendre*
	(ɔ̃) as in the French word	*bon*
	(ɔ̃:) as in the French word	*trompe*
	(œ̃) as in the French word	*un*
	(œ̃:) as in the French word	*humble*

Diphthongs

(ei) as in the English word	*day*
(ou) as in the English word	*show*
(ai) as in the English word	*my*
(au) as in the English word	*loud*
(ɔi) as in the English word	*boy*
(iə) as in the English word	*here*
(ɛə) as in the English word	*there*
(uə) as in the English word	*moor*

Consonants

(p) as in the English word	*pay*
(b) as in the English word	*bay*
(t) as in the English word	*tea*

Consonants

(d)	as in the English word	*dad*
(k)	as in the English word	*cake*
(g)	as in the English word	*game*
(m)	as in the English word	*mad*
(n)	as in the English word	*nod*
(ŋ)	as in the English word	*bring*
	or in the French word	*agneau*
(f)	as in the English word	*fair*
(v)	as in the English word	*vine*
(θ)	as in the English word	*thin*
(ð)	as in the English word	*thine*
(s)	as in the English word	*since*
(z)	as in the English word	*busy*
(l)	as in the English word	*land*
(ʃ)	as in the English word	*sugar*
(ʒ)	as in the English word	*vision*
(r)	as in the English word	*rat*
(h)	as in the English word	*here*
(×)	as in the English word	*ugh*
	or in the German word	*doch*
(ç)	as in the German word	*ich*

The International Phonetic Alphabet (IPA) is a useful tool for the student of singing since it provides internationally accepted guides to the pronunciation of foreign languages. What it fails to provide, however, is a feeling for the nuance and texture of the language as it is spoken.

Interpretation: the exposition of a creative concept or work of art.

The role of the interpreter is to convey the composer's intent, as indicated by the symbols appearing on the printed page and through the aid of the text, as faithfully as possible. To become a valid spokesman for the composer, the singer must identify with the work being performed on three levels: 1) kinesthetic, or an ability to identify with those sense impressions gained by changes (through movement) in the internal state of the body; 2) musical, involving sensitivity of phrasing and a knowledge of musical form and tradition, and 3) poetic imagination, or the ability to evoke mood and atmosphere and be a good storyteller. In its best sense, interpretation means self-identification with the composer and his work, not the presumption inherent in self-expression.

While it is essential that vocal, musical and linguistic skills are developed, it is nevertheless true that none of the mechanical aspects of an interpretive effort (correct tempi, sensitive phrasing, accurate intonation, good tone quality, correct diction, and knowledge of tradition) necessarily ensures an effective performance. Not even a magnetic personality is enough, although it helps overcome many shortcomings. As is also true with the mechanics of good manners, just being correct is not enough. Certainly the essence of a musical experience must lie elsewhere.

INTERPRETATION

The substance of an effective performance is rhythm. Rhythm is inseparable from tempo (movement) and is instrumental in tracing the design of a musical phrase. It is also a factor in tone quality, since the vibrato oscillates in rhythmic patterns. Rhythm, synonymous with movement, is also associated with emotional expression. Thus, tempo, phrasing, tone quality and emotion may be said to possess a rhythmic essence from which the character of each is derived and without which vocalization would be empty and meaningless.

Rhythm forms an important link between technique and interpretation. Through rhythm, contact is made with those natural reflexes relevant to organic movement, to the stimulation of involuntary muscles (in particular, those comprising the vocal mechanism), and to the production of vocal tone. Organic rhythm encourages natural movement, gains contact with the deepest layers of emotion, and is instrumental in the correction of technical faults as well. Interpretive skills, therefore, rely heavily on rhythmic sensitivity and economy of movement. Ease of execution, tonal purity, the ability to sustain long phrases, flexibility, durability, and a natural, even vibrato are all expressions of this economy. When the vocal muscles are poorly coordinated, or restricted in their movement because of psychic tensions, the mechanism will exhibit functional deficiencies in all of these areas. These deficiencies ultimately limit the singer's ability to transform interpretive concepts into a rewarding communicative experience.

Considerable technical facility must be achieved before sophisticated interpretation becomes a serious concern—especially since the young singer is often in the process of "building" or "rebuilding" his instrument, *i.e.*, restructuring the technique by changing the coordinative process that adjusts both the vocal folds and the larynx. To think in terms of pure aesthetics at such a time serves no practical purpose. Good musicianship serves to sustain and even improve the technique when the voice is already well formed, but for the singer who has vocal problems it does virtually nothing but expose his weaknesses.

Several advantages are to be gained by stressing technique: 1) the student will discover a correspondence between stimulus and response and gain an insight into functional mechanics; 2) the freed mechanism will of itself indicate the path to be taken for its continued growth, and 3) the singer will have at his disposal greater technical command (and consequently greater interpretive command) over his instrument. Thus, he will be able to refine his phrasing, "color" the vowels, and phonate without having to "produce" his voice or "make" resonance. In brief, he will have conscious knowledge of the tools at his disposal for the creation of legitimate musical and vocal effects.

The art of singing and the core of a moving interpretation may consequently be found to combine the mechanical aspects of music-making with the kinesthetic sense impressions to which they legitimately correspond. When these factors are balanced with intelligence and imagination, musical performance becomes transformed into art. To help bring the student to the point at which he is able to identify with the expressive movements initiated within the deepest recesses of his being is the ultimate challenge of vocal pedagogy. Emotion, awakened through free organic and muscular movement, guided by intelligence, refined by sensitivity and taste, and directed with imagination and understanding, comprises the essence of an effective interpretation. Free rhythmic articulation binds function, intelligence

164

emotion and musical material into an entity—and, as Ffrangcon-Davies (1855–1918) put it so succinctly, "The whole muscular system from head to feet will be in the wise man's singing, and the whole man will be in the tone."

In the Voice: an expression used to imply that a tone, passage, song, or aria (generally one with which the singer has previously encountered difficulty) has been practiced to the point that its successful execution becomes an anticipated reality.

Music that is described as being "in the voice" is that for which a viable coordinate relationship has been established between aesthetic goals and appropriate muscular responses.

Intonation: fidelity to pitch; the ability to reproduce accurately a single pitch or series of pitches. In earlier centuries, intonation was used to indicate tone quality, as for example "purity of intonation."

Precise intonation depends upon several factors:

1. Auditory perception, or the ability to distinguish accurately among the various vibratory sensations received by the ear;
2. The capability of the inner ear to separate frequencies and space them equally along the basilar membrane;
3. Emotional attitudes, such as acceptable limits of pitch distortion and functional identification with certain emotional types of sound, and
4. Physical coordination among the vocal muscles as they respond to neurological impulses.

Precise intonation requires a total integration of all these elements. Those few who achieve this high level of technical efficiency do not have to concern themselves with singing in tune, as do those of lesser skill, but treat accuracy of intonation as an accepted fact.

See Off-Pitch Singing

Intrinsic Muscle Fibers: the thyrovocalis and the aryvocalis fibers contained within the vocal folds.

Although the intrinsic fibers are known to assist in maintaining the vocal folds in an approximated, parallel position, it is likely that they also influence other elements of the phonative process, particularly the vowel.

Intrinsic Musculature of the Larynx: those muscles or muscle groups whose points of origin and attachment are contained within the larynx (as opposed to the extrinsic muscles, which originate in the larynx but extend to other parts of the body).

The intrinsic muscles of the larynx are the cricothyroids, the posterior and lateral cricoarytenoids, the transverse and oblique arytenoids, and the thyroarytenoid muscles. Others sometimes considered to be part of the intrinsic systems are the aryepiglottic and the thyroepiglottic muscles, since, as their names suggest, they find their point of insertion within the larynx.

Intuition: the power or faculty of possessing direct knowledge or insight without rational thought or inference.

See Vocalis Muscles

See Instinct

Intuition and instinct are two of the most important weapons in the singer's arsenal.

In Voice: being in good vocal form.

Involuntary Movement: muscular contractions that occur spontaneously and not as a result of volitional control or overt stimulation.

Involuntary Muscle: a muscle whose contraction is not stimulated by volition or other overt means.

The fact that most of the muscles comprising the vocal mechanism are involuntary is one of the reasons why learning to sing is so difficult. A successful training program is one that stimulates these involuntary muscles into improved patterns of response without attempting to act upon them directly.

See Indirect Control

Isolated Registration: a condition in which the two register mechanisms, the chest register and the falsetto, function without coordinate relationship.

See Register

J

Jaw Lock: a form of jaw tension marked by fixed mouth positions, oral immobility, and a protruding jawbone (mandible).

A jaw lock is frequently caused by predetermined tonal concepts ("forward placement," "nasal resonance," *etc.*) that encourage singers to use the mouth and sinuses as resonators, purposes for which they are ill suited.

See Jaw Tension
Laryngeal
Suspension
Register

Jaw Tension: muscular interference by the jaw muscles during phonation.

Jaw tension is caused either by throat constriction or because of mouth "resonance." The former is a result of poor coordination among the laryngeal muscles, particularly among those that prepare the vocal folds for vibration (registration) and among those that position the larynx and pharyngeal cavities for tonal amplification (resonance). The latter variety of jaw tension results from attempts to utilize a cavity for resonance that provides neither suitable surfaces nor the relatively fixed position required for that purpose. Although many believe that the hard palate meets the necessary requirements, it is entirely surrounded by fleshy tissue and reflects rather than resonates sound. Furthermore, the mouth must remain free and mobile for articulatory purposes.

Jaw tension can be corrected as follows: 1) by instituting procedures which will permit the tone to resonate in the laryngeal and pharyngeal areas, as it should, and 2) by having the student relinquish all predetermined tonal objectives centered on "forward placement" and quality. Registration is a key factor in correcting those conditions which lead to jaw tension, as the principles upon which the basic mechanisms operate afford direct access to the source of the problem.

See Cavity Tone
Theory
Laryngeal
Suspension
Register
Resonance
Standing Wave

Exercises for relaxation of the jaw muscles are useless, since the jaw muscles cannot relax as long as throat constriction is present. Energy properly directed at the core of the vocal process (the laryngeal musculature) through proper exploitation of the vocal registers should eliminate both throat and jaw tension.

Jaw Tremolo: an extreme form of jaw tension in which the tongue and jaw muscles move in tetanic rhythm with a tremulous tonal pulse.

A jaw tremolo is caused by an improperly adjusted larynx and/or a "mixed" registration. This causes a general disruption of the coordinative process, especially the adjustment of the thyroid cartilage. The result is that compensatory tensions are transmitted to the tongue, jaw, lips, and facial muscles.

See Tremolo

Jerking: an overly energized attack followed by an immediate compensatory recoil.

Jerking demonstrates a fundamental misconception concerning the attack: that the onset of phonation requires direct, conscious action. To avoid an overly energized attack, which so often results in jerking, the singer should merely open his mouth in a natural way, think the vowel and musical pattern, and, without moving, *allow sound to vibrate within the thought form.* This procedure will be less aggressive and ensure an attack as precise as the current functional capabilities of the mechanism will permit. Once this pattern has become habitual, the attack will not be "jerky," but move on a rhythmic élan to reveal an innate and completely unsophisticated musicality.

See **Attack**
    Innervation
    Interpretation
    Rhythm
    Vibrato

Jones' Phonetic Vowels: a phonetic guide to the pronunciation of vowels devised by Daniel Jones and published in 1918 under the title *An Outline of English Phonetics.*

Jones classified each of the many vowel sounds in spoken English by the tongue and mouth position required for its proper articulation. His system has little, if any, special value for the student of singing, since by design it was based upon speech sounds, and therefore does not deal with the modifications needed to adjust the pharyngeal cavities for tonal amplification. What it does provide, however, is a basis for pronunciation that avoids regional accents and establishes a model for correct spoken English.

Judder: an erratic movement of the jaw and mouth during phonation.

The judder is a symptom of extreme vocal abuse and can result from severe throat constriction, a "mixed" registration, and/or a faulty laryngeal suspension. Whether or not a judder can be corrected is questionable.

See **Tremolo**
    Vibrato
    Wobble

K

Kinesthesia: Greek *kinein,* "to move," and *aisthesis,* "perception;" an awareness of movement through sense impressions caused by changes in the internal state of the body.

Since kinesthetic sensory impulses are transmitted to the cerebellum rather than to the cortex, they produce no conscious sensations. However, being detected by muscle receptors, perception of their movement constitutes a special kind of organic "knowing," regardless of the qualitative aspects of the physical activity involved.

The muscle systems whose movements lie below the threshold of consciousness are recognizable on many levels. Anxiety, for example, is accompanied by a physical uneasiness *felt* rather than understood. Another more subtle area of kinesthetic awareness is implicit in expressions such as "I feel it in my bones," when experiencing feelings of revulsion, or when one claims to have a "gut" reaction to a person, an event, or an idea. These visceral feelings, indeed, extend into many realms, particularly that of aesthetics, where preference and taste are as much a matter of organic identification as cultivation through intellectual development. Instinct is largely a product of kinesthetic awareness, and singers who rely upon the right "feel" of the tone for guidance understand their own voices in a very special way.

Kinesthesia explains why the subjective sensations experienced by one cannot be effectively passed on to another. Since few of the important involuntary muscular movements occuring during phonation produce sensations which are capable of reaching the level of consciousness, it is evident that those consciously experienced and controllable are those which fail to probe to the heart of the vocal function. To make the pedagogic problem even more difficult, those sensations that do succeed in reaching the conscious level would appear to be associated with wrong tension. A perfect tone production, like perfect health, produces no localized sensations. Therefore, unless principles are utilized which succeed in stimulating reflexive, involuntary movements that produce no conscious sensations, the conscious symptoms associated with wrong tension will be mistakenly acted upon, and worse, passed along to others as a direct object of study.

The pre-eminence of kinesthesia during phonation prompts the need for a shift in emphasis in current training procedures. This is especially true with regard to directives addressed to peripheral areas (tongue, lips, jaw and breathing techniques) and suggestions to replicate or imitate specific symptoms of vibration (to achieve "mask" resonance or "placement," or to "feel the throat passageway open enough to permit a large grapefruit to pass through"). Although symptoms answering this description may sometimes reach the conscious level, they are not reflections of, nor do they constructively influence, the behavior of those muscle systems recorded as a sense impression in the cerebellum. Assuming the symptoms mentioned above to be the product of a desirable technical condition, they are nevertheless a by-product rather than the cause of kinesthetic movement.

Access to those muscle systems resulting in kinesthesia is made possible by the proper development and integration of the vocal registers. An indispensable adjunct to the execution of exercises designed to exploit these mechanisms is rhythmic commitment. By allowing the mechanism to *respond,* as opposed to being acted upon, the kinetic energy set in motion as a consequence of a rhythmic impetus will result in natural movement. Through natural movement, the mechanism will find its own freedom without the institution of conscious controls, and solve its own problems by an innate capacity for self-regulation.

By observing the obvious correlations that occur between stimulus and response during training, both teacher and pupil should grow into a deeper and more perceptive understanding of "voice," and, through kinesthetic awareness, reconcile taste and aesthetic judgment with functional health in the process.

Kinetic Energy: Greek *kinetikos,* meaning "to move;" that energy which results from movement.

Kinetic energy is potential, or stored, energy that has been transformed. In shooting an arrow from a bow, for example, the potential energy of the archer is transferred to the stretched bowstring. When the arrow is released and takes flight, potential energy is transformed into kinetic energy. Kinetic energy is a prime factor in singing. As muscular movements take place, the vocal folds (like the arrow in flight) move without being moved, and become self-vibratile through a combination of kinetic energy and neurological impulses generated by will power. Thus, a well-used voice seems to sing itself.

Potential energy swiftly transformed into kinetic energy requires that the vocal muscles be in equilibrium and well coordinated. Those few singers who reach this level of technical advancement produce vocal tone quite differently from those who, because of the presence of some degree of muscular interference, must use overt muscular force to generate sound. When a tone is correctly produced, for example, the breath inspired is not required to act as a source of pressure to activate the vocal folds, but becomes a source of oxygen supply to provide the combustible element which infuses energy into the muscles and body substances. In this way the vocal muscles are innervated by electrical impulses transmitted through the nerve fibers from the brain, with the result that the mechanism moves without having to be moved volitionally. A kinesthetic awareness of rhythmic movement is essential to this process, and it is the singer's ability to identify with this type of coordination, kinetically and neurologically energized, which keeps the vocal mechanism functioning freely and effortlessly.

Viewed from this perspective, it is evident that energy loss in singing is similar in principle to that sustained through the pull of gravity in a free swinging pendulum. With the pendulum of a clock, this loss is made up by energy supplied by a spring or weights (maintained movement), whereas in singing it is achieved through air compression, provided the mechanism is in equilibrium. The amount of compensatory energy that must be used as compression is reduced during phonation, and the consequent breath loss is equivalent to the amount of kinetic energy that has been dissipated. When the mechanism is not in equilibrium, this principle no longer holds true, and breath pressure or other alternative energy sources must be substituted. The result of this misapplication of energy is forcing.

It is kinetic energy, operating within the framework of a properly functioning vocal technique, which makes the well-used voice seemingly free and effortless in its production.

See Breathing
     Breath Control
     Conditioned Reflex
     Energy
     Register

L

Labia: the lips.

Labial: of or pertaining to the lips.

Labial Consonant: a consonant whose articulation is dependent upon the participation of one or both lips.

See Consonants

Labial Orifice: the space between the lips; the anterior opening of the oral cavity (or mouth) whose shape is determined by contractions of the lip, jaw, and facial muscles.

The shaping of the labial orifice has a profound influence upon both the facial aspect and the shaping of the pharyngeal orifice (the posterior opening of the mouth), which, in turn, influences those adjustments made by the laryngo- and oropharynges and the nasal pharynx for tonal amplification. A correct technique of tone production, however, does not rely upon fixed mouth or lip positions for its effectiveness. When the pharyngeal resonators function precisely, articulatory activities are independent of the tonal form, and facial expressions can be natural, mobile, and consonant with the emotional content of the text.

See Cavity Tone Theory
Consonants
Laryngeal Action

Large Throat: See Enlarged Pharynx.

Laryngeal Action: those muscular movements which adjust the vocal folds to the requisite length, thickness and tension to accommodate varying combinations of pitch, intensity and vowel. Also involved are the muscular contractions which "set" the laryngeal position so that this cavity can perform effectively as one of the primary resonators of vocal tone.

The larynx and its associated musculatures lie at the heart of the vocal process and form its core; its position potential (high, low, medium, collapsed, open-throated) affects both the timbre and the character of the tonal emission, and also influences functional activities as a whole. A correct laryngeal action compensates for many seemingly serious technical errors. One can breathe improperly when the larynx is well positioned without deleterious effect, and it is noteworthy that many great singers not only employ different breathing techniques, but indeed often breathe incorrectly. If one's posture is poor, a well-positioned larynx will still function properly, if with some slight inconvenience (witness the stance of Rigoletto, Tosca singing "Vissi d'arte" while lying prone, or Amneris languishing on her chaise longue). The feeling of tonal support depends upon a correct laryngeal adjustment and seemingly places the vocal instrument under the singer's control. Under these conditions, mouth positions become important only to the extent that they serve the sense and meaning of the words.

The mobility of the larynx presents a difficulty. As part of the swallowing mechanism, it responds easily to movements which disturb the vocal function. Since phonation involves the entire respiratory tract, psychological factors also constitute a problem, for emotional tension is immediately recorded in the laryngeal area in the form of throat constriction.

A correct laryngeal action equates with functional efficiency. If the vocal folds assume the right length and tension for the pitch and intensity being sung, and the larynx, together with the oropharynx, is properly adjusted to resonate the vowel, all peripheral activities, *i.e.*, breathing, concepts, tone quality, posture and mouth positions, will fall into line. Unless activity within the laryngeal area is functioning properly, all other parts of the mechanism will suffer a disruption of free, natural movement.

Laryngeal Buzz: a vibratory sound created by pressure variations within the respiratory tract.

The laryngeal "buzz" results from tiny puffs of air escaping between the undulating vocal folds, which are acted upon by certain peculiarities of resonance, not wholly undesirable, which in turn cause the tone quality to emerge with slightly rough edges, or to be somewhat out of "focus."

Laryngeal Control: mastery over the laryngeal muscles that yield vocal tone (particularly those responsible for drawing the vocal folds into tension and for positioning the larynx), which is gained through indirect control.

The inhibiting factor in the achievement of effective laryngeal control is that the muscle systems subject to volitional control are those engaged in peristalsis. Peristaltic movement, however, and all muscular movements associated with swallowing, are essentially constricted and inimical to the functional needs of the vocal mechanism. Thus, volitional efforts to regulate the physical dimensions of the vocal folds, to open the throat and to position the larynx, will invariably exacerbate an already difficult problem, *i.e.*, learning to sing without throat constriction.

The solution to the problems encountered when instituting measures designed to bring the vocal mechanism under effective control involves, therefore, procedures which stimulate a broad complex of involuntary muscles without engaging those within the throat parts that are voluntary. Such procedures cannot be instituted without utilizing those principles known to govern registration.

Laryngeal Function: the activity of the larynx and its accompanying musculature.

The natural function of the larynx is to keep foreign matter (in particular, food and liquids) from entering the lungs and to perform as an integral element of the digestive and respiratory systems. Laryngeal functions also include affective expressions, such as laughing, crying, cooing, screaming, coughing, *etc.*, all of which, like singing, communicate an emotional state or condition by means of sound.

Singing, however, is an overlaid function that requires a considerable degree of muscular and coordinative sophistication. This complexity is the reason why so few voices work well naturally as singing instruments, and why the majority of voices must be trained.

See Affective Expression

Laryngeal Mechanism: See Larynx.

Laryngeal Position: the product of adjustments made by the suspensory musculature of the larynx as the vocal muscles become innervated.

Among the possible adjustments which the suspensory muscles are capable of making while positioning the larynx are 1) an elevation or depression of the larynx itself, 2) an inward or outward tilting of the thyroid cartilage, and 3) any combination of these movements.

The position of the larynx cannot be dissociated from other functional elements with which this tonal generator must coordinate. For example, unless the vocal folds reflexively adjust with great precision to accommodate the needs of the melodic pattern being sung, laryngeal stability will be endangered and with it a vital source of resonance. What makes the solution to this problem most difficult is that neither the suspensory muscles nor the physical dimensions assumed by the vocal folds are volitionally controllable. Thus, any effort made to "set" the mechanism by raising or lowering the larynx, by tonal "placement," or by attempts at "nasal resonance," merely superimpose new constrictions on those already present. Fortunately, this difficulty can be overcome, since the laryngeal position and the physical conformation of the vocal folds can be successfully stimulated by applying those principles known to govern registration.

Since the larynx and its associated musculatures represent the core of the vocal process, improved efficiency within this area is crucial to technical development. How skillfully the involuntary muscular systems are stimulated will determine whether or not the larynx will be stabilized, a factor which will profoundly influence the activity of peripheral movements involving the tongue, the jaw, the lips, and the adjustment assumed by the pharyngeal cavities, as well as outlying portions of the breathing mechanism.

Laryngeal Suspension: a term used by Frederick Husler and Yvonne Rodd-Marling to describe the positioning of the larynx within the throat by the suspensory musculature.

Husler and Rodd-Marling refer to the larynx as a mechanism flexibly suspended within the throat by a type of "elastic" muscular scaffolding, and held in balanced tension by opposing muscular systems called "elevators" and "depressors." Directionally speaking, the terms are somewhat misleading, since, in addition to moving the larynx upward and backward, the suspensory muscles are capable of pulling the larynx forward and backward as well.

There are a number of muscles engaged in stabilizing the larynx. The thyrohyoid, a paired muscle whose contraction elevates the larynx, draws it directly upward toward an imaginary "twelve o'clock." Its antagonist, the paired sternothyroid muscle, pulls the larynx in the opposite direction—but more toward seven o'clock. The stylopharyngeal muscle, an elevator, pulls toward one o'clock, while the cricopharyngeal muscle pulls in the direction of three o'clock. To quote Husler:

The various paired muscles of the suspensory mechanism pull on the larynx in four different directions. Each of these directional pulls is able to alter substantially the shape and the degree of tension of the vocal folds, and of the laryngeal cavity above. Each one changes the tonal character of the voice, its possible variations being almost limitless.[58]

[58]Frederick Husler and Yvonne Rodd-Marling, *Singing: The Physical Nature of the Vocal Organ* (New York: October House, 1964), p. 25.

Since the soft palate forms an integral part of the resonating system and is a primary factor in vowel formation, the palatolaryngeal muscle should also be considered an elevating part of the suspensory mechanism. Also of particular interest is the sternothyroid muscle, whose contraction tilts the thyroid cartilage forward and consequently enlarges the laryngeal orifice. Thus, it should be clear that the possibilities for laryngeal positioning and for interadjustment among these various muscle groups are indeed "almost limitless."

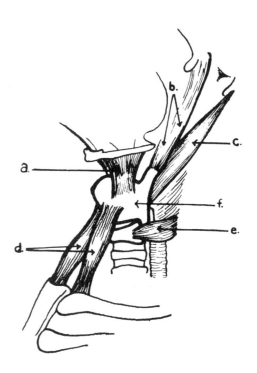

Figure 5. The suspensory mechanism: a) thyrohyoid; b) muscles of the palate; c) stylopharyngeal; d) sternothyroid; e) cricopharyngeal; f) thyroid cartilage. Each of these muscles plays an important role in adjusting and stabilizing the larynx, a factor essential to the maintenance of a general equilibrium of forces throughout the vocal mechanism. (Diagram after Husler and Rodd-Marling.)

Yet another factor of great importance is the interconnection between the suspensory system and that system of muscles which stretches, opens, and closes the vocal folds, *i.e.*, the muscles which account for the process referred to by Husler as "inspanning." As a consequence of this interdependence, an imbalanced registration will disrupt that laryngeal adjustment, while an improper laryngeal suspension will prevent the successful coordination of the two basic register mechanisms.

Husler's concept of laryngeal suspension is synonymous with "resonance adjustment," since the balance of tension shared among the muscle groups comprising this system determines the physical dimensions of the laryngo- and oropharynges, and hence the resonance characteristics of the tone production. Husler logically considered resonance to be a secondary functional manifestation, its qualitative properties being a reflection of the precision with which the cavities are moved into position by the suspensory muscles. This concept stands in direct opposition to generally accepted views of resonance, which contend that resonance can be intensified by "placing" the voice into the nasal passages (where little if any resonance is to be found) and by acting upon the sound, a postulate which violates the known laws of acoustics and physiology.

A correctly suspended larynx affords many technical advantages: it allows the natural tonal beauty of the voice to emerge; it causes the voice to "ring;" it assures tonal steadiness, ease of production, and flexibility, and it gives all tones (even the softest) a "carrying power" that could not be achieved by other means. It further creates the acoustic and kinesthetic illusion that the voice is "well supported" and "focused." Without an effective laryngeal suspension, these qualities would either be entirely lacking, or lacking to such a degree that aesthetic goals would have to be compromised.

Pedagogically, a well-positioned larynx must first be approached through the mechanics of registration, since an effective resonance adjustment is largely dependent upon a precise muscular interplay between the two vocal registers.

See Bel Canto
   Cavity Tone Theory
   Energy
   Register
   Resonance
   Suspensory
      Mechanism
   Standing Wave

Laryngeal Tension: the contraction of the various muscles situated within the larynx and laryngeal pharynx.

The term "laryngeal tension" is frequently confused with "laryngeal tenseness," or constricting tensions. All musical sound, however, depends upon tension: the vocal folds must be tensed to become vibratile, the suspensory muscles must come into tension to stabilize the larynx, and the inspiratory and expiratory muscle systems must be maintained in equilibrium through tension. Proper tensing of these muscle groups gives the *impression* of ease and relaxation, but in reality the condition is symptomatic, indicating the presence of a state of balanced tension and an absence of tenseness. Poor physical coordination reverses this equation, tension being replaced by tenseness.

Another source of wrong laryngeal tension are those muscular contractions which occur in response to fear and anxiety. In the latter instance the throat muscles will constrict even though they are physically ready to coordinate effectively. Constructive training procedures address themselves to these and other problems related to tenseness, not by overt attempts at relaxation, but through the inculcation of new concepts, and consequently by rechanneling the singer's energy resources.

See Anxiety
   Coordination
   Emotion
   Register

Laryngeal Vibration: pressure variations or sound waves caused by a periodic motion of the vocal folds.

Vocal tone, the product of laryngeal vibration, is a complex musical sound, *i.e.*, it consists of a fundamental frequency and varying numbers of harmonic partials or overtones, whose frequencies are integral multiples of the former. There have been numerous theories advanced concerning the mechanics of laryngeal vibration, but as yet none provides a wholly satisfactory answer.

Denis Dodart, a seventeenth century French scientist, was the first to recognize the connection between vocal vibration and pitch. He found that the vocal folds open and close repeatedly because of subglottal pressure, each segment allowing rapid puffs of air to escape through them. The rapidity of these emissions, according to Dodart, is responsible for the phenomenon of pitch in singing. This theory was reinforced by later investigators, who compared the vocal mechanism to a reed instrument in which air escapes between the vibrating reeds in a series of rapid puffs, the pressure variations producing sound waves heard as pitch.

While acoustic similarities between reed instruments and the human voice do in fact exist, the parallels are not exact. In reed instruments the resonator *consistently* dominates the vibrator, whereas the vocal mechanism incorporates in varying relationships a composite of acoustic laws which also includes those pertaining to vibrating strings and wind instruments. Laryngoscopic observations, for example, prove conclusively that the vibrator adjusts to varying lengths and thicknesses purely as a response to pitch and intensity (similar in principle to the vibrating string theory), just as physicists have shown that the acoustic laws operative during the playing of wind instruments also apply to the voice (*i.e.*, equalization of pressure on opposite sides of the player's lips because of the cup design of the mouthpiece, which creates a standing wave).

A more conventional explanation of the nature of laryngeal vibration is the "breath pressure theory," which claims that the vocal folds' resistance to air pressure directed against them by the respiratory musculature during expiration forces them to become vibratile. Whether or not this is true when the mechanism is in equilibrium, which is rare, is an open question. The French scientists J. Piguet, G. Decroix and J. Libersa[59] concluded from their experiments that the vibrations of the vocal folds are *independent* of the strength of subglottal pressure, indicating that some other sort of pressure system must be in effect. While this judgment has not been widely accepted, it seems far more reasonable than the breath pressure theory, for if it is true that the vocal folds are agents whose function is to resist subglottal pressure (which would require breath pressure to be countered with equal but opposing vocal fold tension), this function would inevitably deprive them of the very elasticity essential to their flexibility.

Another French scientist, Raoul Husson, offered a different explanation when he advanced his neurochronaxic theory, which contends that the vocal folds become self-vibratile in response to neurological impulses transmitted by the brain. Like all theories, this, too, has its weakness (for example, that motor responses cannot be stimulated in excess of 100 impulses per second). The plausible feature of Husson's theory is that if the coordinative process is precise, it accounts for the effortlessness so apparent among those who sing correctly.

All of the theories proposed offer at least a partial insight into the nature of laryngeal vibration. Until a scientific consensus is reached, however, no definitive answer to the question of laryngeal vibration and its physical causes can be given.

Laryngectomy: surgical removal of the larynx.

Laryngitis: inflammation of the larynx.

Laryngitis is symptomatic of a physical disability (a cold, viral infection, or

[59]J. Piguet, G. Decroix and J. Libersa, *Comptes Rendus* Vol. 242 (Paris: Academy of Sciences, 1956), p. 1223.

See Bernoulli Effect
      Breathing
      Equilibrium
      False Vocal Cords
      Neurochronaxic
        Theory
      Puff Theory
      Register
      Resonance
      Standing Wave

allergic reaction), vocal abuse, or a poor vocal technique. In the last two instances, laryngitis is often accompanied by visible physical distortions (congestion, facial grimaces, tongue and jaw tremolo, *etc.*).

Laryngology: the branch of medicine that deals with diseases of the larynx and nasopharynx.

Laryngopharynx: the area of the throat between the upper surface of the vocal folds and the tip of the epiglottis.

Because the shape of the laryngopharynx can be adjusted to maintain relatively fixed positions, it is highly influential in tonal amplification or resonance. In an efficient vocal technique, the laryngopharynx is consistently adjusted to energize those frequencies in the range of 2800—3200 cycles per second (frequencies that produce the so-called tonal "ring"), while the oropharynx is tuned to those frequencies necessary for the proper articulation of the vowel.

The consistent tuning of the laryngopharynx to an unchanging band of frequencies, which produces "ring," makes this cavity the prime resonator of vocal tone, and additionally is the factor which makes legato singing possible.

Laryngoscope: an instrument for examining the interior processes of the larynx.

The laryngoscope, a fairly simple mechanism consisting of two mirrors, was invented in 1854 by Manuel Garcia. The smaller mirror, which is attached to the end of a long, slender shaft, is inserted through the mouth, poised beneath the ceiling of the nasopharynx, and positioned so that its reflecting surface faces the vocal folds. The larger mirror is then arranged externally (it is frequently attached to a headband worn by the examiner) to cast light upon the smaller mirror, whose illumined surface carries a reflection of the vocal folds.

Although the laryngoscope is most commonly used for laryngological examinations, Garcia's original intent was that it would serve as a means for observing the adjustments made by the vocal folds during phonation. As such, the laryngoscope has at best produced mixed results, for these reasons:

1. It is very difficult to sing normally when the apparatus is in place;
2. Visibility is obstructed by the tongue, whose attachment to the hyoid bone and epiglottis conceals the anterior portion of the vocal folds;
3. Much of the data collected has resulted from observations of those with vocal problems (few who sing well have subjected themselves to laryngoscopic examination), and thus provides visual evidence of the way the vocal folds should *not* work, and
4. Investigators have by and large examined their own students, and consequently look for and "see" different things.

Recent improvements in the laryngoscope have provided an unobstructed view of the vocal folds. Instead of metal and glass, modern instruments are made of a slender fiber-optic tube that is inserted through the nose. This procedure does not interfere with normal vocal functioning, and at the same time provides an unobstructed view of the interior of the larynx. Although there is always the danger of misinterpretation, these examinations could significantly enhance pedagogic understanding of the vocal process.

Laryngoscopic Examination: the observation of the larynx by means of a laryngoscope.

Laryngoscopic examinations are essential to the diagnosis of vocal abnormalities (*e.g.*, nodules); however, they are useless in correcting the faulty coordination and/or misconcepts that may have given rise to these conditions.

Larynx: Greek, "upper part of the trachea;" the musculo-cartilaginous structure, lined with mucous membrane and housing the vocal folds, that forms the upper part of the trachea or windpipe; the vocal generator, or voice box.

The larynx is suspended within the pharynx by seven sets of suspensory muscles and is affixed, at either end, to the trachea and hyoid bone (to which the base of the tongue is also attached). Its natural function is to keep foreign matter (in particular, water and food) from entering the lungs and to allow air to pass into and out of the lungs for respiration. Speech and singing are both overlaid functions, that is, activities to which the mechanism can readily adapt but for which it was not primarily designed. Both are physical possibilities only because the larynx and entire respiratory mechanism of which it is a part can adapt their natural functions to meet the three functional requirements of a musical instrument: 1) an energy source (the lungs and brain); 2) a vibrator (the vocal folds), and 3) a resonator (the larynx and surrounding pharyngeal cavities).

LARYNGEAL FRAMEWORK

The cartilaginous framework of the larynx is composed of nine distinct parts:

1. Two paired arytenoid (Greek, "ladle-shaped") or "pyramid" cartilages;
2. Two paired cornicular (Latin, "hornlike") cartilages—also called "cartilages of Santorini;"
3. Two paired cuneiform (Latin, "wedgelike") cartilages—also called "cartilages of Wrisberg;"
4. The epiglottis (Greek, "over the glottis");
5. The cricoid (Greek, "finger ring") cartilage, and
6. The thyroid (Greek, "oblong shield") cartilage.

Of these, the cricoid, thyroid, and arytenoid cartilages are most closely associated with the phonatory act. The cricoid or "ring" cartilage forms the base of the larynx. The thyroid cartilage is attached to the framework of the larynx at a point of cleavage formed by its upper and lower extensions. Each of the posterior extensions has a *cornu,* or "inferior horn," that fits over and is attached to the rear of the cricoid ring. The assembly of these parts leaves a gap between the two cartilages that can be closed by contraction of the cricothyroid muscles. The arytenoid cartilages are positioned between the upper posterior portion of the cricoid ring and the inferior horns of the thyroid cartilage. Attached to the arytenoids are three processes or prongs which extend to the thyroid notch, or "vocal process." The facets upon which the arytenoids rest permit contractions of the cricoarytenoid and arytenoid muscles to pull the arytenoids closer together, to leave them separated, to tilt them forward, or to tilt them backward.

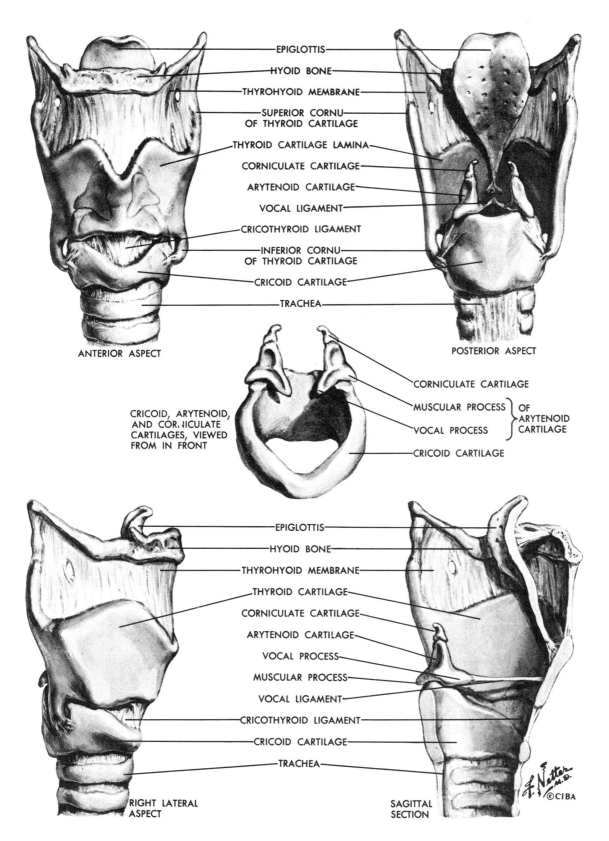

EPIGLOTTIS
HYOID BONE
THYROHYOID MEMBRANE
SUPERIOR CORNU
OF THYROID CARTILAGE
THYROID CARTILAGE LAMINA
CORNICULATE CARTILAGE
ARYTENOID CARTILAGE
VOCAL LIGAMENT
CRICOTHYROID LIGAMENT
INFERIOR CORNU
OF THYROID CARTILAGE
CRICOID CARTILAGE
TRACHEA

ANTERIOR ASPECT

POSTERIOR ASPECT

CRICOID, ARYTENOID,
AND CORNICULATE
CARTILAGES, VIEWED
FROM IN FRONT

CORNICULATE CARTILAGE
MUSCULAR PROCESS } OF
ARYTENOID
VOCAL PROCESS } CARTILAGE
CRICOID CARTILAGE

EPIGLOTTIS
HYOID BONE
THYROHYOID MEMBRANE
THYROID CARTILAGE
CORNICULATE CARTILAGE
ARYTENOID CARTILAGE
VOCAL PROCESS
MUSCULAR PROCESS
VOCAL LIGAMENT
CRICOTHYROID LIGAMENT
CRICOID CARTILAGE
TRACHEA

RIGHT LATERAL
ASPECT

SAGITTAL
SECTION

Figure 6. The cartilaginous structure of the larynx. Reprinted from CIBA Clinical Symposia: The Larynx, *Volume 16, Number 3, 1964.*

181

LARYNGEAL MUSCULATURE

The muscles associated with laryngeal activity are of two types: 1) the intrinsic muscles that originate from and connect to points of attachment on or within the laryngeal framework, and 2) the extrinsic muscles that originate from a point on or within the larynx and connect to another body part, such as the sternum, hyoid bone, mandible, or styloid processes. The names assigned indicate the specific cartilages or bones to which the muscle is attached (*e.g.*, the sternothyroid muscles extend from the thyroid cartilage of the larynx to the sternum or breastbone). The contraction of the intrinsic musculature is responsible for all movements of the cartilaginous laryngeal framework and for intralaryngeal activities (including the approximation and vibration of the vocal folds); the contraction of the extrinsic or suspensory musculature positions the larynx and regulates its movements within the pharynx.

INTRINSIC MUSCULATURE

The cricothyroid, posterior and lateral cricoarytenoid, oblique arytenoid, and thyroarytenoid muscles are paired, intrinsic laryngeal muscles; the transverse arytenoid is an unpaired intrinsic muscle. Pedagogically, the most useful of these (in that their behavior and movement potential can be influenced indirectly by conceptualized musical stimuli) are the thyroarytenoid, cricothyroid, and cricoarytenoid muscles. The thyroarytenoid muscles form the mechanism known as the "vocal cords" and function as a valve to prevent foreign matter from entering the trachea and reaching the lungs. The thyroarytenoids consist of two distinct parts: 1) the internal thyroarytenoids (also called "vocal folds" or "vocal lips"), and 2) the external thyroarytenoids ("vocal bands"). The thyroarytenoid muscles, along with the aryvocalis and thyrovocalis ("vocalis") muscle fibers that crisscross through them, are capable of contracting independently to completely close the glottal space.

EXTRINSIC MUSCULATURE

The extrinsic muscles of the larynx serve to either elevate or lower the larynx. Those muscles whose contractions raise the larynx are the thyrohyoid, palatolaryngeal, and stylopharyngeal muscles. Their natural antagonists are those muscles that lower the laryngeal position: the omohyoids, the sternothyroid and the cricopharyngeal muscles. There are, of course, muscles whose contraction elevates or depresses the hyoid bone and (since the larynx is connected to the hyoid bone) the larynx. These muscles, referred to as the "suprahyoid" and "infrahyoid" systems, therefore, also affect laryngeal positioning. The suprahyoid muscles (the geniohyoid, stylohyoid, stylothyroid, and digastric muscles) contract to raise the hyoid bone and larynx, whereas the infrahyoid muscles (the sternothyroid, sternohyoid, thyrohyoid, and mylohyoid muscles) contract to lower their position.

MUSCULAR FUNCTION

The primary function of all laryngeal muscles is either respiration or digestion (in particular, deglutition or swallowing, and peristaltic movement, or muscular reflexes which direct the contents of the alimentary canal toward the point of exit). Singing is an overlaid function and often requires movements contrary to the habitual movements mentioned above, which are essentially constrictive. Only when

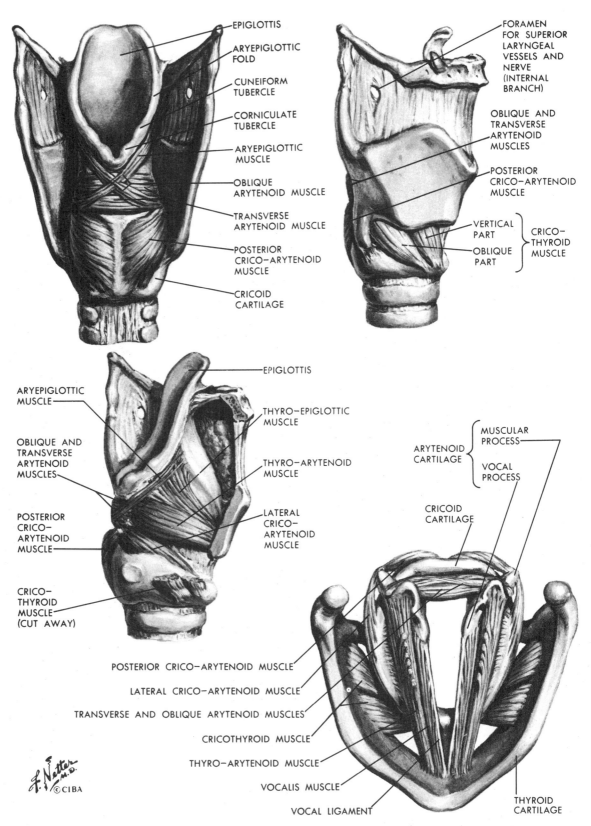

EPIGLOTTIS
ARYEPIGLOTTIC FOLD
CUNEIFORM TUBERCLE
CORNICULATE TUBERCLE
ARYEPIGLOTTIC MUSCLE
OBLIQUE ARYTENOID MUSCLE
TRANSVERSE ARYTENOID MUSCLE
POSTERIOR CRICO-ARYTENOID MUSCLE
CRICOID CARTILAGE

FORAMEN FOR SUPERIOR LARYNGEAL VESSELS AND NERVE (INTERNAL BRANCH)
OBLIQUE AND TRANSVERSE ARYTENOID MUSCLES
POSTERIOR CRICO-ARYTENOID MUSCLE
VERTICAL PART
OBLIQUE PART
CRICO-THYROID MUSCLE

ARYEPIGLOTTIC MUSCLE
OBLIQUE AND TRANSVERSE ARYTENOID MUSCLES
POSTERIOR CRICO-ARYTENOID MUSCLE
CRICO-THYROID MUSCLE (CUT AWAY)

EPIGLOTTIS
THYRO-EPIGLOTTIC MUSCLE
THYRO-ARYTENOID MUSCLE
LATERAL CRICO-ARYTENOID MUSCLE

ARYTENOID CARTILAGE
MUSCULAR PROCESS
VOCAL PROCESS
CRICOID CARTILAGE

POSTERIOR CRICO-ARYTENOID MUSCLE
LATERAL CRICO-ARYTENOID MUSCLE
TRANSVERSE AND OBLIQUE ARYTENOID MUSCLES
CRICOTHYROID MUSCLE
THYRO-ARYTENOID MUSCLE
VOCALIS MUSCLE
VOCAL LIGAMENT
THYROID CARTILAGE

Figure 7. Intrinsic musculature of the larynx. Reprinted from CIBA Clinical Symposia: The Larynx, *Volume 16, Number 3, 1964.*

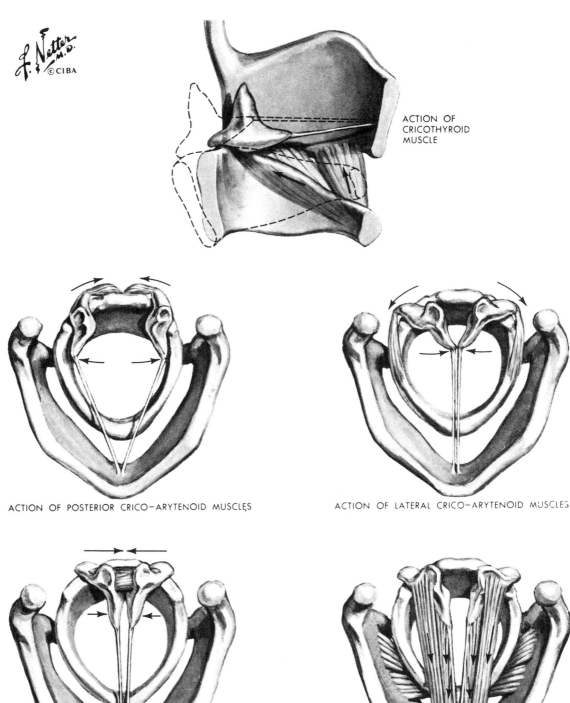

ACTION OF
CRICOTHYROID
MUSCLE

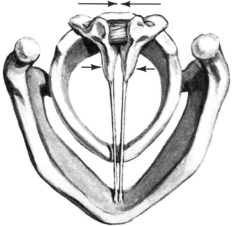

ACTION OF POSTERIOR CRICO-ARYTENOID MUSCLES

ACTION OF LATERAL CRICO-ARYTENOID MUSCLES

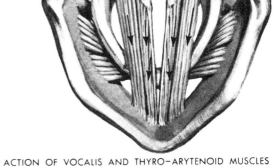

ACTION OF ARYTENOIDEUS MUSCLE

ACTION OF VOCALIS AND THYRO-ARYTENOID MUSCLES

Figure 8. Action of the intrinsic muscles of the larynx. Reprinted from CIBA Clinical Symposia: The Larynx, *Volume 16, Number 3, 1964.*

the four muscular systems controlling laryngeal movement are maintained in a state of balanced tension can a proper relaxation of the swallowing muscles be achieved and genuine open-throated resonance be established.

There are many difficulties to be overcome in eliminating the constricting influence of the swallowing muscles over those muscular movements required during phonation. For example, since the swallowing muscles are subject to volitional control and the "throat openers" are not, all acts of will tend to activate, rather than deactivate, constrictor tensions. In addition, the inferior, middle, and superior constrictor muscles form the posterior wall of the larynx, and the lower constrictor is directly related (by its similar attachment to the oblique ridge of the thyroid cartilage) to the cricothyroid muscles, whose contraction yields sounds commonly recognized as "head voice." Furthermore, both the cricothyroid and thyropharyngeal muscles attach to the lower edge of the inferior constrictor muscle and are innervated by the same branch of the superior laryngeal nerve as is the lower constrictor. As a result of this association, the natural tendency of the cricothyroids is to constrict; it is for this reason that the development of the head voice is so dependent upon a well-developed chest register, which tends to open the throat. Since, however, the thyroid cartilage tilts forward (a throat-opening phenomenon) in response to cricothyroid contraction, and since the contraction of the arytenoid and cricopharyngeal muscles tends to keep the larynx from rising, it is possible to influence the behavior of the suspensory muscles, and ultimately establish open-throated resonance through those techniques associated with register isolation, development, and unification.

The core of the functional process is the intrinsic musculature of the larynx. Energy properly directed moves from core to periphery, and, given a healthy state of physical coordination, the quality of intralaryngeal activity will be reflected in both peripheral activities (*e.g.*, breathing) and the ultimate tonal product.

An effective voice-training program is one that solves problems related to intrinsic muscular coordination by indirect means, that is, one that stimulates involuntary muscles to move more efficiently without resorting to volitional control. An arbitrary positioning of the larynx to enhance resonance characteristics, for example, is useless. A more constructive pedagogic approach would be to work through the dynamics of registration, whereby the vocal folds and intrinsic musculature respond to selected patterns of pitch, intensity, and vowel in predictable ways. When these movements are well coordinated, all peripheral activities will be free to respond to an innate functional logic, and the larynx will position itself reflexively. Instinctual responses to musical stimuli result in fine-tuning; volitional efforts, at best, result in mere approximations.

SUMMARY

In rather simplistic terms, the vocal folds become vibratile by means of antagonistic muscular tension among the intrinsic muscles of the larynx: in particular, among the thyroarytenoid, cricothyroid and arytenoid muscles. The ratio of tension between the last two results in the phenomenon of registration. Concurrently, the laryngeal pharynx is moved into a position favorable to resonance by the infra- and suprahyoid muscle groups. The combined effect of registration and adjustments made for resonance involving these processes determines the quality of the ultimate tonal product.

See Control
Energy
Kinesthesia
Natural Movement
Laryngeal
  Suspension
Register
Resonance
Swallowing
  Muscles
Vocal Folds

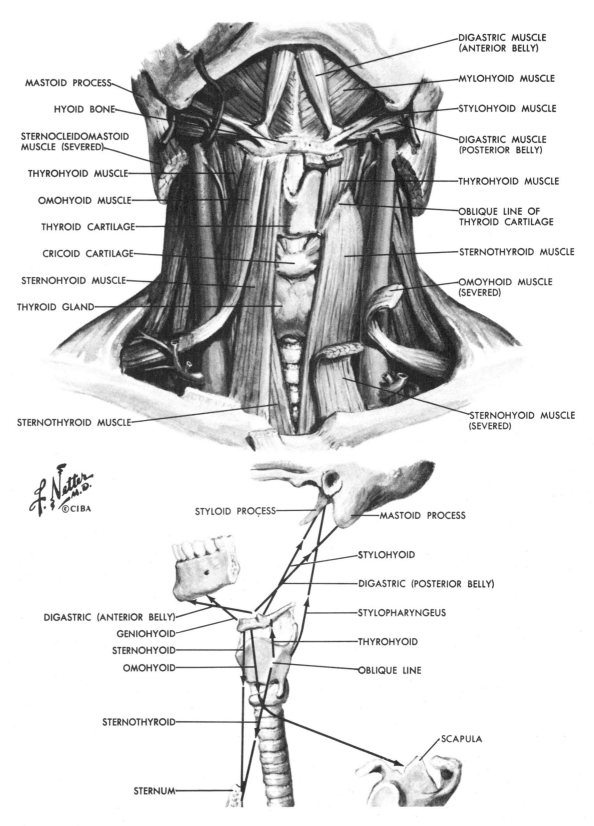

DIGASTRIC MUSCLE (ANTERIOR BELLY)

MYLOHYOID MUSCLE

STYLOHYOID MUSCLE

DIGASTRIC MUSCLE (POSTERIOR BELLY)

THYROHYOID MUSCLE

OBLIQUE LINE OF THYROID CARTILAGE

STERNOTHYROID MUSCLE

OMOYHOID MUSCLE (SEVERED)

STERNOHYOID MUSCLE (SEVERED)

MASTOID PROCESS

HYOID BONE

STERNOCLEIDOMASTOID MUSCLE (SEVERED)

THYROHYOID MUSCLE

OMOHYOID MUSCLE

THYROID CARTILAGE

CRICOID CARTILAGE

STERNOHYOID MUSCLE

THYROID GLAND

STERNOTHYROID MUSCLE

STYLOID PROCESS

MASTOID PROCESS

STYLOHYOID

DIGASTRIC (POSTERIOR BELLY)

STYLOPHARYNGEUS

THYROHYOID

OBLIQUE LINE

DIGASTRIC (ANTERIOR BELLY)

GENIOHYOID

STERNOHYOID

OMOHYOID

STERNOTHYROID

SCAPULA

STERNUM

Figure 9. Extrinsic muscles of the larynx and their action. Reprinted from CIBA Clinical Symposia: The Larynx, Volume 16, Number 3, 1964.
© Copyright 1964, CIBA Pharmaceutical Company, Division of CIBA-GEIGY Corporation. Reprinted with permission from Clinical Symposia, illustrated by Frank H. Netter, M.D. All rights reserved.

186

Maladjustments within any of these muscular complexes have an adverse effect upon natural functioning, particularly upon the manner in which the vocal folds adjust their length, thickness and contour in response to a projected musical figure. As a result, compensatory tensions are introduced that interfere with healthy functional activities, causing a loss of freedom and tonal vitality. Since none of the muscles involved in phonation can be acted upon directly, a constructive training program must seek to improve muscular responses by stimulating natural, reflexive movement.

Lateral Breathing: costal or rib breathing.

See Breathing

Lateral Cricoarytenoid: a paired muscle whose contractions assist in approximating the vocal folds and closing the glottal space.

The lateral cricoarytenoids are part of the intrinsic musculature of the larynx, and consequently are not subject to volitional control.

See **Intrinsic Musculature of the Larynx**

Latissimi Dorsi: large, flat muscles that extend from either side of the lower back to the armpits, shoulders, and lower ribs.

The contraction of the latissimi dorsi (commonly called "lats") draws the arms backward and downward, rotates the front of the arms toward the body, and assists in respiration.

Overconcern for these muscles during phonation leads to "body consciousness" and is inhibitory.

Law of Reversed Effort: a phenomenon of physical activity by which effort expended to control involuntary muscular movement becomes counterproductive.

The law of reverse effort is frequently operative during training with those who try too hard, *i.e.,* those who are overly conscientious, diligent, or ambitious. To avoid this danger, the student must learn to "try without trying," *i.e.,* to "let" things happen rather than attempt to "make" them happen. Too often, striving means struggle, and both must be abandoned in favor of a more relaxed approach to problem solving.

Lax: relaxed, limp, or flaccid.

Muscles are referred to as "lax" when they are inactive (*i.e.,* not tensed) or when they are in poor tone. Lax vocal muscles, in the latter sense, reflect either disuse or misuse and result in weak, undeveloped tonal qualities.

Lax Vowels: See Vowel, Lax and Tense.

Learning to Sing by Singing: a procedure based upon a premise that technical problems can be overcome and vocal improvement made by just singing.

In keeping with most statements concerning vocal development, the contention that one can learn to sing by singing is both true and false. However, if the question "What is learning?" is raised, the proposition "learn to sing by singing" can be brought into proper perspective.

If learning is acquiring a skill that one did not formerly possess, then one cannot learn to sing at a high level of technical proficiency by "just singing." Real learning is a process whereby the vocal mechanism is to a greater or lesser extent being restructured, since the mechanism requires reconditioning to enable it to respond more efficiently. This cannot be accomplished unless principles, and techniques related to their application, are utilized and applied with understanding of individual needs. Such a program requires time, patience, talent, a desire to improve, and a willingness to change. Technical revisions, therefore, cannot be made by "just singing," which, in most instances, becomes a repetition of those habits and practices whose built-in limitations assure their permanence.

The Golden Age of Singing records that at least four years of concentrated technical study were needed before the student was permitted to address himself to even simple songs. On the other hand, many of the world's greatest singers (Bjoerling, Flagstad, Galli-Curci, and Ponselle being notable examples) never studied at all; they possessed natural, God-given voices and trusted their instincts. Since a properly functioning mechanism is intrinsically musical, such singers can indeed reinforce and develop a sense of technical security by just singing a wisely selected repertoire musically.

A comprehensive training program takes these and other factors into consideration, each student being evaluated in terms of individual needs, ambitions, ability, and circumstances. At all levels of technical expertise, getting the "feel" of singing is important. Understanding how the mechanism works (even when it works very well), however, is equally crucial to the care and preservation of one's technical resources.

Legato: Italian, "connected;" connection between two or more tones of a musical phrase.

A true legato reflects a constant, precise resonance adjustment for all tones and is inseparable from good singing. It is the result of a dual resonating system: the one, which finds the laryngeal pharynx tuned to energize those frequencies which cause the voice to "ring;" the other, where the oropharynx is tuned to energize those frequencies necessary to a proper defining of the vowel. With a true legato, the mouth and articulatory processes (the tongue, lips, teeth, *etc.*) are only minimally involved in tonal amplification, and consequently remain free to articulate the text.

An inability to sing a true legato indicates the presence of muscular interference within the coordinative process. These constricting influences must be removed by improving the muscular movements that adjust the length, thickness, and contour of the vocal folds (registration), and those that position the larynx as the prime resonator of vocal tone (resonance).

See **Register**
Resonance
Vowels

Levator: a muscle which raises an organic or skeletal structure, as for example the ribs, the shoulders, the lips, the soft palate and the larynx.

The various levator muscles can be directly influenced during phonation by smiling, by the cultivation of bright tone qualities, by those devices associated with nasal "resonance" (which serve to elevate the larynx, lower the soft palate, and on an acoustic level strengthen the higher partials), by lip rounding and a dropping of the jaw (which lowers the larynx, elevates the soft palate and darkens the tone quality), or by special breathing techniques.

Whether used advisedly or inadvisedly, however, none of the practices mentioned are more than marginally beneficial. All fail to address themselves to the real point at issue, namely, the development and integration of the vocal registers and the release of constricting tensions within the throat parts.

See Bocca Ridente
Lowered Larynx

Liaison: the linking together or redistribution of various phonemes in speech or singing.

Liaison is a common feature of many spoken languages. It frequently occurs in Italian, for example, between words that end with vowels and those that begin with vowels (*e.g., poichè in, scena ancor*). In French, it occurs in the following instances:

1. Between words whose final consonants are generally not pronounced and those that begin with vowels (*e.g., ils arrivent*);
2. Between words whose final consonants are generally not pronounced and those that begin with a mute *h* (*e.g., bon homme*), and
3. For contractions derived from words that end in vowels and those that begin with vowels (*e.g., c'est*).

See Consonants

Lift: a pitch upon which transference is made from one register balance to another; the transference from one register balance to another; the kinesthetic impression derived from such a movement.

While "lifts" can definitely be perceived in the area of register transition (the so-called "break"), they may also be perceived, more subtly, at various segmenting points throughout the tonal range. These points coincide with major physiological readjustments in the length, thickness and elasticity of the vocal folds, *i.e.*, with changes in registration. The relative position of lifts (segmenting points) within the tonal range is shown in Figure 18 (page 331).

Significantly, it is on those pitches which define the borders of the pure and the coordinated falsetto, or head voice, in relation to the chest register that lifts are recognizable. The falsetto, which extends from B below middle C to the octave above, holds the key to an understanding of the subtle transitions exposed by lifts. Success in introducing some degree of coordinate action between this mechanism and the chest register is reflected both in qualitative modifications and in an outward extension in the range of the falsetto in both directions, which transforms it into the head voice. Thus, the lift points closest to the register "break" are identifiable with the pitches at which the pure falsetto terminates, whereas the lifts on the far side of the "break," F below middle C and the F lying an octave and a fourth above middle C, mark the outer boundaries of the coordinated falsetto.

Both the "break" and the lift points within the tonal range will vary somewhat in relation to the weight of the voice and the strength and development of the chest register. Ideally, the chest register should terminate at E—F above middle C. Heavier voice types, however, tend to move this mechanism higher, while on the other hand, lighter voice types often neglect its use entirely.

How the falsetto coordinates with the chest register, therefore, determines to a considerable extent the position of the lift points in the tonal range. Depending upon the type of register balance currently in effect, lift points among the various voice types can vary as much as a major third. Lift points reflect a functional condition and do not provide a suitable point of reference for estimating natural range, tessitura, or voice type. To invest these transitions with an importance they do not possess leads to serious theoretical and procedural miscalculation.

In acknowledging the various segmental points falling within the tonal range, it is also important to recognize that these interadjustments must take place within the framework of an unchanging resonance adjustment. A stable laryngeal position is basic to a correct technique of singing and must be maintained despite changing ratios of registration. If the total range of the voice is to be negotiated smoothly and evenly there must be, rather than a "lifting up and over," a continuous feeling of connection from below, with the tonal flow moving uninterruptedly from the lowest to the uppermost tones of the voice on a perfect legato.

The presence of lift points within the tonal range is neither desirable nor undesirable. More significant is the information they provide about the technical condition of the mechanism as it is reflected in the tone production.

Lift of the Breath: a sensation of reapplied breath pressure often experienced at the various segmenting points throughout the tonal range.

The so-called "lift of the breath" is a sensory illusion created when transference is made from one register balance to another. The term itself, however, is dangerously misleading, since it implies that the singer can exercise direct control over this activity. It is frequently associated with another fallacious concept, "up and over."

Ligament: Latin *ligamentum,* "a band or tie;" a short band of tough, flexible, fibrous tissue that joins bones and/or cartilages and thereby assists in supporting the skeletal framework.

Light Mechanism: the head voice.

Physiologically, the "light" mechanism is a series of sounds produced because of a reduction in the size of the glottal space. This reduction is a result of adjustments made in the length, thickness, and contour of the vocal folds by the cricothyroid and arytenoid muscles, which draw them into tension.

Light Singing: singing characterized by a buoyant tonal texture and low levels of intensity.

Light singing is frequently associated with "marking" or "saving the voice." Continued over protracted periods of time, this practice can become injurious (since in most instances it encourages singing with a collapsed larynx) and arrest vocal development.

Light Voice: a voice characterized by a buoyant tonal texture and limited power.

Although tonal buoyancy is more common among lyric tenors and sopranos, all voice types should be able to sing lightly and buoyantly.

Limbic System: that part of the rhinencephalon, or olfactory brain, which, through its connection with the hypothalamus (the regulator of the autonomic nervous system), regulates the reflexes associated with emotional and behavioral responses (*e.g.,* pleasure, pain, *etc.*).

See Falsetto
 Laryngeal
  Suspension
 Legato
 Register
 Register Segments
 Upper "Break" or
  Upper Passaggio

See Anchored in
  the Chest
 Lift
 Register Segments
 Up and Over

See Head Voice
 Register

See Half Voice
 (To) Mark

190

Because singing is so intimately associated with emotional expression, the limbic system is an integral part of the nervous and muscular systems that comprise the vocal mechanism. Unless the limbic system, or "visceral brain," as it is sometimes called, can function harmoniously with the other elements, learning to sing can be extremely difficult. Anxiety, for example, is a reflection of disruption between the voluntary and involuntary muscular systems, and between the vegetative and nervous systems involved in phonation. It not only fragments the singer's personality, but also limits his capacity for personal expression. Consequently, it interferes with vocal progress.

Limited Range: a tonal compass of less than two octaves.

Any well-used voice extends over a range of at least two to three octaves. A limited range is a result of faulty muscular coordination rather than inherent physical limitations. Frequent causes of restricted tonal range are a "mixed" registration and its constant companion, throat constriction.

Line: legato tonal flow that gives a musical phrase the impression of possessing a linear dimension.

Correct vocalization and good music-making in general depend upon a melodic line, which, when infused with a rhythmic élan, helps the vocal mechanism function at its best.

Lingual: of or relating to the tongue.

Linking: See Liaison.

Lip Falsetto: a term sometimes used to describe a thin, constricted falsetto, possibly because it reflects a certain tenseness of the vocal lips. Since the lip falsetto is incapable of growth or development, it must be considered pedagogically useless.

Lip Rounding: a conscious shaping of the lips to avoid producing tone qualities that are "too open" or "spread," and in general to enhance the quality of the ultimate tonal product.

Lip rounding is usually associated with vowel modification, especially in changing from so-called "open" to "closed" vowels (*e.g., ah* to *oh* or *uh*). It is also used to accomplish the following objectives:

1. Exploit the natural correlation between mouth positions and registration (a smaller mouth opening induces more head register participation; a larger mouth opening induces more chest register participation, *etc.*);
2. Induce the oropharyngeal opening to reflexively assume a shape and form similar to that of the mouth opening;
3. Adjust the mouth and oropharynx so that the low formant is set at its lowest point (about 500 cps), and
4. Influence the ratio of registration by forcing the vocal folds to a length and thickness consonant with the frequency of the pharyngeal cavities.

The acoustic result of these relationships is that the pitch and formant frequencies are brought into closer proximity, an arrangement that does not "tune" the resonators very sharply. It is possible that lip rounding may also position the interior surfaces of the mouth (the hard palate and the ridges behind the upper and lower teeth) to provide the acoustic baffling essential to the formation of a standing wave, which, when present, creates the sensation of "drinking in the tone."

In assessing the importance of lip rounding to phonation, one must also consider the effect it might have upon those muscular systems not subject to volitional control that form the core of the functional process, *i.e.,* the cricothyroid and arytenoid muscles that stretch the vocal folds, the suspensory muscles that stabilize the larynx, and those muscles that adjust the pharyngeal resonators. Since the movement of these muscular systems cannot be sufficiently isolated by lip rounding to strengthen them when they are weak, or to more than marginally improve them when their interaction is imprecise, this practice cannot be considered more than a helpful tool and an occasionally useful device.

The acoustic "set" introduced by lip rounding is a valuable aid in modifying resonance characteristics and in compensating for an overly dominant chest register. An excessive dependence upon lip rounding limits effective vocal communication, since facial expressions must remain independent of tonal needs if the verbal text is to be expressed spontaneously and naturally.

Lip Trill: a rapid oscillation of the lips executed while phonating a tonal quality resembling a hum.

The lip trill has been advocated as an antidote for physical tenseness and lack of coordination among the vocal muscles. However, since it embraces no functional principle, its value is dubious. Although it sometimes enables the singer to phonate higher or lower pitches than usual, the lip trill produces no fundamental or permanent change in a prevailing technical status. Once legitimate phonation is resumed, the vocal muscles revert to their former, habitual (and frequently unwanted) patterns of response. The lip trill is essentially a relaxation exercise, and while relaxation may be a useful point of departure for vocal study, it provides no basis for making those changes essential to technical growth and development. The lip trill serves no purpose other than to raise expectations of progress that are unrealistic and ultimately frustrating to the student.

The primary activities that the lip trill neither improves nor attempts to improve are those muscular movements that account for the phenomena of registration and resonance. Most obviously, execution of the lip trill involves no discernible vowel quality; the pharyngeal resonators whose "tuning" is responsible for selecting and energizing those frequencies which determine and define vowel quality, therefore are either not positioned at all or poorly positioned. To further complicate matters, execution of the lip trill precludes adequate chest register participation at the moment of tonal inception, and consequently makes effective resonance an impossibility (since one of the chest register's prime functions is to serve as a throat opener). Furthermore, since the chest register is inactive and the head register is encouraged to predominate in a tonal area where the latter should remain passive, the chest register is free to "wander" throughout the upper extensions of the voice. In fact, the chest register is actively *encouraged* to do so, since some degree of coordinate activity is required for the articulation of pitches in the upper part of the range. Not only does the lip trill fail to improve an existing technical condition, therefore, but it actually "mixes" the registers and constricts the throat. The inevitable consequence of the lip trill, when used over a protracted period of time, is "white," colorless singing.

The only pedagogic advantage to be gained by using the lip trill is that it offers momentary encouragement to the student by allowing him to produce pitches that he cannot otherwise produce legitimately. Compared to the long-lasting benefits to be derived from procedures designed to regulate the subtle interplay between stimulus and response, *i.e.*, registration, the lip trill is of little pedagogic value. A more constructive training program quite clearly requires a more perceptive understanding of vocal mechanics, kinesthetic sensitivity, conceptual sharpness, and listening acuity. The lip trill and similar devices fail to address themselves to these areas of development.

See Kinesthesia
Laryngeal
   Suspension
Modern Methods
Register
Resonance
Standing Wave
Vocal Study
Vowel

Liquid: a tonal impression created by a lyric, smoothly flowing vocal line and characterized by an evenly pulsating vibrato.

See Vibrato

(To) Listen: to attend closely for the purpose of auditory cognition.

Listening is an intermediary stage of auditory perception between hearing and understanding: one can, for example, hear without listening and both hear and listen without understanding.

For the student of singing, there are three kinds of listening: 1) aesthetic, 2) functional, and 3) emotional. Aesthetic listening is that concerned with the qualitative evaluation of vocal tone. Functional listening, a capability which is refined through experience and training, is the ability to associate various tone qualities with the underlying mechanical processes which have produced them. Emotional listening is that form of auditory perception influenced by predetermined tonal concepts (prejudice for or against a certain type of sound, the quality of a certain artist, *etc.*).

Learning how to listen is indispensable to both teaching and technical training. Through intelligent listening and a strong sense of kinetic rhythm, the singer can grow into an understanding of his own voice, and ultimately into an understanding of himself as a person.

See Auditory Feedback
Emotional
   Listening
Kinesthesia
Functional
   Listening
Self-Listening

Localized Effort: a concentration of energy into one part of the vocal mechanism to the neglect of other functional elements that are equally, if not more, important.

Localized effort results from muscular imbalances within the vocal mechanism which necessitate the introduction of compensatory activities. While many of the expressions of interfering tension are due to natural technical limitations, they are often exacerbated by training methods which attempt to gain direct control over the vocal apparatus by means of breath "control," voice "placement," tonal "support," nasal "resonance," and similar directives. By relying upon these and similar control mechanisms, energy is artifically channeled, *i.e.*, wrongly directed, a situation which inevitably results in tonal forcing.

Localized effort results in a gradual diminution of vocal powers, a loss reflected in tonal unsteadiness, tremulous movements of the jaw and tongue, a flushed face, distended veins, facial grimaces, and a shaking body. To eliminate such distortions, the natural equilibrium of the mechanism must be restored. By discarding all

See Breathing
Equilibrium
Holistic Pedagogy
Kinesthesia
Laryngeal
   Suspension
Muscular
   Independence
Placement
Register
Relaxation
Resonance

processes based upon localized effort, it will be possible to release the vocal mechanism so that it can respond in accordance with its reflexive nature.

Loft Voice: a term used by speech pathologists and phoneticians to refer to the vocal "register" thought to be responsible for the production of higher fundamental frequencies.

While the term "loft voice" was coined to clarify traditional terminology (falsetto, head voice, *etc.*), it is in fact less specific in its connotation than the terms it was designed to replace. The objection to this concept is that the term has no functional basis, since, unlike falsetto, it refers to a pitch range rather than to a separate and distinct physiological adjustment.

The falsetto extends from B below middle C to the octave above. When it is combined with the chest register, it is transformed into the head voice, a type of register balance whose range includes that of the falsetto and extends both above and below it. The so-called "register" referred to as "loft voice" is the head voice and not a basic register mechanism.

"Loft voice" is but one of many descriptive titles introduced since the turn of the century to denote what has been commonly recognized for well over two hundred years as the "head voice." It is neither a needed addition nor an improvement over the more traditional nomenclature.

Long Reed Mechanism: the chest register.

Long Vowel: a vowel phoneme sustained for emphatic purposes; a phonetic vowel type.

Longitudinal Tension: that force, a result of cricothyroid contraction, which elongates the vocal folds.

Longitudinal tension is responsible for pitch in singing. As longitudinal tension is increased by the pull of the cricothyroids, pitch rises, and *vice versa*. The precision with which the cricothyroids and other laryngeal muscular systems coordinate largely determines the quality of the ultimate tonal product.

Longitudinal Wave: a compression wave which travels through an elastic medium on a relatively horizontal plane. For example, a tuning fork struck and made to vibrate causes the air particles nearest the vibrating fork to expand and contract with greater energy than is the case in the air space either above or below the fork.

Loose: See Lax.

Loosely Coupled: See Coupling.

Loss of Voice: an inability to phonate.

Loss of voice can be brought on by pathological disturbances (severe colds, tumors, cancer, *etc.*), or by abuse of the vocal organs (faulty technique, consistent oversinging or undersinging, inappropriate repertoire, *etc.*). When loss of voice

See **Bel Canto**
Falsetto
Falsetto or
   Head Voice
Middle Register
Register

See **Vowel**

a result of the former, one must consult an appropriate medical specialist; when it is a result of the latter, one must consider changing teachers.

Loudness: a quantitative aspect of intensity.

The perception of loudness in singing is a complex phenomenon dependent upon physical and psychological variables in both singer and listener, including the following:

1. Intensity;
2. Tonal quality;
3. The harmonic spectra of the tones produced;
4. The acoustic properties of the room;
5. The degree of fatigue of both singer and listener;
6. Hearing acuity;
7. Interest, and
8. Psychological and tonal predilections.

See **Exercise**
  Hearing
  Intensity

Low Formant: the lower of the two frequency bands activated in a harmonic series, *i.e.*, a fundamental and its overtones.

Low Formant Vowels: vowels whose quality is determined by a strong second formant. For example, *oo* is a low formant vowel.

See **Formants**
  Vowels

Low Register: a more appropriate name for what has been traditionally recognized as the chest register, or those tones lying below the register "break."

See **Register**

Low Voice Press: a dubious method for developing the extreme low tones of the bass voice by lowering the chin and depressing the larynx.

Lower Constrictor: synonymous with inferior constrictor, a paired muscle (of which there are three separate groups) which serves to narrow the pharyngeal wall.

Lower Mechanism: another (and more appropriate) name for the so-called "chest register."

Lowered Larynx: an adjustment which finds the larynx in a position lower than that assumed when in its natural state of rest; in contemporary pedagogy, a term virtually synonymous with "covering."

The teaching of singing with a lowered larynx first appeared on the vocal scene in France (1830), when Duprez astonished the music-loving public with his declamatory and *couverte* tone production. Several advantages accrue from the use of this technique: 1) the "darker" tone quality energizes the fundamental more strongly; 2) there is an immediate increase in tonal volume, and 3) it is possible to bring certain aspects of laryngeal functioning under direct control.

The popularity of Duprez' singing style quickly gave way to the more highly prized liquidity of Bel Canto, and it was not until the close of the century, when the more heavily orchestrated music being performed in the opera houses of the Western world demanded greater opulence of tone and a broader spectrum of tonal "coloring," that singing with a lowered larynx again became an issue. Manuel Garcia was among the first to confront this new development, recognizing that every voice possessed two basic timbres, which he described as "closed" and "open." The closed, "dark" (*sombre*) quality he described in his *Hints on Singing* as being produced when the larynx assumed a slightly lower position than its normal state of rest, an adjustment accompanied by a reflexive elevation of the soft palate and an overall enlargement of the throat cavity.

A fundamental distinction to be made between Duprez' technique and that advocated by Garcia is that with the former the larynx was *volitionally* lowered, whereas with the latter it lowered in response to a natural coloring of the voice through emotional identification. This distinction is important, since, as history records, Duprez' singing style was solely declamatory and deprived the voice of its natural flexibility. Garcia, on the contrary, was emphatic in stating that "dark" and "bright" tonal qualities (synonymous with "closed" and "open" timbres) were essentially the same. He believed that the lowering of the larynx for "closed" timbres caused a general enlargement of the pharyngeal area in all its dimensions, an adjustment which permitted the singer to move freely from "darker" to "brighter" timbres without a fundamental shift in the tonal "set."

In keeping with earlier tradition, Garcia's solution to the heightened demands for power and a broader range of emotional expression was not accomplished at the expense of flexibility and the fine nuances of the *messa di voce,* whereas Duprez' volitional lowering of the larynx led to tonal stiffness, inflexibility, premature vocal decline, and a rather monochromic delivery of both music and text.

Procedures for developing vocal skills by deliberately assuming a low laryngeal position came into greater prominence during the third decade of the twentieth century. This revival of interest is attributable to the fact that by "darkening" the voice, a weight is added that might otherwise be lacking or too difficult to achieve by more legitimate means, *i.e.,* by the patient, time-consuming processes which result in a fine tuning of the pharyngeal resonators and a precise balancing of the vocal registers while the larynx is maintained in its normal position.

The disadvantage of a volitional lowering of the larynx and an artificial darkening of the tone quality is that these procedures inevitably force the vocal folds to adjust to a greater length than is ideal for the pitch, intensity and vowel pattern being sung. Such an adjustment requires greater physical effort and the expenditure of an excessive amount of breath pressure to maintain the vibratility of the vocal cords. An inevitable consequence of this artificial darkening of the tone quality is that it affects the suspensory muscles adversely, upsetting a desired equilibrium between the infrahyoids, which contract too strongly, and their natural antagonists the suprahyoids, which become too relaxed. In addition, other suspensory muscles which also depress the larynx, notably the sternothyroids and the cricopharyngeals are similarly forced out of their natural condition of balanced tension. When excessive, the imbalances resulting from this breakdown of equilibrium cause the larynx to lower, the soft palate to rise, and the pharyngeal cavities to expand abnormally; these adjustments are associated with the negative aspects of "co ering." Once this occurs, the throat parts become stiff, a symptom characteristic of those who have been encouraged to sing with a low larynx.

The immediate, if transitory, benefits to be derived from a deliberate lowering of the larynx are the following:

1. Instant contact with the larynx as a resonator, and consequently contact with what is known as the "core" of the tone;
2. An energizing of the low formants, which reflexively (because of the cavity coupling with which they are associated) introduce more head voice;
3. Greater tonal opulence due to the excessive lengthening and broadening of the pharyngeal cavities, and
4. An improved "set" of the head, which sometimes juts forward to alleviate the discomfort experienced when the larynx rises in response to a "mixed" registration.

An additional advantage is that together with breathing, a lowering of the larynx is one of the few elements involved in tone production subject to direct control. This persuades the unwary that because something is being "done," much is being accomplished.

Among the negative aspects of a lowered laryngeal position are the following:

1. A loss of flexibility;
2. An approximate tuning of the pharyngeal resonators, which requires force to achieve and sustain tonal brightness (a long resonating column does not amplify higher pitches efficiently);
3. A higher rate of breath expulsion;
4. A disproportionate amount of chest voice, causing a "locking" of the registration;
5. A certain amount of vowel distortion because of an imprecise tuning of the pharyngeal cavities;
6. A further distortion of the vowel because the registers have been "locked" into a static adjustment and the pharyngeal resonators are forced to induce the necessary changes in registration, *i.e.*, *ah* having to be modified to *oh* at the point of register transit, a practice known as "covering;"
7. A tendency to overbear the upper tonal range, causing a weakness in the production of low tones, "pushing," tonal unsteadiness in the upper middle range, and an inability to swell and diminish smoothly and evenly, especially in the area of the register crossing, and
8. A misconception that the pharyngeal enlargement accompanying a lowered larynx assures an open-throated resonance adjustment.

From the standpoint of practical pedagogy, the negative by-products of singing ith a lowered laryngeal position far outweigh any merits such a procedure might herwise possess. The adjustment does not facilitate the production of pure vowel ualities, promote breath economy, make possible an evenly graded scale, or cure nal unsteadiness. Perhaps the greatest shortcoming inherent in this practice is at, while it enlarges the throat column, it does not necessarily free it from conricting tensions or "tune" the resonators precisely.

A low laryngeal adjustment (which can be simulated by yawning) is a volitional t every singer is capable of making. Were constricting tensions to be so easily released, the achievement of an open-throated resonance adjustment would no longer be a major obstacle to the development of vocal skills. Since most vocalists are now exposed to training procedures which encourage a low laryngeal adjustment, it would follow that throat constriction would be either uncommon, or a problem easily eliminated. However, it is obvious that few vocalists in the world sing without some degree of throat tension (those who do are considered "exceptional"), and it is evident that a volitional lowering of the larynx is not the answer to the problems encountered when working toward an open-throated technique of singing. Furthermore, if the traditional execution of the *messa di voce* is considered the ultimate criterion of a correct tone production, the concept of the lowered larynx must be rejected, since it is impossible to swell and diminish smoothly and evenly when the larynx is changing from a lower to a higher position (as it must if high tones are to be sung softly) when at the same time the vocal folds embedded within are shifting their ratio of tension. This inability is common among singers who consistently rely on a lowered laryngeal position, especially one that has been assumed deliberately.

Theoretical explanations to justify the practice of singing with a lowered larynx reflect a general unfamiliarity with this technique and its significant features. According to surveys made by Victor Alexander Fields and John Carroll Burgin, pedagogic viewpoints during the first half of the century concerning the desirability of singing with a lowered larynx were evenly divided. While most seem to have agreed that singing with an elevated larynx is incorrect, the reasons given for singing with a lowered larynx are not convincing. What is clearly evident from the study is that up to this time few teachers of singing had given the matter much thought.

A typical sampling of the opinions expressed in these and other studies cover a wide range. Astolfo Pescia (1948) contended that the "larynx must lie in the low lying position where Nature has placed it." Charles Kennedy Scott (1954) was more explicit, believing that the larynx lowers when producing "dark," lugubrious tones but he did not consider this position ideal for normal tonal coloration. This differ from an earlier pronouncement by the same author (1933), who then believed that the larynx should always assume a "rather low" position. After extensive research Joel J. Pressman concluded in 1942 that the larynx should not be maintaine consistently in any fixed position, implying that its maneuverability, while sligh was related to tone "color," and minimally to pitch. The results of more recer scientific studies are more dogmatic, the consensus being that the lowered laryn or "singer's formant," as it is sometimes called, produces the most satisfacto tonal results under all conditions of vocalization.

On the basis of scientific research conducted during the past half century, it the consensus of investigators that singing with a lowered larynx is a permane good. Essentially, however, their findings report on the measurable properties a current fashion in vocal technique without questioning whether or not this tec nique is consistently employed by those singers who are generally classified "exceptional." Whether or not singers of the caliber of Bjoerling, Domingo, Flagsta Ponselle, Galli-Curci, Pavarotti, and Corelli (to name but a few) employ or er ployed a low laryngeal adjustment is a question that has never been raised. It wou be of great interest to know, for example, if professional singers uniformly ado this practice, and if they do, whether it is by virtue of the training received or as part of their natural endowment.

Other questions must be answered before a correct value judgment can be placed on a lowered larynx as a permanent good. If some great singers have had great careers not utilizing a low laryngeal adjustment, and others equally successful sing with a low larynx, can it be said that any particular laryngeal adjustment fulfills an essential functional requirement? Is it possible that those who succeed professionally have done so *because* of singing with a low larynx, or *in spite* of it? Are those who sing well with a low larynx proficient because of that, or because of other factors, *e.g.,* a well-balanced registration and a relative absence of inhibiting constrictions? Did they sing with a low larynx both before and after training? Has the era of the low larynx in singing produced singers of the caliber of those who were pre-eminent during the great Golden Age of Song? If not, can the difference in vocal skills be attributed to a difference between the low laryngeal tone production now fashionable and a more normal positioning of the larynx? Is it possible to "build" voices of exquisite technical excellence (as was done in former times) when this technique forms the basis of instruction, or is success reserved for those who already have naturally well-formed voices? Do talented students of average ability prosper under this regimen, or is real progress reserved for the very few?

If the above questions cannot be answered in the affirmative (and it is evident that they cannot), then is it not true that a volitional positioning of the larynx is an arbitrary and negative procedure for the singer with serious vocal problems? Concern for a proper positioning of the larynx, as the teachers of the Golden Age of Song knew so well, would seem to be a matter best left to nature and a natural organic response to those mechanical principles which, when sensibly applied, adjust the vocal mechanism with a precision not to be achieved by overt acts.

One of the hidden errors in research into this and other phases of the vocal function is that the studies are based upon the "average" singer, or perhaps the technical status of professional singers who are no longer in their best vocal estate, *i.e.,* no longer employing the technique that was operative when their voices were fresh and spontaneously produced. What is not considered is that singers of average ability are often "average" because they use their voices, to some degree, in violation of nature's laws. Since singing with a lowered larynx is something one *does,* it is likely that this technique violates those laws.

Another consistent error in published reports of studies made on laryngeal positioning is that the singers used are divided into two groups, trained and untrained, with no distinction made as to the qualitative properties of their technical status. Logically, this results in placing the above-named artists under the "untrained" classification, since their formal training was either negligible or nonexistent. Oversights of this kind also fail to take into account the general acceptance of the curious dichotomy between the technique of those who are known to be "natural" singers and those whose technical limitations put them in the unflattering category of "trained" singers. Until studies are made of the exceptional singer who uses his voice "naturally" rather than sounding "trained," the value of such studies will be questionable.

The general thrust of scientific analysis up to the present purports to prove that singing with a low larynx is superior to other techniques. Because it enlarges the throat cavities, the technique is looked upon as "open-throated." This reasoning, by extension, implies that those who do not sing with a low larynx perform less efficiently and/or suffer from some degree of throat constriction. Both physically and acoustically, this premise appears to be false. A longer vibrating column does not resonate higher tones efficiently, nor does the fact that most professional or trained singers employ this technique make it right; it only means that the techique is popular.

Placed within a historical perspective, it would appear that concepts related to larngeal positioning vary with time and place. The Italians prefer a stable laryngeal adjustment yielding a more "open" tone quality. The French, with their adoption of the *voix mixte*, advocate a slightly elevated laryngeal adjustment, while German teaching methods favor the more "closed" vowel form and a lowered larynx. In the age of Bel Canto, where flexibility and tonal brilliance went hand in hand with tonal opulence, the lowered laryngeal position was most definitely neither reflected in the musical style nor included in published accounts of the instruction given.

Fashions and cultural attitudes as they affect functional principles do not provide a sound basis upon which to build a viable vocal pedagogy. Until such time as attention is addressed to discovering what is functionally more natural and effective, only those who are exceptionally gifted will transcend their cultural limitations. Unless training procedures are so constructed that singers sound "natural" rather than "trained," all theories must be questioned and studied with care. To date, this has not been done.

Lung: either of the paired, spongelike, thoracic sacs that constitute the basic respiratory organ.

Lyric: a term derived from the Latin *lyra,* or "lyre," an ancient musical instrument possessing light, flowing tonal qualities; a voice type possessing these tonal characteristics; a text set to music.

As applied to singing, the term "lyric" refers to any voice of lighter weight and texture. Thus, the so-called "lyric soprano," "lyric tenor," and "lyric baritone" are characterized by lighter tonal textures than those of their dramatic counterparts. (For some reason, the "lyric bass" is generally referred to as a *basso cantante,* or "singing bass.") The Italian *lirico spinto,* or "pushed lyric," is a somewhat ambiguous vocal category (usually a soprano or tenor) possessing both lyric and dramatic (full-bodied) qualities.

Regardless of vocal weight, repertory, or temperament, all voice types should sing lyrically. This is especially true of dramatic voices, whose possessors tend to rely too heavily on the chest register for their heroic effects, and often resort to forcing.

See Bel Canto
Covering,
  (To) Cover
Formants
Modern Methods
Natural Movement
Open Throat
Register
Resonance
Vocal Training
Vowel
Vowel Modification

See (To) Force
Spinto

M

Maintained Vibration: an oscillating movement sustained by an external or auxiliary source of energy.

When a pendulum is allowed to swing freely, its arc is gradually diminished by friction and the pull of gravity. If its oscillations are to remain constant, an auxiliary source of energy (*e.g.*, a wound spring) equal to these resisting forces must be applied. When this occurs, the pendulum's movement is transformed from free vibration to maintained vibration.

The vocal function is another example of maintained vibration. When the technique is efficient, the vocal folds are maintained in vibration by neurological impulses generated by the brain in response to conceptualized musical stimuli. In order for vocal vibration to be so maintained, there must exist a state of muscular equilibrium throughout the entire tract. In all other instances (*i.e.*, when the technique is faulty), vocal vibration must be maintained by breath pressure, regulated by various types of breath "management," and/or manipulated by other forms of overt physical activity.

See **Breathing**
Energy
Equilibrium
Puff Theory

Male Alto: a man who sings the alto part in a choral composition; a falsettist.

See **Countertenor**

Mandible: the lower jaw.

Manipulation: the use of manual and/or mechanical means to assist the vocal mechanism to adjust more efficiently.

Although it is physically possible to adjust the position of the tongue, and consequently the position of the larynx, and to move the shield cartilage ("Adam's apple") away from the ring cartilage by manipulatory means, it should go without saying that these practices are extremely dangerous.

Mannerisms: eccentricities of action, bearing, or treatment.

Vocal mannerisms are generally manifested by facial expressions, postures, and gestures that have no relevance to the text or music being sung. Frequent examples are exaggerated inspiratory preparation, fixed tongue and mouth positions, a constant, artificial smile, and the so-called "singer's stance."

Most vocal mannerisms develop out of attempts to gain direct control over the vocal function; all induce muscular interference and inhibit effective communication at every level of performance.

See **Mechanistic**
Training

MANUFACTURED TONE

Manufactured Tone: a vocalized sound whose seemingly artificial tonal characteristics result from the imposition of will over function.

"Manufactured" tones are the result of training methods which persuade the singer that he can improve his tone quality by overt preparations, such as these:

1. Assuming the so-called "singer's stance;"
2. Presetting the tongue, mouth, or lips;
3. Maintaining a constant facial expression;
4. Breathing with an elevated rib cage or protruding abdomen;
5. Directing vocal vibrations (tonal "placement," *etc.*);
6. Identifying with and reinforcing specific symptoms of vibration (*i.e.*, "resonating" vocal tone in the head, chest, sinuses, or facial mask), and
7. Adjusting the pharyngeal cavities (as in "covering") or adding "ping."

See **Bel Canto**
Functional
  Listening
Laryngeal
  Suspension
Modern Methods
Register
Vocal Study
Vowel

Such procedures ignore the fact that vocal tone is primarily the product of involuntary muscular activity, and assume that desirable aesthetic goals can be realized by a combination of static procedures. Their natural consequence is tone qualities that sound contrived and artificial ("manufactured") rather than spontaneous and natural. At best, voices taught by these means sound "well trained."

(To) Mark: to "save the voice" by singing softly or taking upper notes down an octave.

As is true of all vocal matters, marking can be either beneficial or harmful; it can be done correctly or incorrectly; it can save the voice or it can ruin it. How and when it is done, if at all, depends in large part on the voice type, its functional condition and general inclination, as well as the amount of singing to be concentrated into a short period of time. As a rule of thumb, the vocal mechanism, like the body, remains comfortable when it has not been maintained too long in a rigid mold. Each singer, therefore, must discover for himself the best way of marking. For some, sustained soft singing will be detrimental, since their technique is so structured that the laryngeal suspension cannot be maintained at lower levels of intensity. For them, the only useful form of marking is to drop octaves.

See **Mezza Voce**
(To) Save the
  Voice

Each singer must learn how to "nurse" his voice, and each must learn by experience when and how to mark effectively. There are no hard and fast rules.

Masculine Voice: a tone quality produced by the vocal organs when the chest register functions as the dominant mechanism.

A masculine voice quality is not exclusively a male attribute. Functionally, the vocal mechanism is asexual, the apparent difference between male and female voice types being one of age and tonal range. Those qualitative differences commonly recognized between male and female voice, therefore, are attributable to physical changes which occur during puberty, at which time the enlargement of the male larynx causes the natural pitch range to lower by approximately one octave. Since, however, the natural tonal range of men lies in a pitch area which readily activates the chest register, the expression "masculine voice" has become virtually synonymous with that mechanism. Conversely, since female voices do not drop an octave as they grow into maturity, women normally speak and sing in the head voice, and the softer textures associated with this mechanism are looked upon (regardless of sex) as being more feminine.

The proximity of male and female vocal ranges to the chest register and head voice, respectively, makes their reliance upon one or the other mechanism both logical and predictable. Cultural attitudes and sociological trends also play an important role in the conscious or subconscious selection of "masculine" or "feminine" pitch ranges and tonal textures. In the latter part of the nineteenth century, for example, "ladies" and "gentlemen" (*i.e.,* those in the upper socioeconomic strata) set themselves apart, vocally, from other members of society by elevating the pitch level of their speaking voices—often to the point of affectation. George Bernard Shaw's delightful *Pygmalion* dramatizes the correlation between speech habits and social status: Eliza Doolittle is transformed from a belting, lower register-dominated "guttersnipe" to a soft-spoken, genteel young lady.

The cultural history of the past three centuries reveals undeniable parallels between accepted modes of personal expression (manners, dress, sexual identity, age, *etc.*) and pitch levels as these affect voice quality. The assignment of roles in operatic literature provides an insight into the specific nature of these parallel relationships, and it is more than coincidence that at the present time (with the growing tendency toward unisex) phoniatrists have observed that the pitch ranges of the speaking voices of males and females have also moved closer together.

Regardless of cultural and psychologically motivated attitudes which lean toward the adoption of one voice characteristic over another, it is evident that a masculine voice is the product of function and register balance rather than gender. Consequently, insofar as the male voice occupies a position in the overall pitch range which includes a high percentage of chest register-oriented tones, those who use this mechanism (whether male or female) are now said to have a masculine voice.

See Castrato
      Register

Mask: French *masque,* meaning "mask" or "countenance;" the facial area around the nose and eyes behind which are located the antra and sinuses.

Many theorists, following the lead of Jean de Reszke and Ernest G. White, believe that the cavities behind the facial mask are the principal resonators of vocal tone. This misconception arises from an awareness of the symptoms of vibration produced in this area by the radiation of vibratory impulses that travel from the tonal source by means of bone conduction. The laryngeal and oral pharynges, however, are the primary sources of cavity resonance during phonation.

See Cavity Tone Theory
      Dans la Masque
      Resonance

Mask Brilliance: resonance characteristics sought and admired by those who advocate training procedures such as "placement," the cultivation of tonal "ping," and nasal resonance.

The tonal brilliance rather easily acquired by conventional practices is false, since it is produced by throat constriction rather than by a proper positioning of the larynx and pharyngeal cavities, which alone yield genuine tonal resonance and "ring."

See Focus
      Placement
      Nasality
      Resonance
      Twenty-Eight
        Hundred

Masking: an acoustic effect created when the frequency and intensity of one sound make indistinct or imperceptible those of another.

The effect of masking results when, as more than one auditory stimulus reaches the nerve fibers of the basilar membrane at the same time, the fibers vibrate sympathetically with the stronger impulse and transmit it to the center of hearing in the cerebral cortex, where it is interpreted as sound; the weaker stimuli are perceived, if at all, only dimly.

Masking has been used in scientific experiments related to singing (in particular, those of Dr. Donald Maxwell of Midwestern State University, Texas) by supplying singers with electronic signals (commonly called "white noise") through earphones to study the relationship between internal and external hearing perception. The purpose of these experiments has been to determine the degree to which hearing during phonation is influenced by auditory feedback and the extent to which vocal functioning can be improved by masking.

To date, the result of masking and its possible benefit to vocal training is promising, if inconclusive.

See Auditory Feedback
    Energy
    Hearing
    Mental Concept
    Self-Listening
    White Noise

Mechanistic Training: procedures whose purpose is to influence and improve involuntary muscular movements by acting upon those which are directly accessible, *i.e.*, the tongue, breathing mechanism, the mouth and facial expressions.

In their most extreme form, mechanistic training methods resort to the use of tongue depressors and hand manipulations of the thyroid cartilage. Since, however, the essential functions of the vocal mechanism are inaccessible to such controls, it may readily be understood why such methods consistently fail of their purpose.

See Bel Canto
    Modern Methods
    Vocal Study
    (To) Yawn

Mellow Tone: a vocalized sound whose "warm," "rich" tonal characteristics result from the concentration of energy within the lower formants of the harmonic spectrum.

See Formant

Mental Attitude: an emotional and intellectual stance taken when becoming involved in the creative process.

Mental attitudes largely determine the success or failure of vocal study. When talent, personality, and a healthy mental attitude are brought into proper perspective, vocal success is reasonably attainable. A healthy mental attitude not only involves self-knowledge, but also appreciating (though not necessarily agreeing with) the creative strivings of others.

Mental Concept: a perception of pitch, vowel quality, variations of intensity and other musical factors which prompts physical responses resulting in vocal tone.

Phonation begins with a mental concept. In its broadest aspect, the concept involves a number of subjective physical and psychological factors such as hearing, judgment, self-image, aesthetic goals and imagination. What emerges as tone quality is a reflection of the clarity or opaqueness of the concepts that have been formed and of the physical capability of the vocal organs to transform those concepts into sound. The purpose of training is to regulate the various conceptual, physical, and psychological variables that influence the ultimate tonal product, and, by using each to improve the other, bring all of the complex elements into a harmonious functional relationship. Since the body obeys and carries out what the mind conceives, it is with mental concepts that the voice-training process both begins and ends.

As a cognitive organ, the mind, during phonation, plays a dual role: while on the one hand it "hears" a tonal form prior to its physical transformation into sound, it also hears and evaluates the resulting tonal product after the vocal organs have made that transformation. The former process is conceptualization; the latter is self-listening. Since in all but the rarest cases the vocal muscles are imperfectly coordinated, and consequently translate the tonal concepts inaccurately, there is an ever present discrepancy among singers between intent and result, *i.e.*, between subjectivity and objectivity.

There are three interrelated factors to be mentioned in connection with lost objectivity: taste, tension and conditioning. In many areas where contact with the world is established through the five senses, conditioning is almost preordained. What may appear exotic and foreign to one will be natural and delightful to another. Value is attached to a thing simply because one has become accustomed to it, or because it is commonly approved. We can also "learn" to like things, and this is often true of certain foods, decor, painting and music, as well as tone qualities.

All of this may be acceptable in many areas of aesthetics, but not in developing vocal skills. In a correct technique of singing there is only one valid concept of the natural: the view that the functional capability of the vocal organs should operate in conformity with nature's laws. Unfortunately, when the vocal technique does not so conform, one can easily be conditioned to like many types of tone quality which are far from being either functionally correct or aesthetically pleasing. This is especially likely to happen with those who are psychologically geared to look for security in a "method" and to "grasp" an idea, in which case objectivity can be lost completely. It is through the capacity of the mind to form a prior concept and then register another impression *after the vocal organs have responded* that dramatic technical improvement can be made.

Alterations in the prior concept can be brought about because the vocal organs react involuntarily to selected patterns of pitch and intensity. By combining these in such a way as to induce a response not pictured in the preconcept, the singer is left open to the possibility of making sounds which he has neither made before nor associated with himself. The mental impressions recorded by the singer can thus be influenced, controlled and reformed. By understanding the processes which evoke a particular type of reflexive tonal response, the teacher can promote changes which the cognitive powers of the talented should be quick to recognize.

A practical means for developing new conceptual images is consequently available. The student need only concentrate on the pitch, intensity, vowel and rhythmic patterns projected by the teacher and respond freely without regard for aesthetic goals. In essence, the student must respond *exclusively to the stimulus* rather than to specific qualitative concepts. Thus, quality expressed in terms of "my quality," "forwardness," "point," "ping," "nasal resonance," or any other imagery that interferes with the vocal process must be ruthlessly discarded. Left unencumbered by outer-imposed disciplines, the vocal organs will then react in a manner more in keeping with their functional potential. Through reliance upon natural rhythmic movement, changes in quality and in the textural properties of the registration will occur—*changes which will be anticipated by the teacher, but not by the student.*

Natural quality, a product of natural movement, depends upon evaluations which must agree not with taste, but with nature's laws. This means that objective and subjective concepts are to be brought into agreement not only with each other, but also with the functional logic by which the vocal organs are governed.

Mental Control: the conscious attempt to exercise restraining or directing influences over physical, emotional and/or psychological responses.

Mental control is frequently used to produce desired results in many human activities. Vocal health, however, like general health, while influenced by thinking, is nevertheless a psychophysical state of being, and neither mental control nor external constraints can stimulate desired responses from the vocal muscles when they are poorly coordinated. Thus, while the mind can and should direct the vocal process, it cannot effectively *will* things to happen unless the vocal muscles are able to respond as directed.

Right mental control must work within the framework of functional possibilities based upon an understanding of natural movement. Wrong mental control is an imposition of the will over function. By pursuing those training procedures which stimulate an involuntary muscular system, the singer is able to grow into an understanding of the nature of legitimate mental control. The concepts developed out of this procedure will then be in keeping with the functional logic by which the movement potential of the vocal muscles is governed.

Among the positive contributions that the effective use of mental control can make during training are the following:

1. Promotion of a correct posture;
2. The regulation of musical elements (changes in pitch, intensity, vowel, *etc.*);
3. The articulation of tonal textures related to the phenomenon of registration (falsetto, chest register, *etc.*), and
4. The ability to respond to general descriptive terms such as "round," "spread," "bright," "dark," "open," "covered," and various sensations of vibration.

See **Kinesthesia**
Mental Concept
Register
Rhythm
Self-Regulation
Sensations of
Vibration

Proper juxtaposition and manipulation of the elements noted above is sufficient to ensure the proper development and coordination of the vocal mechanism. For those willing to discard preconceived aesthetic objectives, and who are able to respond with some measure of spontaneity, the vocal exercises projected will succeed in stimulating the vocal muscles into improved response patterns. The result is that the singer will become gradually informed as to the kind of mental control he should ultimately exercise.

Messa di Voce: Italian, "to put forth, or bud;" to "place" (in the sense of everything being *in* place); according to Domenico Corri, a pupil of Porpora, "to prepare the voice for a crescendo;" in singing, a vocal ornament consisting of the gradual swelling and diminishing of a single tone.

The *messa di voce* was widely used both as a musical ornament and as a pedagogic exercise throughout the Bel Canto era. Indicated by the symbols < > over and under a note, it is common in printed vocal music (including the early operas of Verdi) through the middle of the nineteenth century. As a musical ornament its successful execution was considered the epitome of the singer's art and indicated a complete mastery of vocal technique. As a pedagogic exercise, the *messa di voce* was used to join the two register mechanisms (the falsetto, and the *voce di petto*, or "chest voice") in the area of register transition (E—F above middle C).

Successful execution of the *messa di voce* is marked by the gradual swelling and diminishing of a single tone from *pianissimo* to *fortissimo* and back to *pianissimo* with little or no change in vowel quality.

Metallic Tone: a vocalized sound whose "hard," "bright" tonal characteristics are the result of a rigid pharyngeal adjustment and a preponderance of high partials (many of which are inharmonic, *i.e.*, "noise") within its harmonic spectrum.

Metallic tone qualities are a manifestation of vocal misuse.

Method: a pedagogic procedure based upon the orderly and systematic presentation of materials relevant to a particular subject or discipline (*e.g.*, learning to sing).

Every voice is as unique as its possessor, each of whom has a different personality, temperament, and vocal condition, and whose specific needs must be addressed in a special way. So-called "vocal methods," such as those of Bordogni, Concone, Nava, Vaccai and others are static, sterile approaches to training the singing voice, and consequently are incapable of meeting individual needs and solving individual problems (*e.g.*, a "mixed" registration, throat constriction, *etc.*). While there are some basic functional principles and immutable natural laws that apply to all voices, nevertheless, in constructive vocal training there are as many "methods" as there are pupils.

Some have cited the intrinsic musical value of the vocal methods mentioned above as justification for their inclusion in the pedagogic process. However, as opposed to former times, there is now a wealth of musical literature available for study which serves the same purpose, and which possesses the added advantage of being suitable for performance.

Mezza Voce: Italian, "half voiced;" phonation characterized by lower levels of intensity.

Mezza voce singing can be of several kinds: 1) open-throated and full-bodied, a type which indicates that the larynx is functioning effectively as a resonating agent and that the chest register is holding synergetically against the pull of the head voice; 2) shut off, because the pharyngeal passageway is constricted, and 3) rather bodiless and "unsupported," a technical condition which finds the suspensory muscles that stabilize the larynx to ensure a clear, "floating" tone quality improperly balanced.

Since *mezza voce* singing is impossible unless the head voice performs as the dominant register mechanism, it is natural that *mezza voce* singing reflects the tonal characteristics associated with that register, tones so produced being softer and sweeter in texture than those heard in full-voiced singing.

Mezzo-Contralto: a very rare voice type whose tonal characteristics and tessitura are lighter and higher than those of the contralto, yet fuller and lower than those of the mezzo-soprano.

See Bel Canto
Falsetto
Falsetto or
Head Voice
Middle Register
Register

See Energy
Kinesthesia
Larynx
Modern Methods
Register
Resonance
Vocal Training
Vowel

See Laryngeal
Suspension
Register
Synergy

Mezzo Falso: Italian, "half falsetto;" an archaic expression synonymous with the lower portion of the male head voice.

The *mezzo falso* is a tone quality which indicates that the pure falsetto (falling within the tonal area extending from B below middle C to the octave above) shares some degree of coordinate relationship with the chest voice, a technical condition marking the first step in the development of the head voice and the ultimate fusing of the two register mechanisms into a functional unit.

While the use of the term *mezzo falso* has long since fallen into disuse, an examination of its meaning is useful in that, like *mezzo petto* (half chest), later to become the *voix mixte,* it is a special kind of coordinated registration. Caccini, Tosi, Mancini, Garcia, and other notable teachers of an earlier period clearly stated that all voice types, male and female, possessed a register called "falsetto." The presence and purpose of the *mezzo falso* was explicitly considered by them to be an important intermediate step in combining this mechanism with the chest register.

Failure to understand that the *mezzo falso* is a composite of two contributing and partially fused elements has led to current misunderstandings surrounding the "middle" register. While the expression may be archaic, it nevertheless indicates the important role of the falsetto in developing the *voix mixte* and full-bodied head voice tone qualities, without which the mechanism is incapable of functioning efficiently.

See Bel Canto
Falsetto
Falsetto or
Head Voice
Middle Register
Modern Methods
Register
Resonance
Vowel

Mezzo-Soprano: a female voice type whose tonal characteristics are weightier than those of the dramatic soprano, yet lighter than those of the contralto, and whose range extends from F below middle C to the second B above middle C.

The mezzo-soprano is a frequent victim of vocal misclassification, since her range is virtually identical (a semitone lower) with that of the dramatic soprano. Many fine mezzo voices have been destroyed by acting upon the assumption that they can safely assume soprano roles.

Vocal classification must be based upon tone quality, and since an intrinsically natural quality and tessitura is in most instances dubious until a high state of technical advancement has been reached, judgment must be reserved until such time as technical problems have been solved.

See Vocal Classification

Middle Pharyngeal Constrictor: one of three muscles whose contractions narrow the pharyngeal isthmus to assist in peristaltic movement (swallowing).

All muscles involved in swallowing should remain relaxed during phonation since their contraction invariably induces throat constriction.

Middle Register: a series of vocalized sounds occupying a position which straddles the register "break" in women's voices, and whose distinctive tonal characteristics have led many to conclude that they are the product of a third, separate mechanism rather than a combination of the two basic register mechanisms, the chest register and the falsetto.

The concept of a third, or middle, register is a nineteenth century invention; all seventeenth and eighteenth century sources (Italian: Caccini, Tosi, Mancini, Manfredini; German: Mattheson, Agricola, Marpurg, Hiller, von Engelbrunner, Lasser) recognized but two registers. Most of these authorities considered the "falsetto or head voice" to be the same mechanism, although Agricola (1720—1774) offered a detailed discussion of the *Fistelstimme* (German, "falsetto"), which, however, within the obvious context of his meaning, referred to what is now recognized to be the flageolet voice, or "flute" voice, located above the soprano high C.

Two teachers living in France were the first to suggest a third, or middle, register. Jean Paul Egide Martini (1741—1816), born Schwarzendorf, believed the voice to consist of a *voix de poitrine* (chest voice), *voix du gozier* (throat voice, recognized by the Italians as the falsetto, or *voce di gola*), and the *voix de tête* (head voice). Mengozzi, an Italian, found these divisions to exist in female voice types, but considered the male voice to be comprised of but two registers.

While it might be argued that the difference in the number of registers is a question of gender or differences between male and female sopranos, the prevailing attitude in Italy was summed up by Mancini, who contended that the two-register theory applied equally to all voice types, soprano, alto, tenor and bass. In view of the fact that the term *voix du gozier*, which equates with the Italian falsetto, throat, or "feigned" voice, lies in the mid-tonal range of both the *castrati* and female sopranos as the registers were positioned from the seventeenth to the end of the eighteenth centuries, it is possible that the expression "middle" to designate a register originates from this source.

The concept of a third or middle register received encouragement during the latter part of the eighteenth century because of the concurrent decline of the Rococo vocal style and the development of the *stile parlante,* the declamatory operas composed by Gluck (1714—1787) and Cherubini (1760—1842), which prompted the emergence of the *prima donna.* As sheer volume became a factor, it was evident that special treatment was necessary to build up the strength of the falsetto, a build-up that lowered the position of the pitch range in which both registers had formerly been located. Whereas in former times the *voce di petto* had been considered to terminate at C on the third space of the treble clef, the register "break" (or dividing point which separated and defined the two register mechanisms) now terminated by general agreement at E above middle C.

Since the chest register responds to higher levels of volume and "fattens" as intensity is increased, it is obvious that this mechanism, which shifts slightly with voice weight, took on a depth and richness with women at the beginning of the nineteenth century which made it qualitatively different from the same mechanism as it was used by the *castrati* and the lighter women's voices popular at an earlier time. That this shifting of the "break" area is possible is evident from the performance of those who specialize in singing folk songs, as well as certain "pop" singers who now often take their chest voices to the same upper limits (although in a different way) as did those who performed during the seventeenth and eighteenth centuries. Once it is realized that, like taffy, the chest register can be stretched and thinned out to an inordinate length, one may perceive that the upper limit of this mechanism is variable, and fixed by intensity quite as much as it is by pitch.

Two teachers of extraordinary gifts and influence emerged during the nineteenth century—Francesco Lamperti (1813—1892) and Manuel Garcia (1805—1906)—to reinforce the concept of a third or middle register. In keeping with Martini and Mengozzi, both Lamperti and Garcia made a distinction between the voices of males and females, asserting as did their predecessors that male singers have but two registers, while females have three. The terminology, however, was altered. Lamperti called the lowest and middle registers the "chest" and "mixed;" the highest-pitched "head" voice was reserved for the exclusive use of women because it lies well above the range of tenors and basses. Lamperti's allocation of these "registers" to specific positions within the tonal range is shown in Figure 10.

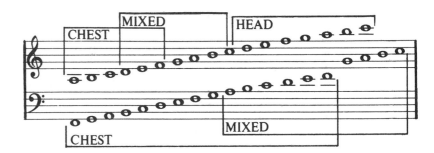

Figure 10. The concept of registration as described by Francesco Lamperti in his book The Art of Singing *(1877).*

By his use of the term "mixed", Lamperti implied (without naming the ingredients) that pitches lying within the vicinity of the register "break" owe their special qualities to the combined action of two elements, thereby reinforcing earlier ambiguities relative to the use of the expression "falsetto or head voice."

Garcia was apparently more aware of the origins of the "mixed" or "middle" register: he referred to this pitch area as the "falsetto" and considered the head voice (because of its high position in the tonal range) to be a remnant of the boy's voice. Since the falsetto is not a legitimate "voice," this explanation created a problem. He surmounted this difficulty by coining the phrase *mezzo petto* (half chest), or, as it is recognized today, the *voix mixte*. By 1894, however, he concluded that men had only two registers, and that the three divisions of women's voices were chest, falsetto, and head. These are shown in Figures 11 and 12, below.

Garcia's most illustrious pupil, Mathilda Marchesi (1821—1913), who taught only women, solidified the concept of a "middle" register in the following statement:

> The three registers of the female voice are the *Chest*, the *Medium*, and the *Head*. I use the term *Medium* and not *Falsetto* (the word used for the middle register by some professors of singing), firstly, because the word *Medium* (middle) precisely and logically explains the position that this register occupies in the compass of the voice, and, secondly, to avoid all confusion that might be caused by the term *Falsetto*, which belongs exclusively to men's voices.[60]

Marchesi specifically rejected the two-register theory as inappropriate to women's voices:

> This grave error has been endorsed by several eminent modern physiologists, who have persuaded themselves that they have established this theory, after their observations with the laryngoscope, but who are incapable of making comparative experiments with their own vocal organs.[61]

[60]Mathilde Marchesi, *Bel Canto: A Theoretical and Practical Vocal Method,* edited by Philip L. Miller (New York: Dover Publications, Inc., 1970), p. xiv.

[64]*Ibid.*

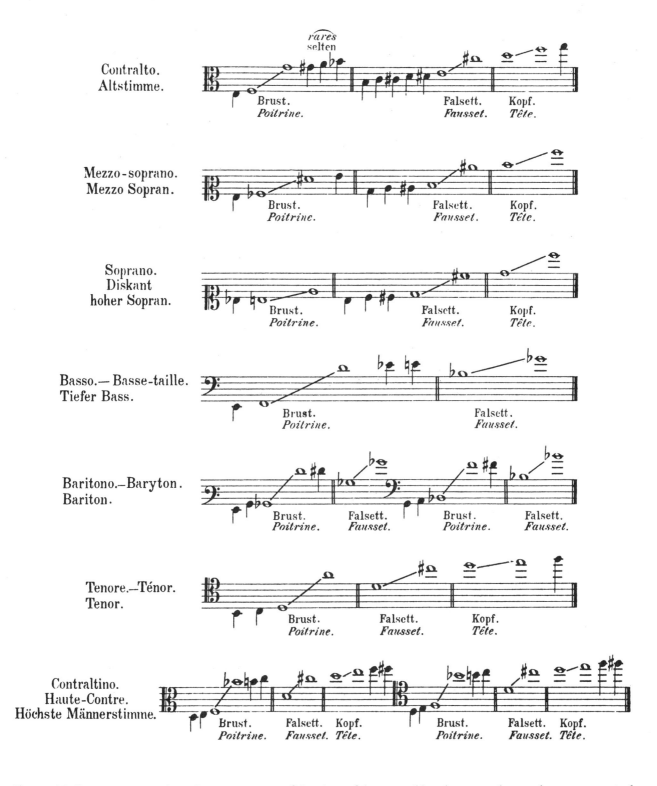

Figure 11. Demonstrating the relative positions of the chest, falsetto and head voice in the tonal range, reported by most early writers as being applicable to all voice types, male and female. (From Garcia, Garcia's Schule, oder Die Kunst des Gesanges.)

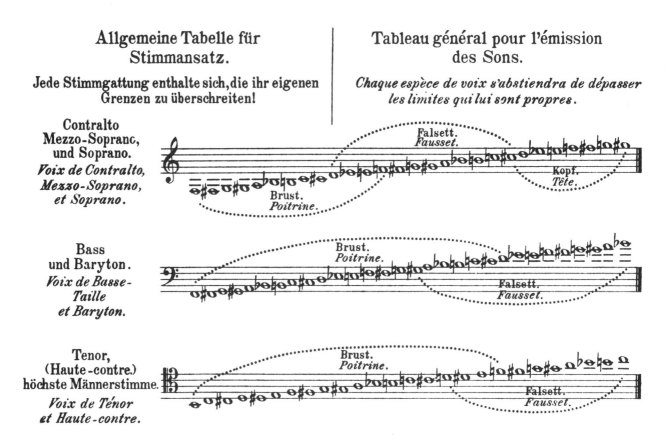

Figure 12. Showing the approximate pitch ranges of the chest register, falsetto and head voice as these are positioned in the great scale. (From Garcia, Garcia's Schule, oder Die Kunst des Gesanges.)

According to Marchesi, the uppermost limit of the chest register was F above middle C, a pitch marking the beginning of the "middle" register, which she believed to terminate an octave above. Such sharp divisions, however, ignore the fact that for three centuries, the lower tones of the falsetto, "mixed," or "middle" register were known to descend to A below middle C, sharing at least a fifth in common with the chest register, and consequently not commencing on the first space of the treble clef.

At earlier stages of technical development, therefore, the term "middle" could not be said to "logically explain the position that this register occupies in the compass of the voice," since it overlaps the tonal range belonging to the chest register. It is only after the two basic register mechanisms, the chest and the falsetto, have been coordinated that the "middle" register as defined by Marchesi appears. The evolution of the concept of a "mixed" or "middle" register from the early part of the nineteenth century to the beginning of the twentieth is shown in Figure 13.

While Marchesi obviously judged the mid-tonal range of female voices on the basis of special quality characteristics, she was still very much aware of its functional origins. Addressing herself to the problems encountered in bridging the "break" in the voice, she made the following statement:

Every effort expended upon the highest notes of a register increases the difficulty of developing the power of the lower tones in the next register, and therefore of blending the two registers, until eventually it becomes impossible.[62]

[62]Mathilde Marchesi, *Bel Canto: A Theoretical and Practical Vocal Method*, edited by Philip L. Miller (New York: Dover Publications, Inc., 1970), p. xv.

A. MIXED REGISTER OF LAMPERTI (from reprint, 1877).

B. FALSETTO REGISTER OF GARCIA (1856),
   later to become MEDIUM REGISTER (1894).

C. MEDIUM REGISTER OF MARCHESI (undated, circa 1901).

Figure 13. Showing the modifications of terminology during the nineteenth century that subsequently led to the neglect of those mechanical principles which operate as control factors in combining the vocal registers, the chest and the falsetto, and that caused the terms "mixed," "middle" and "medium" to become functionally meaningless.

There are two points of interest to be noted in the observation quoted above: 1) that intensity is an important control factor in bridging the registers, and 2) that if Marchesi did not understand the register mechanisms at their primitive level as isolated mechanisms, this was because she had her choice of pupils, and hence did not have to work with beginners or those with serious technical problems. Her most distinguished pupil, Nellie Melba, for example, studied with her less than a year before making her brilliant debut, and problems are not solved in that short space of time.

Unfortunately for subsequent generations, Marchesi's view concerning a "middle" register has gained almost universal acceptance, with the result that the subject of registration has been thrown into an almost hopeless state of confusion. This subsequently led to a belief that all concepts relating to registration were baseless, and that a register was a product of vocal fragmentation, and consequently improper technique.

The inherent fallacy in Marchesi's reasoning is that it fails to take into consideration the fact that a register is not exclusively a tonal range or a tonal quality, but, as defined by Garcia and others, *a series of homogeneous qualities resulting from a particular type of mechanical (muscular) adjustment taking place within the laryngeal pharynx.* Consequently, since no muscular system exists to account for more than two basic types of adjustment, there can be, by definition, no third or "middle" register. While it is true that by combining the chest register with the falsetto a third and distinctive tonal quality will be produced, to assume that this quality constitutes a register is as logical as saying that green is a primary color because it differs from yellow and blue.

On the basis of anatomical structure alone, the three-register hypothesis is untenable. Examination of excised larynges by investigators since the turn of the century has demonstrated that the sole difference between the vocal organs of males and females is one of size, a difference which sets the natural pitch range of female singers an octave above that of their male counterparts. Since but two muscular systems (the cricothyroids and the arytenoids) are involved in drawing the vocal folds into tension to account for the phenonemon of registration, and since no other muscular system exists to account for the presence of a third or "middle" register, the hypothesis upon which this twentieth century concept has been founded is false.

The confusion growing out of a belief in the existence of a third or "middle" register is disruptive to the pedagogic process and makes it impossible to foster and develop effectively those techniques designed to isolate, develop and coordinate the two basic vocal registers (the chest and the falsetto), and thereby restructure a faulty vocal technique. From the standpoint of practical pedagogy, it is obvious that nothing is to be gained by treating a nonexistent mechanism as though it operated upon a valid functional principle.

Middle Voice: a reference, made without regard for functional principles or mechanical derivation, to the middle tonal range of a given voice.

The term "middle voice" refers neither to a particular type of muscular adjustment (register) nor to a particular tonal area, since the "middle" of a well-used voice might encompass the entire range of a voice that is poorly used. The term, therefore, rather vaguely refers to any group of tones in the midrange of a given voice.

Minimal Air: that amount of air remaining in the lungs after they have collapsed.

The term "minimal air" has also been used to refer to the amount of breath that escapes through the glottis under optimum vocal conditions.

Mixed Falsetto: See Falsetto, Mixed.

Mixed Registration: See Registration, "Mixed."

Modal Register: a group of pitches identified and recognized by some scientific investigators as a basic vocal mechanism because it includes those fundamental frequencies *normally* used in phonation (both speech and singing).

The term "modal register" (along with "pulse register" and "loft register") was coined by science in an attempt to clear up the confusion created by the various pedagogic interpretations of the traditional terms "chest register," "head voice," falsetto, and "middle register." Closer examination of its implications, however, indicates that it is more likely to achieve a result diametrically opposed to its intent and purpose.

214

The problem central to any discussion of vocal nomenclature is adequately defining and interpreting the term "register." If a vocal register is interpreted as a series of like tonal qualities resulting from a particular type of muscular adjustment, as Garcia suggested, then there can only be two vocal registers. Based on this premise, those tones alluded to by the term "modal" are products of neither register but of a combined form of both mechanisms.

The great failing of the term "modal register" is that it refers not to a specific type of laryngeal muscular adjustment, but to a "normal" or "average" pitch range for a "normal" or "average" speaking or singing voice. Consequently, the following objections must be raised:

1. While there is tremendous pedagogic confusion surrounding the traditional terms "chest register," "head register," falsetto, *etc.*, there is general agreement upon the distinctive *types* of tonal quality referred to by these terms, and "modal" fits none of these categories;

2. To the 100 or more terms coined since the invention of the laryngoscope to describe or refer to the vocal registers, several more ("modal," "pulse," "loft," *etc.*) have now been added;

3. While tonal qualities cannot be accurately verbalized, and while any system of terminology is subject to misinterpretation, terms such as "vocal fry," "pulse register," "modal register," "loft register," and "stroh" have little meaning to anyone but the scientists who invented them; they are mere words to most studio practitioners;

4. Pitch alone does not constitute a register, nor does it solely influence the workings of the two basic register mechanisms. For example, six pitches ("B" to "e") are common to both registers, and there are innumerable ways in which the two basic mechanisms can be combined to produce any pitch (particularly in the midrange). Furthermore, in the tonal area referred to by the term "modal," it is intensity as well as pitch which exerts a controlling influence over the balance of registration;

5. The "normal" or "average" speaking range is neither qualitatively nor quantitatively common to all voice types and persons. Each individual's tonal quality, for example, is largely determined by the manner in which the two basic register mechanisms are combined in the area of register transition (middle C to the fourth above). Furthermore, the tonal range that is "normal" or "average" to the speech of women is quite obviously not the same as that common to the speech of men;

6. No direct correlation exists between speech and singing, and the "normal" or "average" range of these two phonatory processes is widely divergent. For example, a good soprano's midrange usually extends from "f^1" to "f^2," but she would never speak on any of those pitches unless she were extremely angry, calling someone, or abusing her vocal mechanism. Furthermore, speech is a function of a *detuned* resonating system, whereas singing involves fine *tuning* of the various pharyngeal cavities. Only in theatrical speech and religious chanting (both of which have pitch, duration, and a relatively fixed resonance adjustment) are similar functional processes involved, and

7. The use of the term "modal" to refer to the middle of the voice reinforces the common misconception that there are more than two basic register mechanisms. However, while the vocal folds assume varying lengths and thicknesses, these dimensions are caused by muscular contractions brought to bear by the crico-

thyroid and arytenoid muscle systems to which they are attached. Since there are but two muscle systems, there can be but two register mechanisms. What confuses the issue is the fact that, just as the primary colors yellow and blue can be combined to produce infinite shades of green, the two basic mechanisms can also combine to produce infinite tonal hues, and the functional characteristics of tones in the midrange are products of this mixture.

While it is important that nomenclature be well defined, it is also important that it be derived from valid scientific or empirical data. The term "modal" fails to achieve this goal, and a further proliferation of terms, especially if they are without physiological basis, is unnecessary.

Ultimately, one must learn to hear the relationship between a given tonal quality and the probable muscular activities that yield it, and to develop a system of terminology that accurately reflects this relationship.

Modern Methods: voice training procedures which evolved during the latter part of the nineteenth century, differing radically from early training in aesthetic goals, approach to development, basic principles, and philosophical insights. Before the first two decades of the twentieth century had passed, both the shift in pedagogic interest and the new "principles" which were adopted had become securely entrenched to form the basis of what now constitutes modern methods.

Three seemingly unrelated events acted as catalysts in the transition from earlier practices and beliefs to modern methods: 1) the decline in popularity of the *castrati* and the concurrent ascendancy of the *prima donna*; 2) the invention of the laryngoscope by Manuel Garcia in 1854, which made it possible, for the first time, to examine the vibrating vocal folds, a procedure carried out with the expectation that the information provided would expedite the learning process, and 3) a demand for "big" voices to match the sonorous orchestral textures of late nineteenth century operatic compositions. These three events precipitated a virtual break with so-called traditional training methods, which had been formulated empirically and passed down from teacher to pupil for almost three centuries (roughly 1600—1850).

The demise of the *castrati* was brought about because of a strong moral revulsion towards the practice of castration, and was perhaps inspired by the naturalistic philosophy of eighteenth century Enlightenment, with its concern for individual liberty and freedom. At the same time, a new development in the operatic form—the opera buffa—where mythological subjects were replaced by characters taken from real life, pointed a new direction. With the growing popularity of this genre, there were few roles of any consequence left for the *castrati*, and their career opportunities gradually became restricted to singing in cathedral choirs. It was under these circumstances that women's voices (always a part of earlier tradition, with many achieving equal stature with the *evirati*) assumed a position of prominence which, once taken, was never to be relinquished.

With the rise of the *prima donna*, the two-register theory (chest register and falsetto), formerly agreed upon by most theorists as being applicable to all voice types, male and female, was gradually modified. The tonal breathiness which often appeared when singing in the area of the register "break" (a condition betraying the influence of the falsetto, whose essential characteristic is breathiness) had long posed a serious problem, even with the *castrati*. Since the upper tones of the chest voice are strong and robust, the difficulty, as Mancini and others carefully noted, was in uniting the disparate parts so that the passage from one to the other was "imperceptible." During the process of reinforcing this weakness in the lower tonal range of the falsetto, a quality transformation was found to occur that introduced a third tonal texture, one that later came to be misnamed "middle register."

Before speculating as to the possible reason for the belief that the female voice possessed a third register, it is necessary to point out that without exception, examination of excised larynges has proved that the vocal apparatuses of men and women are, apart from size, fundamentally identical. Since a register is a series of homogeneous tone qualities produced by one mechanism (muscular system), differing essentially from another group of equally homogeneous tone qualities produced by another mechanism (or muscular system), and since in all aspects the laryngeal musculature and its associated cartilages in men and women are identical, then the assertion that there are but two registers in the male voice and three in the female voice must be without substance.

A satisfactory explanation of the three-register theory necessarily involves an understanding of the falsetto and its relationship to the chest register. The falsetto, like the chest register, is the product of a separate mechanical arrangement in which the laryngeal musculature participates to effect an approximation of the vocal folds. Until the turn of the present century, theorists agreed that the falsetto lies immediately adjacent to the chest register, overlapping that mechanism by some five or six tones which they share in common. It was further agreed that the falsetto is restricted in range, breathy in quality, without vibrato, inflexible, and incapable of being sustained; in short, a literally false tone quality.

When, however, the falsetto becomes integrated with the chest register and functions as a coordinate unit, its quality characteristics undergo a change. The result of this juncture is a new series of homogeneous tone qualities which differ essentially from the textural properties associated with the tonal range both above and below the outer boundaries of the falsetto. In this transformation, the mechanical principles which govern and determine registration were gradually sacrificed for aesthetic evaluations, with the result that the mechanical laws which, when applied, evoked a particular type of register response, were gradually forgotten and ultimately lost.

The techniques used prior to the nineteenth century to transform the falsetto into a legitimate tone quality were designed to modify its rudimentary sound, causing it to evolve into what was called the "feigned" voice. While it may be argued that the feigned voice was specifically structured to solve the problems encountered in training the *castrati*, this does not appear to be substantiated by the facts. There were many celebrated women singers appearing before the public when the *castrati* were at the pinnacle of their fame, yet not one of the prominent teachers responsible for their training cited any difference in the principles, methods, or procedures employed in that development. The register "break" (E—F above middle C) is common to all voice types, and the difficulties to be overcome in joining the two mechanisms are quite similar. It is evident, therefore, that the unique textural properties of the feigned voice must have been recognized as applicable not only to the *castrati* but to the voices of women as well. There is little doubt that it is the developed feigned voice which, with the emergence of the *prima donna*, later became more familiarly known as a "middle" register.

That this new nomenclature was but another way of saying the same thing is indicated by the transitional use of the term "mixed" to denote these special tonal properties. Francesco Lamperti (1813—1892) was the first to use the term "mixed" within this context, describing the female voice as being comprised of three registers, "chest," "mixed" and "head," and describing men's voices as having but two, "chest" and "mixed." Apparently Lamperti assumed that everyone was familiar with the basic register mechanisms that were to be combined or "mixed" to yield a tonal texture separate and distinct from those belonging to the pitch ranges lying immediately above and below.

The connection between the falsetto, the "feigned voice" and the "mixed" or "middle" register has been explained in detail by Garcia (1805—1906). Garcia's formulation, which was in direct conformity with traditional beliefs, placed the falsetto in all voice types in a tonal range lying immediately above the chest voice; the head voice was located above the falsetto. As a consequence of the lowered tonal range of the male voice after puberty, Garcia considered the head voice (with the exception of the countertenor) to be a "remnant of the boy's voice." He further concluded that "in comparing the registers, we see that in the male, the chest register descends lower than in the female; that the falsetto is common to both; and that the head voice of the female exceeds that of the male in extent."[63]

The thinking of Garcia profoundly influenced Mathilde Marchesi (1821—1913), who trained Melba, Calvé, Eames, di Murska, and other successful artists. Her response to the ambiguities inherent in the earlier postulate of "falsetto or head voice" differed somewhat from Garcia's. In her opinion, what was formerly considered a developed falsetto (in the sense of its being a legitimate tone quality coordinated successfully with the chest voice to become the feigned voice) constituted a separate mechanism, or "middle" register. Her explanation follows:

> The three registers of the female voice are the *Chest*, the *Medium*, and the *Head*. I use the term *Medium* and not *Falsetto* (the word used for the middle register by some professors of singing), firstly, because the word *Medium* (middle) precisely and logically explains the position that this register occupies in to compass of the voice, and secondly, to avoid all confusion that might be caused by the term *Falsetto*, which belongs exclusively to men's voices. Falsetto, which signifies *Falso* (false), that is, *in place of the true*, is a term that has been used in Italy from the earliest period in the history of the art of singing, to indicate certain *piano* effects in the high tones of the tenor voice.[64]

The information supplied by Garcia and Marchesi is patently false when it is judged in the light of scientific evidence and earlier theoretical opinion, which considered but two registers to exist in all voice types, soprano, alto, tenor and bass. What the substance of their observations suggests, however, is an abandonment of the two-register theory and the functional principles upon which this concept had been based. By the invention of a third so-called register, they and others came to rely exclusively on an evaluation based upon aesthetic judgment. Since an

[63]Manuel Garcia, *The Art of Singing. Part I* (Boston: Oliver Ditson & Co., c.1855), p. 5.

[64]Mathilde Marchesi, *Bel Canto: A Theoretical and Practical Vocal Method*, edited by Philip L. Miller (New York: Dover Publications, Inc., 1970), p. xiv.

aesthetic judgment involves many variables, *i.e.*, taste, conditioning, and emotional predisposition, training methods became unreliable, and the ability to learn how to sing (in the sense of acquiring skills and abilities not formerly possessed) became a somewhat forlorn hope.

A contemporary of Marchesi, William Shakespeare (1849—1931), who was an exponent of the teaching of Giovanni Battista Lamperti, pointed out some of the problems which had arisen because of a misplaced reliance upon aesthetics. Discussing some of the uncertainties encountered in dealing with the "medium" register, he made this comment:

> There is undoubtedly considerable difficulty experienced in the production of the higher notes of the medium register; so much so, that this register has been subdivided by some into upper medium and lower medium. If we venture on this subdivision at all, it is not so much to suggest a difference in the mechanism employed, as to lay stress on the fact that these notes are the most difficult to sing, and their acquisition forms the key, not merely to the highest notes of the tenor, but especially to the head voice of women.[65]

[65]William Shakespeare, *The Art of Singing* (Bryn Mawr, Pa.: Oliver Ditson Co., 1898), p. 25.

Unlike Marchesi, Shakespeare apparently remained acutely aware of the "mechanisms" essential to a proper joining of the chest and head voices. What all of these statements suggest, however, is an ongoing confusion concerning the subject of vocal mechanics. The *castrati* had virtually disappeared from the vocal scene, and once it was recognized that women's voices were qualitatively superior to those of men, they soon became numerically superior. As more or less qualified teachers took over the responsibilities of an older generation, the parallels between the voices of the *castrati*, who had vocal organs comparable in size to women's encased in men's bodies, were either forgotten or ignored, and the training given women took a different course. For many, the subject of registration had long since become a clouded issue, and once the functional principles upon which this concept had been based became obscured, the question of the definition and enumeration of the registers became a subject badly in need of clarification. It was at this time in vocal history that Garcia invented the laryngoscope (1854), hoping at one stroke to facilitate the learning process and provide the basis for a more secure pedagogy. It also marked the beginning of modern methods.

LARYNGOSCOPE

The invention of the laryngoscope by Manuel Garcia set the stage for further changes in pedagogic thought and practice. By being able to see the interior parts of the vocal mechanism, it was anticipated that a better understanding of the physical processes taking place would lead to both an acceleration of progress and a stronger theoretical position with respect to registration. The device itself was very simple, consisting of two mirrors, the smaller of which was attached to a long, slender shaft. When the smaller mirror was inserted into the mouth with the reflecting surface directed toward the vocal folds, the larger mirror, fastened to a headband, was positioned to throw light rays upon the smaller. In this way, the movement of the vocal folds could be seen and studied by the operator of the device.

Several difficulties were encountered during the course of laryngoscopic examinations which limited the effectiveness of this apparatus. First, while phonation was in progress it was impossible to position the small mirror close to the uvula without disturbing the natural movement of the laryngeal musculature and its associated structures. Additional problems were presented by the bulkiness of the base of the tongue, which blocked the view anteriorly, and the inward folding of the epiglottis, which obstructed the view when an *ah* vowel was being sung. Second, since only those areas above the vocal folds were visible, both subglottal activities and movements involving the intricate muscular systems which connect the vocal folds with other elements of the respiratory function were completely obscured.

As a result of these difficulties, concepts related to holistic pedagogy were endangered, and a situation created which fostered the accumulation of questionable data. Despite these limitations, certain activities could be seen through the laryngoscope that had been previously left to conjecture. Perhaps the most important visual evidence to be noted was the varying lengths and thicknesses assumed by the vocal folds to accommodate changes in pitch. These changes were considered by many viewers to be a register, but their conclusion about these segmentations was made without reference to the muscular systems whose contractions were known to be responsible for bringing these changes about.

From this relatively narrow field of inquiry, many divergencies of opinion came to be expressed, since each viewer "saw" different patterns and advanced a theory to justify his observations. During the latter part of the nineteenth century, Sir Morell Mackenzie (1837—1892) described the situation as it existed after the invention of the laryngoscope: "the immediate effect of the laryngoscope was to throw the whole subject into almost hopeless confusion by the introduction of all sorts of errors of observation."[66] Madame Emma Seiler, a distinguished pupil of Helmholtz, was aware of these discrepancies, and attributed them to the fact that the singers observed had not been properly trained and that the correct vocal action was not taking place.

[66]Sir Morell Mackenzie, *Hygiene of the Vocal Organs* (Belmar, N.J.: E. S. Werner & Co., 1928), p. 195.

Emil Behnke (1836—1892), a noted teacher and authority on the physiology of voice, was another who formulated a new theory about registration based upon laryngoscopic observation. His conclusion was that there are three registers, "thick," "thin," and "small," and he subdivided these into special groupings, which he called "lower thick and lower thin," "upper thick and upper thin," and "small." A number of authorities who agreed with his findings chose to substitute the expressions "long reed" and "short reed" for "thick" and "thin," a change which probably encouraged later theorists to compare the functional elements of the vocal mechanism to the acoustic properties of reed instruments.

Madame Seiler held a different opinion, calling the registers "first and second chest" and "first and second falsetto," and suggesting that all tones lying above these four groups belonged to the "head" voice; her postulate was an interesting reconciliation between traditional viewpoints and newer concepts. Dr. Heinrich Reimann (1850—1906) recognized four registers, the "chest," "middle," "head," and "sombre." Lost in the confusion of these "observations," the concept of the vocal registers as understood and practiced in earlier times became meaningless.

The theories that evolved on the basis of laryngoscopic evidence were based solely upon the different lengths and thicknesses assumed by the vocal folds, without reference to the muscular systems responsible for drawing them into tension.

Abstract reasoning is often less convincing than visual evidence, and those who did consider the anatomical possibilities (Mackenzie, Holmes, Howard and others) found their theoretical objections falling on unreceptive ears. It was the contention of these dissenters that since the vocal folds are drawn into tension, and their lengths and thicknesses vary because of the contraction of two muscle systems, the cricothyroids and the arytenoids, there can be but two register mechanisms. This appraisal has been verified in the twentieth century by Dr. Douglas Stanley and William Vennard, although Vennard, apparently in an effort to effect a compromise with popular opinion, denied the logic of his own findings by stating "for all practical purposes, however, we must consider there to be three."

With the gradual erosion of traditional concepts and a proliferation of theories concerning registration, an increasing number of those who entered the profession came to reject the idea in its totality, and consider the voice to be comprised of but one register, or in effect no registers at all. To a certain extent, of course, this latter argument is supportable, since all of the constituent parts of the mechanisms should work as a harmonious entity, *i.e.*, in balanced tension. If there were but one register mechanism, however, the possibility of isolating, developing and recoordinating any of the basic involuntary laryngeal muscular systems whose movements determine the qualitative properties of the ultimate tonal product would be remote, and the training program would be severely restricted in scope.

The one-register or no-register theory is viable with well-formed voices, where the training objective is to obscure all of the transition points in the tonal range and preserve a seamless scale. This is a vocal ideal, however, and the problems faced in vocal training are not concerned with ideal situations but with those related to malfunction. Were there but one register, the voice would be seamless, and its mechanical operation would be inaccessible and consequently impervious to fundamental change. Unless it were possible to stimulate certain of the muscular systems exclusively, there would be no need for vocal study as a learning process, and no possibility for restructuring a faulty technique or transforming (as Mancini noted when he commented upon the development of Bernacchi) a "bad" voice into one of exceptional distinction. In the absence of functional mechanics, vocal training would be restricted to studies in musicianship and interpretation.

The effect of the diverse theoretical opinions advanced on the basis of laryngoscopic examination did not filter down to the average teacher of voice until near the end of the nineteenth century, when the scope of opera broadened and created a demand for "big" voices with higher decibel ratings. This development led to a shift in emphasis from registration to special breathing techniques and concerns for resonance.

"BIG" VOICES

The transition to modern methods was further accelerated by an increasing demand for "big" voices. Larger halls were constructed, the orchestra was dramatically increased in size (the brass section was moved into a position of greater prominence), and disputes concerning the number of registers, having grown tedious, were shunted aside for what appeared to be more pressing problems. Foremost among these were "resonance," voice "placement," and "breath control."

That resonance was not considered a factor until the early part of the twentieth century is clear from a statement of Herbert Witherspoon, a prominent teacher

[67]Herbert Witherspoon, *Singing: A Treatise for Teachers and Students* (New York: G. Schirmer, Inc., 1925), pp. 21, 35.

[68]Herman Klein, *The Bel Canto* (London: Oxford University Press, 1923), p. 20.

and singer (1875–1935), who spoke of this "comparatively new bug-a-boo, resonance." He further remarked "it is an interesting fact that the term nasal resonance I have never found in one of the old books upon the art of singing, either in this country or in Europe."[67] It is also significant that in Garcia's *Hints on Singing* the subject of resonance is not mentioned, and equally noteworthy that his pupil Herman Klein felt compelled to assert "the old Italian teachers had no trouble in obtaining a bright, ringing tone. Resonance, therefore, may not have entered very largely into their theory, but was far from being ignored in their practice."[68]

The growing interest in resonance was not solely a matter of devising a means for increasing tonal volume, but also of developing a technique for relieving the vocal mechanism of the apparant strain to which it was being increasingly subjected. It was during this period that the British physicist E. W. Scripture introduced his so-called "vortex theory," which directed attention to the nasal passages and sinuses as possible resonators of vocal tone. Dr. H. Holbrook Curtis, a noted throat specialist and friend of Jean de Reszke, likewise became deeply concerned about the situation. His observation that the vocal folds are too fragile and poorly designed to effectively resist the strong breath pressure directed against them while singing heavy, dramatic roles prompted him to advocate singing *dans la masque*, *i.e.*, to resonate vocal tone "in the facial mask." Ernest G. White went a step further by declaring that the vocal folds have absolutely nothing to do with the production of vocal tone and that all aspects of tone production and amplification actually occur within the sinus cavities. Another group of theorists, led by Charles Lunn, suggested that the false vocal cords serve as a counteractive point of resistance to the breath pressure exerted against them. According to this theory, the vocal folds would not have to resist breath pressure, and they would therefore be able to maintain their elasticity without stiffening.

At the same time Dr. Curtis and de Reszke were advocating their theory of nasal resonance, Lilli Lehmann (1848—1929) adapted Scripture's vortex theory, writing extensively about the "swirling eddies" that move through the nasal passages, and stressing the sensations of vibration to be experienced in that part of the vocal tract. In her book *How to Sing*, separate chapters are devoted to "Resonance of the Head and Sinus Cavities," "Sensations of the Palate," "Sensations of the Nose," and "Sensations of the Tongue;" she entertained the conviction that a voice was properly "placed" when swirling eddies of sound successfully found their way into the upper resonators and nasal cavities.

This new understanding of voice represented a fundamental departure from traditional beliefs and practices. With the subject of the vocal registers brought to an almost hopeless state of confusion because of the contradictory information supplied by laryngoscopic examination, pedagogic attention was easily diverted to these new ways of thinking. By the beginning of the twentieth century, all had become so well entrenched that even the subject of breathing, heretofore loosely based upon the dictum "He who knows how to breathe knows how to sing" (no authority went into the matter any further than to advocate a correct posture and a slightly elevated chest position), became a controversial subject.

CHANGING PERSPECTIVES

The transition from traditional theories to modern methods was facilitated by similarities more apparent than real. The by-products of registration, for example, create the impression that some tones are "resonating" in the chest, others in the head, and that strong vibratory sensations often appear to be concentrated in the facial mask. To act upon these impulses, *i.e.,* vocal tone itself, through "placement" promised to offer a tangible means for improving desirable tonal characteristics.

The inherent disadvantages in the above approach far outweigh any merits these procedures might otherwise appear to possess. At best, voices well formed as a gift of nature will sometimes marginally progress until reaching the age of thirty-five before this type of misapplied energy reveals itself in the form of vocal difficulties. However, progress and fulfillment of potential are quite different aspects of accomplishment, and viewed in this light, progress of this kind is neither real nor lasting.

An appraisal of training methods based upon "placement" and the replication of sensations of vibration includes the following reservations: no functional principles are involved; symptoms are treated as causes; all vocal problems, regardless of their nature and origin, are addressed alike; such methods harbor an implicit misconception of the significance of tone quality. The latter misconception is particularly significant and points up the errors inherent in the former. Quality should be regarded as a representation of the condition of the functioning mechanism rather than an intrinsically natural tone quality. Invariably, the object of study is to change both the conceptual and the physical identification with the phonative process in a very fundamental way. To "place" a characteristic tone quality, to add nasal "resonance" to vitalize tones which are intrinsically lacking in vitality, or to replicate the specific sensations of vibration thought to be of permanent value, is to leave unchanged the physical coordination responsible for inherent functional deficiencies which limit the technique.

Once developmental programs based upon nasal resonance and placement had been put into effect, additional miscalculations became standard pedagogic practice. For example, when throat constriction was present, tones were thought to be placed "too far back," which immediately confused registration with pharyngeal adjustments made for resonance. When attempting to correct this type of aberration by placing the voice "forward," "higher," or "in the facial mask," it was thought that poorly coordinated laryngeal activities would benefit vicariously, but that procedure failed to differentiate between the ends and the means. With tongue and jaw tension a visible manifestation of wrong throat tension, it was further anticipated that by "relaxing" these parts it would be possible to get at the cause of the difficulty; this proposition overlooked the fact that the singer does not deliberately tense the tongue and jaw, but does so unavoidably.

Since all of the above practices fell short of their objective, other refinements were introduced. Among those more common were directives to "focus" the tone and/or add "ping" and "point" to inject a "ringing" quality and make the voice "project." The more recently introduced "yawn-sigh" is a more successful device for alleviating throat constriction. It is limited, however, because it relieves without changing the condition; with the yawn-sigh, once the mental and physical processes that initiate vocal tone are again set in motion, the wrong tensions more often than not reassert themselves.

All of the above directions contain an inherent fallacy. What is heard as sound is the rhythmic motion of air particles. These cannot be placed or focused, and vibrations which appear to concentrate in the facial mask, chest, or head are present because they have radiated through the skeletal framework of the body from the tonal source (the laryngeal pharynx) by means of bone conduction. Therefore, vibratory impulses cannot be intensified, augmented, or made to resonate in these areas of the anatomy unless a greater amount of energy is generated at the tonal source. Concepts related to "ping" and "point" err in another direction, and find expression by a constriction of the pharyngeal cavities, particularly the nasopharynx. Tonal additives of this description succeed in strengthening the high partials to give the voice a cutting edge, but are incapable of changing or reversing muscular activities within the throat parts and are therefore inappropriate solutions.

The inevitable result of these aberrant practices has been to 1) divert energy from the tonal source (the vocal folds and laryngeal musculature), 2) avoid the laryngeal resonance which provides a genuine "ring" (or those frequencies science finds to be strongly energized within the range of 2800—3400 cps), and 3) substitute an inefficient resonating system (the highly damped, virtually closed, nonadjustable nasal passages and sinuses) remote from the vibratory source for those whose unique construction enables them to resonate the fundamental (one of the crucial aspects of good resonance) and select and energize a diversified band of frequencies necessary to the vitalization of a wide spectrum of vowel qualities (the laryngo- and oropharynges).

With the subject of the vocal registers brought to an almost hopeless state of confusion because of the contradictory information supplied on the basis of laryngoscopic evidence, pedagogic attention turned from functional mechanics to matters pertaining to aesthetics. Questions about the nature of the vocal registers (what they are, how many there are, and what causes them to respond) were virtually discarded from the lexicon. The new questions demanding an answer were as follows: How is nasality to be avoided when encouraging nasal resonance, and what constitutes the difference between the two? Assuming tone can be "placed," where is the right place? The hard palate? The nasal passages? Behind the upper or lower teeth? At the lips? How are tonal vibrations to be concentrated in one area to the exclusion of another? What mental images or concepts can be inculcated to enable the student to produce his voice in "swirling eddies which find their way into the nasal passages and sinuses?" Satisfactory answers to these questions have not yet been advanced.

The quest for greater tonal opulence also had the immediate effect of creating demands upon the breathing apparatus that could not be comfortably accommodated by those whose technique was less than secure. As a result, breath loss and tonal unsteadiness became a problem, and the proposed solution was tonal "support" and breath "control." This stands in direct contrast to the belief of Manuel Garcia, who felt impelled at the age of eighty-nine to remark "As to breathing, do not complicate it with theories, but take an inspiration and observe Nature's laws."[69] The attitude expressed by Garcia could hardly be said to establish breathing techniques as the cornerstone upon which a great vocal tradition had been founded.

The presumed advantage to be gained through regulation of the respiratory function is that this system, unlike the laryngeal musculature which draws the vocal folds into tension, can be acted upon directly. Furthermore, because breath loss is one of the continuing problems with those who sing incorrectly, it seemed logical to conclude that a direct effort to control the rate of breath expulsion would

[69]Manuel Garcia, *Musical Herald,* London (August, 1894).

reduce breath loss and simultaneously correct the faulty muscular coordination which caused it. This promised to place the instruction on a very practical basis, since both teacher and pupil were readily persuaded that by "doing something" much would be accomplished.

It soon became evident, however, that breathing techniques alone, even when based upon "nature's laws," could not adequately compensate for functional deficiencies. As a result, emphasis came to be placed upon more aggressive methods, such as the abdominal tuck, the intercostal lift, the protrusion of the abdomen (strengthened by lying prone with books piled upon the midriff), a forced outward expansion of the rib cage, the inspiration of excessive amounts of air, and a general bracing of the body somewhat in the manner of a weightlifter. None of these practices conform either to early tradition or to the functional needs of the mechanism. They mainly succeed in avoiding the central issue, promoting self-consciousness and perpetuating the very problems they were designed to cure.

With the voice now having to be "supported" by the breath, the greater amount of physical energy used exposed difficulties which had been solved by earlier generations through other means. The problem of the vocal registers and the "break" separating them (especially when singing at higher levels of intensity) was a continuing problem. One solution was to "hook" from the chest voice to the head voice somewhat in the manner of a sophisticated yodel. Another device to gain wide acceptance (introduced by Duprez in 1830 and subsequently rejected as aesthetically objectionable and physiologically debilitating) was the practice of "covering."

The correlation between covering and the need for greater breath expenditure has been convincingly demonstrated by Luchsinger and Arnold[70] and by Douglas Stanley.[71] Stanley's investigations, especially, proved that none of the breathing techniques tested improved the motor response of the vocal organs or materially altered the rate of breath expulsion. On the contrary, the studies indicate that it is function which regulates breath flow, and that breathing techniques (of whatever kind) do not effectively regulate or control breath expenditure and have no positive effect on tonal quality.

While modern training programs have generally included some or all of the practices which evolved during the final decade of the nineteenth century as viable procedures, others have turned to more simplistic methods and advocate singing "naturally," forgetting that nature can be both a good friend and a harsh enemy. More often than not, such concepts preserve a status quo, and propose that one should sing within one's limitations and accept them as being a sign of an inferior natural endowment.

Those who believe in a "natural" approach advise students to assume a good posture, "sing as you speak," and "sing on the breath," or they confine their efforts to matters concerning style and interpretation. Poetic imagery is also used by those who adopt this "natural" approach. While a regimen based upon singing naturally will often help those whose technique is already well advanced, especially in the area of interpretation, it precludes any possibility of learning skills and abilities not formerly possessed.

Up to and including the present, the procedures outlined above continue in one form or another to be embraced both in theory and in practice by a majority of voice teachers. Aware of the limitations of poetic imagery, many have chosen to

[70]Richard Luchsinger and Godfrey E. Arnold, *Voice-Speech-Language* (Belmont, California: Wadsworth Publishing Co., Inc., 1965), pp. 106, 107.
[71]Douglas Stanley, *The Science of Voice* (New York: Carl Fischer, Inc., 1929), p. 52.

solve vocal problems by means of imagery whose purpose is to directly influence function. A sampling of this approach to problem-solving appeared in *Opera News* (November and December, 1978); each teacher asserted that his imagery "works." Some examples are listed as follows:

1. "You take a profound breath, behind the nostrils, with the mouth closed, almost like a snore just before falling asleep."
2. "From armpits to waist is a barrel; now fill it with beer, or whatever you like. As you breathe, imagine the slats bursting."
3. "Think of a grapefruit growing down your throat."
4. "When you sing, a big red flower opens in your breast and the fragrance drifts up into the throat and a teapot blows a stream of steam out through the very tip-top of your head."
5. "You swallow an umbrella, and the handle of the umbrella you keep anchored here, in the pelvis. You sing up the stem of the umbrella and when you have sung well, it opens."[72]

[72]Deborah Seabury, "The Singer's World," *Opera News* Vol. 43, No. 5 (November, 1978), 41–7, and Vol. 43, No. 8 (December 16, 1978), 15–23.

These "solutions" are self-evident absurdities which rely upon the student's natural gift and instinct for vocal expression for any marginal technical improvement that might be made.

In addition to the practices and theories outlined above, there are also those teachers who address themselves to the cure of vocal problems by direct or mechanistic means. Those in this category utilize tongue depressors to "open the throat" and resort to such devices as manipulating the space between the thyroid and cricoid cartilages by using the fingers to effect the desired position. Another device commonly practiced is to have the student sing while the instructor holds the end of the tongue and draws it some distance out of the mouth. All such practices are dubious in value, dangerous, and above all unnecessary.

The great teachers of the past solved vocal problems by gentler means, by employing those principles known to stimulate the vocal registers into improved patterns of response. In this they were most successful, developing remarkable voices which were extensive in range, resonant, flexible and freely produced. Since this goal was accomplished without the use of imagery, without recourse to mechanistic methods and without utilizing such constructs as "placement," nasal resonance, or systems devoted to breath management, it is evident, in view of the extraordinary success of earlier instruction and the failure of currently popular practices, that none of the latter are pertinent to the issue of vocal development.

Just how far voice training practices have departed from earlier concepts related to the vocal function is evident from a statement of Gordon Holmes, a noted nineteenth century physician and throat specialist, who touched upon the mechanical essence of the vocal problem in this statement:

[73]Dr. Gordon Holmes, *The Science of Voice Production and Voice Preservation* (New York: R. Worthington, 1880), p. 100.

> Voice is generated mainly as the result of two consecutive and specially contained movements, the one primary and vital, namely, activity of muscle, the other secondary and material, *viz.*, motion of air. To these two relations may be traced all the physiological effects of vocal exercise.[73]

The correctness of Dr. Holmes' insight is undeniable, and it is apparent that contemporary training has failed to address itself to solutions which would exercise a positive effect either upon the "activity of muscle" so primary and vital to a free tone production, or upon the "motion of air" which is determined by and reflects the efficiency of the muscular and mental processes that have been set in motion.

NEW DIRECTIONS

Shortly after World War I there was a resurgence of interest in vocal matters which promised to place training methods on a more sensible footing. Perhaps the first to form a link between scientific investigation and practical pedagogy was Douglas Stanley. By establishing a direct connection between vocal physiology and what Garcia referred to as a "group of homogeneous sounds produced by one mechanism differing essentially from another group of homogeneous sounds produced by another mechanism," Stanley, in agreement with Dr. Holmes, provided what must be considered the most satisfactory definition of a register yet proposed:

> There are two groups of muscles: the arytenoid and the cricothyroid groups, which act as tensors of the vocal cords. The preponderance of effect of one group over the other determines a register. There are, consequently, two, and only two, registers in the human voice.[74]

Another to forge a vital link between science and vocal pedagogy was Wilmer T. Bartholomew, who conducted his researches at the Peabody Conservatory of Music. Like Stanley, Bartholomew found no evidence to validate the dogma of nasal resonance, voice placement, support, breath control, or the metaphysical concepts associated with imagery, particularly acoustics.

As a consequence of his investigations, Bartholomew postulated that the larynx was the primary resonator of vocal tone and that it alone was capable of energizing those frequencies in the range of 2800–3400 cps, or what has since become known as the singer's formant. Bartholomew also pointed out that the singer's formant matches the natural or "meatus resonance" of the ear canal, a postulate based upon a discovery of Helmholtz, who considered this area of high sensitivity to extend from 2460–3168 cps. Both Bartholomew and Stanley related variations of intensity to changes in the amplitude of the vibrato (which is desirable), making a careful distinction between it and the tremolo and the wobble (which are not).

Other serious teachers of voice emerged to continue and supplement the work of Stanley and Bartholomew. One of the most influential among this group was William Vennard of the voice faculty of the University of Southern California. Vennard also acknowledged a register to be a tone quality produced as the result of a particular type of mechanical arrangement within the laryngeal pharynx, but in an obvious attempt to justify many shades of theoretical opinion on the subject, quickly shifted emphasis away from the concept of "mechanisms" to various "approaches."

In treating the subject on this level, Vennard admitted the existence of three possibilities: 1) "the ideal approach," or one-register theory; 2) the "hypothetical approach," or two-register theory, and 3) the "realistic approach," or three-register theory. He was then able to conclude that "the more sensitive one becomes register-wise, the more registers one is likely to isolate, but we may generalize and say there are three."[75]

[74]Douglas Stanley, *The Science of Voice* (New York: Carl Fischer, Inc., 1929), p. 7.

[75]William Vennard, *Singing: The Mechanism and The Technic* (New York: Carl Fisher, Inc., 1967), p. 69.

In justifying three mutually contradictory premises concerning the number of registers, Vennard failed to pursue his own logic to its ultimate conclusion. If Stanley's definition (which meets in accord with Dr. Holmes' statement concerning the essence of "voice") is accepted as reasonable, then both a direct correspondence and a mechanical principle have been established to certify the presence of two register mechanisms and no more. Since this formulation agrees with the empirical precepts formed as early as the fourteenth century, when the mechanisms were known as the *vox integra* (true voice) and *vox ficta* (false voice), and with the precepts of Tosi, Mancini, Manfredini, *etc.*, who advanced the postulate of the *voce di petto* (chest voice) and falsetto or *voce di testa* (head voice), a substantial body of evidence has accumulated to support the two-register theory.

To explain the apparent logical misconceptions concerning the number of vocal registers that is prevalent among both scientific investigators and practical teachers of voice, it is helpful to remove the subject from its present context and view the matter from a different, less emotionally charged perspective. It has long been recognized, for example, that there are but three primary colors. Suppose two of these, yellow and blue, are used analogously with those properties of tone quality known to be produced when each register mechanism functions in its isolated form. By combining these two colors, a third, green, appears. While possessed of a distinctive hue, green cannot be said to be a primary color, nor can the distinctive tone quality which emerges when the two basic register mechanisms are combined (significantly referred to as a "middle" register) be considered a third register.

Furthermore, when the colors yellow and blue are combined, their influence is sensed by the perceptive eye, but the color remains green, and the depth of the color is related to the proportion and strength of the two primary elements. Thus, green can range from deep to pale, from yellow-blue to blue-yellow, and "color control" is maintained by a proper blending of the two elements.

The same principle is applicable to the integration of the vocal registers. Depending upon how each primary element is blended, the voice may appear to be seamless or uniform in color (depending on one's viewpoint, "no registers" or "every pitch a separate register"), or comprised of two, three, or, since "the more sensitive one becomes register-wise, the more registers one is likely to isolate," four, five, and occasionally six. Since no functional principle can embrace all of these propositions, all but one must be incorrect. Like the two primary colors in the example above, there are only two primary muscle systems which form or constitute the two basic register mechanisms, the cricothyroids and the arytenoids. The multiplicity of tone colors often designated as registers is merely the result of the combination of the two.

CURRENT INVESTIGATIONS

The failure to perceive "voice" and define it has always complicated the investigations of scientists, but no more so than in the present. Because of the absence of a precise definition and a general lack of consensus, there has again been a proliferation of terminology almost identical with that which occured shortly after the invention of the laryngoscope. In this new development, the terms "long reed," "short reed," "lower thick-lower thin," "heavy and light," *etc.*, have been replaced by "vocal fry," "pulse," "modal," "growl," "loft," and "stroh," a nomenclature which further confuses an already confusing area of pedagogic thought.

The new terminology introduced by scientists has surfaced on the basis of pitch-quality relationships, without reference to a corresponding physical arrangement between the two muscle systems which draw the vocal folds into tension, and without considering intensity to be a factor. This is made clear by Marianne Mörner, F. Fransson and Gunnar Fant:

> The terminology with regard to voice pitch levels, *i.e.*, registers, suffers from the existence of an abundance of terms and an ambiguity of their use. It is not the purpose of the present report to discuss registers from a physiological point of view. . . .The only secure common denominator for defining a register is by means of its range on the musical scale. It has therefore been attempted to summarize the terminology used in the literature by placing each author's term within one of the five basic registers which M. Mörner suggests to be referred to in English as the *deepest range*, the *deep-level*, the *mid-level*, the *high-level*, and the *highest range*. . . . It is hoped that this display shall contribute to a better understanding of various terminologies and forward the discussion on suitable terms.[76]

[76]Marianne Mörner, F. Fransson and Gunnar Fant, *Voice Register Terminology and Standard Pitch* (Stockholm, Sweden: Speech Transmission Laboratory, Royal Institute of Technology, 1970), p. 20.

The fundamental misconception in the above proposal is that it studies pitch as though it were produced in a vacuum. Pitch is merely a rhythmic disturbance of air particles as perceived by the listener, and since it is the product of other functions and has no mechanical function of its own, but only acoustic properties, the conclusions reached by the authors quoted bear no relevance to the traditional definition of a register as being "a series of homogeneous sounds produced by one mechanism, differing essentially from another group of equally homogeneous sounds produced by another mechanism." Without physiological justification, registers cannot be properly defined or analyzed, and from the standpoint of vocal pedagogy, cannot be isolated, developed as separate entities, or made to combine or coordinate in a functionally efficient way. Furthermore, since pitch cannot be extracted from intensity, the impact of intensity on an involuntary muscular system must be evaluated conjunctively with pitch.

Other concerns of recent investigations, most of which have been based upon studies of the speaking rather than the singing voice, center on the properties of tonal resonance, the significance of sensations of vibration, and a minute detailing of tongue, lip, jaw, uvula and other volitionally controllable articulatory processes and their effects upon the singer's formant. This is graphically illustrated in a scholarly book by D. Ralph Appelman, Professor Emeritus at the University of Indiana, in which he offers the following suggestions concerning vowel formation:

> Each vowel represents certain well-defined, physiological positions involving the tongue, labial orifice (lips), velum, mandible, and larynx, which have been determined by X-ray photographs and cinefluorography. *Tongue.* To produce the basic vowel, the tip of the tongue must be placed against the bottom front teeth during phonation (production) of all vowel sounds sung on pitches within the area of stability. *Lips.* In the high frontal, mid-frontal, and low frontal vowels, the lips are more spread than rounded. In the lowback, mid-back, and highback vowels, the lips are rounded progressively more than from lowback to highback positions. *Larynx.* The laryngeal position is more lowered during phonation than the passive position assumed during normal breathing.[77]

[77]D. Ralph Appelman, *The Science of Vocal Pedagogy* (Bloomington, Indiana: Indiana University Press, 1967), p. 231.

The premise upon which the adjustments advocated by Appelman are based lacks spontaneity and naturalness; if positioning these parts in the prescribed manner would cure throatiness, nasality, breath loss, lip, jaw and tongue tension, increase flexibility and extend the tonal range, learning to sing would be quite an easy matter. Learning to sing well is a skill not easily mastered, however, and manipulation of the articulators is not an important factor in promoting technical growth. This is because, neurologically, coordination with respect to articulation is subject to intellectual control, whereas the respiratory mechanism, particularly the diaphragm, the vocal folds and their associated musculatures are functions perceived via kinesthesia. This means that their movement produces no conscious sensations and their coordination within the broader framework of phonation can only be improved by freeing autonomous involuntary processes not subject to intellectual control.

While phonation can sometimes be marginally improved by adjusting the articulators, it is unlikely that a dependency upon such procedures will accomplish the purpose such manipulations were designed to serve. On the contrary, a proper positioning and free movement of the articulators is impossible unless functional activities taking place below the level of consciousness, *i.e.*, coordination within the laryngeal area, have first been brought to a reasonably high level of efficiency.

The mechanistic approach implicit in Appelman's formulation disregards such important factors as the singer's instinct and capacity for hearing and feeling, without which phonation would be impossible. Berton Coffin directed his attention to this phase of the subject when he invented the Echophone, a piece of equipment designed to help the student find, hear, feel and learn to "sing on resonance." Another device to achieve this end was the Radioear Vibrator, based upon the principle of isochronal electromechanical tone massage introduced by the great Russian physician Malyutin in 1897. Coffin's gadgets differ somewhat from earlier inventions (many of which have been developed at the Berlin Clinic for Speech Disorders) in that concepts related to resonance and tuning of the laryngeal cavities for the vowel are regulated by holding the Echophone "in front of the mouth with the vocal cords together—no air passing through them." The subject must then "pronounce the modifications of the vowels indicated . . . until they come in loud and clear, somewhat as though 'tuning' a radio. The vowel-color which resonates is the 'mental color of the vowel' which you must think when you sing on that pitch."[78]

Whether or not the use of the Echophone or the Radioear will materially improve a functional condition within the throat parts when the muscles reflect the influence of bad habits, and are undeveloped and poorly coordinated, awaits the test of time. Neither the processes advocated nor the devices employed, however, appear to confront any of the problems related to the restoration of lost motility within the vocal tract (especially the laryngeal generator), and therefore merely help the singer do the best he can with what he has to offer under a present set of technical conditions. To tune a radio is quite easy, but when the mechanical parts are deficient, precise tuning and clear reception is impossible. Moreover, it is impossible to "sing on resonance;" while a precise tuning of the pharyngeal cavities in response to the vowel amplifies the vibrations generated within the larynx, it correspondingly

[78]Berton Coffin, "The Instrumental Resonance of the Singing Voice," *NATS Bulletin* Vol. 31, No. 3 (February-March, 1974), 28.

dissipates that same energy. Thus, if sound is to continue to "resonate," energy must be replenished at the point of delivery, *i.e.*, the glottal area. How this energy is to be replenished has not been considered in the above formulations.

Vocal cosmetics are not the answer to vocal problems, and with rare exceptions singers (even those well established as professionals) have serious limitations which must be addressed in a serious way. Until modern methods are reconstituted to embrace procedures based on valid functional principles, they will fail to fulfill their intended purpose.

CONCLUSION

Vocal pedagogy, it would seem, has moved further and further away (since 1900) from traditional principles and practices. Today, earlier models have for the most part been entirely rejected, and the functional principles upon which they were based have been forgotten. However, a thorough and objective analysis of the results of modern pedagogic methods shows, as a whole, little success: too many gifted students try and fail, and too many start out with well-formed voices only to lose them prematurely. The old way may at first appear to be longer and harder, but historical evidence indicates clearly that in the long run it is shortest and best. Mancini was correct when he urged his readers "not to distrust the inclinations in regard to nature, which, when overlooked, make every attempt to overcome or correct by the aid of art, futile."[79] It is far better, in every way, to rely upon pedagogic techniques designed to stimulate natural movement than to rely upon those designed to replicate "well defined physiological positions." An instinctual approach to singing must never be stifled by mechanistic methods: to do so is to substitute artifice for art.

Whether modern methods have succeeded or failed, or are superior or inferior to those adopted by several generations of teachers who produced a great Golden Age of Song, is an emotionally charged issue each individual must resolve to his own satisfaction. It is well to bear in mind, however, a statement by Frederick Husler and Yvonne Rodd-Marling:

> We no longer have at our disposal the acute sense of hearing once possessed by great teachers of singing. . . . Our ears have lost that strange kind of intuitive, almost somnambulistic intelligence, together with its extraordinary accurate discriminating faculty.[80]

The "intuitive, almost somnambulistic intelligence" possessed by the great teachers of an earlier era cannot be attributed to anything but a knowledge of functional mechanics, which enabled them to recognize the physical origins of the tone qualities being produced, as well as the techniques to be employed to stimulate the mechanism into improved patterns of response. This was a very different kind of perception from that based upon aesthetic judgment. Can it be, therefore, that the "acute sense of hearing once possessed by great teachers" came about, not because their hearing faculty was superior, but because they were trained listeners whose attention was directed to something quite different, and that modern pedagogy is pointed in the wrong direction?

See **Bel Canto**
Breath Control
Breathing
Covering,
(To) Cover
Energy
Falsetto
Falsetto or
Head Voice
Kinesthesia
Laryngeal
Suspension
Larynx
Middle Register
Modal Register
Register
Resonance
Standing Wave
Vortex Theory

[79]Giam Battista Mancini, *Practical Reflections on Figured Singing,* translated by E. Forman (Champaign, Ill: Pro Musica Press, 1967), p. 115.

[80]Frederick Husler and Yvonne Rodd-Marling, *Singing: The Physical Nature of the Vocal Organ* (New York: October House, 1964), p. xiii.

Modulation of Vowel Quality: See Vowel Modification.

Momentum: Latin, "movement;" the identifying property of motion; impetus; the kinesthetic impression derived from movement.

Rhythmic momentum allows body movement to be free and spontaneous. When the vocal function is efficient, it becomes the driving force behind most of the muscular activities that collectively yield vocal tone.

See Emotion
   Energy
   Kinesthesia
   Rhythm

Monotone: a succession of syllables, words, or sentences uttered on one unvaried pitch.

A person who speaks or sings in a monotone is frequently referred to as being tone deaf. However, whereas the latter condition is the inability to *distinguish* between variations in musical pitch, the former is the inability to *produce* variations in musical pitch. Both conditions, in the strictest sense of their meanings, are extremely rare. Most persons who speak or sing in a monotone or who are "tone deaf" merely have difficulty coordinating aural and physical processes. This skill, however, is one that can generally be acquired.

Monotony in singing is often reflected, in less extreme cases, by tonal and inflectional "sameness" and general musical insensitivity.

Motivation: an inner prompting, conscious or subconscious, that compels one to act.

Motivation in singing is the urge to express oneself through vocal tone. It is an integral part of vocal talent but must be tempered by the formulation of realistic and worthwhile artistic goals.

Motor: that which causes motion or produces energy; in singing, impulses transmitted from the central nervous system by means of nerve fibers which innervate a muscle or organic system(s); the vocal mechanism which generates those vibrations perceived as vocal tone. It is the efficiency of these motor responses which determines the efficiency of the tone production.

See Holistic Pedagogy

Mouth Resonance: See Resonance, Mouth.

Mouthy Tone: a vocalized sound whose "thick," "muddy," nonresonant tonal characteristics result from some degree of reliance upon the oral cavity or mouth for resonance.

Under correct technical conditions, vocal tone is resonated primarily within the laryngo- and oropharynges. The mouth is involved in tonal amplification only to the extent that its shape affects, to a certain degree, the shape of the oropharynx. When vocal tone is resonated in the mouth, the phonation of pure vowels becomes an impossibility, and verbal and emotional communication is extremely difficult. "Mouthy" singing is the aural manifestation of these undesirable qualities.

See Resonance

Movement: a physical act that distinguishes animate nature from the inanimate and that reflects the manner in which an organism expends energy.

Movement, especially rhythmic movement, is the medium through which man makes contact with his inner being, with fellow humans, and with the universe at

232

arge. Vocally, it is the medium through which the singer becomes aware of the "feel" of his voice and the causative factors which assure him of its functional rightness.

Rhythmic movement is the essence of the pedagogic process. Only through rhythmic movement is it possible to eliminate faulty muscular tensions, refine, and in many cases, redefine mental concepts, and rechannel stored energy into spontaneous physical activity. The purpose of technical training is to encourage natural rhythmic movement, and by so doing pave the way for physical and emotional spontaneity.

When functional principles that encourage natural movement are applied, the vocal mechanism itself will indicate how it prefers to adjust: an inner logic will prompt it to move this way rather than that. By utilizing techniques designed to stimulate natural movement, "studying" voice becomes a process in which all concerned *observe* the obvious parallels between stimulus and response and grow into a kinesthetic and conceptual knowledge of the vocal mechanism—its needs, abilities and limitations. As a result of an increased freedom of response and a sharpening of mental concepts, the "voice" that emerges no longer has to be "acted upon" to manufacture that which is lacking, but will be *intrinsically* "well focused," properly "placed," "well supported," clear, qualitatively unique and distinctive, and highly adaptable to the requirements of musical and verbal communication. Were it impossible to stimulate natural movement, all hope of learning to sing would have to be abandoned: singing would be an art reserved for those few whose prowess already conformed to the natural laws that govern the vocal process.

In the final analysis, techniques for stimulating natural movement through rhythmic identification must supersede all other pedagogic considerations.

See Energy
   Equilibrium
   Kinesthesia
   Natural
      Movement
   Register
   Resonance
   Self-Regulation
   Vowel

Mucous Membrane: a mucus-producing lining found in those body passages (the mouth, throat, nose, trachea, lungs, alimentary canal, reproductive organs, *etc.*) that open to the external world.

Mucus: a clear, thick secretion produced by mucous membranes which lubricates and protects those body passages (the mouth, throat, nose, trachea, lungs, alimentary canal, reproductive organs, *etc.*) that are openly accessible to the external world.

Muscle: a stringy bundle of body fibers connecting bones, cartilages, and other muscles whose contraction causes movement.

Muscles are named after their points or origin and insertion. For example, the thyroarytenoid muscles are attached at either end to the thyroid and arytenoid cartilages. When brought into tension, muscular movements are of two kinds, voluntary and involuntary. Those most important to singing fall within the latter category.

Most muscle systems, including those that collectively comprise the vocal mechanism, are balanced by natural antagonists, or opposing muscles whose contractions reverse or counter their natural movements. This antagonistic muscle system permits a highly sophisticated and varied degree of movement potential and allows a natural equilibrium, or balance of tension, to exist among the various body muscles and muscular systems.

The vocal muscles require effective antagonistic resistance if their movements are to be well coordinated. When these movements are precisely balanced, there exists a state of muscular equilibrium throughout the entire vocal tract, which extends from the abdominal floor to the palatal muscles. However, when coordination among the vocal muscles is faulty, muscular interference and unrelieved tension are produced. These phenomena are manifested, respectively, by compensatory tensions and throat constriction, and by the characteristic tonal movement known as the "tremolo."

Muscular Antagonism: See Antagonistic Muscle(s).

Muscular Control: See Control.

Muscular Development: the strengthening of body muscles by systematic exercise in ways which conform to their natural movement potential.

Building an efficient vocal technique from the ground up (a process that does not totally apply to those whose voices are already well formed) involves 1) the isolation, separation, development, and ultimate coordination of the two basic register mechanisms, the chest register and falsetto, and 2) the development of the pharyngeal musculature that positions the throat cavities for tonal amplification or resonance. Both processes are accomplished by the skillful manipulation of musical stimuli (pitch, intensity, and vowel) to elicit from the involuntary vocal muscles responses more in keeping with their natural movement potentials.

Time is an equally important consideration in developing, recoordinating, and increasing the tonicity of the vocal muscles. Tradition has it that a period of seven to nine years is required (even for the acknowledged master teachers of the Bel Canto era) to bring a voice to its fullest state of development. Furthermore, full vocal maturation is not reached until about the age of forty. Provided that one sings correctly, has not abused the mechanism and maintains good health, however, the singer's vocal prime should last at least twenty years—from age forty to sixty.

Muscular Glottis: the part of the glottis that is bounded by the vocal ligaments.

Muscular Independence: the ability to contract one muscle or muscle group to the exclusion of others (*e.g.,* an isometric exercise).

Singing is a complex coordinative activity involving the contraction of many involuntary muscles. Attempts to establish muscular independence during phonation, therefore, while not impossible, are certainly ill advised. Localized effort invariably becomes localized tenseness. Any attempt to establish direct control over specific muscles (*e.g.,* contracting the abdominal muscles, "lifting" the diaphragm, raising the uvula, widening the pharynx, fixing the tongue, or setting the jaw) is bound to fail of its purpose and engender muscular stiffness within the laryngeal area, breathing apparatus, facial muscles, and/or mouth.

Muscular Movement: physical activity that results from the contraction of body muscles in response to neurological stimuli.

The muscles of the body work somewhat in the manner of a complex system of pulleys, in which each muscle or muscle group has a natural antagonist whose

See Emotion
  Energy
  Kinesthesia
  Movement

See Laryngeal
    Suspension
  Register

See Coordination
  Localized Effort
  Muscular Tension

contraction effects a recovery of movement or countermovement. Thus, when a muscle contracts it causes the bones and/or cartilages to which it is attached to move in one direction or another, and the contraction of its antagonist restores these elements to their original position or pulls them in the opposite direction.

Muscular movement is of two types: voluntary, or movement that results from conscious neurological processes, and involuntary, or movement generated by the autonomic nervous system, which is beyond the realm of conscious control.

Since "voice" is largely the product of involuntary muscular movements, effective conscious control over the vocal mechanism is virtually impossible. The essential difficulty in voice-building is to find ways and means to stimulate involuntary muscles to move more efficiently without trying to establish conscious or direct control, a process which invariably engenders muscular stiffness and compensatory tensions. This can only be done through the mechanics of registration. Since both registers respond involuntarily and predictably to specific patterns of pitch, intensity and vowel, the skillful teacher can manipulate these musical elements to elicit more efficient responses from the vocal mechanism, and thereby pave the way for real technical rehabilitation and progress.

See Autonomic Nervous System
Kinesthesia
Limbic System

Muscular Process: the projection of the arytenoid cartilage to which various muscles are attached.

The muscular process and the vocal process are collectively engaged in those movements that close the glottal space and consequently approximate the vocal folds.

See Vocal Process

Muscular Tension: that stress or force resulting from the contraction and elongation of a muscle or muscle system.

Muscular tension is frequently confused with muscular "tenseness," or the stress resulting from muscular interference. Vocal tone, however, cannot be produced without tension. The pedagogic concern, therefore, is to develop a technique in which the vocal muscles tense *properly, i.e.,* in conformity with nature's laws and without the interference of muscles that should remain passive during phonation.

See Coordination

Musical Tone: sounds whose vibrations are both regular and rhythmic as opposed to those that are erratic (noise).

Mutation: (archaic) the pubescent transition from a boy's voice to a man's; also used with reference to the joining, or coordinating, of one register mechanism to another.

Mutation of Registers: See Register Blending.

Mutational Chink: a small, triangular opening between the arytenoids which occurs during phonation.

The mutational "chink" is responsible for those breathy tonal characteristics typified by immature and undeveloped voices, and is a result of an imbalanced registration in which the chest register fails to participate adequately in the coordinative process.

Myasthenia: Greek *mys*, "muscle;" in singing, a weakness of laryngeal functioning that results from vocal abuse.

Mylo-: Greek *mylai*, "molar teeth;" a prefix that refers to the floor of the mouth.

Mylohyoid: the flat, triangular muscle that forms the floor of the mouth, whose contraction pulls the tongue and hyoid bone forward.

Mylopharyngeal: that part of the superior constrictor muscle which attaches to the lower jaw.

The mylopharyngeal muscle is part of the swallowing mechanism and consequently should remain passive during phonation.

Myo-: Greek *mys*, "muscle;" a prefix that refers to body musculature.

Myoelastic-Aerodynamic Theory: a widely accepted postulate advanced by Johannes Müller (1843), who demonstrated that the frequency of the vibratory impulses perceived as vocal tone is caused by the following factors: 1) movement of air from the lungs and trachea, *i.e.*, subglottal breath pressure, and 2) contraction of the intrinsic laryngeal muscle systems that adjust the vocal folds to the requisite length, mass, and tension for the pitch, intensity, and vowel pattern being sung.

An understanding of the myoelastic-aerodynamic theory reveals the nature of one of the basic problems confronted when attempting to enhance and develop vocal skills, namely, how to bring a highly complex and largely involuntary muscular system into balanced tension. Unless pedagogic procedures and the principles upon which they are founded effectively stimulate these muscular systems into improved patterns of response, the acquisiton of technical skills not formerly possessed is clearly impossible.

See Bel Canto
    Modern Methods
    Reflex

Myoelasticity: the stretching capability of muscles.

N

Nares: the nasal passages; a cavity lined with mucous membrane whose opening communicates posteriorly with the nasal pharynx, and anteriorly to the outer atmosphere by its external openings, or nostrils.

Narrow Voice: a voice lacking "roundness" because of youthfulness, lack of register development and/or throat constriction. A narrow voice is usually "white" and colorless.

See Register
    Voix Blanche
    Voix Sombre

Nasal Cavity: that portion of the pharynx bounded at either end by the posterior nares and the nostrils, and divided by the septum into two fossae.

Many theorists and teachers of voice believe that the fossae, together with the antra and sinuses, are critical factors in resonance. Out of this belief has grown a method of tone production known as "nasal resonance." Since, however, the nasal fossae are small, fixed cavities far removed from the tonal source, they possess none of the qualifications necessary to effective tonal resonation, a fact verified by scientific investigation.

See Cavity Tone Theory
    Nasality
    Nasopharynx
    Resonance

Nasal Consonant: a voiced consonant phoneme (*e.g., m, n* or *ng*) which may be produced with or without nasality.

The proper articulation of so-called "nasal consonants" is subject to the same rules that apply to the correct production of nasal vowels. Each requires a high level of technical proficiency if nasality is to be reduced to a minimum, and depends upon the adoption of procedures whose purpose is to establish the laryngeal pharynx as a primary resonator of vocal tone.

A physical arrangement important to the successful nonnasal execution of nasal consonants is the position of the palatal arch, which must be broad and flat. Otherwise, should the velum be raised, and the larynx correspondingly lowered, the tone quality becomes "darker" and "covered." Such a technique makes nasality more difficult to avoid even when the laryngeal pharynx is engaged as a resonator.

The difficulties inherent in the nonnasal production of nasal consonants can be overcome if the concept of vowel purity so admired by those who established the Bel Canto tradition is adopted and made to replace the current fad of "mask resonance" and forward "placement."

See Bel Canto
    Consonants
    Formant
    Hum
    Nasality
    Sensations of
      Vibration
    Twenty-Eight
      Hundred

See Nasality
    Open Throat
    Resonance

Nasal Resonance: See Nasality; Resonance, Nasal.

Nasal Tone: a vocalized sound whose thin, "twangy" tonal characteristics are the result of throat constriction.

Nasal Vowel: a vowel phoneme (*e.g.,* the French *in, en, an, on, etc.*) whose articulation tends to introduce some degree of nasality, and consequently throat constriction.

Nasality: unpleasant, "twangy" tonal characteristics that are engendered by throat constriction.

The cause of nasality has been the subject of a long-standing controversy among theorists. The dispute centers on whether or not the nasal passages should be open, partially open, or completely closed during phonation. Scientific studies devoted to the subject generally support the contention that the nasal passages should be closed, but with exceptions. To quote Croatto and Croatto-Martinelli:

> On the whole, radiological research has led most of the authorities to favor complete occlusion in the oral phonemes. Some of them meanwhile present evidence that it is not always produced in hermetic fashion.[81]

[81]Lucio Croatto and Caterina Croatto-Martinelli, "Physiopathologie du voile du palais," *Folia Phoniatrica* 11 (1959), 137.

The nineteenth century scientist Passavant, after whom Passavant's ridge was named, demonstrated in his experiments (by inserting tubes of varying size into the nose to alter the interior dimensions of the passageway) that nasality only occured when the opening was excessive. In this century, George Oscar Russell published data based upon X-rays taken of professional singers; this data contended that tone quality was not affected adversely when the nasal port was open, and that no apparent correlation existed between nasality and either the opening or closing of the nasal passages.

Another nineteenth century investigator, Sir Morell Mackenzie, proposed a do-it-yourself type of experiment to clarify this issue, testing whether or not the nasal passages had an effect on tone quality by pinching the nostrils intermittently while the subject sang a sustained vowel quality. In conducting this test, he proposed the following hypothesis: should the nasal passages be a factor in resonance, or even in phonation itself, the closure of the nostrils would produce a marked change in the tone quality; if the passages were already closed, the closure of the nostrils would make no appreciable difference.

On the basis of these and other experiments, Mackenzie concluded that the nasal passages should not be open during phonation. However, he did go on to report the following:

[82]Sir Morell Mackenzie, *The Hygiene of the Vocal Organs* (Belmar, N.J.: E.S. Werner & Co., 1928), p. 215.

> In the human voice, it seems probable that greater volume can be obtained by opening the nasal passage, but at the cost of adding a constant group of nasal resonances to those of every vowel sound. This, to my ear, gives a disagreeable monotony to all of the vowel sounds.[82]

238

Is not clear why authorities concerned with the problem of nasality feel that when the conditions are right the nasal passages should behave consistently. What does emerge with clarity, however, is the fact that under certain conditions the passages should remain open, while under another set of conditions they should remain closed. This is evident from the fact that the so-called "nasal" consonants and vowels (*e.g., ng, m,* and *n*), and particularly the hum, can be produced without a trace of nasality and yet cannot be sounded unless the nasal passages are open. On the other hand (as Mackenzie's nostril test proves), the closure of the passages neither increases nor decreases the amount of nasality present. This response would not be expected were effective resonation of nonnasal qualities dependent upon an open passageway.

Several conclusions suggest themselves with respect to the function of the nasal port and its relationship to nasality and a correct tone production:

1. The nasal passages, whether open or closed, are not germane to the issue of nasality;
2. Nasality must owe its being to the manner in which other elements engaged in the phonative process participate in adjusting the upper palatal region, and
3. If, as some authorities contend, the nasal port is closed much of the time, then the concept of nasal resonance (since a closed cavity cannot act as a resonator) is merely a sensation produced by some other type of activity.

If neither the closing nor the opening of the posterior nares (and consequently the nasal passages) is a significant factor in nasality, it is necessary to look elsewhere for the cause of this distressing vocal fault. In view of the fact that phonation is a secondary, overlaid function, the inconsistent behavior noted above must be attributable to either a violation of, or a conflict with, a primary organic activity. The obvious source of this conflict between vocalization and a primary organic activity is swallowing, where food and liquids are passed downward to the digestive organs in a series of wavelike movements. In singing, these constrictive movements must be reversed if the pharyngeal tract is to maintain a constant open-throated resonance adjustment.

In view of the difficulties encountered in adapting the alimentary canal to the vocal process, it is not surprising that an open-throated tone production is rare, while throat constriction in varying degrees is extremely common. This is because the palatal muscles (which are active in both vowel formation and swallowing) meet with the superior constrictors (which form a horizontal half-ring across the posterior pharyngeal wall) at the level of the hard palate, known as Passavant's ridge. Since the superior constrictors interconnect with the middle and inferior constrictors, and the latter to the cricothyroid muscle system in front (the stretchers of the vocal folds) and to the thyroid cartilage behind, and since all of these muscle systems communicate readily with other members of the pharyngeal tract (namely, the palatalpharyngeals, the salpingopharyngeals, and the stylopharyngeals, which connect the soft palate with the tongue), all of which are essentially constrictive, their prevailing tendency is to interfere with rather than assist the vocal process.

The result of the combined activities of these muscle systems is to tilt the thyroid cartilage inward (which reduces the interior dimension of the larynx) and to narrow the space between the tongue and the posterior pharyngeal wall. When this occurs, the wavelike motion natural to peristalsis is arrested in its beginning phase and the muscle systems become rigid. Nasality is the product of this type of physical coordination, and technically it is one of the more serious vocal faults.

As is true with other impressions of vibratory sensation, *i.e.*, those which appear to resonate in the head and chest, or which impress as being "forward" or "back," the symptoms associated with nasality are misleading. Sir Richard Paget investigated this phase of the subject quite thoroughly, constructing a resonator "formed of a rubber tube (about 1 inch in diameter) attached to an organ reed and fitted with a cork tongue." One of the interesting developments resulting from this experiment was the discovery that

> . . . if, while the reed was sounding, the tube was suitably pinched, near the opening from the reed . . . an appreciable twang was added to the vowel-sound. This experiment indicates that a part, at least, of the so-called nasal quality . . . is probably due to a constriction of some part of the pharynx.[83]

[83]Sir Richard Paget, *Human Speech* (New York: Harcourt, Brace & Co., 1930), p. 96.

Nasality and nasal "twang," therefore, are not essentially related to an opening or closing of the nasal passages, but, as Wilmer T. Bartholomew later confirmed, are products of unrelieved tension within the pharyngeal tract, the degree of nasality corresponding exactly to the amount of constriction engendered.

When Manuel Garcia warned about being "deceived by mere appearances" he was referring to breathing, but he could well have expanded the concept to include nasality and illusions experienced with respect to resonance. Despite appearances, as has already been shown, nasality is a product of wrong throat tension, and the nasal passages play a negligible role in producing this quality. Furthermore, the nasal cavities are not a factor in tonal amplification, as Warren B. Wooldridge (1954) has so conclusively proven. To understand the nature of this paradox, and to understand nasality itself, one must consider the manner in which sound is transmitted.

Sound waves are known to travel most efficiently through a tensed or dense medium. When the pharyngeal musculature is constricted during phonation, the vibratory impulses generated at the tonal source are provided with a medium through which they can travel efficiently. The result is that the impulses generated radiate upward through the tensed pharyngeal musculature until they terminate at Passavant's ridge, immediately adjacent to the posterior nares. The impression derived from this type of constriction is that the tone is "pinched," "caught in the throat," or "nasal." When the pharyngeal walls are free of constricting tension, sound waves concentrate along an alternate route and radiate through the bone structure.

The difference between nasality and the appearance of nasal resonance, therefore, is in a physical sense essentially one of muscular coordination. When the tone quality is nasal, the vibratory impulses *traverse the wrongly tensed pharyngeal muscle systems involved in peristaltic movement;* vibratory impulses which are free of nasality are *transmitted through the skeletal framework by means of bone conduction.* When the amount of wrong tension is slight, the resultant tonal product creates the impression that "resonance" is concentrated in the facial mask. When the constriction is excessive, the tone quality becomes nasal. When there is a complete absence of muscular interference, the tone quality is not nasal, nor does it appear to possess nasal "resonance," but is clear, "ringing," and full-throated.

In recent years science has provided a more perceptive insight into the nature of vocal resonance, recognizing that the vocal tract itself, *i.e.*, the laryngo- and oropharynges, is the primary resonator of vocal tone. The conclusion of Johan Sundberg, the Swedish scientist, is that

> a number of factors that are often cited as determinants of excellence in singing: the nasal cavity, head and chest resonances, breathing and so on . . . have not been mentioned simply because they seem to be not relevant to the major acoustic properties of the vowel sounds produced in professional operatic singing. Our research suggests that professional quality can be achieved by means of a rather normal voice source and the resonances of the vocal tract. . . . Resonance outside the vocal tract, such as in the head or in the chest, cannot contribute appreciably to the singer's acoustic output in view of the great extent to which sound is attenuated as it passes through tissues.[84]

[84]Johan Sundberg, "The Acoustics of the Singing Voice," *Scientific American* (March, 1977), 23.

The distinction between nasality, "nasal resonance" and a full-throated tone production points up an interesting dichotomy between nineteenth and twentieth century aesthetics. Prior to the twentieth century, "purity of intonation," *i.e.*, vowel (tonal) purity, was considered one of the prerequisites of a correct vocal technique, a concept which stands in direct opposition to the "disagreeable monotony in all vowels" noted by Mackenzie. This change in attitude came about when Dr. H. Holbrook Curtis and Jean de Reszke advanced their theory of "nasal resonance," a postulate which promised to achieve greater tonal opulence and help the voice cut through the more heavily orchestrated works being mounted. While this practice added "ping" and "point" to the tone by strengthening the higher partials, it was accomplished at the expense of tonal purity by adding a "constant group of nasal resonances to every vowel sound."

It might be contended that nasality is unavoidable when producing so-called "nasal" phonemes (*e.g.*, the French sounds *in, an, on,* and the "nasal" consonants *m* and *n*), but this overlooks the fact that vowel sounds (even those which appear to require nasalization) can be produced to better advantage and without nasality by a combined tuning of the laryngo- and oropharynges. To sing a perfect legato and maintain resonance characteristics which are common to all vowels (regardless of the language being sung) requires a continuity of tonal energy independent of those adjustments necessary to accommodate vowels which are loosely and inaccurately described as nasal, "foward" and "back."

Legato singing is impossible unless the laryngeal pharynx consistently energizes those frequencies (quite independent of the formants which, when energized, define the vowel) ranging from 2800 to 3400 cps. Since this frequency range has been shown by science to yield a ringing tone quality, any effort to "place" or "resonate" the tone in the facial mask inevitably diverts energy from the tonal source (the laryngeal pharynx) and introduces the very constrictor tensions which result in nasality. When the technique is so structured that the larynx provides a continuing source of resonance, it becomes possible to produce a nasal "color" without the tone possessing even a suggestion of nasality.

A nasal tone "color" can be produced free of nasality by simulating its harmonic spectrum, and since any harmonic spectrum can be created by properly adjusting the pharyngeal cavities, it is evident that the effective production of nasal phonemes is not dependent upon the nasal passages. Hence, the functional difference between aesthetically acceptable nasal phonemes and nasality is one of pharyngeal cavity adjustment.

When de Reszke proclaimed to a waiting world that "the tone should be in the nose, but the nose should not be in the tone," he dealt a severe blow to the hopes and aspirations of succeeding generations of singers, who have been taught to take his statement seriously. A directive of this kind is flawed for these reasons:

1. It embraces no functional principle;
2. It is incapable of stimulating the pharyngeal musculature (largely involuntary) into improved patterns of response;
3. It neglects to take into account the fact that the nasal passages are incapable of performing effectively as resonators;
4. It is impossible to arbitrarily "place" the tone in one pharyngeal cavity to the exclusion of another, and
5. It "acts" upon a tone quality whose essential properties have already been determined at the onset of phonation.

Exercises commonly in use to concentrate tonal energy in the facial mask or nasal passages (*i.e., hng-ah, ngah, etc.*) patently encourage nasality and should be avoided, since nasality and the "twang" with which it is associated is both a product and a promoter of throat constriction.

Nasopharynx: a small cavity positioned behind the nose, above the level of the soft palate, and opposite the posterior nares (nasal openings); also known as the mesopharynx.

The nasopharynx can either be included or excluded as a member of the vocal resonating system by 1) a lowering or elevation of the velum, and 2) the presence or absence of a sphincter action involving the superior constrictors. Like the nasal passages, however, the relatively fixed dimensions of this cavity reduce its effectiveness as a resonator, since it cannot be adjusted, or "tuned," and is generally excluded from the resonating system because the nasal port is seldom open during phonation.

At one time the nasopharynx was thought to be responsible for energizing the higher partials in the tonal spectrum (to add brilliance to the tone quality), but this function is now recognized to originate within the laryngeal pharynx.

Natural Breathing: the biological function that maintains organic life through the inhalation and oxidation of air, and the exhalation of carbon dioxide and other wastes.

In natural breathing, the vocal folds open reflexively with each inhalation and exhalation, and close briefly between cycles. Inasmuch as the phonative act requires the folds to approximate for vibration (*i.e.,* to become parallel without touching), it is obvious that there exists a natural contradiction between the inspiratory and expiratory tension of natural breathing and the approximation of the vocal folds as they position themselves to create the pressure variations necessary to the production of vocal tone. Essentially, the problem with natural breathing is that it forces the vocal folds apart, whereas in order to phonate properly they must come together.

A practical remedy often proposed to solve this problem is to initiate phonation just before the completion of the inspiratory cycle. This will curb the reflexive opening of the vocal folds by inhibiting the normal shift of inspiratory tension to expiratory tension, *i.e.,* it will establish a balance between the "in" and "out" movements of the breathing muscles. Consequently, the glottal space will remain closed without being forced to do so by the registration, by constricting the throat, or by tensing the neck muscles.

Natural breathing is not a factor in sustained phonation because 1) it interferes with the desired neuromuscular approximation of the vocal folds, and 2) it under-oxygenates the muscle systems involved.

See Gesture of
    Inhalation
    Breathing

Natural Frequency: the time rate at which a freely oscillating member (*e.g.,* a pendulum) passes through a given point; an acoustic property latent within a cavity whose fundamental frequency, determined by its size and physical dimensions, will vibrate sympathetically when brought into proximity to a sound wave set in motion by a vibrator whose natural speed of vibration is the same.

In singing, the vibratory pattern of the vocal folds produces a fundamental and its corresponding overtones. When the cavities immediately adjacent are so adjusted as to be "tuned" to the same frequencies, the air within them responds sympathetically to create a condition known as resonance. Since the vocal folds are not freely oscillating and there are several cavities (the trachea, the laryngo- and oropharynges, and the mouth) which can be tuned either separately or together in a great variety of ways, a mathematical working out of the resonance potential of the vocal organs with respect to natural frequency is extremely complicated. What is clearly evident, however, is that the vocal mechanism becomes an efficient sound-producing instrument when these two phases of technique, vocal fold vibration and cavity dimension, are precisely tuned to one another.

See Cavity Tone Theory
    Coupling
    Formant
    Frequency
    Fundamental
    Laryngeal
      Suspension
    Register
    Resonance
    Standing Wave
    Sympathetic
      Vibration
    Vowel

Natural Method: a training program founded upon principles whose purpose is to innervate the vocal organs and help them to respond in accordance with their natural movement potential.

The essential property of a "natural" method of vocal training is that the procedures adopted succeed in stimulating spontaneous, uncalculated response patterns without reliance upon outer-imposed disciplines. Such a program is difficult to institute because 1) it requires a knowledge of those functional principles which prompt an involuntary muscular system to react in a predictable manner, and 2) the vocal organs are respiratory and digestive mechanisms, and singing is a secondary, overlaid function. In the latter instance, because the primary functions possess those elements necessary to the creation of musical tone, *i.e.,* an actuator (neurological impulses and breath), a vibrator (the vocal folds) and a resonator (the pharyngeal cavities), it is possible to adapt them to the vocal process.

When phonation is "natural," the muscular activities that collectively yield vocal tone must conform to the laws governing their primary function, *i.e.*, respiration and the ingestion and digestion of food and liquids. Since, however, these organic systems are almost always capable of operating efficiently when performing their primary functions, they are seldom disposed to do so during phonation. Consequently, singing at a high level of technical efficiency is in most cases an acquired skill resulting from successful vocal study, the focal point of which centers on the stimulation and coordination of a complex system of involuntary muscles. A natural method is one which succeeds in adapting these muscle systems to the vocal process without recourse to methods of direct control.

Unless the directives given during the course of instruction are based upon principles which recognize the vocal mechanism to be one that *reacts*, and that it is therefore essentially incapable of being *acted upon* effectively, the training given cannot be said to constitute a natural method. Judged on this basis, suggestions to inject "ping" or "nasal resonance," to "place" the voice "forward," or "up and over," or to "manage" the breathing apparatus, being examples of outer-imposed disciplines, cannot legitimately be included in a natural method of voice training.

If vocal study is to have any relevance, it is necessary to remove all outer-imposed disciplines and encourage natural functioning. An ingredient essential to this process is spontaneity, and spontaneous reactions are impossible unless the student is instructed to abandon the learned responses listed above, and helped to learn how to respond. None of the above directives fulfill this requirement. By their very nature they discourage spontaneity and inhibit the natural (correct) movement potential essential to the development of a free vocal technique.

The goal of all constructive pedagogy is to discover and develop to the fullest the natural resources of the vocal mechanism and to ensure that it operates in accordance with nature's laws. To achieve this goal, it will be found that there are as many "methods" as there are pupils. Unless, however, principles are employed which reject outer-imposed disciplines and effect an inner release, the method cannot truly be said to be natural.

See Bel Canto
   Control
   Holistic Pedagogy
   Kinesthesia
   Modern Methods
   Movement
   Register
   Standing Wave

Natural Movement: a spontaneous organic or muscular reflex that conforms to the natural laws governing the functioning of that organism or muscle.

Natural movement is an integral part of the vocal process. If phonation is to be "natural," therefore, the proper stimulation of those involuntary muscular activities that collectively yield vocal tone must be considered one of the primary goals of technical training. Free, natural movement depends upon the removal of all blockages caused by physical and psychological tensions, and cannot be achieved by the imposition of outer-imposed disciplines.

The principles incorporated into the training methods which developed the singing style known as Bel Canto appear to conform more closely to the natural movement potential of the vocal organs than do those introduced at the beginning of the twentieth century, to which they are diametrically opposed.

See Bel Canto
   Conditioned Reflex
   Control
   Instinct
   Modern Methods
   Kinesthesia
   Reflex
   Register

Natural Quality: that property of tone, apart from pitch and intensity, determined by its harmonic structure (the relationship established between a fundamental and its overtones, or partials), by temperament and anatomical structure, and revealed only when the mechanism is free of constricting tensions, *i.e.*, with all its constituent parts finely "tuned" and well coordinated both physically and conceptually.

One of the frequent misconceptions with regard to natural quality is that the tonal product assumed to be a true representation of an intrinsically natural quality is merely a reflection of the condition of the functioning mechanism. Consequently, by accepting the habitual as being natural, and a temporary condition as a permanent attribute or limitation of potential, the hoped-for revisions essential to progress cannot be made. Such revisions and progress can only be made when "natural" is taken to mean "correct."

To successfully dissociate qualitative concepts and physical responses from the habitual and familiar, it is necessary to institute changes through the stimulation of natural movement: change from qualitative properties which reflect the presence of vocal faults (*i.e.*, an abbreviated tonal range, tension and tremulous movements of the tongue and jaw, poor flexibility and defective resonance characteristics), and change from poorly coordinated reflexes to those free of muscular interference and compensatory tensions. Unless this can be done, those properties associated with a natural quality will remain latent and unrealized.

See **Bel Canto**
  Breathing
  Control
  Kinesthesia
  Modern Methods
  Movement
  Register
  Vowel

Natural Range: the total compass of pitches that a given vocal mechanism is potentially capable of producing.

The potential or natural range of most voices is approximately three octaves, of which at least two should be negotiated with comfort and ease. Although range is frequently used to categorize voices, it should not be a primary consideration until the technique has been stabilized. Too often, what appears to be a natural range is merely a reflection of the condition of the functioning mechanism. Thus, neither range, tessitura, nor the qualitative properties of the tone production are reliable indicators of a potentially natural range.

A constructive training program proceeds from the known to the unknown. What are known are the vocal faults (the type of constriction and the general character of register imbalances) and those principles which govern function. By applying functional principles and working toward the elimination of known vocal faults, the natural range, tessitura and voice quality will manifest themselves when the program has been successfully carried out. To accept range as "natural," especially when the vocal compass is limited, only ensures the continuance of those faults which represent the limiting factor in the technique.

To establish voice categories on the basis of what appears to be a natural range is a dangerous presumption. This is especially true when the natural range and tessitura of many voice types are hardly more than a semitone apart (for example, mezzo- and dramatic sopranos, lyric baritones and robust tenors), and consequently not easily classified. Vocal faults obscure natural range, tessitura and vocal quality, and must be eliminated before accurate assessment of a vocal potential is possible. Hasty judgments inevitably lead to serious errors in both repertoire and training procedures in general.

See **Register**
  Vocal
    Classification

Natural Register: See Register.

Natural Singing: phonation in which the vocal mechanism operates in conformity with nature's laws and within the legitimate movement potential of the vocal muscles.

Natural singing is always free, expansive, and efficient from the standpoint of energy economy, and expressive of inner thoughts and feelings. Natural singing, however, must not be confused with singing "naturally," or sounding "well trained." Too often the first merely suggests "singing with what one has" in the way of voice, which is merely a tone production based upon habit; the second is frequently the result of outer-imposed disciplines ("placement," breath "control," "nasal resonance," *etc.*), which by definition lack spontaneity and place the mechanism under the subjection of the will.

Natural singing may either be a gift or the result of a developmental process which corresponds to, and agrees with, natural order, *i.e.*, those forces, known and unknown, which operate upon and within us and to which we should all be responsive. Concepts, the use of energy, emotion, hearing and listening, together with the positioning of the vocal muscles, which occurs as the respiratory organs are made to adapt to the vocal process, must all be in equilibrium if the vocal technique is to be consonant with nature and if it is to function freely.

If singing is to be truly natural, spontaneous and free, all outer-imposed disciplines must be removed from the instruction, and principles applied which, by stimulating natural movement, awaken the singer's instinctive responses. In this way, an innate organic capability for self-regulation and self-correction will assert itself, with the result that the mind will be instructed as to the nature of functional needs, and learn to help develop and utilize the resources of the mechanism intelligently. On these terms, natural singing becomes a matter of fulfilling a latent functional potential that is primarily based upon an understanding of the logical movement potential of the organic systems involved.

See **Kinesthesia**
Natural Method
Register
Self-Regulation

Natural Voice: a technical status in which coordination among the various muscular systems involved in phonation is both precise and uncultivated; an attribute of a vocally untutored individual whose exceptional capabilities have been endowed by nature; also, a synonym for chest voice.

Those who have naturally well-formed voices obviously possess technical skills others less fortunate must strive for years to attain. However, they also face the danger of exploitation (*e.g.*, choral singing at an early age, oversinging, inappropriate repertory, excessive technical demands, *etc.*), and must learn to resist the temptation of being pushed too far and too fast. The human voice capable of singing naturally, whether by gift or by training, possesses a priceless personal and cultural asset which must be nurtured carefully. Time is not a factor in this process; fulfillment of potential and career longevity is. Since a singer's real vocal prime begins at the age of forty and extends (depending upon physical health and intelligent management of vocal resource) into the early sixties, the urge to overaccomplish is as pointless as it is self-defeating. A conservative approach is especially advisable for those who possess opulent voices capable of singing dramatic roles.

Growth into artistic maturity is a slow, gradual process, even for the exceptionally gifted. Those who desire to preserve the integrity of their natural abilities, or are obliged to develop them, are well advised to concentrate during the formative years on the study of a musical instrument (particularly the piano), languages, the rudiments of music history and theory, and be content to sing on their vocal interest rather than exhaust their capital. If abused, a natural voice will soon lose most of those characteristics commonly associated with naturalness.

Nature's Laws: those universal principles, known and unknown, that govern and determine the function of an organic or mechanical system.

When the vocal mechanism operates in accordance with nature's laws, all movements engaged in by the various muscles and muscle groups that collectively comprise the mechanism are precise, necessary, and within the domain of their natural movement potentials. As a result, the vocal organs display an economy of movement which represents a fulfillment of vocal potential, and singing becomes free, apparently relaxed, and responsive to the expressive desires of the singer.

If, on the other hand, the technique does not conform to nature's laws, the mechanism displays characteristic symptoms of misuse, notably shortness of breath, fatigue, throat constriction, an abbreviated tonal range, a lack of resonance and flexibility, tongue or jaw tremolos, *etc.* These deficiencies can only be eliminated by replacing faulty muscular movements that do not conform to nature's laws with those that do.

A technique developed in accordance with nature's laws assures career longevity, exploits the fullest resources of the mechanism, and places at the singer's disposal those essentials necessary to effective communication.

Neck Muscles: muscular systems that connect the head to the shoulders and chest.

The neck muscles that can potentially influence the vocal process are the splenius, the semipenalis and longissimus capiti, the salpingopharyngeal, the sternomastoid, and the sternocleidomastoid muscles, all of which, in various ways, join the occipital bone, the mastoid process, the temporal bone, and the upper four thoracic vertebrae to the trunk of the body.

Two of these muscle groups, the sternomastoids and the salpingopharyngeals, actively participate in phonation, since, when tensed, they serve as conduits for the radiation of phonatory vibrations to the inner ear. The former set arises from the sternum (breastbone) and clavicle (collarbone), meeting and attaching to the outer surface of the mastoid process; the latter interconnects the Eustachian tube (the air passage between the nasopharynx and ear), the wall of the pharynx, and the palatopharyngeal muscle.

Neck Tension: improper engagement during phonation of those muscles that connect the head to the shoulders and chest.

The flushed face and visible distortion of the neck when the technique is faulty provide visible evidence of the strain to which the vocal mechanism is being subjected. The adverse physical effect of such tension is that the natural equilibrium between the supra- and infrahyoid muscle systems (those that stabilize the larynx during phonation) is upset, with the immediate result that the base of the tongue is either drawn down and back or pulled forward. When this occurs,

See Bel Canto
Mechanistic
Methods
Modern Methods

See Bel Canto
Breathing
Control
Energy
Formant
Kinesthesia
Laryngeal
Suspension
Movement
Register
Resonance
Vowel

See Carrying Power
Larynx
Sensations of
Vibration
Standing Wave
Tongue

the throat constricts, the tongue stiffens and the jaw becomes locked, the chest rises excessively and becomes tense, and the vocal folds are unable to vibrate freely.

The various types of malfunction revealed by the symptoms outlined above also create a partial blockage of the Eustachian tubes. This interference disrupts communication between the nasopharynx and the tympanic membrane, with the result that the singer's hearing perception becomes untrustworthy. It is this blockage which accounts for the off-pitch singing contributed by those whose hearing acuity is otherwise quite exceptional. Furthermore, since the sternomastoid muscles serve as conduits for the radiation of vibratory impulses to the mastoid bone behind the ear, neck tension causes many who sing incorrectly to "hear" their voices as being large and resonant, when in fact they are "noisy," diffused, and lacking in carrying power.

Although conventional practices for the release of neck tension (*e.g.,* special breathing techniques, exercises for loosening the jaw, manipulating the tongue, shaking the head from side to side, *etc.*) may help momentarily, they are without permanent value and fail to address themselves to the root of the problem. Unless energy is redirected, and activity within the laryngeal pharynx is successfully re-channeled, neck tension and its deleterious effects will continue to act as an impediment to free vocalization.

Necktie Tenor: a male singer plagued by throat constriction. So-called "necktie tenors" sing with a high laryngeal position and frequently display those visual and tonal symptoms associated with choking.

Nerve: a fiber (or fibers) that originates in the brain or spinal cord, connects various parts of the nervous system with other organs, and conveys neurological impulses throughout the body.

Neural Connection: a neurological impulse that originates in the cerebral cortex, energizes the phonatory process, and establishes intercommunication between the larynx and the respiratory system, the ear, and the facial muscles.

Neurochronaxic Theory: a theory advanced by the French scientist Raoul Husson which states that the frequency of vocal vibration is determined by the chronaxy of the recurrent nerve (rather than by muscular tension or breath pressure).

Working with excised larynges, Husson discovered that the vocal folds could be stimulated electrically to vibrate and establish pitch. From this experiment he concluded that the length, thickness, and contour of vocal fold vibrations are determined by motor impulses generated from the central nervous system, and that the vocal folds are therefore virtually self-vibratile.

To understand the full implications of Husson's theory, it is first necessary to examine the relationship between breathing and singing. Animate life (movement) is totally dependent upon oxygen. During inspiration, air is taken into the lungs, where it is oxidized; during expiration, respiratory waste (carbon dioxide) is eliminated from the lungs. The purpose of breathing, therefore, is to replenish the oxygen used to create energy and to rid the system of organic waste.

If Husson's theory is correct, the combustible energy that is generated from oxidation and transferred to the vocal mechanism by neurological impulses is the force that vitalizes the muscular activities that yield vocal tone. If this is true, technical skill in singing must be considered the product of precisely formed concepts and efficient coordination (equilibrium) among those muscles that transform these concepts into vocal tone. Thus, the neurochronaxic theory stands directly opposed to the widely accepted belief that breath *pressure* constitutes the actuating force in the generation of vocal tone.

The flaw in Husson's theory would appear to be that the innervation of the vocal folds defies a general rule in neurophysiology; namely, that motor responses cannot be stimulated more than 50 to 100 impulses per second. According to Husson, however, impulses with a higher frequency can be accommodated by being diverted to second, third and fourth nerve fibers with parallel arrangements. This view conforms precisely to those neurological processes that occur in reflexive movement, and it may well be that the objections to Husson's theory are based upon a consideration of procedures which *act* upon the mechanism, as opposed to those which stimulate it into reflexive movement.

The pros and cons of Husson's theory have been widely debated by scientists, but the consensus is that it is flawed and leaves too many questions unanswered to be completely satisfactory.

See Breath Control
Breathing
Energy
Laryngeal
Suspension
Reflex
Natural Movement
Register

Neutral Resonance: resonance characteristics which, independent of changing patterns of pitch, intensity and vowel, cause vocal tone to sound uniform and evenly produced.

Neutral resonance is made possible by the ability of the laryngeal pharynx to tune consistently to frequencies in the range of 2800—3400 cycles per second, *i.e.*, those frequencies that infuse vocal tone with so-called "ring." These characteristics underscore the entire musical phrase and make possible legato singing and uniformity of tone quality.

See Coupling
Resonance
Twenty-Eight
Hundred

Neutral Vowel: a "muddy" vowel quality which lacks definition and results in a loss of tonal and textural clarity.

Neutral vowels are caused by imprecise concepts and/or faulty technique. The common pedagogic remedy to alleviate this condition is the overstressing of consonants, which further promotes textural distortion and skirts the central issue. If the vowel quality is ill defined, then it is vowel purity, not overarticulation of consonants, that merits attention when restoring or acquiring lost tonal and textural clarity.

Phoniatricians believe that there are fifty or more discernible vowels in the English language alone. Since each can be produced clearly and precisely, concepts that refer to a neutral vowel have to do with a faulty tone production rather than a genuine vowel type.

See Consonants
Laryngeal
Suspension
Register
Resonance
Schwa
Vowel

No-Register Theory: a viewpoint which contends that the vocal mechanism is a muscular complex that should always be treated as a functional entity, and that vocal registers, if they exist, are merely manifestations of malfunction.

Those who subscribe to the "no-register theory" either ignore the mechanical origin of vocal tone, believing that by training the end product of an organic activity, *i.e.*, voice itself, these activities can be improved, or believe that the diverse muscular activities involved in phonation must be strengthened and integrated without disturbing the unitary function of the mechanism. This logic is perhaps unassailable as an ultimate objective, since the diverse parts of any mechanical system that utilizes energy and generates power should for all practical purposes be viewed as a totality. Under optimum conditions, when each of the constituent parts works efficiently, the system as a whole will work efficiently. In such instances the system need not be disturbed.

The vocal mechanism is no exception to this rule. When it functions efficiently, all of its constituent parts (the muscles that adjust the length, thickness, and contour of the vocal folds; the suspensory muscles that position the larynx within the pharynx for tonal amplification; the respiratory muscles; the tongue; the palatal muscles, *etc.*) coordinate precisely to yield vocal tone that is vital, resonant, of beautiful quality, and free. When these muscle systems fail to do so, however, as is usually the case, the efficiency of the motor (organic) response is undermined. Under these circumstances the vocal technique, like any other motor system, will betray the specific nature of the malfunction by the sound it produces, as well as by showing other symptoms. In such instances the concept of training the mechanism without disturbing the unitary function of its integral parts must be abandoned, to be replaced by procedures aimed at reconditioning and "rebuilding" the mechanism.

A program designed to promote a functional reconditioning and restructuring of the vocal mechanism is impossible unless essential elements can be relatively isolated, developed independently, and reintegrated into the technique. The success of such a procedure is totally dependent upon a knowledge and understanding of the mechanical principles which govern registration. To proceed on the basis of a "no-register theory" when the vocal technique is faulty is to presuppose that the voice itself is at best one of limited potential, and that it is incapable of real technical growth.

The danger inherent in "fragmenting" any motor system (*i.e.*, in isolating its functional components) is that, unless the mechanical principles upon which it operates are clearly understood, its performance can be worsened rather than improved. Thus, it is evident that proponents of the "no-register theory" choose to solve the problem either by ignoring it, or by remaining unfamiliar with the mechanical principles by which the vocal mechanism, like all mechanisms, is governed.

Most teachers of singing have recognized that the voice tends to divide itself into two distinct parts (the chest register and the falsetto, which are separated by a "break") and that, in order for a singer to sing effectively, these disparate parts must be united. However, it is irresponsible to conclude that these divisions are the result of a faulty tone production, and not the natural manifestation of the mechanism's intrinsic functional elements, and to deal with register-related problems as though they did not (or should not) exist by "disguising" or smoothing over the area of the "break" at any cost. To say that the voice naturally divides itself into fairly obvious parts, and to attempt to understand the relationship between these parts is one thing; to say that this division is the product of a faulty vocal technique is quite another, especially when it is evident that most of the world's great singers fall into this category.

In the final analysis, the "no-register theory" is a reflection of aesthetic predispositions (*e.g.*, that the chest register is "unfeminine" or the falsetto "unmasculine") which limit the teacher's ability to understand the mechanical principles involved, and which, unfortunately, limit the student's technical progress. As long as a highly complex mechanism such as that which produces "voice" is approached and treated as a functional entity, the particular combination of virtues and faults that yields the qualities associated with that mechanism will remain uncorrected. If the registration is "mixed," for example, it will remain so, regardless of the pedagogic principles employed, until the chest register and falsetto have been isolated and independently developed.

By skillfully "fragmenting" the functional entity, drastic changes can be made in the coordinative process. Like the skilled mechanic who can disassemble a faulty motor, clean and perfect its constituent parts, and reassemble it to function more efficiently, the skillful voice teacher must be able to follow a similar—if less extreme—procedure. This kind of restructuring process is impossible, however, as long as the "no-register theory" is adopted and followed to its logical conclusion.

See Aesthetics
   Bel Canto
   Energy
   Holistic Pedagogy
   Modern Methods
   Register
   Vocal Study

Node: Latin *nodus*, "a knot or callus;" acoustically, zero displacement, or a state of rest in a vibrating body that occurs at the intersection or crossover point between two or more loops.

Nodule: a blister, corn or callus on the vocal fold that is caused by friction.

Nodules, or nodes, are without exception the product of a faulty vocal technique, misuse of the instrument, and training procedures either wrongly applied or based upon wrong principles. To repair the damage caused by nodes through rehabilitation requires great care and considerable patience, since to duplicate the procedures that caused them will assure their return.

A nodule condition can be corrected by surgical removal, or in mild cases by a long period of rest. Unless a new approach to vocal training is taken, however, there is every reason to believe that the condition will recur.

See Bel Canto
   Modern Methods
   Vocal Study

Noise: those sounds that consist of erratic pulsations and possess poorly defined or disagreeable characteristics of pitch, intensity, duration, or quality.

Singers who opt for loudness over quality introduce elements of noise into their singing and lose much of the potential beauty and carrying power of their voices.

See Quality
   Resonance
   Sonance
   Timbre
   Tone
   White Noise

Normal: the usual or customary condition of things.

The average singing and speaking voice is used incorrectly, and is therefore far from normal from the standpoint of physiological health and the most efficient use of the instrument. Within this context, "normal" is not "average," but exceptional.

The great singer is exceptional in that the way he uses his vocal organs conforms to nature's laws and the functional logic by which the movement potential of those organs is governed. He may actually be the possessor of an "average" instrument, but by using it extremely well he appears to be exceptional. From a functional point of view, therefore, the great singer should be considered "normal," since his vocal technique exemplifies the most efficient and economical way in which the vocal organs should be used.

Nose: the respiratory organ responsible for olfaction and the filtering of micro-organisms and dust from inspired air.

As filters, the mucous membranes of the nose assist those of the mouth, pharynx, and trachea in protecting the lungs from intrusion and infection.

There are no cavities in the nose, however, suitable for the resonation of vocal tone.

See Breathing
    Nasality
    Pharynx
    Resonance

Nose Breathing: See Breathing, Nose.

Nota Filate: Italian, "spun tone;" a disturbance of the air particles surrounding the vocal folds that is set in motion by the movement of the vocal folds, and which creates the impression that the tone is being "spun." Such an impression indicates that the voice is being effortlessly produced and that the vocal folds are being maintained in a state of self-vibratility. To seemingly "spin" the tone reflects the attainment of a high state of technical excellence.

See (To) Spin a Tone

Nota Mentale: Latin, "mental tone;" the mental preparation of the tonal form, an integral part of a concept dealing with the onset of phonation whereby the vocal folds and pharyngeal cavities are positioned mentally *before* sound is emitted.

The specific procedure to be followed when practicing the *nota mentale* is as follows: 1) stand with comfortable posture, erect but not stiff; 2) "think" the tonal form (the pitch, intensity and vowel pattern, the appropriate balance of registration expressed as texture) while the mouth is shaped as though one were singing; 3) breathe calmly and easily, and 4) phonate by *hearing* vibrations emerge out of the thought form. The result will be a gentle onset, a reduction of constrictor tensions, and a much freer and more natural tonal emission bereft of the unpleasant associations often connected with the concept of tonal "attack."

See Attack
    Mental Concept
    Onset

Note: a pitch, musical tone, expressive quality, or musical symbol used to indicate pitch and/or duration.

See Tone

Note Connection: See Legato.

Nuance: a subtlety of muscial expression.

Nuances are achieved by variations of volume, intensity, rhythm, timing (*rubato*), phrasing, and emotional or tonal coloration. All these factors are dependent upon a free vocal technique for effective execution.

O

Oblique Abdominus: a paired respiratory muscle on either side of the midriff which rises and falls during inspiration and expiration.

When the vocal mechanism is maintained in equilibrium during phonation, contractions of the oblique abdomini counterbalance each other and prevent the abdominal wall from collapsing.

See **Breathing**

Oblique Arytenoid Muscle: a paired muscle at the rear of the larynx whose function in the phonative process has not yet been determined.

Oblique Ridge: the ridge formed by the wings of the thyroid cartilage to which various muscles are attached.

(To) Occlude: to close with the cusps fitting together (*e.g.*, the vocal folds or teeth); to approximate.

The occlusion or approximation of the vocal folds during phonation permits vocal vibration and prevents breath loss.

Off-Pitch Singing: faulty intonation during phonation; the imprecise articulation of musical patterns that results from a lack of hearing acuity, ill-formed concepts, inappropriate repertoire and/or poorly coordinated vocal muscles.

Physically, off-pitch singing occurs when the vocal muscles are either incapable of or unaccustomed to "tuning" the mechanism precisely, a deficiency which must generally be overcome by the use of greater or lesser degrees of physical force or mental insistence. Under these circumstances, consistently accurate intonation is a difficult, if not impossible, achievement. Off-pitch singing, therefore, reflects a breakdown in the lines of communication between concept and response, and consequently is almost always the result of technical faults and conceptual misjudgments rather than a perceptual limitation.

In correcting problems related to off-pitch singing, attention should not be addressed to pitch *per se*, but to those factors which make precise intonation impossible, *i.e.*, a poorly developed and imbalanced registration, throat constriction, facial grimaces, bodily stiffness and its causes, and faulty concepts with regard to quality. It is also important to challenge and re-evaluate the training procedures which either led to, or failed to correct, the underlying faults which resulted in off-pitch singing.

See **Constriction**
   Covering,
      (To) Cover
   Eustachian Tube
   (To) Force
   Functional
      Listening
   Hearing
   Modern Methods
   Nasality
   Register
   Resonance
   Vowel

253

Old Italian School: the name given a vocal tradition which defined an era (circa 1650—1880), and produced a musical style and pedagogic techniques which laid the foundation for Western vocal culture.

Although the teachers who established traditional training techniques could hardly be said to have founded a "school" or to have adhered to a specific "method," they included Caccini, Tosi, Porpora, Corri, Mancini, Agricola, Tenducci, Praetorius, Manfredini, Francesco Lamperti, Garcia, and many others.

The Old Italian School devised training procedures founded upon extremely concrete and elemental functional principles, including registration, purity of intonation (synonymous with vowel purity), precise articulation, a perfect legato, agility, correct posture, supervised practice, and, to a lesser extent, breathing. The principles formulated during this era were generally abandoned around the turn of the twentieth century for so-called "modern" methods (*e.g.,* concern for resonance *per se,* "nasal resonance," "placement," "breath control," *etc.*), which constitute a radical departure from earlier theory and practice.

See Bel Canto
     Modern Methods

Omohyoid Muscle: a paired suspensory muscle that connects the shoulder blades (scapulae) to either wing of the hyoid bone and influences the movement of both the larynx and the tongue.

The contraction of the omohyoids is instrumental in lowering the larynx and, together with the contraction of the arytenoids and sternohyoids, in approximating the vocal folds.

See Laryngeal
        Suspension
     Larynx
     Suspensory
        Mechanism

On the Breath: a directive founded on a belief that the singer "has no throat" and that tone is carried on a breath stream.

The notion that vocal tone is "supported" by the breath or carried "on the breath" arises from a misconception that tone is "vocalized breath," or an air stream. Vocal tone, however, is merely an aural perception experienced because of a rhythmic disturbance of the air particles as vibratory impulses move through the vocal tract into the surrounding atmosphere. These impulses, or rapid condensations and rarefactions, occur at a frequency identical to that of the pitch being sounded. Consequently, it is physically and acoustically impossible for vocal tone to be literally carried on the breath or sustained by a breath stream.

Imagining that one is singing on a steady breath flow, however, can sometimes be used as a psychological ploy. A constricted technique, for example, produces a false "ring." Since constrictor tensions cannot be released volitionally, it is often useful to encourage their reflexive release by asking the student to "sigh" through a tone. When this sighing effect is combined with other procedures (such as improving the balance of registration or precisely tuning the pharyngeal cavities), a gradual breakdown of deeply rooted throat constriction can often be achieved. Thus singing "on the breath" can be used on occasion as a constructive functional catalyst. However, it is at best an expedient and must never be considered a functional principle, or pursued as an ultimate pedagogic objective.

See Cavity Tone Theory
     Energy
     Laryngeal
        Suspension
     Larynx
     Movement
     Register
     Resonance
     Yawn-Sigh

Onset: the attack, or the initiation of vocal tone.

There are two types of onset or attack: the "hard" and the "soft." The former which is that advocated by Manuel Garcia in his commonly misunderstood term *coup de glotte,* may be safely used for dramatic emphasis—provided that the suspensory muscles are capable of being maintained in equilibrium throughout the duration of phonation. If they are not, a "hard" attack will cause the mechanism to recoil and constrict.

A "soft" attack is that advocated by the Italian directive *con slancio* ("with abandon") and by the French *laissez vibrer* ("let it vibrate"). This type of onset results in a "launching" or self-induced initiation of vocal tone.

See **Attack**
Con Slancio
Coup de Glotte

Openers: a term used by Husler and Rodd-Marling to refer to the cricoarytenoid dorsalis muscle, or posticus, whose contraction enlarges the glottal space for inspiration and expiration.

The posticus may also assist in vocal functioning by holding against the pull of the cricothyroids during the production of the pure falsetto.

See **Falsetto**
**Falsetto or
Head Voice**
Middle Register
Register

Open Hum: a modified hum produced with the mouth slightly open and the nasopharynx and nasal passages closed (rather than open, as with the closed-mouth hum).

The so-called open hum can be used effectively in high-lying phrases where a literal closing of the lips would make phonation difficult. High-lying phrases rely upon the head voice, a mechanism produced when the cricothyroids, or stretchers of the vocal folds, come under tension. The cricothyroids, however, join to the inferior constrictors, whose primary function is peristaltic movement (swallowing) rather than phonation. With little or no mouth opening, it is extremely difficult to engage a sufficient amount of arytenoid (chest register) tension to counteract this tendency, with the result that the larynx rises, the pharyngeal cavities narrow, and the swallowing mechanism becomes rigidly set from the palatal region above to the larynx below. Consequently, humming (whether with open or closed lips) tends to invite the very constricting tensions that the singer should seek to avoid.

Humming in both forms has been used in an attempt to "bring the tone forward," or to induce those kinds of "frontal resonance" characteristic of French nasal phonemes (*e.g., en, an, on, etc.*). These attempts fail of their purpose, however, since all genuine resonance is produced within the laryngo- and oropharynges rather than in the mouth, nose, or facial mask.

Both the open- and closed-mouth hum should be looked upon as technical difficulties, inhibitory rather than helpful to the development of vocal skills and an open-throated vocal technique.

See **Hum**
Nasality
Register
Resonance
Vowel

Open Throat: an adjustment of the laryngo- and oropharynges that is free of constricting tensions (muscular interference).

A belief that open-throated singing is desirable is shared by almost all teachers of voice. What kind of attention should be directed toward effecting this openness, and exactly how open the ideal opening is, as well as the means to be employed in moving toward that objective, are details upon which opinion is sharply divided. The solution for many is to depend upon imagery ("feel as though a large grapefruit is passing down the throat," *etc.*). Others advocate a volitional widening of the pharyngeal walls to create space, the practice of the "yawn-sigh" or "sigh" tones, or the use of tongue depressors and manipulation of the external parts of the larynx with the fingers. In what is mistakenly thought to be more traditional practice, some teachers instruct their students to achieve an open throat by means of voice "placement," "bringing the tone forward," or "directing" tonal energy into the facial mask. Another group relies upon those principles associated with self-regulation, recognizing that the physical coordination within the laryngeal musculature can be influenced (and the throat freed of constricting tension) through the mechanics of registration, *i.e.*, correlative patterns between stimulus and response which induce the vocal muscles (because of spontaneous movement) to move in a natural way.

One of the continuing misconceptions with respect to open-throated phonation is that the pharyngeal cavities should be enlarged. This viewpoint is encouraged by the current popularity of "covering," a practice which requires a lowering of the larynx and a corresponding elevation of the soft palate, *i.e.*, pharyngeal enlargement. Prior to the twentieth century, however, covered singing was not an approved vocal practice; a more compact pharyngeal adjustment was favored. While the latter type of tone production is a skill more difficult and time consuming to acquire, it is superior to all others from the standpoint of energy economy, ideal open-throated resonance, aesthetics, and career longevity.

Volitional or mechanistic attempts to enlarge the pharyngeal isthmus in an effort to "open the throat" can be extremely dangerous, since it is impossible to make such an adjustment without engendering compensatory tensions unless the throat parts are already free. A truly open-throated resonance adjustment is extremely rare—even among professional singers.

Open Timbre: a vocalized sound whose bright, clear tonal characteristics result from a precise, narrow tuning or positioning of the pharyngeal resonators (particularly the oropharynx); a *voix claire* (French, "clear voice") tone as opposed to a *voix sombre*, or "dark voice" tone.

Prior to the turn of the twentieth century, timbres and vowels were considered the products of pharyngeal adjustment. This concept has subsequently been verified by scientific research, which has conclusively proved that each modification in the shape of the oropharynx (whether it be made larger, smaller, wider, or narrower) produces a corresponding change in the harmonic spectra by selecting and energizing specific frequencies that yield recognizable tonal characteristics (such as "dark," "bright," "closed," "open," "warm," "steely," "mellow," "edgy," and "nasal"). The famous nineteenth century pedagogue Manuel Garcia clearly recognized this phenomenon when he stated that "The result of this mutual dependence between pharynx, timbres and vowels is that a change in one produces a corresponding change in both the others."[85]

To facilitate the development of pharyngeal resonance, specific exercises were devised to ensure that both "bright" (*claire*) and "dark" (*sombre*) timbres, which were used primarily for expressive purposes, maintained a common resonance adjustment. Garcia further insisted that each vowel, on a single pitch with a constant level of intensity, was to be modified from "bright" to "dark" and *vice versa* as:

ah	oh	ah;
eh	eu (as in the French *peu*)	eh;

[85]Manuel Garcia, *Hints on Singing*, translated by Beata Garcia (New York: Edward Schuberth Co., Inc., 1894), p. 12.

ee	*ü* (as in the French *tu*)	*ee;*
oh	*oo*	*oh, etc.*

"Open timbres" or "bright" tonal qualities are produced by a narrowing of the oropharynx. However, this narrowing must not be achieved by more than a slight elevation of the larynx, since elevation of the larynx invariably engenders tongue constriction and disturbs the natural equilibrium that must always be encouraged among the various muscles that collectively comprise the vocal (respiratory) mechanism. Singing with a raised larynx is dangerous, as it tends to result in qualities that lack the genuine tonal "ring" characteristic of sounds resonated with a stable laryngeal adjustment.

A laryngeal adjustment that does not elevate the larynx, and at the same time assists in narrowing the oropharyngeal isthmus, is the forward tilting of the thyroid cartilage (*i.e.*, the proper contraction of the cricothyroid muscles). This movement also eliminates tracheal resonance, shortens the length of the vibrating tube, and, when accompanied by a slight lowering of the velum (as it usually is), makes the voice bright, vibrant and flexible.

In many ways, the exercises invented by Garcia, and timbral gradations in general, are vocal continuums similar to the *messa di voce*. The essential difference is that in the former the resonance adjustment (oropharyngeal dimension) varies with minimal change in the balance of registration, whereas in the latter, the balance of registration varies with minimal change in the resonance adjustment.

True, well-resonated "open timbres" are spontaneous tonal qualities that reflect the attainment of a high level of technical proficiency, a status which implies that the registration is well balanced and that the pharyngeal resonance adjustment is precise. Since modern pedagogic procedures no longer include those principles essential to the development and integration of the vocal registers and a successful tuning of the pharyngeal resonators (nor the practices with which those principles are associated), the options formerly available with respect to timbres are now difficult, if not impossible, to acquire through training.

Open Tone: a vocalized sound (especially one in the area of register transition) whose "shouty," aesthetically unpleasing tonal characteristics result from a predominance of chest register participation; a trait common to male singers, as women's voices tend to "spread" in the upper tonal range.

Open tones must not be confused with "open timbres" or "open-throated" tones, both of which are legitimate features of a correct tone production. Technically, both open timbres and open-throated tones are produced by a precisely tuned, though different, pharyngeal resonance adjustment and register balance. On the other hand, "open" tones (which should actually be referred to as "overly open" or "poorly resonated" tones) result from a crudely formed resonance adjustment and an excessively energized chest register operating too high in the tonal range. Consequently, because of the unavoidable tonal forcing that accompanies this type of muscular imbalance, neither the laryngo- nor the oropharynges are capable of adjusting properly, and the vowel (tone) quality becomes distorted.

See **Bel Canto**
 Coupling
 Covering,
  (To) Cover
 Modern Methods
 Nasality
 Register
 Resonance
 Twenty-Eight
  Hundred
 Vowel, Dark and
  Bright

Overly open tones are functionally disruptive. When habitual, the head voice is progressively weakened and unable to balance equitably with the chest voice. This sets up a condition in which it is virtually impossible to sing at lower levels of intensity without constricting the throat. In such instances, it is essential to do the following:

1. Isolate and develop the pure falsetto (using the *oo* vowel exclusively);
2. Exercise the coordinated falsetto on inverted scale patterns (using the *ah* vowel);
3. Restore lost vitality to the lower tones of the chest register, and
4. Use octave jumps to straddle the register "break" (singing *ah* on the tonic, and changing to *oo* on the upper octave, each pitch being sung vigorously).

When correctly utilized, these exercises will develop the weaker mechanism, restrain the excessive vigor of the chest register, and at the same time prepare the way for the desired emergence of the head voice.

The problems arising from a habitual use of "open" tones must ultimately be solved by rebalancing the registration, particularly in the "break" area. This involves the skillful manipulation of intensity, and during early stages of development, the use of so-called "closed" vowels. Intensity, however, is the most important element, for when the intensity is lowered, both the ratio of registration and the vowel quality will modify reflexively. Quiet, restrained phonation is impossible unless the registers coordinate, and coordination of the registers is the first step to be taken when learning to produce aesthetically pleasing sounds.

By attacking the problem of "open tones" at the source (by procedures which establish the head voice as the dominant mechanism, with the chest voice holding synergetically against its pull), the difficulties encountered in the "break" area (which often cause "overly open" tone qualities and other vocal faults) are capable of being solved to what should be the ultimate satisfaction of both the executant and the listener.

See Coupling
     Covering,
       (To) Cover
     Register
     Resonance
     Synergy
     Vowel Modification

Oral Cavity: that cavity commonly known as the mouth.

The mouth is bounded anteriorly by the teeth and lips, laterally by the interior walls of the cheeks, and posteriorly by the constricted aperture, or isthmus, formed by the pillars of the fauces, that leads into the oropharynx. Its roof is formed by the hard and soft palates, and its floor, by the tongue muscles and mucous membranes.

Although many theorists consider the mouth a primary resonator of vocal tone, it is not well suited for this purpose, since it consists almost entirely of fleshy tissue and must remain highly mobile during phonation to assist the articulatory processes. Attempts to use the mouth as a resonator invariably lead to tongue and jaw stiffness and throat constriction.

However, the oral cavity does affect vocal functioning to some degree, since an open mouth position tends to induce reflexively more chest register participation whereas a smaller mouth opening brings in more head voice. Likewise, an open mouth position is more suitable for the phonation of higher levels of intensity, and a smaller one for lower levels. The oral cavity is also influential in shaping the oropharynx for the resonation of different vowel phonemes, a smaller mouth open ing corresponding in size to the more compact adjustment required to resonate so-called "closed" vowels, a larger one corresponding to the more ample oropharyngeal adjustment necessary for the resonation of "open" vowels.

The essential ingredient in an efficient vocal technique, however, is not a prescribed or fixed mouth position, but the proper coordination of those interior muscular processes that adjust the vocal folds (registration) and stabilize the larynx. Mouth positions influence tone production, but do not control functional activities.

Oral Falsetto: See Falsetto, Oral.

Oral Resonance: tonal amplification mistakenly attributed to adjustments made in the shape of the oral cavity or mouth.

See **Cavity Tone Theory**
   Laryngeal
      Suspension
   Mouthy Tone
   Quality
   Register
   Resonance

The small amount of resonance generated by the oral cavity, and its general unsuitability for this purpose, would seem to disqualify the mouth as a potential resonator of vocal tone. An effective resonator must have firm reflecting surfaces and must be capable of remaining relatively fixed during phonation, since a constant vowel quality is dependent upon an equally constant cavity adjustment. The mouth meets neither of these criteria, since its lateral walls (the cheeks) and floor are formed by soft, fleshy tissue, and it must remain highly flexible and mobile during phonation to assist the articulatory processes. Furthermore, the formant regions that must be energized for the precise articulation of vowel phonemes are reinforced by energy concentrations within the laryngeal pharynx and the oropharynx—not within the mouth.

The laryngo- and oropharynges are the source of all genuine tonal resonance. They are ideally suited for this purpose, since they are bounded by firm reflecting surfaces capable of reinforcing the higher partials (2800—3400 cycles per second) that infuse vocal tone with genuine tonal "ring;" they can be positioned to maintain relatively fixed adjustments without disturbing the articulatory processes, and they house or are adjacent to the vibrating vocal folds.

See **Cavity Tone Theory**
   Coupling
   Helmholtz
   Resonance
   Twenty-Eight
      Hundred

Organ of Corti: a gelatinous mass encased within the cochlea (the snail-shaped part of the inner ear that is imbedded within the temporal bone) which converts mechanical impulses (*e.g.*, frequencies, intensities, and timbres) into electrical impulses, and transmits the latter to the auditory nerve and ultimately to the auditory centers of the brain.

The organ of Corti is essential to hearing, or the perception of sound. Discovered by Alfonso Corti in 1851, it contains a mass of cells upon which tiny hairs are arranged in four orderly rows.

See **Hearing**

Oropharynx: the pharyngeal cavity directly behind the oral cavity or mouth, directly above the laryngeal pharynx, and directly below the nasopharynx.

The oropharynx is bounded anteriorly by the pillars of the fauces, uvula, and base of the tongue, and laterally and posteriorly by the interior walls of the pharynx. Its lower boundary terminates with the tip of the epiglottis.

The oropharynx is essential to both vowel formation and resonance. It can be tensed to provide a firm resonating surface, and it can either be tuned independently or coupled to the tuning of the laryngeal pharynx. Not only is the oropharynx responsible for the proper articulation of vowel phonemes, but, along with the phenomena of radiation and bone conduction, it is also responsible for sensations of vibration experienced by many singers in the area of the facial mask. Awareness of these sensations has led to the doctrines upon which modern methods such as "placement" and "nasal resonance" have been founded.

(To) Oscillate: to move or travel back and forth between two points; to move backward and forward like a pendulum; to vibrate.

Fluctuating tonal movements (*e.g.,* the vibrato) and vocal vibration itself are examples of oscillating movements.

(To) Overblow: to sound the harmonic or partial of a fundamental tone by using excessive breath pressure.

Overblowing is loosely used to describe a tone production characterized by the use of excessive force and a consequent dissipation of energy. It results from an absence of equilibrium (*i.e.,* a lack of precise coordination) among the vocal muscles.

Overlaid Function: an adaptive use of an organic or muscular system for purposes other than its primary function.

Singing is an overlaid function, since the primary purpose of the vocal organs is to assist in respiration and ingestion. Because these organs possess all of the attributes necessary for sound-making (*i.e.,* an actuator, a vibrator and a resonator), they are readily adaptable for use as a musical instrument.

In all but the rarest instances, the voice must be trained in order to achieve technical proficiency, since singing is not "natural" in the sense that respiration and ingestion are natural. The procedures adopted during training, therefore, must employ principles which succeed in bringing the coordinative process yielding sound into harmony with those laws governing the natural movement potential of the respiratory musculature.

Overtone: a harmonic partial, or pitch whose frequency is an integral multiple of a fundamental tone.

The arrangement, points of concentration, and general distribution of overtones within the harmonic spectrum of a vocalized sound determine its quality characteristics. These variables are, in turn, dependent upon the skill with which the resonating cavities (the laryngo- and oropharynges) are "tuned," as well as the ratio of tension shared between the muscle systems which enable the vocal folds to become vibratile. The efficiency with which these processes respond is reflected in the qualitative properties of the ultimate tonal product and its overtone structure.

Overtone Theory: See Harmonic Theory.

Overtraining: a condition of staleness brought about because a musical composition, phrase, or vocal exercise has been repeated to the point that all inspiration and meaning have been lost.

Overtraining occurs most frequently because the vocal exercises selected lack variety. Monotonous repetition of scale patterns, regardless of their intrinsic value, is detrimental to progress. The vocal mechanism (like all muscle systems in a complex organism) is capable of performing a variety of tasks, and must learn to do so. Consequently, these systems must be trained to become flexible and not "set" rigidly by scales and exercises practiced by rote. To acquire this flexibility, training programs must be based upon procedures which encourage natural, spontaneous movement and avoid those associated with overtraining.

The psychological factors which lead to overtraining result from an insecurity which demands constant reinforcement and feedback, excessive ambition, and/or the desire to achieve too much too soon. These are serious impediments, and it is important to realize that time is an important factor in any learning experience. In singing, particularly, there is no short road to success. The prudent course is to make haste slowly.

See Anxiety
    Exercise
    Practice
    Natural Movement
    Rhythm

Oxidation: the combustive chemical process by which inspired oxygen is transformed into energy.

The energy derived from oxidation during respiration vitalizes all body substances and activities.

See Energy
    Emotion

Oxygen: the colorless, tasteless gas that enters the blood stream by means of the respiratory process and serves as the combustible element which generates energy.

See Energy

P

Palatal Register: a term sometimes used to refer to those mid-range vocalized sounds whose tonal characteristics are believed to be influenced by contractions of the palatal muscles during phonation.

Although the contraction of the palatal muscles elevates the posterior portion of the larynx and consequently influences registration, the palatal muscles do not act upon the vocal folds directly, and therefore they cannot be said to contribute to the formation of a separate register.

Theories formulated in an attempt to explain the special textural qualities peculiar to the mid-tonal range of the voice are without foundation unless there is operative a mechanical principle or muscular system which directly affects the manner in which the vocal folds are drawn into tension. The so-called "palatal register" does not meet these criteria.

Palate: the upper wall or "roof" of the mouth, which separates the oral cavity from the nasal pharynx.

The palate is generally considered to be composed of two distinct surfaces: 1) the so-called "hard" palate, which terminates anteriorly with the gums and posteriorly with the so-called "soft" palate, and 2) the soft palate or velum, which terminates posteriorly with the fleshy lobe known as the "uvula."

Although many believe that it is the elevation of the uvula that closes off the nasopharynx, this closure is in fact the product of the combined contractions of the superior constrictor and the levator and tensor palati muscles.

Palatoglossus Muscles: those paired muscles attached to either side of the soft palate and tongue which serve to elevate the tongue and narrow the pillars of the fauces.

Palatopharyngeal Muscles: the paired muscles that form the posterior portion of the pillars of the fauces, extend downward from the soft palate to merge with the stylopharyngeal muscles, radiate into the inner lining of the pharynx, and ultimately attach to the larynx itself.

The contraction of the palatopharyngeal muscles performs three important functions during phonation: 1) it raises the larynx; 2) it lowers the soft palate or velum, and 3) it narrows the pillars of the fauces. Thus, the palatopharyngeal muscles, along with the stylopharyngeal and palatoglossus muscles, are instrumental in

See Covering,
    (To) Cover
Larynx
Nasality
Open Tones
Palate
Pharyngeal Voice
Register
Suspensory
    Mechanism

See Nasality
Passavant's Ridge
    (Cushion)

See Larynx

See Coupling
Laryngeal
    Suspension
Larynx
Resonance

263

positioning the larynx and in shaping (tuning) the oropharynx for the articulation of various vowel phonemes.

Pancostal Breathing: costal or rib breathing.

Parallel Relationship: a corollary connection between two things or activities; the connection that exists between a specific stimulus and its natural response.

Many parallel relationships can be observed in singing: for example, that between pitch-intensity patterns and registration; that between registers and corresponding tonal textures; that between registration and vowel qualities (and *vice versa*); that between throat constriction and tremulous tonal movements; that between "pushing" and tonal unsteadiness (*e.g.,* the wobble); that between interior muscular tenseness and visible signs of strain; that between inner psychological tenseness and vocal mannerisms; that between open mouth positions and high levels of intensity, and so forth.

Of the parallels noted above, those known to exist between pitch-intensity patterns and registration (*e.g.,* lower levels of intensity to coordinate the registers, higher levels when isolating the chest register and the falsetto, and more complex relationships as development becomes increasingly sophisticated), and between vowel phonemes and registration (*oo* and *ee* reflexively induce more head register participation than do *oh* and *ah, etc.*) are levels of understanding crucial to the successful development of vocal skills. Once these parallels have been observed and studied, the mechanical principles governing function will become self-evident, and vocal training will become what it can and should be: an adventure in learning.

Paranasal Sinus: one of the cavities in the bones of the skull near the nose that communicates with the nasopharynx and contains air.

Although the paranasal sinus is frequently considered the source of so-called "nasal" or "mask" resonance, it (like all other sinus cavities—the ethmoid, frontal, maxillary, nasopharyngeal, and sphenoid) is not well suited for this purpose, being highly damped with mucus and nonadjustable. While it is frequently contended that the sensations of vibration often experienced in the facial mask "prove" that these cavities perform as resonators, these sensations are present because vibratory impulses have radiated from the tonal source (*i.e.,* the vibrating vocal folds) and resonate within the pharyngeal cavities through the medium of bone conduction.

Partial: literally, a "part" of a tone; one of the higher frequencies reinforced by the sounding of a fundamental tone to comprise a complex musical tone; an overtone.

Partials whose frequencies are integral multiples of the fundamental frequency are referred to as "harmonic" partials; those whose frequencies are not are called "inharmonic." Harmonic partials are generally recognized as musical tones; inharmonic partials are perceived as noise. The qualitative characteristics of complex sounds are primarily determined by the number, frequency and relative intensity of the partials that comprise their harmonic spectra.

Most musical tones contain both harmonic and inharmonic partials, and possess some element of noise. While the presence of these partials modifies quality characteristics, they may yet be perceived as aesthetically pleasing. Individual voices, as a matter of fact, are recognized more readily because of their faults and the inharmonic partials present (*i.e.*, nasality, "mouthiness," unsteady voice movement, shrillness, *etc.*) than they are because of those qualitative properties which result when the partials are harmonic, or integral multiples of the fundamental. The manner in which the harmonic and inharmonic partials are arranged and reinforced within the harmonic spectra to form the ultimate tonal product is also influenced by the anatomical and physiological structure of the singer, and by temperament.

See **Complex Tone**
　　Fundamental
　　Laryngeal
　　　Suspension
　　Quality
　　Register
　　Resonance
　　Timbre

Passaggio: Italian, "passageway;" an early frame of reference used to indicate that portion of the tonal range, or "break" (E—F above middle C), where it is necessary to cross from the chest voice to the head voice smoothly and evenly.

Although developmental procedures must be designed to lay the foundation for an ultimate smoothness in negotiating the *passaggio*, such attempts should never be incorporated into early training procedures. The smooth and easy negotiation of the *passaggio* without loss of range, resonance, or flexibility is the hallmark of technical mastery.

See **Bel Canto**
　　Break
　　Falsetto
　　Falsetto or
　　　Head Voice
　　Messa di Voce
　　Middle Register
　　Register

Passavant's Ridge (Cushion): literally, the knuckle put forth by the first cervical vertebra to facilitate mobility of the head; a pharyngeal barrier formed by the superior constrictor and levator palati muscles whose contraction raises the velum, or soft palate, to close off the nasopharynx.

See **Nasality**

Pear-Shaped Tone: a term sometimes used to describe a well-formed vocalized sound.

In all probability, "pear-shaped" alludes to a pharyngeal adjustment whose conformation is similar to the tapered end of a pear, while the larger oral cavity resembles the fuller end. The tone quality that emerges from this type of resonance adjustment is a pear-shaped tone.

Imagery of this description represents a purely subjective judgment and can mean different things to different people. It embraces no functional principle, and at best merely describes an ultimate qualitative objective without specifying how that objective is to be achieved. The concept of a pear-shaped tone, like most imagery, is of questionable pedagogic value and contributes little or nothing to the voice-building process.

See **Bel Canto**
　　Imagery
　　Modern Methods
　　Register
　　Resonance
　　Vowel

Pelvic Diaphragm: the funnel-shaped pelvic floor formed by the paired levator ani muscles.

During inhalation, the pelvic diaphragm helps support the abdominal viscera, which are compressed by the contraction and lowering of the diaphragm proper, *i.e.*, the muscular partition that separates the thoracic and abdominal cavities.

Pelvic Girdle: the bony basin that surrounds the pelvis and serves as the point of attachment for numerous thoracic, abdominal, spinal, and leg muscles.

Pelvis: the basin-shaped cavity formed by the pelvic girdle and lower spine that separates the abdomen from the genitalia.

Since numerous respiratory muscles are attached to the pelvic girdle and lower spine, the pelvic floor or diaphragm is, in a sense, the lowest extreme of the vocal mechanism.

Pendular: resembling the movement of a pendulum.

Pendulous: poised without visible support; suspended so as to swing freely; vascillating.

Pendulum: a regularly oscillating body whose movement potential is determined by momentum and the force of gravity.

Perception: awareness of external or internal environmental stimuli through the medium of physical sensations (hearing, sight, smell, taste, or touch).

Perception is strongly influenced by psychological factors (*e.g.,* anxiety, emotional attachment, suppressed anger), and the degree to which perception reflects the reality of events is largely determined by the degree to which these factors have encouraged or countered sensory blockages.

See Anxiety
     Emotion
     Kinesthesia
     Movement

In most instances, perception is as much *believing* that something has happened, or is happening, as it is responding to actual environmental stimuli. Consequently, perception generally represents an evaluation of stimuli and sensations. How one perceives, reacts to, and identifies with sensations is the composite result of the quality of stimulation, and one's experience, reason, cognition, cultivated tastes, and judgment.

Period of Vibration: the amount of time which elapses between the beginning and end of a tonal oscillation; a cycle.

Periodicity: the quality or state of being regularly recurrent.

Musical tone is periodic, and it travels as regularly recurrent waves or cycles. Pitch or frequency, therefore, is usually expressed as "cycles per second," or cps.

Peristaltic Movement: the progression of materials through the alimentary canal during swallowing, ingestion, digestion, and excretion, by successive involuntary contractions of the muscles that form the walls of the canal.

Obviously, peristaltic movement is more "natural" than, and diametrically opposed to, the pharyngeal expansion that must be established for open-throated singing. Consequently, the natural tendency of the pharyngeal musculature to constrict is one of the greatest obstacles to be overcome during vocal training.

Personality: Latin *persona,* "mask;" the complex of behavioral, intellectual and emotional characteristics that distinguishes one human being from another.

The possessor of a pleasing, magnetic or charismatic personality holds a certain advantage in the performing arts over those who are not so fortunate, but without musical and poetic insight, a lively intelligence, creative imagination and genuine human warmth (which unfortunately do not necessarily go hand in hand with an ingratiating personality, a great voice, or a correct vocal technique), this advantage is not sufficient to excite and hold the interest of an audience. At best, a person who possesses an attractive personality but who lacks those requisites can become a good colleague and a competent performer, but he can never become an artist.

Personality factors complicate the learning process at all levels, and reflect psychological and psychosomatic tendencies which can either be favorable or unfavorable to technical training, one's ability to communicate, and vocal health. Studies have shown, for example, that nodules and polyps develop in aggressive personalities, whereas their occurrence is rare among those who are more passive and well-mannered, even when they have been subjected to the same training regimen. Not infrequently it has also been found that many personalities are so structured that they prefer to fantasize a great career, only to collapse in the face of reality when the possibility presents itself. A surprising number become alarmed at the emotional freedom and lack of inhibition that accompanies the restoration of lost motility as they progress (an unavoidable corollary to a relaxation of inner tension), and when the "mask" has been removed through expansive movement, they reject this growth into emotional maturity to cling to the false security upon which they have relied for so long a time.

An inner desire to express thoughts and feelings spontaneously and freely is a personality trait which must be accepted and willingly shared by those who strive to become artists. Personal charm, musical and poetic insight, creative imagination and personal warmth are natural endowments, however, which, while they can be fostered and developed through training, cannot be acquired. For those who possess exceptional gifts, a charismatic personality, and a willingness to work, singing becomes a spiritually elevating experience which enriches not only the artist but all mankind.

See Emotion

Pharyngeal: related to, located in, or produced in the pharynx.

Pharyngeal Cavity: the throat.

See Pharynx

Pharyngeal Falsetto: See Falsetto, Pharyngeal.

See Mucous Membrane
Mucus

Pharyngeal Membrane: a mucus-secreting tissue which lines the entire pharyngeal tract.

Pharynx
Phlegm

Pharyngeal Tract: the throat.

See Pharynx

Pharyngeal Voice: a term sometimes used to refer to the coordinated falsetto or head voice.

The term "pharyngeal voice" was coined by the twentieth century Englishman E. Herbert-Caesari to describe the tonal quality that results when the falsetto is in the process of being transformed into the head voice. Herbert-Caesari accurately believed the so-called "pharyngeal voice" to be the combined product of a special type of vocal fold formation and a "tuned" oropharyngeal resonance adjustment. With the assistance of a laryngoscope, he determined that in producing this quality the vocal folds are adjusted to present a slightly shorter and somewhat thinner vibrating surface than for the production of so-called "chest" tones, and he correctly deduced that this adjustment eliminates the "drag" of the chest register and makes it possible for the singer to sustain a higher tessitura. He also correctly set the lower extension of this adjustment for all voice types, male and female alike, at E above middle C, the point of register transition.

Herbert-Caesari described the pharyngeal voice as "bright," "bouyant," "highly flexible," and capable of articulating absolutely pure vowels, especially the so-called "bright Italian *ah*," without modification or distortion. In advocating the technique which led to this type of tone production, Herbert-Caesari discounted the need for breath "support," believing that the pharyngeal voice "by a willed nervous-mental energy would translate itself into muscular action."[86]

[86]E. Herbert-Caesari, *The Voice of the Mind* (London: Robert Hale, 1951), p. 346

The concept of the pharyngeal voice as formulated by Herbert-Caesari would seem to be identical with the "feigned voice" described by Isaac Nathan in his *Musurgia Vocalis,* and is quite clearly a device for combining the two register mechanisms, the chest register and the falsetto. Pedagogically, the development of the coordinated falsetto or "pharyngeal voice" is most desirable, since the combined activity of the two register mechanisms significantly reduces the amount of energy needed to produce upper tones, greatly enhances vocal flexibility, and ultimately leads to upper tones of rare freedom and beauty. Developmental procedures, however, must be restricted to those students whose techniques are well advanced, since premature attempts to coordinate the two basic register mechanisms can be limiting and often harmful.

The term "pharyngeal voice" has also been used to refer to "pharyngeally resonated" tones, or those vocalized sounds properly resonated within the laryngo- and oropharynges. Manuel Garcia (1805—1906) introduced this concept to vocal pedagogy with respect to resonance when he observed that the pharynx is "the real mouth of the singer" and the source of all genuine resonance.

Pharynx: that portion of the respiratory tract and alimentary canal situated immediately behind the mouth and the esophagus; the throat.

The pharynx is comprised of three distinct but interconnecting chambers or cavities: 1) the laryngeal pharynx (or laryngopharynx), that portion of the pharynx which houses the vocal folds, the so-called "false vocal cords," and the ventricles of Morgagni; 2) the oropharynx, which extends from the hyoid bone to the terminating point of the soft palate and opens into the mouth, and 3) the nasopharynx, which lies directly behind the nose and above the level of the soft palate.

Of the three pharyngeal cavities, the laryngo- and oropharynges (since they are immediately adjacent to the vibrating vocal folds) serve as the primary resonators of vocal tone. They are perfectly designed for this purpose. Their walls can be either firmed or softened, and they can be adjusted or "tuned" in a variety of ways to select and energize those frequencies responsible for defining the vowel. An added benefit provided by a proper tuning of the pharyngeal resonators is that this frees the articulators, so that the tone does not interfere with the articulation, nor the articulation with the tone.

The natural or primary function of the pharynx is to assist in the processes of ingestion and respiration; phonation is an adaptive or overlaid function. Consequently, peristaltic movement (swallowing) and an inhibition of respiration brought on because of psychological tension are constrictive tendencies which must be reversed if an effective resonance adjustment is to be established for singing. Pharyngeal adjustments free of constricting tensions are the functional equivalent of what has come to be recognized as "open-throated" singing.

Phase: periodic changes in the harmonic motion of a sinusoidal wave, or the fraction of a period that has elapsed since a moving body has passed through a median point to form a node. Phase is only considered a component of a sound wave when two or more sine waves are present.

When the alternate expansions and contractions of air particles set in motion by a vibrator oscillate at a uniform rate, the musical tone produced is said to be "in phase." Phase differences, however, have no discernible effect on the ear, since quality depends upon the relative energies of the various harmonics present, and not on their phase differences.

Phlegm: Latin *phlegma,* "flame" or "inflammation;" viscid mucus secreted in abnormal quantities by the mucous membranes of the respiratory tract.

Phlegm sometimes accumulates on the vocal folds during phonation. These secretions result either from pathological conditions (*e.g.,* allergic reactions to certain substances) or from irritation of the vocal folds brought on by muscular interference. In either event, if the condition is not chronic, there is little reason for concern, since an occasional accumulation of mucus or phlegm is not extraordinary.

Friction is often the cause of excessive phlegm. The vocal mechanism is made up of a complex set of mutually antagonistic muscle groups, and when a more efficient pattern of response has been stimulated in opposition to habitual and less efficient patterns, the pharyngeal membranes will reflexively release secretions of mucus, their natural lubricating agent. This is both healthy and natural, since under normal circumstances the throat must be maintained in a comfortably moist condition. The annoying problem of excessive mucus should disappear once the constricting tensions no longer interfere or conflict with the throat openers.

Should excessive phlegm remain a continuing problem, one should seek competent medical advice to determine if the condition is pathological. If it is not, the difficulty lies with a faulty vocal technique, and the training procedures to which the mechanism has been subjected should be challenged and re-evaluated.

See **Mucous Membrane**
Mucus

Phon: Greek *phōnē,* "voice" or "sound;" an acoustic unit of measurement often used to measure the difference between loudness and intensity.

The phon is established on a scale beginning at zero, for the faintest audible sound a listener can perceive, and extending in logarithmic measure over thirteen decibel powers to the threshold of pain, or one hundred and thirty phons. The number of phons of a given sound is equal to the decibels of a standard tone of one thousand cps.

Phonasthenia: general weakness of the vocal organs brought on by misuse or abuse.

Phonasthenia, which impairs singing but not speech, is a strong possible indication that no direct functional parallel exists between speaking and singing.

Phonation: Greek *phōnē*, "voice" or "sound;" the articulation of vocalized sound.

Strictly speaking, all vocalized sounds (including sighs, whimpers and grunts) are products of phonation. However, the term is customarily used to refer more specifically to vocal activities that result in speech or singing.

Phoneme: Greek *phōnēma*, "speech sound" or "utterance;" a speech sound; a member of the smallest units of sound that collectively comprise a linguistic or phonetic system.

There are two types of phonemes: 1) consonants, or phonemes produced by or with the assistance of the articulatory processes, and 2) vowels or sonants, phonemes produced without the assistance of the articulatory processes. The distinguishing, qualitative characteristics of each phoneme (with the exception of the so-called "unvoiced" consonants, whose articulation does not involve vocal vibration) are products of the combined effects of the processes of registration, or the manner in which the vocal folds are adjusted as they become vibratile, and resonance, or the manner in which the pharyngeal cavities are adjusted for tonal amplification.

See **Consonants**
    Vowel

The term "phoneme" is occasionally used to indicate the physical position assumed by the pharyngeal cavities for the articulation of a specific vowel.

Phonemic: of, relating to, or having the characteristics of a phoneme.

Phonemics: a branch of linguistic analysis involving the study of phonemes.

Phonetic: of or relating to spoken language, speech sounds (phonemes), or the science of phonetics.

See **International Phonetic Alphabet**

Phonetic Alphabet: a set of symbols used for phonetic transcription.

See **Sing As You Speak**
    Vowel Migration

Phonetic Pedagogy: the use of existing speech patterns in an attempt to achieve skill in singing.

Phonetic Transcription: the process of representing or recording the sounds and other phenomena of speech or sung texts by written symbols.

Phonetics: the study and systematic classification of speech sounds (phonemes).

Phonic: of, relating to, or producing sound; of or relating to the sounds of speech or phonics.

Phonics: the science of speech; a method of teaching beginners to read and/or pronounce words or texts of songs by learning the phonetic values of letters of the alphabet and their various combinations.

Phonogram: a written symbol used to represent a phoneme, syllable, or word; a succession of such symbols that occurs with the same phonetic value in several words of a language (*e.g., ight* or *bright, fight, light, might, tight,* etc.).

Phonology: the science of speech sounds (phonemes) concerned with the history and theory of sound changes in a language or related languages; the phonetics and phonemics of a language.

Phrenic Nerve: the neurological fiber that conveys impulses between the brain and the diaphragm.

See Breathing
Diaphragm

Pianissimo Singing: extremely soft singing.

Functionally, there are two types of *pianissimo* singing: 1) "legitimate," in which both basic register mechanisms, the falsetto and chest register, coordinate efficiently in an open-throated resonance adjustment, and 2) "detached" or "disembodied," in which the head voice predominates, but without sufficient connection with the chest register to keep the throat open.

Although "detached" *pianissimo* singing can occasionally be used for special vocal effects (especially by "light" sopranos and lyric tenors), its tonal characteristics, in general, are excessively "sweet" and uninteresting, and its production invariably involves some degree of throat constriction. "Legitimate" *pianissimo* singing, on the other hand, along with the correctly produced *messa di voce*, represents a high level of technical proficiency and is very rare, since if the throat is not to constrict, both the registration and the resonance adjustment must be precise.

See Laryngeal
Suspension
Messa di Voce
Open Throat
Register

Piercing Tone: a vocalized sound whose shrill, unpleasant tonal characteristics are products of throat constriction and a particular type of "mixed" registration.

The "mixed" registration resulting in piercing tone qualities is one in which the chest register has been made to intrude too high into the tonal range, with the result that the tone quality is strong, but "thin" and "edgy." Because of the abnormal register balance, the upper partials are overenergized, the pharyngeal resonators become excessively narrow and too hard-surfaced, the base of the tongue stiffens, and the voice sounds "driven." Since under these conditions there is some degree of laryngeal connection and the head voice is strongly active, the singer is nevertheless able to "lean on" his voice and expend considerable energy without physical fatigue or breath loss. One of the more regrettable tendencies of the piercing voice is to sharpen the pitch.

The piercing voice, on first hearing, often seems considerably more advanced technically than it actually is, especially since its possessor is often able to undertake advanced repertoire.

See Constriction
Registration,
"Mixed"

Pillars of the Fauces: muscular partitions, formed by the palatoglossus and palatopharyngeal muscles, that extend the velum into the sides of the throat and serve as a line of demarcation between the oral cavity, or mouth, and the oropharynx.

See Larynx

Pinched Tone: a vocalized sound whose "thin," harmonically impoverished tonal characteristics are products of severe throat constriction.

See Constriction
Open Throat

Ping: a "focused," "biting," slightly metallic tonal characteristic often confused with genuine "ring."

A natural, ringing tone quality cannot be accurately described as having "ping," and to "produce" this quality by overtly acting upon the vocal mechanism is a serious misjudgment. To conceptually impose a tone quality not present at the moment of tonal inception merely succeeds in producing that which, by definition, is "made" and therefore artificial. By failing to confront the real issue—namely, the reason why the tone lacks "ring"—procedures cannot be set in motion that, when correctly applied, are the only possible means of correcting such problems.

The suggestion to put "more ping" into the tone is a directive which moves away from naturalness and spontaneity. As soon as the vocal folds become vibratile and the pharyngeal cavities take form, all effective control related to vowel definition and tone quality has already been lost, and any subsequent effort to influence tone quality is a question of too little too late. Outer-imposed disciplines, whether physical or conceptual, can never lead to vocal freedom.

Pitch: that property of musical tone determined by the frequency of the sound waves producing it; the position of a sound in a musical scale.

Vocal tone is the product of 1) concepts developed out of perceptions related to aural phenomena, 2) neurological stimulation of the vocal muscles in response to these conceptualizations, and 3) a movement capability of the muscle systems involved (in particular, those responsible for the phenomenon of registration and adjusting the pharyngeal cavities) to respond to these neurological impulses. Consequently, vocal pitch, a property of all vocal tone, is the product of these processes, and includes the following physical activities:

1. The contraction of the thyroarytenoid, aryvocalis, and thyrovocalis muscles (all of which are embedded within the vocal folds), which initiate vocal vibration;
2. The creation of air pressure variations by the emission of tiny puffs of air through the vibrating vocal folds;
3. Adjustments made in the physical dimensions of the vocal folds (registration) that determine the shapes of the resulting wave forms;
4. Adjustments made in the physical dimensions of the laryngeal, oral, and nasal pharynges and the oral cavity (mouth) for tonal amplification or resonance, and
5. The regulation of breath pressure.

In a correct tone production, the functional activities listed above coexist in a state of balanced tension or equilibrium. Under these circumstances the pitch will always be an exact duplication of the conceptualized version.

The most common acoustic references to pitch are the following:

1. *Centered Pitch,* a series of frequencies that oscillates evenly around a fixed center (often used to refer to "in tune" singing);
2. *Mean Pitch,* a frequency imagined by the listener as an average or midpoint between the crest and trough of a continually oscillating sound wave (*e.g.,* a vibrato). When tonal oscillations are precise, a "mean" pitch sounds "centered" or "in tune," and
3. *True Pitch,* an exact frequency determined by measurement or by objective judgment.

While pitch is measurable and can be mathematically defined with precision in terms of radiation, frequency and intensity, perception of pitch is a subjective evaluation based upon a sensation, an evaluation influenced by loudness, quality, timbre and emotion. Conditioning, training, and an innate sensitivity are also factors in determining how pitch is perceived, and all of these perceptions in one form or another establish the parameters within which conscious or subconscious judgments are made with respect to intonation.

See **Frequency**
Kinesthesia
Off-Pitch Singing

Pitch Control: a conscious or subconscious attempt to regulate intonation through a reliance upon conceptual and perceptual disciplines.

Singing in tune is a reflexive event which occurs whenever there is perfect consonance between concept and mechanical response. Ideally, therefore, accuracy of intonation does not require control, but is a self-regulatory aspect of function. When the technique is efficient, intonation will always be a duplicate of the tonal concept that has set the physical forces in motion.

Concern for pitch control diverts attention from important matters related to functional mechanics, and when pitch problems exist, it fails to provide an answer to an obvious vocal problem.

See **Off-Pitch Singing**
Self-Regulation

(To) Place the Voice: an effort to "direct" vocal tone or reinforce sensations of vibration in various parts of the body; to attempt to improve vocal functioning by this method.

Two powerful figures in the musical world of the late nineteenth century, Lilli Lehmann and Jean de Reszke, were responsible for introducing and promoting concepts related to "placing the voice." The solution to vocal problems proposed by Lehmann was to replicate sensations of vibration thought to be desirable; that advocated by de Reszke was to approach the problem by means of nasal "resonance." Lehmann's directives were the more elaborate of the two, depicting through drawings the precise spot each note in the tonal scale should be "placed." Low tones were placed against the alveolar ridge, and as the scale rose, placement angled progressively toward the top of the head. A sampling of her more complex theories as to how tone is to be placed follows:

> As soon as the nose is adjusted by the breath-jerk and with it the *a* is placed by the larynx, the *ye* position must be joined to the *a*, this brings the tone forward toward the nose and lets it ring over the lowered palate, as by means of the *ye* the tongue compels the larynx to take a higher backward position and thus constricts the cavity of the mouth. The sensation would appear thus: −a− horizontally alone and *aye* joined to it. The *y* and the *e* are felt firmly at the nasal wall. The slanting ⌐a⌐ which represents the frontal lowering of the larynx, pushes with its *a* strength toward the chest muscles in the front and so, always replaced and rearticulated, comes to be placed under the strongly tensed nasal wall where it must always remain.[87]

[87]Lilli Lehmann, *How to Sing*, translated by Richard Aldrich (New York: The Macmillan Company, 1941), p. 96.

Directives of this description mark a radical departure from traditional training methods, and at best record subjective impressions which have little or nothing to do with the processes involved in *developing* vocal skills. Lehmann herself tells that, as little children, she and her sister Marie could strike the fourth line G above the treble staff a hundred times in succession and trill on it for a long time, and that they used to sing the aria of the Queen of the Night from Mozart's *The Magic Flute*, a feat few singers in the world are able to accomplish even as adults. Madame Lehmann's vocal coordination was natural rather than acquired, and her entire sensitivity was obviously bound by the subjective "feel" of the mechanical adjustments involved.

De Reszke's proposal was much more simple, both in concept and execution, and therefore has become widely accepted. It required only that the tone be "directed" toward the nasal passages, mainly by use of the voiced consonants such as *hng-ah* and *m*. The obvious fallacy in both of the formulations is that, since "voice" is merely the orderly disturbance of air particles set in motion by the vibrating vocal folds, vocal tone cannot be "placed" or directed. A second fallacy is the implicit assumption that by replicating symptoms, whether by imitation or other means, it is possible to bring about fundamental changes in the physical processes that are responsible (through radiation by means of bone conduction) for generating these symptoms.

Although the "doctrines" advanced by Lehmann and de Reszke appear to represent radical departures from traditional training procedures, this is not so. Registration, the idea of which had included references to the chest voice and the head voice, had always been recognized to possess properties of resonance which appeared to center in the anatomical regions after which they had been named. Since the head occupies the position in the body higher than the chest, the fact was inescapable that the symptoms associated with either the chest or the head voices would create the impression of tonal height and/or depth. This sense of higher or lower "position" was recognized by preceeding generations of teachers to be an effect, not a cause. Furthermore, it was known that the proper symptoms could not be evoked unless those muscle systems which produced them had been stimulated into improved patterns of response by projecting exercises which embraced the principles known to govern registration.

As a consequence of the formulations advanced by Lehmann and de Reszke, the techniques for stimulating and improving muscular responses at the tonal source, expressed by the Bel Cantists in terms of mechanical principles related to registration, were neglected, forgotten, and ultimately lost to subsequent generations of teachers. The continuing decline in vocal skills and a present inability to "build" voices is directly attributable to the currently wide acceptance of the Lehmann-de Reszke "doctrines" as a procedural basis for vocal training. Unless attempts to "place the voice" are abandoned, this state of affairs will continue to deprive students of their rightful vocal legacy.

Placement: in twentieth century thought, a concept which holds that vocal tone can be "directed" and tonal energy concentrated in various parts of the anatomy, usually "forward," in the facial mask, or in the head; in terminology extant during the eighteenth and nineteenth centuries, a concern for the proper initiation of vocal tone by concentrating energy into the laryngeal area, by singing into the instrument.

One of the early exercises for developing a correct tonal placement (as described by Gaetano Nava, a master teacher of Bel Canto during the eighteenth and nineteenth centuries) was the *vibrazione*. The direct object of this exercise (to be performed on a single tone, and identical in its execution to the second phase of the *messa di voce*) was to cultivate an awareness of laryngeal vibration for the express purpose of establishing effective control over laryngeal functioning. In addition to the *vibrazione*, another reference to "placement" was *imposto* (Italian, meaning "placed"), which may have derived from *impasto* (literally, "paste"), an obscure and rarely used expression which, according to Mancini, indicated a full-throated tone production. It is quite possible that *impasto* was also used in conjunction with *messa*, as in *messa di voce* (taken in its original meaning, signifying that everything is *in* place and complete). However, just as with the passing years *messa di voce* came to be known as the swelling and diminishing of a single tone, *impasto* became *imposto* or "placed." Thus, *impasto*, *messa di voce* and *imposto* could be taken to mean, by implication, "complete," with the singer adopting an attitude of readiness by, as Domenico Corri, the distinguished pupil of Porpora, expressed it, "preparing the voice for a crescendo," *i.e.*, for phonation.

One of the first references to "placement" as it is understood in contemporary pedagogy was made by G. B. Lamperti (1840—1910), who, as quoted by William Earl Brown, emphasized this sense of completeness by describing a "placed" tone as one "that is felt in the mask or the face, as well as high in the head, in the pharynx and deep in the throat, and on low tones in the chest." These he described as "placement sensations," a concept carried to extravagant lengths by Lilli Lehmann (sensations of the nose, tongue, palate, *etc.*). This concept marked the first point of departure from traditional Bel Canto beliefs by shifting emphasis from those principles known to stimulate the vocal mechanism and produce "registers," to their accompanying symptoms, *i.e.*, sensations of vibration concentrated in the "head" and "chest."

Whether or not Lamperti was merely "climbing on the bandwagon" and going along with a current trend is an open question. Certainly his views concerning placement were not shared by his illustrious pupil William Shakespeare, who believed that a tone was properly produced by "placing or balancing the larynx over the breath (to) retain it in its appropriate position." This depends (according to his account) on what Husler and Rodd-Marling later described so perceptively in their discussion of the suspensory muscles which govern laryngeal movement: an effective interaction between the supra- and infrahyoids and their associated musculatures. Describing this aspect of phonation, Shakespeare made the following statements:

> This outer shield [referring to the larynx] . . . must be steadied by the combined action upwards and downwards of appropriate muscles, which enable the adjoining tuning muscles to contract more vigorously when producing the higher notes of the scale. This invests the tongue-bone with no slight importance, and suggests that some support is necessary *to it*. There are powerful sets of muscles proceeding from this bone to the undersurface of both sides of the jaw and others to the sides of the chin, and also connecting (to the clavicle). These together help to firm the floor of the mouth. Again, several muscles pass from the tongue-bone to the skull at the back of the mouth.[88]

All these lend support by pulling the tongue-bone, to which is attached the larynx, not only *upward*, but *forwards* or *backwards*, while at the same time [other] connecting muscles are pulling the vocal instrument *downwards toward the chest bone*.

[88]William Shakespeare, *The Art of Singing* (Bryn Mawr, Pa.: Oliver Ditson Co., 1898), p. 19.

PLACEMENT

[89]William Shakespeare, *The Art of Singing* (Bryn Mawr, Pa.: Oliver Ditson Co., 1898), p. 20.

The larynx is thus steadied, and displacement is prevented whenever the tuning muscles vigorously contract for the production of high notes.[89]

Thus the registers seem to be influenced by different sets of placing muscles; the latter through interchange of action balance the larynx in the exact position necessary to any note, high or low, loud or soft; simultaneously, the muscles inside bring about the infinite and remarkable modifications in the length and breadth of the vibrating vocal cords to which reference has already been made. *The control over the placing, tuning, and register changes should be unconscious.*[90]

[90]*Ibid.*, p. 21.

Shakespeare's explanation of "placement" is reasonable and conforms directly to those beliefs entertained by the great teachers of the Bel Canto era. Subsequent concepts regarding placement, however, represent a radical departure from this postulate. Whereas according to Shakespeare, "voice" was considered to be the product of vibratory impulses set in motion by muscular activities taking place at the tonal source (the laryngeal pharynx), "placement" is now considered a question of "singing on resonance;" it is to be achieved by replicating and intensifying sensations of vibration in parts of the anatomy which, of themselves, are incapable of either initiating or augmenting vocal tone. It may readily be seen, therefore, that the original concept of placement and resonance, whether *impasto, imposto* or *messa,* held that a well-placed tone was the product of function. Specifically, this function was a precise tuning of the pharyngeal cavities in response to the vowel (which implies laryngeal stability), together with those muscular processes which contract to meet the requirements imposed by pitch and intensity, and which regulate and determine the physical conformation of the vocal folds.

Contemporary versions of placement differ substantially from that described by Shakespeare. In the 1930's Frank Hill defined it as "the directing of each vocal sound so that it can be properly reinforced." In *Grove's Dictionary of Music and Musicians* (fifth edition), Franklyn Kelsey contends that it is "the directing of a stream of sound toward one part of the anatomy or another," but goes on to declare that in a literal sense such an event is a physical and acoustic impossibility. When scientific authorities continued to expose the fallacy of the above postulates, modifications occured in both theory and practice. In a pamphlet published in 1969 by the American Academy of Teachers of Singing, placement is defined as "a product of perfect mental and physical coordination." Vennard takes another position and describes it as "the illusion that tones of different timbre are in different parts of the body." The consensus now appears to be that "placement" is, as one writer put it, "the integration and coordination of the voice as it applies to the particular individual."

Despite the tempered quality of the above definitions, a great many teachers still incorporate the visual imagery associated with placement into their training procedures. The specific suggestions involved in this practice include advice to "direct the tone against the hard palate," to "put it in the facial mask," to "direct it forward toward the lips, or behind the front teeth," to "feel it resonate in the head or in the chest," and other euphemisms. As concrete proposals, these are no less absurd than asking a violinist to produce a beautiful tone by "directing" the sound produced by his instrument to the ceiling, floor, or third row of the orchestra.

The proponents of "placement" have failed to recognize 1) that "voice" is merely an orderly disturbance of air particles that cannot be acted upon, and 2) that it has no mechanical function of its own, but is the product of other activities.

A proper view of placement, therefore, is one which recognizes that the sensations experienced by many singers in various parts of the body (the head, chest, facial mask, *etc.*) are symptoms which appear because vibratory impulses have radiated from the tonal source through the skeletal framework by means of bone conduction. Consequently, they merely reflect the quality of the functional activities (notably, registration and resonance) occurring within the laryngeal pharynx. Although the intensity with which these symptoms appear reflects the efficiency of the coordinative process yielding vocal tone, that efficiency cannot be improved by attempting to increase the intensity of the symptoms. Nor can symptoms be made to appear (except as figments of the imagination) unless they are already the product of a present technical status.

"Placement" is a concept without basis in fact. It embraces no mechanical principle, it is impossible to execute in practical physical terms, and it overlooks the fact that all effective control over tone quality is lost once the vocal folds become vibratile. Pedagogic procedures based upon "placement" or the imagery with which it is associated should be categorically eliminated if training procedures are to be constructive.

See Bel Canto
Bone Conduction
Focus
Imposto
Kinesthesia
Laryngeal
  Suspension
Modern Methods
Movement
Register
Resonance
Vowel

Pleura: the serous membrane lining each half of the thorax that folds back over the surface of the lung of that side.

Pleural Capacity: See Vital Capacity.

Pleural Cavity: that area of the thorax containing the lungs.

Plosive: a consonant phoneme articulated by the stoppage and sudden release of sound.

Plosives are formed with the assistance of one or more of the articulatory processes, and are named for that process primarily involved in their articulation. They can be either "voiced" (involving vocal vibration) or "unvoiced." For example, there are "bilabial plosives" involving both lips (voiced, *b;* unvoiced, *p*); "lingual plosives" involving the tongue (voiced, *d;* unvoiced, *t*), and "palatal plosives" (voiced, *g* as in "goat;" unvoiced, *k*).

See Consonants

Point: an imagery designed to "focus" an otherwise diffused tone quality by means of tonal "placement."

Since all effective control over "voice" has been lost once the vocal folds have become vibratile and the impulses set in motion have moved beyond the pharyngeal cavities, it is inevitable that procedures based upon "point," "ping," "focus" and similar imagery, because they rely upon overt controls to bring an involuntary muscular system under subjection, serve no other end than to induce varying degrees of throat constriction.

A pure, unblemished tone quality is not "pointed," nor does it have "ping" or

See Nasality
(To) Place the
  Voice
Placement
Production, Tone
(To) Project
Purity of
  Intonation
Vocal Study

similar ascriptions; such concepts are at variance with the "roundness" typical of an unblemished, pure tone quality.

Pointed Vowel: a term used to refer to a vowel phoneme (*e.g., ee* or *ay*) whose tonal form seems to lack "roundness" (*i.e.,* in contrast to phonemes such as *oo, oh,* or *ah*).

See Placement
    Vowel

       The term "pointed vowel" is not to be taken literally, since in reality vowels are neither "round" nor "pointed," but merely possess different harmonic structures.

Polyp: in vocal hygiene, a growth on the upper or lower surface of the mucous membrane lining the vocal folds.

See Nodule

       The term "polyp" is often used interchangeably with "nodule." However, a nodule is a growth or blister on the edge of the vocal folds that generally results from vocal abuse, whereas a polyp is often of pathological origin.

See Consonants

Post-Dental Consonant: a consonant phoneme articulated with the tongue and alveolar ridge, or area behind the upper teeth; a lingua-alveolar consonant.

Posterior: pertaining to the rear, as opposed to the anterior, which pertains to the front; dorsal (as opposed to ventral).

Posterior Cricoarytenoid: See Posticus.

Posticus: a paired muscle that attaches at one end to the cricoid cartilage and pulls upon the muscular processes of the arytenoids; the posterior cricoarytenoid muscles.

See Breathing
    Cricothyroid
       Muscle
    Falsetto
    Register

       Contraction of the posticus widens the space between the vocal folds. While some consider this contraction to be active only during silent breathing, and thereby unrelated to vocal functioning, others believe that it assists the cricothyroids in the production of falsetto tones.

Postural Muscle: any of those body muscles whose contractions collectively resist the pull of gravity and allow the body to be maintained in an upright position.

       Although many muscles might be considered "postural" (including those of the legs, pelvic girdle, back, shoulders, and neck), the term "postural muscle" is usually used to refer to any of those dorsal muscles that articulate with the oblique abdominals.

Posture: the position or carriage of the body, whether characteristic or assumed for a specific purpose.

       Although good posture during singing is visually attractive, and although it facilitates the functional process and helps maintain vocal health, it cannot of itself improve the vocal technique, the efficiency of which is dependent upon how well a broad complex of laryngeal muscles coordinate (in particular, those responsible for the phenomena of registration and resonance). What good posture can do is improve one's appearance and maintain the body in a state of balanced poise, or readiness to respond. Within the latter context, good posture is highly desirable—especially during earlier periods of technical development.

When the vocal muscles are well coordinated, however, one can sing quite correctly in almost any position. In opera, for example, singers are required to perform difficult music in what would normally be considered an awkward or poor posture. Nevertheless, a good baritone singing the role of Rigoletto is not restricted vocally by having to assume the posture of a hunchback; nor does a vocally proficient Tosca sing "Vissi d'arte" less effectively while lying prostrate on the stage. Although a normal posture might be more comfortable and attractive, and pose fewer problems, extremes of posture should not act as an impediment to a correct tone production when the singer has been well schooled.

The crucial factor in tone production is physical coordination within the throat parts. Posture helps, but it is not essential to that coordination.

Posturing: a bodily affectation.

Posturing during phonation is either a result of a self-consciousness or of training procedures designed to bring the vocal mechanism under direct or overt control. Methods founded upon specialized breathing techniques, tonal "placement," prepared or "fixed" mouth positions, and a desire to "make" or "produce" a particular tone quality are common sources of posturing. Posturing can also occur as a defense reaction to the anxiety that often surfaces when technical improvement establishes contact with deeper layers of feeling.

See **Anxiety**
Emotion
Movement
Singer's Stance

Regardless of its origin, posturing is unsightly and precludes any possibility of either singing or learning to sing correctly.

Power: the intensity with which a sound radiates through space.

In singing, the term "power" is usually reserved for those "big" voices capable of sustaining high levels of intensity and ideally suited to the singing of heavy, dramatic roles. Power, however, is but one component among many (namely, an ability to vary intensity with control and finesse, to sing legato and sustain long phrases, to execute rapid passages easily and accurately and to produce high levels of volume without forcing) without which artistic singing is impossible. Power, in the absence of other essential ingredients, merely degenerates into loud singing.

Voices potentially capable of undertaking dramatic roles and singing with power must be nurtured carefully. Considerable muscular tonicity is required to sustain high levels of volume without forcing or overextending one's resources, and such a capability is not reached until about the age of forty. Those voices which are potentially ideal for the singing of heavy roles are well advised to restrain their ambition until such time as the required tonicity has been built up and the art of legato singing has been completely mastered.

See **(To) Force**
Legato
(To) Push

Training procedures which make power the direct object of study are damaging to the mechanism and assure a limited career.

Practice: repetition of a musical composition or parts thereof, or of specific vocal exercises, to improve technical proficiency.

Basically, there are two kinds of practice: 1) learning by rote or repetition, and 2) applying specifically designed exercises or musical patterns to work through a particular problem.

Rote practice is mindless and rarely leads to improvement, since in all but the rarest cases, the concepts, physical coordination, kinesthetic awareness, and aesthetic goals of the singer are in some way faulty. Thus, in most instances, rote practice merely tends to reinforce or "lock in" those very concepts and patterns of physical response which the singer should be working to correct.

Practice, therefore, can be either constructive or destructive, and until the singer's technique is well established, it generally should be done under the direct supervision of a competent teacher. Learning to sing is not a matter of consolidating a status quo, or bringing the mechanism under subjection, but developing new concepts and response patterns which free the mechanism. Furthermore, intelligent self-help in the form of practice requires an objectivity and an understanding of functional mechanics no student presenting himself for instruction possesses; otherwise he would not be a student.

The study material and exercises employed during both supervised and unsupervised practice should serve to accomplish the following objectives:

1. Refine concepts;
2. Develop an awareness and understanding of the mechanical principles at work in the vocal process, and of inherent functional limitations;
3. Recoordinate the laryngeal muscles so that they can perform more efficiently, and
4. Achieve some degree of spontaneous movement through rhythmic identification with the musical patterns projected.

Since each individual possesses unique personality traits, aptitudes, and vocal problems, no practice manual, ritual, or set of exercises will meet all of the needs of all students. Just as individual problems and aspirations differ, so, too, must the proposed remedies. For those whose voices are well formed as a gift of nature, practice should be limited to exercises for "warming up," the best vocal study for them being the cultivation of an innate "singer's instinct." There is a vast musical literature appropriate to one's age and vocal needs to be learned and performed, all of which, if wisely selected, will further both musical and vocal progress.

See **Bel Canto
Exercises
Production, Tone
Register**

Preparatory Effort: a mental and physical attitude assumed prior to the inception of vocal tone.

The essential features of tonal preparation are as follows: the singer need only assume a natural and comfortably poised stance, inspire the required amount of air without effort, and respond to the directives implicit in the music or exercise pattern to be executed. On this level, proper preparatory effort is a mental and physical readiness to respond to a thought process which conceptualizes the vowel, the musical figure, and the intensity level to be sung, and causes what appears to be spontaneous vibrations to appear within the thought form.

Conscious, volitional preparatory efforts (*e.g.*, expanding the rib cage, elevating the chest, taking an unusually large breath, breathing through the nose, tucking in or protruding the abdomen, assuming a "set" facial expression or mouth position, raising the soft palate, lowering the larynx, *etc.*) more often than not promote self-consciousness and body stiffness, and constitute measures which inhibit free, spontaneous movement. Paradoxically, the art of preparing for phonation is in essence the art of learning how to prepare without preparing.

See **Attack
Mental Concept
Movement
Rhythm**

Prephonatory Tuning: a reflexive approximation of the vocal folds that occurs in response to neurological stimuli before any movement of air below the glottis has taken place. This postulate was advanced by Dr. Barry Wyke of Yale University, and it contributes significantly to an understanding of vocal functioning.

See **Air Stream**
Bernoulli Effect
Breath Pressure Theory
Holistic Pedagogy

Pressed Tone: a vocaized sound whose hard, inflexible tonal characteristics result from excessive and misdirected energy expenditure.

"Pressed" tones either disturb, or are caused by a disturbance of, the natural equilibrium that should exist between the suspensory muscles which stabilize the larynx and those which, when properly tensed, enable the vocal folds to maintain an easy vibratility. This misapplication of energy causes the larynx to "slip" (*i.e.,* be raised or lowered to an unnatural position), with the result that the throat parts constrict and stiffen, the breathing muscles become overtaxed, and the tone quality becomes hard and unwieldy.

"Pressed" tones often result from conscious attempts to increase the size or weight of a voice beyond its current capabilities. Thus, "pressed" tones represent misuse of the vocal organs, and originate not only in a misunderstanding of functional mechanics but also in faulty aesthetic concepts.

See **Coordination**
Energy
Register

Pressure: force applied to something by something else in direct contact with it.

In singing, pressure is applied to the vibrating vocal folds by escaping breath. However, the amount of breath pressure needed to form and sustain vocal tone varies in inverse proportion to the functional capabilities of the mechanism. Thus, when the vocal muscles (in particular, those responsible for the phenomena of registration and resonance) are efficiently coordinated, very little breath pressure is needed to initiate and sustain vocal tone. When, on the other hand, the vocal muscles are poorly coordinated, interfering tensions must be overcome by excessive breath pressure.

See **Breathing**
(To) Force

Primary Register Change: that point in the tonal range at which the chest register ceases to be, and the head register becomes, the predominant mechanism; the point of register transition; the register "break."

Although the specific point of register transition varies somewhat with vocal weight and voice type, the primary register change in all voice types, male and female alike, is in the vicinity of E – F above middle C.

See **Messa di Voce**
Register

(To) Produce: to give being, form or shape to; to make; to manufacture.

See **Production, Tone**

Production, Tone: the manner in which the phonative process is set in motion (articulation); the manner in which the vocal mechanism is used (technique).

The term "production" is a twentieth century invention that places greater emphasis upon the manner in which the phonative process is set in motion than it does upon the use of the mechanism with respect to its ability to respond. It appears to be more than coincidence, however, that both the term and its related conceptualizations emerged during the industrial era. Prior to this era, references to voice training mentioned voice "culture," a concept which recognized the existence of definite parallels between the principles employed to ensure vocal growth and those pertaining to agriculture.

Training methods based upon concepts related to tone "production" generally reflect a preoccupation with procedures which act upon the mechanism, since tone "production" is concerned with special techniques for controlling the breath, proper "placement," and/or devices for "directing" the voice into the nasal passages to vitalize its resonance characteristics.

The negative procedures associated with tone "production" may be more readily comprehended when it is realized that "voice" is nothing more nor less, physically, than the activity of muscles and the movement of air. Proper developmental procedures, therefore, must stimulate the activity of muscles within the throat parts responsible for generating vocal tone into improved patterns of response; this end can be achieved by the selection of scales and exercises which cause them to react spontaneously. Procedures based upon an assumption that tone is "produced" do not address themselves to this or related vocal problems.

(To) Progress: to develop or move toward a higher, better, or more advanced stage.

Vocal progress should be easy to evaluate. When the singer is able, over a period of time, to negotiate a wider range of pitches without forcing; when he has increased his options with respect to dynamics; when he can phonate purer vowels; when he finds his voice more flexible; when he experiences less fatigue; when he can sing with fewer visible signs of effort: then, he has progressed.

Too often, however, vocal progress is confused with musical or aesthetic progress, which, of course, is exceedingly difficult to evaluate, since it is so dependent upon subjective and cultural variables. Thus, what one considers "better" is, more often than not, an opinion reflecting the influence of other factors. This is especially true when the technique has been brought under that kind of restraint commonly looked upon as "control." To be relevant to the voice-building process, however, vocal progress must be judged objectively and extracted from personal, aesthetic, and musical considerations. Vocal progress is not manifested in a singer whose elevated musical taste prompts him to sing with greater control, but over a diminishing technical resource; however, there are many singers who demonstrate this paradox.

Improvement in vocal skills is measurable, and if technical progress is to be evaluated objectively and placed within its proper perspective, it must be judged without reference to other factors.

(To) Project: to produce vocalized sounds possessing sufficient tonal energy to be clearly audible at all levels of intensity from reasonable distances (*e.g.,* the back of a large auditorium); to propel the voice as an act of will, thereby infusing the tone with greater carrying power.

The term "project" is a product of twentieth century pedagogic thought, and like so many modern terms, it implies an ability to act upon the mechanism. Tonal "projection," however, is both a physical and an acoustic impossibility. Physically, vocalized sounds are the product of an essentially involuntary muscular system which cannot be acted upon; acoustically, they are alternate expansions and contractions of air particles set in motion by the vibrating vocal folds. These pressure variations, resonated by the pharyngeal cavities, proceed rhythmically through space in all directions at a constant speed, approximately 1100 feet per second, or 175 miles per hour. Hence, they cannot be hurled through space like a javelin, "projected," "directed," or "placed."

The myth of tonal projection has been perpetuated over the years by notable singers who feel that they are able to "lean on the voice" (Italian, *appoggiare la voce*), and by increasing interior pressure, "move" the voice to the listening audience with greater power and vitality. What actually occurs, however, is that increasing energy output is met by a corresponding increase in those elements which provide an effective source of resistance as an equilibrium is maintained among the muscular processes involved. There are two such sources of resistance located within the vocal organs: 1) the reduced size of the tonal exit created by a narrowing of the false vocal cords, and 2) laryngeal stability. Because of this arrangement there is no dissipation of energy, the tonal vibrations become highly volatile, and the voice appears to "project."

One of the more common pedagogic errors has been to devise substitute measures to achieve this sense of tonal projection by attempting to "place," "focus," or "direct" vocal tone, or to infuse it with "ping," "nasal resonance," or other imagined properties associated with resonance, none of which are capable of bringing the mechanism into equilibrium. These are practices that neither restructure a faulty technique nor set up vibratory patterns which, because they move on a strongly energized rhythmic impulse, possess of themselves both an unusual carrying power and resonance characteristics which create the impression that the voice has been "projected."

See **Appoggiare la Voce**
Carrying Power
Coupling
Focus
Laryngeal
  Suspension
Placement
Resistance
Resonance

Pronunciation: the manner of articulation of the components of spoken language (phonemes).

Pronunciation involves not only the qualitative factors of spoken language (*i.e.*, vowel and consonant quality) but also quantitative factors such as the pitch (or lack thereof), duration, and stress each phoneme receives in relation to other component sounds.

Pronunciation should not be confused with enunciation, which involves the quality of articulation (*i.e.*, the clarity and precision with which each phoneme is articulated).

See **Diction**
Enunciation

Psychological Factors: those mental, emotional and behavioral patterns which cause one to be attracted to, or be repelled by, certain types of external stimuli; the effect of such characterological structures on vocal functioning.

Psychological factors are significant to vocal pedagogy: they are responsible for the formation and development of concepts, for perceptions with respect to hearing, for aesthetic preferences and goals, for one's ability to respond, and for the manner in which energy is channeled. Without exception, inner tensions and the inhibition of respiration (which are the somatic counterparts of anxiety) are the greatest obstacles to vocal development. To a remarkable degree, however, proper stimulation of the vocal muscles through constructive training will, by eliminating throat constriction and other respiratory tensions, release both the muscular interference whose presence "locks in" the vocal mechanism and the hidden fears which brought those tensions into being.

For those who find themselves capable of participating in a dynamic growth

See **Anxiety**
Emotion
Energy
Kinesthesia
Movement
Rhythm

process designed to achieve this objective, two distinct advantages will have been gained: 1) a freeing of the vocal mechanism and the acquisition of a correct vocal technique, and 2) growth into a deeper knowledge of themselves as individuals.

Puff Theory: a pedagogic hypothesis that attempts to explain vocal functioning in terms of the puffs of air that are released through the vibrating vocal folds during phonation.

Theoretical speculations concerning the nature of resonance and the production of vowel sounds originated in the early eighteenth century when the French scientist Denis Dodart (1634—1707) discovered that pitch was determined by tension on the vocal folds and that breath was released in a series of tiny puffs. Subsequent studies carried out by Wilfred Willis (1830), Sir Charles Wheatstone (1837), Hermann L. F. Helmholtz (1885), and E. W. Scripture (1906) verified this observation and resulted in the formulation of two somewhat opposed theories: the harmonic, or Wheatstone-Helmholtz theory, and the puff theory advocated by Scripture.

According to the proponents of the puff theory, subglottal breath pressure causes the approximated vocal folds to burst open in a series of rapid explosions. After each burst, the natural elasticity of the folds, through recoil, moves them to a position below their normal median point. As a result of this recoil and the consequent increase in subglottal pressure, the cycle is again set in motion, and is repeated without interruption until phonation ceases. The aural perception of these puffs (which, when the vocal mechanism responds efficiently, occur at approximately 4.8 to 6.2 times per second) is known as a vibrato.

Acoustically, these puffs and the pressure variations they create excite the air within the pharyngeal cavities; accordingly, they add the harmonic and inharmonic frequencies to which these cavities are tuned, and the inharmonic partials add warmth to the tone quality. Thus, on the basis of this theory, tonal quality is the product of anatomical structure, the character of puffs emitted through the vibrating vocal folds, and the precision with which the pharyngeal cavities are tuned or adjusted to the fundamental frequency.

One of the more interesting aspects of the puff theory is the challenge it presents to conventional twentieth century views concerning the role of breathing in singing. Since it is evident that the puffs of air which periodically burst through the vibrating vocal folds determine the rate of breath expulsion, then it must be concluded that breathing does not control function in singing (as proponents of "breath support" and "breath control" have maintained for nearly a century). On the contrary, it is function that controls the rate of breath expenditure, *i.e.,* muscular coordination as it affects the physical dimensions of the vocal folds and the forceful or willing closure of the glottal space.

See **Bel Canto**
Bernoulli Effect
Harmonic Theory
Modern Methods
Standing Wave
Vibrato
Vowel

The puff theory is now generally recognized to be valid by all members of the scientific community, despite the fact that it stands diametrically opposed to the aerodynamic and other theories. The lack of a consensus, however, is merely indicative of the fact that it is as difficult to explain the human voice as it is to establish mutually agreeable procedures for developing it.

Pulse Register: a term introduced by scientific investigators to refer to vocalized sounds with extremely low frequencies and pulse-like oscillations; a "vocal fry," "glottal fry," "creak," or *Strohbass.*

The concept of a "pulse register" is without value to voice culture for the following reasons:

1. It is a designation based upon acoustic rather than physiological data, and there is no distinct mechanical or muscular system responsible for its articulation;
2. The vibratory impulses it describes have no relevance to the "pulse" or vibrato of a legitimate vocal tone;
3. The vibratory impulses it describes are "musical" only in that they possess measurable pitch; they contain no recognizable vowel phoneme and cannot be swelled or diminished;
4. The sounds to which it refers are "freak" tones with no aesthetic value; like squeaks, groans, screams, and squeals, they should be considered forms of affective expression, and not confused with legitimate vocalization, and
5. The sounds to which it refers have no pedagogic value since they could never be incorporated into, or used to influence or improve, the quality of those tones universally accepted as being legitimate.

The term "pulse register" should be abandoned, since a further proliferation of terminology, even when justified on acoustic terms, simply adds confusion to an already confused area of thinking with respect to the number and origin of vocal registers.

See **Affective
Expression
Falsetto
Loft Voice
Modal Register
Registration
Vibrato
Vocal Fry**

Pure Registration: an ambiguous frame of reference which can indicate either 1) a technical status where the two basic register mechanisms, the chest and the falsetto, are fully developed and perfectly coordinated, or 2) the virtual isolation of these same mechanisms.

Both a perfectly coordinated and an isolated registration are extremely rare. In those instances where the registers are fully developed and perfectly coordinated, there would be an absence of throat constriction. The tone quality would be unblemished, the overall tonal range would encompass approximately three octaves, the voice would move with extreme agility, and the singer would be capable of swelling and diminishing with ease. The production would, in sum, be technically flawless. A pure registration of this description is a virtually unattainable ideal.

A more common reference to a "pure" registration is based upon a hypothesis having to do with total mechanical isolation. In such a case, one would be said to "have no voice" because 1) the highest pitch capable of being phonated would be B above middle C, regardless of sex or voice type, 2) the chest voice, which terminates at E – F above middle C, would be excessively strong, unmusical and rough textured, whereas the lower tones of the falsetto (pitches which are shared in common with the chest register) would be weak in intensity and extremely breathy, and 3) the quality and intensity differential would be so extreme (and aesthetically incompatible) that it would prohibit coordination as long as they were retained in this elemental form.

The concept of a pure registration, however, is most useful to an understanding of functional mechanics and the physical dynamics which underlie vocalization at higher levels of sophistication. In this sense of its meaning, a "pure" registration is an important theoretical postulate.

See **Bel Canto
Modern Methods
Register
Vocal Study**

Pure Tone: a vocalized sound whose lack of tonal imperfections is the product of exquisitely refined concepts and perfect physical coordination; an elemental sound wave, or tone without overtones (acoustics).

In the first sense, "pure" tones are exceedingly rare, since very few singers reach such high levels of technical proficiency. In the acoustical sense, pure tones cannot be produced by the human voice.

Pure Vowel: a vocalized sound whose well-defined resonance characteristics and general lack of tonal blemishes reflect a high level of technical development; a simple vowel phoneme, *i.e.*, one without a diphthong.

The production of pure vowels is impossible unless the conceptual and physical conditions are right. Consequently, the vowel (tone) quality will be impure to the degree that there is throat constriction, a "mixed" registration, or other faults.

While vowel purity is one of the ultimate objectives of training, it is rarely an immediate objective. The preliminary steps to be taken toward achieving vowel purity are those concerned with register development and the elimination of constrictor tensions within the resonating system, procedures which inevitably involve modification of the vowel.

Manipulation of the vowels, therefore, must be considered an unavoidable feature of training until such time as a higher plateau of technical excellence can be reached. Within this context, the oft-quoted statement "He who knows how to pronounce distinctly knows how to sing" should be amended to "He who is *able* to pronounce distinctly and sustain pure vowels knows how to sing."

Purity of Intonation: an expression common to the Bel Canto era (circa 1700— 1880) that refers not to pitch but to quality, and implies that all vowel phonemes are being maintained without blemish or modification over a wide pitch range, especially in the area of the register "break."

Purity of intonation was and should always be one of the primary goals of vocal training, since it is an accomplishment which finds both concepts and physical response precisely tuned and coordinated.

(To) Push: during phonation, to expend energy that is improperly channeled or improperly absorbed by the vocal mechanism.

Pushing is caused by the misdirection of energy during phonation, not by the expenditure of a particular *amount* of energy. It is, therefore, no more characteristic of those who sing vigorously than it is of those who sing quietly and with restraint. It is always present, however, when the registers are "mixed" and the throat is constricted.

When the mechanism is in equilibrium, it is literally impossible to "push."

Pyriform Sinus: any of the pear-shaped cavities between the so-called "collar" of the larynx (*i.e.*, the muscular ring formed by the aryepiglottic folds and the epiglottis, the cartilages of Wrisberg, and the arytenoid muscles) and the thyroid cartilage.

While some theorists claim that the pyriform sinuses are responsible for tonal "ring," this theory seems to be based more on conjecture than on fact. Their actual role in vocal functioning, if any, has not been determined.

Q

Quality: the aspect of musical sound that makes one voice or instrument distinguishable from others; timbre.

Vocal quality is the complex tonal product of numerous factors, including the following:

1. *Mechanical Efficiency and Acoustics.* The shape of each vibratory pattern or sound wave and the manner in which energy is distributed within the harmonic spectrum (*i.e.,* the arrangement, concentration or dispersion, and relative intensity of partials or overtones, both harmonic and inharmonic, in relation to the fundamental tone) are largely responsible for both tonal quality and vowel quality. These acoustical properties, in turn, are the product of muscular movements that adjust the length, thickness, and contour of the vocal folds (*i.e.,* those responsible for the phenomenon of registration) and among those that position the larynx and adjust the pharyngeal cavities for tonal amplification (*i.e.,* those responsible for resonance). When these muscles are precisely coordinated, the resulting tonal product will be free and spontaneous, and it will reflect the natural, intrinsic qualities of the mechanism (*i.e.,* those determined solely by anatomical and psychological factors).

2. *Tonal Pulse.* Good vocal quality is impossible without a regular tonal pulse, or vibrato, which introduces a regular rise and fall in both pitch and intensity, and creates the impression of centered or "constant" pitch. Regularity of tonal pulse adds beauty and richness to vocal tone by ensuring that both the fundamental and its corresponding overtones are in a state of continual flux while both the pitch being sung and the overall quality of the tonal product seem to remain constant. Thus, every well-produced vocal tone (except an extremely soft *pianissimo*) contains constantly changing factors that enrich the tone harmonically and also a constant factor that creates the impression of uniform pitch.

   Since very few voices are sufficiently well coordinated to possess a vibrato, most exhibit, to a greater or lesser extent, erratic tonal pulse patterns that result from register imbalances and/or throat constriction. Although less severe examples of these erratic movements merely yield vocal tones that are less than satisfactory, extreme forms (commonly recognized as a "tremolo" or a "wobble") are qualitatively objectionable.

3. *Resonance Characteristics.* Vocal quality is determined not only by the vibratory patterns set in motion by the vocal folds, but also by the manner in which these vibrations are modified by the surrounding resonance cavities. Thus, the size and shape of the vibrating air column, the capability of the laryngo- and oro-

pharynges to function as both coupled and uncoupled resonators, and the relative firmness of the pharyngeal walls all influence vocal quality.

Firmly tensed pharyngeal walls energize higher frequencies within the tonal spectrum and yield ringing, or metallic, tonal characteristics; lax pharyngeal walls select lower frequencies and yield warm, mellow tonal characteristics (excessively lax walls are responsible for tones that sound dull and lifeless). Maximum tonal richness is achieved when the pharyngeal walls are neither overly tensed nor overly lax, but are maintained in a state of optimum tonicity.

4. *Anatomical Structure.* Anatomical factors, such as sturdiness of bone structure and the size, shape, and dimensions of the pharyngeal cavities and vocal folds also influence vocal quality. Although these factors ultimately determine whether the voice will be large or small, and whether it will be soprano, alto, tenor, or bass, there is no assurance that a singer who possesses superior anatomical structure will also possess that unique sense of physical coordination, when generating vocal tone, that is necessary to the attainment of a high degree of technical proficiency. Conceptual sharpness and a gift for physical coordination, not anatomical structure, are prerequisites to efficient phonation and beautiful tone quality.

5. *Psychological Factors.* Individual emotional characteristics, personality, temperament, perception, musicality, taste, and general characterological structure are important determinants of vocal quality. Since psychological predispositions generally determine the type of tone qualities to which one will be instinctively drawn, each individual "produces" or learns to produce those qualities he finds emotionally satisfying while rejecting those which are less attractive or even threatening, even though the latter may be more healthy and vital.

6. *Aesthetic Considerations.* While one's conception of tonal beauty is largely a product of cultural influences, psychological predisposition, training and temperament, it is a force which exerts the strongest possible influence on both tonal perceptions and the manner in which the vocal organs are stimulated. Psychological factors and aesthetic goals are virtually one and the same; the sole exception occurs when one feels frustrated in the attainment of those desired goals because of technical inadequacy.

See   Bel Canto
      Coupling
      Functional
        Listening
      Modern Methods
      Natural Movement
      Pitch
      Register
      Resonance
      Vibrato
      Vowel

Although the acoustic properties of quality can be analyzed and reduced to mathematical formulae, they remain a tonal perception judged by the listener on the basis of psychological predisposition and taste, as these are conditioned by training, experience and culture. However, in estimating a singer's quality it is important to recognize that quality is a product of function, and that evaluations such as "good" or "bad" are purely subjective. In order to arrive at a more objective viewpoint, therefore, it is necessary to make a distinction between qualities which are intrinsically "natural" and those which merely reflect the present condition of the functioning mechanism.

The difficulty of adopting a proper attitude toward quality during training is one of the major stumbling blocks to progress.

Quality and Its Functional Derivatives: Tone quality is the end result of a mental and physical process, and consequently it is subject to analysis on both levels. As all tone qualities are a composite of tonal textures which originate in registration and adjustments made for resonance, it is possible for the trained ear to recognize technical difficulties at their source and set in motion the necessary procedures for correcting them. The following table, Figure 14, lists a wide variety of functional possibilities and indicates how they influence quality.

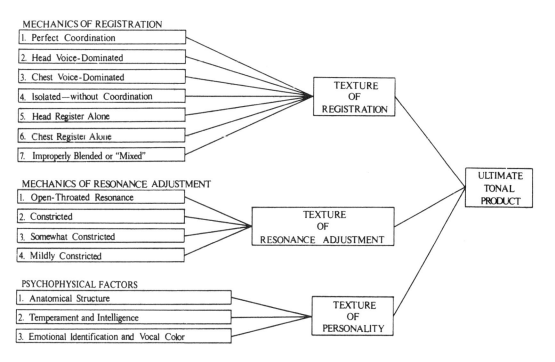

Figure 14. *Quality and Its Functional Derivatives.*

All three of the categories mentioned below are of special interest. Each is important functionally, and most are subject to modification and change. By selecting one category out of each group, it is possible to assess with considerable accuracy the nature of the vocal faults either present or absent. The first category has been planned to indicate the seven most common physical arrangements of the registration. These arrangements are as follows:

1. A rare state of perfect coordination where both registers have been fully developed and smoothly joined;
2. A divided registration whose action is dominated by the upper register, or "head" voice;
3. A divided registration whose action is dominated by the lower register, or "chest" voice;
4. A condition where both registers are used, but with an audible gap separating them. In this arrangement, the registers are often so widely separated as to prohibit free passage from one to the other. This makes singing difficult, if not impossible. If the gap is narrow, the technique is ready to move into either one of the higher categories. Of all the categories listed, this is the broadest, and within it the technical status of the singer can be anywhere from the primitive to the fairly advanced;
5. A condition where the falsetto, or "head" voice, is used alone while the lower

register is excluded entirely from discernible participation. This situation is not likely to be encountered with the male voice;

6. A condition where the "chest" register is used exclusively, while the "head" register is neglected. This condition is common to the male voice, less so to the female unless she is "belting," and

7. An improper blending or "mixture" of the registers in which they have been smoothly joined in a wrong balance. This introduces muscular conflicts which can never be resolved without disengaging the registration. The problem here is that the procedures necessary to the correction of one fault will often intensify another, making a just solution impossible. For example, in order to break down the constrictor tensions always associated with a mixed registration, the chest register must be re-established in its rightful place. But if the mixture of the registers is too severe, the vigor required to make this mechanism operative will merely serve to fortify the very constrictions it is supposed to dislodge. Thus, what is essential to a successful realignment of the registration will often bring about a worsening of the resonance adjustment. For some types of mixed registration, therefore, no solution exists. Certain mixtures, however, notably those allied with the average lyric tenor, a mixture often mistakenly referred to as the Bel Canto type, are functional to a degree, and with patience, they are subject to correction.

Each of the seven mechanical arrangements of the registration described is accompanied by representative textures which may easily be recognized as belonging to either the "head" register, the "chest" register, or some combination of the two. In addition, there are the resonance adjustments made for tonal amplification, and these fall into four basic categories:

1. An ideal adjustment, where a condition of precise, "open-throated" resonance has been established;

2. A reversal of this ideal adjustment, in which constrictor tensions take over and the tonal resonance becomes "throaty;"

3. A resonance adjustment common to most singers of quality, which, while not particularly noticeable or objectionable, nevertheless inhibits vocal growth and development, and

4. A minimal amount of muscular interference (constriction), which permits distinguished vocalization, but which cannot permit the attainment of the level of excellence reached by those few whose singing is truly open-throated.

All of the classifications so far mentioned represent the several types of coordinative processes commonly met with as the vocal organs respond to pitch-intensity patterns and the vowel. From this it follows that tone quality, i.e., vowel quality and timbre, must in effect be a repository for whatever textural contribution each category of mechanical response has to offer. Evidence may always be found within the tone quality to show the extent of those textural modifications introduced by the character of the coordinative arrangement prevalent at a given moment. Beyond these factors, others must be considered:

1. The influence of individual anatomical structure. This is an unchangeable factor but it nonetheless plays an important role in determining the natural tessitura and textural properties of the voice;

2. The influence of temperament. It goes without saying that qualities of temperament and intelligence play an important role in the infusion of those individual quality characteristics which make every voice distinctive and unique, and

3. The influence on texture of the quality of emotional identification. "Coloring" the vowel to dramatize the emotional import of the lyrics is one of the chief interpretive devices at the singer's disposal.

Most of the subtle adjustments made in "coloring" the vowel are emotionally oriented. They take position as a response to feelings commonly associated with vocal literature such as love, anger, fear, disdain, happiness, longing, grief, jealousy, and the like. However, before the ultimate purpose of singing is confronted, *i.e.,* to convey with great sensitivity a full range of emotional experience episodically, the pure joy of making sound for its own sake must be developed. How the singer relates to this is another important aspect of vocal color, for the *quality* of his identification, his response *to* feeling *through* feeling, will in the long run establish his value as an artist.

The capacity of the singer to relate with emotional sensitivity depends upon functional freedom. Unless the registration is properly balanced and the resonance adjustments well formed, vowel "coloring" must always be contrived and artificial. Functional freedom *awakens* feelings, and when this happens, it is not necessary to "put" feeling into anything. It is there.

From what has been said, the tonal textures heard as the end product of a singer's technique can be evaluated with some accuracy simply by understanding the mechanical relationships between cause and effect, *i.e.,* the effect upon the tonal texture of the anatomical structure, temperament and vowel coloring, together with the coordinative pattern of response offered by the registers and the resonance adjustment. When these elements are placed in their proper perspective, a real understanding of the vocal function will have been gained.

Quiver: an excessively tremulous, erratic tonal movement.

A "quiver" during phonation results from 1) misconcepts with respect to vocal technique, 2) wrongly directed physical energy, which is the natural consequence of such misconcepts, 3) unrelieved muscular interference and the resultant compensatory tensions that cause the throat to constrict, or 4) the deliberate making of special interpretive effects, such as the depiction of age, nervousness, or timidity.

See **Tremolo**
Wobble

R

Range: the compass of legitimate pitches a voice is capable of producing.

The well-used voice possesses a range of at least two octaves, *i.e.*, tones which can be sung with a legato connection. Although ranges of three octaves are not uncommon (particularly with women's voices), those who boast of having four octaves or more invariably possess "breaks" which are indicative of a greater or lesser degree of mechanical fragmentation.

Range must not be used to categorize voices unless the technique is well advanced, since it is primarily a reflection of functional efficiency rather than functional potential. A baritone with a good technique, for example, can often sing higher than a tenor with a poor one. Classification of voices based upon functional inadequacies leads to false presuppositions and serious pedagogic misjudgments. Vocal quality and natural tessitura—not range—are the primary considerations in determining vocal categories.

See **Register**

Rarefaction: the process of making less dense; in acoustics, the part of a sound wave in which the air particles set in motion by a vibrator are moving farther apart.

Ratio of Registration: See Registration, Ratio of.

Raucous Singing: harsh tonal qualities which result from an overly dominant chest register and a lack of genuine tonal resonance.

See **Resonance**

Reaching For a Tone: a physical contortion which results when the larynx rises with ascending musical patterns.

The direct cause of symptoms associated with reaching for a tone is an overly dominant chest register which has been moved too high in the tonal range. This condition invariably forces the larynx to rise, constricts the throat, and results in compensatory tongue and jaw tension. These faults can only be remedied by correcting the imbalanced registration which precipitated them.

See **Register**

Realistic Approach to Registration: a concept which acknowledges that only two muscular systems are responsible for the phenomenon of registration, but which considers the tones the two registers share in common (*i.e.*, the bridging area within the tonal range) to be the product of a separate mechanism.

Such a viewpoint is no more "realistic" than saying that green is a primary color because it differs from yellow and blue. To devise a training program based upon a nonexistent mechanical principle serves no functional purpose and merely leads to pedagogic confusion. In all probability, if the two vocal registers are not understood functionally, their interaction will not be understood either.

See Middle Register

Rectus Abdominus: an expiratory muscle (actually, a band of four flat muscles joined to each other by a tendon) which extends from the pubic bone to the cartilages of the fifth, sixth, and seventh ribs.

Recurrent Nerve: a member of the vagus nerve system whose transmission of electrical impulses causes the vocal mechanism to adjust reflexively to conceptualized stimuli of pitch, intensity and vowel.

Reed Theory: an acoustic theory borrowed from the family of man-made instruments, *i.e.*, the clarinet, oboe, *etc.*, to explain the nature of vocal functioning.

The reed theory is founded upon the principle of forced resonance, which holds that pitch is dependent upon and determined by the natural frequency of the air column rather than that of the vibrator. In this sense, the resonator consistently dominates the vibrator. The reed theory is partially operative during phonation in certain types of tone production where the vocal folds are forced into a conformation dictated by the shaping of the cavity. Unlike reeds, however, the vocal folds are capable of being adjusted to a wide variety of lengths and thicknesses by the muscle systems which draw them into tension. Consequently, there are times when the vocal vibrator will dominate the resonating system (*e.g.*, when tones are "too open") just as they can be dominated by the shaping of the resonating cavities (*e.g.*, when "covering").

See Cavity Tone Theory
   Coupling
   Covering,
      (To) Cover
   Standing Wave

While the interaction between cavity adjustment and vocal fold dimension will vary in response to the needs of tonal "coloring," under ideal conditions neither phonative element dominates the other. Under these technical conditions the vowel (tone) quality will emerge with absolute purity and the mechanism will operate at optimum efficiency.

Reedy Tone: an impure quality whose tonal characteristics are determined by a weak fundamental and strongly reinforced upper partials. Slightly nasal in quality, a "reedy" tone is a product of throat constriction.

Reflex: an involuntary act performed by means of an afferent impulse transmitted to a nerve center located in the brain stem and reflected to an efferent impulse.

Reflexive movements are governed by neurological impulses arising from motor nerve cells which, as they pass along fibers and branches, cause the muscle cells to contract. The branches traversed by the motor nerve cells trace what is known as a "reflex arc," which may be either simple or complex. A reflex arc comprised of three branches, for example, will be comprised of a sensory neuron, a connector neuron attached to the spinal cord, and an effector neuron. The rapidity of reflexive movements, which are far less fatiguing than those which are voluntary, is due the diversity of the pathways traveled by the neurological impulses.

There are two types of reflexive movement: 1) primary or unconditioned, and secondary or conditioned. The knee-jerk test provides an example of the former, while the classic experiment conducted by Pavlov using a bell, food and a dog (the dog learning to salivate at the sound of the bell) is an example of the latter. Most habitual responses belong to the Pavlovian category of conditioned reflex. From the standpoint of vocal pedagogy the distinction to be made between the two is important, since unconditioned reflexes always result in spontaneous, natural movement, whereas secondary reflexes substitute an artificial stimulus for an innate physical reaction by rechanneling impulses along auxiliary neural pathways.

Since it is apparent that a reflexive system cannot be acted upon, the avenues of approach essential to an effective solution to vocal problems are limited. There is a special advantage to be gained through the functioning of a reflexive system, however, namely its ability (when properly stimulated) to respond naturally, rapidly, with absolute precision, and with a minimal amount of fatigue. If this advantage is to be exploited, the principles and practices employed during training must be directed toward the stimulation of those involuntary muscle systems within the vocal tract whose function is directly responsible for the quality of the ultimate tonal product, and yet which cannot be consciously regulated or controlled.

There are other persuasive reasons why vocal training must rely upon procedures designed to stimulate reflexive movement: 1) the ideal position of the larynx is unknown and, like quality, which usually represents a present technical status rather than an intrinsically natural quality, it can only be conceptualized and experienced *after* vocal problems have been eliminated; 2) the mass per unit length, tension, mode and rate of vocal fold vibration are not susceptible to improvement by means of respiratory and/or articulatory controls, and 3) the intricate interpositioning and coordination among the involuntary muscular systems engaged in phonation cannot be replicated either through verbalization or by example.

With such considerations foremost in mind, it is not difficult to understand why the procedural options available for the development of vocal skills are circumscribed. A simple solution would be at hand were special breathing techniques, relaxation, the use of imagery, lowering the larynx, a precise positioning of the tongue, jaw and mouth, and/or emphasis on resonance capable of effecting a desired technical reconstruction. This is not possible, however, because the imposition of volitional controls violates a cardinal rule governing the behavior of all complex muscular activities, namely, that if but one member of a muscular complex is reflexive, *all members of the system must be treated as though they, too, were reflexive.* This principle precludes any hope of attaining a viable solution to vocal problems through recourse to mechanistic methods.

The excitation of reflexive movements during phonation represents the principal means by which the vocal mechanism can be stimulated into improved patterns of response. Of particular significance is the fact that, because they are natural and unlearned, such movements indicate to both teacher and student the functional potential of the mechanism and, by "announcing" themselves, reveal the underlying principles by which they are governed. Traditionally, the tone qualities resulting from the spontaneous activity of the vocal muscles under varying conditions have been incorporated into the concept of "registers," or qualities which emerge as a consistent and predictable reflexive response to specifically arranged patterns of pitch, intensity and vowel.

REGISTER

The accessibility of the vocal mechanism because of registration makes it possible to 1) improve the coordinate relationship among a broad group of involuntary muscles within the throat parts, 2) bring those systems into a higher state of tonicity, 3) institute conceptual controls based upon primary, unconditioned reflexes, 4) achieve an open-throated pharyngeal resonance adjustment, and 5) by stimulating natural movement, awaken the student's latent instinct for singing. Control over the functional elements involved in phonation must not be exercised until such time as they suggest themselves, however, since it is only *after* these reflexive systems have expressed themselves in movement that the mind is able to comprehend them and control their activity conceptually.

It is evident from a study of reflexive movements in phonation that the functional activities associated with an efficient tone production cannot be controlled by direct intervention. The role of the intellect is to observe the parallel relationships between stimulus and response, to become aware of the instinctual processes at work and to trust them, and ultimately to grow into an understanding of natural functioning. Unless training procedures are based upon principles which encourage natural functioning (the stimulation of unconditioned reflexes) as opposed to mechanistic methods (the imposition of artificial stimuli), the singer's vocal potential can never be realized.

Register: a group of like sounds or tone qualities whose origin can be traced to a special kind of mechanical (muscular) action. The term "register" is derivative, being used by organists to describe those changes of tone quality brought about by setting various "stop" combinations. As with the organ, the vocal registers appear to owe their distinctive tone qualities to separate kinds of mechanical action.

Two questions concerning the vocal registers have troubled theorists and pedagogues throughout the centuries: namely, "How many?" and "What do we call them?" Attempts to answer the latter have generally indicated one's attitude toward the former.

Except for a minority viewpoint, which considered the vocal mechanism to be composed of but one register, and registration to be a product of faulty technique, theories have generally fallen into two categories: 1) that there are two vocal registers, or 2) that there are three. The resulting systems of nomenclature reflect this difference in basic concept. Prior to the invention of the laryngoscope (1854), the registers were commonly known as chest and falsetto, or head voice, which is a falsetto-derived tone. Since that time there has been a proliferation of "mechanisms," but in all cases the registers appear to have been named after either their visual appearance, an area of sensual awareness (specific vibratory sensations), acoustic properties, or their position in the tonal scale. "Lower thick," "lower thin," "upper thick," "upper thin," together with "long reed," "short reed," "small," and similar expressions, for example, all report upon the appearance of the vocal folds as seen through a laryngoscope.

Contemporary scientific investigators, primarily interested in acoustic analysis, have introduced the terms "pulse," "modal," and "loft." Those more conservative adopt "lower," "middle," and "upper," terms which cite the position of the registers in the tonal range. "Chest," "middle," and "head" are carry-overs from an earlier nomenclature and indicate both the areas of the anatomy in which vibratory sensations appear to be concentrated, and the amalgamation of these sensual impressions as they fuse together in the mid-tonal range.

All of the foregoing indicates that tone qualities cannot be adequately described, and that most terminology consequently tends to be both inadequate and somewhat misleading. Since there are but two muscular systems to account for a mechanical difference in the vocal function, the cricothyroids and arytenoids, it seems evident, if a register is due to a mechanical adjustment within the laryngeal pharynx, that there can be but two registers as well.

With few exceptions, the two-register theory formed the basis upon which training methods had been founded from the fourteenth century, when they were called the *vox ficta* and *vox integra*, until the invention of the laryngoscope. In commenting upon the increase in register mechanisms reported as a result of laryngoscopic examination, Sir Morell Mackenzie, an eminent surgeon practicing during the latter part of the nineteenth century, had this to say:

> The actual mechanical principles involved are only two. In singing up the scale, the vocalist *feels* that at a certain point he has to alter his method of production in order to reach the higher notes. This point marks the break between the so-called "chest" and "head" registers, or what may be called the lower and upper storeys of the voice. This division of the voice is fundamental, all others being based either on convenience for teaching purposes, or on fantastic notions derived from subjective sensations or erroneous laryngoscopic observations.[91]

Physiologically, a register may be defined as a type of coordination between two groups of laryngeal muscles in which either one or the other of the tensor groups predominates. It is because of the interaction between these systems that the vocal folds adjust so that they become "thick" or "thin," that the impression of "higher" or "lower" tonal placement is created, that symptoms of vibration appear to concentrate in the chest or head, and that the singer becomes aware of the "break" which frequently divides the tonal range into two parts. This division will run anywhere from D to F♯ above middle C, depending upon the functional condition of the mechanism and the level of intensity being sung.

Unless the balance of tension shared between the two muscle groups involved in registration is equitable, neither the physiological symptoms, the acoustic properties, nor the proper length and thickness of the vocal folds will be present. In addition, the ambiguities surrounding the various transition points, especially the register "break," will remain.

From the standpoint of a practical nomenclature, it is advantageous to refer to the two registers in their primitive (isolated) form as chest register and falsetto, as distinguished from chest voice and head voice, which implies that some measure of coordination between the two exists, and that the tones produced possess acceptable musical properties.

The term "register" has also been used, somewhat imprecisely, to indicate tessitura or vocal range. Thus, a coloratura soprano is often described as singing "in a higher register," whereas a bass is said to sing "in a lower register." Although this usage is not scientifically accurate its reasoning is basically sound, since higher voices, regardless of sex, tend to settle into a head register-dominated balance.

[91]Sir Morell Mackenzie, *The Hygiene of the Vocal Organs* (Belmar, New Jersey: Edgar S. Werner & Co., 1928), p. 89.

The coloratura, for example, is seldom required to use the chest register, since her natural tessitura lies so far above the pitch range of that mechanism. Similarly, the bass sings in a chest-dominated registration and rarely employs the head register (except in its coordinated form and when singing softly). In each instance, however, both registers should always be present and work together as a coordinate unit.

BASIC REGISTER MECHANISMS

The basic register mechanisms are the chest and the falsetto. Qualitatively they are opposites. Both are inflexible, but the chest register sounds masculine and rough textured, and is produced by strength, whereas the falsetto is extremely breathy, toneless, "hooty," and of limited power.

The intensity pattern of each register is similar, increasing rapidly as the scale is ascended, but with the falsetto proportionately weaker throughout its range. Because the lower and weaker tones of the falsetto overlap the upper portion of the robust chest register by a fourth, the two mechanisms appear to be widely separated, and it is this awkward juxtaposition of high and low intensities that is responsible for the "break" in the voice.

The basic register mechanisms have been defined as a series of tones produced by the same mechanism, distinguishable because they differ qualitatively from another series of homogeneous sounds produced by another mechanism. Photographs taken of the vocal folds in motion substantiate this claim, proving that the sounds called "registers" correspond to extreme differences in the physical appearance of the vibrator. For example, in an isolated (pure) falsetto the edges of the vocal folds separate and look like an inverted Roman numeral V, whereas in the chest register their edges are drawn into a parallel position. They further show that these adjustments, which also involve differences in the length and thickness of the vibrating surface, correspond to specific patterns of pitch, intensity and vowel. It is, therefore, the manner in which the vocal folds are drawn into tension, and their resultant physical dimensions, that produces the contrasting qualities called "registers."

The importance of the concept of registration to the voice-building process is this: since the muscle systems involved react in a predictable manner to specific patterns of pitch, intensity and vowel, it is possible to control their function by manipulating these tonal elements. Normally, the two registers interact, for in order to sing, the cricothyroids and arytenoids (whose contraction maintains vocal fold tension) must combine their activity and function, well or badly, as a coordinate unit.

The location of the basic mechanisms, the chest register and the falsetto, is shown in Figure 15, together with the tonal areas established after they have combined to become the chest voice, the male "mixed" voice (*voix mixte*), the female "middle" voice (often mistakenly referred to as a "middle register"), the head voice, and the altissimo "flute" voice.

Of particular interest in this proliferation of "voices" is their proximity (with the exception of the flute-voice) to the register "break," a fact which indicates that they are not separate mechanisms, but the result of a particular type of interaction between the primary mechanisms, *i.e.*, the chest register and the falsetto. Certainly

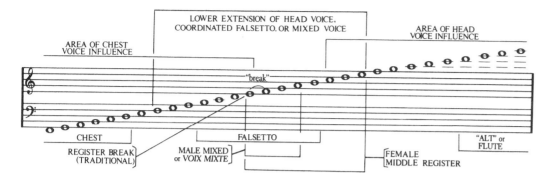

Figure 15. The basic register mechanisms and their areas of influence within the tonal range after they have been combined. Like the shades of green that appear by mixing blue and yellow, special tonal textures are attributable to a mixing or blending of the chest register and the falsetto. Each requires special treatment because of the wide discrepancy between their textural properties and intensity patterns in the area of the register "break."

the weakness in the lower extension of the female head voice, especially when noting its characteristic breathiness, betrays its affiliation with the falsetto and justifies the claim that it is a falsetto-derived tone quality. On the opposite side of the "break," the chest voice (male and female), unless it is isolated and becomes ugly and "shouty," reflects some degree of coordinate relationship with the lower extension of the falsetto, a condition erroneously referred to as "chest resonance."

Garcia used the expression "*voix mixte*" to indicate this juncture with male voices, an obvious reference to a process involving a joining of the basic register mechanisms. In more recent times the *voix mixte* has come to be known as the "head voice." This modification in nomenclature reveals a startling change in viewpoint between pre-twentieth century and contemporary methodology. Access to the head voice is now gained by a device known as "covering."

With women's voices, the strengthening of the lower octave of the head voice (pitches shared in common with their falsetto, B below middle C to its octave) encouraged a belief that this tonal area constituted a third or "middle" register. There are four weaknesses in this theory:

1. No separate mechanism exists to merit this designation;
2. The "middle" register, unlike the chest and falsetto, has no fixed boundaries, since the midrange of a well-used voice often embraces the entire range of one that is poorly produced;
3. Unlike the chest and falsetto registers, the "middle register" cannot be isolated, and
4. The mid-tonal range of women's voices, as of men's, shifts in accordance with the natural tessitura of each individual voice type, the midrange of the contralto being widely removed from that of the coloratura soprano.

For these and other reasons, the midrange of the various voice types cannot be considered a register. A "mixed" registration, in particular, would be easy to cure if a third register existed. Since it does not, such a cure is impossible unless the two register mechanisms which are improperly coordinated (the chest register and the falsetto) are restored to their rightful place in the tonal range. If a "mixed" registration is to be corrected, the wrongly combined parts, like a broken limb that has been improperly set, must be isolated in order to be reintegrated. Were the unique properties of the mid-tonal range, and particularly the area of the register "break," attributable to the presence of a third register, then by isolating this mechanism, correction of this fault would be far less tedious and time consuming. In the absence of a third mechanism, therefore, the postulate of a third register is a concept based on aesthetics rather than function.

If quality is used as the sole criterion for justifying the existence of a register, then there is some reason for believing that a "middle" register exists in women's voices. Smoothing the register "break" does transform the quality of the pitch range occupied by the lower extension of the head voice to give it special properties, a difference which led many early theorists to conclude that women's voices were comprised of three registers, while male voices had but two.

Mathilde Marchesi summed up the attitude of those empiricists who based their opinions upon what Mackenzie described as "notions derived from subjective sensations" in this statement:

> Empiricism, which in these days appears to struggle more than ever against the incessant progress made by all the sciences connected with the phenomena of the voice, as well as against all rules of modern pedagogy, has put in circulation, among other absurdities, the assertion that the female voice only possesses *two* registers, viz: Chest and Falsetto. This grave error has also been endorsed by several eminent modern physiologists, who have persuaded themselves that they have established this theory, after their observations with the laryngoscope, but who are incapable of making comparative experiments with their own vocal organs.[92]

[92]Mathilde Marchesi, *Bel Canto: A Theoretical and Practical Vocal Method* (New York: Dover Publications, Inc., 1970), p. xiv.

Marchesi's position is unsupportable, however, since examination of excised larynges has proven that the vocal organs are asexual, the sole difference between the mechanisms of men and women being one of size. Once the relationship of these qualities to their functional derivatives (the chest register and the falsetto) was lost, training procedures used in developing vocal skills came to depend almost exclusively on metaphysical concepts, imagery, and/or aesthetics. This emphasis has led in recent years to an almost exclusive concern for the art of singing, to the neglect of those processes involved in learning how to sing.

How the chest register and the falsetto interact, the stimuli to which they respond, as well as the general dynamics of the developmental process, are summed up under the subtitles that follow.

REGISTERS AND RANGE

The range of the basic register mechanisms is confined within prescribed limits. The upper extension of the chest register terminates at E above middle C. Its lower extension depends upon the voice type, male or female, and the classification to which it belongs—tenor, baritone, basso, contralto, mezzo-soprano or soprano. Thus, its lower extension can terminate anywhere from G below middle C, with women's voices, to the C two octaves below, with the lowest male voice, *i.e.*, the basso. The range of the pure falsetto is identical for all voice types, beginning a

B below middle C and extending to the octave above. When either of these mechanisms appears in its isolated form, it is incapable of producing aesthetically pleasing sounds.

Range extension occurs when the two register mechanisms combine to function as a coordinate unit. Under ideal technical conditions the overall range can include three full octaves, although two octaves of usable range is usually sufficient to accommodate the needs of most arias. However, range extension is not the sole criterion of vocal excellence, since the adjustment assumed by the pharyngeal cavities to resonate the vowel determines the qualitative properties of tone production. Nevertheless, without the coordinate activity of the two basic register mechanisms, aesthetically pleasing tone qualities and range extension are both impossible.

REGISTERS AND FLEXIBILITY

Vocal flexibility is totally dependent upon a registration dominated by the head voice, *i.e.*, a developed and integrated falsetto. Of the two basic mechanisms, the head voice alone is inherently agile; the chest register supplies solidity, strength and character to the tone quality, and serves as a throat-opening agent. All voice types, regardless of sex, weight or tessitura, depend upon a head voice-dominated technique for flexibility.

Weightier voices, usually of lower tessitura, inadvertently tend to overstress the stronger mechanism and underutilize the head voice. Consequently, male singers generally find it more difficult to acquire agility than do women. Overdependence upon the strength and vitality provided by the chest voice results not only in a loss of vocal flexibility and freedom, but also in tonal unsteadiness and an undesirable dependence on physical force.

REGISTERS AND INTENSITY

The relationship between registers and intensity is most obvious when attention is focused on the area of the register "break." One of the outstanding features of the "break" area is that the lower tones of the falsetto, and the head voice as well, noticeably weaken as they approach and overlap the chest register. Since the upper tones of the chest register become more powerful as they move upward into the *passaggio*, some accommodation must be made if the two parts are to work together as a harmonious unit. Intensity is one of the keys to effecting this compromise. For example:

1. High levels of intensity must be used to engage or isolate either register (with the falsetto, it will appear at first to be energy rather than intensity);
2. Lower levels of intensity tend to combine the registers—especially in the area of the break, and
3. All high tones, regardless of their intensity level, engage both mechanisms, and variations of intensity in this area reflect the ratio of tension shared by the two mechanisms.

The discrepancies of intensity within the break area noted above also affect the resonance adjustment negatively, since the laryngeal suspension is disturbed when the muscles stretching the vocal folds fail to coordinate properly. This disruption of normal function, together with the imbalanced registration indicated by the "break," accounts for the traditional difficulty singers have experienced in developing a seamless register transition.

Intensity is a key factor in remedying register imbalances, for since the upper tones of the chest register overpower the lower tones of the falsetto and head voice, the gap must be bridged by lowering the intensity of the chest register while gradually increasing the strength of the weaker mechanism.

REGISTERS AND PITCH

The frequency range (pitches) that can be articulated varies with the physical dimensions of the vocal folds. Tension brought to bear on the vocal folds, therefore, is expressed in patterns of adjustment which correspond basically to the low, medium, high, and highest pitch ranges of the singing voice. These changes in conformation take place as follows:

1. Lower Pitch Levels. For the lowest pitches of the singing range, the vibrating surface of the vocal folds must meet two requirements—length and thickness, the thickness of the surface being more important than its length. To accommodate these needs, the thyroarytenoids contract to increase the mass of the vibrating surface as a reflexive response to the singer's desire to sound a low pitch. Simultaneously, the arytenoids contract strongly, almost without resistance from the cricothyroids, their natural antagonists. The increase in vibratile mass resulting from this dominance of arytenoid tension introduces a homogeneous tonal texture commonly recognized as the "chest register."

2. Medium Pitch Levels. At medium pitch levels, a complex combination of muscular contractions changes the general contour of the vocal folds so that they become longer, somewhat thinner, and capable of supporting increased tension from the intralaryngeal and suspensory musculature. Each rise in pitch is met by a corresponding increase in tension on the lateral cricoarytenoids, the posterior arytenoids, the cricothyroids and the inner fibers of the vocalis muscles. The contracted cricothyroids, attached to the thyroid cartilage, cause the upper part of the larynx (the "Adam's apple") to tilt slightly forward. These complex muscular responses enable the vocal folds to adapt to the increase in tension and frequency necessary for the production of pitches lying in the mid-tonal range.

When the vocal folds have adjusted in the manner described, there emerges a new tonal quality, one which has been variously referred to as the "middle range," the "middle register," or the "middle voice." A more suitable analysis, however, would be to recognize this quality as a combination of the two basic mechanisms, the chest register and the falsetto, which are operating for the first time as a functional unit.

In the medium pitch range the vocal folds vibrate freely at their fullest length, although the contracted inner fibers of the vocalis muscles have caused a reduction in mass, or thickness. As pitch continues to ascend, however, there is a point at which the longer, thinner adjustment will also have outlived its effectiveness, since higher pitches and increased tension require another change in the contour of the vibrating surface. To meet these needs, the vocal folds assume yet another ad justment, one having an effect similar to the "stopping," or shortening, of a vibrating string. In phonation, this shortening of the vibrating surface is achieved by a process called adduction.

3. Higher Pitch Levels. To sing at higher pitch levels, the vibrating surface of the vocal folds must become shorter and thinner. An important feature of this rearrangement is adduction, a process in which the posterior portions of the vocal folds approximate and press together, thereby shortening the anterior segment left free to vibrate. This adduction is achieved by the combined action of the transverse arytenoids, the oblique arytenoids and the lateral cricoarytenoids. When brought under tension in response to rising pitch levels, greater portions of the vocal folds adduct and make contact; hence, the glottal space becomes smaller and the vibrating surface thinner. An exact parallel to this process is the working of the common zipper, which, when made to close, gradually reduces the aperture above the adducted parts. An unforced adduction of the vocal folds is essential to the free production of high tones and is largely dependent upon two factors: 1) a well-developed, properly integrated registration, and 2) a proper laryngeal suspension.

4. Altissimo ("Flute-Voice"). Tones beginning at the second C above middle C in the female voice, or altissimo, are qualitatively of two kinds: 1) those tones which sound "whistly" or flute-like, and 2) those which are full-bodied and can be swelled and diminished. Although the former are risky when permanent, they are extremely useful as the first step in a general filling-out process. Even those voices which never have occasion to use these notes can benefit from their study, since the flute-voice, as it is sometimes called, can be an important factor in the reduction of excessive tonal weight. Through skillful handling, this quality can reduce the "drag" in the voice which makes floating, effortless, soft high tones impossible to produce.

Physiologically, there is no special mechanism in the female vocal apparatus to account for these distinct qualities. Like all other sounds produced by the singing voice, these qualities are the product of cricothyroid and arytenoid muscular contractions. The "whistly" quality is the result of the larynx having been made to assume an abnormally high position by the contraction of the hypothyroid muscle, a contraction which pulls the larynx upward towards the hyoid bone. At the same time, the pyramid cartilages to which the arytenoids find their point of attachment are drawn forward, and the glottal space becomes extremely small. The overall effect is an abnormal elevation of the larynx, and consequently a narrowing of the laryngeal isthmus. Aesthetically, the tone quality emitted lacks fullness and power.

When the flute-voice is properly developed, the laryngeal suspensory muscles will hold with greater firmness at the second C above middle C to prohibit the larynx from rising, the arytenoids will brace against the increased pull of the cricothyroids, and the glottal space will become longer. Under these conditions, the "whistly" quality will disappear, the voice will fill out, and pitches in altissimo will become legitimate extensions of the tonal range.

REGISTERS AND RESONANCE

Effective resonance depends upon a precise tuning of the pharyngeal cavities. Since the larynx must be maintained in a stable adjustment (neither elevated nor lowered) to facilitate this tuning, how its affiliated muscle systems coordinate becomes a matter of crucial concern. Vocal fold tension, for example, either contributes to or inhibits laryngeal stabilization. Consequently, when these systems are poorly coordinated, and the registration is therefore imbalanced, the suspensory muscles (the thyrohyoids, stylopharyngeals, sternothyroids, and cricopharyngeals) cannot maintain an equilibrium. This imbalance disrupts the normal processes necessary to healthy function. As a result, resonance characteristics lack vitality, nasality becomes a problem, and the voice loses warmth and richness.

The most vital source of resonance is the laryngeal pharynx, a cavity which infuses the tone with "ring." To adjust it and other cavities making up the resonating system is impossible unless the registers are well balanced.

REGISTERS AND THE VOWEL

The response of the laryngeal musculature to vowel concepts necessarily involves changes in the ratio of registration, or balance between the chest voice and the head voice, assumed by the vocal folds. These changes can be heard by the attentive listener and are commonly recognized as being "vocal" sounds, or textures which "belong" to a particular pattern of pitch and intensity when different vowels are produced. One of the more obvious differences is that between "open" vowels and those that appear to be more "closed." Even to the casual listener it will be evident that the *ah* tends to be "too open," while the *oo* vowel seems not "open enough" and too "covered."

Tomograms (X-ray pictures which can exclude all those parts not in the axis of its rotation by having both the plate and the X-ray tube rotate during the exposure, thus isolating specific functional activities) taken by V.E. Negus, P.J. Rousselot, Dr. Friedrich Brodnitz, and others, clearly indicate that the physical conformation of the vocal folds is partially responsible for these changes, quite as much as it is for pitch and intensity. Indeed, even the ventricles may be observed to alter their dimension, being larger for the *ee* vowel than for any of the others, and larger for a "covered *ah*" than for open vowels that are "uncovered." Since the physical dimension of the vocal folds is determined by the ratio of tension assumed by the arytenoid and cricothyroid muscle systems that draw them into tension, *i.e.*, registration, it is evident that vowel production depends upon the physical conformation of the vocal folds, and not solely on resonance or cavity formation.

As is so often the case, the area of the register "break" dramatically emphasizes the relationship between the vowel and registration, and it is here that the natural inclination of the so-called "closed" vowels to minimize the thrust of the more aggressive chest register is quite apparent. Almost all teachers of voice agree upon the necessity of bridging the register gap, or developing the upper tonal range, by "covering" or changing from an "open" vowel to one more "closed." Since open vowels invite stronger chest register participation and the closed vowels more head voice, it is evident that the physical conformation of the vocal folds is affected by both registration and the vowel, and that "covering" may be used to induce greater head voice participation. (To consider "covering" within this context as a permanent good, however, is to deny the possibility that all vowels can be phonated with absolute purity within all pitch areas at all levels of intensity. What covering does indicate is that the different vowels can indeed alter the register balance in various ways, even when the same levels of pitch and intensity are being sung.)

Whether the pedagogic objective is to unify the registers or to separate them to correct an improper "mixture," a judicious matching of appropriate vowels to correct pitch-intensity patterns is crucial. The practical significance of specific vowels to registration and general technical development can be summed up as follows:

1. *Ah* requires more chest register participation than any other vowel and is easily activated, especially in lower tonal areas, by singing loudly with the mouth open. When the purpose of instruction is to separate the mechanisms, *ah*, sung at a level of high intensity and low pitch, is the most suitable exercise;

2. *Oo* is falsetto-oriented and is reluctant to join properly with the chest register. When used on a single tone and sung firmly with an excessively high rate of breath expulsion, it is most helpful in separating the registers and/or isolating the pure falsetto. Lowered intensity reflexively transforms the falsetto into the head voice. To introduce more head voice into the coordinate relationship when singing *ah*, one need only preface the exercise with an *oo*, i.e., *oo-ah*. Matching the texture of the *ah* to the *oo* will reflexively decrease the domination of the chest voice and incorporate more head register into the *ah*. Conversely, if the technique is dominated by an excessively strong head voice, the procedure should be reversed (*ah-oo*). Doing so should immediately supply more body and solidity to the tone, and

3. *Ee* tends to coordinate the registration, but if resonated improperly through a dependence on the mouth form, it will constrict the throat. All vowels, including the *oo*, should be resonated pharyngeally. The practical way to do this is to let the *ee* vowel migrate toward a more open *ih* or *eh*, and sense the vibrations within the identical area in which the *ah* resonates. The next step is to close the vowel gradually until the *ee* is phonated clearly and distinctly, but with the same tonal vitality as the *ah*.

While the various vowels can legitimately be considered important aids to technical efficiency (especially to registration), it is important to remember that vowels can only be as pure as the coordinative process will allow. They cannot, of themselves, improve the registration when the registers are insufficiently developed and respond improperly. When the registers are "mixed," vowels will continue to remain impure, and the registration will remain relatively unaffected by vowel manipulation. In the final analysis, careful, precise enunciation of the vowels will make the most of a present stage of development, but unless the technique is well advanced, it will do no more.

Register Balance: the proportion of tension distributed between two muscular systems, the arytenoids (chest register) and the cricothyroids (falsetto), as they contract when bringing the vocal folds to the requisite length, thickness and elasticity for the pitch, intensity and vowel pattern being sung.

The type of contraction brought to bear by these two systems determines whether or not they will counterbalance each other effectively, *i.e.*, maintain themselves in equilibrium. The quality of this relationship may vary in many ways, producing a spectrum of adjustments ranging from favorable to unfavorable. Each mechanism may be fully developed and properly integrated, each may be well developed as an independent unit, yet fail to work harmoniously with the other, or, either or both may be undeveloped or disproportionately developed in a variety of ways.

REGISTER BLENDING

To speak of a register balance, therefore, it is necessary to employ a descriptive modifier, as, for example, well-balanced, poorly coordinated, unevenly balanced, chest or head voice-dominated, or imbalanced.

Register Blending: the process which forms the two register mechanisms, chest and head, into a functional unit.

A "blended" registration is the opposite of a "mixed" registration: the former implies proper development and juncture, the latter, improper. Register blending should not be attempted until both register mechanisms are well developed and ready for integration. An indispensable exercise for the blending of the registers is the *messa di voce,* or the swelling and diminishing of a single tone. Register blending is synonymous with register mutation.

See Messa di Voce
    Register
      Development

Register "Break:" the point of separation between the two register mechanisms. Although the break is generally found in the vicinity of E to F above middle C, its exact position is dependent upon several variables, *i.e.,* the weight of the voice, the levels of intensity being sung, the vowel, and the general technical condition of the mechanism.

The abrupt tonal change occuring during a register "break" represents a physical adjustment that indicates a dramatic shift from one type of laryngeal muscular coordination to another. After the "break," the vocal folds, instead of maintaining their former position of approximation, readjust their dimensions and angulation in one of two ways. The first alternative, more common with men's voices, will find the vocal folds acquiring sharp, tautened edges and separating slightly. This adjustment decreases the amplitude of movement (the normal, pleasant vibrations that introduce a "singy" quality to the voice), sharply reduces the intensity, and permits excessive amounts of air to escape unchecked. The resulting tones become straight, breathy, weak in the lower extension of their range, and lacking in harmonic richness—qualities peculiar to the pure falsetto. The second alternative finds the vocal folds maintaining their position of approximation, but becoming longer and thinner, an adjustment qualitatively associated with the head voice.

The division between the two registers is easily detectable, therefore, because of a noticeable discrepancy between the texture and intensity of the upper tones of the chest register (a texture usually identified with masculinity and high levels of intensity) and that of the lower tones of both the falsetto and the head voice (each of which possesses the softer texture and lower intensity levels associated with femininity).

Unless the technique is well advanced, vocal training begins with the disengagement of a wrongly combined registration. This means that the "break" must be opened up so that each mechanism can be strengthened independently before the process of unification is begun. Premature obliteration of the break seals in errors and results in technical stasis. The "break" area can be said to be smoothed over correctly when it becomes possible to execute a *messa di voce* on all tones within that and other areas, without loss of range, resonance, or flexibility.

Skillful handling of the pitch-intensity patterns to effect changes in the register balance within the "break" area is essential if manipulative control over the involuntary muscles of the vocal apparatus is to be gained. When handled correctly, the result will be a distinct qualitative improvement in the eventual tonal product.

Register Change: an abrupt transition from one register balance to another that causes a break in the tonal flow.

A register change is justified 1) when the break is essential to the development of each register in its separated form before blending, and 2) for purposes of dramatic emphasis and "coloring."

Dramatic arias, as well as many songs, frequently demand noticeable register changes. The danger in using a divided registration, however, is that it can conceivably split the mechanism apart, ultimately causing a vocal breakdown. Such a failure is always traceable to a misuse of functional principles. The vocal norm involves a constant adding and subtracting, rebalancing, or coordination between the two mechanisms in order to establish a smooth juncture. Those who possess a well-developed vocal technique thus have at their disposal the option, rather than the necessity, of using the two mechanisms either separately or together.

See Registration,
Ratio of
Register Rotation

Register Coordination: the process of combining the two registers, the chest and the falsetto, and training them to work as a functional entity.

The benefits derived from the proper coordination of the registers include extended range, greater dynamic contrast, increased flexibility, and improved resonance, *i.e.*, those attributes generally associated with fine singing. Premature coordination of the registers (*i.e.*, complete juncture before each mechanism has been fully developed independently) seals in vocal faults and virtually precludes the possibility of further improvement. Physiologically, a coordinated registration finds an equitable distribution of tension among the following muscle groups: the lateral cricoarytenoids, the posterior arytenoids, the thyroarytenoids, the cricothyroids, and the vocalis muscles.

Register Development: the exercising and refining of those muscular processes which yield the two series of dissimilar tone qualities termed "chest" and "falsetto."

The purpose of register development is to bring all of the physical elements engaged in phonation into equilibrium, and thereby to balance an imbalanced mechanism. Generally, there are three stages involved in this process: 1) separation of the registers; 2) strengthening of each mechanism as an independent unit, and 3) subsequent unification. The necessity for each stage depends on the technical condition of the vocal mechanism, a condition which has little to do with the singer's length of previous study or professional status.

Register Isolation: a process designed to separate the chest register and the falsetto.

Register isolation is essential when the two registers are wrongly combined ("mixed"), and must occur before their independent development and realignment can take place. Isolation of the registers, therefore, represents an elemental or transitional stage in vocal development.

Although complete isolation of the registers is theoretically interesting, it is a questionable procedure pragmatically because of the limitations it would impose. A more practical solution is to encourage a small gap between the registers, thereby leaving the mechanism in a condition which permits it to continue functioning, while at the same time maintaining the separation necessary to independent development.

Register Mechanism: the muscular systems which yield tone qualities commonly recognized as chest register and falsetto.

The two primary muscular systems involved in registration are the cricothyroids and the arytenoids, which, together with their auxiliaries, respond reflexively to the pitch, intensity and vowel patterns conceptualized by the singer. Since these muscles move involuntarily and cannot be directly acted upon, their movement, and the manner in which they coordinate, must be influenced indirectly.

In a larger sense, the register mechanisms are part of the entire respiratory tract, since the elasticity of the folds is designed to answer the needs of respiration rather than vocalization. Much of the respiratory tract also functions as a digestive system, and it is the natural peristaltic movement associated with the act of swallowing that makes free vocalization so difficult.

Vocally, it is the manner in which the vocal folds are brought into tension for the pitch, intensity and vowel quality being sung which must be considered the basic register mechanism. The precision with which these movements occur determines the success or failure of the vocal process, and especially the laryngeal suspension so important to good resonance.

See Indirect Control
Laryngeal
    Suspension
Registration

Register Mutation: See Register Blending.

Register Overlap: a group of tones, ranging from B below middle C to the E natural above, that can be produced by either the chest register, the falsetto, or the head voice.

A successful balancing of the registers in the overlapped area produces a quality frequently identified as a middle register. Since, however, no separate muscular system exists to account for a third, or middle, register, this concept is without merit. Proper handling of the register overlap is similar in principle to the solution of those problems encountered in the area of the register "break."

See Middle Register
Register Break
Registration

Register Rotation: an aural perception of the textural changes which occur when the voice moves from one extreme of the tonal range to its opposite, when swelling and diminishing, or when negotiating larger intervals.

Every pitch, every level of intensity, and every vowel requires, ideally, a special setting of the vocal folds with regard to their length, thickness and elasticity. Each of these dimensions produces modifications of texture which are identifiable with either the chest voice or the head voice.

Since the symptoms associated with these mechanisms correspondingly create vibratory impulses centered in the chest and the head, both the change in registration and the symptoms aroused give the impression that the voice "rolls," or rotates, from one type of sensation and one locale to the other. Those who do not experience this feeling suffer to some extent from a "locked" registration, one in which a given setting of the vocal folds is maintained for several pitches rather than changing and rebalancing with each.

Register Segments: in singing, noticeable points of transition in the tonal range caused by a shift in the length and thickness of the vocal folds.

Since the same pitches can often be sung with the tautened vocal folds either shorter and thicker, or longer and thinner, these transitional points will vary somewhat. Roughly speaking, they coincide with the terminating point of the outer extremes of the pure falsetto (B below middle C to its octave) and the outer extremes of the coordinated falsetto, or head voice (F below middle C to its octave above, where the register "break" is located).

Women experience additional segmenting points at the upper F above middle C, and another at C# above high C. While these segmenting points can be obliterated, or disguised so as to be imperceptible, they nevertheless exist, and the careful listener will detect slight changes in the tonal texture as the singer passes from one segmenting area to another.

Segmenting points are also recognized as "lifts," but when this terminology is used there is seldom any connection made with registration.

See Segment

Registration: referring to the condition of the two register mechanisms, the chest and falsetto, whether they are working separately or together, the relative strength of each participating element, and the influence of these elements on the laryngeal suspension and resonance adjustment.

Most references to registration require a descriptive modifier for clarification, as, for example, isolated, well or badly coordinated, "mixed," or unified. Certain of these terms merit special attention and are discussed below under the appropriate headings.

ISOLATED REGISTRATION: a condition which finds each of the two register mechanisms, the chest register and the falsetto, functioning without coordinate relationship. A principle feature of an isolated registration is the wide "break" which separates the two register mechanisms. A truly isolated registration is rare and is found only with those who are said to have "no voice." Such voices are short-ranged, unable to sustain a legato line, inflexible, and without tonal beauty. However, by understanding how the registers work in their more primitive form (their textural properties and the special pitch-intensity patterns which evoke their response, as well as their reaction to different vowels), it is possible to grow into a fuller understanding of their potential interaction at more sophisticated levels of vocalization.

"MIXED" REGISTRATION: the product of an improper coordinative relationship between the two registers which results in compensatory muscular interference, throat constriction, and other serious vocal faults.

The registration is said to be "mixed" when the roles of the two basic mechanisms become reversed: that is, when the falsetto is overdeveloped and operates too low in the tonal range, while the chest voice thins out and moves too high into the upper-middle portion of the voice. Vocally, a "mixed" registration is comparable to a pianist who is forced to play his repertoire cross-handed instead of in the conventional manner: not only are serious technical limitations imposed, but sustained artistic expression is virtually impossible. Most singers are trained into a "mixed" registration by proponents of the one-register, or no-register, theory. The tonal range and intensity characteristics of a "mixed" registration are shown in Figure 16, below.

There are three kinds of "mixed" registration: 1) a chest register-dominated balance with the head voice improperly joined; 2) a coordinated head voice with a

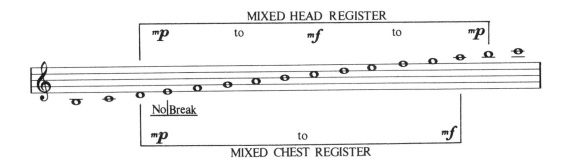

Figure 16. Showing the limited range and intensity of a "mixed" registration. Because the muscle systems which account for a "mixed" registration are severely imbalanced, they are unable to function properly, and throat constriction inevitably results.

deficiency of chest register development, and 3) a total mixture which obliterates the textural properties of both registers, leaving the voice short-ranged and incapable of withstanding pressure. Thus, if the textural properties of both registers cannot be detected in the tone produced, the registers are "mixed."

To correct a mixed registration, the registers must be separated, strengthened independently, and ultimately reunited in a more viable coordinate relationship. To effect the separation, each must be re-established firmly within its natural tonal range. Single, sustained tones sung at a firm *forte* will be most effective in each case: a loud, breathy *oo* will reinforce the falsetto within its proper tonal range (B below middle C to the octave above), and a strong, sustained *ah* in the low tonal range will encourage the isolation of the chest register. After the registers have settled into their rightful tonal areas, they must be strengthened independently through exercise, and gradually reunited.

RATIO OF REGISTRATION: the proportionate tension shared by the two muscle groups which adjust the length, thickness, and contour of the vocal folds in response to changing patterns of pitch, intensity and vowel.

Since the physical dimensions of the vocal folds should vary for each pitch, intensity and vowel pattern, the balance or ratio of tension shared between them must vary correspondingly. Under these circumstances, an untrained listener might perceive the voice to possess but one characteristic tone quality, or "one register." Most voices, however, are improperly balanced, and discrepancies in the ratio of registration are readily observable as "breaks," or more subtly, as points of segmentation, sometimes referred to as "lifts."

UNIFIED REGISTRATION: a complete, "seamless" juncture of the two register mechanisms.

If the registers are both highly developed and properly integrated, a unified registration is ideal: the voice will respond freely and precisely over a wide range of pitches (at least two and a half octaves), at any dynamic level, and, with the exception of women's upper voice range, on any vowel. If the voice is seamless, but fails to meet any of the above criteria, the registers are to a greater or lesser degree "mixed" and must be separated, strengthened independently, and ultimately reunited.

Registration and Sexual Identity: a relationship between organic systems and their functional potential, and the manner in which these systems are employed when used as a vehicle for self-expression, especially as these goals are conditioned by psychological factors and cultural conditioning.

Concepts identifiable with registration extend far beyond mere vocal mechanics and include attitudes of personal and sociological significance. As George Bernard Shaw so perceptively dramatized in his play *Pygmalion,* transforming the social status, dress and personality of Eliza Doolittle was inconceivable without a radical change of speech habits. One of the essential features of this transformation was a change from a chest register-dominated speaking voice to the higher pitched head voice, a registration which, at the time, was considered more feminine and "ladylike." It is of further interest to note that today, with emphasis on women's liberation and a trend toward unisex, the general pitch level of the male and female speaking voices has drawn closer together, those of men moving slightly higher and those of women considerably lower.

Similar parallels between general cultural trends and common modes of personal expression (manners, dress, vocal qualities, *etc.*) can be observed historically, indicating that a direct link exists between pitch levels (both spoken and sung), registration and sexual identity. In this regard, Dr. Friedrich S. Brodnitz, the noted throat specialist, wrote concerning the Baroque era that

> voices mirror not only individual characters but the spirit of a period as well. In this sense, the voice of the *castrato* personifies the bisexual ideal with its unity of a female voice in a man's body. In the mythological atmosphere of the Baroque opera, the *castrato* portrayed Gods and mythological persons who presented male and female characteristics in a vocal hermaphroditic combination.[93]

Opera provides many fascinating examples of vocal hermaphroditism, sexual and cultural stereotyping, and confused sexual identities, all of which involve registration. Thus, early eighteenth century operas (particularly those based upon the librettos of Metastasio) often used *castrati* to portray mythological characters, such as Jove and Venus, and metaphysical "non-persons," such as the Muses, Love, *etc.* Later, *castrati* were used to portray mortals popularly thought to be almost superhuman, an example of such a character being Handel's Giulio Cesare. Mozart, attempting to fulfill his lifelong dream of composing a successful *opera seria* (although by the last quarter of the eighteenth century they were virtually obsolete), assigned the role of Idamante in *Idomeneo* to a *castrato.*

More subtle and interesting, however, are the many examples of vocal sexual and social stereotyping, such as the frequent association of youth and nobility with higher voice types (Lucia-Edgardo, Violetta-Alfredo, Tristan-Isolde, *etc.*); the association of dominant masculine figures with baritones (Don Giovanni, Figaro, Escamillo, *etc.*); the association of lower female voice types with earthiness and sensuality (Princess Eboli, Carmen, Dalila, *etc.*); that of lower male voice types

See **Falsetto**
    Falsetto or
      Head Voice

[93]Friedrich S. Brodnitz, "The Age of the Castrato Voice," *Journal of Speech and Hearing Disorders* Volume 40, Number 3 (August, 1975), 294.

with paternalistic figures (Georgio in *I Puritani*, Rigoletto, Miller, Hans Sachs, King Marke, Wotan, *etc.*); that of comic basses with grotesqueness and social satire (Don Basilio, Falstaff, Beckmesser, Baron Ochs, *etc.*), and so forth. These stereotypes, although less common in a democratic society, nevertheless continue to occupy a place in a wide segment of the popular imagination.

As in real life, however, not all sexual identifications are so cut and dried, yet these, too, inevitably involve tone qualities associated with registration. Among the many examples of confused sexual identity in opera are the so-called "trouser roles" (Cherubino, Romeo in *I Capuleti ed i Montecchi*, Arsace in *Semiramide*, Octavian, *etc.*) and the use of special register effects to assume unexpected masculine or feminine characteristics (*e.g.*, Marcello's falsetto response to Rodolfo's invitation to dance in the last act of *La Bohème*). One of the most complex, interesting, and humorous examples of confused sexual identity is Octavian's masquerading, during the first and third acts of *Der Rosenkavalier*, as the delightful young maid Mariandel. In these scenes, we find a mezzo-soprano portraying a male teenaged knight-lover, who in turn is masquerading as a young female servant, *i.e.*, a female playing a male playing a female.

It may be seen, therefore, that concepts related to masculine and feminine are closely associated with the pitch ranges and textural properties yielded by the vocal registers, and that these, in turn, are identifiable with specific emotional and psychological attitudes. In more sophisticated form, these characteristics are perceivable in the singer's interpretative efforts, since the tone colors used to "orchestrate" a song or aria similarly derive their vocal properties from those tonal textures contributed by either of the two basic register mechanisms, or by some combination of them.

The functional importance of registration transcends issues exclusively concerned with tone production, since efficiency in that area merely provides the mechanical means to express individual thoughts and feelings. By placing his vocal skills at the service of communication, each singer makes a personal statement concerning himself and the material which he has chosen to perform. On these terms, he becomes a spokesman for all humanity, articulating thoughts and feelings pertinent to his time and place. While such statements can be made and received on many levels, they will nevertheless mirror, as Dr. Brodnitz so perceptively remarked, both the individual and the spirit and emotional climate of a period. Registration and sexual identity play a prominent role in determining the specific pattern of that identification.

Rehearsal Voice: soft singing whose purpose is to reduce vocal wear and tear; "marking."

Marking must be executed with an energy level sufficient to maintain an open-throated resonance adjustment, with the head register strongly dominant. If prolonged or done incorrectly, it can be extremely detrimental, reinforcing an improper coordination, promoting throat constriction, and thereby fatiguing the voice prematurely. Paradoxically, those who consistently "save" their voices are frequently the first to lose them.

See **(To) Mark**

Reinforcement: acoustically, the amplification of the natural frequency of a vibrator by an adjacent resonator tuned to the same frequency.

In singing, tonal reinforcement, interference, and phase are products of the wave forms generated by the vibrating vocal folds, and of the dimensions of the pharyngeal cavities which amplify these vibrations.

Relative Pitch Theory: an acoustic theory based upon the premise that the dominant partial or partials of a musical tone are always relative to the frequency of the fundamental.

Scientists have advanced numerous theories which partially account for the sound-producing capacities of the human voice. None of these, however, provides the complete answer.

See **Fixed Pitch Theory**
Formants
Harmonic Theory
Puff Theory

Relax the Throat: a directive which is at best a physical impossibility during phonation, and at worst a source of throat constriction.

Relaxation does not eliminate incorrect muscular tension (*i.e.,* tenseness), nor does it rechannel energy within the coordinative process; it is merely a prephonatory condition of readiness. Vocal tone is the product of energy, muscular tension, and resistance. All three are required to maintain an open-throated resonance adjustment, and must be properly utilized if the mechanism is to function efficiently. To deliberately attempt to relax the throat by whatever means (wagging the head from side to side, *etc.*) may afford momentary relief while silent, but unless a radical change in approach is made, the throat stiffness it was intended to relieve will recur with the resumption of phonation.

Advice given to "relax the throat" addresses itself to a symptom, and when acted upon, reverses the intention of the directive.

Relaxation: the release of muscular or nervous tension; the lengthening that characterizes inactive muscles.

A frequent antidote for tenseness, the pedagogic directive "Relax" implies that, since effort is being misdirected, it is better to do nothing. Relaxation, however, is merely a preliminary condition of readiness: it is essential to free response, but not part of the response itself. Correct affirmative action, *i.e.,* tension within the coordinative process without tenseness, is the cause of the apparent relaxation and ease of execution so common to great singers.

Muscles cannot contract without tension. Since the vocal mechanism is wholly comprised of muscle and cartilage, and must assume a wide variety of adjustments to meet phonative needs, it is evident that vocal tone is impossible without tension. Tension, however, must not be confused with tenseness, nor relaxation considered an antidote for poor physical coordination.

Reserve Breath: inspired air which remains in the lungs after a normal cycle of inspiration and expiration is completed. Reserve breath accounts for about 60% of the 3-quart capacity of normal or average lungs.

Reserve breath helps maintain the respiratory equilibrium characteristic of good singing. To sustain vocal tone, air compression in the lungs must be built up and maintained to ensure that reserve breath is not drawn upon at the end of a musical phrase. When the technique is inefficient, or if the singer overextends himself, reserve breath must be used. When this happens, air compression and the energy supplied to the muscle systems through oxidation are dissipated. As a result, the

See Breathing
    Energy

natural respiratory equilibrium essential to a correct tone production is lost, only to be recovered after a brief period of rest.

Residual Breath: inspired air which cannot be voluntarily expired from the lungs.

Accounting for about 25% of the 3-quart capacity of average human lungs, residual breath remains in the lungs even after forced exhalation; it only escapes completely when the lungs are deflated. Residual breath is often confused with reserve breath; neither should be used in singing.

Resistance: the action of one force or source of energy against another.

Resistance is an important element in phonation. Among its positive contributions is the bracing of one muscle or muscle system against the contraction of another (known as synergy) in order to maintain the vocal mechanism in equilibrium. Another has to do with energy, which, if it is to be conserved, must meet with resistance. Examples of this type of resistance can be observed in the steam-boiler, the sails that harness energy to move a boat through the water, and, hypothetically, in a situation where an irresistible force meets an immovable object. In singing, resistance is provided because the approximated vocal folds close the laryngeal exit to build up lung compression. Another source is the false vocal cords, whose narrowing offers what Charles Lunn described as a "point of resistance."

Since resistance is functionally essential to energy economy, a qualitative distinction must be made between proper and improper muscular resistance. In the latter instance, a more correct term to describe this condition would be "interference."

See Anxiety
    Emotion
    Energy
    Natural Movement

The expression "resistance" is also used with reference to psychological attitudes which, because of a fear of expansive movement, result in a partial immobilization of the muscle systems essential to phonation.

Resistance, Point of: a term introduced by the nineteenth century theorist and teacher Charles Lunn, and championed by Edmund J. Myer, to describe the function of the false vocal cords in resisting breath flow.

It was Lunn's contention that the elasticity of the vibrator must be perfectly uniform to ensure regularity of vibration, and consequently steadiness of tone. Uniformity of air supply, he found, could not come from the vocal folds, since he believed them to be dependent for their motion on the breath, and therefore unable to control it. On the other hand, if the false vocal cords present both a narrow and a constant opening, it is they which are able to most effectively control the breath flow, steady the tone, and, as with a lock in a canal, create a counterforce, or supraglottal pressure system. Thus, as the pressure variations set in motion by the vocal folds become more ample, the backward and downward pressure caused by air impounded within the ventricular sacs (due to a narrowing of the space between the false vocal cords) will increase correspondingly to ensure tonal steadiness at all levels of intensity.

The current pedagogic neglect of Lunn's formulation doubtless stems from the fact that there appears to be no practical mechanical control available to directly effect this narrowing movement. It is likely that Lunn's theory is correct, but that this point of resistance produced by a narrowing of the false vocal cords depends upon other factors in the coordinate relationship of the functional parts involved, such as respiratory equilibrium, registration and a proper laryngeal suspension.

Resonance: a spontaneous reinforcement and amplification of tonal vibrations which occurs whenever a cavity is tuned to the natural frequency of the pitch being sounded.

An important fact of resonance is that the column or cavity does not create energy, but merely causes energy to be absorbed at an increased rate; by making the tone louder, this increase dissipates energy more rapidly. Thus, a tuning fork, for example, will continue to vibrate for a longer period of time when it has been made to vibrate independently than when it has been made to excite a cavity or another vibrator. While an increase in loudness during phonation is due to an increase in the delivery of energy at the tonal source by neurological innervation, vocal fold tension and breath compression, it is nevertheless essential to the production of well-defined vowels that the cavities of the throat and mouth are "tuned," or adjusted, to select those frequencies in the absence of which vowel definition would be impossible.

The efficiency with which vibratory impulses set in motion by the vocal folds are absorbed and amplified is not solely a matter of cavity tuning, but is also attributable to forced and sympathetic vibration. However, while both forced and sympathetic vibration add a certain vitality to the tonal product, these must be recognized as resultant acoustic properties whose character is determined by 1) the quality and intensity of the energy input at the sound source, 2) the physical dimensions of the cavity or cavities serving as resonators, and 3) the weight and solidity of one's bone structure.

Since the neurological and muscular activities involved in generating energy and adjusting the pharyngeal cavities can either be well coordinated or poorly coordinated, the problem of obtaining optimum resonance must be addressed by devising techniques for stimulating the appropriate muscle systems so that a physical condition exists which *creates resonance spontaneously.* In the absence of such physical coordination, the singer is obliged to rely upon devices and practices which attempt to "make" resonance, and which must inevitably be contrived and artificial.

To energize the frequencies necessary to define both pitch and vowel over a wide tonal range, the cavities employed for tonal resonation must be flexible rather than fixed, as they must accommodate a wide variety of different frequency combinations. The three cavities most suitable for this purpose are the larynx and the laryngo- and oropharynges. Of these, the larynx is especially important, since the muscle systems which tense the vocal folds and connect with other elements of the respiratory process meet there, and any disturbance of its natural equilibrium disturbs other related functions as well. With the larynx stabilized, the laryngopharynx is able to consistently tune to resonate those frequencies ranging from 2800 to 3400 cycles per second to produce the "ring" in the voice. Inasmuch as this phase of tuning is independent of changing vowel patterns or articulatory movements, the voice is capable of sustaining a pure legato flow of tone.

It may be seen, therefore, that if the tuning of the larynx and the laryngopharynx is consistently "set" to resonate a frequency range extending from 2800 to 3400

See **Breath Pressure Theory False Vocal Cords**

cps, the oropharynx must be responsible for selecting and concentrating the energy generated at the sound source into those frequency bands, or formants, which differentiate the numerous vowel sounds. The oropharynx is ideally equipped for this task, since it is easily adjustable within its own boundaries, capable of being made firmer or softer, and capable of being raised or lowered, arched or widened.

Since eighty to ninety percent of all tonal energy is concentrated within well-defined vowel bands, or formants, and since formants are selected by adjusting the pharyngeal cavities in response to the vowel, it is evident that skill in producing beautiful, resonant tones has to do with physical coordination within the throat parts. How to include or exclude tracheal resonance, how to respond to or reject those influences exerted by ever-changing mouth positions, and how to change the response patterns responsible for these adjustments, are questions that have to be answered satisfactorily if the singer is to acquire vocal skills commensurate with his talent potential.

Extensive research carried out by Paget, Sundberg and others substantiates this concept of resonance, and demonstrates that the laryngo- and oropharynges operate as a double resonating system. In this type of resonation, two or more cavities can be tuned either separately or together. When a single cavity is used as a resonator, it must present firm reflecting surfaces and be lightly damped, but this condition does not necessarily apply to a double resonating system. What is particularly striking in the above findings is the fact that when two cavities are coupled, their physical dimensions are relatively inconsequential, neither the exact shape, cross section nor surface quality (hard or soft) noticeably affecting the resonance characteristics.

Even more far-reaching in importance, it was found, is the manner in which these cavities interact in conjunction with the vibratory pattern and physical conformation of the vocal folds. Depending upon their muscular tonicity (high or low), whether they are well coordinated or poorly innervated, those muscle systems (the supra- and infrahyoids and the palatals) which stabilize the larynx and adjust the pharynges to resonate the vowel cannot avoid constricting. Resonance, therefore, is not solely a matter of precise cavity adjustment (tuning) for the vowel, but equally one of coordination involving vocal fold tension.

Two facts of unusual importance to pedagogic practice emerge from an understanding of cavity resonance: 1) that the amount of energy produced by a vibrator (*e.g.*, a violin string or the vocal folds) is dissipated in inverse proportion to the amount of resonance generated, and 2) that neither a proper shaping of the mouth nor an arbitrary positioning of the tongue and palate, *etc.*, addresses itself to basic technical needs.

In the first instance it is evident that in order to increase resonance, energy must be concentrated within the vocal generator. This fact is substantiated by the acoustic presence of a standing wave, which finds the pressure oscillations at their optimum point of amplitude at the glottis (or vibrator), and at their minimum amplitude at the lips and teeth. Raoul Husson noted this in his experiments, finding that a mere twenty percent of the vocal intensity generated at the sound source (the laryngeal area) passed beyond the mouth of the singer. Consequently, to issue directives such as "bring the tone more forward," "get it in the facial mask," and "up and over," fails to increase the delivery of energy at the tonal source, and as a result decreases rather than increases resonance.

In the second instance cited, it goes without saying that a proper positioning of the articulators is totally unrelated to problems concerning the development of the muscle systems noted above. It utilizes no principle geared to the stimulation of reflexive, natural movement among those laryngeal and pharyngeal muscles which cannot be volitionally controlled, and upon whose movement tonal freedom and efficient resonance is wholly dependent.

Ideally, resonance (used in conjunction with the manipulation and selection of different vowel phonemes) and registration are of equal importance during training. In actual practice, however, the course of the instruction will often require a shift in emphasis. With poorly formed voices, registration is always more crucial, because a well-tuned resonance adjustment is impossible when the registers are either imbalanced or poorly developed. On the other hand, when the technique is advanced, the resonance adjustment demands greater attention than the registration, since the efficiency of the registration can be enhanced under certain conditions by concentrating on the resonance adjustment. During intermediate stages of development there will be a dual emphasis; each lesson will include those exercises designed to correct the registration, as well as those whose intent is to refine the resonance adjustment.

COMMON MISCONCEPTIONS

The vibratory impulses generated at the sound source and amplified by adjustments made within the vocal tract create impressions of resonance which are misleading, and that result in pedagogic practices based upon symptoms rather than the causative factors to which they owe their being. These are discussed under the headings that follow.

CHEST RESONANCE: a term used to describe sensory perceptions experienced by many singers in the thoracic area. The expression is, of course, a misnomer, since there are no cavities in the chest suitable for tonal amplification. In fact, the chest is a cage filled with spongy materials that dampen, rather than reinforce, tonal vibrations.

Undoubtedly, the sensations of vibration experienced by many singers in the chest arise from two characteristics of resonance: 1) the participation of the trachea and bronchi in the tonal amplification of lower pitches, and 2) vibrations radiating through the skeletal framework by means of bone conduction.

HEAD RESONANCE: vibratory sensations experienced in the facial mask or in various parts of the head.

There is little or no resonance in the head and sinus cavities. The entry into the sinuses is small and the cavities themselves are heavily damped with mucous membrane. An additional negative factor is that their structure admits no possibility for adjustment or readjustment. Scientific investigators have repeatedly disproved the validity of head resonance by stuffing the nasal passages with gauze to dampen the reverberation, and then recording the absence of a measurable effect on the resonance characteristics.

The symptom of vibration that appears to resonate in the facial mask is doubtless caused by forced vibrations which are conducted through the bone structure and experienced in various parts of the anatomy. An awareness of localized vibration, however, does not necessarily indicate that a condition of genuine resonance exists, but merely that vibratory impulses are being transmitted. Furthermore, the transmission of vibration is not under the direct control of the singer. He does not transmit the impulses, he merely sets the vibratory pattern in motion.

Since the transmission of sound is more efficient through a tensed medium, the sensation of vibration felt in the head can often indicate the presence of false tension, and therefore an undesirable technical control. A perfectly free tone production, like the perfect golf swing or tennis stroke, is notable for its absence of localized tension; the exhilarating sense of free movement transforms all activity into a harmonious totality free of localized sensation.

Symptoms of vibration mistakenly attributed to head resonance are inseparable from a falsetto-derived tone quality or head voice. Whether the resonance characteristics can be described as "good" or "bad," however, depends upon the condition of the registration and the quality of the pharyngeal adjustments formed by the singer. All tones produced possess some characteristic of resonance, and it is easy to confuse these characteristics with the type of registration currently in effect. Thus, when the singer experiences strong sensations of vibration in the facial mask, or appears to be singing in the so-called "head" or "chest" voice, the symptoms must be attributed to bone conduction. The strength of the symptoms transmitted depends upon the amount of energy generated by the vibratory impulses originating within the laryngeal area.

MOUTH RESONANCE: a belief that by forming the oral cavity properly, the vowel will be both purified and vitalized; an objective usually associated with such directives as "get the tone out of the throat."

The measurable resonance characteristics that can justly be attributed to the mouth cavity are so negligible as to eliminate this postulate from serious consideration.

To act as a tuned resonator, a cavity must present firm yet adjustable surfaces, and these must be capable of maintaining a stable position if the vowel is to be kept from migrating. The mouth cavity offers no such advantage. The cheeks are soft and fleshy, its floor is comprised of muscle and cartilage, and during the articulation of consonants, it is in a constant state of flux. Mouth-resonated tones "lock" the mechanism and are synonymous with impure vowels and "mushy" tone qualities.

The mouth, therefore, must be considered no more than a housing for the articulators, and one of the primary goals of training should be to detune it as a resonating agent. When this has been successful, the laryngo- and oropharyngeal cavities will be free to perform, as Manuel Garcia so aptly put it, "as the real mouth of the singer."

Pharyngeal resonance is indispensable to the sustaining of constant vowel qualities, since any change in cavity dimension alters both the resonance characteristics and the vowel. Proper coordination among the muscle groups which position these cavities, as well as the adjustments assumed by the vocal folds, represent the basic functional elements which determine the efficiency of the vocal process. Attempts at mouth resonance promote muscular interference, tense the jaw, tongue, and facial muscles, and generally disturb the smooth interaction between tone and text.

To a certain extent, the mouth cavity, while not a resonator, may be considered a superficial aid in effecting improvements within the laryngeal musculature; while it is true that all vowels should be resonated pharyngeally, the fact remains that the pharyngeal cavities do tend to pattern their form after a mouth position. It is also true that registration is somewhat affected by the character of the mouth position. A wider opening is more favorable to the production of so-called "open" vowels, and induces a higher percentage of chest register response. Conversely, a narrower mouth position will facilitate the production of the more strongly head register-dominated "closed" vowels. Neither a "mixed" registration nor throat constriction, however, is materially improved or corrected through a dependence upon prepared mouth positions or mouth resonance.

NASAL RESONANCE: sensations of vibration experienced in the nasal passages, or facial mask, brought on by radiation, bone conduction, sympathetic and/or forced vibration.

Neither the nasal cavities themselves nor the sinuses (six in number) can be considered resonators, and that possibility has been widely discredited by scientific investigators. Contrary to the usual sensory impression, scientists have found that a stronger concentration of energy exists in the laryngeal area even when the singer perceives the resonance characteristics to be centered in the facial mask, or head.

The illusion which persuades the singer that his voice is resonating in the head cavities is due to bone conduction and forced resonance, by means of which vibratory energy is transmitted from the laryngeal source into outlying areas. Extrinsic muscular tension (stylohyoid, palatopharyngeal, sternothyroid, hyoglossus, cricopharyngeal, and omohyoid) is largely responsible for this phenomenon, and these systems, through their connection with the spinal vertebrae, transform the entire body into a complex vibrator. The precise arrangement of the tension potential involved accounts for the different types of sensation experienced by the singer.

SOUNDING BOARD RESONANCE: a form of forced resonance whereby vibratory impulses generated at the sound source (a tuning fork, the strings of a piano or violin, the vocal folds) are amplified.

Unlike cavities whose selectivity varies with the size of the opening, the dimension of the cavity, and the type of surface (hard or soft), a sounding board will amplify a broad range of frequencies indiscriminately, its resonance characteristics being determined by the size, mass and surface of the board. It is probable that the skeletal framework of the body acts as a sounding board, since it is apparent that vibratory impulses generated at the sound source are transmitted through the various bone structures. Singers have perceived these sensations, referring to them as "chest" and "head" resonance, but such perceptions are rather subjective, and it is unlikely that the amplification of vibratory impulses through bone conduction is more than marginally significant.

The hard palate may conceivably be considered a vocal sounding board, but its effectiveness in this capacity has yet to be verified. It is important to remember, however, that the reflection of vibrations by the hard palate, if it occurs, does not amplify or resonate the tone, but merely aids in its transmission.

See Cavity Tone Theory
  Coupling
  Double Resonator
  Fixed Pitch Theory
  Forced Vibration
  Formants
  Laryngeal
    Suspension
  Relative Pitch
    Theory
  Register
  Resonance Cavity
  Sympathetic
    Vibration
  Twenty-Eight
    Hundred
  Vowel Manipulation
  Vowel Modification

RESONANCE ADJUSTMENT

Resonance Adjustment: a positioning process involving the cavities of the throat and mouth which occurs as the respiratory and digestive tract is transformed into a sound-producing instrument.

The movement from relaxation to balanced tension is known as the "attack," and it is at this moment that the larynx and pharyngeal cavities reflexively position themselves to form a resonance adjustment.

Resonance Cavities: those cavities of the throat and mouth which, by a process of tuning, amplify the tonal vibrations set in motion by the undulating vocal folds and act as selective resonators of the vowel.

For a cavity or cavities to act as selective resonators, they must meet certain requirements. Foremost among these is an ability to adjust and interadjust and to lie in close proximity to the vibrator. In addition, they should possess reflecting surfaces capable of being firm or soft, of being made longer or shorter, of being enlarged or narrowed without engaging constrictor tensions, and of maintaining their stability without interfering with the articulatory processes.

There are six cavities which can be considered a potential source of vocal resonance. Listed in the order of their position within the vocal tract, lower to higher, these are the following: 1) the trachea; 2) the larynx; 3) the laryngopharynx; 4) the oropharynx; 5) the nasopharynx, and 6) the mouth.

THE TRACHEA: a tube lying below the larynx that conveys air into the lungs. The trachea is made up of eighteen flexible cartilages forming a three-quarter circle, the posterior circumference being completed by transverse fibers known as the trachealis muscle. The dimension of the trachea is decreased by the contraction of the trachealis, and enlargement of the trachea takes place when these muscle fibers relax, a condition most favorable to the resonation of low tones.

The value of the trachea as a resonator is sometimes discounted because of the fact that this cavity lies below the larynx, and tone does not pass through it when moving into the surrounding atmosphere. However, every time a compression wave is formed above the glottis, pressure below is correspondingly decreased, and a rarefaction wave is formed. Consequently, the vibratory pattern both above and below the glottis moves in phase, and the trachea then functions as a resonator. Subglottal pressure within the trachea nevertheless constitutes a problem because it interferes with the resonation of higher pitches. Fortunately, this cavity is easily detuned, a process set in motion by the contraction of the cricothyroid muscles. The contraction of those muscles increases as the pitch rises, and causes the thyroid cartilage to tilt forward. This shuts off all tracheal resonance and eliminates the sympathetic vibrations emanating from that source. Thus, the trachea can be coupled or uncoupled by means of tonal concepts.

THE LARYNX: a valve guarding the entrance to the trachea, designed to keep food, liquids and other foreign substances from entering the lungs. Its lower border connects with the tracheal rings, while its upper boundary terminates at the epiglottis. Divided into an upper and lower portion by the glottis, or space between the vocal folds, it is also used as a vocal organ. The larynx houses the vocal folds and provides an area for the build-up of both subglottal and supraglottal pressure

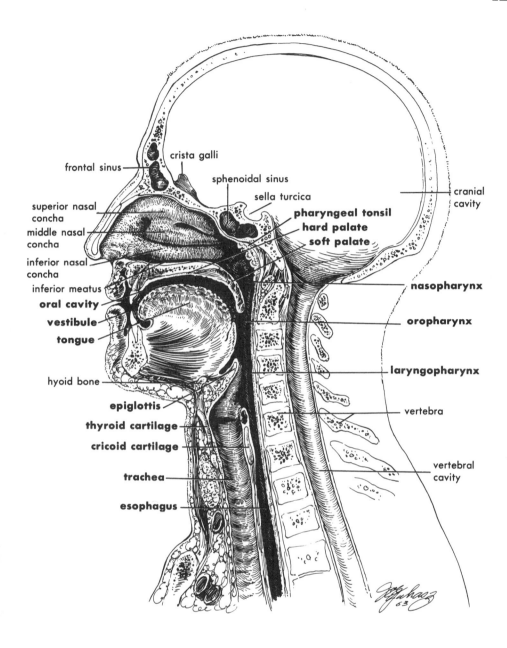

Figure 17. Showing the cavities of the throat and mouth capable of being used for the resonation of vocal tone. From James E. Crouch, Functional Human Anatomy, *Third Edition (Philadelphia: Lea and Febiger, 1978). By permission.*

THE LARYNGOPHARYNX: the upper portion of the larynx, beginning at the superior surface of the vocal folds and ending at the upper tip of the epiglottis. Thus, the upper portion of the larynx and the lower area of the laryngopharynx are one and the same. Immediately above the true vocal folds lie the oft-forgotten false vocal cords. These perform an important function during phonation: when they narrow to check the breath flow, air is impounded within the ventricular sacs (the pouches between the true and false vocal cords) to create a supraglottal pressure system.

Since every alteration in the size, shape, width and/or length of aperture alters the resonance characteristics, as well as the qualitative properties of the tone produced, the narrowing of the false vocal cords, the inflation of the ventricular sacs, and the manner in which the larynx, the laryngopharynx and oropharynx are formed and adjusted in response to the singer's tonal concepts become matters of crucial technical importance. The laryngopharynx serves as the primary resonator of vocal tone and is responsible for introducing the "ring" into the voice.

THE OROPHARYNX: a highly adjustable cavity ideal for tonal resonation. Located at the back of the mouth, the oropharynx is bounded above by the nasopharynx and below by the laryngopharynx. Because of its innate flexibility, it is responsible for the production and resonation of numerous vowel sounds. A further advantage is that it can be tuned either separately or collectively with the larynx.

The oropharynx is directly influenced by the movement of the larynx, especially when the thyroid cartilage tilts forward, as is normally the case when the scale is ascended. When the uvula is slightly raised and the soft palate area expanded, there is a corresponding enlargement of the throat parts, an adjustment essential to the production of "dark" tone qualities. This process can also be reversed without constricting to produce "bright" tone qualities, and it is a combination of these adjustments which produces a wide variety of tonal "colors." The oropharynx and the resonance it generates are affected negatively when the larynx either rises or descends excessively.

THE NASOPHARYNX: lying immediately above the oropharynx, it is a poor resonator, being highly damped, and nonadjustable; because of the tiny opening joining it to the cavities below, it is virtually inaccessible.

THE MOUTH: a most inefficient resonator. It is too involved with articulation, too mobile and too fleshy to answer the needs of genuine resonance. Apart from articulation, its role is largely that of adjusting to a form that assists proper pharyngeal activity, and to a considerable extent, the registration. X-ray studies of professional singers made by George Oscar Russell (1931) prove rather conclusively that the mouth is not an important phonative factor, either in vowel formation or in resonance.

While the oral cavity cannot be considered a resonator, its adjustment inevitably influences the physical dimensions of the laryngo- and oropharynges, and without doubt alters the resonance characteristics of the vocal tract. Since, however, neither the exact shape, cross section, nor length of the cavities is of consequence in double resonating system (as Sir Richard Paget proved in his experiments), it possible, and even desirable, for movements within one area to take place while leaving the function of the other undisturbed. This can be demonstrated on a pragmatic level, because it is not at all difficult to sing a well-defined *oo* vowel while the mouth is maintained in a smiling position.

Although a larger or smaller opening of the mouth, lip rounding, a smiling p sition and/or a pursing of the lips may be useful devices, they are, when the technique is correct, matters of choice rather than necessity, since neither the size of the mouth opening nor its physical conformation is of any real importance to the production of either pure vowel phonemes or tonal resonation.

Resonating System: the cavities of the throat and mouth (the larynx and laryngopharynx, the oropharynx, and mouth) which amplify the vibrations set in motion by the vocal folds to produce a singing tone.

Resonation: a re-sounding or amplification of the initial source of vibration set in motion by the vocal folds when the natural frequency of the cavity and that of the vibrator coincide.

Respiration: the life-sustaining physical process in which an organism takes in oxygen, distributes and utilizes it in oxidation, and releases carbon dioxide or other waste.

Respiration is one of the few areas of the functional process over which the singer can exercise volitional control. Consequently, various pedagogic procedures have been developed to "control" breath expenditure, inspiration, expiration, and the working of the diaphragm, whose contraction and relaxation coincide with and reflexively assist the respiratory process. The functional benefits of these procedures, however, are questionable.

See Breathing

Respiratory Air Stream: See Air Stream.

Respiratory Scaffolding: a physical condition and natural posture maintained during phonation which indicates that a state of balanced tension or equilibrium exists between the postural muscles (*i.e.*, those of the neck, back, lower abdomen, and buttocks) and the respiratory musculature.

A correct respiratory scaffolding is helpful, but it does not ensure an efficient vocal technique, since if the laryngeal musculature is well coordinated, all peripheral activities (such as posture and a proper respiratory scaffolding) will either accommodate or balance themselves reflexively.

See Posture

Respiratory Tract: the life-sustaining system of organs, muscles, and cartilage which extends from the pelvic floor to the frontal sinuses.

Since the respiratory system contains an actuator, a vibrator and a resonator, it can be transformed into a musical instrument to become a vocal mechanism. Correct use of the mechanism, however, requires that the adaptation obey those laws by which its natural movement potential is governed.

Rhythm: 1) movement; 2) an ordered, recurrent alternation of strong and weak elements in the flow of sound; 3) the manner in which tone progresses through a musical phrase within a given meter, and 4) the orderly pressure variations set in motion by the vibrating vocal folds.

Vocal study is primarily concerned with rhythm as movement, since the stimulation of natural movement within an involuntary muscular system is the key that opens the door to technical progress. Rhythmic movement brings the vocal muscles into equilibrium, eliminates constricting tensions, develops muscular tonicity, refines concepts, and ultimately increases self-awareness, dispensing with and rendering unnecessary those procedures designed to act upon the instrument. Once a freer rhythmic response is achieved, the mechanism itself will dictate how it should respond—an inner impetus will prompt it to move *this* way and not *that way.*

The logical sequence of events growing out of rhythmic movement is as follows: rhythmic movement fosters natural movement; natural movement promotes spontaneity, and spontaneity encourages the mechanism to respond in terms of an innate functional logic. Thus, the properties of natural singing can be discovered through natural rhythmic movement. Were it not possible to stimulate natural movement, all hope of rechanneling misdirected energy within the vocal mechanism (an involuntary muscular system) would have to be abandoned.

See Energy
   Kinesthesia
   Natural Movement
   Register
   Vocal Study

In the final analysis, it is the stimulation of natural movement *through rhythmic identification,* rather than technical details usually concerned with tone "production," which sustains the voice-building process and fosters continued technical growth.

Rhythmic Energy: energy contained within movement itself, or kinetic energy, as opposed to overt energy; the element which makes it possible to move without directly acting upon the processes involved in movement.

See Energy
   Reflex

Rhythmic energy is the source of motor power, which, in reponse to neurological impulses generated by the will, enables the vocal mechanism to respond naturally and in terms of an innate functional logic.

Rhythmic Training: a discipline designed to gain contact with, and knowledge of, the involuntary muscular movements responsible for the production of vocal tone. The essence of rhythmic training centers on response—the singer must learn to *allow* his voice to respond, rather than *making* it respond. This process is achieved in the manner described below.

The singer must do the following:

1. Assume a natural, comfortably erect posture;
2. Conceptualize the musical pattern (pitch, intensity, vowel) to be sung;
3. Open his mouth and *think* the vowel form;
4. Inspire and phonate in response to the mental concept (*i.e.,* by "hearing" the tonal vibrations appear—not by making them), and
5. Conceptualize the inner rhythmic pulsations (vibrato), energize them, and move them through the musical patterns.

The exercise should be performed legato, without giving any note of the pattern special emphasis and without moving the body.

By adopting this procedure, the vocal mechanism will yield tonal qualities as a direct response to musical concepts without physical or conceptual interference. It fosters natural movement, which promotes spontaneity, and encourages the mechanism to respond in terms of an innate functional logic. Where inadequacies exist, this process of natural response exposes them and indicates the proper corrective measures to be taken.

Training in rhythmic response, used in conjunction with principles governing registration, makes it possible to restructure and revamp all aspects of vocal technique, and it constitutes one of the basic training procedures. Unlike pedagogic practices which attempt to directly regulate the tonal product ("nasal resonance," "tonal placement," *etc.*), rhythmic training allows the tone-producing mechanism to react. Because interfering tensions have been removed, the mechanism restructures itself, thereby refining the singer's tonal concepts and coordinating the muscle systems involved, as well as releasing many physical and psychological impediments to the communicative experience.

See Energy
Kinetic Energy
Laryngeal
  Suspension
Natural Movement
Register

Rib Breathing: See Breathing, Costal and Intercostal.

Ribs: the twelve paired, curved bones that enclose the thorax.

Collectively, the twenty-four ribs, the sternum (breastbone) to which they are attached, and the muscles and cartilage that separate the ribs and connect them to various structures, form a "rib cage," which protects the visceral organs contained within the thorax.

The rib cage reflexively expands during inspiration as the lungs fill with air, a process which is reversed during expiration. Although some pedagogic methods recommend a conscious expansion of the rib cage prior to the onset of phonation, this procedure, like all attempts to impose mechanistic controls, induces exaggerated, self-conscious posturing and general body stiffness, and it also has a deleterious effect on the ultimate tonal product.

See Breathing,
  Costal and
  Intercostal
Mechanistic
  Training

Rich Tone: a sound whose harmonic spectrum is enriched by the proper reinforcement of both higher and lower partials or overtones.

Rigidity: muscular or nervous tenseness which inhibits motion, and therefore free tone production—not to be confused with tension.

Rigidity, or limited motility, is a condition which finds the vocal organs unable to adjust quickly and easily to the vocal process. There are several reasons for this disability: 1) a lack of "singer's instinct;" 2) muscular interference engendered because of poor vocal training, and 3) psychological tensions which "lock" the mechanism. One, or a combination of all three of these factors, contributes to conceptual and physical rigidities which are extremely difficult to correct.

Relaxation exercises, a common panacea for the relief of rigidity, are a useless device, since by failing to innervate the mechanism in a positive way, they do nothing to correct the problem.

See Energy
Kinesthesia
Natural Movement
Register

Rima Glottidis: Latin, "crack of the glottis;" the space which separates the vocal folds.

See Glottis

Ring: a vibrant tone quality reflecting the presence of strong upper partials in the harmonic spectrum, especially those within the frequency range of 2800 to 3400 cycles per second.

Ringing tones are associated with laryngeal resonance and can be of two kinds: 1) open-throated, and 2) constricted. The first type of resonance is very rare, and is a tonal property which makes great singers so exceptional. Since the muscular system responsible for an open-throated ring cannot be acted upon voluntarily, any effort to "make" the voice ring, or imitate a ringing quality, will merely serve to promote interfering tensions, and consequently some degree of throat constriction. While it may appear logical for young singers to "produce" a ringing tone quality, it is nevertheless a temptation to be avoided.

Ring Shield Muscles: the cricothyroid muscles which attach to the thyroid cartilage or "Adam's Apple." It is the ring shield muscles whose contractions are responsible for the tone qualities recognized as falsetto, or its derivative, the head voice.

Rolled Non-Fricative: the phoneme articulated by "rolling the tongue" (*e.g.,* an Italian *r*).

Roof of the Mouth: the hard palate.

Round Tone: a quality whose resonance characteristics give the impression of tonal warmth and roundness.

Although the term "round" accurately describes the physical adjustment frequently assumed by the lips and oropharynx in resonating "round" tones, such subjective descriptions should generally be avoided, since they invite misinterpretation and pedagogic confusion.

S

Salpingopharyngeal Muscle: the muscle that connects the lower border of the Eustachian (auditory) tube with the posterior border of the pharynx. When contracted, the salpingopharyngeal muscle opens the Eustachian tube, elevating the pharynx and narrowing its sides.

(To) Save the Voice: to sing lightly in rehearsal in an effort to prevent vocal fatigue; to "mark."

Saving the voice is frequently attempted by singing "half voice" (*mezza voce*), or by singing higher tones an octave lower or in a coordinated falsetto. The successful adoption of these practices depends in large measure upon those conditions peculiar to a present technical status. Each singer, therefore, must discover which of the available alternatives, if any, is right for himself.

The most efficient conserver of vocal resources is a healthy technique. No form of behavior, however prudent it may be, can "save" the voice of a singer whose technique is faulty.

See **(To) Mark**

Scapula: either of the paired "shoulder blades," or *scapulae*, which are often raised during high chest breathing.

Because the omohyoid muscles connect the shoulder blades and hyoid bone, any raising of the shoulder blades during phonation inevitably disturbs the natural equilibriumm of the laryngeal musculature.

See **Breathing**

Schwa: German, "dull;" in phonetics, a vowel type.

The so-called "schwa vowel" (*e.g.,* "a*bove*") is associated with weak, unstressed syllables in speech and in singing. The seeming insignificance of these syllables (like the small notes in music) encourages singers and speakers to neglect the proper delineation of the phonemes they contain. However, no vowel is intrinsically dull, and each should be energized to produce tones that are vital and clear.

See **Neutral Vowel**
Vowel
Vowel Modification

Scientific Approach: pedagogic procedures based on findings of the various sciences (*e.g.,* acoustics, neurology, and physiology) which deal with specific aspects of the vocal mechanism and function.

Although scientific information is useful for exposing the fallacy of unsound pedagogic theories and practices, it contains little that can be applied in studio practice. It is interesting and informative, for example, to know the following:

1. Inefficient function dissipates energy;
2. An "ideal" tonal pulse (vibrato) is 5.0—6.2 oscillations per second;
3. The tonal spectrum (*i.e.*, overtone content in relation to the fundamental) determines vocal quality;
4. The shape of the pharyngeal cavities (in particular, the laryngo- and oropharynges), determines resonance characteristics;
5. The larynx is raised, lowered, and tilted by a complex of suspensory muscles;
6. The positioning of the vocal folds for vibration is determined by the contraction of two basic muscular systems, and
7. All muscles associated with peristaltic movement (including the tongue) are antagonistic to those required for open-throated singing.

Information of this description contributes little to the central pedagogic problem: how to stimulate involuntary muscles to move more efficiently so that the ultimate product, voice, will emerge freely over a wide range of pitches and dynamics with beautiful, vibrant quality. Admittedly, even from the standpoint of pure analysis, the vocal mechanism does not readily lend itself to scientific scrutiny. Pitch, for example, cannot be extracted from intensity and vowel quality nor from the muscular activities that yield it, and since the processes involved in respiration and the ingestion of food and liquids employ the same muscle systems as those used in phonation, the movement of these parts is so complex as to make most judgments (even when reasonable) somewhat speculative.

One of the major limitations of scientific studies (although essential to research) is that they reflect an absence of interdisciplinary communication, without which the various bodies of knowledge cannot be synthesized into a comprehensive holistic pedagogy. The acoustician, for example, concentrates on the harmonic components of the tonal product without reference to the concepts, the culturally influenced aesthetic values, or the quality of the muscular activities which have prompted their emergence. Similarly, the neurologist is almost exclusively concerned with the role of the brain and central nervous system in stimulating muscular movements. Psychological attitudes and other areas vital to the phonative and creative process have rarely been taken into consideration.

A less excusable error among investigators has been to produce data based upon an as yet undefined terminology. As a result, oscillating movements of diverse kinds have been lumped under the general heading of a vibrato, without reference to their functional derivatives. Equally serious has been a proliferation of the number of registers (for example, fry, modal, pulse, loft, the deepest range, the mid-level, the higher level, and the highest range) for which no accounting can be made in terms of a separate mechanical (muscular) system, which alone determines a register.

Furthermore, much scientific data has been recorded without reference to the type of training, if any, given the subjects, or to their level of accomplishment or aesthetic preferences as these are influenced by temperament, *i.e.*, a tendency to favor "covered" techniques by vocalists of northern climes, a more "open" production by southern Europeans. Another limiting factor is that the subjects have, in general, been students or professionals of average ability. Consequently, the data is untrustworthy, commenting upon what *is* rather than what *should be*. One of the more glaring errors has been to establish a "trained" *vs.* an "untrained" category.

In the absence of a category for "natural" voices, Placido Domingo and many other notable artists would have to be considered "untrained" rather than "trained," since they never have had vocal study.

Historically, it is obvious that scientific knowledge is not a prerequisite to good teaching: the greatest teachers of singing, those responsible for the so-called Golden Age, possessed no scientific knowledge. What they did possess, however, was an awareness of those relationships between stimulus and response which prompted a broad complex of involuntary muscles to move in accordance with nature's laws. Additionally, the principles and terminology were mutually agreed upon and carefully defined.

Obviously, scientific investigation and its value to vocal pedagogy should not be discounted, since it exposes the inherent weaknesses and fallacies of the metaphysical concepts and imagery upon which so much modern methodology has been structured. Certainly, reasonable, orderly theorizing based upon precise data gives structure and reinforcement to the learning process. It is not, however, the essence of that process.

See **Bel Canto**
Holistic Pedagogy
Modern Methods

Scoop: a slurring from one note to another—particularly from a lower to a higher one.

The scoop, unlike the portamento, a legitimate artistic effect, is a habit resulting from one or more of the following functional or artistic aberrations:

1. A faulty sense of pitch;
2. An imbalanced registration in which a preponderance of chest register makes the voice heavy and unwieldy;
3. An overt attempt to maintain a full-throated resonance adjustment formed on lower pitches, inadvertently "locking" the registration, and
4. An aesethetic misconception of musicality that results from imitating a singer with one of these deficiencies.

Scooping is an unmusical and technically deleterious habit and should be conscientiously avoided.

(A) Seamless Voice: a vocal mechanism whose constituent parts are so integrated that all "breaks," gaps and/or transition points within the tonal range are undetectable.

The even gradation of tonal textures for which the seamless voice is notable is somewhat analogous to the playing of stringed instruments such as the violin, where each pitch matches (or can be made to match by proper fingering), yet differs slightly in quality from that of its neighbors. Individual notes sounded by the piano, to cite another example, are produced by strings of varying length and tension, physical differences which result in subtle textural modifications that qualitatively distinguish one pitch from another.

Technically, a seamless voice is one in which each changing pattern of pitch and intensity is met by a corresponding change in the physical dimensions of the vocal folds, which meet these requirements by becoming thicker or thinner, longer or shorter. These changes, even though the pharyngeal adjustments made to form and define the vowel remain constant, are responsible for producing modifications of quality which are barely perceptible as the voice moves stepwise through its tonal range. If these graduated textural modifications do not take place, or are prohibited from taking place, the muscular systems "lock" and lose their flexibility.

The concept of a seamless voice has persuaded many theorists that the vocal mechanism is comprised of but one register, or as it is sometimes described, a "separate register for every note." While this concept is not without a certain validity, it does, however, fail to take into account the fact that all motor systems, mechanical or human, are comprised of parts which can be separated or isolated. If this possiblity did not exist, reconditioning a faulty motor system would be impossible. From the standpoint of vocal pedagogy, therefore, a seamless voice, while an ultimate good, is not desirable until all of the working parts are capable of functioning at optimum efficiency.

Pedagogic procedures designed to develop a seamless voice without regard for the condition of the participating muscular systems "seal in" vocal errors, thus permanently arresting technical development.

Second Break: See Upper "Break" or Upper Passaggio.

Segment: a division of a vibrator into two or more parts; one of the characteristic arrangements assumed by the vocal folds when adjusting their length, thickness, and contour in response to changing patterns of pitch, intensity and vowel.

In addition to the register "break," there are five legitimate segmenting points located in diverse parts of the tonal range. (See Figure 18.) These transition points can be smoothed over completely, isolated for special "color" effects, or (like the "break" itself) emphasized for dramatic purposes. The manner in which they are treated, however, is a basic pedagogic concern whose solution depends upon a thorough understanding of the mechanics of registration.

Segmental Vibration: that portion of a vibrator (*e.g.*, a string of the piano or the violin) whose frequency ratio is a common fraction of the fundamental frequency, or those vibrations set in motion by the full length of the string.

Segmental vibrations are the sum of a complex of simple sound waves, the nature of which can readily be perceived by observing the "stopping" of a stringed instrument. If, for example, the point of stoppage falls at an integral fraction of the entire length of the string, the frequency of vibration will increase in inverse proportion to the decrease in length. Thus, when the string is vibrating as a whole, it is simultaneously vibrating in halves, thirds, fourths, fifths, *etc.*, each vibrating segment contributing its sound to the total harmonic structure. More familiarly, segmental vibrations are known as partials. These may either be harmonic or inharmonic, the first partial representing the fundamental frequency.

The human voice produces many partials which, depending upon one's hearing acuity, can be perceived in excess of 16,000 cps, although those frequencies below 10,000 cps are sufficient to accurately define quality.

Selectivity: the cavity adjustments made in response to a tonal image whose purpose is to enhance the resonance characteristics generated at the sound source.

See Bel Canto
Modern Methods
(To) Progress
Register
Resonance
Vocal Study
Vowel

See Register

See Coupling
Fundamental
Harmonic
Partial
Quality
Resonance
Standing Wave
Timbre

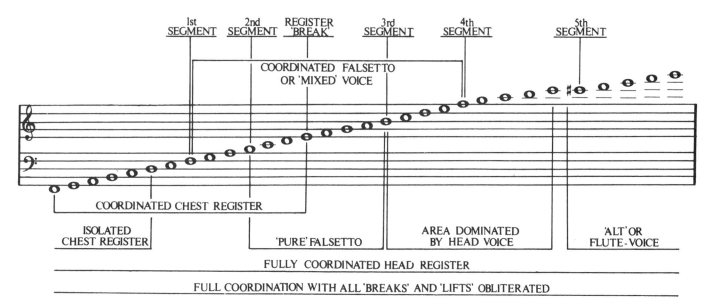

Figure 18. Showing the five segmental points as they evolve out of a coordinate relationship between the two basic register mechanisms—the chest register and the falsetto. Those who possess well-formed voices (having at least two or more octaves of tonal range) will have little difficulty in recognizing the textures and the transition points which define the boundaries recorded above.

Of the several cavities available to serve as potential resonators of the vowel (the trachea, the laryngeal pharynx, the oropharynx, the nasopharynx, the mouth, and the sinuses), only the laryngo- and oropharynges are capable of performing effectively as selective resonators. Several factors—adjustability, proximity to the vibrator, and the relationship between the physical dimensions of these cavities and the frequency of the pitch being sung—influence selectivity. For example:

1. Cavity size. Lower frequencies require larger cavities for tonal amplification; higher frequencies require smaller cavities;
2. Length of aperture. Lower frequencies require larger openings; higher frequencies require smaller openings, and
3. Texture of cavity walls. Soft-lined cavities tend to dampen upper partials and reinforce lower ones; hard-walled cavities tend to reinforce upper partials and add tonal brilliance.

These considerations and the need to provide a uniform resonance adjustment for a wide range of pitches, intensities, and vowels demonstrate the need for firm-walled, adjustable resonators whose dimensions can be varied in length and width and whose relatively fixed positions are independent of the frequent adjustments made by the articulatory processes. The laryngo- and oropharynges fulfill these requirements admirably. The trachea, nasopharynx, sinuses and mouth do not, and must be discounted as selective resonators.

See Cavity Tone Theory
Coupling
Resonance

Self-Listening: the use of auditory feedback to evaluate the ultimate tonal product against a preconcept; a shifting of concentration from a preconcept to the sound actually being produced.

The inhibiting factors in self-listening are built in, and arise because of perceptual values which, long before vocal study has begun, find expressive urges, talent, intelligence, psychological attitudes and musicality merged to form a vocal self-image whose special quality characteristics become personalized into "my quality."

"My quality" and the quality of self-listening may therefore be seen to rely heavily upon subjective aesthetic impressions, which are manifestly unreliable. Since, in all but the most exceptional instances, "my quality" merely represents the condition of the functioning mechanism rather than an intrinsically natural potential, the pedagogic objective must be to institute measures which will 1) by-pass preconcepts which are without relevance to potential, 2) stimulate the vocal organs into improved patterns of response (which will be new to the student but anticipated by the teacher), 3) reconcile subjective impressions with objective reality, 4) lessen a dependency upon auditory feedback, and 5) help the student learn what to listen to and for.

None of the objectives mentioned above can be achieved through self-listening in terms of "my quality," and if they are to be gained at all, quality must be looked upon as an unknown variable, the "X" in an equation which must be solved before the answer can become known. A primary element in any such formulation is learning to hear functionally, that is, learning to do the following:

1. Recognize the textural properties that are yielded by each of the two basic register mechanisms;
2. Estimate the strength and relative development of each;
3. Discern the contribution of each to a particular register balance;
4. Identify and evaluate the textural contribution of the resonance adjustment, *i.e.,* open-throated or constricted, and
5. Recognize the relationship and desirable independence between vowel formation and the articulatory processes.

Another obstacle to an objective quality appraisal through self-listening is the discrepancy which exists between sound waves perceived by interior hearing processes and those that reach the basilar membrane through the external ear. Among the conflicts to be resolved are the following:

1. Differences in frequency and phase between sound waves transmitted through bone tissue (or internal hearing) and those which reach the external ear through the outer atmosphere;
2. Misinformation supplied because of muscular constriction within the throat parts, which provide a tense medium favorable to the transmission of vibratory impulses, and
3. Distorted impressions caused by a sphincter movement of the pharyngeal musculature which closes the Eustachian tube, thus blocking the transmission of signals to the inner ear.

It is because of the diverse and conflicting bodies of information supplied to the brain through these sources that objective self-listening, and therefore self-listening as a useful pedagogic device, is unreliable.

If singers are to learn to listen perceptively, therefore, subjective impressions must be reconciled with objective reality. This requires a "third ear," without which functional disorders, wrong mental concepts, distorted hearing, often ill-advised interpretative and aesthetic goals, and an entrenched self-image cannot be rectified.

Preliminary scientific studies indicate that experienced singers are much less dependent upon self-listening, or auditory feedback, than those who are inexperienced. Since it is impossible to hear one's own voice objectively, it is obvious that the experienced singer relies on other factors for aesthetic guidance, notably kinesthesia, tonal textures as these are related to registration, and conditioned reflexes, rather than quality.

Self-Regulation: the inherent ability of an organism to recognize and respond favorably to a congenial environment; a self-corrective tendency which, when conditions are right, takes place spontaneously.

In singing, the external environment consists of primary musical elements. This concept, whether it be a simple scale or a complete melody, constitutes, in effect, a stimulus to which the vocal organs respond. If the stimulus (environment) is such that it promotes healthy reflexive movement, then the respiratory organs will adapt successfully to the vocal process. When a stimulus is projected which violates an innate functional logic, natural movement gives way to restricted movement, and the laryngeal musculature must be *made* to move. Forcing movement makes the voice sluggish and dissipates energy.

Self-regulation is an intrinsic characteristic of natural movement and can best be described as vocal self-interest. When exercises selected during training are thoughtfully constructed, the organic system will move spontaneously and willingly—it perceives that its best interests are being served and responds accordingly. The tendency of an organism to regulate itself, therefore, is simply a response which indicates that the demands placed upon it can be successfully carried out within the framework of its movement potential. Organic systems may thus be said to be capable of recognizing a distinction between use and abuse.

Unless correction of a vocal problem is based upon an understanding of self-regulation, training procedures run the risk of losing contact with functional naturalness. Such a failure precludes any hope of inducing a correct laryngeal suspension and leads to serious errors, both as to procedure and theory. Furthermore, an absence of contact with natural organic movement leaves tonal concepts at the mercy of cultural attitudes, teacher-imposed taste, a vocal fashion growing out of a prevailing emotional climate, conditioning, and the often deleterious influence of linguistic and ethnic peculiarities.

Opposed to this, an understanding of the procedures associated with self-regulation, together with a firm grasp of the principles governing registration and adjustments for resonance, will encourage natural and functionally correct response patterns which transcend limitations of this description. In this process, if the vocal exercises selected represent the kind of "exercise" the vocal organs require to achieve greater stabilization, the singer's instinct for creative expression should be awakened. By combining instinctual knowledge with an understanding of functional laws, there should be a corresponding increase in artistic growth, as well as in technical skills.

See **Auditory Feedback**
Bone Conduction
Functional
Listening
Hearing
Kinesthesia
Quality
Sensations of
Vibration
Vowel

See **Kinesthesia**
Natural Movement

Semi-Consonant: a consonant whose articulation requires a subsequent vowel phoneme (*e.g., b*); a voiced consonant.

As is true of all semi-consonants, the plosive must be articulated before the sounding of the vowel. This is particularly true in medium and upper pitch ranges, where it is impossible to establish an open-throated resonance adjustment with the lips closed.

Semi-Roll: an *r* phoneme articulated by a single roll (trill) of the tongue; an "Italian *r*."

Semi-Vowel: a sustained consonant (*e.g., l, m, n*) which, because it is preceeded by a vowel phoneme, requires muscular movements characteristic of the production of both consonants (articulatory noise) and vowels (laryngeal vibration).

Semi-vowels present no real difficulty in the lower and mid-ranges, since the mechanism is not under sufficient tension to affect the pharyngeal resonators adversely. They are more difficult to produce in the upper tonal range, however, because it is next to impossible to maintain an open-throated resonance adjustment with the lips either partially or completely closed. To overcome this difficulty, it is necessary to articulate the consonant just before the vowel is sounded.

Sensation: an impression conveyed by an afferent nerve to the sensorium, or seat of sensory nerve receptors in the brain. These nerve impulse excitations can be of three basic types:

1. *Primary*, as in the conscious awareness of pain, taste, smell, heat, *etc.,* by the direct stimulation of a sense organ or a sensory nerve;
2. *Secondary*, or *referred*, as in the case of vibrations radiated throughout the skeletal system by bone conduction, and
3. *Phantom*, as when sensations of pain or pressure are "felt" in limbs that have been amputated, an instance in which the brain perceives sensations that have no actual point of stimulation.

The ability to feel, record and evaluate different sensations as they are awakened during training is a primary factor in developing technical skills, provided that the sensation is observed and not acted upon, generated, or overtly intensified. Vocally, a sensation is the product, not the cause of muscular movement. Therefore, if a particular sensation is thought at a given time to be more desirable than another, it must be brought into being by duplicating the process to which it owes its being. This process involves the principles governing registration, applied in conjunction with vowel modifications whose purpose is to correct tonal blemishes and improve the overall mechanical function of the instrument.

Sensations of Vibration: kinesthetic impressions aroused during phonation which seem to be located either at the sound source (the larynx) or in peripheral areas of the body, notably the chest, the facial mask, or nasal sinuses.

Vibratory excitation of sensory (afferent) nerves can be of two origins:

See **Consonants**
     Plosive
     Semi-Vowel

See **Consonants**
     Hum

See **Kinesthesia**
     Register
     Resonance
     Vowel

334

1. Muscular movements, either voluntary or involuntary, which occur in response to efferent nerve stimuli and actually produce the vibration, or
2. Radiation of already produced vibrations to other parts of the body through bone conduction.

There are many sensations of vibration with which singers may readily identify. For example, an awareness of tones being "high" or "low" stems from a kinesthetic identification with muscular movements associated with changes in registration that occur as pitch is raised or lowered, causing chest register-dominated tones to "feel" different from those dominated by the head voice.

Vibratory sensations answering these descriptions are easily identifiable. Less traceable are those influences contributed by the various types of laryngeal adjustment (high, low, open-throated or constricted), by the vibratory pattern of the vocal folds (whether they approximate by force due to wrongly applied energy, or willingly because of precise coordination), and by the amount of compensatory tension engendered in order to overcome muscular interference.

Sensations of vibration are often deceptive since they offer little indication of the source of the symptom. An awareness of "mask resonance," for example, will often be experienced by those who possess a free vocal technique, while others who are aware of similar sensations (although perhaps less intense) can only be described as vocal cripples. What must be taken into consideration when evaluating these and other symptoms is that, while all vibratory impulses radiate through the skeletal framework because of bone conduction, their transmission is modified and conditioned by the particular type of muscular tension present in the technique. Since the physical factors that give rise to vibratory impulses can combine in an almost infinite variety of ways, the quality and intensity of the vibratory sensations moving through the skeletal framework are not, of themselves, trustworthy guides.

The qualitative factors inherent in all sensations of vibration experienced by the singer, therefore, obviously possess both positive and negative aspects. Jaw tension, a stiffening of the neck muscles, throat constriction, a "mixed" registration, and numerous other components of a faulty tone production often yield sensations not totally dissimilar to those generated when the resonance adjustment is open-throated and the registration is well balanced. Consequently, the fact that one "feels" these vibrations in what is thought to be a desirable locale is not truly significant, especially when these sensory impressions are commingled with those aroused by the presence of vocal faults.

To rely on directives which focus attention on a specific symptom of vibration during training avoids the central pedagogic issue. Treatment addressed to symptoms cannot cure a "mixed" registration (which always lies at the root of technical difficulties), nor can the right physical sensations be intensified by this means until this malfunction has been alleviated or corrected. Attempts to replicate sensations of vibration experienced by those who sing correctly are equally futile, and sensations cannot be "willed" into being. Reliance upon imagery and imagination to conjure up a sensation never yet experienced is self-deluding, especially when no functional principle is being applied.

The admixture of positive and negative sensations is often of such a kind that, when the technique is poor, the negative symptoms will obliterate those generally acknowledged to be desirable. This does not mean that they no longer radiate or are absent, but simply that they have been overpowered by stronger negative tensions concentrated in, or dispersed throughout, other areas of the anatomy. In view of the diversity of influences, good and bad, which through muscular movement excite the sense organs during phonation, it is evident that attempts to replicate sensations of vibration approach the problem from the wrong direction. If sensations of vibration are the product of muscular movement, then it is obvious that training procedures should not be directly concerned with symptoms, but focus on procedures which stimulate the involuntary muscular systems producing them into improved patterns of response.

The confusion of concepts employed to rectify mechanical deficiencies without attacking the source of the problem may be seen from the variety of images students are often urged to act upon: "place the tone forward," "direct it against the front teeth," "feel it almost in, but not quite in the nose," "feel the vowel between the eyes," "resonate in the facial mask," "sing the tone as though it were going out of the back of the neck and heard by someone standing behind you," "focus the tone with the uvula," "feel it deep and in the throat," and/or "feel it in the head cavities."

The concepts related to sensations of vibration noted above embrace no functional principle. They confuse ends with means, and merely prove that different physical sensations are the product of different kinds of physical coordination, each being comprised of certain positive attributes and limitations, and nothing more. Impressions are no substitute for physical reality, and unless sensations of vibration are properly identified with their causes, they do not merit serious consideration as a basis for developing vocal skills.

Some "impressionistic" solutions detailed above have unfortunately become standard pedagogic practice, "nasal resonance" and voice "placement" being foremost among them. That these solutions are without substance, however, is evident from the results of experiments, conducted by Charles Frederick Lindsley (1932), which have proven that the illusion of vibration is often more real than the reality itself. The falsetto, for example, which appears to resonate exclusively in the "head," he found to excite more response at the point of the larynx and trachea than in the head cavities. Another startling exception is the impression that vibratory impulses are resonated in the nasal sinuses, or "mask." This illusion was dispelled by Warren B. Wooldridge (1954), who, having filled the nasal passages with cotton gauze to dampen them, discovered no loss in tonal vitality. While vibratory sensations can be "felt" in the facial mask, they are due, quite clearly, to bone conduction rather than resonance.

Facts more pertinent to a just evaluation of sensory perception during phonation are as follows:

Tonal vibrations are generated within the laryngeal pharynx. They are amplified by the cavities through which they pass, and radiate through the bone structure to all parts of the skeletal framework. To intensify the vibrations experienced in the facial mask, the vitality of the vibratory impulses must be increased at the generating source, *i.e.,* the larynx. Attempts to intensify tonal vibrations at terminal points or peripheral areas of the resonating system will therefore not only fail to enhance the resonance characteristics, but effectively diminish their intensity because energy is being diverted from the tonal source.

To elevate specific sensations of vibration to the status of a functional principle is therefore pedagogically improper, because

1. Sensations are the product and not the cause of muscular movement;
2. It is impossible to describe accurately the nature of subjective impressions;
3. Bone conduction and muscular tension cause vibrations, like ripples on the water, to radiate through the cavities of the throat and mouth to all parts of the skeletal framework. In essence, they are everywhere;
4. The extent to which vibratory sensations are experienced in peripheral or terminal areas is proportionate to the amount of energy concentrated at the generating source, the larynx. Attempts to strengthen vibratory impulses at their terminal points invert this process;
5. Since symptoms are to a certain extent the product of muscular impedence combined with healthy functional activity, the qualitative difference in symptom is dependent upon the quality of the physical coordination within the throat parts. The difference between "good" and "bad" tensions constitutes the essential difference, for example, between tone feeling "forward" or "too far back;"
6. Since the vibratory characteristics will change or modify with changing technical conditions, *i.e.*, physical coordination within the throat parts, to insist on reproducing the same symptoms, thinking them to be a permanent good, is to preclude any possibility of real technical improvement, the symptom being the parallel expression of the physical coordination;
7. To successfully duplicate the symptoms of vibration thought to be ideal, whether projected conceptually or by imitation, is impossible without first having duplicated the identical set of physical conditions, *i.e.*, technique, and
8. While the technical status will express itself in terms of specific vibratory sensations, the equation is not reversible—physical coordination cannot be instituted or modified, except with negative results, by attempting to work from the symptom to the cause.

On a pragmatic level, the singer's primary concern during training is to develop a technique which permits freedom of movement and expression. Consequently, to overemphasize the importance of particular sensations of vibration at any point in the learning process is to neglect the reaffirmation of those functional principles which form the very foundation of a correct voice production.

The sensory impressions present in all vocalization are valuable guides to an intelligent use of the vocal mechanism. These impressions, however, should not center on locale, but on an awareness of the internal state of the body. A mental awareness of the specific nature of the manner in which the bodily organs respond to a musical stimulus requires that the singer consider his relationship to the communicative experience as a totality. To concentrate on isolated areas of vibratory sensation moves away from this objective. Therefore, if a particular sensation is thought at a given time to be more desirable than another, it must be brought into being and introduced to the pupil's consciousness with a concern for process rather than the replication of symptoms. This process involves the employment of those principles governing registration, applied in conjunction with vowel modification, whose purpose is to correct tonal blemishes and improve the overall mechanical function of the instrument.

Pedagogic reliance upon sensation to effect a technical improvement usually

See Bel Canto
Kinesthesia
Modern Methods
Register
Resonance

develops weaknesses, since the sensations experienced by most singers are too closely associated with their problems to provide a solution.

Separated Formants: a term referring to the tonal spectrum of a vowel phoneme whose first two frequency bands are widely separated.

See Coupling
Formants

Septum: the cartilaginous partition (the so-called "bridge of the nose") that separates the nasal port into two fossae, or cavities.

Many pedagogues believe that the area directly behind the septum (the nasopharynx) is the source of so-called "nasal resonance," or resonance "in the mask." The usefulness of the nasopharynx as a resonator, however, has been thoroughly discounted by scientific investigation.

See Nasality
Resonance

Shake: a trill (archaic); now sometimes used to describe the defect known as "tremolo."

See Tremolo

Shallow Breathing: See Breathing, Shallow.

Shallow Tone: a vocalized sound whose harmonic spectrum lacks strong lower partials.

"Shallow" tones are usually the result of singing with an elevated larynx and an absence of chest register connection.

See Anchored in the
Chest
Laryngeal
Suspension

Sharp: a symbol (#) denoting the augmentation of an interval; a descriptive term referring to vocalized sounds whose frequencies are higher than the true pitch.

A sharpening of the true pitch will occur when an excessive amount of breath pressure is used for the pitch-intensity pattern being sung, as, for example, when the vocal mechanism is "tightly" coupled acoustically. Another cause of this distressing vocal fault is a technical condition in which some degree of throat constriction is present in combination with a head voice-dominated register balance. This is especially likely to happen when singing at higher levels of intensity in the upper pitch range. Only in the rarest instances is sharp singing attributable to faulty hearing perception.

See Coupling

Sharp Vowels: the so-called "bright" vowels (*eh, ee, etc.*).

Aesthetically, "sharp" vowels merely represent one aspect of tone "color," although if they are produced with absolute consistency it indicates the presence of some undesirable constrictor tensions. Acoustically, a sharp tone quality is caused by an overenergizing of the frequencies in the range of 3000–4000 cps at the expense of lower harmonics.

See Formants
Vowel, Dark
and Bright

Shearing Action: an auditory function (involving the organ of Corti and the basilar and tectorial membranes) that generates and transmits electrical impulses to the brain through the auditory nerves.

See Ear
Hearing
Organ of Corti

Sheen: a bright, shimmering tonal quality.

Tonal "sheen" usually indicates correct technical use of the mechanism and the presence of a true vibrato, although certain types of incipient throat constriction can exhibit a similar characteristic.

See Tremolo
Vibrato

Shield-Pyramid Muscles: the thyroarytenoid muscles (a term that was used by Marchesi).

Shock of the Glottis: See Coup de Glotte.

Short-Reed Voice: (archaic) the falsetto.

Short Vowels: brief, unaccented vowels; "vanishing" vowels.

See Schwa
Neutral Vowel

Shortness of Breath: a physical condition that results from expending energy for muscular activity faster than it is derived from oxidation.

There are many mechanical causes for shortness of breath. Among them are the following:

1. A "mixed" registration;
2. Tonal breathiness, due to a failure of the vocal folds to approximate;
3. A condition in which the vocal folds are forced to approximate;
4. A lack of resistance to subglottal pressure because the false vocal cords have failed to narrow;
5. An imbalanced registration, which finds the "break" between the two mechanisms too great, making the transit awkward and effortful;
6. The assiduous observance of a special breathing technique (which promotes "breath consciousness" and stiffens the body), and
7. Any energy applied which does not contribute to the maintenance of a functional equilibrium.

When the vocal mechanism functions efficiently, the singer will never experience shortness of breath, since virtually all of the energy will have been converted into vocal tone. It cannot be assumed, however, that a voice capable of sustaining long phrases necessarily possesses a secure vocal technique or is being used correctly. Certain voice types (usually those which are slightly tremulous, bright in color and somewhat constricted) are frequently capable of sustaining long phrases without difficulty. Consequently, an absence of breathing problems does not indicate that one sings freely or is without technical faults.

See Breathing,
    Shallow
Energy
Registration,
    "Mixed"
Tremolo
Vibrato

Shoulder Blade: See Scapula.

Shoulder Breathing: See Breathing, Clavicular.

Shouty Tone: an unattractive vocalized sound (commonly described as "too open"), usually most prominent in the area of register transition, E to F above middle C, caused by an aggressively energized chest voice functioning without coordinate relationship with the head voice.

Shrill Tone: an "edgy," piercing tonal quality caused by a high laryngeal position (*i.e.*, throat constriction) and a consequent spreading of the oropharynx.

Shut Off: a term used to describe a constricted tone quality.

Shut Voice: a reference to the almost forgotten Bel Canto practice of performing vowel sequences with the mouth in a half open position.

The pedagogic significance of the "shut voice" (*voce chiusa*) is that its practice detunes the mouth as a resonator and encourages genuine laryngeal resonance (or, as the Bel Canto masters referred to it, "anchoring the tone in the chest"). Thus, this device was considered an important step in detuning the mouth as a resonator and freeing the tonal form (resonance adjustment) from the articulatory processes and *vice versa*.

Sibilant: a consonant comprised of hissing sounds (*e.g., s, z, sh, zh, etc.*).

Sibilate: to pronounce with an initial sibilant.

Sigh Tones: a technical device for effecting the release of throat tension.

The sigh is nature's own way of relieving constriction, whether it be due to anxiety or other causes. The production of tones in the manner of a heavy sigh by releasing rather than pushing out or controlling the breath serves to eliminate many problems caused by muscular interference. This is particularly true with respect to the difficulties encountered in the area of the register "break."

Silent Breathing: See Breathing, Silent.

Simple Sound: the sound emitted by a vibrator whose regular oscillations produce no partials or overtones (*e.g.,* that produced by a tuning fork).

Many simple sounds moving together make up the complex sounds heard in vocal and instrumental tone.

Simultaneous Attack: the precise, immediate articulation of vocalized sound without breathiness, glottal noise, or any other form of tonal interference; the act of bringing the vocal folds, the suspensory muscles which position the larynx, and the palatal and pharyngeal muscles from a state of relaxation into balanced tension.

A simultaneous attack requires a high order of technical precision if a hard onset is to be avoided. It is synonymous with the original intent of the *coup de glotte*.

Sine Wave: the wave form of a simple sound; that wave form whose graph reflects the mathematical relationship in which its sine represents the perpendicular.

Acoustic analysis is based upon the findings of the French scientist J.B.J. Fourier (1768—1830), who mathematically explained the periods of rarefaction and compression of air particles in various simple and complex sound waves.

Sing As You Speak: a pedagogic directive intended to encourage spontaneity during phonation and to avoid the posturing which makes tone production "arty" and unnatural; a postulate based upon the assumption that good speech habits will effect an overall improvement in the vocal technique.

As long as the advice to "sing as you speak" is given to discourage grimaces, posturing, and the tracing of inflectional patterns with corresponding movements of the body and head, this concept is constructive. When it is used to suggest that a direct parallel exists between speech and singing, however, it overlooks fundamental differences between the two methods of communication. These differences are as follows:

1. The mechanics of normal speech require neither sustained vibrations nor a tuned resonance adjustment, whereas singing is impossible without relatively fixed resonators which can be tuned separately or "coupled." Thus, to tune the resonators in speech is to "put on" voice. To fail to tune them in singing is unmusical;
2. Increased intensity in speech correlates with rising pitch levels, but without recourse to a vibrato; in singing, increases and decreases in intensity are regulated by a graduated increase and decrease in the amplitude of the vibrato;
3. Duration is a minimal factor in speech, whereas in singing a constant vowel quality must be sustained;
4. The range of pitches used in speech is extremely narrow (unless one resorts to shouting), whereas in singing at least two octaves of pitches must be produced under effective control;
5. The amount of airflow in speech is considerably higher than it is when one sings correctly, breathflow in singing using but 36 cc of air per second;
6. According to spectrographic analysis, spoken and sung phonemes are not the same, and
7. Physiologically, speech does not require the active participation of the cricopharyngeal muscle, whereas singing depends heavily upon its contraction to insure laryngeal stability, the release of tongue and jaw tension, and optimum stretching of the vocal folds.

The sum of these differences indicates that the only factors common to both speech and singing are laryngeal vibration (although of different kinds), the articulation of consonants, and the combining of vowels and consonants to form syllables and words. These differences have been clarified by the research of Luchsinger and Arnold, who concluded that

the difficulty in assigning certain functions of the pharyngeal resonator to audible patterns of the voice may be found in the fact that the influence of the throat on the voice has little to do with the logical-conceptual levels of language. Instead, it is closely linked to the phylogenetically *older levels of emotional expression.*[94]

[94]Richard Luchsinger and Godfrey E. Arnold, *Voice-Speech-Language* (Belmont, California: Wadsworth Publishing Co., Inc., 1965), p. 116.

Singing, therefore, is an intrinsic natural form of affective expression used from birth, whereas speech is a culturally imposed phenomenon that must be learned. Consequently, to "sing as you speak" reverses a fundamental principle, subjecting natural processes to domination by the intellect instead of using the intellect to bring all things into consonance with nature.

On a pragmatic level, the absence of a functional correlation between speech and singing can be revealed by examining the speaking voices of those who sing extremely well and *vice versa:* the greatest singers sometimes have mediocre speaking voices, while those who possess speaking voices of exceptional quality frequently sing either poorly or not at all. Consequently, it is obvious that no direct correlation exists. The development of a beautiful speaking voice, however, depends upon the utilization of the mechanical principles used to train the singing voice; neither a good singing voice nor a good speaking voice can be developed through speech.

A continuing problem in vocal pedagogy is the absence of absolutes (which makes structured learning difficult, if not impossible) and a prevalent tendency to make generalizations on the basis of subjective experiences. It is out of this background that an imagined functional identity between speech and singing has gained wide acceptance. There is some justification for this assumption, however. The professional singer is a pragmatist, and he is concerned with oneness, with having all of the pieces of the vocal puzzle fit neatly in place. For him, his tone production, projection of the text, sense of musical syle, acting, stage presence, facial expression, *etc.*, must fuse into a total artistic package. He is more concerned with the appearance of reality than with reality itself.

The concern of the professional singer, therefore, is with "putting it all together." These concerns, however, are not those of the student interested in developing his vocal technique. If the projection of text is not to interfere with the tone production, it is essential that the intellectual processes associated with speech and the instinctual identification with vocal tone as a sophisticated form of affective expression be treated, for a considerable period of time, as two separate and distinct functional entities. This procedure formed one of the bases upon which the art of Bel Canto was founded, where "purity of intonation," *i.e.,* vowel purity, was a fundamental training objective. During this era, it was only after a protracted period of study that *solfeggio* was introduced to combine tone with text. Permission to sing a rather elementary song literature came much later.

The advice to "sing as you speak" may therefore be seen to be a useful fiction to the professional singer, but when evaluated from the standpoint of developing vocal skills it is an inhibitory doctrine, since it treats the voice-building process in superficial terms and employs no functional principles that are designed to effect an improvement of the activities taking place at the sound source. Because of its limitations, the advice to "sing as you speak" cannot be considered a useful pedagogic tool.

See Coupling
    Natural Singing
    Register
    Resonance
    Vowel

Sing on the Breath: See On the Breath.

Singer's Stance: an alert, pleasantly erect posture, uncaricatured and devoid of mannerisms, indicating that the body is in a state of poised readiness to initiate and sustain phonation.

Adopting the singer's stance, while helpful, is not an essential part of tonal preparation, and should be viewed as a consequence rather than the direct cause of a correct tone production. Those who sing well usually "look right" because the complex muscular movements within the laryngeal pharynx are well coordinated.

Judged on this basis, the singer's stance, like ripples moving in concentric circles on the surface of a body of water, must be considered a peripheral and visual manifestation of correctly applied core energy, a condition which implies a proper stimulation and efficient response of the vocal muscles.

See Laryngeal
    Suspension
    Larynx
    Modern Methods
    Posture
    Register
    Resonance
    Vowel

Singing Sense: an innate ability to make sounds which are physiologically healthy and aesthetically satisfying; an instinct for making vocal tone that exceeds intellectual comprehension; a spontaneous collaboration between concept and function.

See Kinesthesia
    Limbic System

Single Formant Vowel: a vowel phoneme in whose harmonic spectrum the first two formants are so close together that the resulting quality registers as the average of the two frequencies.

See Coupling
Formant

Sinus: a cavity in the skull that contains air and opens into the nasopharynx.

Although scientific investigation has repeatedly denied the value of the sinuses to tonal amplification, the paranasal sinuses are frequently considered the source of "nasal" or "mask" resonance. Since, however, they are small, muted, virtually inaccessible (because of their small apertures), and nonadjustable, they are categorically unsuited for this purpose.

See Cavity Tone Theory
Resonance

Sinus of the Larynx: one of the two ventricular sacs on either side of the passageway between the vocal folds and the false vocal cords; the ventricular sacs.

The sinuses of the larynx are formed by the drawing together of the false vocal cords during phonation, an act that provides supraglottal resistance to the subglottal pressure exerted by escaping breath, and thereby allows the vocal folds (under ideal technical conditions) to remain self-vibratile within a pressure-balanced equilibrium.

Research by Husson (1935), Luchsinger (1949) and van den Berg (1955) indicates that the shape of the ventricles alters slightly to accommodate various vowel positions. Beckmann (1956) demonstrated an additional function through careful experiments with excised larynges. He found that the exclusion of the ventricles (which he plugged with cotton to eliminate their effectiveness as a resonator) caused a marked reduction in higher harmonics, and consequently a reduction in tonal brilliance. These experiments show that the false vocal cords are important to vowel formation and resonance characteristics on account of their influence on the shaping of the ventricular sacs.

See Bernoulli Effect
Breathing
False Vocal Cords

Sinus Tone Production: a theory of tone production advanced by the English pedagogue Ernest G. White, who postulated that vocal tone is determined, not by the vibration of the vocal folds, but by the selective circulation of air currents within the sinuses and pharyngeal cavities above the larynx. He further contended that the currents of air, starting from the highest point in the sinus cavities, spiraled downward and were emitted through the nostrils. He described the basic tonal counterpart of these spiraling currents as "a tiny sound generally known by that foolish term 'falsetto.'"

White seemed confident that his theories were in agreement with nature's laws, since he believed that plants and animals were composed of various spiral nebulae. He based his theories on the unassailable premise that all organic and inorganic matter is similarly constructed and that its various forms are interdependent, complemental, coordinated, and conditioned. His theories, though extreme, were founded on earlier premises, notably those of Galen in the second century, Dodart in the seventeenth century, and Scripture in the early twentieth century.

Although White acknowledged that air is emitted through the vocal folds in a series of puffs, and that the dimensions of the folds determine the character of these puffs, he dismissed them as being unimportant either as vibrators or for their effect upon cavity resonance. His theory is wanting in that it makes no provision for the muscular processes at work in tensing the vocal folds. Thus, while he believed that "registers most positively exist," he thought them to be "controlled by making a definite and selective use of the different cavities of the sinuses and head."[95] White's theories did not lack supporters—mainly because of the belief (fairly common in the early part of this century, and proven by scientific experimentation) that the vocal folds are neither properly constructed nor sturdy enough to effectively resist the breath exerted against them, especially during forceful singing.

Various theories were concurrently advanced to relieve the vocal folds of the strain to which they were thought to have been subjected, such as those of Dr. H. Holbrook Curtis and Jean de Reszke ("nasal resonance"), Lilli Lehmann (*Wirbeln* or "eddies"), and others. While none of these can be taken seriously scientifically (since sound is merely the alternate compression and rarefaction of air particles— not whirling currents or eddies), they were all attempts to clarify the crucial problems relevant to vocal fold tension.

White's conviction that the vocal folds cannot effectively resist breath pressure exerted from below when strongly applied, his recognition of the important role played by the false vocal cords as resisters, and his belief that the mechanism is controlled neurologically, are major contributors to the advancement of vocal theory.

Sinusoid: a sine curve, or a curve which traces and records simple harmonic motion.

Sitting on the Breath: a phrase used to describe sensations accompanying the impounding or momentary retention of air within the lungs; one of the many "vocal tricks" to develop a sense of breath "support."

The specific technique for identifying with the feeling of sitting on the breath is to inspire quickly and deeply, hold the chest high, and follow this action by an exceedingly slow and deliberate exhalation. The purpose of this method is to counterbalance intercostal and diaphragmatic tensions through abdominal tension, described by Vennard as being similar in feeling to "sitting on a beach ball."[96] The value of this and other practices concerned with breath control is questionable, since too great a concern is shown for individual parts of the functioning mechanism, to the detriment of the whole.

Small Register: the series of vocal sounds or tonal qualities lying above the soprano high C; the so-called altissimo or "flute-voice."

"Small register" is a term introduced by late nineteenth century theorists based upon laryngoscopic observation of the vocal folds. If one "looks" at the vocal mechanism instead of listening to it, then the expression "small" is a fitting comment on an observable phenomenon, since it accurately describes the physical conformation of the folds for this particular tonal area. No separate muscular system exists to justify setting the notes in altissimo apart as a separate "register," however, nor does "small" properly identify tonal qualities located in this pitch range.

Snarl: a twangy, nasal vocal quality which is the product of throat constriction.

Proponents of "nasal resonance" frequently advocate the use of the "snarl" to

[95]Ernest G. White, *Sinus Tone Production* (London: J. M. Dent & Sons, 1938), p. 8.

See **Bernoulli Effect**
    False Vocal Cords
    Feigned Voice
    Register
    Resonance,
      Nasal
    Vortex Theory

See **Bel Canto**
    Breathing
    Imagery
    Modern Methods

[96]William Vennard, *Singing: The Mechanism and the Technic* (New York: Carl Fisher, Inc., 1967), p. 145.

See **Flageolet Register**
    Register
    Whistle Register

increase what is considered to be a desirable resonance characteristic. However, while the advice may be well intentioned, it is neither aesthetically nor functionally desirable, since the nasality it encourages is produced by a constriction of the pharyngeal cavities. To increase resonance, vibratory sensations must be energized at their source (within the laryngo- and oropharynges), not by attempting to intensify symptoms. To follow the latter course is to promote muscular interference and invite throat constriction.

See Nasality
Sensation
Sensations of
Vibration

Soaring Tone: a vocalized sound that is free, lyric, and possesses those qualities associated with fine singing.

"Soaring" tones are indicative of a well-balanced registration, a precise resonance adjustment, and general vocal health.

Soft Palate, or Velum: a fold of muscular tissue covered by a mucous membrane, from the center of which dangles the uvula.

The soft palate forms the anterior boundary of the oropharynx and the posterior extension of the hard palate. Its movement is governed by five muscle systems: the glossopalatini and pharyngopalatini, which depress it, the levator veli palatini and uvular, which elevate it, and a depressor-tensor, the tensor veli palatini.

The soft palate performs two primary functions: 1) to relax during respiration in order to open the passageway from the nose into the nasopharynx, and 2) to perform a sphincter action to effect a separation between the alimentary canal and the nasal port during the act of swallowing. When adapted to the vocal process, the walls of the soft palate, as part of the oropharynx, assume a shape and dimension appropriate to the selection and energizing of those frequencies necessary to define and resonate a wide spectrum of vowel qualities. In "dark" or "covered" singing, for example, the soft palate becomes elevated (accompanied by a corresponding lowering of the larynx), while for the production of "bright" tone qualities it lowers as the larynx rises. The soft palate also controls the opening and closing of the nasal port, and the reason mid-tonal range humming is often utilized as an exercise during training is that, apart from its tendency to disengage the chest register from its coordinate relationship with the head voice, and to partially relax wrong throat tension, it ensures a desired opening of the nasal passages.

Because of the various roles played by the soft palate (swallowing, articulation, resonance and vowel formation), its coordinate relationship with other laryngeal and pharyngeal activities determines in large part the success or failure of the phonative process. Like most elements of the vocal function, the soft palate should never be acted upon directly, but be allowed to form and adjust in response to the concepts by which it is innervated.

See Arched Palate
Formants
Hum
Laryngeal
Suspension
Mental Concept
Modern Methods
Register
Resonance
Standing Wave
Vowel

Soft Singing: sustained phonation at low levels of intensity.

Correct tone production at low levels of intensity is difficult. Unless the technique is highly efficient, the throat parts easily revert to their natural valvular action and constrict, a tendency difficult to reverse. To sing softly without constricting, the chest register musculature (the arytenoids) must hold synergetically in direct proportion to the strength of the contraction of the antagonistic system which produces the head voice. If, however, the chest register is energized, this mechanism (which responds reflexively to high levels of intensity) will stiffen as the intensity is lowered, causing the larynx to rise and the tongue and jaw to "lock" and become tremulous.

The head voice (which corresponds to cricothyroid tension, a muscle system faceted at one point to the lower constrictors), on the other hand, must perform its pulling action without engaging the swallowing muscles to which it is attached. Without a proper balance between these two mechanisms, therefore, the laryngeal suspension cannot maintain a position of open-throated resonance and will collapse. Thus, open-throated soft singing is an extremely difficult technical accomplishment.

In view of the difficulties encountered in maintaining an open-throated resonance adjustment when singing at lowered levels of intensity, it is evident that soft singing is potentially dangerous, especially when it is sustained for protracted periods of time. Traditionally, the legitimacy of soft singing was tested by swelling a single tone from *piano* to *forte*. If the full voice did not expand willingly and smoothly out of the soft beginning, then something was held to be wrong with either the registration or the resonance adjustment (as expressed in vowel quality), or both. The deceptive property of soft singing is that it can often be aesthetically pleasing when it is not being properly produced.

From an interpretive and aesthetic viewpoint, it is advantageous to consider that lowered levels of intensity are a special type of tonal texture, and that opposite extremes of intensity represent the more obvious aspects of tone "color." In full-voiced singing, where both register mechanisms are under optimum tension, the voice will take on a "ringing" quality, whereas in soft singing the same tones will be more mellow and sweet. Thus, while correct soft singing is possible because of a shifting balance in the registration, it continues to share the identical resonance characteristics that prevail during full-voiced singing; the sole difference between the two extremes of texture and intensity is that the energy required to sustain open-throated soft singing often appears disproportionate to that needed when singing full voice. This paradox can be explained, however, by the fact that laryngeal stabilization and an open-throated resonance adjustment must be fed the same amount of energy regardless of the intensity level being sung.

See **Breath Support**
Building on the Soft
Carrying Power
Energy
Messa di Voce
Register

One of the common misconceptions about laryngeal stabilization is that this equilibrium is maintained by means of breath and/or tonal support. An equilibrium, however, is self-supportive and does not need "shoring up" or muscular "propping" to ensure its continuance. More pertinent to the issue is the fact that the muscular systems being held in balanced tension are sufficiently oxygenized to sustain this equilibrium during both loud and soft singing.

Solar (or Celiac) Plexus: a network of nerves and ganglia (groups of cell bodies located outside the central nervous system) situated behind the stomach; sometimes referred to as the "abdominal" or "visceral brain;" the so-called "pit of the stomach."

See **Anxiety**
Autonomic Nervous System
Kinesthesia
Vocal Organs

As a part of the autonomic nervous system concerned with visceral and involuntary functions, the solar plexus performs as an internal environmental control system which responds to emotional stimuli. Thus, its nerves and ganglia are not subject to intellectual control, but react to external environmental pressures.

Since the solar plexus does not connect with the recurrent nerve which innervates the laryngeal musculature, it is not a significant factor in phonatory control. It is a factor, however, in "performance nerves" and their control mechanisms.

Solfège: French, derived from the Italian *solfeggio;* vocal exercises based upon the tonic sol-fa system. In France, a distinction is still made between solfège and a vocalise; the latter is borrowed from the Italian *vocalizzo,* denoting an exercise or vocal composition without syllables. The custom in Italy is to combine the two under the single heading *solfeggi.*

Solfège, a derivative of Solmization (a method of musical notation using syllables based upon the Greek hexachord), was developed by Guido d'Arezzo in the eleventh century. Upon hearing a hymn composed in the year 770 by Paulus Diaconus for a text written in praise of St. John Baptist, Guido observed that the syllables beginning on the first note of six successive phrases coincided with the six pitches of the natural hexachord C, D, E, F, G, A. The text is as follows:

Ut queant *Re*sonare fibris,
*Mi*ragestorum *Fa*muli tuorum,
*Sol*vi polluti *La*bii reatum,
Sancte Joannes.

About the year 1600, it was felt that the hexachord should be extended by one note to become a heptachord. Consequently, *si* was added, apparently by combining the first letters of Sancte Ioannes, as John was spelled in Adonic verse. The syllable *ut* was later replaced by *do,* since many felt the substitution would add greater sonority to the voice than that offered by the original.

The tonic sol-fa system was an important inclusion in early training programs, being used to combine sight-singing with ear training and tone production. From the standpoint of vocal development, both in France and in Italy, its essential purpose was to coordinate tone and articulation so that one would neither conflict with nor diminish the effectiveness of the other. The study of solfège and *solfeggi,* therefore, was considered an important preliminary step toward readying the student for his first venture into song literature, and ultimately, opera.

The most famous corpus of solfège ever assembled was composed in 1796 by professors of the Conservatoire de Paris under the direction of Cherubini. Of particular interest in the many volumes constituting this opus is the fact of their extraordinary difficulty. Given their thoroughness, it is clear that the Golden Age of Song which followed was not an historical accident, but the product of finely honed teaching skills, a desire to exploit the functional potential of the human voice, and sensitivity to musical style. Especially noteworthy is the fact that the music of the time did not require the extreme virtuosity contained in the solfège and vocalises. That fact supports the conclusion reached by many that the great operatic age which followed, and the seemingly excessive technical demands it placed upon the singer, was but a logical consequence of the availability of a great number of highly disciplined performers able to exploit the new music.

In reviewing the history of solfège, it is apparent that these studies helped build a great vocal tradition. What is imperative, if the level of technical skill associated with that era is to be attained again, is that these exercises, together with the principles upon which the training methods of the time were founded, should be restored to use. It is undeniable, of course, that the study necessary to achieve the goal of technical excellence obviously extant during the early part of the nineteenth century required a considerable amount of self-sacrifice and dedication, a prospect not easily contemplated in this age of shortcuts. The road is nevertheless well worth the traveling even when one falls short of the ultimate objective (as the majority of those who try inevitably must).

Solfeggio: See Solfège.

Somatic: of, relating to, or affecting the body and its organs.

Body condition, emotional attitudes, and suppressed subconscious responses are frequently expressed somatically through "body language." Observation of the latter, therefore, can frequently be of significant pedagogic value.

Somatic Nervous System: a component of the central and peripheral nervous systems responsible for controlling finely differentiated muscular movements.

In singing, the somatic nervous system collaborates with the autonomic nervous system (those nerves concerned with such vital involuntary processes as digestion, circulation of the blood, and breathing), but its primary function is to convey information along afferent and efferent pathways to and from the central nervous system. Thus, volitionally controllable movements are recorded and controlled by the somatic nervous system.

Sombre: French, "dark" or "deep."

Sombre is the term Manuel Garcia used to refer to tonal qualities produced with a fully coupled resonance adjustment: that is, with a raised palate and a slightly lowered laryngeal position. In recent years, "dark" tones have been equated with so-called "covered" tones, which clearly was not Garcia's intent. While "covering" will darken the tonal quality somewhat, it does so by introducing varying degrees of vowel distortion (*e.g., ah* to *uh*), and unless used with discretion, it promotes throat constriction.

The conceptual confusion inherent in these two terms is due to the problems encountered in the area of the register "break," where the chest voice is commonly pushed (especially with weightier voices) beyond its natural boundaries. The result is tones which appear "too open." While covering will alleviate this condition, its value remains open to question for many reasons:

1. A smooth transition from "covered" tones to bright vowels is impossible except by constricting the throat;
2. The resonance adjustment lacks precise tuning;
3. It distorts rather than modifies the vowel, and
4. True *sombre* qualities are difficult to produce in the "break" area, especially at high levels of intensity, since higher pitch levels require a delicately balanced registration and a *shortened* resonance column for precise tuning.

Thus, covering is at best a temporary expedient, not a permanent solution.

See **Bel Canto**
   Modern Methods

See **Afferent**
   Autonomic
      Nervous System
   Limbic System

Dark tone qualities, therefore, especially when associated with covering, are not favorable to a correct resonation of pitches lying in the higher tonal range. On the contrary, a proper "rounding" of tones falling within the "break" area depends upon a successful joining of the two register mechanisms. This is accomplished by lowering the intensity of the chest voice while simultaneously (conceptually) increasing the pull of the head voice. When this rebalancing has been brought about without disturbing the resonance adjustment, it will be possible to modify dark tones to bright tones unaccompanied by a radical change in the resonance adjustment.

To mistake the roundness characteristic of a head voice-dominated technique in the tonal area under discussion for "darkening" or "covering" is a serious pedagogic mistake. Neither dark tones nor those considered covered are essential to the production of high tones under ideal technical conditions. While they are useful during intermediate stages of training, their value also extends to the area of interpretation.

See Covering,
  (To) Cover
  Register
  Resonance
  Vowel, Dark
    and Bright

Sonance: the aural sum of the physical properties (*e.g.*, pitch, intensity, timbre, harmonic spectrum, *etc.*) of vocal tone.

Sonority: the aural sum of the resonance characteristics of vocal tone.

An opulent or rich tonal sonority is indicative of an open-throated resonance adjustment.

Soprano: a term derived from the Italian word *sopra*, meaning "above;" also thought by certain authorities to be derived from *sovrana,* meaning "sovereign, chief, or highest;" a voice of high range and bright quality; the highest of the three divisions into which women's voices are classified. Also included among soprano singers are boys whose voices have not yet changed, and the *castrati,* who dazzled audiences during the seventeenth, eighteenth and early nineteenth centuries.

Originally, voices were classified as soprano, alto, tenor, or bass, but with the growing popularity of opera and a corresponding advance in technical skills, new categories were added. The earliest additions were *soprano leggiero* (light soprano), lyric soprano, and dramatic soprano. During the latter part of the nineteenth century, new additions included the *spinto,* a lyric soprano capable of sustaining the rigors of singing dramatic roles; the *acuto,* or coloratura soprano; the Falcon, named after Marie Cornélie Falcon (1812—1897), whose special qualities were probably the French equivalent of an Italian *spinto;* the *soprano assoluta,* one who essays all roles from dramatic to *leggiero,* and the Wagnerian soprano.

The total tonal compass of the above-mentioned voice types extends from G below middle C to the G above high C. Each category is potentially capable of developing a range of two and a half octaves which can be sung smoothly and with flexibility, and with ample carrying power.

Sotto Voce: Italian, "under voice;" softly; whispered.

An interpretive effect in which the resonance characteristics associated with the chest and head voices are deliberately neutralized.

Sound: movements of the air particles set in motion by a vibrator; vibratory sensations relayed from the ear by the auditory nerve and perceived by the brain. Sound is separated into two broad categories—noise, or nonperiodic vibrations, and tone, or vibrations which are periodic or regular.

The qualitative properties of sound are determined by its harmonic structure, the hearing acuity of the listener, and such diverse factors as sociological and cultural influences, psychological constitution, and aesthetic preferences developed during training.

Sound Wave: the movement of particles within an elastic medium (as, for example, air) that travel outward from a vibratory source in concentric spheres of condensation and rarefaction. A sound wave, whether simple or complex, is comprised of four basic elements: 1) frequency, 2) amplitude, 3) duration, and 4) form. Taken together, these elements are perceived as musical tone.

Sounding Board: a rigid but elastic surface which, in proportion to its size and general conformation, amplifies the sound waves produced by a vibrator.

In order for a sounding board to amplify the frequencies set in motion by a vibrator, the impulses must be transmitted through direct contact, as for example by pressing a tuning fork against it, or through a conducting agent such as the bridge of a violin. There are, however, no anatomical parts in the human body capable of functioning as a sounding board, and this type of amplification is not a factor in singing.

Sounding Board Resonance: See Resonance, Sounding Board.

Spectrum: in acoustics, a visual representation of the component parts (sinusoids, or simple sound waves) of a complex sound. This is usually plotted on a graph recording two variables, as for example the strength of various harmonics, or partials, *versus* the fundamental tone, amplitude *versus* frequency, or frequency *versus* formant strength.

(To) Spin a Tone: to produce a vocalized sound that creates the illusion of soaring freely through space; a shimmering tone quality which usually indicates the presence of a true vibrato.

Spinto: Italian, "pushed" or "stretched."

The term *spinto* is used to describe a voice type (usually soprano or tenor) that is genuinely lyric, but large enough to sing dramatic roles. A *spinto,* however, is not capable of the tonal intensity of its dramatic counterpart. Accepted at face value, the term would appear to have a negative connotation, since when used correctly the voice is never pushed in order to produce powerful tones.

Spontaneity: unconstrained, unpremeditated muscular movements which occur in response to conceptual or environmental stimuli.

Spread Tone: a vocalized sound whose tonal characteristics reflect reinforced inharmonic partials and the diffusion, rather than concentration, of sound impulses.

"Spreading" is usually caused by the excessive dominance of the chest register, *i.e.*, an imbalanced registration, coupled with an elevated laryngeal adjustment, a condition often encouraged by a habitual "smiling" mouth position and oversinging in an effort to achieve tonal "brightness" and/or "ring."

Although there is nothing essentially wrong with adopting a pleasant facial expression while singing, raising this procedure to the status of a functional principle merely serves to distort the vocal process. The ultimate result of spreading is a premature loss of vocal skills.

See **Bocca Ridente**

Stable Vowel: a vowel phoneme that is considered acoustically ideal and used pedagogically as a standard of comparison for other vowels; a concept designed to enhance textual intelligibility through phonetics, with stress placed upon the physiological aspects of vowel quality, and the articulators in particular, rather than vocal imagery, or the utilization of techniques based upon principles which stimulate an organic system into predictable patterns of response.

The concept of a stable vowel is based upon phonemic identification, or as described by D. Ralph Appelman, the establishment of "a steady state characteristic of a vowel with well-defined boundaries in its proper acoustic position." Such a process involves an awareness of phonemic changes at two levels: 1) a perception of vowel quality as it agrees with or departs from a basic or primary vowel, and 2) the articulatory adjustments, such as tongue-backing and lip-rounding, which accompany such changes.

The perception of vowel quality as advocated by phoneticians includes concepts related to pure vowels, basic vowels, vowel migration, and quality alternate vowels. These perceptions are purportedly accomplished by "imitating the basic vowel and quality alternatives from recorded sound, matching the timbre [being] accomplished by concentrating upon the phoneme and disregarding the timbre. If the recorded phoneme is matched, the quality or timbre of the vowel will be more nearly similar within each pitch range and intensity variation."[97]

There are four fundamental weaknesses in the phonetic solution to the problem of textual intelligibility as it relates to singing: 1) it falsely assumes that a proper positioning of the articulators effects a corresponding improvement in the mechanical response of the vocal organs; 2) it ignores the influence of laryngeal muscular activity on the ultimate tonal product; 3) it fails to take into account the fact that spoken phonemes, as proven by spectrography, are not the same when they are sung, and 4) to remain stable, all primary vowels must be restricted to a pitch range of scarcely more than an octave. It is evident, therefore, that these formulations are based on acoustic phenomena rather than events which transpire at the sound source (the laryngeal pharynx). Consequently, the mechanical processes within the throat parts, which yield "stable" and other vowels, are ignored along with the spontaneity which is so crucial to the stimulation of natural movement.

In the absence of any functional principle, the phonemic controls proposed, as well as the mechanistic implications of the process itself, while undoubtedly useful in the study of foreign languages, must be looked upon with suspicion when considered from the standpoint of voice-building and the development of technical skills. As a theoretical postulate, it neither explains the cause of the textural differences noted, nor accounts for the modifications of tone quality both above and below those pitches upon which a stable vowel can be articulated, nor does it

[97]D. Ralph Appelman, *The Science of Vocal Pedagogy.* (Bloomington, Indiana: Indiana University Press, 1967), pp. 223, 229.

address those problems encountered in eliminating throat constriction or in correcting a "mixed" registration.

Another serious conceptual error is to consider stable vowels to be "pure," and to imply therefore that all others are impure derivatives. In reality, all properly produced vowels are equally pure, each having its own individuality. Since to produce any vowel "purely," *i.e.*, without tonal blemish, requires an exceedingly high level of technical proficiency, refined concepts, and a precisely coordinated laryngeal musculature, the question must be raised as to whether or not the mechanistic procedures utilized in concepts related to stable vowels are more than marginally beneficial, if at all, as aids in achieving that proficiency.

Staccato: Italian, "short," "detached;" a short, detached vocalized sound possessing true pitch and well-formed resonance; the musical figure that elicits such a response.

Accepting Garcia's genuine intent for his term *coup de glotte*, staccato might be defined as "a reiteration of the *coup de glotte*;" that is, the rapid reiteration of a precise opening and closing movement of the vocal folds. For a properly executed staccato, these movements will occur within an open-throated resonance adjustment. The ability to execute staccato figures indicates a high level of technical proficiency.

Since the muscular movements involved in staccati must occur with great rapidity, it is essential that reliance is placed upon reflexive responses, rather than overt muscular activity, to execute this musical effect. Therefore, staccati should never be attempted by initiating a series of diaphragmatic contractions or "abdominal tucks." The diaphragm is without proprioceptive nerve endings and cannot be controlled volitionally, while the abdominals are far too sluggish in movement to coordinate with the rapid opening and closing of the glottal space required by successive staccati. What the successful execution of staccato figures does require is a head voice-dominated technique resonated within a poised and stabilized laryngeal adjustment.

Standing Wave: a pattern of vibratory motions or pressure oscillations whose optimum point of amplitude occurs at the glottis, or vibrator, with its minimum point of amplitude at the lip opening. In singing, a standing wave is produced when a vibratory pattern is reflected back toward the tonal source, to combine with the newly injected waves set in motion by the movement of the vocal folds.

The formulations of acousticians with respect to a standing wave are best understood by examining the vibratory pattern of the sounds produced by wind instruments. In the brass family, a standing wave is created when acoustic energy is returned toward the mouthpiece by the flare of the bell, a principle which was clearly understood as early as the mid-nineteenth century. Depending upon the interaction between the injected and returning sound waves moving through the tubing, pressure variations can either be increased or decreased. According to A. H. Benade, these variations are known to have a positive effect upon the lip movements of the player, to a certain extent (when the technique is correct) making the lips self-vibratile.[98]

While there is no direct parallel between the acoustic properties of brass in

[98]Arthur H. Benade, "The Physics of Brasses," *Scientific American* (July, 1973), 44–55.

struments and the human voice, it is nevertheless evident that certain acoustic similarities, while not exact, do in fact exist.

The first indication that brass instruments and the human voice share certain acoustic principles resulted from experiments conducted by Raoul Husson.[99] Of unusual interest is the fact that the vocal intensity leaving the singer's mouth amounts to but 20% of the energy generated within the larynx. When evaluated in conjunction with Husson's neurochronaxic theory (which holds that the vocal folds are relatively self-vibratile because of electrical impulses generated by the will), this new piece of evidence is most significant. What appears to suggest itself as a possibility is that the 80% of tonal energy that does not move beyond the mouth of the singer is, like the reflected acoustic energy within the tubing of a horn, returned to the tonal source to be converted into a standing wave. There is also an undeniable parallel between the degree of self-vibratility of the horn player's lips when a standing wave is present, and the self-vibratility of the vocal folds when the vocal mechanism functions efficiently.

Johan Sundberg arrived at a similar conclusion when he incorporated the concept of the standing wave into his acoustic explanation of the movement of sound waves through the vocal tract, finding this phenomenon to exert a profound influence on the structure of the formants.[100] When the expansion and contraction of the pharyngeal cavities occur at a point where the standing wave is at maximum or minimum amplitude, the formant frequencies will rise or lower accordingly. Consequently, the physical dimensions of the resonators as they respond to the vowel determine whether or not optimum pressure oscillations will center within the glottal area. Since the greatest amplitude of oscillation in a standing wave occurs at the vibratory source, and properly energized formants are a product of a precise pharyngeal cavity tuning, it would appear that the relationship between the two is more than coincidental.

It is probable, therefore, that it is the close association between the formant frequencies and the standing wave that determines the quality and intensity of the tone produced. When the cavities are properly adjusted, the energy expended by the singer is both economical and in inverse proportion to the dynamic level of the sound emitted. Unless, however, the pharyngeal cavities are adjusted so as to place the maximum amount of pressure at the sound source (the area immediately adjacent to the vibrator, *i.e.*, the vocal folds), the optimum amount of resonance potential cannot be realized, and greater physical force must be used to compensate for the deficiency.

By acknowledging the presence of a standing wave in the vocal tract, Sundberg tacitly admits the existence of an indirect acoustic parallel between brass instruments and the human voice. If each formant is associated with a standing wave, it is evident that some agency or agencies above the glottis must be responsible for energizing the formants and reflecting some of the waves backward. Sundberg, in common with most teachers of voice, believes that the position of the jaw, the body and the tip of the tongue, together with lip formations, creates the formant frequencies, and that a standing wave is created by a specific type of positioning of these parts.

A more recent research paper by Krzysztof Izdebski and Thomas Shipp tends to refute Sundberg's contention with regard to the importance of the articulators.

[99]Raoul Husson, "Rôle de la fourniture laryngée dans la formation du timbre des voyelles parlées et chantées et genèse des passages et des régistres de la voix," *Rev. franc. Phoniat.* (1935).

[100]Johan Sundberg, "The Acoustics of the Singing Voice," *Scientific American* (March, 1977), 16–23.

STANDING WAVE

[101]Krzysztof Izdebski and Thomas Shipp, "The Effect of Vertical Laryngeal Position on Singers' Sustained Vowel Formants," *Journal of Research in Singing* Vol. II, No. 2 (July, 1979), 8.

[102]Charles Lunn, *The Philosophy of Voice* (New York: G. Schirmer, 1903). [103]Edmund J. Myer, *Vocal Reinforcement* (Boston: The Boston Music Co., 1891).

Izdebski and Shipp state in their conclusion that "our data shows no interaction between vertical laryngeal positions and either fundamental frequency or formant frequency in the singers studied, either with the jaw free to vary, or when it was held fixed."[101] On a pragmatic level, the latter viewpoint seems more practical than Sundberg's formulation, since it is evident that the jaw, tongue and lips are in relatively constant motion when the articulators are involved in communicating the verbal text, indicating that the resonation of the vowel and the articulation of consonants are two separate functions.

Sundberg's choice of the expression "sound source" is noteworthy, for if the amplitude of oscillations is greatest at the vibratory source, and, as Husson suggests, only a fraction of the total energy moves into the outer atmosphere (as is true with the standing wave), then tonal energy must to a certain extent be "bottled up" within the pharyngeal resonators. This implies that the vocal mechanism, like other power generators, *e.g.*, the steam boiler, is in its own way designed to provide an essential balance between pressure and resistance in order to intensify the tonal energy at the vibratory source. As is true with other generators, pressure must be built up and partially contained; otherwise, energy expenditure will be uneconomical. The question arises as to how this is to be accomplished vocally.

Two possibilities exist to assist in the creation of a standing wave: 1) a narrowing of the false vocal cords, which permits some of the sound waves to emerge while redirecting a certain percentage of the tonal energy downward, and 2) an adjustment of the mouth cavity, which can conceivably function somewhat in the manner of the flared bell of the trumpet.

The most likely source of resistance to internal pressure, as pointed out by Lunn,[102] Myer[103] and others, is provided by the false vocal cords. By their position of relative approximation during phonation, the false vocal cords cause the ventricular sacs to inflate; the type of inflation, according to investigators, depends upon the type of technique being employed. Thus, together with the movements of the vocal folds themselves, the vibrations pulsating within the ventricular sacs reinforce the downward movement of the vibratory pattern toward the tracheal area, thereby equalizing both sub- and supraglottal pressure. The effect of this arrangement is to maintain the optimum pressure oscillations associated with a standing wave within the glottal area. Under these technical conditions the vocal folds, like the lips of the horn player, become relatively self-vibratile.

While the mouth cavity is looked upon by many theorists as a source of supraglottal pressure, this concept must be discarded, since there is virtually no pressure build-up in an open-ended cavity. If the function of the mouth cavity, however, is considered to be acoustically parallel with the flared bell of the horn, it can assume a more practical role in tone production. Although this is pure conjecture, it is probable that the hard palate and the areas behind the upper and lower teeth are responsible (when positioned correctly) for reflecting the vibratory impulses, and by returning a certain percentage of them toward the glottal area, creating a standing wave.

Speculation upon the importance of the standing wave to the vocal function is particularly interesting since it conceivably rationalizes some of the traditional and rather metaphysical concepts that have been so difficult to teach and almost impossible to acquire through either imitation or volitional acts. It is quite possible that directives such as "directing the tone toward the hard palate," "placing the voice behind the upper teeth," and "drinking in the tone" are kinesthetic indicators of the presence of a standing wave. While directives of this description have no reality either conceptually or physically for those singers whose technique is faulty, these sense impressions can be very real for those who sing at a higher level of technical efficiency.

From a pedagogic standpoint, practices designed to replicate a symptom without first setting up those conditions which yield that particular symptom are futile. It is not that the symptoms are without reality, but simply that they cannot be realized until such time as the physical coordination within the throat parts is so arranged as to yield those symptoms.

The presence of a standing wave is an important acoustic factor in a correct tone production. As Sundberg was so careful to point out, however, its presence is due to a specific shape and design of the pharyngeal cavities. If a standing wave is to be created, therefore, training techniques must turn away from metaphysical concepts and a dependence upon imagery, and employ those functional principles which alone will establish the physical prerequisites which account for its presence. This improvement can best be brought about by establishing a well-balanced registration and a resonance adjustment within the laryngeal pharynx which is free of constricting tensions.

See Coupling
Formants
Drink In the Tone
Modern Methods
Neurochronaxic
Theory
Register
Resonance
Vowel

Static Adjustment: a general rigidity of the vocal musculature that impedes spontaneous, natural movement.

Training based upon voice "placement," "breath control," and "nasal resonance" inadvertently encourages tonal uniformity and static physical adjustments, and it consequently promotes throat constriction.

Stationary Air: that breath which remains in the lungs after expiration.

In expansive breathing (such as that required when singing or in other physical exercise), stationary air is referred to as "residual breath," whereas in normal, or "tidal" breathing, it is called "reserve breath."

See Breathing
Dead Space

Steely Tone: a vocalized sound whose hard, "edgy" tonal characteristics result from excessive force and from tongue and throat constriction.

Invariably, "steely" singing can be ultimately traced to an energized chest register driven too high in the tonal range, causing the throat to stiffen. In a correct technique of singing, the chest register should always respond synergetically, in which case a steely tone quality is almost impossible to produce.

See Register
Synergy

Stentorian Voice: an unusually loud or powerful voice.

The term "stentorian," derived from the name of a loud-voiced Greek herald in the time of the Trojan War, carries no qualitative implications other than volume.

Sternocleidomastoid Muscles: part of a muscular triangle located in the neck whose medial wall is formed by the hyoglossus and thyrohyoid muscles and the middle and inferior constrictors; the muscles that rotate the head on its axis.

The sternocleidomastoids originate at the mastoid bone behind the ear and attach to the clavicle (collarbone) and the sternum (breastbone), and when tensed, elevate these two parts of the skeletal framework. Consequently, they are active in high chest (clavicular) breathing.

The essential function of the sternocleidomastoids is postural control. Because they are in such close proximity to the larynx (which is positioned between them) and the extrinsic laryngeal muscles, however, they can, when tensed, seriously interfere with the phonative process. As a rule, relaxation of the chest and shoulders will neutralize the negative tensions engendered by this muscle system.

See Neck Tension
    Posture

Sternohyoid Muscles: a paired muscular system that connects the breastbone, or sternum, with the hyoid bone at the base of the tongue.

The contraction of the sternohyoids and omohyoids (which connect each wing of the hyoid bone with the shoulder blades) is an integral part of the inspanning of the larynx, a process that slightly lowers the base of the tongue and the laryngeal position, closes the glottal space, and helps transform the respiratory tract into a singing instrument.

See Larynx

Sternothyroid Muscles: a paired muscular system that connects the breast-bone, or sternum, with the thyroid cartilage.

The contraction of the sternothyroids pulls down on the thyroid cartilage, a procedure that lowers the larynx and serves as a natural antagonist to the contraction of the cricothyroids, which are the muscles responsible for the tonal qualities commonly recognized as head voice or falsetto. When the sternothyroids fail to hold against the pull of the cricothyroids, the interior vocalis muscles are forced to make up for the deficiency by acting as surrogate antagonists to cricothyroid tension. This fairly common functional imbalance results in tonal unsteadiness, inflexibility, "chesty" tonal characteristics, and difficulty in managing the upper tonal range. It is a condition common to those who are overly zealous to develop so-called "big" voices, and to those who prematurely attempt heavy operatic roles.

See Larynx
    Lowered Larynx

Sternum: the compound ventral bone to which the ribs are attached; the breastbone.

Movement of the sternum is dependent upon intercostal muscular contractions that expand or contract the rib cage during inspiration and expiration.

See Breathing
    Ribs

Stiff Throat: a rigidity of the vocal mechanism brought on by throat constriction.

Throat constriction is usually a symptom of an imbalanced registration and/or a faulty laryngeal position (too high, too low, or "collapsed"). However, it is also the result of the subconscious suppression of anxieties (hence, the expression "choked up"), and is a natural concomitant of peristaltic movement (swallowing). One of the difficulties in forming an efficient resonance adjustment is the achievement of a relatively fixed, "open-throated" laryngeal adjustment to counter the latter tendency.

Another occasional source of throat constriction is the constant repetition of the same vocal exercises, which tends to "overtrain" one kind of muscular movement at the expense of others. This is why changing voice teachers is sometimes immediately and noticeably beneficial: the mere changing of exercise patterns offers welcome relief to a "bored" muscular system. Unless the new exercises satisfy the functional needs of the mechanism, they too will ultimately bring on stiffness, rigidity, and constriction.

See **Throat**
    Constriction

Stimulus: an agent that evokes muscular movement, sensory excitation, or glandular secretion from a living organism.

Successful training procedures depend upon the proper stimulation of the vocal musculature through appropriately designed patterns of pitch, intensity and vowel. When managed skillfully, such programs stimulate natural movement and supersede all attempts to gain direct control over the mechanism (*e.g.*, "breath control," "nasal resonance," "placement," *etc.*).

When the vocal function is efficient, no energy need be expended in "placing" the voice, for the voice will "place" itself; resonance need not be artificially "made," for vocal tone will be intrinsically resonant, and breath need not be "controlled," for breath expenditure will be controlled by the efficient and economical use of energy. Stimulation of the mechanism through proper concepts provides the best solution to these and related problems.

See **Breathing**
    Energy
    Laryngeal
      Suspension
    Register

Stop Plosive: a consonant or combination of consonants whose articulation requires a momentary interruption of tonal flow prior to the articulation of a plosive (*e.g.*, "te*sts*").

To sound the example cited above, the speaker or singer articulates the first sibilant (implosion), momentarily interrupts the tonal flow (plosion), and concludes by articulating the *ts* (explosion). When the pattern comes before a vowel phoneme, it is called a "plosive;" after a vowel, it is called a "stop."

The mechanics of the stop plosive are more properly a concern of the speech therapist than of the student or teacher of singing.

See **Consonants**

Straight Tone: a vocalized sound that lacks tonal pulse (whether vibrato, tremolo, or wobble).

"Straight" tones make the mature voice sound lifeless, and go against the grain of natural function and health. Although they can be effectively used to create special interpretive effects (fatigue, old age, grief, mysticism, unearthliness, *etc.*), their habitual use is an indication of a subconscious preference for or reliance upon intellectual processes rather than upon genuine, spontaneous feeling.

Although a relatively straight tone production usually provides cleaner harmonic definition in choral singing, its use, even in this instance, is a compromise, for if all the members of an ensemble were to possess a correct vocal technique, the combined natural tonal pulse (vibrato) of the group would be regular, and consequently unobtrusive.

A true vibrato is a natural corollary of an efficient vocal function.

See **Tremolo**
    Vibrato
    Wobble

Strained Tone: a vocalized sound that reflects muscular interference and compensatory tensions resulting from abuse of the mechanism.

Both conceptual refinements and mechanical improvements are required to alleviate vocal strain.

Strap Muscles: muscles which connect to the hyoid bone above, to the sternum (breast bone) below, and to the pharyngeal musculature behind. The muscle systems comprising this group are the thyrohyoid, the sternohyoid, the sternothyroid and the laryngopharyngeal.

The "strap" muscles are so named because of their shape. Their function in singing is to stabilize the larynx.

Stress: See Anxiety; Consonants.

Stretchers of the Vocal Folds: the cricothyroid muscles, whose contraction brings the ring and shield cartilages together and makes the vibrating surface of the vocal folds longer and thinner.

Except for the contraction of the interior vocalis muscles, the vocal folds depend almost entirely upon the contraction of the cricothyroids, and their opposers the arytenoids, for the elasticity and tension needed for the production of vocal tone.

Stretching of the Vocal Folds: adjustments made in the length, thickness, and general contour of the vocal folds during phonation by the contraction of two muscle systems, the cricothyroids and the arytenoids, which are capable of functioning either independently or in any combination of shared responsibility to produce qualities commonly recognized as "vocal registers."

The stretching of the vocal folds is exceedingly complex, but since muscular antagonism is essential, there may be said to be two muscle systems, the cricothyroids and the arytenoids, which are most critical. Because these systems can be stimulated to respond either independently or as a coordinate unit, their activity falls into three broad categories of adjustment: 1) cricothyroid tension alone; 2) arytenoid tension alone, and 3) a sharing of tension, which, expressed in terms of ratio, offers a wide variety of alternatives, only one of which is ideal for the pitch intensity and vowel pattern being sung.

While it is possible to produce pitches of recognizable quality within relatively narrow pitch ranges when either of the above muscle systems functions alone, these qualities (familiarly known as falsetto and chest register) are aesthetically unattractive and too limited to be considered a legitimate form of singing. Because they can be isolated, exercised as independent units, and combined in a variety of ways, however, it becomes possible to restructure a faulty vocal technique, a process known prior to the twentieth century as "cultivating" the voice.

Since the ratio of tension shared between the cricothyroids and the arytenoids influences the textural properties of the ultimate tonal product, it becomes possible to estimate the degree to which each of the muscle systems involved is participating through their aural equivalents. Thus, by knowing the formulae for stimulating the two muscle systems so that they will either separate or combine, and by recognizing the tonal equivalents of these various arrangements, a considerable body of involuntary muscular activities taking place at the sound source (larynx) can be developed and integrated into a technique of singing which ultimately becomes a concrete kinesthetic and conceptual reality.

The interrelationship between the cricothyroids and the arytenoids (which equate with the falsetto and the chest registers, respectively) is summarized as follows:

In a pure falsetto, the cricothyroid muscles contract with virtually no opposition either from their natural antagonists, the arytenoids, or from the interior vocalis muscles. Under these conditions the tonal range is limited to an octave, beginning at B below middle C. As the range and/or intensity is increased, however, cricothyroid tension is increased proportionately, a tension countered by either a bracing action or energized activity from their antagonist, the arytenoids.

The coordinate activity of the cricothyroids and the arytenoids in response to range extension further invites the participation of the sternothyroids and the thyrohyoids. This "stretching of the vocal folds" immediately transforms the tonal quality, yielding characteristics commonly recognized as the coordinated falsetto or head voice. As the range and/or intensity increases, the coordinated falsetto is further modified by the contraction of the sternohyoids and omohyoids to assist in effecting a partial closing of the glottal space, a coordination which eliminates the tonal breathiness characteristic of the pure falsetto. Thus modified, the tone quality becomes clear and musical, indicating that contact has been made with the so-called "full voice." Further range extension and/or increases in intensity are accomplished by a contraction of the palatal and cricopharyngeal muscles, movements that result in the appearance of a more fully developed head voice.

Even a well-developed head voice, however, is weak in its lower tonal range, since the pure falsetto (from which the head voice is derived) extends only from B below middle C to its octave. Below the area of the "break," therefore, the head voice must be strengthened by combining it with the chest register, that is, by increased arytenoid tension. The arytenoids (in particular, the crico-, lateral, and transverse arytenoids) narrow the glottal space and, by holding against the contraction of the cricothyroids, eliminate the breathiness in the lower extension of the head voice.

A complete closing of the glottal space, however, depends upon the activity of the crisscrossed aryvocalis and thyrovocalis muscles, whose contractions "fatten out" the central portion of the vocal folds, which, like overstretched rubber bands, thin out in the middle when the antagonistic contractions become strong. The glottal space in the lower extension of the head voice cannot, in fact, be completely closed without the assistance of the vocalis muscles, although their participation is dependent upon a favorable balance of tension having first been established between the cricothyroid and arytenoid musculatures.

A correct ratio of tension between the primary muscle systems which draw the vocal folds into tension is not only crucial for adjusting them to the right length, thickness and tension for the pitch, intensity and vowel being produced, but is also profoundly beneficial in promoting laryngeal stabilization (without which the resonance characteristics would be deficient). Another advantage is that it strengthens and vitalizes the vibratory impulses delivered to the pharyngeal cavities lying immediately above them, and upon which continuity of resonance is wholly dependent.

See Falsetto
Falsetto or
Head Voice
Head Voice
Laryngeal
Suspension
Register
Resonance
Vowel

Strident Tone: a vocalized sound that has harsh, shrill, or "edgy" tonal characteristics.

"Strident" tones are the result of the high laryngeal position and tongue constriction characteristic of a "mixed" registration.

See Registration,
"Mixed"

Striving versus Letting: opposing tendencies, one of which overtly acts upon the vocal mechanism while the other allows it to respond reflexively.

To strive is to struggle, and singers who try too hard often reinforce difficulties that would resolve themselves with little or no effort under more relaxed circumstances. Inadvertently, those so disposed frequently undermine their own technical development.

See **Natural Movement**
Register
Registration,
"Mixed"

Although as a general practice it is advisable to "let" the mechanism respond to an inner rhythmic impetus in order to encourage natural, spontaneous movement, there are times when students should be urged to respond aggressively, and in effect, "try." An example of this need for positive action is the necessity for exercising the chest register vigorously, either to develop it in its relatively isolated form to help break down compensatory tensions, or when correcting a "mixed" registration.

As is true of most things pertaining to vocal pedagogy, there are times when one should "try," and times when one should "let." There are no absolutes.

Stroke of the Glottis: See Coup de Glotte.

Styloglossus Muscles: muscles that connect either side of the tongue with the styloid processes, the wedge-shaped bones at the base of the skull.

The contraction of the styloglossus muscles, which elevates the larynx, assists in peristaltic movement or swallowing. Because of this association (a constrictive pharyngeal movement), these muscles must remain passive during phonation if open-throated resonance is to be established and maintained.

Stylohyoid Muscles: muscles that connect the hyoid bone at the base of the tongue with the styloid processes (cranium).

See **Nasality**
Larynx

The contraction of the stylohyoid muscles, which pulls the tongue upwards and backwards, assists in peristaltic movement or swallowing. Since this process is constrictive, these muscles must remain passive during phonation if open-throated resonance is to be established and maintained.

Stylopharyngeal Muscles: a muscle system which originates in the base of the skull and enters the pharynx between the middle and superior constrictors.

See **Twenty-Eight**
Hundred
Voix Claire

Through their attachment to the thyrohyoids, the stylopharyngeals elevate the larynx, and concurrently distend the pharynx. Tension on the stylopharyngeals during phonation accounts for the false "ring" in the tone that is one of the distinguishing features of throat constriction.

Subglottal Pressure: pressure exerted during phonation by air particles impounded in the portion of the larynx located below the glottis, including the upper section of the trachea.

Subglottal pressure conceivably functions as 1) an actuating force directed against the vocal folds to set them into motion, 2) a reservoir for storing the oxygen essential to animate life, and 3) a source of self-generating energy, because breath has been compressed into the lungs. Each of these possibilities has its supporters; the majority believes that the vocal folds resist the subglottal pressure directed against them to produce a fundamental, *i.e.*, pitch. According to the breath pressure theory, the rate of breath expulsion is subject to regulation and control by conscious manipulation of the abdominal and intercostal muscle systems.

A more interesting hypothesis is the neurochronaxic theory, which holds that the vocal folds are innervated neurologically and become vibratile independent of breath pressure. While assuring the self-vibratility of the vocal folds, this theory is for all practical purposes inoperative unless there is an equalized pressure system both above and below the glottis to preserve an essential respiratory equilibrium. The possibility for creating such a system exists, however, since air can be trapped within the ventricular sacs by a narrowing of the false vocal cords.

There is some scientific evidence to support the above hypothesis. Experiments by J. Piguet, G. Decroix, and J. Libersa, reported in an article published by the Academy of Science (Paris, 1956), and earlier studies conducted by J. Ewald in Germany, seem to prove that the frequency of the vibration of the vocal folds is independent of the strength of subglottal pressure. If this is true, the importance of the false vocal cords to a correct tone production would be crucial, since without a source of supraglottal pressure to counter subglottal pressure, the equalization of opposing pressure systems essential to the self-vibratility of the vocal folds would be impossible. The spin-off effect would inevitably disturb other elements of the respiratory process, and necessitate the introduction of compensatory tensions. However, few present-day theorists share this viewpoint; most believe that both subglottal pressure and laryngeal functioning can be effectively influenced by regulating the respiratory process through the employment of various techniques of breath control.

In all probability, the reason for the popularity of systems based upon respiratory controls is that, in a mechanical age, mechanical solutions appear to be both logical and attractive. This approach becomes even more appealing in light of the difficulties encountered in bringing an involuntary muscular system into equilibrium, as is necessary when sub- and supraglottal systems are equalized.

See Bernoulli Effect
Breath Pressure
Theory
Energy
False Vocal Cords
Mechanistic
Methods
Neurochronaxic
Theory
Sinus Tone
Production
Supraglottal
Pressure
Vortex Theory

Subglottal Vibrations: vibratory sensations experienced during phonation that occur below the larynx (*e.g.*, "chest resonance").

Subglottal vibrations, like supraglottal vibrations, are the product of vibratory patterns set in motion by the vocal folds. These subglottal vibratory movements occur because with each compression wave formed above the glottis, pressure is decreased below. The result is that alternate compressions and rarefactions take place both above and below the vocal folds, and it is this which accounts for subglottal vibrations.

The intensity of the vibrations experienced in the subglottal cavities is minimized by a forward tilting of the thyroid cartilage as the scale is ascended. Since the tracheal rings are flexible, the effect of this tilting action is to cut off much of the lower area that would otherwise be brought into vibration. This adjustment shortens the resonance column and leaves the vocal mechanism in an ideal "set" for the production of tones in higher pitch ranges.

The symptoms of vibration experienced in the region of the chest, however, should never be thought of as "chest resonance." Those vibrations which appear to be reinforced during the singing of low tones are present because of radiation and bone conduction, not resonance; while the trachea does possess hard reflecting surfaces reasonably well suited for tonal amplification, its capacity for selectivity is too limited to respond to more than two or three pitches effectively.

The qualitative properties of the vibrations felt below the larynx, therefore, are determined by the quality of those above the larynx. These, in turn, depend upon the efficiency of those laryngeal muscular activities which draw the vocal folds into tension, laryngeal stabilization, and the quality of the pharyngeal adjustments made for resonance.

See Cavity Tone Theory
      Coupling
      Resonance
      Vowel

See Aerodynamic
      Theory
      Bernoulli Effect
      Breathing
      False Vocal Cords

Suction: the pull exerted by discrepancies in atmospheric pressure caused by the movement of air from a low to a high pressure system; one of the factors which, according to many scientists, approximates the vocal folds and closes the glottis.

Superimposed Function: a muscular or organic activity extraneous to the primary function of that muscle or organism; a muscular or organic adaptation.

Both speech and singing are superimposed functions, since the primary functions of the vocal muscles are respiration and the ingestion of foods and liquids. This is one of the reasons that natural, free vocalization is so rare: phonation is not a "natural," but an adaptive or overlaid function. For practical purposes, however, "natural" must be taken to mean "in accordance with nature's laws." Any superimposed function is natural, therefore, if it does not violate those laws by which a primary function is governed.

See Nature's Laws

Superior Fold: the upper portion of the thyroarytenoid muscles, which connects the arytenoid cartilages with the thyroid cartilage and the cricothyroid ligament.

The underside of the thyroarytenoid muscles (or the inferior fold) forms the vocal folds.

Superior Laryngeal Nerve: that branch of the tenth cranial nerve which innervates the cricothyroid muscles and (along with the recurrent laryngeal nerve) all other reflexive movements associated with phonation.

See Vagus Nerve

Supplemental Breath: the air that remains in the lungs (about 3 pints) after a tidal, or normal, respiratory cycle is completed.

Supplemental breath should never be called upon during phonation, since it must be expelled by physical effort, resulting in a severe disturbance of the respiratory equilibrium. Singers who have experienced a need to draw upon their supplemental breath to complete a musical phrase are familiar with its slow recovery rate, as well as the loss of poise and control that results when reliance upon supplemental breath is necessary.

When recourse to supplemental breath becomes habitual, either the composition being sung is beyond one's present abilities, or there is something seriously wrong technically.

Support: See Breath Support.

Supraglottal Pressure: a pressure system created by a narrowing of the false vocal cords, which causes the ventricular sacs to inflate, thus countering subglottal pressure; also viewed by many theorists as a property of the oral cavity, although this would hardly appear likely with an open-ended cavity.

See Bernoulli Effect
False Vocal Cords

Suprahyoid Muscles: the digastric muscle, consisting of two fleshy bellies—the one drawing the hyoid bone forward and up, the other, backward and up, or, when contracted simultaneously, drawing the hyoid bone directly upward; the my-lohyoid, which elevates the tongue and the floor of the mouth, consequently raising the larynx; the hyoglossus, which retracts and depresses the tongue, and the sty-lohyoid and stylopharyngeal muscles, which connect the styloid processes to the tongue and draw the hyoid bone upwards and backwards.

The suprahyoid muscles, also called the "supralaryngeal muscles," elevate the tongue and larynx and assist in peristaltic movement, or swallowing. Because of their association with this process (a constructive pharyngeal movement), these muscles must remain passive during phonation if open-throated resonance is to be established and maintained.

See Swallowing
Muscles

Surd: Latin, *surdus*, meaning "deaf" or "mute." In acoustics, a voiceless sound (as opposed to a sonant, or voiced sound).

Suspended Resistance: a balance of tension maintained between the inspir-atory muscles and their natural antagonists, the expiratory muscles.

Unless a state of suspended resistance or equilibrium is established during phonation throughout the entire respiratory system, energy will be dissipated, the vocal function inefficient, and the resulting tonal product impure.

See Breathing

Suspensory Mechanism: the extrinsic laryngeal musculature that positions the larynx for tonal amplification or resonance.

The suspensory muscles can be divided into three groups:

1. Those that elevate the larynx: the palatal, stylopharyngeal, and thyrohyoid muscles;
2. Those that depress the larynx: the cricopharyngeal and sternothyroid muscles, and
3. Those that tilt the larynx: the omohyoid and sternohyoid muscles. (See Figure 19, below.)

The manner in which these involuntary muscles interadjust determines to a great extent the overall efficiency of the vocal function. When they are not in a state of balanced tension or equilibrium, compensatory muscles are activated. This source of muscular interference manifests itself in the form of throat, jaw and tongue constriction, and/or in an excessively elevated or lowered laryngeal position.

Attaining a proper laryngeal suspension, or resonance adjustment, is the most difficult technical problem to be surmounted during training. Whereas the upper pharyngeal resonators can be tuned to the vowel, and, together with the registra-tion, induced to respond in predictable ways, the resonance characteristics gen-erated within the laryngeal area, which are determined by the quality of the laryngeal suspension, are less manipulable. One difficulty is that the suspensory muscles and the laryngeal muscles responsible for the phenomenon of registration) are involuntary, and at the same time closely associated with the muscular system

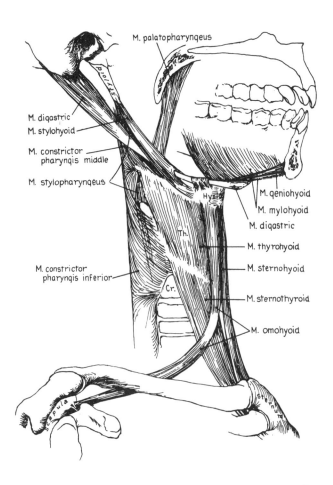

Figure 19. Suspensory muscles of the larynx and the neck in relation to neighboring structures. From Wallace O. Fenn and Hermann Rahn, Editors, Handbook of Physiology, *Section 3: Respiration, Volume 1 (Baltimore: American Physiological Society).*

responsible for swallowing, or peristaltic movement, which is a constrictive process. Unlike registration, however, where the "ear" can easily perceive differences between the various types of falsetto, head voice and chest voice, the singer's concepts related to laryngeal adjustments are preconditioned, and therefore he is without conceptual alternatives. In effect, he is bound by concepts related to tone qualities with which he has become familiar, and which for both physical and psychological reasons he identifies with as being "my quality."

Attempts to develop an open-throated resonance adjustment require not only that an involuntary muscular system be stimulated into more expansive movement, but also that this movement be induced without involving the more habitually reflexive activities associated with swallowing. It is for this reason, among others, that the common practice of deliberately lowering the larynx (or raising it) is particularly dangerous, since by definition all volitional acts involving the throat parts are constrictive.

See **Laryngeal**
    Suspension
    Lowered Larynx
    Register
    Vowel

Sustained Breathing: See Breathing, Sustained.

Swallowed Tone: a vocalized sound whose quality is the product of throat constriction and whose harmonic spectrum lacks upper partials.

"Swallowed" tones, or tones that appear to be "caught in the throat," indicate the presence of interference from the muscles that assist in swallowing, or peristaltic movement. This muscular interference is generally the result of the following factors:

1. An imbalanced registration;
2. A faulty laryngeal suspension, and/or
3. Psychological armoring.

The first two functional deficiencies can be reversed by the proper stimulation of the involuntary muscles that adjust the length, thickness, and contour of the vocal folds (registration), and of those that position the larynx for the amplification of vocal tone (resonance). Psychological armoring, on the other hand, often makes it exceedingly difficult, if not impossible, to establish contact with movements that are free and natural. It is, therefore, a serious pedagogic concern.

See **Anxiety**
Breathing
Energy
Natural Movement
Register
Resonance

Swallowing Muscles: those muscles which assist in peristaltic movement or deglutition.

In swallowing, the physical dimension of the pharyngeal isthmus is reduced by an exceedingly complex process that involves a sphincter movement, which in turn is caused by the following factors:

1. A backward and upward movement of the soft palate made possible by the joint action of the tensor and levator muscles;
2. A contraction of the epiglottis and the aryepiglottic folds, and
3. An elevation and closure of the larynx, which presses against the back of the tongue.

It is in this manner that food and drink are directed downward over the dorsum of the tongue and passed into the esophagus. Also involved in this process is the digastric muscle, whose anterior belly connects the jaw and hyoid bones, and whose posterior belly joins the hyoid bone to the mastoid process of the temporal bone. The infrahyoid muscles, because of their attachment to the hyoid bone, also participate in peristaltic movement. The elevators and depressors of the jaw, the mylohyoid, the geniohyoid, the temporal, and the masseter, are other important constrictors.

The muscles of the pharynx (whose upper portion is attached to the skull, whose lower portion is attached to the tissues in front of the cervical spine, and whose fibers blend below with the esophagus and connect to the larynx by means of the thyropharyngeal and cricopharyngeal muscles) work cooperatively with those muscles noted above whose contraction narrows the oropharynx. These muscle systems surround the pharynx to form a semicircle with a frontal opening, and are three in number: the superior, middle, and inferior. (See Figure 20, below.)

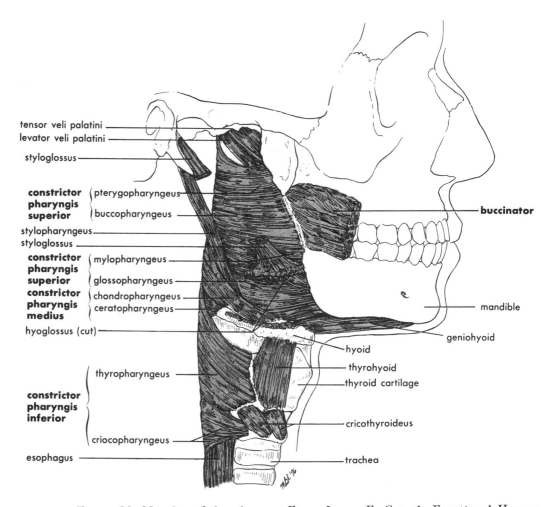

Figure 20. Muscles of the pharynx. From James E. Crouch, Functional Human Anatomy, *Third Edition (Philadelphia: Lea and Febiger, 1978).*

It is extremely difficult to avoid bringing the numerous constrictor systems into tension during phonation. The stylopharyngeal muscle in particular, which enters the pharynx between the upper and middle constrictors and connects with the thyroid cartilage, adds to the complexity of the problem. This is especially true since it also connects with the styloglossus muscle, which raises the tongue, as well as with the longitudinal fibers of the esophagus, which terminate at the top of the cricoid cartilage. Thus, the larynx itself participates in the swallowing process and is psychologically and physically caught up in peristaltic movement, both by conditioning and by general character structure.

The magnitude of the difficulty faced when developing vocal skills can be comprehended when it is realized that the constrictive mechanisms associated with swallowing lie in very close proximity to the throat openers. Consequently, whether intentionally or inadvertently engaged, they intrude almost naturally on the process of phonation and act as an impediment to free vocalization. When they interfere, as is so often the case, the cure is to be found not only in those areas of technical development (primarily registration) which will release inner creative strivings but also in the process of learning to respond rhythmically, spontaneously, and naturally to the stimulus contained in the musical scale or exercise pattern presented, instead of simply developing "learned responses." This process should encourage expansive movement and reverse the constrictive tendencies present in peristaltic movement. To volitionally lower or raise the larynx to relieve constriction is inadvisable, since to do so inevitably worsens the condition that this procedure was intended to cure.

See **Emotion**
Energy
Open Throat
Natural Movement
Register
Rhythm
Resonance

Sweet: an implicitly derogatory expression used to describe voices that are monochromatic, somewhat constricted, limited in range and power, and unable to withstand pressure.

"Sweet" voices are the products of a "mixed" registration. Although frequently attractive initially, their soft tonal characteristics and limited capacity for emotional expression generally become tedious after two or three songs.

No well-used, fully developed voice would ever be described as "sweet."

See **Registration,**
"Mixed"

Syllabic Consonants: consonants whose articulation contains a syllable without a vowel (*e.g.,* char*m*, chai*n*).

See **Consonants**

Sympathetic Vibration: an amplification of sound occuring whenever a secondary vibrator or cavity is tuned to the same natural frequency as that of the primary source of vibration, *e.g.,* the vocal folds and the cavities of the throat and mouth, or two strings, when the natural speed of vibration of one is an integral multiple of the other.

For example, when a key on the piano is silently depressed and its lower octave sounded with the damper pedal held down, its pitch will be clearly audible. The reason for this sympathetic response is that the frequency of the upper octave is an integral multiple (a harmonic) of the fundamental. While the singing voice operates at a much more sophisticated level, general tonal reinforcement through sympathetic vibration remains an essential feature of its acoustic system.

See **Cavity Tone Theory**
Damping
Fixed Pitch Theory
Formants
Register
Relative Pitch
Theory

Synergy: muscular activity which results in a muscle or muscle group holding in balanced tension against the contraction of its natural antagonist.

In a properly balanced registration, the arytenoids (*i.e.,* those muscles responsible for tonal qualities commonly recognized as chest register) hold synergetically against the pull of the cricothyroids (those responsible for tonal qualities recognized as head voice). In early stages of development, however, the chest register must be strongly energized, since its potential must be fully exploited if it is to function synergetically at optimum efficiency. As stretchers of the vocal folds, the cricothyroids should never be used synergetically.

See **Register**
Stretchers of the
Vocal Folds

Synthesized Support: respiratory equilibrium.

The term "synthesized support" was probably coined to justify the concept of "tonal support" or "breath support." However, an equilibrium is self-sufficient and does not have to be "supported;" nor does tone (the displacement of air particles by a vibrating mechanism); nor does breath (*i.e.,* inspired air).

See **Breath Support**

T

Talent: inherent physical, artistic, or creative ability.

Vocal talent might be defined as "the inherent ability to conceptualize a musical idea, to transform that conception into vocal tone, and to perceive that tonal product as an integral part of a communicative experience of artistic value." Among the general indicators of vocal talent are the following:

1. Musical aptitude and insight;
2. A physical instinct for producing vocal tone;
3. Personality and general intelligence, and
4. An urge to communicate thoughts and feelings with sensitivity.

Rarely are these elements equally strong in a given singer, but, as indicators of vocal potential, they should average out. For example, dramatic or even musical deficiencies can be overcome by a remarkable vocal presence; likewise, exceptional musical perception and dramatic sense can compensate for obvious vocal short-comings. Since every performer is less proficient in certain areas than in others, the aspiring artist must struggle to overcome deficiencies, but at the same time maintain a high level of proficiency in those areas most congenial to his natural gifts.

Teaching: the art of instilling knowledge, developing insights and sensitivity, and assisting in the acquisition of technical skills not formerly possessed in those who seek guidance and help.

In the fullest sense of the word, good teaching releases inherent creative instincts within a student and helps bring him to a fulfillment of his personal, as well as his artistic, potential. Neither personal charisma nor the aura of success are important factors in this interchange, although these virtues are not to be discounted. Far more important is an inquisitive mind, a knowledge and love of subject matter, an ability to be caught up in the excitement of making new discoveries, and a willingness to admit the possibility of error, whether in theory or in practice, or both.

Teaching is a gift, and one of the more curious aspects of teaching is that some know much and impart little, whereas others who know less are not only able to impart that which they know, but also able to stimulate a desire in others to search for more complete and satisfying answers. Among the positive traits associated with teaching are the following:

1. Patience;
2. A knowledge of vocal mechanics;
3. An ability to relate on a human level;
4. An ability to "hear" empathetically;
5. A capacity for explaining abstract concepts and simplify them;
6. An intuitive identification with the voice as a musical instrument, and
7. A basic knowledge of repertoire and vocal classifications, and the ability to select from the latter that which is appropriate to each student's level of technical development.

Negative aspects which undermine effective teaching are the following:

1. Encouraging students to attempt that which is too far beyond their present level of achievement;
2. Lack of understanding and sympathy concerning the difficulties to be surmounted in the development of vocal skills;
3. Patronizing attitudes;
4. The imposition of one's own aesthetic preferences;
5. Intruding into the student's personal life and affairs;
6. Living vicariously through the student to the detriment of both parties, and
7. A subconscious desire to keep the student a "student."

The art of teaching is an outward expression of an inner vision, a growth process in which horizons are expanded, ideas tested, and limitations removed, all of which involves change. To grow is to change, and while all change does not necessarily mean improvement, nevertheless, consistency (lack of change) cannot be considered a virtue as long as technical problems remain. Growth is a matter of ontology, and the teacher's responsibility is to goad, to guide, to suggest, and to direct the student into a growth pattern unique to his abilities.

A common fault to be avoided when participating in a dynamic growth process is to employ static procedures, or "method." Each individual is unique. His problems, abilities, expressive goals and world view are, or should be, peculiar to himself. To turn him into a carbon copy of his teacher, however estimable he or she may be, is destructive. For a teacher to project his vocal problems onto the student who does not share them is equally damaging.

In a vital teaching experience, both teacher and pupil should be caught up in an ontological process, a process of becoming. As in all such processes, the paths are largely uncharted. It is the mutual seeking out of these new paths that makes teaching not a science but an art.

Technique: the manner in which a physical activity (*e.g.*, phonation) is executed and used to accomplish a desired aim (*e.g.*, artistic expression); a particular way of doing things.

Vocal technique is the manner in which the vocal mechanism responds; it is the physical link between artistic intent and artistic expression. A technique or function that conforms to nature's laws is efficient; one that violates those laws is inefficient. The ultimate goal of vocal training, therefore, is to establish a technique which fulfills and agrees with the movement potential of the muscular and organic systems involved in the phonative process.

Teeth: the hard, enameled appendages seated in the gums of both jaws and used for the prehension and mastication of food.

Teeth, primary elements of the digestive system, are used only for articulating consonants during phonation (*e.g.,* "*th*at"). Although some pedagogues have considered the teeth resonators of vocal tone, they are singularly unsuited for that purpose. Others have considered the teeth fixtures against which the tip of the tongue should be placed during phonation. Even this minor role, however, must be denied, since the tongue must remain free during phonation to articulate consonants without disturbing the pharyngeal adjustments made for resonation of the vowel.

Tenor: the highest male voice type.

A well-used tenor voice has a range of at least two octaves: C below middle C to the octave above middle C. The category "tenor," however, is commonly divided according to relative vocal weight and timbre into several subcategories, including "lyric," *spinto,* "dramatic," *robusto,* and *Heldentenor.*

See Countertenor

Tenorino: an implicitly derogatory expression used to describe a lyric tenor whose faulty technique displays characteristics associated with a "mixed" registration: soft texture, undeveloped chest register, throat constriction, and an inability to withstand the rigors of vigorous singing.

See Registration, "Mixed"

Tense Vowels: See Vowel, Lax and Tense.

Tenseness: body stiffness engendered by faulty muscular coordination.

The term "tenseness" is associated with faulty tone production and must not be confused with "tension," which carries no such pejorative connotation. Vocal tone (or, for that matter, the product of any other physical activity) without muscular tension is an impossibility.

See Register
Relaxation

Tension: the act or condition of being stretched; stress resulting from the contraction of an elastic body (*e.g.,* a muscle).

Muscular tension is essential to vocal tone. It is required both for respiration and for the two basic functional activities that yield vocal tone: registration (the physical adjustments made in the length, thickness, and contour of the vocal folds for vibration) and resonation (the positioning of the pharyngeal cavities for tonal amplification). When the vocal function is efficient (*i.e.,* in equilibrium), a diverse combination of mutually antagonistic muscles coordinates their movement, with the result that there is a balance of tension (or a lack of "tenseness") throughout the entire respiratory (vocal) tract.

See Laryngeal
Suspension
Register
Resonance
Vowel

Tensor Veli Palatini: muscles whose contraction positions the velum, or soft palate; also known as the tensor palati.

As an opposer to the levator palati, the function of the tensor palati is to tense the soft palate, and to a certain extent, to depress it. The tensor palati is often regarded as being instrumental in opening the auditory (Eustachian) tube. Its probable role in phonation is to narrow the pharyngeal isthmus in the production of bright, ringing tone qualities.

See Arched Palate
Eustachian Tube
Larynx
Swallowing
Vowel, Dark and
Bright

Tensors of the Vocal Cords: the interior thyroarytenoid, or vocalis muscles, that form the vibrating surface or "lip" of the vocal folds.

See **Laryngeal
Suspension
Register
Stretchers of the
Vocal Folds
Vocalis Muscles**

"Tensors" is a term introduced by Frederick Husler and Yvonne Rodd-Marling to refer to the ary- and thyrovocalis muscles imbedded within the vocal folds. While these muscle fibers are capable of autonomous movement, they nevertheless depend upon the contraction of the cricothyroids and the arytenoids, as well as the suspensory muscles responsible for laryngeal stabilization, to perform effectively.

One of the most important functions of the tensors is to effect a full approximation of the vocal folds, a closure which would otherwise be impossible.

Terminology: technical language or expressions used in a specific art or science.

Vocal terminology is often arbitrary, subjective, misleading, and self-serving. These undesirable characteristics usually result from one or more of the following:

1. Subjective impressions of sensations of vibration;
2. Observation of inefficient vocal functioning;
3. The lack of a thorough understanding of the vocal function and of the natural laws that govern it, and
4. Futile attempts to define vocal qualities which are essentially indefinable.

To define is to limit, and since the vocal function is a totality of mental, conceptual, emotional, and physical responses, its product, vocal tone, cannot be precisely defined. Nevertheless, if order is to be restored out of chaos, a terminology must be decided upon, and anchored in concrete reality rather than aesthetic, metaphysical and/or subjective impressions, whereby intelligence relating to the development, care and preservation of the voice can take its place with other disciplines without embarrassment.

Tessitura: Italian, meaning "texture;" a reference to a particular kind of tonal coloration and voice quality that determines voice classification; in more recent times, a term used to indicate that portion of the vocal range (high, medium, or low) within which the majority of pitches in a given opus are concentrated. Tessitura may also refer to the pitch range a singer is capable of producing with the greatest comfort and ease regardless of technical limitations; this is commonly referred to as a "natural" tessitura.

Since vocal training is concerned with the development of a latent potential, the relationship between tessitura and voice quality is an issue of paramount importance. Within this context, the concept of tessitura (texture) equates with natural quality; most especially it equates with that quality which distinguishes a mezzo-soprano from a dramatic soprano, a lyric baritone from a dramatic tenor, *etc.*, rather than the quality which distinguishes one individual voice from another. Even at best, there exists a certain inconsistency in all tonal colorations. The soprano's voice, for example, is generally brighter in quality than that of her mezzo-soprano counterpart. However, although all sopranos and mezzos possess bright or dark textural properties that define their voices, it will often be found that the natural quality of some mezzos is brighter than that of many sopranos because of differences in temperament, technical skill, and ethnic background. On the other hand, when a singer's natural coloration is obscured by vocal faults such as "thickness," "nasality" and other forms of throat constriction, it becomes imperative to look elsewhere for a more reliable basis upon which to form value judgments.

To ensure that the textural properties (tessitura) of the tone production are intrinsically natural from a functional standpoint, two essential procedures must be adopted: 1) purification of the vowel quality without regard for other aspects of quality, and 2) balancing and integration of the two basic register mechanisms, the chest and the falsetto, which alone makes the goal of vowel purity an obtainable objective. On these terms, it is not important that a voice is dark or bright; it is only important that the balance of registration proper to each pitch, intensity and vowel quality is operative. When it is, the singer's natural tessitura will reveal itself in terms of both range and quality, and errors growing out of premature classification of voices into "categories" will be avoided.

One of the common mistakes during training is to classify voices with respect to tessitura on the basis of range. However, it is texture, not range, which is the ultimate determinant of a singer's voice classification. Questions of voice classification and natural tessitura will be answered only after procedures based upon those principles known to govern registration have been adopted, and when emphasis has been placed upon purification of the vowel quality.

Tetanic: pertaining to rapid muscle spasms.

Thick Tone: a vocalized sound whose tonal characteristics are "dark" and "muddy."

"Thick" tones are always the result of faulty technique, usually because of a "mixed" registration or a dependency on mouth resonance. Although the term is occasionally misused to denote the chest register, "thick," in this instance, probably refers more to thickness of vibrating surface than to faulty function.

See **Mouthy Tone**
Resonance

Thin Register: a term coined by the nineteenth century theorist Emil Behnke to refer to the male falsetto and female midrange.

See **Middle Register**
Register

Thin Tone: a vocalized sound lacking fullness and body, and consequently one that is harmonically impoverished; a tone quality that is deficient in chest register participation.

Since arytenoid tension is required to establish an open-throated resonance adjustment, its absence results in both thin tonal characteristics and the throat constriction characteristic of this type of tone production.

Thoracic Breathing: See Breathing, Intercostal.

Thorax: the chest.

The thorax houses the heart, lungs, and other vital organs. These are sheathed and protected by various thoracic bones and cartilages, including the ribs, clavicle ("collarbone"), sternum ("breastbone"), and xiphoid process, a point of attachment for the abdominal musculature.

Threshold of Audibility: the weakest sound that can be heard (zero decibels); the lowest frequency that can be heard (15—16 vibrations per second).

Throat: a passageway lying between the oro- and nasopharynges and the thorax (chest), containing most of the elements essential to respiration and the ingestion of foods and liquids.

The extraordinary capability for interaction among the diverse throat parts (the presence of hard and soft resonating surfaces, possibilities for lengthening, shortening, broadening and/or narrowing the pharyngeal tract, the adjustability of the soft palate, which permits two types of opening for the pharyngeal outlet, the changing cavity dimensions caused by movements of the base of the tongue and the mouth, two valves which can open or close the passageway, *etc.*) makes it possible to articulate a great number of frequencies (pitches) and their corresponding overtones over a wide range of intensities. Vibratory impulses are generated by the vocal folds within this area (referred to by scientists as the sound source), and these are shaped into vowel qualities (formants) by the surrounding laryngeal and pharyngeal cavities, which also resonate them.

Many misconceptions surround the role of the throat in phonation. Although one of the laryngeal valves (the vocal folds) is capable of propagating sound waves, and the primary resonators of vocal tone are located within that area, numerous authorities continue to advise singers to "get the tone out of the throat" and/or "relax the throat." Such directives, obviously intended to alleviate throat constriction, fail to recognize that 1) the sound waves set in motion by the vocal folds move through space by rhythmic compressions and rarefactions of the surrounding air particles, and 2) tone is inseparable from tension. The pedagogic solution, therefore, is not to "place" or "direct" the pressure variations heard as "voice," or to "relax the throat," but to discover a means whereby the involuntary muscular systems functioning at the sound source can be made to coordinate more effectively, *i.e.*, to assume tension without becoming tense.

With the exception of the articulators, all of the mechanical processes involved in the production and resonation of vocal tone are located within the throat. Unless procedures are adopted which succeed in stimulating the appropriate laryngeal muscular systems without recourse to methods of direct control, the acquirement of vocal skills not formerly possessed will remain an impossibility.

See Cavity Tone Theory
Formants
Laryngeal
Suspension
Register
Resonance
Vocal Study
Vowel

Throat Voice: See Feigned Voice; Pharyngeal Voice; Falsetto.

Throaty Tone: a vocalized sound whose "swallowed," "dark," "tight," "covered," or "pinched" tonal qualities are caused by constrictor tensions within the throat parts.

Among the reasons throaty tones appear to be "too far back," or "caught in the throat," are the following:

1. Failure of the suspensory muscles (thyrohyoid, palatal, stylopharyngeal, sternothyroid and cricopharyngeal muscles) to maintain a proper laryngeal adjustment—neither too high nor too low;
2. A poorly developed and imbalanced registration;

3. Faulty breathing habits (high chest, overexpansion of the rib cage, protrusion of the abdomen, abdominal tuck, or breathing through the nostrils without opening the mouth);
4. Using the mouth as a determinant of the vowel and resonance;
5. An absence of balanced tension between the suprahyoid muscles (genioglossus, stylohyoid, mylohyoid, digastric and genioglossus), which through their attachment to the hyoid bone raise the larynx, and the infrahyoid group (sternohyoid, sternothyroid, thryohyoid and omohyoid), which depress it;
6. Tension of the neck muscles, particularly the sternomastoid, and
7. Anxiety.

The complex interplay among the muscle groups mentioned, as well as that among the cricothyroid, arytenoid and other muscle systems operating within the larynx, is the sole determinant of the qualitative properties of the physical processes involved in phonation. When these muscle groups are in equilibrium, both with themselves and with each other, the vocal mechanism is able to function without muscular interference, *i.e.,* it is well coordinated and open-throated.

In a throaty tone production, the above-named muscle systems are impeded in their movement. As a result, the vocal folds are not precisely adjusted to accommodate the pitch, intensity and vowel patterns being sung, the palatal muscles constrict the oropharynx, and the infra- and suprahyoid muscles responsible for stabilizing the larynx are incapable of functioning properly. The degree of throatiness in the tone production, therefore, is directly proportionate to the degree to which these muscle systems conflict.

One of the negative by-products of throatiness is an abnormal disruption of subjective hearing. The reason for this is that the sternomastoid muscles, when tensed, press against the pharyngeal arch and conduct the vibrations generated within the larynx up to the mastoid bone, seemingly intensifying their strength. Thus, the voice (while smaller) appears to be disproportionately large to the singer himself. Those who like to "hear" their own voices resonate encourage this symptom, and consequently perpetuate the "throaty" condition. Throatiness introduces a false "ring" in the tone, deprives the voice of its natural freshness and beauty, and fatigues the mechanism.

Attempts to alleviate the inner tensions which are the physical counterparts of throatiness often involve conscious efforts to "relax the throat" and to "bring the tone forward" to "get the tone out of the throat." These practices, however, fail to address themselves to the central issue. Vibratory impulses cannot be set in motion without tension. The solution to problems related to throat constriction, therefore, is not to be found in relaxation exercises, but in rechanneling energy so that wrong tension is eliminated.

Stimulation of the vocal organs into a fundamentally different type of physical response can only be accomplished through the mechanics of registration, which, when properly utilized, will stimulate the movement of those muscles which tauten the vocal folds and position the larynx without engaging constrictor tensions. Thus, through positive emphasis upon the stimulation of muscular movements which are in keeping with an innate functional logic, the mechanism will respond with greater freedom.

Throatiness is a difficult, although common, vocal problem. If it is to be solved,

THYROARTENOID MUSCLE

pedagogic procedures must be based upon valid functional principles, and not, as is so often the case, aesthetic impressions and patent remedies.

Thyroarytenoid Muscle: one of two complex muscles covered by an elastic membrane; more familiarly, the vocal folds.

The thyroarytenoid is named after its two points of attachment; it arises out of the thyroid cartilage at one end and attaches to the vocal processes of the arytenoid cartilage at the other. Its function is to connect the thyroid cartilage and the cricothyroid ligament with each of the two arytenoids. The thyroarytenoid is divided into two parts: 1) the vocalis muscle, or internal thyroarytenoids, and 2) the external thyroarytenoids.

The vocalis muscle performs multiple functions. It can draw the arytenoid cartilage forward (which relaxes the full length of the vocal folds), or, because the insertion of the fibers along the rim of the glottis is such that they transverse each other, it can draw certain portions of the folds forward to increase their tension, *i.e.*, adduct them, or relax them for abduction. Thus, because they are capable of independent action, yet capable of working in conjunction with the cricothyroid and arytenoid muscle systems, the vocalis muscle fibers are important factors in regulating the size of the glottal slit. In view of the complexity of these and other laryngeal muscular systems, the possibilities for adjustment and interadjustment within the vocal mechanism are virtually limitless.

The external thyroarytenoid arises on the inner surface of the thyroid cartilage and draws the arytenoid cartilage forward as it tenses in opposition to the contraction of the cricothyroids, thus shortening the vocal folds. Some fibers of the external thyroarytenoid muscle connect to the lateral border of the epiglottis, where they become known as the thyroepiglottic muscle.

The fact that all of the above muscle systems are involuntary indicates the magnitude of the difficulty encountered in voice training.

See **Indirect Control**
Intrinsic Musculature of the Larynx
Ventricular Bands
Vocalis Muscles

Thyroepiglottic Muscle: a band of muscular tissue comprised of thyroarytenoid fibers that penetrate the epiglottic fold and reach the epiglottis itself.

This muscle fiber plays an important role in closing the glottal space and in determining the length, thickness and elasticity of the vocal folds. It is known that during the sounding of the vowel *ah* the epiglottis partially closes the vestibule of the larynx; it is probable that the thyroepiglottic fibers are responsible for this closure.

Thyrohyoid Ligament: a band of muscular tissue lying between the hyoid bone and the thyroid cartilage.

Thyrohyoid Muscle: a muscle that pulls each wing of the thyroid cartilage to a side of the hyoid bone.

The thyrohyoid muscle is constrictive by nature, since when under contraction it causes the larynx to rise.

Thyroid Cartilage: Greek, meaning "shield-shaped;" the large anterior laryngeal cartilage commonly known as the "Adam's apple."

See **Larynx**

376

Thyrovocalis Muscles: muscle fibers within the vocal folds which extend through the main fleshy body of the vocal folds to the margins of the vocal lips; the interior thyrovocalis muscles; the so-called "vocalis muscles."

The contraction of the cricothyroid and arytenoid muscles causes the vocal folds, like stretched-out rubber bands, to become somewhat thinner in their middle portion. To correct this limitation, the thyrovocalis muscles and their crisscrossed counterparts, the aryvocalis muscles, tense to "fill out" the eliptical separation between the vocal folds, thus effecting a complete closure of the glottis.

Since each vocalis fiber is capable of working alone, in conjunction with other vocalis fibers, or with the cricothyroid and arytenoid muscle systems, nature has provided a very sophisticated system—capable of infinite variations—for approximating the vocal folds. It is, in the final analysis, due to the contraction of the vocalis muscles that the two register mechanisms can be coordinated into one functional unit, and that the midrange of the voice can be produced without loss of tonal vitality.

See Intrinsic Musculature of the Larynx
Thyroarytenoid Muscle
Vocalis Muscle

Tidal Breath: the amount of air (about one pint) that passes into and out of the lungs during normal respiration.

The amount of oxygen contributed to body tissues from tidal breathing is sufficient for sustaining life, but not for building up the compression and energy level necessary to sustained vocalization, which requires what is known as complemental breath.

See Breath
Breathing
Vital Capacity

Tight Tone: a vocalized sound produced while the throat parts are constricted, creating the impression that the voice has been "caught in the throat." Acoustically, "tight" tones have weak lower formants and excessively energized high partials.

"Tight" tones result from a faulty technique, muscular rigidity that is symptomatic of anxiety, or a combination of the two. The general lack of motility and stiffness throughout the mechanism is felt, heard and empathetically perceived as "tightness."

See Anxiety
Formants

Tightly Coupled: See Coupling.

Tilt of the Thyroid: a forward and downward pulling upon the thyroid cartilage that, in turn, stretches the vocal folds, a movement caused when the cricothyroids are contracted.

Timbre: the wave form or complex harmonic structure of a sound as expressed in quality; the "color" of sound.

The timbre of a vocal tone depends upon 1) the number of the harmonic partials or overtones present in the tonal spectrum, 2) the location of those partials within the tonal spectrum, and 3) the relative strength of each partial in relation to other partials and to inharmonic, accessory "noises." These factors are determined both by the resonance characteristics present and by the physical dimension of the vocal folds, *i.e.,* registration. While anatomical peculiarities and cavity resonance have long been known to affect timbre, it has only been in recent years that the physical conformation of the vocal folds has likewise been considered influential. This was proved in the mid 1920's by the German scientist R. Schilling, who demonstrated that for marked differences in vowel color of the same basic vowel phoneme, the vocal folds displayed distinct differences in their adjustment and vibratory pattern. Shortly after, J. Tarneaud of France also demonstrated that timbre was influenced to a considerable extent by the physical conformation of the vibrator.

Individual voices are readily distinguishable by timbre, which is determined by such factors as 1) the efficiency of mechanical response, and 2) natural physical characteristics (size and arrangement of resonance cavities, bone structure, muscular tonicity, general physical health, *etc.*).

Differences in timbre can be perceived both objectively and subjectively: in the former instance, by aesthetic impressions of vocal tone (for example, "clear," "sweet," "round," "dark," "shrill," *etc.*), and in the latter, by harmonic data recorded by scientific instruments.

Tired Voice: See Fatigue.

Tonal Beauty: that quality of vocal tone deemed aesthetically pleasing.

The main variable in evaluating tonal beauty is the aesthetic judgment of the listener. Obviously, what appeals to one may not appeal to another. Thus, every aesthetic judgment is prejudiced by the sociological, cultural, emotional, temperamental, and educational or pedagogic experiences of the listener. It is for this reason that acquiring a technique that conforms to nature's laws should be the single goal of vocal study, for when the technique is correct, it can be adapted to any aesthetic purpose that does not violate its natural, inherent functional logic.

Tonal Brilliance: See Brilliance.

Tonal Color: See (To) Color the Voice.

Tonal Textures: See Quality; Quality and Its Functional Derivatives.

Tone: a sound possessing characteristics of pitch, duration, and intensity produced by a vibrating mechanism; a vocalized sound that possesses these characteristics; the physical condition of an organic or muscular body in which its functions are responsive to appropriate stimuli and are performed with requisite vigor.

In the latter sense of its meaning, the vocal mechanism can be said to be "in good tone" when the muscular system responds rapidly, and "in poor tone" when it responds sluggishly.

Tone (Big): See Big Voices.

Tone Consciousness: an attitude towards singing whereby attention is concentrated on "producing" the voice and "making" quality.

Tone consciousness precludes any possibility of spontaneous movement and leads to habits that reduce singing to a contrived, calculated skill. It also inhibits the development of a free, natural vocal technique.

Tone consciousness is frequently a by-product of such practices as voice "placement" and "nasal resonance," which attempt to act directly upon the mechanism to "make" an admired tone quality, and which confuse "voice" and function.

See Cavity Tone Theory
(To) Color the
Voice
Coupling
Resonance
Quality
Vowel

See Aesthetics

See Manufactured Tone

Tone Deafness: an inability to distinguish differences in pitch.

Although tone deafness is a familiar complaint of those who cannot sing, it is, in reality, a rare dysfunction. The essential difficulty with those thought to be tone deaf is a lack of coordination between hearing and physical response.

Tone Kernel: See Core.

Tone, "Made:" See Manufactured Tone; Tone Consciousness.

Tone Production: See Production, Tone.

Tongue: the fleshy, movable organ occupying the floor of the mouth, and comprised of several muscles and fibers that are attached to the jaw, hyoid bone, pharynx, and soft palate.

The highly mobile tongue possesses sensory organs and digestive glands, and is active in chewing, tasting, and swallowing. Its secondary function is to assist in the articulation of consonants and to alter the shape of the pharyngeal cavities during the production of vowels. It is divided into two parts by the terminal sulcus (a groove or furrow). The larger, anterior part belongs to the floor of the mouth, while its root forms the forward part of the oropharynx.

The muscles comprising the tongue may be divided into two groups: the extrinsic and the intrinsic. The extrinsic muscles originate outside the tongue and are named after their point of origin. They include the styloglossus, hyoglossus, palatoglossus and genioglossus muscles. The intrinsic lingual (tongue) muscles originate and insert entirely within the tongue and are named according to the three spacial dimensions in which their fascicles run: the longitudinal, vertical and transverse muscles. By the combined efforts of the extrinsic and intrinsic musculature the tongue can, at will, become more concave or convex, move from side to side, and be protruded, retracted, elevated, or depressed.

Since the root of the tongue is fastened to the hyoid bone (a horseshoe-shaped arch from which the larynx is suspended), the ratio of tension distributed between the supra- and infrahyoid muscle systems raises and lowers not only the hyoid bone but also the tongue, to which it is attached. These systems also coordinate with other pharyngeal muscles (especially the stylopharyngeals, with which the palatopharyngeals and the salpingopharyngeals merge) to form a complex communication between the soft palate, the thyroid cartilage, the upper, middle and lower constrictors, and consequently the cricothyroid and arytenoid muscles, whose contraction determines the ratio of tension brought to bear on the vocal folds. The root of the tongue is, therefore, intimately associated physiologically with the functional processes of the larynx and the laryngo- and oropharynges. The primary function of the root of the tongue during phonation, then, is to form the forward wall of the oropharyngeal cavity, and as a result, to become an active participant in tonal resonation.

While the root of the tongue differs structurally, functionally, and in appearance from its forward part, it is also supplied by different cranial nerves, *i.e.*, the hypoglossal and vagus, rather than the trigeminal nerve, which governs the movement of its forward portion. In addition, the hypoglossus system innervates the intrinsic laryngeal musculature as well as the suspensory (strap) muscles. Thus, the possibility exists that the forward and posterior portions of the tongue can be made to move either separately or conjunctively. This proves ideal from the standpoint of combining vocal sounds with a verbal text, since it enables each of the two portions of the tongue to perform their specific tasks without interference, *i.e.*, the pharyngeal resonation of vowel sounds and the lingual articulation of consonants.

Other nerve systems govern sensory perception, notably the seventh cranial nerve, which relays the neurological activity necessary for sensory awareness to the anterior part of the tongue, the ninth cranial nerve, which supplies the posterior portion of the tongue, and which, in addition, conveys sensation to the fauces, tonsils, pharynx and soft palate, and the tenth cranial nerve, which supplies sensory impulses to the pharynx, larynx, trachea and other organs. It is due to the neurological impulses moving through these systems that the singer becomes kinesthetically aware of the "feel" of his voice.

As part of the oropharynx, the base of the tongue plays an important role in determining vowel (tone) quality, since the selection of the formants (frequency bands) depends upon the shape of the laryngo- and oropharynges. It is obviously impossible, therefore, to pronounce different vowels distinctly without altering the shape of the base of the tongue, and, by so doing, changing the shape of the oropharynx. To sing an *ee* vowel, for example, there must be a forward arching of the tongue, which, by partially separating the laryngo- and oropharynges from the mouth, "tunes" the resonating system so that it selects and energizes the frequency bands which are responsible for yielding that vowel quality. The precision with which this takes place (dependent in large part on the precision with which the vocal registers coordinate) involves a complex of muscular activities that forms the very core of the functional process. It is when these processes are helped to coordinate more effectively that the tongue performs properly and positions itself correctly without having to be acted upon. The tongue will never present a problem when the registration and resonance adjustment are in good order.

As stated previously, the tongue functions in a dual capacity during phonation. Its forward part, or blade, must be free-moving for the articulation of consonants, whereas its root area, which forms the forward wall of the oropharynx, must maintain a constant adjustment in order to sustain a constant vowel quality. It is this physical and neurological independence that enables the singer to produce a legato flow of tone which does not interfere with the articulatory processes, and that prevents articulation of consonants from interfering with the free flow of vocal tone.

Many have suggested that the position of the tongue during phonation should be volitionally set in order to improve or ensure a correct tone production (*e.g.*, by grooving the tongue, making it lie flat on the floor of the mouth, or by placing it against the back of the lower teeth). This, however, does not seem reasonable. If activities within the throat parts could be successfully manipulated and controlled by adjusting the position of the blade of the tongue, the acquisition of vocal skills would be greatly simplified. But any expectation of improved function by adopting this practice is unrealistic. The inception of vocal tone takes place within the larynx, and once constricting tensions have been engendered, the mechanisms associated with peristaltic movement take over. When this occurs (as it must when the tone production is faulty), no act of will, manipulation, or setting of the tongue can, of itself, reverse the process.

One of the most common symptoms growing out of the manipulative practices noted above is tongue stiffness. Tongue stiffness, however, while it can be induced, does not usually originate with the tongue itself, but is caused by constrictor tensions within the throat parts. Until these have been relieved, the tongue cannot be made to relax, nor can any manipulation or positioning process relieve undesirable tensions at the sound source when the latter are pre-existent. It is only when the vocal mechanism functions without muscular interference that the tongue will be mobile and relaxed, in which case it will reflexively assume its own natural position in response to the needs of the tonal form.

There is no evidence to justify a belief that by adjusting the tongue the tone production will be free. The fact that the tongue has been adjusted to the "right" position, *i.e.,* "grooved," "relaxed," or "placed gently against the lower teeth," does not certify that the functional activities taking place within the larynx will also be correct. To position the tongue is easy; to coordinate the laryngeal musculature so that its movement is facile and free is difficult, and indeed, involves procedures which do not directly concern the tongue at all.

Tongue Bone: slang for hyoid bone, to which the base of the tongue finds its point of attachment.

Tonicity: the normal tension or condition of an organic or muscle system when at rest; the elastic condition of healthy muscle tissue.

The body is said to be in a high state of tonicity when the muscular systems respond rapidly, in a low state of tonicity when they respond sluggishly. Exercises employed to effect technical improvement, therefore, should be designed not only to perfect the coordination among those muscle groups responsible for registration and resonance, but also to bring these same muscles to a high level of tonicity.

To a certain extent, muscular tone is dependent upon physical maturation and muscular development. It is for this reason that young singers, regardless of their precocity, must resist the temptation to undertake heavy operatic roles too soon. Generally speaking, no singer under the age of thirty-five has had time to build up the muscular tonicity needed to sustain this kind of singing without straining the mechanism.

Too Far Back: a term used to describe vocal qualities produced when the throat is constricted.

The awareness of a tone being "too far back" is a sense impression both heard and felt. As a description of reality, however, it is somewhat misleading. All vocal tone is generated and resonated within the laryngo- and oropharynges, those well formed being the result of a precisely coordinated laryngeal musculature. When, as is frequently the case, the tone production reflects some degree of throat constriction and the voice appears to be caught in the throat, the pedagogic solution lies with the employment of principles which will stimulate the appropriate laryngeal muscle systems into improved patterns of response, not with advice to relax or bring the tone "forward."

In reality, a tone described as "too far back" is not back far enough. If, as science has proven, the laryngo- and oropharynges are the most important resonators, then

See **Bel Canto**
Cavity Tone Theory
Consonants
Formants
Modern Methods
Register
Resonance
Standing Wave
Vowel

See **Hyoid Bone**
Tongue

until constrictor tensions have been released and a condition of open-throatedness established, the wealth of resonance back, down and below the constricted area will remain untapped. Thus, the problem is not that the tone is too far back, but that there is a constriction too high in the pharyngeal tract.

The use of the term "too far back" to indicate a constricted tone quality is one of the many examples of the loose terminology that afflicts the vocal profession and makes intelligent intercommunication with other disciplines almost impossible.

Too Open: a phrase used to describe vocalized sounds whose "shouty," "spread" tonal characteristics result from an overly dominant chest register in the "break" area (E—F above middle C).

Singing that is "too open" unavoidably results in vowel distortion and is "colorless." It is always due to an imbalanced registration, and consequently faulty technique.

Toothy Singing: vocal performance characterized by a visible display of the teeth.

"Toothy" singing is a by-product of the early Italian pedagogic tradition that a smiling countenance infuses clarity and "brightness" into vocal tone and is visually pleasing. A toothy smile, however, quickly becomes tedious—especially when it has nothing to do with the sentiment being expressed.

Since it offers no real technical advantage over other facial expressions, and since, in fact, it may actually encourage vowel distortion and "spreading," a constant smiling mouth position during phonation should not be encouraged.

Trachea: the main trunk of a muscular membranous tube that connects the lower part of the larynx with the bronchi and through which air passes into and out of the lungs; known in the vernacular as the "windpipe."

The trachea is made up of approximately eighteen cartilaginous rings placed one above the other and separated by a fibrous membrane. These are joined posteriorly by fibrous tissue and unstriated (smooth) muscles which contract during exhalation and relax during inhalation. This reflexive movement accounts for the known inability of the vocal mechanism to tolerate high levels of energy input when phonating pitches in the lowest tonal range, since a reduction of the circumference of the passageway because of excessive expiratory pressure "shuts off" much of the resonance potential.

Trachoma of the Vocal Cords: a chronic, contagious conjunctivitis marked by inflammatory granulation or nodes on the conjunctival surfaces of the vocal folds.

Nodes or nodules on the vocal folds result from friction caused by poor muscular coordination.

Transition Points: See Register "Break;" Segment.

Transverse Arytenoid: a muscle whose contraction approximates the two pyramids to which the arytenoid muscles are attached.

The contraction of the transverse arytenoid is essential to a complete approximation of the mid-portion of the vocal folds (*i.e.,* a complete closing of the glottal space).

Transverse Muscles: muscles that are extended on a more or less horizontal plane across the body.

Tremolo: a tonal movement generally produced by unrelieved muscular tension and/or nervousness; an interpretive effect used to depict old age, nervousness, or anxiety.

The acoustic characteristics of the tremolo are 1) rapid tonal oscillations (approximately 7.0—8.0 times per second), and 2) a constant amplitude (the distance between the peak and trough of an oscillation), *i.e.*, an amplitude which fails to increase or decrease proportionately to increases or decreases in intensity. Tremulous tones are harmonically impoverished, nervous in aspect, qualitatively monotonous, and functionally unhealthy.

Curiously, the tremolo is not always undesirable. A release of unrelieved tension, for example, will exhibit symptoms similar to those recorded before tension has been released. A direct analogy to this type of muscular reaction is the trembling of the arm which commences with the relaxation that takes place *after* discharging a heavy package. To make a subtle distinction of this kind with reference to tremulous tonal movements, however, requires experience, a knowledge of functional mechanics, and the objective guidance of an experienced teacher.

See **Vibrato**
Wobble

Trill: an accelerated movement of two musical tones; the rapid articulation of one speech organ against another (*e.g.*, the touching and releasing of the tip of the tongue against the ridge of the teeth as with a rolled *r*).

As a musical ornament, the trill is usually a rapid fluctuation between two distinct pitches of a diatonic scale, a major or minor second apart. In earlier times, it was often customary to trill on intervals of a third, fourth, or even a fifth.

The proper execution of a trill is a most difficult technical feat. During early stages of training, however, the trill can be used (without any expectation of executing it properly) to relieve throat constriction: that is, like the performance of rapid scales, to *release* controls rather than to *impose* them by attempting to execute the figures precisely. This relief of tension and loss of control allows things to happen which lie beyond conceptual limitations. Obviously, in early stages of development, there will be little semblance of a trill. With the passing of time, however, and the concurrent development and integration of the registration, the emerging tonal oscillations will gradually represent a rapid alternation between two distinct notes (*i.e.*, a trill).

See **Exercises**

Troughed Tongue: a tongue grooved or furrowed down the middle.

A troughed tongue has been deemed by some to be a desirable adjustment for the production of a well-formed tone. Since, however, the tongue must remain highly mobile during phonation for articulatory purposes, any fixed position will cause it to stiffen, and undermine articulatory freedom.

See **Tongue**

True Cords: the vocal folds whose vibration disturbs the surrounding air particles to establish pitch, as opposed to the false vocal cords, which lie immediately above them.

See **False Vocal Cords**
Larynx
Vocal Folds

See **Falsetto**
Falsetto or
  Head Voice
Middle Register
Register

True Falsetto: a pure falsetto; a type of tone quality which is produced when the cricothyroids tense without opposition from their mutual antagonists, the arytenoids.

The pure falsetto in all voice types is a breathy, straight, "hooty" sound that cannot be sustained for more than two or three seconds. It extends from B below middle C to the B an octave above. As it coordinates with the chest register, the falsetto is transformed into what is commonly recognized as the "head voice."

True Ribs: the top seven ribs, which are attached to the sternum or breastbone.

Twangy Tone: a vocalized sound whose tonal characteristics are strongly nasalized.

Acoustically, a "twangy" tone is caused by pharyngeal constriction, a condition that results in the resonators being too lightly damped, and that consequently leads to the overenergizing of the higher partials. Many feel that this helps the voice to "cut through" a full orchestra, and they encourage this quality by practicing what is known as a "snarl" tone.

"Twangy" tones reflect a strange aesthetic preference and are abusive to the vocal mechanism.

See **Damping**
Nasality

Twenty-Eight Hundred: the frequency band (actually an area in the vicinity of 2800—3400 cycles per second) into which energy is concentrated when vocal tone possesses "ring."

The connection between tonal "ring" and "2800" was first discovered by Helmholtz as early as 1875. He found this quality characteristic to be the result of "dissonant" partials, noticing that they only became audible when the sound intensity and the expenditure of physical energy were both high. His report, however, appears to make no qualitative distinction between various types of tonal brilliance, *i.e.*, metallic or shrill tones, or brilliance combined with warmth. Later investigators have produced evidence to indicate that "2800" is a product of resonance generated within the laryngeal pharynx. One of the more fascinating aspects of aural perception relative to "2800" is the fact that this band of frequencies corresponds exactly to the center point of the peak frequencies to which the ear is most sensitive.

The reason why the ear is especially sensitive to this particular band of frequencies lies within the structure of the ear canal itself. As sound waves move through the canal to the eardrum, the pressure variations are intensified, the result being a dramatic reinforcement of energy as the sound waves reach the eardrum. Thus, for frequencies between 2000 and 5500 cps, it has been shown that the pressure on the eardrum is almost double the amount of pressure introduced at the open end of the canal, *i.e.*, the external ear.

Whether the "ring" in the voice associated with strongly energized frequencies in the range of 2800—3400 cps represents a desirable aspect of technique has not as yet been determined. So far, scientific investigators have only established that this frequency band, when energized, produces a "ringing" tone quality. Since however, both an open-throated and a constricted tone production possess this characteristic (although in the two cases they are qualitatively different), establishing "2800" as an ultimate good must be viewed with suspicion.

The fact that a tone will ring solely on the basis of its having gained some degree of "2800," regardless of its qualitative properties, is evident from experiments conducted by Sir Richard Paget:

> If, while the reed was sounding, the tube was suitably pinched, near the opening from the reed . . . an appreciable twang was added to the vocal sound. This experiment indicates that a part, at least, of the so-called nasal quality . . . is probably due to a constriction of some part of the pharynx, so as to produce an additional resonator of high pitch, though the presence of nasal resonance seems to be indicated.[104]

Paget attributed this "ring" to energized frequencies in the range of 2732 cps. Other experiments conducted by Dayton C. Miller and George Oscar Russell have been quoted by William Vennard with reference to "squeezing" pipes and the dramatic effect this had in altering tone quality. Russell contended the high partials were responsible for producing a typical New England "twang."

Until such time as a qualitative distinction has been made between the false ring associated with throat constriction (twang and nasality) and the genuine ring (brilliance) heard when the tone quality is open-throated and freely produced, "2800," for all practical purposes, must remain an intriguing catch phrase rather than a useful pedagogic tool.

[104]Sir Richard Paget, *Human Speech* (New York: Harcourt, Brace and Co., 1930), p. 96.

See **Nasality**

U

Unification of Registers: a pedagogic procedure designed to coordinate the two basic register mechanisms, the chest register and the falsetto, into a harmonious functional unit.

The pedagogic key to this procedure is an understanding of the mechanical principles responsible for the phenomenon of registration. These principles and the needs of the particular mechanism dictate the musical pattern required to bring about their perfect juncture. The skill with which the two register mechanisms, the chest voice and the falsetto, are fused into an entity determines the ultimate efficiency of the vocal technique.

See Register

Unused Register: that mechanism which remains inoperative in a divided or isolated registration.

Although the "unused" register is generally the falsetto in male voices and the chest register in female voices, the situation is frequently reversed for singers who specialize in so-called "pop" music.

Unusual Voice Types: those voices 1) that are not easily classified, or that are rare and uncommon, 2) whose superior anatomical structure makes them ideally suited to produce qualities of exceptional beauty and opulence, 3) that function at a high level of efficiency, and 4) whose tonal characteristics do not appear to conform to the functional laws that govern conventional voice types, *i.e.,* those voices in a special group that can be said to have a "freak" tone production.

While some voice categories may be rare because there are few voices that fall into them, there is no such thing as an unusual voice type. Apparent departures from the "norm" are notable because of the special techniques employed, *e.g.,* countertenors who sing in a "mixed" head voice with a considerable amount of throat constriction, male altos who sing in a "mixed" falsetto, or voices capable of negotiating a range (never smoothly connected) of four or more octaves.

All voices, regardless of classification or unusual qualities, function in accordance with immutable physical laws, and while many unusual and exotic tone qualities can be produced without violating those laws (*e.g.,* the yodel), most do. Sophisticated singing as developed in Western civilization admits the possibility of a legato tone connection throughout all parts of the tonal range, a potential ability to swell and diminish on all pitches falling within a tonal range of at least two octaves of usable notes, extreme flexibility of movement, and an ability to sustain long musical phrases without breath loss or fatigue.

Given a healthy vocal technique, the "unusual" element in an artist's performance is temperament, cultural orientation, intelligence, imagination, charisma, and other special properties associated with personality. When these attributes are combined in one whose vocal technique is totally responsive, the singer so fortunate is not only unusual but rare.

Up and Over: a directive issued in order to gain access to the head voice; synonymous with "lifts."

The necessity for lifting "up and over" exists because of an overly energized chest register, which, because the approach to the register "break" and the "upper *passaggio*" minimizes the "pull" of the head voice, prohibits smoothness of access to the upper tonal range without forcing. Unless the energy used in lifting "up and over" is expended in such a way as to utilize those principles known to govern registration, however, this directive, when followed, will affect the vocal mechanism adversely. To maintain an open-throated resonance adjustment, the chest register must hold against the pull of the head voice, a synergetic activity which is impossible unless the approach notes to the "lift" point are softened.

The lift points where it is often felt that the directive "up and over" is appropriate always reflect the presence of an imbalanced registration, and consequently must be cured by rectifying that imbalance. When the voice is seamless, indicating that the registers are precisely balanced, the directive "up and over" is neither appropriate nor necessary.

See Falsetto or
Head Voice
Head Voice
Lift
Register
(A) Seamless
Voice
Synergy

Upper "Break" or Upper Passaggio: a transition point in women's voices lying between the last note of the so-called "middle" register and the "head" voice.

The upper "break" or upper *passaggio* is situated one octave above the actual point of register transition, or primary "break," and corresponds to a segmenting point where the vocal folds present a shorter, thinner vibrating surface to accommodate the pitches to be sung from F (top line of the treble clef) to high C.

There is a fundamental functional difference between these two breaks. The primary break occurs within a pitch range where the two register mechanisms overlap, a condition which exists when arytenoid tension is high, causing the chest register to dominate the weak lower extension of the head voice. As a result, the singer is obliged to *change from one mechanism to the other.* Thus, the gap between them (or "break") logically represents an absence of coordinate activity in that crucial area.

The muscular dichotomy noted above does not apply to the so-called "upper break." If access to higher pitch levels is to be gained, tension on both mechanisms must be simultaneously engaged. Consequently, the upper tonal range, regardless of fluctuating intensities, cannot be articulated when the registers function as isolated entities. Thus, pitches positioned an octave higher than the primary break, the so-called "upper break" or upper *passaggio*, require the participation of *both* register mechanisms at all times. A distinguishing difference between the two is that the primary register break represents a dramatic mechanical change from one muscle system to its antagonist, while these same systems (the cricothyroids and the arytenoids) *always* function as a coordinate unit both above and below the upper break.

The primary register break may therefore be seen to represent a change from one relatively isolated mechanism to its counterpart, whereas the upper *passaggio* results from a discrepancy in the ratio of tension shared between these same mechanisms in their coordinate form, *i.e.,* faulty coordination between two muscle systems which have already been fully engaged but imprecisely balanced. Since the excessive weight characteristic of this imbalance cannot be moved higher than the top line of the treble staff, the singer must resort to manipulative devices ("lifts," "up and over," *etc.*) to gain access to her higher tonal range. The awkwardness experienced in negotiating this transition is directly proportionate to the discrepancy in the registration.

Adoption of devices such as "lifting up and over" fails to take into consideration the fact that the upper break is a secondary functional manifestation whose disappearance depends upon a proper alignment of the registers at the primary break. It is by shifting emphasis to the isolation, development and reintegration of the chest and head voices that the imbalances causing the upper break will disappear, initially by a slight lowering of the intensity on the approach notes and ultimately through reflexive activity. As a consequence of this rebalancing, the segmentation of the vocal folds will occur smoothly and naturally, making all manipulative devices unnecessary.

The appearance of an upper break, therefore, is due to an imbalanced registration. With the chest register unanchored, the lower tones of the female head voice become weak. To compensate for this weakness, energy is wrongly applied when moving into the upper mid-tonal range. As a consequence, the chest register, instead of responding synergetically to the pull of the head voice, must be acted upon, causing it to lose its identity by "thinning out." Its presence is betrayed, however, by the "too open" quality characteristic of this mechanism when it is energized. Under these circumstances it is no longer possible to phonate a pure *ah*, with the result that tones have to be "covered" in order to force the vocal folds to assume a more suitable dimension.

In a correct tone production, the chest register (except for an occasional dramatic effect) should always respond synergetically to the pull of the head voice. Thus, when the arytenoid muscle systems (which yield qualities recognized as "chest" register) contract energetically, they interfere with the function of the cricothyroids (the stretchers of the vocal folds), which yield tone qualities recognized as "head" voice. At certain pitches, therefore, the muscular interference caused by the contraction of the arytenoids becomes intolerable, with the result that the voice tends to "break."

It has only been in recent years that problems related to an upper break have appeared on the vocal scene, and it is noteworthy that this appearance coincides with the neglect of the principles known to govern registration. Difficulties in handling the second break, therefore, will disappear once the functional laws pertaining to the development and use of the mechanism are correctly utilized.

See **Anchored in the Chest**
Bel Canto
Falsetto
Falsetto or Head Voice
Middle Register
Modern Methods
Register
Segment
Stretching of the Vocal Folds
Synergy

Upper Constrictor: the superior constrictor muscles, whose sphincter-like contractions close off the entry into the nasopharynx.

See **Nasality**

Upper Diaphragm: a term used to refer to the mylohyoid muscle, which forms the floor of the mouth, and pulls the hyoid and the tongue upward and forward. It is part of the muscular systems used in peristaltic movement, and is thus essentially constrictive.

Upper Mechanism: the higher of the two register mechanisms; the falsetto.

See Falsetto or
    Head Voice

Upper Process: a term occasionally used to refer to the higher of the two register mechanisms, the falsetto; loosely stated, this could include the head voice.

See Falsetto
    Falsetto or
      Head Voice
    Head Voice

Upper Register: the mechanism responsible for tonal qualities generally recognized as head voice or falsetto.

Those who deny the existence of the vocal registers occasionally use this term to refer to those pitches lying in the upper extension of the tonal range.

Uvula: the small, membranous appendage that terminates the posterior portion of the velum, or soft palate.

Neither voice teachers nor scientists seem to agree on the importance of the uvula, if any, to phonation. Some believe it should be volitionally raised to shut off the entrance into the nasal cavity and thus prevent nasality, while others maintain that neither a higher nor a lower adjustment is significant.

Perhaps the most convincing argument against raising the uvula to block the entrance into the nasal passages is that this is the first step in peristaltic movement, which is constrictive. The natural affinity between a raised uvula and swallowing presents fairly conclusive proof of the undesirability of this practice. Certainly from the standpoint of good pedagogy it is unwise to volitionally fix its position, since it will position itself naturally and correctly when the internal laryngeal functions are well coordinated..

See Hum
    Nasality

Volitional attempts to control the position of the uvula inevitably tend to stiffen the mechanisms and produce tonal rigidities through self-consciousness. It is conceivable, however, that the uvula, by its curious design, could, along with the pillars of the fauces, form the final barrier or point of resistance to the breath and tonal flow before vocal tone passes into the mouth cavity.

V

Vagus Nerve: either of the tenth pair of cranial nerves (also called the "pneumogastric nerves"), which supplies sensory and motor nervous impulses to the viscera and various parts of the respiratory system, including the lungs and the recurrent, superior and inferior laryngeal nerves which stimulate the vocal muscles. Thus, the vagus nerves are the chief transmitters of the neurological impulses which eventually yield vocal tone.

The superior and inferior branches of the vagus nerve perform two functions. The superior, which is primarily sensory, innervates the cricothyroid muscles, which stretch the vocal folds, while all other intrinsic muscles of the larynx are supplied by the inferior branch. Thus, it is evident that the internal muscles of the larynx responsible for adjusting the vocal folds are involuntary, and controlled not so much by muscle sense as by hearing, a fact which accounts for the rather monotonous tone quality observable with those whose hearing is seriously impaired.

In the absence of motor sensitivity among the intrinsic muscles of the larynx, it would appear that hearing, and concepts developed through hearing, provide the sole means by which vocal skills can be developed. Fortunately, there is another alternative. While neurological innervation of the vocal mechanism in response to concepts prompts an organic response over which the singer has no volitional control, it is nevertheless possible to overcome both conceptual and physical limitations by encouraging natural, spontaneous movement and avoiding those concerns having to do with quality *per se*. Through the skillful selection and juxtaposition of elemental scale patterns, it becomes possible to by-pass the student's tonal preconceptions, stimulate natural movement, treat the mechanism as a unit or as isolated elements, and for all practical purposes gain what amounts to direct control over the coordinative process by indirect means.

See **Afferent**
 Hearing
 Holistic Pedagogy
 Indirect Control
 Kinesthesia

Vegetative: affecting, arising from, or relating to involuntary body functions; those muscular and organic functions controlled by the autonomic nervous system.

See **Autonomic Nervous System**

Veiled Tones: those vocalized sounds whose breathy tonal characteristics are the product of improper register and resonance adjustments.

See **Falsetto**
 Nodule

Velocity: quickness of motion; speed.

Velocity of tonal movement, or agility, is a by-product of the general flexibility which results when the vocal mechanism functions efficiently. The velocity of the sound produced, however, is not a factor in singing.

Velum: the soft palate; that part of the pharynx which forms the posterior portion of the mouth, from which it is separated by the uvula and the pillars of the fauces. Since the velum includes the upper portion of the oropharynx, it is important to the formation and resonation of vowel phonemes.

Velvety Tones: vocalized sounds whose tonal characteristics are frequently referred to as "rich," "warm," and "smooth."
   A "velvety" sound is usually a reflection of temperament but can be consciously produced for interpretive purposes. Acoustically, it is a tone quality reflecting the presence of strongly energized lower partials.

Ventricles of Morgagni: the cup-shaped ventricular pouches which separate the vocal folds from the false vocal cords, or ventricular bands.
   Although the role of the ventricles of Morgagni in phonation has not been established scientifically, there is some evidence to support the contention that the contraction of the ventricular bands and the consequent cupping of the ventricles of Morgagni establish a supraglottal pressure system to counteract the subglottal pressure exerted by the escaping breath, by narrowing the aperture at the point of exit. If this is proven to be true, it will lend greater credibility to the opinion of those theorists who reject the breath pressure theory.

Ventricular Bands: the false vocal cords; the muscular bands which form the upper border of the ventricular pouches, or ventricles of Morgagni.
   As a middle laryngeal sphincter, the ventricular bands close to block the point of exit during coughing, weightlifting, and defecation. A pathological condition exists, however, when these bands are used during phonation as a vibratory mechanism, an abuse causing ventricular dysphonia, or chronic hoarseness. Anxiety in times of acute emotional stress creates similar symptoms and is know as hyperkinetic dysphonia.

Vertebra: one of the bony and cartilaginous segments composing the spinal column.

Vestibule of the Larynx: that part of the laryngeal pharynx lying above the ventricular bands, or false vocal cords.

Vibrating String Theory: a mathematical formula advanced in the seventeenth century by a friar of the Order of St. Francis, Père Marin Mersenne, to explain the physical properties of sounds produced by a vibrating string with respect to its length, tension and mass, its wave length, manner of segmentation and the frequency of the resultant sound wave; in singing, a pedagogic theory which attempts to compare the vibrational pattern of the vocal folds with that of tautened strings (*e.g.,* those of the violin or the piano).
   The vibrating string theory is not directly analogous to the function of the vocal

folds, although one direct parallel may be drawn, *i.e.*, that each vibrating mass is of a specific length, tension and elasticity related to pitch, and that each produces a fundamental and a series of overtones. Among the important differences are the following:

1. Strings do not alter their tension, whereas vocal fold tension is constantly being varied by the contraction of a complex laryngeal muscular system;
2. Intensity is controlled and regulated in a stringed instrument by the strength of the bowing, plucking, or stroke of a hammer, whereas vocal fold pressure must be decreased at higher levels of pitch and intensity if the elastic rebound of the folds is not to be counteracted;
3. The physical dimension of strings is uniformly graduated from thicker, for the lowest tones, to thinner, for the upper tones, whereas the vocal folds are not, being (a) short and thick for the lowest tones, (b) longer but thinner and under higher tension for the mid-tonal range, and (c) shorter, thinner and more highly tensed for the upper tonal range, the mass of the folds decreasing after adduction;
4. Strings vibrate simultaneously along their full length, forming loops and nodes, whereas the vocal folds open anteriorly, and until they adduct (become so tautened that their vibration is reduced to their medial margins) they move in undulating pulsations toward their posterior attachments, and
5. Strings divide into segments, whereas the vocal folds release subglottal pressure in a series of rapid puffs.

Attempts to compare the human voice acoustically and functionally with members of the instrument family once promised to provide information potentially useful to the development of a viable vocal pedagogy. Such analogies, however, are inexact, and in addition fail to include physiological and psychological phenomena, which, for the teacher of voice, lie at the very heart of the pedagogic problem. For him, understanding the mechanical principles which make it possible to build or reconstruct a vocal technique is far more important than knowing that the vocal mechanism belongs, more or less, to the string, reed, or wind instrument family.

See Bel Canto
Coupling
Harmonic Theory
Modern Methods
Neurochronaxic Theory
Puff Theory
Resonance, Sounding Board
Standing Wave

Vibration: a rhythmic oscillation or molecular movement in the atmosphere that is perceived as sound.

There are four basic kinds of vibration:

1. Free vibration, in which a vibrator moves freely within an elastic system until its energy is dissipated by friction, heat, or the pull of gravity;
2. Maintained vibration, in which the energy dissipated by friction or gravity is replaced by an independent source so that the original vibration continues at its own natural frequency (*e.g.*, the spring of a clock);
3. Forced vibration, in which 1) a vibrator imposes its natural frequency on that of a rigid but resilient surface (*e.g.*, the sounding board of a piano or the violin), and 2) a vibrator either dominates or is dominated by an adjacent resonating system, in which case the resultant frequency will represent a compromise between that natural to each had they been vibrating independently, and
4. Sympathetic vibration, in which the natural frequencies of both the vibrator and the resonator are identical.

To a greater or lesser extent, all of the above-named vibrational modalities participate in tone production. Taken in reverse order, sympathetic vibration occurs when the pharyngeal resonators share the same natural frequency as that of the vocal folds. Forced vibration occurs when 1) the vibratory mass of the vocal folds is too great for the pitch-intensity pattern being sung, causing the tone to sound "too open," a condition which finds the vibrator dominating the resonator, and 2) the physical dimensions of the cavity are so arranged that the resonator dominates the vibrator, as in "covering," where the larynx is lowered and the velum elevated. Maintained vibration is the result of either breath pressure or breath compression, combined with a neurological stimulation of the involved muscle systems. Free vibration is a form of sympathetic vibration, which must be maintained because the pharyngeal cavities possess no energy of their own.

All of the above types of vibration must, of course, be maintained. However, under ideal technical conditions, this maintenance (like the small amount of energy supplied by the weights of a timepiece to compensate for the loss of momentum in the movement of the pendulum) must be considered marginal. While there is limited data to support this hypothesis, the late nineteenth century German physicist Ewald explored this possibility, demonstrating by his experiments that the vocal folds could be made to produce definite pitches without breath pressure solely by electrical stimulation, a postulate elaborated upon in this century by the French scientist Raoul Husson.

When all of the muscular forces involved in phonation are in equilibrium, the vocal folds are sustained by neurological energy and some combination of all of the above vibratory motions. The extent to which any one of these predominates, especially free vibration, is determined by the presence or absence of muscular interference, *i.e.*, a perfect consonance between well-formed mental concepts and precise physical coordination.

Vibrato: a tonal oscillation above and below a mean pitch that imparts vitality, buoyancy and harmonic richness to vocalized sounds.

Leopold Mozart, an eminent violinist and the father of Wolfgang, was perhaps the first to comment upon a vibrato, noting that "Nature herself suggested it to man." There are many distinguishable types of tonal oscillation, however, only one of which can truly be called a vibrato, the others being an admixture of the vibrato, the tremolo, and the wobble. When it is considered that all vocal sound waves are propagated because of muscular movement, it is evident that the differences among these three classifications represent varying aspects of technique.

A true vibrato, like an absolutely pure tone quality, is a product of refined concepts and mechanical (muscular) processes that function in a state of equilibrium. The balanced tension among the muscular systems involved in phonation peculiar to this type of tonal movement are not present in the tremolo and the wobble. The tremolo, whether combined with some elements of the vibrato or in its pure form, results from greater or lesser degrees of unrelieved tension within the throat parts, a condition visually betrayed by a fluttering action of the tongue and jaw. The wobble, a less acute technical problem is due 1) to a shifting of tension from the arytenoids to the cricothyroids, creating a conflict between the two basic register mechanisms that causes the tonal oscillations to become too slow and erratic, and

2) failure of the infra- and suprahyoids to suspend the larynx properly and thereby stabilize its position.

On the basis of the data presently available, it may be said that there are two special properties of a vibrato: 1) a periodicity (the duration of one complete cycle of recurrent pitch changes), which remains constant regardless of the changes in amplitude made to accommodate increases in intensity, and 2) an amplitude, which increases and decreases in direct proportion to the rise and fall of intensity. Neither the tremolo nor the wobble, nor any combination of the two, meets these criteria.

One of the earliest scientific formulations concerning the vibrato was advanced by Sir Wilfred Willis (1830), who based his postulate upon the glottal puff theory. It was Willis' contention, shared by other notable scientists, that these puffs travel to the pharyngeal isthmus and return again repetitively to the sound source; this view coincides with the presence of a standing wave as explained by Johan Sundberg. This acoustic phenomenon, in conjunction with the influence of the resonance characteristics potentially present within the trachea, the laryngo- and oropharynges, and the ventricular sacs, consists of compression waves that move to and fro between the upper and lower portions of the vocal tract, the oscillations of which result in a tonal pulse recognized as a vibrato. If the sound waves propagated by the puffs are not in phase with the loops and nodes of the standing wave, the evenness of the tonal pulse will be disturbed. The audible properties of such disturbances are perceived aesthetically as a tremolo or wobble.

More recent studies of the vibrato by Thomas Shipp and Rolf Leanderson (1982) reinforce earlier findings of Douglas Stanley (1945), which attribute the presence of a vibrato to laryngeal functioning. In the Shipp-Leanderson experiments, the cricothyroids (that system reponsible for yielding tone qualities commonly recognized as the falsetto or head voice) were found to be the most important regulatory mechanism, and a vibrato was found to result when this system works out of phase with the mylohyoids, which, when tensed, elevate the palate. The Shipp-Leanderson postulate is substantially in accord with earlier investigations conducted by Robert Mason and Willard Zemlin (1966).

Scientific opinion with respect to the measureable aspects of the vibrato expresses a reasonable consensus, although there are certain disparities. Howard B. Rothman, Kenneth Nielsen, and James W. Hicks, Jr. (1979) found that the frequency rate of the vibrato (in the judgment of selected professional singers, teachers, scientists and physicians) was most agreeable when confined within a range of 5.0 to 6.0 cycles per second. Tonal movements exceeding these parameters, whether faster or slower, tremulous or unsteady, were judged to be displeasing. Shipp and Leanderson arrived at a similar conclusion, observing a normal frequency rate of 4.8 to 6.0 times per second. Earlier studies conducted by Carl Seashore (1938), however, extended the vibrato rate from 6.0 to 6.8, while Douglas Stanley (1945) stated that it should only vary from 6.0 to 6.2. In a study made in collaboration with S. K. Wolfe and W. J. Sette, Stanley (1935) reported the vibrato to range from 4.5 to 6.4 cycles per second, a compass approximating the findings of Shipp and Leanderson.

Whether or not the measurements made of characteristic tonal pulses during the past four decades can lead to a just evaluation of the functional properties of a given tone quality (as is the case with harmonic analysis) is open to question.

To a certain extent it would apper to be possible, but in reality, since a great number of singers afflicted with a trembling of the jaw and tongue, symptoms which are visually indicative of constricting tensions within the upper vocal tract, exhibit a pulse rate falling within the 5.0 to 6.2 range, it would seem that unless all oscillations are studied with reference to their harmonic structure and the type of muscular activity at the sound source, the only conclusion to be reached is that tonal pulses within a prescribed range are aesthetically pleasing, while others outside that range are not. Thus, just because the tonal pulse is pleasing and/or unobtrusive, it cannot be assumed that the vocal technique is functionally healthy and is yielding a true vibrato.

Several possible explanations suggest themselves to account for the different rates of frequency reported by science. Perhaps the most convincing of these is the fact that tonal pulses rarely fit comfortably into the exclusive categories assigned them in research. Just as a pure hysteric and a pure compulsive are considered ideal clinical cases in psychology, so must those afflicted with a pure tremolo and/ or wobble be considered ideal clinical cases in singing. To continue the analogy, those who could be said to be completely free of all neurotic traits are as rare as those who have a pure vibrato, and each represents an aspect of human perfection. Most singers, being human, display some combination of all three of the above elements, both in their singing and in their characterological structure. If suitable categories are to be established, therefore, clinical cases exculsively representative of each type of tonal movement must be sought out and studied if the findings are to be valid. Moreover, when aesthetic judgment is involved, it must further be established whether or not an aesthetic norm is functionally normal, or, as in "pop" singing, whether it is to a greater or lesser degree an acceptable vocal aberration.

Stanley recognized that most of the singers tested in his experiments did not fit exclusively into any of the three general categories set up, and as an accommodation added what he called a "tremolo-vibrato." However, in view of the wide range of tonal oscillations that have been studied (exhibiting extreme differences in amplitude relative to frequency, which is often of itself erratic), not even this addition is sufficient to cover the range of possibilities. Indeed, it is questionable whether precise categories can be established at all unless the vibrato, tremolo and wobble can be linked to their functional origins.

Other possible impediments to the use of vibrato tracings as an objective method of rating technical efficiency are the following: 1) qualitative tastes, which often change with changing cultural attitudes; 2) the awkward positioning of the subject (tongue protruded, *etc.*) necessary for laryngeal photography; 3) sensitivity of equipment; 4) the type of training subjects have received, and 5) analysis based upon perceptual evaluations and/or taking an average of all those who have been tested. In view of the rarity of a true vibrato, it is evident that vibrato tracings are extremely unreliable determinants of technical excellence.

A feature common to all voice types has been observed to be a rhythmic activity of the diaphragm, which, together with a slight rippling of the walls of the vocal tract and its mucosal lining, moves synchronously with each tonal pulsation. Indeed, many training procedures are based upon the presumption that the vibrato is controlled by directly acting upon the diaphragm. However, the diaphragm is without proprioceptive nerve endings, produces no conscious sensations, and consequently cannot be consciously controlled. Moreover, as the British neurologist Barry Wyke has pointed out, the mechanical processes involved in phonation result from the integrated activity of some forty or more muscles (mostly involuntary), which must be precisely regulated over a time scale often measured in less than a millisecond. To overtly control these integrated activities by energizing any one phase out of context, especially with the intent of improving general response patterns and overall coordination, is both practically and neurologically impossible.

There are additional reasons why the vibrato, and indeed most of the functional elements involved in phonation, cannot be directly acted upon: 1) the ideal position of the larynx is unknown, and like quality, which usually represents a present technical status rather than an intrinsically natural quality, it can only be conceptualized *after* vocal problems have been eliminated; 2) the mass per unit length, tension, mode and rate of vocal fold vibration are not susceptible to improvement by means of respiratory and/or articulatory controls, and 3) the desirable position of the involuntary muscular systems engaged in phonation cannot be replicated either through verbalization or by example. It is apparent, therefore, that control over the vibrato (except for the imposition of negative tensions) is impossible until such time as technical faults have been eliminated and the mechanism is totally responsive to conceptual and emotional stimuli.

In the absence of overt control systems, the question arises as to how the vibrato and other tonal oscillations come into being. Perhaps the most reasonable answer is that advanced by Ernest Gardner (1975), who attributed all tonal movements to excitatory and inhibitory mechanisms within the cerebellum. He believed that these on-off impulses were directed by way of the deep cerebular nuclei to other parts of the nervous system and then transmitted to the appropriate muscle systems responsible for generating vocal tone. Since neurological activity of this nature stimulates all of the respiratory muscles, the theory would appear to provide a hypothesis upon which a valid accounting can be made of the varying types of tonal movement. The theory also lends further support to the contention of many that effective training procedures must address themselves to problems related to the proper stimulation and coordination of a highly complex laryngeal muscular system, and encourage reflexive movements which are spontaneous and natural, if ever discriminating concepts are to be brought to fruition.

From the standpoint of function, a true vibrato is the result of a combination of several factors: 1) the ratio of tension shared among the complex muscular systems which tauten the vocal folds and determine their physical dimensions; 2) the conformation of the trachea, larynx, and the laryngo- and oropharynges in relation to themselves and each other as these adjustments affect the formant structure; 3) a state of balanced tension among all of the respiratory (vocal) muscles, and 4) conceptual clarity. When these elements are finely tuned and precisely coordinated, a true vibrato results. It is an equation which cannot be reversed, however, since a vibrato is merely an outward expression of an inner functional condition, a result and not the cause of finely integrated physical processes.

If the vibrato is a disturbance of air particles resulting from the activity of a vocal "motor" that is finely tuned, then it follows that the focal point of instruction should be directed toward improving those functional activities, not toward the vibrato itself. As stated earlier, if technical faults are present, both natural quality and the precise interpositioning of the vocal muscles are unknown. This means that at most stages of development concepts are conditioned by function, and do not operate as the controlling factor. Thus, while conceptual controls play an important role in developing vocal skills, they are not (or should not be) concerned with the character of the tonal movements *per se,* but with procedures which, through the mechanics of registration, improve the performance of those muscular systems responsible for generating vocal tone. It is through the employment of techniques designed to stimulate reflexive, natural movement that concepts are refined to the point where they are capable of controlling the character of tonal movements. Within this context, the intellect observes and studies the nature of the reflexive movements taking place within the vocal tract, an aspect of training that usually lasts until a high level of technical excellence has been reached.

Attempts to overtly control the vibrato have taken many forms (tonal support, special breathing techniques, *etc.*), none of which have proved successful. Most singers are victims of tonal unsteadiness of one kind or another that is rarely of their own choosing. In tacit recognition of the fact that erratic movements cannot be corrected by controlling the movements themselves, advice is often given to produce "straight" tones to alleviate the problem. This merely exacerbates an existing problem, usually adding another dimension to those vocal faults already present.

The singing of "straight" tones occasionally serves a useful interpretive purpose, since by making the voice lifeless, they are ideal for depicting age, world weariness, despair, innuendo and hate. There are also those who prefer straight tones for choral repertoire, especially when women are required to sing without any vibrato in an attempt to imitate boy sopranos. This preference usually extends to the singing of music composed during the Baroque era.

From the standpoint of acceptable aesthetic norms, the vibrato is an indispensable element in musical tone. It makes the voice buoyant and vibrant, ensures a legato vocal line, reflects emotion, infuses the voice quality with harmonic richness, causes the pitch to sound "centered," promises flexibility, and is a major factor in executing a trill and *messa di voce* (although a trill must not be considered an exaggerated vibrato, but two separate and distinct pitches). The vibrato is also an important factor in minimizing vocal fatigue because of the on-off neurological impulses by which it is innervated. Because it is a reflection of correct vocal technique, *i.e.*, reflexive organic activities based upon an innate functional logic, the vibrato awakens and gains contact with those instinctual processes without which one could not be a singer. The vibrato, therefore, is an indispensable adjunct of a correct vocal technique.

See **Attack**
    Control
    Formants
    Functional
       Listening
    Kinesthesia
    Onset
    Reflex
    Register
    Self-Regulation
    Standing Wave
    Tremolo
    Wobble

Viscera: the internal organs of the body, especially the heart, lungs, kidneys, liver and intestines located in the great cavity.

The term "visceral" is occasionally used to describe those instincts which are organic or "gut" reactions to an idea or an event.

See **Kinesthesia**

Vital Capacity: the maximum amount of breath that can be inhaled and exhaled in a single respiratory cycle; the sum of complemental, tidal and supplemental air.

Vital capacity has little relevance to tone production, since, when the technique is efficient, only 36 cc per second of a total capacity (which, for men, averages 225 cubic inches, or 3600 cc and for women, approximately 150 cubic inches) is lost. Consequently, the pedagogic problem is not to improvise techniques designed to "control" or regulate breath expenditure, but to effect a natural closing of the glottal space by bringing the laryngeal muscular activities which approximate the vocal folds into a state of balanced tension, an equilibrium achieved by employing those principles known to govern registration.

Vocalization is so commonly thought of in association with breath pressure or breath compression that the essential function of respiration is frequently over-looked. Essentially, the natural function of the respiratory mechanism is to supply oxygen to the body substances and muscle tissues to provide the combustible element necessary for the production of energy. Since, in singing, such a small amount of breath is lost when the technique is efficient, there is always a substantial amount of residual air left in the lungs after the completion of even the longest musical phrases. Consequently, a fresh supply of air is inspired because of a lack of oxygen rather than loss of breath.

Vital capacity, therefore, is not a factor in phonation. Excessive breath expenditure is a matter of poor laryngeal muscular coordination rather than an inadequate breath supply or a faulty method of "control."

See Breath
 Breathing
 Control
 Dead Space
 Laryngeal
  Suspension
 Puff Theory
 Register
 Resonance
 Vowel

Vitality: that characteristic which distinguishes the living from the nonliving.

In singing, "vitality" is used to refer to those tonal properties which reflect buoyancy, self-vibratility, a true vibrato, tonal richness, and other aspects associated with a free production. Thus, tonal vitality is a sign of vocal health.

Vocal Bands: See Vocal Folds.

Vocal Classification: the assigning of voices to categories or voice types (*i.e.,* soprano, alto, tenor, or bass).

Originally, because of limited technical skills, most singers fell comfortably within one of these four basic voice types. Since the middle of the nineteenth century, however, the four categories have been expanded and subdivided to indicate not only the singer's approximate range, but also the relative weight of his voice, and in many cases, the type of music for which he is particularly suited (*e.g.,* *soprano leggiero,* "dramatic soprano," *Heldentenor,* and "Verdi baritone"). Today, the original four generic terms are used most frequently in choral music.

Voices should never be categorized prematurely, since the natural range, quality and tessitura are unknown quantities until existing faults have been removed. Therefore, proper pedagogic procedures address themselves to the problem of removing those faults that are known, rather than looking for or attempting to develop a quality that is unknown. As the great sculptor Rodin once remarked, "Finding the beauty of an object is easy. Starting with a great block of marble, all one must do is cut away the unnecessary parts." On these terms the voice, too, will reveal its natural classification once impediments in the form of muscular interference have been removed.

The tones produced by the average singer rarely represent an intrinsically natural quality, but reflect the condition of the functioning mechanism. To establish one's natural tone quality and voice classification, therefore, it is necessary to recondition the mechanism by correcting impurities of vowel and imbalances within the registration, and by achieving a condition of full-throated resonance. When vocal faults are removed and the mechanism becomes physically well coordinated, the voice classification will be self-evident, and the speculative errors so frequently associated with premature voice classification will be avoided.

Vocal Compass: range; the extent of notes that can be phonated.

Vocal compass is frequently confused with "practical" or "usable" range. Although the compass or total extension of a well-used voice should be about three octaves, the practical range (particularly with males) may be no more than two octaves. This is because the falsetto is not generally considered aesthetically acceptable for males, and because females are allowed to use the chest voice in either a combined or a relatively isolated form. Considering the fact that both the falsetto and the chest voice are integral parts of the mechanism, and that ideally they can be coordinated into the usable range, a three octave compass does not seem excessive. The pedagogic problem, of course, is *how* to combine these two elements into an effective functional unit.

Vocal Cords: the lower portion of the thyroarytenoid muscles, which projects into the cavity of the larynx and whose movement creates the pressure variations responsible for pitch. Theorists now substitute the word "folds" for cords, since the older usage suggests that a parallel exists between the vibratory characteristics of the vocal folds and the strings of the violin; such a suggestion is both untrue and misleading.

Although no conclusive explanation has been advanced, the most common theories related to the function of the vocal folds are the following:

1. The "breath pressure theory," which contends that pitch is produced by the vocal folds' resistance to the pressure exerted by expired breath;

2. Registration, whose adherents believe that the length, thickness, and contour of the vocal folds are adjusted by two antagonistic muscle systems, the cricothyroids and the arytenoids, to meet changing conditions of pitch, intensity, and vowel. Those who support this theory can be further divided into 1) a group which combines the functional principles of registration with the breath pressure theory, and 2) a minority which believes that the vocal folds and their associated musculatures are energized by oxidization and respond freely to neurological impulses transmitted through the central nervous system;

3. The neurochronaxic theory, which holds that the vocal folds are set in motion by motor impulses from the central nervous system to create pressure variations which, in turn, produce pitch;

4. A "double-valve theory," which maintains that the vocal folds and false vocal cords create a system of sub- and supraglottal pressure that enables the vocal folds to become self-vibratile and respond freely (provided the mechanism functions in equilibrium) to neurological impulses;

5. The aerodynamic theory, or "Bernoulli effect," which states that the vocal folds approximate by a sucking action due to air flow;

6. A theory that complex contractions of the ary- and thyrovocalis muscle fibers running through the vocal folds approximate the midportion of the vocal folds and narrow the glottal slit, and

7. The "sinus tone theory," which claims that vocal tone is produced by the direction of currents of air into the sinus cavities and their consequent emission through the nasal passages (this theory assigns no role to the vocal cords in phonation).

While these theories may appear confusing and contradictory, perhaps all, to a greater or lesser degree, explain in part the function of the vocal folds. Some, of course, can only be true under ideal technical conditions; others may be either compensatory or indispensable. The breath pressure theory, which is the most universally accepted, does not seem practical, since the angulation of the vocal folds is not conducive to resistance, and, were they to resist, such resistance would cause them to lose their elasticity. Sinus tone production does not seem to offer a sensible solution.

See **Bernoulli Effect**
     Breath Pressure
       Theory
     Neurochronaxic
       Theory
     Sinus Tone
       Production
     Vocal Folds

Vocal Deterioration: a decline in mechanical efficiency resulting from abuse, misuse or overuse of the vocal mechanism.

The physical manifestations of vocal deterioration are fatigue, singing out of tune, an inability to sustain long phrases, and a reduction in range, resonance, and flexibility.

See **Vocal Study**

Vocal Discipline: the ability to make artistic choices suitable to one's current functional needs and capabilities.

Vocal discipline demands that the singer be content with deliberate, thorough preparation, and that he reject a tendency toward compulsive practice, oversinging, and a desire to work on an unsuitable repertoire. Learning how to sing correctly and the development of a professional career are time-consuming processes, and to force progress defeats both purposes. Vocal discipline is also necessary if the singer is to protect himself against premature career promotion and professional exploitation. Too much too soon has ruined many promising careers.

A successful training program requires a realistic goal, a workable pedagogic plan for achieving that goal, and a good sense of timing. Additionally, one must have good work habits and the vocal self-discipline that is essential to the care and preservation of the voice.

See **(To) Mark**
     Vocal Study

Vocal Dynamics: variations and contrasts in vocal intensity that generally range from very soft to very loud.

In a correct technique of singing, vocal intensity can rise to fifty decibels, or twice the capability of the average speaking voice.

See **Vibrato**

Vocal Endurance: an ability to sing for protracted periods of time without fatigue or deleterious aftereffects.

Vocal endurance is the product of a correct vocal technique, and it indicates that the vocal muscles are well coordinated and responsive to refined concepts.

See **(To) Mark**
     (To) Save the Voice
     Vocal Discipline

Vocal Exercises: See Exercises.

Vocal Faults: flaws due to 1) correct principles wrongly applied, 2) procedures based upon sensory illusion rather than substance, 3) wrongly directed effort because of qualitative misconcepts, and 4) poor physical coordination.

VOCAL FOLD VIBRATION

The most common faults are "throatiness," a "mixed" registration, and an improper laryngeal suspension (*i.e.*, resonance adjustment). Their aural manifestations range from shortness of breath, limited range, devitalized resonance and an inability to swell and diminish, to general inflexibility. While vocal faults can be present because of natural disabilities or acquired by imitating respected artists, they can also be a product of pedagogic mismanagement, either because of correct principles inexpertly applied, or general misconceptions pursued to their logical conclusion.

Vocal Fold Vibration: a movement of the vocal folds essentially conditioned by the manner in which the total laryngeal musculature coordinates.

The normal function of the vocal folds during phonation is to alternately open and close the glottal space. During the closed phase of its cycle, the air compression built up within the lungs presses against the vocal folds, and, in conjunction with neurological stimuli, sets them in motion. As a counterbalance to the build-up of air compression below the vocal folds, the upper valve of the larynx (the false vocal cords) narrows. This limits and controls the rate of airflow, and by so doing, inflates the ventricular sacs to create a supraglottal pressure system. Because of the counterbalance between sub- and supraglottal pressure, the vocal folds are not obliged to resist the pressure that might otherwise be directed against them, and in the absence of this requirement, they become self-vibratile. At the same time, breath expulsion is reduced to a minimum and tonal unsteadiness is eliminated.

Due to the natural elasticity of the system, the vocal folds oscillate both above and below their median position. At the crest of their wave-like motion, a tiny burst of air escapes, after which the folds spring back to normal. Like a pendulum responding to the pull of gravity, however, the folds overshoot the mark in reversing their path, causing a descent below their median point. This increases subglottal pressure and causes the cycle to repeat itself. In the well-used voice, these oscillations occur at an approximate rate of 6.0 to 6.4 cycles per second. It is because of the frequency of the vibratory motion of the vocal folds that the pitch of a given note is established.

When phonation begins, the glottal opening occurs at the anterior portion of the vocal folds and moves rearward to the arytenoids. The lower lips of the vocal bands open first, followed by the upper lips, and close again in the same order, a fact which accounts for the "rolling" expressed in the vibratory pattern of the glottic rims when they have been set in motion. Thus, there are three influences at work in the initiation and sustaining of a vibratory pattern: 1) the concepts which innervate the muscular activities involved; 2) the self-stretching ability of the internal thyroarytenoids, and 3) the contraction of the cricothyroid and the arytenoid muscle systems.

Vocal Folds: a muscular valve lined with mucous membrane; also known as the thyroarytenoids and the vocal cords.

The vocal folds are formed by the upper free margins of the conus elasticus (a cone-shaped structure of elastic tissue attached below to the upper borders of the cricoid cartilage, in front to the thyroid cartilage, and at the rear to the arytenoids) and are fastened anteriorly to the notch of the thyroid, and at the rear, to the arytenoid cartilage. Since they merge with the vocal processes, they can, when drawn together, completely close the entrance into the trachea. Because the vocal folds are elastic and can be brought into tension, they are capable, when vibratile, of creating pressure variations at a frequency equivalent to the fundamental of the tone being produced.

The vocal folds are made up of two parts: 1) the internal thyroarytenoids, the vocal lips or vocalis muscles, and 2) the external thyroarytenoids, an outer longitudinal muscle which terminates with the conus elasticus to form the vocal band. The terms vocal lips and vocal bands, therefore, are not synonymous, but represent separate parts of the vocal folds.

The vocal lips are embedded in the vocal folds and are composed of two fibrous muscle bundles that crisscross each other: 1) the thyrovocalis, and 2) the aryvocalis. Capable of being tensed or relaxed either separately or together, these fibers, some of which extend upward to the epiglottis, others to the ventricles of Morgagni (sacs between the true and false vocal cords), are essential to a full closing of the glottal space.

The vocal bands into which the vocalis fibers radiate are comprised of the longitudinal strands of the conus elasticus that cover most of the inner muscles of the internal thyroarytenoids. Due to the presence of the vocalis fibers, a close functional connection is maintained between these two vibrating members. Unlike the vocal lips, the vocal bands are not capable of setting themselves in motion, and they must rely upon the contraction of the cricothyroids and arytenoids to be drawn into tension.

There are, therefore, two muscle systems responsible for adjusting the vocal folds to the required length, tension and elasticity: the cricothyroids, and the thyro- and cricoarytenoids. When the ratio of tension distributed between these two muscle systems, and others with which they must coordinate, are in equilibrium, the mechanism will assume tension without becoming tense. When they, or the cartilage to which they are attached, become rigidly "set" so that a rapid change of balance becomes impossible, the voice will "break." A break of this description is not to be confused with a register break, since the two types differ radically both as to cause and effect; the difference between the two characteristically different phenomena is obvious to the trained listener.

The involuntary movements made by these muscle systems constitute the essence of the vocal function. Whether or not they coordinate effectively determines the quality of the tonal emission, as does the manner in which the larynx is maintained in an adjustment favorable to resonance. How to change the response pattern of these involuntary muscle systems when they are poorly coordinated constitutes the direct objective of vocal study. Since the vocal folds cannot be acted upon directly, their behavior patterns must be changed by the rhythmic execution of specially designed scales and exercises which evoke a predictable reflexive response.

See Bernoulli Effect
Energy
Kinesthesia
Natural Movement
Neurochronaxic
Theory
Puff Theory
Register
Resonance
Rhythm
Vocal Cords

Vocal Freedom: the ability to articulate a wide variety of pitch, intensity and vowel patterns with ease and flexibility.

Vocal freedom is the primary goal of vocal study, since concerns related to tone production can be relegated to the subconscious, permitting the singer to concentrate his energies on the spontaneous expression of his thoughts and feelings.

Beautiful tone quality, while a natural corollary of a correct technique, is not the sole objective of vocal study, as it is evident that harsh and even ugly tone qualities can be produced correctly. Thus, vocal freedom is essential to free, natural, unaffected vocal communication over a broad spectrum of emotional expression.

Vocal Fry: in phonetics, a rough, squeezed vocalized sound produced by an upward movement of the larynx accompanied by a corresponding lowering of the epiglottis; in singing, a tonal quality resembling a death rattle that is heard only in the lowest pitch range of the voice.

Concepts related to vocal fry originated with linguistic specialists in Semitic languages, who described it as a "laryngeal voiced fricative" produced by laryngeal constriction. Within this context, concepts related to vocal fry are inimical to a free, open-throated tone production.

Evaluated on the basis of the form in which it has been adapted to vocal training, vocal fry is not a laryngeal voiced fricative, but a tone quality producible only in the tonal range directly below that of the chest register. The positive aspect of this quality is that its characteristic vibrations cannot be produced unless the muscles that constrict the tracheal rings are relaxed, and as a consequence it momentarily serves to engender a sense of throat freedom.

Among the negative factors that limit the usefulness of vocal fry as a tool in developing technical skills are the following: 1) it can neither be swelled nor diminished; 2) it possesses no identifiable vowel quality as vowel quality is recognized in Western voice culture; 3) it is completely inflexible; 4) it is unrelated to other mechanical functions such as the chest register and falsetto, and 5) no separate mechanism or muscular system exists to justify the acceptance of vocal fry as either a vocal register or a legitimate tone quality.

See **Glottal Register**
Register
Vocal Study
Vowel

Therefore, vocal fry is of minimal importance to the development of an aesthetically acceptable, open-throated tone production.

Vocal Function: the efficiency with which the vocal musculature transforms concepts related to musical tone into vocalized sound.

The basic functional activities include the following:

1. The cerebral conceptualization of musical stimuli and the transformation of these concepts into nervous impulses;
2. The transmission through the central nervous system of energy derived from oxidation to activate the vocal musculature;
3. The involuntary muscular contractions that adjust the length, thickness, and contour of the vocal folds in response to these conceptual images (*i.e.*, registration), and
4. The involuntary muscular movements which position the larynx and pharyngeal cavities for tonal amplification (*i.e.*, resonation).

See **Imagery**
Register
Resonance
Vocal Study

When these processes work harmoniously together, and when their muscular movements are precise and efficient, the vocal function is free and operates in accordance with nature's laws.

Vocal Generator: See Generator.

Vocal Hygiene: living habits and training procedures as these relate to the care and preservation of the singing voice.

Unless there are special problems concerning general health, vocal hygiene is a matter of common sense and rational living habits. Exercise, moderation in eating and drinking, avoidance of the indiscriminate taking of antibiotics and other prescribed medications, and adequate rest are all important aspects of vocal hygiene.

The most critical area of vocal hygiene, however, is the proper cultivation and nurturing of the voice. Misuse is destructive and overuse is dangerous. Combining sensible living habits with a correct technique of tone production is the best vocal hygiene and goes a long way toward achieving physical, mental and vocal health.

Vocal Ligament: a tough, fibrous tissue which forms the edge of the vocal folds and the underside of the conus elasticus.

The vocal ligament, which fastens the vocal folds to the cricoid cartilage and cricothyroid muscle, is essential to the stretching action that adjusts their dimensions to accommodate changing patterns of pitch, intensity and vowel.

See **Vocal Folds**

Vocal Limitations: restrictions in the use of the vocal mechanism.

There are two kinds of vocal limitation: natural and imposed. The natural limitations of the human voice are generally a range of two and a half to three octaves and a maximum intensity of about fifty decibels. Within these limitations, the well-developed voice should be able to produce all notes at any dynamic level and on any vowel (with the exception of the upper extension of women's voices) with tonal vitality, and it should exhibit a perfect legato, flexibility, the ability to swell and diminish at will, and ease of execution. The degree to which these capabilities are lacking in a voice is the degree to which the technique is limited.

Natural limitations can be overcome by training to the degree that the instruction is sound and one's talent and instinct for singing permits. Imposed limitations, whether conceptual or present because of muscular interference, may either result from instructional inadequacies or be self-imposed because of psychological blockages and limitations of talent.

See **Bel Canto**
Modern Methods
(To) Progress
Vocal Study

Vocal Lips: See Larynx; Vocal Folds.

Vocal Mechanism: the muscles, cartilages and organs belonging to the respiratory system and alimentary canal that, adapted to the vocal process, give rise to "voice."

Since the respiratory system and alimentary canal contain within themselves all of the properties requisite to the sounding of musical tone, *i.e.,* an actuator (neurological impulses and/or breath pressure), a vibrator (the vocal folds), and a resonator or series of resonators (the trachea, larynx, oropharynx and mouth), they are readily adaptable for service as a tone-producing musical instrument. These vocal *organs*, as they have come to be called, are capable of producing the widest variety of tone qualities ranging from the ugly to the beautiful, and when used with skill, musical sensitivity and poetic imagination, are superior to all mechanical instruments.

See **Bel Canto**
Breathing
Larynx
Modern Methods
Register
Resonance
Vocal Study
Vowel

VOCAL ORGANS

Since singing is a secondary, overlaid function, the principles applied in developing the tone-producing resources of the vocal mechanism must not violate any of those laws which govern its primary functions.

Vocal Organs: those portions of the respiratory system and alimentary canal, namely, the lungs, trachea, larynx, pharyngeal cavities, and the articulatory processes and their associated musculatures, whose structure and movement potential make them readily adaptable to the production of vocal tone.

While the elementary processes noted above sustained life for over twenty-three million years, it was not until about one hundred thousand years ago, with the emergence of intelligent *Homo sapiens*, that speech and singing developed. While it might be argued that singing began as affective expression, singing as it is now recognized in its sophisticated form is either a "gift" or a skill acquired through study.

See Affective
Expression
Vocal Mechanism

In view of their origins, the organs of voice should be considered a vocal mechanism both in speech and singing.

Vocal Pedagogy: the art or science of training the vocal mechanism.

Vocal Process: a projection of the anterior part of the arytenoid cartilage, which, when rotated by the contraction of the lateral cricoarytenoids, assists in closing the glottis.

Vocal Progress: See (To) Progress.

Vocal Range: See Range; Register.

Vocal Reflexes: those involuntary muscular contractions characteristic of most of the muscular systems involved in phonation.

Among the muscular reflexes essential to phonation are those which 1) tauten the vocal folds, 2) stabilize the larynx, 3) adjust the pharyngeal cavities for resonation of the vowel, and 4) raise and/or lower the palate. In view of the fact that most of the movements associated with these muscle systems cannot be directly acted upon, training procedures adopted for the development of technical skills must in large part center on techniques which stimulate a broad complex of involuntary muscles without violating their natural movement potential.

Giovanni Battista Mancini (1716–1800), one of the great teachers of the Bel Canto era, described the type of process necessary to an effective stimulation of the vocal reflexes involved in phonation by comparing the cultivation of vocal skills to agriculture. His comment follows:

[105]Giam Battista Mancini, *Practical Reflections on Figured Singing*, translated by E. Forman (Champaign, Ill.: Pro Musica Press, 1967), p. 115.

> Art consists in knowing where nature directs us, and to what we have been destined. By understanding the gifts of nature, and by cultivating them easily, man can perfect himself. How sure is harvest for the attentive farmer who has observed and understood the different seeds which are fecund in the diverse types of earth.[105]

If pitch, intensity and vowel are substituted for soil, sunlight and moisture, the parallels between voice culture and agriculture may be seen to be exact, and

406

the vocal mechanism may be seen to be part of a microcosmic ecological system. As is true with plant growth, vocal growth occurs through cooperation with, and an understanding of, a natural, healthy interplay between external stimuli and internal organisms.

Since the vocal registers and their associated tonal textures respond reflexively to specific patterns of pitch, intensity and vowel, and correspondingly determine the length, thickness and elasticity of the vocal folds, these elements are capable of acting as a catalytic agent in establishing the growth pattern of the vocal organs, and in the process, changing the response pattern of a broad complex of involuntary muscles situated within the throat parts. An understanding of the reflexive and predictable response of the vocal muscles to specifically designed exercise patterns is the key to a successful technical restructuring of the vocal mechanism.

See **Laryngeal**
Suspension
Limbic System
Mental Control
Reflex
Register

Vocal Sensations: vibratory feelings of one kind or another that accompany the production of most vocalized sounds.

Different physical adjustments produce different sensations. "Forward" vibrations (those perceived in the facial mask) generally reflect a healthier adjustment than do those that are "too far back," which invariably represent throat constriction. However, since vibratory sensations can only be effectively transmitted through a tensed medium, and a well-produced tone gives the impression of being the product of relaxed effort, *i.e.,* tension without muscular interference, then it is evident that all sensations of vibration are to a greater or lesser extent signs of the presence of some degree of compensatory tension.

The highest state of technical proficiency occurs when the mechanism is in equilibrium, at which time the vibratory sensations are distributed evenly throughout the system and all localized sensations disappear. To be aware of an overall feeling of free tonal emission is both admirable and desirable. To concentrate on and energize any specific areas of vibratory sensation to the exclusion of the whole is the first step toward a decline in technical skills.

A principle cause of vocal decline, therefore, is the misuse of concepts related to vocal sensations. If the voice is well formed, the sensations of vibration, by definition, must be substantially correct and not in need of change. When the mechanism is in equilibrium, however, localized sensations disappear, since they are distributed equitably throughout the entire body. Consequently, all efforts to reinforce or intensify "mask" resonance and "forward placement" introduce subtle changes in the overall coordinative process that mark the first step toward functional disintegration. For the student afflicted by vocal problems (*e.g.,* the voice appearing to be produced "too far back," or "caught in the throat"), the sensations of vibration experienced merely indicate the area within which functional changes have to be made.

To attempt to exchange one type of sensation for another as an act of will is to attempt the impossible. Effective changes within the coordinative process involve functional principles and are brought about by a realignment of the registration and a more correct use of the laryngo- and oropharynges in establishing an adjustment favorable to resonance. Since mask resonance is a symptom of compensatory tension, to require a student already a victim of throat constriction to produce this effect is to request him to superimpose a new layer of wrong tension upon another already present.

VOCAL STRAIN

See **Cavity Tone Theory**
Larynx
Register
Resonance

Vocal sensations, therefore, should never be cultivated as a direct object of instruction. While some symptoms are more desirable than others and represent a higher state of technical proficiency, none embody a functional principle or provide a direct means of access to the core of the functional process. Vocal sensations are products, not causes, and as such, must be considered indicators of a vocal condition rather than functional elements of the vocal mechanism itself.

Vocal Strain: abuse that results from an inability to successfully transform the energy directed to the mechanism by means of neurological impulses into vocal tone.

The misapplication of energy that is characteristic of vocal strain is the result of faulty concepts, poor muscular coordination, or both. Most commonly, muscular coordination is the problem, with the spill-over of misapplied energy being diverted into varying forms of compensatory tension. Regardless of its origin, however, excessive force must be used to compensate for the deficiencies arising from a misuse of energy. Vocal strain is always due to a faulty vocal technique. Correction of this condition necessitates a thorough revision of tonal concepts and aesthetic goals, as well as a dispassionate re-examination of the pedagogic procedures which led to this form of vocal abuse.

The physical manifestations of vocal strain are a tendency toward early fatigue, loss of range, power, and/or flexibility, and some degree of throat constriction.

See **Bel Canto**
Energy
Modern Methods

Vocal Study: a program ideally designed to gain a more perceptive insight into the functional logic by which the vocal organs are governed, based upon procedures designed to remove taste and aesthetic preferences from value judgments related to tone production.

Vocal study is essentially concerned with the technical aspects of tone production, observing those natural reactions characteristic of a mechanical or organic system. A basic knowledge of acoustics, physics, and anatomy, combined with a solid musical background and singing experience is extremely helpful if this project is to be carried out successfully. Factual knowledge, however, cannot supersede in importance an instinctual understanding of the human voice and its functional needs, or an "ear" for vocal mechanics. The founders of the art of Bel Canto, for example, were completely ignorant of the scientific aspects of phonation, yet, relying on empiricism alone, they developed the most extraordinary vocal technicians, and also provided a solid technical foundation upon which future generations of teachers and singers were able to build.

Vocal study begins with the asking of the right questions and the adoption of an "I don't know, let's find out" attitude. Some of the possible questions are the following:

What is "voice," and what influences are at work in determining quality? Is quality attributable to cause or effect? Is tone the product of a voluntary or an involuntary muscular system? If involuntary, how can these muscles be stimulated?

Does the tone production always yield a smooth scale, and are there "breaks" or transition points? If so, what is the underlying cause of these breaks in the legato line? Is there a discrepancy in quality and intensity between tones on one side of the break and its opposite? Is a noticeable difference in resonance characteristics to be discerned between them? Can these differences in quality and intensity, if they exist, be attributable to different kinds of mechanical action within the throat parts? If so, what muscular systems could be involved to account for these differences? Is an even scale desirable under all circumstances, or do "breaks" sometimes reflect a higher or more healthy technical status? Are these associated with any specific arrangement of pitch, intensity and vowel?

Does the larynx rise when singing in the chest voice or in the head voice? Does it depress? Which of these adjustments is more correct, or are they sometimes correct and at other times incorrect? Why?

Does the tonal texture remain the same when different vowels are sung at the same level of pitch and intensity? If so, why? If not, why not?

Is a wider mouth opening associated with loud singing or soft singing, or neither? Is the vowel dependent upon any particular mouth position, or is it independent? In either case, why? Does the vowel quality modify when swelling from soft to loud? Is there any association between singing loudly with the mouth wide open and chest register response? If true, need this always be true? Are there textural differences in tone quality to be noted between loud and soft singing? If so, what is the cause?

Does one method of breathing or the practice of breath control possess special advantages over other breathing methods? Do these free or stiffen the mechanism? Does a special technique of breathing regulate and control function, or does function (precise muscular coordination within the throat parts) control the expenditure of breath? Does a controlled method of breathing improve the resonance, range, flexibility and tone quality? Does it reduce the fatigue element? Is relaxation of the tongue and jaw immediately reflected in an improvement in tone quality or freedom? Is it permanent? Is tongue and jaw tension a cause or an effect?

When looking at photographs of the vocal folds, could it be said that their physical dimensions can be established or improved by means of tonal "placement" or breath control, or are the adjustments they assume working at cross purposes with normal respiration? If so, and if breathing techniques are important, must they necessarily be abnormal or unnatural? Is singing itself "natural"?

Is it true or false that a fixed cavity such as the nasal pharynx can resonate a wide range of pitches, or is a fixed cavity restricted to the resonation of a fixed frequency? If a fixed cavity can only resonate a fixed band of frequencies, what other cavities are available to provide a more efficient resonating system?

When a tone is said to be "too far back" or "caught in the throat," is this literally true, or does it only appear to be so? Is an "open" tone desirable? If it is, then under what conditions is a tone "too open"? Do these qualities have anything to do with "registers"? Why are some vowels thought to be "forward" and others "back"? Can they truly be said to answer this description? If so, how does this relate to pharyngeal resonance? How is "placement" affected by different tonal patterns? Does it affect those patterns at all? Does it affect them negatively? Is it possible to "place" the voice?

Finally, do the theories subscribed to, regardless of source, square with the accepted laws of physics, acoustics, physiology and common sense?

The answers to the questions listed above require an open-minded approach to the subject. By studying the parallel relationships that exist between stimulus (the exercise pattern) and the reflexive response of the vocal organs, information is yielded which reveals the functional principles that govern the vocal mechanism. When, through vocal study, training procedures succeed in bringing the coordinative process into agreement with nature's laws, the end result, "voice," will display marked improvement.

Teachers who find answers to the above and other questions should have the tools at their disposal to "build" the already healthy voice, and, as is frequently necessary, restructure the technique of those less fortunate. Opinions arising out of this experience will then be founded upon fact rather than, as now, expressions of personal taste and prejudice. Only in this way will the failure syndrome inherent in modern methods (the passing along of techniques that caused the teacher to fail to develop his own potential) be replaced by a system that assures vocal growth and career longevity.

Vocal Tract: the entire respiratory system, which extends from the pelvic floor to the palatal muscles.

Vocal Training: a procedure designed to achieve what are usually, in the beginning, two separate and ofttimes mutually contradictory activities: 1) the process of learning to sing, and 2) the art of singing.

The technical purpose of voice training (the process of learning how to sing) is to extend the tonal range, promote greater flexibility, bring out the fullest resonance potential of the instrument, and at the same time enhance the beauty of the ultimate tonal product.

Since "voice" as perceived by the listener is nothing more than a series of rhythmic expansions and contractions of air particles set in motion by muscular activities taking place within the throat parts, it is evident that voice training in the highest sense of its meaning must address itself to problems related to effecting an improvement in the physical coordination among those muscle systems.

The scope of vocal training includes the following: 1) the isolation, development and proper integration of the two register mechanisms; 2) growth into a kinesthetic awareness of the laryngo- and oropharynges as primary resonators of vocal tone; 3) the development of a true legato; 4) concern for posture, and 5) the refinement of concepts related to vowel purity and timbre, or tone color.

Realization of the objectives outlined above depends upon techniques designed to stimulate and release natural, reflexive muscular responses within the pharyngeal area, particularly the laryngo- and oropharynges. By recognizing correlative patterns, it becomes possible to eventually understand the functional laws by which the vocal mechanism is governed and to distinguish between those responses which are healthy and those which are not.

The development of technical skills depends upon the guidance of a qualified teacher. Supervised practice rather than self-help is essential if the program is to be carried out successfully. It is the teacher's responsibility to bring a sound knowledge of functional mechanics to the voice-building process, since it is through his ability to stimulate (through the design of the exercise patterns selected) a complex of involuntary muscles so that they can be made to respond in conformity with an innate functional logic, that real progress is made. The student who participates in a developmental program of this description should not only improve technically, but also, by tuning in to the sensory and aural impressions experienced, understand his voice as a mechanism, and above all, "know" himself as a person.

Vocalis Muscles: the crisscrossed aryvocalis and thyrovocalis muscle fibers that form the interior portion of the thyroarytenoids or vocal folds. As their name suggests, the ary- and thyrovocalis muscles find their points of attachment to the arytenoid and thyroid cartilages, respectively.

The torsion action of the vocalis fibers is responsible for the closing of the glottis after the cricothyroid, thyroarytenoid and arytenoid muscles have prepared the vocal folds for phonation. Since their ability to assume tension is limited because of the gelatinous substance in their connective tissue, the influence of the vocalis muscle fibers is restricted to the mid-tonal range of the voice. The contraction of these muscle fibers is essential both to the elimination of breathiness in the lower tonal range of the head voice and to the unification of the two register mechanisms.

The transverse fibers constituting the vocalis muscle system are subject to neurological stimulation exclusively, a fact which would appear to lend support to Raoul Husson's neurochronaxic theory.

See Larynx
Neurochronaxic
Theory
Thyroarytenoid
Muscle
Vocal Fold
Vibration
Vocal Folds

Vocalise: a vocal exercise.

Vocalises form the essence of materials used in the development of vocal skills. An effective vocalise is one designed to meet an immediate pedagogic objective. Thus, effectiveness is determined by two criteria: timeliness and functional needs. Any vocalise executed routinely or mindlessly serves no pedagogic purpose.

The standard vocalises of Bordogni, Concone, Nava, Vaccai, *etc.*, have little pedagogic value, since they center on the art of singing and rarely address themselves to a specific problem. Although claims have been made for their musical worth, this is negligible compared to the wealth of important vocal literature available for musical study.

See Laryngeal
Suspension
Register
Resonance
Solfège

Vocalization: the act of exercising the vocal mechanism.

Vocalization is used both 1) to "warm up" the vocal mechanism (*i.e.*, to re-establish a consonance between mental concepts and physical responses), and 2) to change or improve characteristic patterns of response. Effective vocalization (*i.e.*, the use of an exercise to achieve a specific objective at an appropriate time) is essential to vocal progress and development.

Although most singers prefer to adhere to patterns with which they feel comfortable, any melodic material should theoretically suffice for warming up the mechanism. Those who sing correctly should require only five or ten minutes to "get the mechanism going," although further vocalization frequently serves as psychological reassurance. Those who sing incorrectly, of course, require longer periods of time, since a technique that violates nature's laws subjugates the mechanism and necessitates a constant reinforcement of mind over matter.

Vocalized Breath: a device whose purpose is to free the throat of wrong tension and control the ultimate tonal product by regulating the respiratory function.

Taken in the literal sense of its meaning, the concept of vocalized breath is without basis in fact. Air does not "stream" or flow evenly through the vocal folds, but is released in a series of tiny puffs. Furthermore, the vibratory impulses perceived as "voice" are transmitted through space (like all sound waves) because their periodic motion, or rapid expansions and contractions, disturb successive layers of air in the surrounding atmosphere. These disturbances, perceived as sound, travel at a speed of slightly more than 1100 ft. per second, or in excess of 750 miles per hour. Thus, if tone were "vocalized breath" or if it moved on a stream of air, it would be expanding through space at gale force.

Pedagogically, the concept of vocalized breath can sometimes be of marginal value since it offers an image which superficially reduces throat constriction by having the singer concentrate on *releasing* rather than *producing* his voice. At best, however, it deals with a status quo without changing the physical coordination within the laryngeal musculature to any noticeable extent.

See **Air Stream**
Focus
On the Breath
Puff Theory
Yawn-Sigh

If "voice" is produced because of the activity of muscles, concepts based upon "vocalized breath," "carry the tone on the breath," "focus," and similar directives do not address themselves to this crucial aspect of phonation, and are but marginally useful to the development of vocal skills.

Voce di Finte: See Feigned Voice.

Voce di Gola: See Falsetto.

See **Falsetto**
Register

Voce di Petto: Italian, "chest voice." A reference to the lower of the two register mechanisms commonly recognized to exist by the founders of the art of Bel Canto.

See **Register**

Voce di Piena: Italian, "full voice."

Voice: the movement of air particles; sound(s) perceived by the faculty of hearing whose vibratory characteristics are determined by the movement of the vocal folds and conditioned by the shaping of the surrounding pharyngeal cavities.

In a literal sense, "voice" is nothing more than rapidly expanding and contracting air particles. It has, therefore, no mechanical function of its own, but is the product of other functions. This fact is pedagogically significant, since all effective control over "voice" is lost once the vocal folds become vibratile. Consequently, to act upon vocal tone after its character has been formed merely succeeds in misdirecting energy and in undermining the clarity of the concepts so essential to a correct tone

See **Bel Canto**
Modern Methods
Register
Resonance
Vocal Training

production.

"Voice" is the end product of a mechanical process which takes place within the laryngeal pharynx. To consider it the process itself is to confuse ends with means, and to make an assumption that will result in the commission of serious pedagogic errors, both theoretical and practical.

Voice As Mind: a theory of voice training based upon a belief that vocalized sounds, because they are the product of concepts, can be regulated and controlled by the mind, essentially with the aid of imagery and imitation.

The fact is undeniable that learning potential in singing is dependent upon an ability to perceive sounds and to make pitch and qualitative distinctions with great sensitivity. Because of such diverse factors as hearing acuity, emotional listening, conditioning, training, and psychological predisposition, as well as the ever-present dichotomy between objectivity and subjectivity, the mind (while it sends out a complex of neurological messages) must itself be trained if concepts and the reality of experience are to meet in reasonable agreement. This requires a very special kind of interplay between concept and response, one which acknowledges that in its movement potential the vocal mechanism, like all organs of the body, possesses an innate functional logic, and consequently, what the body knows the mind must learn. On these terms, relationships between stimulus and response, and cause and effect, must be carefully observed.

The premise upon which "voice as mind" is founded tacitly admits that the muscle systems responsible for setting in motion those vibratory impulses recognized as "voice" are not subject to volitional control. This severely limits its effectiveness as a pedagogic principle, since it overlooks several factors:

1. The limited extent to which involuntary movements can be influenced by concepts, *i.e.*, the release of constrictor tensions or the isolation and reintegration of the vocal registers;
2. Inaccurate information received with respect to sensory impressions and auditory feedback, each garbled because of interfering tension, and
3. The fact that the quality ultimately desired cannot be conceptualized, since quality reflects the condition of the functioning mechanisms rather than an intrinsically natural quality (which only appears *after* interfering tensions have been removed).

Most voices are flawed, and unless procedures are adopted which attack the problem at its source, *i.e.*, poor laryngeal muscular coordination, neither the mind nor the mechanism will be honed to a sharp edge. Lost motility because of muscular interference within a broad complex of involuntary muscles is the source of most vocal difficulties, and until that motility is restored, subjective concepts will continue to be conditioned by physical limitations.

Restoration of lost motility, elimination of throat constriction, and correction of an imbalanced registration are not susceptible to improvement by "intelligent" use of the voice, but by 1) devising means for stimulating involuntary muscular systems within the throat parts into reflexive, spontaneous movement, and 2) by-passing an entrenched self-image. The achievement of these objectives requires that a sharp distinction be made between the *art of singing* and the *process of learning to sing*. The art of singing (aesthetics), or the use of skill and imagination in the creation of things of beauty, implies that one has utilized the available tools or materials with taste and imagination. The process of learning to sing differs in that it is concerned with the acquisition of skills and abilities not formerly possessed.

The concept of "voice as mind" is supportable, therefore, as long as it pertains to the art of singing, where it is capable of exercising control over the voice within whatever boundaries a present technical status permits. As it participates in the learning process, however, the function of the mind is to be responsive to the instruction given and then to simply observe as objectively as possible the differences, if any, that transpire naturally. The training of both mind and muscle begins with an evaluation of these differences.

It is because the mind is capable of entertaining a prior concept and then forming another impression *after* the vocal organs have responded that qualitative concepts (which are usually misconcepts associated with what should more properly be considered the condition of the functioning mechanism) can be evaluated quite objectively. It is by observing the parallel relationships between a musical stimulus (*e.g.*, a scale or melodic pattern) and the tonal response it evokes that it is possible to form new value judgments on a basis other than aesthetics. As more sophisticated stimuli are projected, the mind will become increasingly aware of the movement potential of the muscular systems involved in phonation, and by noting an increase in options, choose those which are more advantageous to continued growth and development.

Alterations in the prior concept, leading to the ultimate refinement of the concepts themselves, therefore, can be brought about because the vocal organs react involuntarily in different ways to specifically arranged patterns of pitch, intensity and vowel, the basic elements responsible for registration. Since the teacher is able to arrange these in such a way as to by-pass a preconcept, the singer is exposed to the possibility of producing sounds he has never made before nor associated with himself. Moreover, he should immediately become aware of the movement potential of the muscular systems involved in singing, identifying both kinesthetically and conceptually with those that are freer and more natural. Thus, like the successful farmer who knows through experienced observation and study what seeds to plant, when to plant them and at what moment the harvest is ripe, so, in principle, the singer learns to cultivate his voice.

The concept of "voice as mind" as the dominating element in teaching and learning is too restrictive and holistic in approach to be an effective pedagogic tool. Technical development is impossible when the muscle systems are hampered and restricted in their movement because of interfering tensions. In such circumstances, mental controls are useless, and instead of undergoing the needed "building" and restructuring of his technique, the singer is obliged to do the best he can with what he has to offer in the way of physical coordination. Unless concepts related to a present set of conditions can be by-passed, and the integral parts of the mechanism relatively isolated, strengthened, and recoordinated more effectively, tone quality, which (if it is to be free and natural) so largely depends upon precise physical coordination, will remain a poor replica of its potential.

All perceptive learning starts with a confession of ignorance and a desire for knowledge. It is this role the mind must play if the vocal mechanism is to develop to its fullest potential. "Voice as mind" as commonly understood is not founded on such a premise, but presupposes a foreknowledge of organic processes it neither fully understands nor is capable of changing profoundly.

Voice Box: slang, the larynx.

Voice-Building: a training program designed to restructure the coordinative process among those muscle systems responsible for yielding vocal tone.

"Voice-building" as a term, a concept, and a process was in common usage until

See **Affective**
    Expression
    Auditory Feedback
    Bel Canto
    Holistic Pedagogy
    Manufactured Tone
    Modern Methods
    Natural Movement
    Register
    Resonance
    Vocal Study
    Vowel

shortly after the turn of this century. Synonymous with another semi-archaic expression, "voice culture," it implied that vocal skills not formerly possessed could be learned. To "build" a voice is to extend its range, to improve its resonance characteristics, to enable it to swell and diminish over a wide tonal range, and to increase its flexibility.

Voice-building is impossible without an understanding of those mechanical principles which govern the function of the muscle systems involved in phonation, primarily those concerned with registration.

See Bel Canto
Modern Methods
Register
Vocal Study

Voice Culture: (semi-archaic) the careful nurturing of vocal skills based on the premise that the vocal organs are part of an ecological system which, depending upon the quality of the environment (the musical stimulus), provides a climate either favorable or unfavorable to growth and maturation; synonymous with "voice building," which implies technical reconstruction.

The concept of "culture" as applied to the development of vocal skills was popular prior to the twentieth century. Within this context (the word itself is derived from the Latin *culturare,* "to till or cultivate"), it is evident that in former times a rich tonal harvest and a bountiful crop were both recognized to be dependent upon a knowledge of nature's laws, a parallel Mancini (1716—1800) drew when he advised teachers to observe and trust nature, remarking "how sure is harvest for the attentive farmer who understands the different seeds that are fecund in the diverse types of earth." The concept of voice culture and the principles of natural functioning upon which the art of Bel Canto was founded grew out of this understanding.

See Bel Canto
Energy
Modern Methods
Natural Movement

Voice on the Breath: See On the Breath.

Voice Placement: See Placement.

Voice Training: a procedure(s) adopted in order to extend the singer's tonal range, promote greater flexibility, bring out the fullest resonance potential of the instrument, and at the same time enhance the beauty of the ultimate tonal product.

Since "voice" as perceived by the listener is nothing more than rhythmic expansions and contractions of air particles set in motion by muscular activities within the throat parts, it is evident that voice training in the highest sense of its meaning must address itself to the development and precise coordination of those muscle systems. Training programs that attempt to improve the mechanical function of the vocal organs by imposing aesthetic preferences and/or overt control systems avoid the basic pedagogic problem, and consequently fail of their purpose.

See Bel Canto
Modern Methods

Voiced Consonant: a consonant whose production requires laryngeal vibration (*e.g.,* the phoneme *b*).

Voices, Exceptional: See Exceptional Voices.

Voices, Natural: See Natural Voice.

See Lowered Larynx
      Timbre
      Vowel, Dark
        and Bright

Voix Blanche: French, "white voice."

The term "white voice" refers to a tonal quality whose harmonic spectrum is deficient in lower partials because of an improper resonance adjustment. Its white and colorless characteristics reflect mechanical imbalances rather than natural limitations.

Voix Claire: French, "clear voice;" as described by Manuel Garcia, an "open" tone quality produced by a slight raising of the larynx and a corresponding lowering of the soft palate. Because of the narrowed pharyngeal isthmus, care must be taken not to engender constricting tensions when employing this technique.

Voix Mixte: French, "mixed voice;" a combination of two disparate tonal textures derived from the chest voice and the falsetto.

The origin of the *voix mixte* is obscure, but it was probably introduced by Manuel Garcia when he was teaching at the Conservatoire de Paris (1830–1848). He was fluent in French and undoubtedly sympathetic toward the desire of French artists to create a singing style independent of Italian influences, based upon the textures and nuances that are characteristic of spoken French. Functional mechanics do not vary with nationality, however, and the old ambiguities with respect to the meaning of "feigned voice," "falsetto," and "head voice" remained.

Because of his background and training, Garcia's presence at the Conservatoire nevertheless ensured the continuance of the basic features of Italian training. One such feature was the concept of a "mixed" voice, originally introduced by Francesco Lamperti (1813–1892), which, by limiting the head voice to the upper part of the female voice range, assigned but two registers to the male voice: namely, the chest register and the falsetto. With an increasing demand for greater tonal opulence, the "break" between the registers became more of a problem, since the high intensity of the chest register and the comparatively low intensity of the falsetto made it exceedingly difficult to "bridge" the mechanisms smoothly. As a result, with more robust singing, male voice types appeared to require special treatment, with greater attention directed toward, to use Lamperti's term, "mixing" the two basic register mechanisms.

Since the male voice was considered to have but two register mechanisms, the *voix mixte,* as originally conceived, was undoubtedly a combination of the chest register and the falsetto. Moreover, since the falsetto sounds unmanly, it is further evident that for psychological reasons, as well as for the reason that in its coordinated form the falsetto no longer sounds "false," the adoption of the term *voix mixte* to refer to an *end product* was a most reasonable answer to an awkward problem.

The constructive or destructive use of the *voix mixte* depends upon the qualitative condition of the two registers (whether fully, partially, or unevenly developed) and the resonance adjustment (whether open-throated or constricted). The correctness of these relationships was tested in the Italian tradition by requiring the singer to execute the *messa di voce*. For whatever reason, the French school adopted a more laissez faire attitude toward "mixing" the mechanisms, a misjudgment that has led to a type of tone production often referred to as *voix blanche,* or "white voice."

Unless it is utilized correctly, the *voix mixte* will not withstand the rigors of forceful singing, and, as is evident in the technical limitations of those trained in the French School during this century, it causes the voice to be small, overly refined and rather colorless.

While it may be reassuring to experience little or no difficulty with a register transition through the use of the *voix mixte,* a seamless voice is nevertheless not desirable when technical faults and limitations have not yet been removed. While the voice will be seamless, the technical errors will also be "sealed in." The study of the *voix mixte* does not of itself carry any assurance that these undesirable tone qualities will be avoided.

Voix Sombre: French, "dark voice," or a "closed" timbre, a quality described by Manuel Garcia as a tone "color," produced when the space between the tongue and palate is widened, as in the initial stages of a yawn.

The *voix sombre* must not be confused with "covering," since in covering there is a vowel *change* (*e.g.,* from *ah* to *uh* or *oh*) to facilitate a register change in the area of the register "break," whereas the *voix sombre* (according to Garcia's description) is produced by an enlargement of the *same* cavity (vowel) formation. The difference between the *voix claire* and *voix sombre* is solely one of tone "color," not vowel modification in its present meaning.

Volume: in singing, the quantity of sound produced by the human voice.

Volume is a tonal characteristic that represents the sum of frequency, duration, intensity, harmonic structure, and reverberation. Intensity is usually considered to be synonymous with volume, but differs in that it is solely dependent upon the magnitude of the impetus generated at the tonal source. While greater intensity always increases the tonal volume, further increases can also result from an intensification of any of the above-mentioned properties.

Psychologically, volume is a subjective aspect of the hearing process, since the sound waves impinging upon the ear of one listener may be either unpleasantly loud or too soft for another.

Vomit the Tone: a rather graphic directive often used to encourage an open-throated resonance adjustment.

Although the pedagogic value of the suggestion "vomit the tone" is questionable, it is nevertheless an attempt to overcome both physical and psychological barriers to a free tone production. One of the healthy functional manifestations of a correct technique is a reflexive feeling of wanting to regurgitate, a symptom which can accompany a sudden release of throat constriction sometimes experienced in the normal course of vocal development.

Psychophysically, when the throat has been induced to open reflexively for the first time, the singer frequently experiences a surfacing of repressed anxieties, a fear of inner expansion and of "losing control," and a consequent feeling of wanting to regurgitate. This sensation, brought on by expansive movement, is a reversal of what athletes refer to as "choking up," a condition which invariably causes a breakdown of physical coordination.

VORTEX THEORY

See **Drink In the Tone**
     Gag Reflex

Overt attempts to release constrictor tensions by vomiting the tone are of marginal value. When it occurs reflexively, however, the feeling of gagging is a direct result of correctly applied functional principles.

Vortex Theory: a formulation first brought to the attention of theorists in the early part of the eighteenth century by Denis Dodart, who spoke of "eddies" moving through the resonators, and later elaborated upon by the British scientist Edward W. Scripture just prior to the beginning of the twentieth century.

Scripture denied the validity of the Wheatstone-Helmholtz overtone theory, finding that the vocal folds did not vibrate in the manner of vibrating strings but produced a series of puffs, which caused the movement of air to proceed in twisting, corkscrew-like currents through the mouth, the nasal cavities, and into the sinuses. Gunnar M. C. Fant, a contemporary Swedish scientist, agrees in part with Scripture's findings, recognizing that the puffs emitted by the vocal folds create pressure variations which produce glottal sound waves, and that these, rather than the vibration of the mechanical folds themselves, account for pitch.

The vortex theory has received support in more recent years by E. Herbert-Caesari and the Reverend Noel Bonavia-Hunt, and is described by the latter in the preface to Caesari's book, as follows:

> The human voice is the product of a main wave modified by a number of subsidiary waves. The main wave takes form immediately in front of the vocal cords of the larynx, and is due to the vortices or rotating cores of air pressure which issue from the vibrant (glottal) slit. It is possible to detect these vortices with the aid of a sensitive electrical instrument. A similar process takes place in the mouthpiece of orchestral brass instruments in which the air column is excited by the player's lips. The vocal cords . . . do not create sound, they produce eddy currents, one eddy at each complete vibration to and fro, just as each vibration of the horn-player's mobile lips shoots an eddy into the mouthpiece.[106]

[106]E. Herbert-Caesari, *The Science and Sensations of Vocal Tone* (London: J. M. Dent & Sons, 1936), p. xii.

What is not offered in the above explanation is the possible existence of an obstruction whose presence would cause a partial blockage of subglottal pressure (as provided by the mouthpiece of a brass instrument, through which energy is funneled into the tubing of the horn), and which would serve to create eddies by returning a considerable percentage of the moving air *back toward the tonal source.* Unless such a resisting agent is to be discovered, the vortex theory would be palpably false.

While no direct parallel exists between the acoustical properties of brass instruments and the vocal mechanism, there does appear to be a strikingly close functional resemblance. Each utilizes an equalized pressure system located on opposite sides of the vibrator and each creates a standing wave which, by increasing the amplitude of oscillations at the tonal source, enables the lips of the player and the vocal folds of the singer to become largely self-vibratile.

With the vocal mechanism, the role of the mouthpiece is assumed by the false vocal cords and the ventricles of Morgagni. Thus, just as air is impounded within the cup of the mouthpiece by the limitations imposed by the small aperture leading into the tubing of the horn, so, too, the false vocal cords, by narrowing, cause the

418

ventricular pouches to inflate. In both instances, the pressure build-up curbs breath expenditure and redirects the energy toward the tonal source.

What can be deduced from the above is this: if the ventricular sacs inflate, as is universally acknowledged, then it must follow that the clockwise and counterclockwise movement of air that results from their inflation creates rapidly moving currents, which could conceivably substantiate the presence of "eddies." If this assumption is true, the vortex theory would no longer stand in open defiance of the known laws of acoustics.

The vortex theory was brought into considerable prominence by Lilli Lehmann (1848–1929), who referred to the whirling currents as *Wirbeln* ("eddies"). She considered a tone well "placed" when these currents successfully found their way into the upper resonators, particularly the nasal passages and the sinuses. At the same time, Dr. H. Holbrook Curtis and Jean de Reszke advanced their theory of nasal resonance, which, while it did not embrace the vortex theory, did focus attention on the sinuses as possible resonators. The concept of sinus tone production was later developed at length by E. G. White, whose extreme position shocked rather than challenged voice specialists. The adaptation of Scripture's theory to practical use by Lehmann, de Reszke and White was perhaps inevitable, since big voices were in demand to sing the more heavily orchestrated and dramatic music of Verdi and Wagner. By "placing" the voice into the nasal cavities and "resonating" it there, it was thought that the vocal folds would be relieved of a considerable amount of pressure, and that they would therefore fatigue less easily.

The difference between Scripture's postulate and that of the voice teachers may be seen to be one of emphasis, the latter expressing an attitude toward the resonance properties of tone, the former expressing an attitude toward movements of air caused by the presence of a supraglottal pressure system. This divergence proved significant: whereas the vortex theory may or may not be ultimately verifiable, its application in the form of nasal resonance and sinus tone production is patently inappropriate. Certainly it is demonstrable that the nasal passages are inefficient resonators. They are small, heavily damped with mucous membrane, and virtually inaccessible because of the tiny openings through which sound must pass as it emerges from the throat cavities. Furthermore, since sound travels by means of alternate expansions and contractions of the air particles surrounding the vibratory source, it cannot be "placed" under any circumstances. On the other hand, it is clear that the movement of air within the ventricular sacs must create eddies, or small whirling currents, because of the downward pressure that counters subglottal pressure, and because of the clockwise and counterclockwise rotation of the air within the sacs.

While the vortex theory may at first glance appear to be somewhat exotic, it is not without the support of an impressive array of scientists and practical teachers of voice. If it is to be understood, however, the principles involved in establishing an equilibrium between two opposed internal pressure systems must not be confused with those pertaining to resonance.

Vowel: a sustained phoneme, or sound produced by an undulating movement of the vocal folds whose vibratory pattern is amplified because of adjustments made by the cavities of the mouth. The word "vowel" is derived from the Lat-

See **Bernoulli Effect**
Breath Pressure
   Theory
Fixed Pitch Theory
Formants
Nasal Resonance
Puff Theory
Resonance
Sinus Tone
   Production
Standing Wave

in word *vocalis,* the adjective form of the noun *vox,* which means "voice" or "sound."

Generally, vowels are introduced, connected, or concluded by consonants. Although consonants delineate vowels to form words, it is generally the vowels that carry the emotional and communicative impact of phonation.

Although vowel phonemes are commonly represented by five verbal symbols— "a," "e," "i," "o," and "u" (sometimes "y" and "w")—phoneticians distinguish more than fifty-six vowel sounds in the English language alone. Potentially, each of these sounds can be produced in a "pure," ideal form which possesses tonal clarity and richness. Thus, in good singing, although some phonemes may be unaccented or intentionally de-emphasized (*e.g.,* "above"), none is intrinsically limited in vitality or clarity. Strictly speaking, there are no schwa (German, "dull") vowels in singing except for interpretive effects.

ACOUSTIC PROPERTIES

The vowel form which results from the adjustments noted above is responsible for creating the harmonic structure of a complex vocal tone, the specific category of vowel quality being determined by the manner in which energy is distributed within the frequency range. Each vowel activates four (sometimes five) areas of frequency, two of which are prominent. These are known as formant regions, and must be strongly reinforced if the resonance and vowel quality are to be well defined.

The formant regions comprise the tonal spectrum and differ for each vowel. In this arrangement, the specific areas of concentration for one vowel may be uniformly higher or lower, while for another they will be more widely separated. The formant regions are also known as frequency bands. As the frequency bands necessary to vowel definition operate independently of the fundamental, the same vowel may be sung on many different pitches.

The characteristic frequencies for a vowel are distributed in such a way as to make the formation of some vowels easier at certain pitch levels than at others. The reason for this is that the fundamental, *i.e.,* the frequency of the pitch being sung, is movable, whereas the areas of energy concentration for the vowel are fixed. Thus, when the position of the fundamental lies below the formants (frequency bands) necessary to articulate a given vowel, that vowel is clearly delineated and pure.

With a constantly shifting fundamental, however, it is not always possible to include all of the harmonics necessary to good vowel definition. For example, it is an acoustic impossibility for a soprano to sing a literal *ee* or *oo* on a high B♭ or C, since the first formant of both vowels lies considerably below the fundamental frequency. To attempt to maintain the literal qualities of the *ee* and *oo* in this range, therefore, is to attempt the impossible.

What is evident here is the natural conflict of relationship sometimes found to exist between the vowel and its fixed area of energy concentration, and a changing fundamental moving over a tonal range of two or more octaves. The vowel, if it is to retain full definition, must always lie within a tonal range where its lowest frequency is higher than the fundamental. Once the fundamental moves above the lowest area of harmonic response, the vowel will be forced to modify. This is precisely what has been cited in the above example. The lowest formant for both the *ee* and *oo* vowels fall below the soprano's high B♭ and C and cannot, therefore, be energized. To insist on maintaining the literal quality of the *ee* and *oo* vowels for high tones with women's voices leads to abuse of the mechanism.

The specific nature of tone quality may be seen to depend acoustically upon its harmonic structure. Included in this structure are certain partials, or overtones, not included in the frequency bands of the vowel proper. According to their arrangement within the harmonic spectrum, these partials impart additional characteristics to the overall tonal quality which range from brilliant to thick, shrill, or nasal. Curiously, when there is a relative absence of partials lying outside the frequency bands which define the vowel, the purer the vowel quality and the greater the similarity between voices. What seems paradoxical is that each voice nevertheless succeeds in retaining its uniqueness.

Purity of vowel, synonymous with correct tone production, implies a precise tuning of the resonators, which, in turn, implies similarities in technique, harmonic structure and, to a certain extent, concept.

PHYSICAL ADJUSTMENTS

Vowels are a product of adjustments within the throat parts made in response to a mental concept of pitch, intensity and vowel, combined with those influences contributed by aesthetic and creative goals. Physically, the resultant vowel quality represents an external expression of an internal functional condition. Thus, for all practical purposes, the terms vowel quality, tone quality, timbre, and quality are synonymous. When the internal adjustment of the vocal mechanism is well coordinated, the tones produced will reveal the intrinsic beauty of the singer's natural quality. Vowel forms, therefore, are created by adjusting the cavities of the throat and mouth in response to the singer's qualitative concepts, and that which is commonly referred to as "tone production" is a matter of physical coordination.

Of the cavities potentially capable of determining vowel quality, only the mouth, the larynx and the laryngo- and oropharynges are adjustable, and consequently only these cavities are areas of interest. Scientific research has demonstrated that the larynx and laryngo- and oropharynges are the cavities most suitable for resonation and formation of the vowel, since they may, through adjustment, be "tuned" in or out, and be coupled or uncoupled for use as either single or double resonators.

The mouth, of course, has some effect on vowel quality through its connection with the pharyngeal cavities directly behind it, but because of its constant involvement with articulation, it should not be considered a constituent part of the vowel form itself. While it should be "detuned" as a resonator, however, its ability to influence the adjustment of the pharyngeal cavities located directly behind it should not be minimized.

In an ideal technique, therefore, the larynx itself is tuned to energize frequencies of approximately 2800—3400 cycles per second (an adjustment which accounts for the so-called "ring" in the tone), the laryngo- and oropharynges are positioned to select and energize those frequencies which define the vowel, and the mouth is used to serve a twofold purpose: 1) to facilitate a proper positioning of the pharyngeal cavities in order to define the vowel and create a resonance adjustment, and 2) to assist in the free articulation of consonants.

VOWELS AND REGISTRATION

A feature peculiar to the human voice is that so many diverse activities must be coordinated. Careful observation of the way a vowel reacts under changing conditions of pitch and intensity, for example, will reveal that the same muscular complex which adjusts the vocal folds for pitch and intensity (*i.e.*, those responsible for the phenomenon of registration) play a prominent role in selecting and reinforcing the band of frequencies essential to the proper delineation and amplification of the vowel. Practical experience has demonstrated, in fact, that an absolutely pure vowel (one unblemished by accessory noises) depends not only upon an ideal resonance adjustment, but also upon a correctly balanced and well-integrated registration. All statements, therefore, concerning vowel purity when the registration is divided or imbalanced must be considered relative: they refer to reasonable vowel definition rather than to vowel purity *per se.*

Vowels are of particular interest to the training program because numerous functional and conceptual imperfections (such as throat constriction, nasality, and a "mixed" registration) are exposed there. Since technical faults must be corrected before concepts can be clarified, work on purifying the vowel must proceed towards two major objectives: 1) improvement of the resonance adjustment and the elimination of muscular interference, and 2) improvement in the registration.

While the various vowels may legitimately be considered important aids in improving the overall technique (especially the registration), it is important to remember that vowels can only be as pure as the coordinative process will allow. They cannot, of themselves, improve the registration when the registers are not reasonably well developed and ready to respond. Similarly, when the registers are mixed, vowels will continue to remain impure, and the registration will be relatively unaffected by vowel manipulation unless combined with the proper pitch-intensity pattern. In the final analysis, careful and precise enunciation of the vowels will make the most of a present stage of development, but unless the technique is well advanced, it will do no more.

See Cavity Tone Theory
     Coupling
     Registration
     Resonance

VOWEL TYPES

Every change made in the shaping of the pharyngeal cavities through which sound travels correspondingly changes 1) the acoustic properties of the tone produced, 2) the aesthetic impression it makes on the listener, and 3) to a certain extent, the form assumed by the mouth and articulatory processes. Thus, vowels are frequently classified as either "front or back," "open or closed," "lax or tense," "dark or bright," "veiled or clear." In the main, these concepts are less useful to teachers of singing than to phoneticians, speech therapists and those who teach foreign languages. Within these latter disciplines, new concepts relative to pronunciation, or the need to overcome physical impediments, logically necessitate the development of a special terminology. The common vowel types are outlined as follows:

DARK AND BRIGHT VOWELS: The concept of "dark" (*voix sombre*) and "bright" (*voix claire*) vowels was first documented by Manuel Garcia during the latter half of the nineteenth century. He associated the dark tone with an enlarged pharyngeal adjustment (a higher position of the soft palate combined with a slightly lowered larynx), and he associated the bright tone with a more compact pharyngeal adjustment (with a lowered soft palate and a higher laryngeal position). Despite its soundness, Garcia's formulation has been abandoned, and dark tones are now considered synonymous with "covering." This change in attitude merits closer examination.

Garcia was careful to point out that the essential difference between a dark and a bright tone was timbre, a vowel coloration within a framework of a pharyngeal adjustment which, while expanding or contracting slightly, retains the same basic configuration. It is due to this uniformity that the skillful vocalist is able to swell and diminish on a single tone simply by increasing and decreasing the amount of pressure being applied, and to link dark and bright tones without distorting the vowel quality. Garcia even invented exercises to develop a vocal technique based upon this concept. A "covered" tone, by contrast, not only alters the tonal coloration but also involves a rather obvious change, even a distortion, of both cavity formation and vowel quality.

When the sole difference between a dark and a bright vowel is recognized to be one of timbre, it then becomes possible to sing all shadings of vowel quality, even in the area of the register "break," without altering the resonance adjustment. If one accepted the premise that "covering" is necessary to negotiate these transitional tones, vowel purity would be impossible. Garcia's concept of timbre modification, on the other hand, makes it possible for all vowels, dark or bright, to be produced in the area of register transition without vowel distortion. This is not true of covered tones. Judged within this context, "covering" is a compensatory device which should be considered at best a temporary expedient rather than a permanent good.

Acoustically, dark vowels may, because of the enlargement of the laryngo- and oropharynges, be considered less finely tuned than bright vowels. The effect of this less precise tuning is to diminish the strength of the upper partials in the harmonic spectrum and thus reduce the "ring" and brightness that would otherwise be present. (One of the reasons "nasal resonance" has become so popular is that its somewhat "snarly" quality causes the voice to "ring," although falsely; it possesses the additional advantage of immediate achievement.) With the clear, bright vowels the reverse is true: the tuning is finer, with the high partials strongly energized. A more normal tonal coloration should, therefore, be considered to lie somewhere between these two acoustic extremes.

The production of dark and bright tone qualities depends in large part upon registration. A lowered larynx associated with dark tone qualities (if they are not to sound "mouthy") is impossible without a strongly activated chest voice. The slightly higher laryngeal position necessary for the production of bright sounds (if they are not to be "shrill") requires a strongly dominant head voice. Neither of these alternatives is desirable on a permanent basis.

In a correct vocal technique, it is the size of the pharyngeal opening that essentially determines whether a tone quality will be dark or bright, the larynx normally assuming an adjustment independent of variations in tonal coloration.

FRONT AND BACK VOWELS: Closely associated with "closed" and "open" terminology, "front" and "back" vowels indicate 1) the relative position of the mouth and tongue, and 2) those symptoms associated with a particular balance of registration. "Front" vowels are generally formed by using a smaller mouth opening (*e.g., oo*); "back" vowels require a larger opening (*e.g., ah*). Among the practices employed to facilitate the formation of vowels because of a dependency upon mouth positions are tonal "placement," "lip rounding," "pursing," and smiling. The tongue adjustments generally advocated are more elaborate and include arching into "high-back," "mid-back," "low-back" positions, "grooving," "flattening," *etc.*, each position being associated with an appropriate vowel phoneme.

The concept of front and back vowels was introduced into the vocal lexicon by phoneticians and is important to the correction of speech disorders or in learning to pronounce foreign languages. Since, technically, speech and singing share little in common, concepts of this nature are of little more than marginal help in developing vocal skills. There are many, however, who believe such a correlation to exist. Among the pedagogic assumptions to grow out of such a belief is that by freeing the articulators, the involuntary muscular systems yielding vocal tone will be vicariously improved, when in fact the reverse is true. Moreover, the concept of "front" and "back" ignores the fact that the laryngeal tuning necessary to energize those frequencies in the range of 3,000 cps (which accounts for tonal "ring") should be constant for all vowels. Also overlooked is the importance of the vocal folds (whose physical conformation is responsible for creating the impression that certain vowels appear to be "front" and "back," "too open," "closed" or "covered"). A further conceptual error is that excessive reliance is placed upon the mouth and the articulatory processes for vowel definition, a practice which makes it impossible for vowels and consonants to be independent yet mutually cooperative elements in the communicative experience.

Concepts related to "front" and "back" are incapable of improving either the registration or the performance of those muscle systems whose contractions adjust the pharyngeal cavities for resonation of the vowel, and indeed tend to undermine their effectiveness. This failure is almost inevitable when the above directives are used in conjunction with tonal "placement" (*e.g.*, "high," "low," "forward," "against the hard palate or teeth," *etc.*); regardless of how they are arranged, such directives preclude any hope of achieving natural, spontaneous movement.

LAX AND TENSE VOWELS: a theoretical analysis of tonal forms which categorizes vowels according to the degree of tension engendered throughout the phonatory tract. Since the degree of tension involving the lips, tongue and pharyngeal walls has a direct effect upon the manner in which overtones are modified, energized, and aurally perceived, it is felt that, in order to brighten the tone quality, these parts of the vocal process should be volitionally acted upon and regulated in terms of greater or lesser tension.

According to this theory, lax vowels (*e.g., ah*) are those which are produced with a low tongue position and which are by nature ringing and vibrant; tense vowels (*e.g., oo*), on the other hand, produced with an elevated tongue position, are considered veiled and more difficult to infuse with vitality.

One of the important pedagogic objectives is to absolve the articulators, the tongue and jaw especially, from tension and unnecessary involvement with tone production. Concepts such as tense and lax vowels force an abandonment of this course by encouraging the singer to act upon a voluntary muscular system, when in fact, his main interest is to learn how to influence and change for the better those involuntary activities within the throat parts which yield and resonate tone.

NEUTRAL VOWELS: "Neutral" vowels are often considered "dull" vowels. However, although some vowels are more difficult than others to produce and infuse with a clear, ringing tone quality, no vowel sound is intrinsically dull. Every vowel in the tonal lexicon is, when the technique is correct, capable of matching all other vowel qualities in tonal clarity, the sole admissible difference being one of greater rather than lesser difficulty. The *a* vowel, as in the word "above," is a typical example of a neutral vowel. Vowels of this type are correctly considered dull in speech, but never in singing. The dullness so often heard in the singing of neutral vowels is due to an absence of pharyngeal resonance and represents an aspect of incorrect technique.

OPEN AND CLOSED VOWELS: The so-called "open" and "closed" vowels are conceptualizations gleaned from aural impressions of quality, generally because of the close association between these qualities and the size of the mouth opening. All vowels, however, are primarily influenced by the physical conformation of the vocal folds, the vibratory patterns they set in motion, and the acoustic coupling of the laryngo- and oropharynges. The central issue, therefore, is not whether the mouth is open or closed, but whether the size of the mouth opening aids or inhibits a proper setting of those cavities within the throat parts that are responsible for defining and resonating the vowel. On these terms, concepts such as "open" and "closed" are without validity.

The role assigned to the position of the mouth with respect to open and closed vowels is a twentieth century invention; earlier viewpoints, as summed up by Manuel Garcia (1805—1906), were that "the pharynx is the real mouth of the singer." However, a belief that the size of the mouth opening is important to the resonation of some vowel phonemes is not without substance. For example, certain vowels (*e.g., ah*) are difficult to phonate unless the mouth is quite open, while others considered "closed" (*e.g., oo*) are produced more easily with a narrower mouth opening.

There are two probable reasons for this shift in emphasis: first, information provided by phoneticians and speech therapists, and second, the broadening of dramatic and aesthetic concepts in the development of opera. Within the latter context, the operatic works of Wagner and the later scores of Verdi, Strauss, *et al.*, created a demand for bigger voices. In response to this demand, those concerned placed greater emphasis on the development and dominance of the chest voice. The effect was, with women's voices, to "mix" the registers (by thinning out the chest voice and carrying it well up into the mid-tonal range to create what is now referred to as a "second break"), and with men's voices, to push chest voice-dominated tones up to the F and F# above middle C. In each case tonal volume increased, but the voices lost much of their flexibility, the mouth was forced to open excessively, and the tone quality in the upper middle range became what is now commonly referred to as "too open." Under these circumstances it was no longer possible to phonate a pure *ah*, and the singer was either advised to "close" the vowel and its corresponding mouth position and/or to "cover" the tone.

It may be seen, therefore, that an "open" vowel sound is not exclusively the province of a particular kind of mouth or tongue position, or an impression of the tone being either "front" or "back," or the vowels being "lax" or "tense," but a symptom produced by a particular type of registration. In the examples cited above, it was due to an overly dominant chest register that the effectiveness of a resonance adjustment was undermined, causing the tone quality to sound "too open."

"Closed" vowels reverse the conditions associated with "open" vowels, because they cannot be produced without a strongly energized head voice and tend to be "bodiless" and lacking in overall vitality. This is immediately apparent when, in phonating an *oo* vowel at high levels of intensity, the relative absence of chest register participation is especially noticeable, since voices that use this technique are unable to withstand the rigors of vigorous singing.

With the obvious correlation between "open" and "closed" vowels and the size of the mouth opening, as well as a "setting" of the pharyngeal resonators and registration, the question arises as to where the pedagogic process begins. Since registration alone among these elements operates on a mechanical principle, it is these principles which exert the profoundest influence on function—mouth positions and concepts related to "open" and "closed" vowels being, at best, aids to an improved positioning of the pharyngeal cavities and a proper tensing of the vocal folds.

VEILED VOWELS: This category refers to a breathy, diffused tone quality to which some vowel sounds adapt more readily than others. The so-called "veiled" vowels (*e.g., oo*) are those that lack the ring and natural vibrancy of the "open" vowels (*e.g., ah*). Technically, veiled vowels result from the tendency of those phonemes which encourage upper register participation to "detune" an open-throated resonance adjustment, thereby sacrificing the "ring" in the voice provided by laryngeal resonance. This tendency results from the inclination of the cricothyroid muscular system, which increases head voice participation, to invite throat constriction because of its close association with the lower constrictors. Those who possess a well-coordinated vocal technique, however, are proof that this tendency can be overcome, since all tones produced by an efficient mechanism (except those employed for special interpretive effects) are ringing and vibrant.

SUMMATION

To categorize vowels and "set" any of the physical elements involved in the phonative process in the manner described above does not constitute good pedagogy. None of these vowel types embraces a functional principle, and to train the voice on this basis can at best effect a superficial technical improvement. In the final analysis, it is more desirable to develop a technique where the tone is independent of both the articulatory processes and the mouth form. Basically, all vowels should be formed pharyngeally, and the entire concept of closed, open, lax, tense, front and back vowels should be properly considered one of misplaced emphasis.

See Cavity Tone Theory
     Energy
     Formants
     Kinesthesia
     Kinetic Energy
     Register
     Resonance

Vowel Bands: the two most prominent of the four or five areas of frequency energized by a specific vowel. Vowel bands are also called "frequency bands" or "formant regions."

See Formants

Vowel Consciousness: the ability to recognize various vowel qualities and to distinguish subtle differences in their tonal textures. Just as pitch discrimination is an integral part of musical development, vowel discrimination is essential both to technical development and to artistic interpretation.

Vowel Form: an adjustment of the pharyngeal cavities responsible for resonation which facilitates the sounding of various vowels.

The pharyngeal cavities which are adjustable and therefore suitable for resonation are the following:

1. The nasopharynx (the area directly behind the nose);
2. The mouth, or oral cavity;
3. The oropharynx (the area directly behind the mouth);
4. The laryngeal pharynx, and
5. The larynx.

Of these, the oropharynx and laryngeal pharynx are the primary resonators of vocal tone. The mouth is not an effective resonator because of the constant readjustments in its shape required by articulation. It does, of course, have some effect on vowel quality because of its connection to the pharyngeal cavities.

In a correct technique, however, the mouth is "detuned" as a resonator so that it can assist in articulating consonants and in influencing the formation of the adjustable pharyngeal cavities lying directly behind it (*i.e.*, the oro- and laryngopharynges) for resonance. The nasal pharynx is a relatively fixed cavity whose lower boundary is determined by the movement of the uvula, which, when it rises, seals the entrance and eliminates whatever properties of resonance might otherwise exist in this enclosure. When the uvula is not retracted, however, this cavity, although heavily damped with mucous membrane, may conceivably increase or conduct vibratory sensations to a minimal extent. The oropharynx, on the other hand, enlarges as it presents a firm surface for tonal reflection, adjusts to define the vowel, and is an important resonator of vocal tone. Perhaps the greatest contribution of the nasopharynx to vocal sound is in the production of semi- or consovowels, (*e.g.*, *ng*).

In an ideal technique, the laryngeal pharynx is tuned to energize vibrations of approximately 2800—3400 cycles per second (a concentration which accounts for the so-called "ring" in a tone), the oropharynx is adjusted to those frequencies necessary to define the vowel, and the mouth is adjusted to meet the needs of the oropharyngeal adjustment and articulatory processes. The vowel form which results from these adjustments is responsible for creating the harmonic structure of a complex tone.

Vowel Formant: the manner in which energy is distributed within the tonal spectrum (*i.e.*, the number, frequency, relative intensity, and duration of harmonic partials) by specific vowel phonemes.

Since vowel formants and vowel quality can only be as well defined as the coordination among the various muscle groups involved in phonation will allow, practical vocal pedagogy is not concerned with vowel formants *per se*, but with the functional principles governing the movements of those muscles responsible for tone quality.

See Fundamental
Partial
Quality
Timbre

Vowel Formant Movement: a pedagogic theory, based upon the principles of speech therapy, which associates effective tone production with the selecting of proper "phoneme positions," or conscious arrangements of the tongue, mouth, and jaw, to assist in the coupling of the various resonance cavities.

In a mechanistic approach, as expressed in the formant movement theory, it is assumed that arbitrary and consciously controlled positions of the above-named parts will cause the emergence of a freely produced tone quality. Such an approach, however, can never be successful in coordinating the intricate complex of muscles involved in singing because most of these muscles are involuntary. The formant movement theory fails in practice to alter in any constructive way the natural movement of those laryngeal muscles whose proper coordination is essential to good tone quality.

See Natural Movement
Vowel Migration
Vowel Modification

Vowel Glide: a diphthong; a direct transition from one vowel phoneme to another. The English word "I," for example, is comprised of a glide from *ah* to *ee*.

Vowel Manipulation: the selection of vowels which, in conjunction with pitch and intensity, serve to facilitate changes in the ratio of registration and/or the resonance adjustment.

Unlike vowel "shading" or vowel "coloring" (qualities which emerge spontaneously in response to a musical and emotional stimulus), vowel manipulation is used to assist in changing a prevailing functional condition. Changes in the physical dimensions of the vocal tract (the laryngo-, oro-, and nasopharynges), for example, alter the formant frequency, a longer column equating with lower frequencies, a shorter column with higher frequencies. It is for this reason that various vowel sounds can be "colored," modified, or made "darker" or "brighter." Thus, formants are strengthened or weakened because of the type of adjustments made within the vocal tract, *i.e.,* a lowering or raising of the larynx and soft palate, a broadening or narrowing of the pharyngeal isthmus, a forward tilting or retraction of the thyroid cartilage, and (marginally) the position assumed by the articulators.

To understand how the formant theory works on a practical level, it is necessary to set up an exercise pattern which permits the vowel to be the changeable element in an otherwise stable environment, for example, by singing successively the five primary vowels on a single pitch at a constant level of intensity, *i.e., ah-aye-ee-oh-oo.* By so doing, it will be obvious that each vowel exhibits distinctive textural properties and that these textures correlate not only with changes within the pharyngeal resonating system, but also with shifting balances of registration, moving progressively from a slightly more chest register-oriented quality when singing *ah* to a more dominant head voice balance for *oo.*

The significance of this predictable reaction is clear: the variable element, the vowel, influences the ratio of registration, just as specifically arranged patterns of pitch and intensity cause the vowel (unless the basic register mechanisms, the chest register and falsetto, are extremely well coordinated) to degenerate, *e.g., oo* to *oh, ah* to *aah.* It is apparent, therefore, that manipulation of carefully chosen vowel phonemes, as well as pitch and intensity, is crucial to technical development.

Once it becomes apparent that the register balance migrates with changing vowels, and that these changes are also associated with so-called "open" and "closed" vowel phonemes, a number of interesting possibilities for technical improvement suggest themselves. To cite one example, the correction of a register imbalance when the tone quality is "too open" (or chest register-dominated) can be made by prefacing the "open" vowel with one more "closed," as *oo-ah, oo-ee*, making certain that the textural properties of the first vowel are retained while phonating the second. Should the tone quality be too "closed" (or head voice-oriented), the same pattern need only be reversed.

Manipulation of the numerous vowel phonemes provides a means for stimulating an involuntary laryngeal muscular system whose contraction 1) regulates the physical dimension of the vocal folds (registration), and 2) adjusts the suspensory muscles which stabilize the larynx (resonance). The importance of vowel manipulation to technical training, therefore, is that it corrects imbalances in the ratio of registration, and at the same time helps purify the vowels, both objectives being accomplished conceptually without recourse to mechanistic methods, *i.e.*, direct control.

Although the possibilities of vowel manipulation are almost endless, especially when used in conjunction with the principles governing registration, several common and predictable reactions are to be observed:

1. That the ratio of registration changes with changing vowels, even if pitch and intensity remain constant;
2. That the reaction of the laryngeal musculature to pitch, intensity, and vowel is identical for both men and women;
3. That the so-called "open" vowels elicit more chest register response;
4. That the so-called "closed" vowels elicit more head register response;
5. That *ah* is useful in bringing the chest register into greater prominence and in exposing inequities of registration;
6. That *ee* tends to coordinate the registration, but at the same time exposes weakness in the resonance adjustment (constrictor tensions are readily detectable with *ee*), and
7. That the proper articulation of *oo*, a phoneme which tends to disengage the chest register, is a difficulty not commonly surmounted even by fine artists.

Since under certain conditions the physical dimensions of the vocal folds adjust to the acoustic properties of the surrounding resonators, it is apparent that vowel manipulation, especially when used in conjunction with the principles known to govern registration, is both theoretically and practically significant to vocal pedagogy.

See Cavity Tone Theory
Control
Covering,
  (To) Cover
Formants
Quality
Reed Theory
Registration
Sensations of
  Vibration
Standing Wave
Vowel

Vowel Migration: the movement of one vowel phoneme away from another, described as a "stable" vowel; the deliberate and conscious regulation of the articulators and the resonating system to facilitate these movements; also known as phonemic migration.

The physiological directives underlying the principle of vowel migration are designed to provide a frame of reference wherein any vowel can be readily identified because of its phonemic relationship to a "stable" vowel. Thus, it is thought, by conscious regulation of the articulators, energy within the sound spectrum can be channeled more efficiently. Conceptually, the selection of one available migratory option over another is made by comparing the vowel sound produced with recorded models, at which point the student will know exactly what vowel has been uttered, and consequently make the required adjustments.

The concept of vowel migration is perhaps helpful when, as an adult, one undertakes the study of a foreign language. It is, however, a mechanistic approach quite without relevance to the development of vocal skills and a poor substitute for the quality modification to which the talented singer adapts so readily as an aural experience. For the singer, who must conceptualize a great number of vowel phonemes in his own as well as foreign languages, these migrations can be clearly discerned as textural changes brought about because of shifting balances in the ratio of registration.

Techniques based upon vowel migration may be important to the student who has difficulty in identifying with vowel phonemes with which he is unfamiliar. The singer's real problem, however, is not one of vowel conceptualization, so much as developing a technique that finds all of the muscular systems involved in phonation brought into equilibrium at a high state of tonicity.

Vowel Modification: a self-modifying process which results from a well-balanced registration; the practice of altering relatively pure vowel phonemes for interpretative or technical purposes, for example, *ah* to *oh* or *uh*. As an interpretative effect, vowel modification is used to "color" key words for comic or dramatic emphasis. Technically, it is used to influence the balance of registration on any given pitch-intensity pattern.

The modification of vowel phonemes has been introduced into vocal pedagogy for two reasons: 1) because of aesthetic considerations, and 2) because of its immediate effect on both the positioning of the pharyngeal resonators and the physical dimension of the vocal folds. Aesthetically, vowel modification depends upon the use of so-called "closed" vowels to darken the tone quality (as in "covering") to avoid "spreading" and/or "too open" tone qualities, and "open" vowels to counterbalance the over-darkening (or excessive "covering") which is an inherent danger when singing "closed" vowels. The physical and acoustic significance of vowel modification is that it can cause 1) the vibrator to dominate the resonator, 2) the resonator to dominate the vibrator, and/or 3) an interaction between the vibrator and the resonator which helps bring the instrument into equilibrium.

With the first of the three available options, it is the excessive length and thickness of the vocal folds which forces the laryngo- and oropharynges out of their proper adustment—*i.e.,* the vibrator dominating the resonator—thus causing the tone to be "too open." The second option reverses this procedure, the use of so-called "closed" vowels altering the physical dimension of the pharyngeal cavities, an event which forces the vocal folds to adjust to a length and thickness which differs from that assumed when phonating vowels often described as "too open," in which case the resonator dominates the vibrator. In both instances, pitch and intensity remain constant, the changing factor being the vowel.

The importance of these manipulative devices to vocal pedagogy is far-reaching and affects the mechanical processes taking place during phonation in the following manner. When a "closed" vowel is selected to correct a tone quality considered "too open," the vocal mechanism readjusts and the physical dimensions of the pharyngeal cavities undergo a change: the larynx lowers slightly; there is a simultaneous elevation of the palate and the epiglottis; the ventricular folds become elongated; there is a widening of the space between the tongue and the epiglottis, and, acoustically, there is a weakened second harmonic, which is compensated for by a strengthened fundamental.

With the production of "open" vowels, both the physical and acoustic arrangements associated with "closed vowels" are reversed. In view of the fact that all of these adjustments are brought about because of muscular contractions within the throat parts, there will be moments and even stages during training when one device will prove more beneficial than another, the wisdom of the choices made determining the rate and extent at which technical progress will be made.

Perhaps the most important event taking place within the pharyngeal cavities because of vowel modification is the effect these altered vowel phonemes have upon the physical dimensions of the vocal folds. When a darker, more "closed" tone production is adopted, the vocal folds increase their length and present a thinner vibrating surface, whereas in a brighter, less "covered" tone production, the length is shortened. The immediate advantage to be gained through the use of "closed" vowels is that tension is reduced on the arytenoid muscular system, a shift which eliminates the "too open" quality in the area of the register "break." In terms of registration, this rebalancing diminishes the strength of the chest voice and permits the head voice to emerge with greater vitality. A choice of "open" vowels reverses these physical adjustments and acoustic arrangements and establishes a condition whereby the chest voice is able to emerge with greater prominence, a procedure essential to the connection of a "mixed" registration.

Aesthetic judgments as to whether or not a tone is "too open," "too closed," or nicely balanced are therefore crucial to the success of any training program. Equally important to that success, however, is an understanding of the physical events that are set in motion because of the suggested modifications. In the final analysis, the question that must be raised is whether dominance by the vibrator over the resonator, or *vice versa,* is a permanent good, or merely a device for overcorrecting imbalances among those muscle systems which draw the vocal folds into tension, stabilize the larynx, and position the pharyngeal resonators.

The third of the available options would seem to provide an answer to this question, and indeed represents a different kind of vowel modification. In this arrangement, the length, tension and mass of the vocal folds correspond to and match the acoustic properties of the pharyngeal cavities as these adjust to define and resonate the vowel. As an ultimate goal of vocal pedagogy, this technical status cannot be reached (unless as a gift of nature) except through the application of those principles known to govern registration, combined with the manipulation of "closed" and "open" vowel phonemes as described above. Thus, like weights placed upon a scale to achieve a perfect balance, the adjustments assumed by the vocal folds and those formed by the pharyngeal cavities must be juggled until they are brought into equilibrium, at which point both the vibrator and the resonators are perfectly "tuned." When this plateau has been reached, the essential difference between the first two types of vowel modification and the third is that, in the latter instance, vowels *do not have to be modified, but modify themselves.*

An example of this capability for self-modification is provided by the artistic effect known as the *messa di voce,* or the swelling and diminishing of a single tone. Here it can be observed that at *pianissimo,* the vibrato is reduced to its minimal amplitude and the tone is sweet and shimmery, whereas in swelling to *forte,* these qualities undergo a change, with sweetness gradually being replaced by a tonal "ring" which increases with the amplitude of the vibrato. Since intensity is the only changing factor in this exercise, it is evident that the resultant subtle, self-modifying properties of the vowel are caused by alterations in the physical dimensions of the vocal folds rather than by alterations in cavity formation. Obviously, this type of vowel modification differs from the others and is literally a textural modification of the same vowel phoneme.

The influence of a vowel on the vocal process has always engaged pedagogic interest, but with the increase in scientific studies since the turn of the century, a considerable body of information has become available that establishes a direct link between the vowel and pharyngeal cavity formation, acoustically known as formants, and adjustments made by the vocal folds. These findings indicate that a vowel's influence results in altering the ratio of registration, and conversely that the ratio of registration, if it does not change with the changing vowel, forces the vowel to modify.

The interdependence of the vowel and registration is readily demonstrable by recalling parallels with which every singer and teacher of voice is familiar. Among the more obvious examples to be selected are the following:

1. The reluctance of the chest register to articulate when (a) women attempt to sing an *oo* vowel loudly in the chest voice, where the so-called "open" vowels are easier to produce, and (b) when men sing the same vowel loudly on their highest tones, baritones tending to resort to "covering," tenors letting the vowel modify because the chest register (at full voice), which has engaged reflexively, injects more "ring" into the tone, modifying the true vowel;

2. A distortion of the vowel quality, which (a) with women often "spreads" their high tones, resulting in a quality which, unless accompanied by a dramatic change of texture, cannot be sung softly, and (b) with men produces qualities described as "too open," a condition which signifies that the chest register is excessively dominant;

3. The difficulty all voice types have in phonating the so-called "closed" vowels at high levels of intensity in the area of the register "break," a problem which cannot be resolved satisfactorily until both registers have been equalized, and

4. A technical inability to phonate absolutely pure vowels throughout the bulk of the tonal range, regardless of the singer's sex; such purity can only be achieved when the registers are perfectly balanced in an open-throated resonance adjustment.

All of the problems listed above arise because of an imbalanced registration, an adjustment of the vocal folds which makes it impossible to produce a true vowel phoneme. Since from the turn of the century the mechanical principles governing registration have either been rejected, ignored, or generally misapplied, correction of these difficulties has led to proposed solutions which, with the regulation of intensity excluded as a control factor, rely exclusively upon vowel modification. Among the more familiar directives introduced on the basis of this sole dependency are "hooking," "lifting up and over," and/or "covering." While these devices may perhaps be useful as a temporary expedient, they are incapable in themselves of correcting imbalances within the registration except by applying greater or lesser degrees of physical force, *i.e.,* "pushing."

From the standpoint of technical development, vowel modification must be viewed as 1) the use of so-called "open" and/or "closed" vowels to raise or lower the formant frequency, and thereby help rectify an imbalanced registration, and 2) the product of a precisely balanced registration, in which case the vowel, rather than being modified, modifies itself. If, however, as in contemporary theory and practice, vowel modification in the form of "hooking" and "covering" is considered a permanent good, both technically and aesthetically, the conclusion is inescapable that 1) the vowel distortion that accompanies these practices represents the highest level of technical skill, and 2) vowel purity on all pitches within the tonal range is an unattainable goal. Both of these propositions are, of course, patently untrue.

Since training procedures currently in vogue fail to take advantage of the obvious parallels between stimulus and response as expressed in registration, the correction of register inequities is now wholly dependent upon those influences brought to bear through an exclusive dependency upon vowel modification. Fortunately, however, pitch and intensity (the regulators of registration) are integral parts of every scale pattern or musical phrase. Consequently, it is often found that many voice teachers, like the hero in Moliere's *The Bourgeois Gentlemen* (who, having come into a sum of money, hired tutors so that he might become educated, and exclaimed, "Think of it! Here I have been speaking prose all my life and never knew it!"), unwittingly manipulate the registers without understanding the mechanical principles involved, relying solely upon their hearing perception and instinct for vocal tone to guide them.

Until such time as technical skills have reached a high level of development, vowel modification in the form of vowel manipulation is a most important teaching tool. At higher levels of technical sophistication, however, when both the pharyngeal resonators and the vocal folds adjust so that neither forces its acoustic properties upon the other, the entire vocal mechanism is in a state of conceptual and physical equilibrium, and all vowels can be produced with absolute fidelity.

See Bel Canto
Cavity Tone Theory
Covering,
(To) Cover
Formants
Harmonic Theory
Messa di Voce
Modern Methods
Quality
Register
Resonance
Vowel

Vowel Purity: vocalized sound possessing no peripheral noises, such as nasality, "twang," "throatiness," shrillness or similar imperfections. Vowel purity is synonymous with beautiful tonal quality.

See Pure Tone
Quality
Stable Vowel

Vowel Quality: See Quality.

Vowel Size: prepared physical adjustments of the articulators and the oral and pharyngeal cavities in response to various vowel phonemes; usually associated with "open" and "closed" vowels.

The concept of vowel size is founded on a mistaken belief that by the lowering of the jaw and, to quote one of its proponents, an "enfoldment of an imagined specific area by the oral cavity," the singer will be provided with "a new sensation of vowel recognition which he must learn to associate with a proper breath pressure ratio." As a result of this "experience," the singer is able to provide himself with a "sensation table" involving vowel recognition, sensation, articulatory position and breath pressure.

Physically, vowel size refers to the degree to which the oropharynx is open, an enlargement corresponding to "darker" tone qualities, a narrower passage corresponding to those that are "brighter." In principle, this concept agrees with Garcia's *voix claire* and *voix sombre,* except that the larger opening is associated with "covering," the smaller with a modified form of "nasal" resonance. The difference between the two is that the *claire* (open) and *sombre* (closed) adjustments permit a swelling and diminishing from one type of timbre and intensity to its opposite, whereas in "covering" and "nasal" resonance this is impossible.

The procedures adopted to stimulate the desired sensations associated with vowel sizes include a pre-setting of the articulators, a particular technique of breathing, and the imposition of a "twangy" vowel quality, as for example *ngyee* or *ngyaa.* Regardless of whether darker or brighter vowel phonemes are selected, the result is the same. As long as the "twang" is encouraged, the palatal muscles will come under wrong tension and cause the throat to constrict. This is especially true when the pharyngeal isthmus is narrowed, where the high tongue position serves to raise the larynx. Since this adjustment is identical to that assumed at the beginning of peristaltic movement (swallowing), throat constriction is unavoidable.

When the concept of vowel size is combined during the learning process with "high-back" and "mid-back" tongue positions, "forward" and "back," "open" and "closed" vowels, an excessive preoccupation with the tongue, "singing with a lowered larynx," breath "support" by means of the abdominal tuck or intercostal lift, "placing the voice into the nasal passages for resonation," and lip rounding, there is an immediate and paralyzing effect on the vocal mechanism.

Vowel Spectrum: the manner in which energy is distributed within the harmonic structure of complex tones; the number, frequency, and distribution of harmonic partials in relation to the fundamental of a complex sound wave.

Vowel Triangle: a geometric figure which results when the first and second formants are presented in graph form; first proposed by C. Hellwag in 1781.

The vowel triangle depicts the acoustic relationship of the basic vowel formants, but does not take into consideration the glottal vibrations, which, depending upon the registration, yield many more partials. Consequently, while it explains the basic vowel quality, it does not include the influence of the higher partials on timbre. The vowel triangle presented by Hellwag, as shown by Luchsinger and Arnold, is illustrated in Figure 21.

The vowel triangle is acoustically interesting, but is an analysis after the fact. What it fails to provide is information pertinent to the stimulation of the muscular movements engaged in positioning the vocal mechanism, *i.e.,* the movements that result in the most economical and efficient means for energizing those frequencies.

See Bel Canto
(To) Bite Into
the Tone
Holistic Pedagogy
Imagery
Modern Methods
Nasality
Sensations of
Vibration
Vocal Study
Vowel
Vowel, Dark and
Bright

See Formants
Register
Quality
Timbre
Vowel

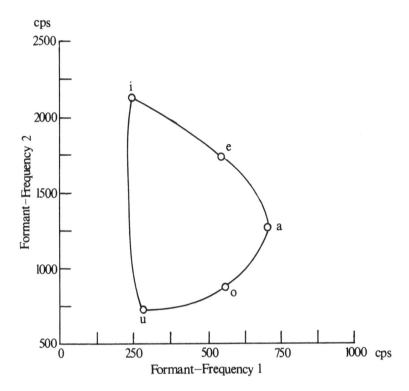

Figure 21. A facsimile of the original graph, or vowel triangle, as drawn by C. Hellwag in 1781, showing the acoustic relationship of the basic vowel formants. (After Luchsinger and Arnold.)

W

Warming Up: a gradual flexing of the vocal muscles to ease them into movement before subjecting them to higher levels of tension.

The length of time necessary to "warm up" the vocal musculature varies with the technical skill of the individual; the better the technique, the shorter the period of time required to bring the mechanism to a condition of readiness. Those who must warm up for thirty or forty-five minutes do so because of anxiety or compulsion, or in order to impose wrong concepts on a reluctant mechanism.

See Anxiety

Wavelength: points of identical phase, or equally spaced node points, in a series of compressions and rarefactions composed of moving air particles.

Wavelength is related both to frequency (pitch) and to the velocity of sound. If velocity increases, the wavelength increases also; both wavelength and velocity increase with temperature. These changes have no effect on pitch, regardless of the medium through which the frequencies are being transmitted.

Weak Voices: vocal mechanisms deficient in muscular tone.

Although not all voices are equally strong or capable of withstanding equal amounts of pressure, "weak" voices are generally the result of a poor vocal technique. If the vocal function is efficient, every voice will be able to absorb the pressure demanded by suitable repertoire.

See Tonicity

(A) Well-Trained Voice: a technical status which finds consistency, control over limitations, an absence of tonal roughness, and a rather ordinary voice quality raised to the level where the tone production itself is considered to be correct, but the instrument is nevertheless one of inferior potential; a judgment given further credence when somewhat meager resources are used "intelligently," *i.e.,* with restraint, and with taste and imagination.

Popular acceptance of a voice as being well trained, as opposed to being natural or "exceptional," is a common fallacy. The end result of all training methods should be a vocal technique which is "natural," unaffected, spontaneous and free. This objective, however, is rarely achieved through study because of the prevalence of mechanistic training methods. These, because the vocal organs have been subjected to outer-imposed disciplines (voice "placement," nasal resonance, breath "control," *etc.*), make the voice sound at best "well trained" rather than natural. The statement, for example, that a voice is of "limited natural ability but well trained," is,

See Bel Canto
    Mechanistic
      Methods
    Modern Methods

437

more often than not, suspect. Voices fitting this description may be well disciplined, but not well trained from the standpoint of sounding spontaneous, natural and free.

Whirling Currents: See Vortex Theory.

Whisper: a vocal sound produced without periodic vibrations; a toneless, breathy vocal quality.

There are four factors which set whispering apart from singing:

1. The vocal folds are incompletely closed, with the glottis shaped like an inverted V;
2. Vocal fold tension is much lower than in phonation, the margins of the vocal folds do not visibly vibrate, and air escapes in nonperiodic frictional turbulence, so that noise is produced instead of tones of variable or measurable frequency;
3. There is an excessive amount of breath loss, and a sharp reduction in subglottal air pressure, and
4. There is a total neutralization of the pharyngeal cavities as tuned resonators.

All of these together contribute to the sounding of tone qualities recognized as whispering.

A whispered sound is produced without a clearly defined resonance adjustment and without the vocal folds being approximated. Because it is fatiguing to produce, it is valueless as a pedagogic device. In those instances where the voice is chronically strained, hoarse or overtired, silence rather than whispering provides the necessary rest and relaxation.

Except for rare interpretive effects, a whispered sound should never be used either in singing or during technical development.

Whistle Register: strictly speaking, not a register at all, but a series of tones sung in altissimo which, because of their high position in the tonal range, require a special adjustment of the vocal folds.

According to experiments first conducted by Carl Müller (1876) and repeated in this century by Richard Luchsinger, the membrane margins of the vocal folds perform vertical vibrations without a horizontal component during the production of whistle tones. What may be concluded from their experiments is that the physiological events which transpire during the production of whistle tones bear no relationship to those taking place during the production of tones considered more legitimate. With whistle tones, no direct relationship exists between amplitude of vibration and intensity, or between the undulating movement of the vocal folds (the "puff" method) and pitch, nor are the horizontal movements which normally interrupt the oscillatory cycle in a lower pitch range present.

For these reasons, and perhaps others, the whistle tone does not appear to be an integral part of most voice types, although with higher voices, it must obviously be regarded as a legitimate component of the tonal range. The whistle voice cannot be considered a "register," however, since no separate muscular system or systems exist to fulfill the necessary requirements.

See Puff Theory
    Register

White Noise: a hissing sound, reproducible electronically, whose unusual acoustic properties result from the equally intense energization of all frequencies within its harmonic spectrum.

White noise, which sounds rather like a waterfall, makes it difficult for a listener to perceive any other sound—especially his own voice—and has been used in scientific experiments to attempt to determine the extent to which hearing during phonation is influenced by auditory feedback, and the extent to which vocal functioning can be improved by masking external stimuli.

According to researchers Donald Maxwell of Midwestern State University (Texas) and E. Ross Ekstrom,[107] the effects of white noise masking on vocal functioning are less significant for those who sing well than for those who do not. Not surprisingly, it was found that the former appear to depend more upon kinesthetic impressions for regulating their tone production than upon auditory feedback. Results concerning the effect of masking upon the efficiency of vocal functioning are, however, still inconclusive.

[107]E. Ross Ekstrom, "Control of Singing Intensity as Related to Singer Experience," *NATS Bulletin* XVII (December, 1960), 8–12.

See **Auditory Feedback**
    Masking

White Tone: a vocalized sound whose shallow, colorless tonal characteristics result from a deficiency of chest register participation and a consequent predominance of head register.

Acoustically, the chest register produces a stronger, more complex overtone series than does the head voice, which, contrary to popular belief, produces very few overtones. (In fact, the falsetto, from which the head voice is derived, produces virtually none.) These acoustic characteristics of the two basic register mechanisms account for the colorless tonal characteristics of "white" tones.

Wild Air: air that is not in a state of vibratory motion; breath that escapes through the vocal folds during phonation.

"Wild air," characteristic of breathy singing, is especially noticeable in the lower-middle tones of the female voice when the two register mechanisms have not been properly coordinated. In general, wild air and tonal breathiness indicate some functional inefficiency.

Sometimes, however, wild air or breathiness is not undesirable: for example, when separating a mixed registration, breathiness is one of the first signs of the emergence of the pure falsetto.

See **Falsetto**
    Falsetto or
        Head Voice
    Register

Windpipe: See Trachea.

Wobble: an erratic tonal movement in which neither the periodicity nor the amplitude of the sound waves produced during phonation is related to the particular pitch-intensity pattern being sung.

There are distinct physiological and qualitative differences between the wobble and other characteristic tonal movements, such as the vibrato and tremolo. The perfectly even pulsations of the vibrato are desirable movements and reflect a proper use of the instrument. The tremolo and wobble, on the other hand, result from poor muscular coordination, and indicate the presence of muscular interference and compensatory tensions.

Whereas the even pulsations of the vibrato are proportionate to and regulated

WOBBLE

by intensity, the irregular and erratic pulsations characteristic of the tremolo and wobble are not, and the latter cannot properly be considered variants of the vibrato. The tremolo is characterized by an excessively fast, "nervous" tonal pulse brought on by severe throat constriction, and muscular rigidity. The wobble, on the other hand, results from an overly dominant chest register forced too high in the tonal range, a fault which disrupts the stability of the laryngeal suspension.

Surprisingly enough, the wobbly tone is relatively free: its prevalence in operatic voices is in itself an indication that the wobble, while distressing to hear, is nevertheless more healthy functionally than the tremolo. Basses and contraltos are particularly prone to tonal unsteadiness and the wobble, and the excessive tonal movements frequently associated with their singing exemplify this vocal fault. The voice suffering from a tremolo, however, fatigues easily, lacks durability and is rarely able to withstand the rigors of an operatic season.

X

Xiphoid Process: a point of attachment for the abdominal musculature.

Y

(To) Yawn: a natural reflex which transpires in response to a deficiency of oxygen; an involuntary reaction to anxiety, boredom, or fatigue; in singing, both a relaxation exercise and a device for inculcating a sense of open-throatedness.

Since phonation is impossible when a yawn is in progress, its value to the voice-building process is limited. As a device, however, it does offer a perfect example of the fundamental difference between a natural approach to training and mechanistic methods. In the first instance, those who recognize the relaxation potential of the yawn exploit it to relieve throat constriction and to engender a sense of open-throatedness by utilizing an area of natural functioning which (like chewing, sucking, swallowing, *etc.*) need not be learned; in the second instance, those who are mechanistically inclined adopt it because it possesses definable physical attributes they associate with vocal freedom, as 1) a lowered larynx, 2) an enlarged pharyngeal isthmus, 3) an arched palate, and 4) a flattened tongue.

See Covering,
    (To) Cover
    Energy
    Laryngeal
      Suspension
    Lowered Larynx
    Mental Concept
    Nasality
    Register
    Resonance
    Vowel

Neither of the above approaches succeeds in fulfilling its intended purpose because each fails to confront the fundamental difficulty. True open-throated resonance requires the careful development and integration of many diverse elements, *i.e.*, concepts, the manner in which the vocal folds are drawn into tension, respiratory equilibrium, and laryngeal suspension . None of these activities, when set in motion, is influenced to any extent by yawning.

Yawn-Sigh: a pedagogic procedure designed to release constrictor tensions and achieve some degree of throat freedom.

The proper execution of the yawn-sigh is not difficult: while maintaining the initial gesture and position of a yawn, the singer must phonate and transform the rather toneless sigh into a "straight," somewhat "breathy," half legitimate quality without altering the pharyngeal adjustment. When executed properly, the feeling of sighing will be stronger than the yawn.

The virtue of the yawn-sigh is that it utilizes a natural reflex to eliminate wrong tension at its source. Another possible advantage is that, like the cat who yawns and stretches, the vocal muscles move out of a rigid "set." The systems involved, however, are being neither exercised nor maintained in equilibrium during such movements, and consequently the yawn-sigh must be considered a relaxing exercise and nothing more.

See Congesting
    On the Breath
    Placement
    Register
    Resonance

YAWN-SIGH

The concept of the yawn-sigh could perhaps be considered an extension of an earlier practice known as "singing on the breath," the essential purpose of each being to deliberately release breath in order to remove the false "ring" associated with throat constriction.

Z

Zero Audibility: the weakest sound that can be heard, or zero decibels (db); those pitches whose frequency is too low to be perceived by the ear.

Zero audibility, along with other aspects of hearing perception, varies with age, individual, and other factors such as protracted exposure to excessive decibel levels in a work or social environment, as for example working in a boiler factory or listening to acid rock. Thus, zero audibility is not so much a question of frequency or energy in the sound as it is the effect of this energy on the sensation of hearing.

The extreme range of audibility extends from 15cps to 20,000 or more, depending upon individual hearing acuity.

Index of Names

Years in italics denote date of publication.

Agricola, Johan Friedrich (1720–1774), *20, 208, 209, 254*

Appelman, D. Ralph (*1967*), *229, 230, 351*

Arnold, Godfrey E. (*1949*), *58, 225, 341, 434*

Arteaga, Estaban (*1785*), *19*

Baker, Elsworth F. (1903–), *12*

Bartholomew, Wilmer T. (*1942*), *91, 227, 240*

Beckmann, G. (*1956*), *111, 343*

Behnke, Emil (*1885*), *220, 373*

Bellussi, G. (*1954*), *127*

Benade, Arthur H. (*1973*), *352*

Bernacchi, Antonio (1685–1756), *21, 31, 221*

Bernoulli, Daniel (1700–1782), *7, 10, 32, 33*

Blanchet, Jean (1724–1778), *20*

Bonavia-Hunt, Rev. Noel (*1977*), *418*

Bordogni, Giulio Marco (1787–1856), *106, 207, 411*

Brodnitz, Friedrich (1899–), *304, 311, 312*

Brown, William Earl (*1931*), *38, 275*

Burgin, John Carroll (*1973*), *198*

Caccini, Giulio (c. 1546–1618), *143, 208, 254*

Caffarelli, Gaetano Maiorano (1710–1783), *57*

Cherubini, Luigi (1760–1842), *209, 347*

Cirillo, Vincenzo (1623–1667), *24, 25, 27*

Coffin, Berton (*1974*), *230*

Concone, Giuseppe (1801–1861), *106, 207, 411*

Corri, Domenico (1746–1825), *20, 113, 121, 143, 144, 206, 275*

Corti, Alfonso (1822–1876), *259*

Croatto, Lucio (*1959*), *238*

Croatto-Martinelli, Caterina (*1959*), *238*

Curtis, H. Holbrook (1856–1920), *86, 222, 241, 344, 419*

Czermak, J. M. (*1859*), *110*

Decroix, G. (*1956*), *41, 178, 361*

DeLucia, Fernando (1860–1925), *79*

De Reszke, Jean (1850–1935), *79, 86, 203, 222, 241, 242, 273, 274, 344, 419*

Di Carlo, Nicole Scotto (*1979*), *67, 89*

Diday, Y. R. (*1840*), *79*

Dodart, Denis (1634–1707), *178, 284, 343, 418*

Duprez, Gilbert-Louis (1806–1896), *78, 79, 82, 195, 196, 225*

Ekstrom, E. Ross (*1960*), *439*

Engelbrunner, Nina D'Aubigny von (*1803*), *20, 113, 208*

Ewald, J. (*1899*), *361, 394*

Falcon, Marie Cornélie (1812–1897), *349*

Fant, Gunnar M. C. (*1970*), *91, 229, 418*

Farinelli, born Carlo Broschi (1705–1782), *57*

Ferri, Baldassare (1610–1680), *30*

Fétis, Francois Joseph (1784–1871), *20*

Ffrangcon-Davies, David (1855–1918), *165*

Fields, Victor Alexander (*1947*), *198*

Fourier, J. B. J. (1768–1830), *129, 130, 140*

Franca, Ida (*1959*), *114*

Fransson, F. (*1970*), *229*

Froeschels, E. (*1952*), *61*

Galen (130–200), *343*

Garcia, Manuel Patricio Rodriguez (1805–1906), *x, 6, 20, 22, 26, 73, 86, 109, 110, 113, 115, 129, 137, 139, 144, 179, 196, 208–210, 213, 215, 216, 218, 219, 222, 224, 227, 240, 254–257, 268, 299, 318, 348,*

352, 416, 417, 422, 423, 425, 434

Gardner, Ernest (*1975*), *397*

Gemelli, A. (*1954*), *127*

Gross, S. (*1909*), *58*

Guido (d'Arezzo) (c. 991–1033), *347*

Hellwag, C. (*1781*), *434*

Helmholtz, Hermann L. F. (1821–1894), *91, 130, 142, 146, 220, 227, 284, 384, 418*

Herbert-Caesari, E. (*1963*), *267, 268, 418*

Hertz, Heinrich R. (1857–1894), *147*

Hicks, James W., Jr. (*1979*), *395*

Hill, Frank (*1938*), *276*

Hiller (Hüller), Johann Adam (1728–1804), *20, 113, 208*

Holmes, Gordon (*1880*), *x, 101, 221, 226–228*

Howard, John, (*1886*), *221*

Husler, Frederick (*1964*), *x, 86, 117, 175–177, 231, 255, 275, 372*

Husson, Raoul (*1935*), *4, 111, 178, 248, 249, 316, 343, 353, 354, 394, 411*

Izdebski, Krzysztof (*1979*), *353, 354*

Jeans, Sir James (*1961*), *74*

Jones, Daniel (*1918*), *168*

Kelsey, Franklyn (*1955*), *276*

Klein, Herman (1856–1934), *222*

Lamperti, Francesco (1813–1892), *92, 144, 209, 210, 218, 254, 416*

Lamperti, Giovanni Battista (1840–1910), *xi, xii, 26, 38, 114, 219, 275*

Lanza, Francesco Giuseppe (c. 1750–1812), *20*

Lasser, Johann Baptist (1751–1805), *20, 113, 208*

Leanderson, Rolf (*1982*), *395*

Lehmann, Lilli (1848–1929), *140, 222, 273–275, 344, 419*

Libersa, J. (*1956*), *41, 178, 361*

INDEX OF NAMES

Bibliography

I. Pedagogy and Related Disciplines

Appelman, D. Ralph. *The Science of Vocal Pedagogy.* Bloomington: Indiana University Press, 1967.

Bacon, Richard MacKenzie. *Elements of Vocal Science.* London: Baldwin, Cradock & Joy, 1824.

Bairstowe, Edward C. and Greene, H. Plunkett. *Singing Learned from Speech.* London: Macmillan & Co., 1946.

Baker, Elsworth F., M.D. *Man in the Trap.* New York: The Macmillan Co., 1967.

Bartholomew, Wilmer T. *A Survey of Recent Voice Research.* Oberlin, Ohio: Proceedings of the Music Teachers National Association, 1937.

Behnke, Emil. *The Mechanism of the Human Voice.* London: J. Curwen & Sons, 1880.

Boone, D. *Voice and Voice Therapy.* Englewood Cliffs, N.J.: Prentice-Hall, 1971.

Brodnitz, Friedrich S. *Vocal Rehabilitation.* Rochester, Minn.: Whiting Press, 1959.

Brower, Harriette. *Vocal Mastery.* New York: Frederick A. Stokes Co., 1920.

Brown, William Earl. *Vocal Wisdom: Maxims of Giovanni Battista Lamperti.* New York: Arno Press Inc., 1931.

Browne, Lennox and Behnke, Emil. *Voice, Song and Speech.* New York: G.P. Putnam's Sons, undated [c. 1885].

Burgin, John Carroll. *Teaching Singing.* Metuchen, N.J.: The Scarecrow Press, 1973.

Burney, Charles. *A General History of Music from the Earliest Ages to the Present Period.* London: By the Author, 1776. Also 2nd ed., with critical and historical notes by Frank Mercer. London: G.T. Foulis & Co.; New York: Harcourt, Brace, 1935.

Campbell, E. J. Moran. *The Respiratory Muscles and the Mechanics of Breathing.* London: Lloyd-Luke, 1958.

Chorley, Henry F. *Thirty Years' Musical Recollections.* (Reprint) New York: Vienna House, 1972.

Clippinger, David Alva. *The Head Voice and Other Problems.* Bryn Mawr, Pa.: Oliver Ditson Co., 1917.

Corri, Domenico. *The Singers Preceptor.* London: Chappel & Co., 1810. Reprinted in *The Porpora Tradition: Master Works of Singing.* Edited by Edward Foreman, vol. 3. Champaign, Ill.: Pro Musica Press, 1968.

Curry, Robert. *The Mechanism of the Human Voice.* New York: Longmans, Green & Co., 1940.

Curtis, H. Holbrook. *Voice Building and Tone Placing.* New York: D. Appleton & Co., 1900.

Dorian, Frederick. *The History of Music in Performance.* New York: W.W. Norton & Co., 1900.

Duey, Philip A. *Bel Canto in Its Golden Age.* New York: King's Crown Press, 1951.

Duschnitz, Marco. *Theorie of the Production of Vocal Sounds.* Philadelphia: J. Schuberth & Co., 1870.

Edwards, Henry Sutherland. *History of the Opera, from Monteverdi to Donizetti*. London: W.H. Allen & Co., 1862.

Eisenson, S. *The Improvement of Voice and Diction*. New York: Macmillan, 1958.

Fant, Gunnar M.C. *Acoustic Theory of Speech Production*. The Hague: Mouton & Co., 1970.

Ferrari, Giacomo Gotifredo. *A Concise Treatise on Italian Singing*. London: G. Schulze & J. Dean, 1818.

Fields, Victor Alexander. *Training the Singing Voice*. New York: King's Crown Press, 1947.

Franca, Ida. *Manual of Bel Canto*. New York: Coward-McCann, Inc., 1959.

Garcia, Manuel. *The Art of Singing. Part 1*. Boston: Oliver Ditson & Co., undated [c. 1855].

——— *École de Garcia: Traité complet de l'art du chant*. Paris: Troupenas et Cie, 1840.

——— *Garcia's Schule, oder Die Kunst des Gesanges*. Mainz: B. Schott's Söhne, undated [c. 1850].

——— *Hints on Singing*. Translated by Beata Garcia. London: E. Ascherberg & Co.; New York: Edward Schuberth & Co., 1894.

Goldschmidt, Hugo. *Die italienische Gesangmethode des XVII Jahrhunderts*. Breslau: Silesian Press, 1892.

Grout, Donald Jay. *A Short History of Opera*. 2nd ed. New York: Columbia University Press, 1965.

Hallock, William and Muckley, Floyd S. *Voice Production and Analysis*. New York: Looker-on Press, 1897.

Helmore, Frederick. *The Italian Registers*. London: J. Masters & Co., 1887.

Henderson, W.J. *Early History of Singing*. London: Longmans, Green & Co., 1921.

——— *The Art of Singing*. By the Author, 1896; Freeport, N.Y.: Books for Libraries Press, 1968.

Herbert-Caesari, E. *The Voice of the Mind*. London: Robert Hale, 1951.

——— *The Science and Sensations of Vocal Tone*. London: J.M. Dent & Sons, 1936; New York: Crescendo Publishing, 1968.

Holmes, Gordon, M.D. *The Science of Voice Production and Voice Preservation*. New York: R. Worthington, 1880.

Howard, John. *The Physiology of Artistic Singing*. Boston: By the Author, 1886.

Husler, Frederick and Rodd-Marling, Yvonne. *Singing: The Physical Nature of the Vocal Organ*. New York: October House, 1964.

Judson, L.S. and Weaver, A.T. *Voice Science*. New York: Appleton-Century-Crofts, 1942.

Klein, Herman. *The Golden Age of Opera*. London: G. Routledge & Sons, 1933.

——— *The Bel Canto*. London: Oxford University Press, 1923.

Kofler, Leo. *The Art of Breathing as the Basis of Tone-Production: The Old Italian Method*. New York: E.S. Werner & Co., 1897.

Kwartin, Bernard. *Fundamentals of Vocal Art*. New York: Omega Music Edition, 1941.

Lamperti, Francesco. *A Treatise on the Art of Singing*. Translated by J.C. Griffith. London: G. Ricordi & Co.; New York: G. Schirmer, undated [1877?].

Lang, Paul Henry. *Music in Western Civilization*. New York: W.W. Norton & Co., 1941.

Lehmann, Lilli. *How to Sing*. Translated by Richard Aldrich. 3rd rev. ed. New York: The Macmillan Co., 1941.

Luchsinger, Richard and Arnold, Godfrey E. *Voice—Speech—Language*. Translated by Godfrey E. Arnold and Evelyn Rohe Finkbeiner. Belmont, Cal.: Wadsworth Publishing Co., 1965.

Lunn, Charles. *The Philosophy of Voice*. 1st ed. London, 1878. 9th ed. New York: G. Schirmer, 1903.

Mackenzie, Sir Morell. *The Hygiene of the Vocal Organs*. London: The Macmillan Co., 1886. (Reprint) Belmar, N.J.: E.S. Werner & Co., 1928.

Mancini, Giovanni (Giam) Battista. *Practical Reflections on Figured Singing*. 1st ed. 1774. Translated by Edward Foreman. Champaign, Ill.: Pro Musica Press, 1967.

——— *Practical Reflections on the Figurative Art of Singing*. Milan: By the Author, 1776. Translated by Pietro Buzzi (ed. 1777). Boston: The Gorham Press, 1912.

Marchesi, Mathilde. *Bel Canto: A Theoretical and Practical Vocal Method*. New York: Dover Publications, Inc., 1970.

——— *Ten Singing Lessons*. New York and London: Harper & Brothers, 1901.

Marchesi, Salvatore. *A Vademecum for Singing Teachers and Pupils.* New York: G. Schirmer, 1902.

Miller, Dayton C. *The Science of Musical Sounds.* New York: The Macmillan Co., 1916.

Mills, T. Wesley. *An Examination of Some Controverted Points of the Physiology of Voice— Especially the Registers of the Singing Voice and the Falsetto.* Cambridge, Mass.: By the Author, 1883.

———— *Voice Production in Singing and Speaking.* Philadelphia: J.B. Lippincott Co., 1913.

Moses, Paul J. *The Voice of Neurosis.* New York: Grune & Stratton, 1954.

Muckey, Floyd S. *The Natural Method of Voice Production.* New York: G. Schirmer & Sons, 1915.

Myer, Edmund J. *Position and Action in Singing.* 1st ed. By the Author, 1897. New ed. Boston: The Boston Music Co., 1911.

————*The Renaissance of Vocal Art.* Boston: The Boston Music Co., 1902.

————*The Vocal Instructor.* Philadelphia: Theodore Presser Co., 1913.

————*Vocal Reinforcement.* Boston: The Boston Music Co., 1891.

————*The Voice from a Practical Standpoint.* New York: Wm. A. Pond & Co., 1886.

Nathan, Isaac. *Musurgia Vocalis.* London: Fentum, 1836. Reprinted in *The Porpora Tradition: Master Works on Singing.* Edited by Edward Foreman, vol. 3. Champaign, Ill.: Pro Musica Press, 1968.

Nava, Gaetano. *Elements of Vocalization.* New York: G. Schirmer, Inc., Library vol. 437, undated [c. 1900].

Pacchiarotti, Gaspare. *Modi Generale di Canto.* Milan, 1836.

Paget, Sir Richard. *Human Speech.* New York: Harcourt, Brace & Co., 1930.

Palmer, E. Davidson. *The Rightly-Produced Voice.* London: Butler & Tanner, 1897.

Parry, C. Hubert. *The Evolution of the Art of Music.* New York: D. Appleton & Co., 1908.

Praetorius, Carl. *The Tone Placed and Developed.* Chicago: Faulkner & Ryan, 1907.

Procter, Donald F. *Breathing, Speech, and Song.* Vienna: Springer Verlag, 1980.

Proschowsky, Frantz. *The Way to Sing.* Boston: C.C. Birchard & Co., 1923.

Redfield, John. *Music: A Science and an Art.* New York: Alfred A. Knopf, Inc., 1926.

Reid, Cornelius L. *Bel Canto: Principles and Practices.* New York: Coleman-Ross Co., 1950. (Reprint) New York: The Joseph Patelson Music House, 1971.

————*The Free Voice.* New York: Coleman-Ross Co., 1965. (Reprint) New York: The Joseph Patelson Music House, 1971.

————*Voice: Psyche and Soma.* New York: The Joseph Patelson Music House, 1975.

Rose, Arnold. *The Singer and the Voice.* London: Faber & Faber, 1962.

Rousselot, P.J. *Principes de Phonetique Experimentale.* Paris: H. Didier, 1924.

Russell, G. Oscar. *Speech and Voice.* New York: The Macmillan Co., 1931.

———— *The Vowel.* Columbus: Ohio State University Press, 1928.

Sachs, Curt. *Rhythm and Tempo.* New York: W.W. Norton & Co., 1953.

Scott, Charles Kennedy. *Word and Tone.* London: J.M. Dent & Sons, 1933.

———— *The Fundamentals of Singing.* London: Cassell & Co., 1954.

Seashore, Carl. *Psychology of Music.* New York: McGraw-Hill Book Co., 1938.

Seiler, Emma. *The Voice and Singing.* Philadelphia: Lippincott Publishers, 1869.

Semple, Armand. *The Voice, Musically and Medically Considered.* London: Bailliere, Tindall, & Cox, 1884.

Shakespeare, William. *The Art of Singing.* Bryn Mawr, Pa.: Oliver Ditson Co., 1898.

———— *Plain Words on Singing, in the Absence of a Master.* New York: G.P. Putnam's Sons, undated [c. 1924].

Smolover, Raymond. *The Vocal Essence.* Scarsdale, N.Y.: Covenant Publications, 1971.

Stanley, Douglas. *The Science of Voice.* New York: Carl Fischer, Inc., 1929.

————*The Voice: Its Production and Reproduction.* New York: Pitman Publishing Corp., 1933.

————*Your Voice—Applied Science of Vocal Art.* New York and Chicago: Pitman Publishing Corp., 1945.

Stewart, George Walter. *Introductory Acoustics.* New York: D. Van Nostrand Co., 1933.

Strunk, Oliver. *Source Readings in Musical History.* New York: W.W. Norton & Co., 1950.

Taylor, David C. *New Light on the Old Italian Method.* New York: The H.W. Gray Co., 1916.

Tenducci, Giusto Ferdinando. *Instructions of Mr. Tenducci, to His Scholars.* London: Longman & Broderip, 1785[?].

Tetrazzini, Luisa. *How to Sing.* Philadelphia: Theodore Presser Co., 1923.

Tosi, Pier. Francesco. *Observations on the Florid Song.* 1st ed. 1726. Translated by J. E. Galliard (1743). London: Reeves Bookseller, Ltd., 1926.

Ulrich, Bernhard. *Concerning the Principles of Voice Training During the a Capella Period and Until the Beginning of Opera (1474–1640).* Translated by John W. Seale. Edited by Edward Foreman. Champaign, Ill.: Pro Musica Press, 1973.

Vennard, William. *Singing: The Mechanism and the Technic.* 4th ed. New York: Carl Fischer, Inc., 1967.

Weiss, D. and Beebe, H. *The Chewing Approach in Speech Therapy.* Basel: Karger, 1950.

Westerman, Kenneth N. *Emergent Voice.* Ann Arbor: Edwards Bros., 1955.

White, Ernest G. *Sinus Tone Production.* London: J.M. Dent & Sons, 1938.

————*The Voice Beautiful in Speech and Song.* London: J.M. Dent & Sons, 1938.

Whitlock, Weldon. *Bel Canto for the Twentieth Century.* Champaign, Ill.: Pro Musica Press, 1968.

Witherspoon, Herbert. *Singing: A Treatise for Teachers and Students.* New York: G. Schirmer, Inc., 1925.

———— *Thirty-Six Lessons in Singing for Teachers and Students.* Chicago: Meissner Institute of Music, 1930.

Wromski, Thaddeus. *The Singer and His Art.* New York: D. Appleton & Co., 1921.

II. Dictionaries

American Standard Acoustical Terminology. Acoustical Society of America. New York: American Standards Association, 1960.

Baker's Biographical Dictionary of Musicians. 4th ed. New York: G. Schirmer, 1940.

Encyclopaedia Britannica. Edited by Walter Yust. Chicago, London and Toronto: William Benton, Publishers, 1958.

Encyclopoedia of Music. Edited by John Weeks Moore. Boston: J.P. Jewett & Co., 1854.

An English Pronouncing Dictionary. Edited by Daniel Jones. New York: E.P. Dutton Co., 1926.

Grove's Dictionary of Music and Musicians. 5th ed. Edited by Eric Blom. New York: St. Martin's Press, 1955.

The International Cyclopedia of Music and Musicians. 3rd ed. Edited by Oscar Thompson. Philadelphia: The Blakiston Co., 1944.

The Oxford Companion to Music. 9th ed. Edited by Percy A. Scholes. London: Oxford University Press, 1955.

A Pronouncing Dictionary of American English. Edited by John Samuel and Thomas Knott. Springfield, Mass.: G. & C. Merriam & Co., 1944.

The Shorter Oxford English Dictionary. 3rd ed. Edited by C.T. Onions. Oxford: The Clarendon Press, 1973.

Webster's New International Dictionary. 2nd ed. Unabridged. Springfield, Mass.: G. & C. Merriam Co., 1960.

III. Technical Books

Bartholomew, Wilmer T. *Acoustics of Music.* New York: Prentice Hall, 1942.

Békésy, Georg von. *Experiments in Hearing.* Translated by E. G. Wever. New York: McGraw-Hill, 1960.

Boudreau, J.C. and Tsuchiatani, C. *Sensory Neurophysiology.* New York: Van Nostrand Reinhold, 1973.

Brazier, M.A.B. *The Electrical Activity of the Nervous System.* London: Pitman Medical Publishing Co., 1960.

Cates, H.A. and Basmajiian, J.V. *Primary Anatomy.* Baltimore: Williams & Wilkins Co., 1955.

Crandall, Irving B. *Theory of Vibrating Systems and Sound.* New York: D. Van Nostrand Co., 1926.

Crouch, James E. *Functional Human Anatomy.* 3rd ed. Philadelphia: Lea & Febiger, 1978.

Culver, Charles A. *Musical Acoustics.* New York: McGraw-Hill Book Co., 1956.

Cunningham's Manual of Practical Anatomy, vols. 2 and 3. 14th ed. Edited by G.J. Romanes. New York: Oxford University Press, 1977–78.

Denes, Peter B. and Pinson, Elliot N. *The Speech Chain.* Bell Telephone Laboratories Science Series. Baltimore: Williams & Wilkins Co., 1964.

Fletcher, Harvey. *Speech and Hearing in Communication.* New York: D. Van Nostrand Co., 1929.

Gardner, Ernest. *Fundamentals of Neurology.* 6th ed. Philadelphia: W.B. Saunders, 1975.

Grant, John Charles Boileau. *A Method of Anatomy.* 5th ed. Baltimore: Williams & Wilkins Co., 1952.

Gray, Giles Wilkerson and Wise, Claude Merton. *The Bases of Speech.* 3rd ed. New York and Evanston: Harper & Row, 1959.

Gray's Anatomy. 36th ed. Edited by Williams and Warwick. Philadelphia: W.B. Saunders Co., 1980.

Hall, Jody and Kent, Earle L. *The Language of Musical Acoustics.* Elkhart, Ind.: C.G. Conn, 1957.

Handbook of Physiology, vol. 1, sec. 3. Edited by W.O. Fenn and H. Rahm. Washington, D.C.: American Physiological Society, 1964.

Helmholtz, Hermann L.F. *On the Sensations of Tone.* Translated by Alexander J. Ellis. London: Longmans, Green & Co., 1875. (Reprint) New York: Dover Publications, 1954.

Hollingshead, W. Henry. *Anatomy for Surgeons.* New York: Paul B. Hoebler, 1954.

International Phonetic Association. *The Principles of the International Phonetics Association.* London: University College, 1961.

Jacob, S.W., Francone, C.A. and Lussow, W. S. *Structure and Function in Man.* 4th ed. Philadelphia: W. B. Saunders Co., 1978.

Jeans, Sir James. *Science and Music.* London: Cambridge University Press, 1961.

Kimber—Gray—Stackpole's—Anatomy and Physiology. 17th ed. Edited by Marjorie A. Miles, Anna B. Drakontides and Lutie C. Lewell. New York: Macmillan Publishing Co., 1977.

Kirchner, J.A. *Pressman and Kelemen's Physiology of the Larynx.* Rochester, Minn.: American Academy of Opthamology and Otolaryngology, 1970.

Ladefoged, Peter. *Elements of Acoustic Phonetics.* Chicago: University of Chicago Press, 1962.

Marshall, Madeline. *The Singer's Manual of English Diction.* New York: G. Schirmer, 1953.

Martinet, Andre. *Elements of General Linguistics.* Chicago: University of Chicago Press, 1966.

Mörner, Marianne, Fransson, F. and Fant, Gunnar. *Voice Register Terminology and Standard Pitch.* Stockholm: Speech Transmission Laboratory, Royal Institute of Technology, 1970.

Negus, Victor Ewings. *The Mechanism of the Larynx.* London: Wm. Heinemann; St. Louis: C.V. Morby Co., 1929.

Potter, Ralph L., Kopp, George A. and Green, Harriet. *Visible Speech.* New York: D. Van Nostrand Co., 1947.

Scripture, E.W. *Researches in Experimental Phonetics: The Study of Speech Curves.* Washington, D.C.: Carnegie Institute, 1906.

Stevens, S.S. and Davis, Hallowell. *Hearing, Its Psychology and Philosophy.* New York: John Wiley & Sons, 1938.

Taylor, Robert M. *Acoustics for the Singer.* Emporia: Kansas State Teachers College, 1958.

Ward, Ida C. *The Phonetics of English.* New York: D. Appleton Century Co., 1929.

Wise, Claude Merton. *Applied Phonetics.* Englewood Cliffs, N.J.: Prentice-Hall, 1957.

Zemlin, Willard R. *Speech and Hearing Science.* 2nd ed. Englewood Cliffs, N.J.: Prentice-Hall, 1981.

BIBLIOGRAPHY

IV. Articles and Dissertations

Ackermann, E.L. "Action of the Velum Palatinum on the Velar Sounds /k/ and /g/." *Vox* 21(1935):2.

Arnold, G.E. "Physiology and Pathology of the Cricothyroid Muscle." *Laryngoscope* 71(1961):687.

———— "Vocal Nodules and Polyps: Laryngeal Tissue Reaction to Habitual Hyperkinetic Dysphonia." *Journal of Speech and Hearing Disorders* 27(1962):205.

Benade, Arthur H. "The Physics of Brasses." *Scientific American* (July, 1973): 44–45.

Brodnitz, Friedrich S. "The Age of the Castrato Voice." *Journal of Speech and Hearing Disorders* 40(August, 1975).

Brown, W.S., Jr. "Supraglottal Air Pressure as a Technique for Studying Speech and Singing." *Transcripts of the Sixth Symposium: Care of the Professional Voice, Part I*, pp. 45–47. Edited by Van Lawrence. New York: The Voice Foundation, 1977.

Calnan, J.S. "Movements of the Soft Palate." *British Journal of Plastic Surgery* 5(1953):286.

Campbell, William M. and Michel, John F. "The Effects of Auditory Masking on Vocal Vibrato." *Transcripts of the Eighth Symposium: Care of the Professional Voice, Part I*, pp. 50–55. Edited by Van Lawrence. New York: The Voice Foundation, 1979.

Cleveland, T. "Acoustic Properties of Voice Timbre Types and Their Influence on Voice Classification." *Journal of the Acoustical Society of America* 61(1977):1622.

Coffin, Berton. "The Instrumental Resonance of the Singing Voice." *NATS Bulletin* 31(1974):28–33.

Coleman, Robert F. and Williams, Robert. "Identification of Emotional States Using Perceptual and Acoustic Analyses." *Transcripts of the Eighth Symposium: Care of the Professional Voice, Part I*, pp. 75–83. Edited by Van Lawrence. New York: The Voice Foundation, 1979.

Croatto, Lucio and Croatto-Martinelli, Caterina. "Physiopathologie du voile du palais." *Folia Phoniatrica* 11(1959).

Curtis, H.S. "Automatic Movements of the Larynx." *American Journal of Psychology* 2(1900):237.

David, E.E., Jr. "The Reproduction of Sound." *Scientific American* (August, 1961): 72–84.

Dew, Robert A., M.D. "The Biopathic Diathesis." *Journal of Orgonomy* 6(1972): 187–200.

Di Carlo, Nicole Scotto. "Perturbing Effects of Overarticulation in Singing." *Journal of Research in Singing* 2(1979): 10–27.

Diday, Y.R. and Pètrequin. "Memoirs sur une Nouvelle Espèce de Voix Chantée." *Gazette Medical* 8(1840): 305–314.

Dodart, Denis. "Sur les Causes de la Voix de l'Homme, et de ses Differens Tons." *Memoires de l'Academie Royale des Sciences* (1700).

Douglas, Jan Eric. "The Ring of the Voice and its Relationship to Resonance." Music Degree Dissertation, Florida State University, 1977.

Ekstrom, E. Ross. "Control of Singing Intensity as Related to Singer Experience." *NATS Bulletin* 17 (1960):8–12.

Faaborg-Andersen, K. "Action Potentials from Internal Laryngeal Muscles During Phonation." *Nature* 178(1956):340.

———— "Electromyographic Investigation of the Intrinsic Laryngeal Muscles in Humans." *Acta-Physiology Scandanavia* 140 (1957): 1–150.

Fairbanks, Grant, House, Arthur S. and Stevens, Eugene L. "An Experimental Study of Vowel Intensities." *Journal of the Acoustical Society of America* 20(1950):457–59.

Fields, V. A. "Review of the Literature on Vocal Registers." *Vocal Registers in Singing*, edited by John Large. The Hague: Mouton, 1973.

Fletcher, Harvey. "Loudness, Pitch and Timbre of Musical Tones and Their Relation to the Intensity, the Frequency and the Overtone Structure." *Journal of the Acoustical Society of America* 6(1934):59–69.

Froeschels, E. "Chewing Method As Therapy." *Archives of Otolaryngology* 56(1952):427.

Furstenberg, A.C. "Evidence of Laryngeal Participation in Emotional Expression: Its Relation to Hysterical Aphonia." *Annals of Otology, Rhinology and Laryngology* 67(1958):516.

Garcia, Manuel. "Observations on the Human Voice." *London, Edinborough and Dublin Philosophical Magazine and Journal of Science* 10 (1855):511–513.

Gemelli, A., Sacerdote, G. and Bellussi, G. "Analisi Electroacoustica della Voce Cantata." *Bollettino della Società Italiana di Fonetica sperimentale, Fonetica biologica, Foniatria, Audiologia* 4(1954):3–4.

Harrington, R. "Study of the Mechanism of Velopharyngeal Closure." *Journal of Speech Disorders* 9(1944):325.

Hartog, C.M. "The Function of the Ventricle of Morgagni." *Acta-Otolaryngologica* 10(1926): 253–56.

Hill, Frank. "Freedom in Song." *The Gazette and Herald*. Blackpool, England (1938).

Hollien, Harry. "On Vocal Registers." *Journal of Phonetics* 2(1974): 125–143.

———— "Vocal Pitch Variation Related to Changes in Vocal Fold Length." *Journal of Speech and Hearing Research* 3(1960):150–56.

Hollien, Harry and Michel, J.F. "Vocal Fry as a Phonational Register." *Journal of Speech and Hearing Research* 11(1968):506–509.

Husson, Raoul. "Étude des phénomès physiologiques et acoustiques fondamentaux de la voix chantée." *Folia Phoniatrica* 3(1950).

———— "A New Look at Phonation." *NATS Bulletin* 13 (1956): 12–13.

———— "Rôle de la fourniture laryngée dans la formation du timbre des voyelles parlées et chantées et genèse des passages et des régistres de la voix." *Rev. franc. Phoniat.* (1935).

Iwata, S., von Leden, H. and Williams, D. "Air Flow Measurement During Phonation." *Journal of Communication Disorders* 5(1972):67–69.

Izdebski, Krzysztof and Shipp, Thomas. "The Effect of Vertical Laryngeal Position on Singers' Sustained Vowel Formants." *The Journal of Research in Singing* 2(1979):1–9.

Kenyon, E.E. "Relocation of Oral Articulative Mats to Speech and Intrinsic Laryngeal Musculature in General to the Function of the Vocal Cords." *Archives of Otolaryngology* 5(1927):481–501.

König, W.F. and Leden, H. von. "The Peripheral Nervous System of the Human Larynx." *Archives of Otolaryngology* 73, No. 1 (1961).

Large, John. "Towards an Integrated Physiologic-Acoustic Theory of Vocal Registers." *NATS Bulletin* 28(1974):18–36.

Leden, Hans von. "The Mechanism of Phonation." *Archives of Otolaryngology* 74 (1961).

Lindsley, Charles F. "The Psychological Determinants of Voice Quality." *Speech Monographs*, vol. 1. Baton Rouge: Louisiana University Press, 1934.

Linke, E. "A Study of Pitch Characteristics of Female Voices and Their Relationship to Vocal Effectiveness." *Folia Phoniatrica* 25(1973):173–185.

Lloyd, W.F., Negus, F.E. and Neil, E. "Observation on the Mechanics of Phonation." *Acta-Otolaryngologica* 48(1958):205–38.

Manfredini, Vincenzo. "Dell'unire la voce di petto colla voce di testa, la quale volgarmente chiamasi falsett." *Regole Armoniche*. Translated by Philip A. Duey. 2d ed. Venice. (See Duey, *Bel Canto in Its Golden Age*.)

Metzger, Wolfgang. "Mode of Vibration of the Vocal Cords." *Psychological Monographs* 38(1928).

Miller, Richard. "A Brief Consideration of Some Registration Practices in National Schools of Singing." *Journal of Research in Singing* 2(1979):2–14.

Miller, R.L. "Nature of the Vocal Cord Wave." *Journal of the Acoustical Society of America* 31(1959):667–679.

Moore, P. and Leden, H. von. "Dynamic Variations on the Vibratory Pattern in the Normal Larynx." *Folia Phoniatrica* 10(1958):205–238.

Mörner, Marianne, Fransson, F. and Fant, Gunnar. *Voice Register Terminology and Standard Pitch*. Stockholm: Speech Transmission Laboratory, Royal Institute of Technology, 1970:17–20.

Pescia, Adolfo. "Singing Means Production: Interview with Myles Fellowes." *Etude* (December, 1948).

Piguet, J., Decroix, G. and Libersa, J. *Comptes Rendus* 242 (Paris: Academy of Sciences, 1956).

Pressman, Joel J. "Physiology of the Vocal Cords in Phonation and Respiration." *Archives of Otolaryngology* 35(1942):355.

———— "Physiology of the Larynx." *Physiological Review* 35(1955):355–378.

Rothman, Howard, Nielson, Kenneth and Hicks, James, Jr. "Perceptual Classifications of Voice Movements." *Transcripts of the Eighth Symposium: Care of the Professional Voice, Part I,* pp. 57–59. Edited by Van Lawrence. New York: The Voice Foundation, 1979.

Rubin, H.J. "The Neurochronaxic Theory of Voice Production—A Refutation." *Archives of Otolaryngology* 71(1960).

Russo, V. and Large, John. "Psychoacoustic Study of the Bel Canto Model for Register Equalization: Male Chest and Falsetto." *Journal of Research in Singing* 1(1978):1–25.

Sacerdote, G. "Researches on the Singing Voice." *Acustica* 7(1957).

Schilling, Richard. "Über die Stimme erbgleicher Zwillinge." *Klin. Wschr.* 15(1936):756.

Seabury, Deborah. "The Singer's World: Voice Teachers I." *Opera News* (November, 1978):41–47.

———— "The Singer's World: Voice Teachers II." *Opera News* (December 16, 1978):15–23.

Shipp, Thomas, Leanderson, Rolf and Sundberg, Johan. "Rate and Extent of Vibrato as a Function of Vowel, Effort and Frequency." *Transcripts of the Eighth Symposium: Care of the Professional Voice, Part I,* pp. 46–49. Edited by Van Lawrence. New York: The Voice Foundation, 1979.

Sonninen, Aatto A. "Is the Length of Adjustment of the Vocal Fold the Same at All Different Levels of Singing?" *Acta-Otolaryngologica* 163(1954):219–31.

———— "The Role of the External Laryngeal Muscles in Length Adjustment of the Vocal Cords in Singing." *Acta-Otolaryngologica* 48(1947):16–25.

———— "The Role of the External Laryngeal Muscles in Length Adjustment of the Vocal Cords in Singing." *Acta-Otolaryngologica,* Supplement 130(1956).

Stout, Barrett. "The Harmonic Structure of Vowels in Singing in Relation to Pitch and Intensity." *Journal of the Acoustical Society of America* 10(1930):137–48.

Sundberg, Johan. "The Acoustics of the Singing Voice." *Scientific American* (March, 1977): 16–23.

———— "Formant Structure and Articulation of Spoken and Sung Vowels." *Folia Phoniatrica* 22(1970):28–48.

Tarneaud, J. "Du rôle fondamental du larynx dans la différenciation du timbre des voyelles." *Comptes Rendus* (Paris: Academy of Sciences, 1941).

Tatsumi, M., Kunisaki, O. and Fujisaki, H. "Acoustic Analysis and Subjective Evaluation of Sung Vowels." Annual Bulletin, *RILP* 10(1976):191–198.

Timcke, Rolf, Leden, Hans von and Moore, Paul. "Laryngeal Vibrations: Measurements of the Glottal Wave." *Archives of Otolaryngology* 68(1958):1–19.

Titze, Ingo. "The Concept of Muscular Isometrics for Optimizing Vocal Intensity and Efficiency." *Journal of Research in Singing* 2(1979):15–25.

Van den Berg, Janwillem. "On the Role of the Laryngeal Ventricle in Voice Production." *Folia Phoniatrica* 7(1955):57–69.

———— "Direct and Indirect Determination of Mean Subglottic Pressure." *Folia Phoniatrica* 7(1956):1–24.

———— "Subglottic Pressure and the Vibration of the Vocal Folds." *Folia Phoniatrica* 9(1957):65–71.

———— "Vocal Ligaments versus Registers." *NATS Bulletin* 20, No. 2 (1963):16–23, 31.

Van den Berg, Janwillem and Tan, T.S. "Results of Experiments with Human Larynges." Reprinted from *Oto-Rhino-Laryngologica* 21(1959).

Van den Berg, Janwillem and Vennard, William. "Toward an Objective Vocabulary for Voice Pedagogy." *NATS Bulletin* (February 15, 1959): 10–15.

Van den Berg, Janwillem, Zantema, T. and Doornenbal, P., Jr. "On the Air Resistance and the Bernoulli Effect of the Human Larynx." *Journal of the Acoustical Society of America* 29(1957):626–631.

Vennard, William. "The Bernoulli Effect in Singing." *NATS Bulletin* (February, 1961): 8–12.

Wiksell, Wesley A. "An Experimental Study of Controlled and Uncontrolled Types of Breath." *Studies in Experimental Phonetics,* edited by Giles Wilkeson Gray. *University Studies,* no. 27. Baton Rouge: Louisiana State University Press, 1936.

William, A.F. "The Nerve Supply of the Laryngeal Muscles." *Journal of Laryngology and Otology* 65(1951):343.

Wolf, S.K., Stanley, D. and Sette, W.J. "Quantitative Studies on the Singing Voice." *Journal of the Acoustical Society of America* 6(1935):255–266.

Wooldridge, Warren B. "Is There Nasal Resonance?" *NATS Bulletin* 13(1956).

Wyke, Barry D. "Neurological Aspects of Phonatory Control Systems in the Larynx." *Transcripts of the Eighth Symposium: Care of the Professional Voice, Part II,* pp. 42–53. Edited by Van Lawrence. New York: The Voice Foundation, 1979.

Zerffi, W.A.C. "Vocal Nodules and Crossed Arytenoids." *Laryngoscope* 45(1935):532.

———— "Vocal Muscular Development." *Archives of Otolaryngology* 62(1955):406.